SECOND EDITION

HUMAN RESOURCE INFORMATION SYSTEMS

SECOND EDITION

HUMAN RESOURCE INFORMATION SYSTEMS

Basics, Applications, and Future Directions

EDITORS

Michael J. Kavanagh
University at Albany—State University of New York

Mohan Thite
Griffith University, Australia

Richard D. Johnson
University at Albany—State University of New York

SAGE | SA SOUTH ASIA

Los Angeles | London | New Delhi
Singapore | Washington DC | Melbourne

Originally published in 2012 by

SAGE www.sagepublishing.com
Los Angeles | London | New Delhi | Singapore | Washington DC | Melbourne

This South Asia edition published in 2012 by

SAGE | SA SOUTH ASIA

SAGE Publications India Pvt Ltd
B1/I-1 Mohan Cooperative Industrial Area
Mathura Road
New Delhi 110 044, India

Published by Vivek Mehra for SAGE Publications India Pvt Ltd and printed at Chaman Enterprises, New Delhi.

ISBN: 978-81-321-0872-6 (PB)

CONTENTS

Preface

This second edition of *Human Resource Information Systems: Basics, Applications, and Future Directions* is written with the objective of improving the content and the usefulness of the content for faculty and students. Our first edition was driven by the need for a comprehensive textbook in human resource information systems (HRIS)[1] that could be used in teaching and serve as a reference. It was personally frustrating for the editors and chapter authors to have to use several books in teaching an HRIS course since the only comprehensive textbook for the academic market was published in 1990 (Kavanagh, Gueutal, & Tannenbaum, 1990) and was soon out of print. Although there have been several books on HRIS published, most authors have focused only on one aspect or dimension of the HRIS field, for example, on e-HR, Web-based HR, or HRIS in a global context. As a result, faculty have had to rely on books of readings, parts of entire HRM and IT textbooks, and HR computer workbooks to cover the entire field of HRIS in their courses. The growing importance of HRIS was due to the recognition by human resources management (HRM) practitioners, academics, and managers that information technology (IT) and information systems (IS) had become a critical aspect of developing and using HRM programs to better manage the human capital of an organization. Thus, a comprehensive education in the HRM field required the knowledge and skills for developing, implementing, and maintaining a human resource information system.

In the preface to the first edition of this book, we note that Kavanagh et al. (1990) stated that "among the most significant changes in the field of human resources management in the past decade has been the use of computers to develop what have become known as human resource information systems (HRIS)" (p. v). We also argue that the introduction of computers and IS/IT concepts to the field of HRM during the 1980s and early 1990s was a *revolutionary* change. That is, HRM paper systems in file cabinets were being replaced by the use of mainframes, PCs, and HRM software to computerize the HRM systems. To keep up with these technological changes in the HRM function, companies were forced to adapt, even though it was quite expensive, in order to remain competitive in their markets.

After these revolutionary changes in HRM during the early 1990s, we have argued, HRM and IT/IS advances have been *evolutionary*; that is, there have been constant improvements in the HRIS field. From stand-alone applications on a PC, the field of HRIS/HRMS now has seen the implementation of enterprise resource planning (ERP) configurations in HRM with extensive use of manager and employee self-portals. The evolutionary changes in the HRIS field have been rapid through the 1900s and 2000s, but as we state in our first edition, "the changes from 1990 on, although very important and requiring more complex technology, [still] represent an evolutionary change" (Kavanagh & Thite, 2009, p. xvii). We based this assertion on the fact that the conception of the operation and role of HRM has not undergone any other fundamental change since 1990 but rather an evolutionary one that involved "a process of continuous change from a lower, simpler, or worse to a higher, more complex, or better state" (p. xvii).

This changed role of HRM has evolved to the point that HRM managers and professionals are now seen as strategic partners, and sophistication in the use of computer technology to improve the delivery of HR programs and activities to management has grown immensely. Most critically, these changes have meant that there have been significant advances in the use of people knowledge in managerial decisions. These advances are due to the fact that people knowledge can be accessed more rapidly now than in 1990, and with a higher degree of accuracy. This marriage of HR with IT/IS in the development and improvement of an HRIS has increased the ability of management to use people knowledge to make better decisions on the human capital of their firms to gain a competitive advantage in the marketplace.

What these changes have meant for the neophyte learner, with a background in HRM or IT and trying to understand the HRIS field, is that it is not sufficient to begin one's study with the improved products and processes that have occurred recently due to evolutionary changes. For example, it would not be wise or fruitful to begin one's study of the HRIS field with a focus on service-oriented architecture (SOA), enterprise portals, N-tier architectures, cloud computing, or the use of Web 2.0 in HRM. This would be like starting with Chapter 17 of this book and then proceeding backward through the book. Unfortunately, many people do, in fact, focus on learning the technological advances in HRIS without understanding the basics first. Since the changes in HRM up though the early 1990s represent a revolutionary way of thinking about the field, one must *first* understand what this revolution represented, that is, how HRM moved from using paper records in file cabinets to the computerization of the HR function. Only then can the learner move on to study, apply, and use the improved IT products developed through the evolutionary process.

NEW ASPECTS OF THE SECOND EDITION

First, a new coeditor has been added to increase the breadth of HRIS knowledge that could be used to improve the second edition. Professor Richard D. Johnson is the new coeditor. Dr. Johnson is an assistant professor of management at the University at Albany, State University of New York and a certified Human Resource Information Professional. For more details, see Dr. Johnson's biographical statement. Professor Johnson's knowledge and experience encompass both the HR and the IT fields, and he was instrumental in adding new cases as well as more recent information about the HRIS field to this second edition. In addition to adding a new coeditor, Sage asked several faculty members who had adopted and used the first edition to provide evaluations of the entire book as well as of each chapter. Their recommendations were very useful and led us to make a number of changes.

In terms of the content of this second edition, there are now 17 chapters instead of 16. We added a chapter by splitting Chapter 6 from the first edition, "Cost Justifying HRIS Investments," into two chapters in this second edition: Chapter 6—"HR Metrics and Workforce Analytics" and Chapter 7—"Cost Justifying HRIS Investments." Naturally, this required major changes in Chapter 7. This decision was based on feedback from the anonymous faculty reviewers as well as on our personal judgment that one of the major uses of an HRIS was to focus better on providing accurate and timely information for managerial decisions, both strategic and operational. HR metrics and workforce analytics are critical to cost justifying decisions to develop and implement an HRIS, as well as to improving its use as a decision tool. Another significant content change was a complete revision of Chapter 10 from the first edition, "Job Analysis and HR Planning," to a more up-to-date Chapter 11 on "Talent Management." This change also reflects today's emphasis on talent management, particularly during the current world financial situation. These changes represent more general revisions throughout the second edition; that is, we updated the chapters so they present a survey of current knowledge and practice in IT, HRM, and HRIS.

Other content changes involved improving the "vignettes" from the first edition, which are now titled "HRIS in Action." New cases were added to a number of the chapters, and we significantly expanded the chapter discussion questions. We did these things to improve the text as a learning and teaching tool—we wanted the text and each chapter within it to present a consistent learning experience. Thus, we established a consistent structure across all chapters. Chapters contain, in the following order, an editors' note, chapter objectives, chapter content, a chapter summary, a list of key terms, chapter discussion questions, and a case with student questions. This consistent structure for all chapters should facilitate the learning process for both faculty and students. The *internal consistency* for each chapter was established by emphasizing the same chapter learning points for the chapter objectives, chapter summary, key terms, and chapter discussion questions. We felt that this within-chapter consistency would aid the learning process of the students and aid the faculty in identifying the important content of each chapter. For the student, the key terms are a guide, in the view of the editors, to the important aspects of the chapter, but they are not a glossary. Nor are all the key terms listed in the glossary, although the glossary in the appendix has been expanded and improved to include additional technical terms. Likewise the Web sites and additional readings in the appendix have been expanded because of recent changes in the field. In determining to make these changes in the book, the three coeditors worked to make the second edition a textbook they would personally be comfortable using to teach their HRIS courses.

In summary, in this second edition, we have described the major advances in the field of HRIS and the relation of HRIS to managerial decision making while, at the same time, exploring the basic concepts of developing, implementing, and maintaining an HRIS. The book represents the intersection of the best thinking and concepts from the two fields of HRM and IS/IT. It was the early intersection of these two fields that changed the role of HR in organizations from record keeper to strategic partner. After introducing the basic concepts of an HRIS combined with new approaches to the operation of HRM in the organization, we then proceed to the more advanced, and evolutionary, technical changes. The basic philosophy of this book is that the integration or harmonization of technology with people management in an HRIS will create a distinct competitive advantage for organizations We hope that you, the reader, gain this understanding and that you enjoy this book.

A password-protected instructor resources site includes PowerPoint® presentations, test banks, detailed lecture outlines, suggested course projects, and a variety of full-text SAGE journal articles selected to support and enhance the content of the book. These materials are available at www.sagepub.com/kavanagh2e.

Many individuals contributed in a variety of ways to provide assistance in the completion of this book, and we would like to thank them. First of all, we would like to thank all the authors who contributed chapters. We know how difficult it is to write a chapter for an edited book, particularly when the editors have defined the philosophy and approach to be used. In addition, special thanks go to those individuals who provided invaluable insights through their evaluations of the first edition of this book and its chapters: Julie Siliven, San Antonio College; Kevin Brown, Florida International University; Marc S. Miller, Manhattanville College; Judy Gilleo, Lindenwood University; Robin Watkins, DeVry University; Neptali Martinez, New York University; and William L. Tullar, University of North Carolina–Greensboro.

Again, we would like to thank Dianna Stone of the University of Texas at San Antonio for her support for the creation of this book and her assistance in helping find authors to write chapters. Our thanks go to the professionals in the International Association for Human Resource Information Management (IHRIM) and the Society for Human Resource Management (SHRM) who patiently listened and responded to our ideas regarding this book. We would also like to thank Lisa Shaw for the understanding exhibited in her interactions with us as well as her suggestions for resolving technical issues we encountered in writing the book. Also, thanks to MaryAnn Vail for her guidance and patience during this long process. Finally, we would like to thank Eve Oettinger, and especially Karen Taylor, for correcting our grammar as needed and finding those mistyped words and grammatical errors that were done by gremlins.

In particular, we would like to thank our families, who provided the warmth and support we needed when frustration and writer's block crept in!

—Michael J. Kavanagh, Mohan Thite, and Richard D. Johnson

NOTE

1. HRIS is sometimes referred to as human resource management systems (HRMS). We feel the terms are synonymous.

REFERENCES

Kavanagh, M. J., Gueutal, H. G., & Tannenbaum, S. I. (1990). *Human resource information systems: Development and application*. Boston: PWS-Kent.

Kavanagh, M. J., & Thite, M. (2009). *Human resource information systems: Basics, applications, and future directions*. Thousand Oaks, CA: Sage.

PART I

INTRODUCTION TO HUMAN RESOURCE MANAGEMENT AND HUMAN RESOURCE INFORMATION SYSTEMS

Chapter 1

Evolution of Human Resource Management and Human Resource Information Systems

The Role of Information Technology

Mohan Thite, Michael J. Kavanagh, and Richard D. Johnson

EDITORS' NOTE

The purpose of this chapter is to provide an introduction to the fields of **human resource management (HRM)** and information technology **(IT)** and to the combination of these two fields into human resource information systems **(HRIS)**. The history of the field of HRM and the impact of computer technology on HRM will be covered, as well as the advent of using a human resource information system and the subsequent effects on both HR and IT professionals. The different types of HR activities will be discussed as well as the different types of information systems used in HRIS. A central focus of this chapter is the use in *managerial decision making* of results and reports from an HRIS. The development of the HRIS field has been seen to have a significant impact on the emergence of strategic human resource management (Strategic HRM), as is discussed in this chapter. This first chapter will lay the groundwork for the remainder of this book, and, consequently, it is important to understand thoroughly the concepts and ideas it presents. This chapter contains definitions for a number of terms in common use in the HRM, IT, and HRIS fields. (Note that a glossary defining these terms is also provided at the back of this book.) The central themes of this book in terms of the development, implementation, and use of an HRIS will also be discussed. A **model of organizational functioning** that shows the relationship of human resources management to the strategic planning of an organization with an emphasis on the use of an HRIS will be covered too. An overview of the entire book will be presented here as well, one discussing how each chapter is an integral part of the entire field of HRIS. Finally, you should note that the "Key Terms" used in this chapter are in bold and contained in a section after the chapter "Summary." The pattern of sections for this chapter will be consistent for all chapters of this book.

CHAPTER OBJECTIVES

After completing this chapter, you should be able to

- Describe the historical evolution of HRM, including the changing role of the human resources (HR) professional
- Discuss the impact of the development of computer technology on the evolution of HRM and HRIS
- Describe the three types of HR activities
- Explain the purpose and nature of an HRIS as well as the differences between the types of information systems functionality in an HRIS
- Discuss how the information from an HRIS can assist in decision making in organizations
- Discuss how the developments in HRIS have led to HRM becoming a strategic partner in organizations and to the emergence of the field of strategic human resource management (Strategic HRM)
- Be able to define Six Sigma, balanced scorecard, and the contingency perspective and fit model of HRM
- Describe the differences between e-HRM and HRIS
- Describe the central themes of the book and how they relate to managerial decision making
- Understand how HRM and HRIS fit within a comprehensive model of organizational functioning

HRIS IN ACTION

Situation Description

To illustrate the importance and use of HRIS in contemporary HR departments, this vignette examines the typical memoranda that may appear in the in-box of HR professionals and managers. Assume you are the HR director of a medium-size organization that primarily maintains and uses manual HR records and systems. This morning, your inbox contains the following memos that require action today.

Memo 1: A note from the legal department indicates that some female staff members have filed an employment discrimination complaint with the local government agency responsible for the enforcement of equal opportunity employment. The female staff members allege that, for the past 10 years, they have been passed over for promotion because they are women. In order to respond to this allegation, the legal department requires historical data on the promotions of both males and females for the past 10 years for all jobs in the company broken down by department. It also needs the training records for all managers involved in personnel actions, such as promotions, to ascertain whether or not they have received training in equal employment provisions, especially in terms of unfair gender discrimination.

Memo 2: The second item is a complaint from employees working in a remote location of the company, about 150 miles away. The employees are complaining that their pay slips are not reaching them on time and that they are finding it difficult to get timely and accurate information on the most recent leave and benefits policies of the company.

Memo 3: A letter from the marketing manager states that he has not received any updated information on the status of his request, made three months ago, to recruit a new salesperson. The failure to recruit and hire a new salesperson has had a negative effect on the overall sales of the company's products over the past quarter.

Memo 4: A letter from the HR professional in charge of the southwest regional office says that she is swamped with HR administrative work, particularly personnel transactions on employees. As a result, she has not been able to meet employees in her region to describe and begin to implement the recent Employee Engagement Initiative as required by corporate headquarters.

Memo 5: A note from one of the production managers indicates that he has received a resignation letter from a highly regarded production engineer. She is resigning because she has not received the training on new technology that she was promised when hired. She notes that most of the other production engineers have attended this training program and have had very positive reactions to it.

Memo 6: A strongly worded note from the director of finance asks the HR department to justify the increasing costs associated with its operation. The note indicates that the HR director needs to develop a business plan for the overall operation of the HR department to include business plans for all of the HR programs, such as recruiting and training. Further, the finance director indicates that unless the business cases can demonstrate a positive **cost-benefit ratio**, the budget for the HR department will be reduced, which will lead to reductions in the HR department professional staff.

As the HR director, your first thought may be to resign since searching for the information required by these memos in the manual records on employees will require several days if not weeks to complete. However, you have just returned from a professional conference sponsored by the Society for Human Resources Management (SHRM) and remember how an HRIS may be what you need! As this chapter and the ones that follow will illustrate, an HRIS enables an HR department to streamline its activities and the demands placed on it by automating the HR data and processes necessary for the management of the **human capital** of the organization. This automation helps develop the capabilities to produce information and reports on the requests contained in the memos in the vignette, and these reports will facilitate efficient and effective managerial decision making. While an HRIS cannot make the judgement calls in terms of whom to recruit or promote, it can certainly facilitate better inputting, integration, and use of employee data, which will reduce the administrative burden of keeping detailed records and should aid and enhance decisions about strategic directions.

Need for an HRIS in Decision Situations

If you read the above memos again, you will recognize that each one has a request for HRM information that will be used in a decision situation. The information requested in Memo I will help the legal department determine the company's potential liability in a workplace gender discrimination situation. This information may help to determine whether the company should decide to rectify the situation in terms of an informal settlement with the female staff members or to defend the company's promotion procedures as valid—in court if necessary. The information required in Memo 2 may help the HR department decide to change its payroll procedures as well as its distribution of benefits information to remote company locations. The information needed to respond to Memo 3 will impact decisions by the HR department to change recruitment and selection programs. Obviously, the response to Memo 4 would greatly support the need for the acquisition of an HRIS. The information required to answer Memo 5 may help in decisions regarding the revision of recruiting and training procedures, especially for new engineers. The information that would be provided in response to Memo 6 will help decide the future of the HR department. As you go through this book, look at information on the capabilities of various human resource information systems, trying to find an HRIS that would allow you (as the HR director) to respond to each of the six memos in one day.

INTRODUCTION

Leading management thinkers suggest that "it is not technology, but the art of human- and humane-management" that is the continuing challenge for executives in the 21st century (Drucker, Dyson, Handy, Saffo, & Senge, 1997). Similarly, Smith and Kelly (1997) believe that "future economic and strategic advantage will rest with the organizations that can most effectively attract, develop and retain a diverse group of the best and the brightest human talent in the market place" (p. 200).

To maintain a competitive advantage in the marketplace, firms need to balance the resources available to the firm to achieve the desired results of profitability and survival. The resources that are available to the firm fall into three general categories: physical, organizational, and human. In discussing how to gain a competitive advantage in the global market, Porter (1990) notes that management of the human resources in the global economy is the most critical of the three. The idea of treating human resources as a means of gaining a competitive advantage in both the domestic and the global marketplace has been echoed by other authors. As Greer (1995) states,

> In a growing number of organizations human resources are now viewed as a source of competitive advantage. There is greater recognition that distinctive competencies are obtained through highly developed employee skills, distinctive organizational cultures, management processes, and systems. This is in contrast to the traditional emphasis on transferable resources such as equipment. . . . Increasingly, it is being recognized that competitive advantage can be obtained with a high quality work force that enables organizations to compete on the basis of market responsiveness, product and service quality, differentiated products, and technological innovation. (p. 105)

The effective management of human resources in a firm to gain a competitive advantage in the marketplace requires *timely and accurate information* on current employees and potential employees in the labor market. With the evolution of computer technology, meeting this information requirement has been greatly enhanced through the creation of HRIS. A basic assumption behind this book is that the effective management of employee information for decision makers will be the critical process that helps a firm maximize the use of its human resources and maintain competitiveness in its market.

The first purpose of this book is to provide information on the *development, implementation, and maintenance* of an HRIS. The second purpose is to demonstrate *how an HRIS can be used in traditional HRM programs,* such as in selecting and training employees, to make these programs more efficient and effective. The final purpose is to emphasize how an HRIS can provide timely and accurate employee information to assist decision makers at both the strategic and operational levels in an organization. As a consequence, the quality of employee information will have a strong effect on the overall effectiveness of the organization.

HISTORICAL EVOLUTION OF HRM AND HRIS

One can analyze the historical trends of the HR function from different viewpoints: the evolution of HRM (human resources management) as a professional and scientific discipline, as an aid to management, as a political and economic conflict between management and employees, and as a growing movement of employee involvement influenced by developments in industrial, organizational, and social psychology. The historical analysis that follows will demonstrate the growing importance of employees from being just one of the replaceable parts in organizations in the 20th-century industrial economy to being a key source of sustainable competitive advantage in the 21st-century knowledge economy.

Since this is a book on HRIS, we will examine the development of the fields of both human resources and information technology in terms of their evolution since the early 20th century. This means examining the evolution of HRM intertwined with developments in IT and describing how IT has played an increasing role in the HRM function. This historical analysis will show how the role of HRM in the firm has changed over time from primarily being concerned with routine **transactional and traditional HR activities** to dealing with complex transformational ones. Transactional activities are the routine bookkeeping tasks—for example, changing an employee's home address or health care provider. Traditional HR activities are focused on HR programs like selection, compensation, and performance appraisal. However, **transformational HR activities** are those actions of an organization that "add value" to the consumption of the firm's product or service. An example of a transformational HR activity would be a training program for retail clerks to improve customer service behavior, which has been identified as a strategic goal for the organization. Thus, transformational activities increase the strategic importance and visibility of the HR function in the firm. This general change over time is illustrated in Figure 1.1 and will become evident as we trace the historical evolution of HRM in terms of five broad phases of the historical development of industry in the United States. For more information on this historical development, you should consult Kavanagh, Gueutal, and Tannenbaum (1990) or Walker (1982).

Figure 1.1 Historical Evolution of HRM

Role of HRM	
Early 20th Century	*21st Century*
Caretaker	Strategic partner
→	
Employee focus Records	Cost-effectiveness Employee development

Pre–World War II

In the early 20th century and prior to World War II, the personnel function (the precursor of human resources management) was primarily involved in clerical record keeping of employee information; in other words, it fulfilled a "**caretaker" function**. During this period, the prevailing management philosophy was called "**scientific management**." The central thrust of scientific management was to maximize employee productivity. It was thought that there was *one best way* to do any work, and this best way was determined through time and motion studies that investigated the most efficient use of human capabilities in the production process. Then, the work could be divided into pieces, and the number of tasks to be completed by a worker during an average workday could be computed. These findings formed the basis of piece-rate pay systems, which were seen as the most efficient way to motivate employees at that time.

At this point in history, there were very few government influences in employment relations; consequently, employment terms, practices, and conditions were left to the owners of the firm. As a result, abuses such as child labor and unsafe working conditions were common. Some employers set up labor welfare and administration departments to look after the interests of workers by maintaining records on health and safety as well as recording hours worked and payroll. It is interesting to note that record keeping is one of the major functions built into the design of an HRIS today; however, there simply was no computer technology to automate the records at this time in history. Of course, paper records were kept, and we can still see paper record HR systems in many smaller firms today.

Post–World War II (1945–1960)

The mobilization and utilization of labor during the war had a great impact on the development of the personnel function. Managers realized that employee productivity and motivation had a significant impact on the profitability of the firm. The human relations movement after the war emphasized that employees were motivated not just by money but also by social and psychological factors, such as receiving recognition for work accomplished or for the achievement of work norms.

Due to the need for the classification of large numbers of individuals in military service during the war, systematic efforts began to classify workers around occupational categories in order to improve recruitment and selection procedures. The central aspect of these classification systems was the *job description,* which listed the tasks, duties, and responsibilities of any individual who held the job in question. These job description classification systems could also be used to design appropriate compensation programs, evaluate individual employee performance, and provide a basis for termination.

Because of the abusive worker practices prior to the war, employees started forming trade unions, which played an important role in bargaining for better employment terms and conditions. There were significant numbers of employment laws enacted in the United States that allowed the **establishment of labor unions** and defined their scope in relationship with management. Thus, personnel departments had to assume considerably more record keeping and reporting to governmental agencies. Because of these trends, the personnel department had to establish specialist divisions, such as recruitment, labor relations, training and benefits, and government relations.

With its changing and expanding role, the typical personnel department started keeping increasing numbers and types of employee records, and computer technology began to emerge as a possible way to store and retrieve employee information. In some cases in the defense industry, **job analysis** and classification data were inputted into computers to better understand, plan, and use employee skills against needs. For example, the U.S. Air Force conducted a thorough and systematic job analysis and classification through its Air Force Human Resources Laboratory (AFHRL), which resulted in a comprehensive occupational structure. The AFHRL collected data from thousands in jobs within the Air Force, and, through the use of a computer software program called the **Comprehensive Occupational Data Analysis Program (CODAP)**, it was able to establish more accurately a **job description** classification system for Air Force jobs.

Personnel departments outside the defense industry were not using computers at this time. Computers were being used for billing and inventory control, but there was very little use for them in the personnel function except for payroll. The payroll function was the first to be automated. Large firms began harvesting the benefits of new computer technology to keep track of employee compensation, but this function was usually outsourced to vendors since it was still extremely expensive for a firm to acquire or develop the necessary software for the payroll function. It was simpler to outsource this function. It is important to realize that computer technology was just beginning to be used at this time, and it was complex and costly. With increasing legislation on employment relations and employee unionization, industrial relations became one of the main foci of the personnel department. Union-management bargaining over employment contracts dominated the activity of the department, and these negotiations were not computer based. Record keeping was still done manually despite the growing use of computerized data processing in other departments, such as accounts and materials management. What resulted was an initial reluctance among personnel departments to acquire and use computer technology for their programs. This had a long-term effect in many firms when it came to adopting advancements in computer technology, even though this technology got cheaper and easier to use.

Social Issues Era (1963–1980)

This period witnessed an unprecedented increase in the amount of labor legislation in the United States, legislation that governed various parts of the employment relationship, such as the prohibition of discriminatory practices, the promotion of occupational health and safety, the provision of retirement benefits, and tax regulation. As a result, the personnel department was burdened with the additional responsibility of **legislative compliance** that required collection, analysis, and reporting of voluminous data to statutory authorities. For example, to demonstrate that there was no unfair discrimination in employment practices, a personnel department had to diligently collect, analyze, and store data pertaining to *all* employment functions, such as recruitment, training, compensation, and benefits. To avoid the threat of punitive damages for noncompliance, it had to ensure that the data were comprehensive, accurate, and up-to-date, which made it essential to automate the data collection, analysis, and report generation process. As you go through the chapters of this book, these varying laws and government guidelines will be covered within the specific HR topics.

It was about this time that personnel departments were beginning to be called human resources departments and the field of human resource management was born. The increasing need to be in compliance with numerous employee protection laws or suffer significant monetary penalties made senior managers aware of the importance of the HRM function. In other words, effective and correct practices in HRM were starting to affect the "bottom line" of the firms, so there was a significant growth of HR departments, and computer technology had advanced to the point where it was beginning to be used. As a result, there was an increasing demand for HR departments to adopt computer technology to process employee information more effectively and efficiently. This trend resulted in an explosion in the number of vendors who could assist HR departments in automating their programs in terms of both hardware and software.

Simultaneously, computer technology was evolving and delivering better productivity at lower costs. These technology developments and increased vendor activity led to the development of a comprehensive **management information system (MIS)** for HRM. The decreasing costs of computer technology versus the increasing costs of employee compensation and benefits made the acquisition of computer-based HR systems (HRIS) a necessary business decision. However, the personnel departments were still slow in adopting computer technology, even though it was inexpensive relative to the power it could deliver for the storage and retrieval of employee information in MIS reports. So, the major issue at this time in the historical development of HRIS was not the need for or capabilities of technology but how to best implement it.

Another factor was the booming economy in most industrialized countries. As a result, employee trade unions successfully bargained for better employment terms, such as health care and retirement benefits. Consequently, labor costs increased, which put pressure on personnel managers to justify cost increases against productivity improvements. With the increased emphasis on employee participation and empowerment, the personnel function transformed into a "protector" rather than a "caretaker" function, shifting the focus away from maintenance to development of employees. Thus, the breadth and depth of HRM functions expanded, bringing about the need for strategic thinking and better delivery of HR services.

Cost-Effectiveness Era (1980 to the Early 1990s)

With increasing competition from emerging European and Asian economies, U.S. and other multinational firms increased their focus on cost reduction through automation and other productivity improvement measures. As regards HRM, the increased administrative burden intensified the need to fulfill a growing number of legislative requirements, while the overall functional focus shifted from employee administration to employee development and involvement. To improve effectiveness and efficiency in service delivery through cost reduction and value-added services, the HR departments came under pressure to harness technology that was becoming cheaper and more powerful.

In addition, there was a growing realization within management that people costs were a very significant part of a company's budget. Some companies estimated that personnel costs were as high as 80% of their operating costs. As a result, there was a growing demand on the HRM function to cost justify their employee programs and services. In one of the first books to address this growing need to cost justify the HRM function, Cascio (1984) indicates that the language of business is dollars and cents, and HR managers need to realize this fact. In a later edition of his book, Cascio (1991) quotes Jacques Fitz-enz (1980), who more accurately states the need for those responsible for human resource management to cost justify their function:

> Few human resource managers—even the most energetic—take the time to analyze the return on the corporation's personnel dollar. We feel we aren't valued in our own organizations, that we can't get the resources we need. We

complain that management won't buy our proposals and wonder why our advice is so often ignored until the crisis stage. But the human resources manager seldom stands back to look at the total business and ask: Why am I at the bottom looking up? The answer is painfully apparent. We don't act like business managers—like entrepreneurs whose business happens to be people. (Fitz-enz, 1980, p. 41)

Even small and medium firms could afford computer-based HR systems that were run by increasingly user-friendly microcomputers and could be shown to be cost-effective. The prevailing management thinking regarding the use of computers in HR was not that their use would result in a reduction in the number of employees needed in HR departments but that employee activities and time could be shifted from transactional record keeping to more transformational activities that would add value to the organization. This change in the function of HRM could then be clearly measured in terms of cost-benefit ratios to the "bottom line" of the company.

Technological Advancement Era and the Emergence of Strategic HRM (1990 to Present)

The economic landscape underwent radical changes throughout the 1990s with increasing globalization, technological breakthroughs (particularly **Internet-enabled Web services**), and hyper competition. Business process reengineering exercises became more common and frequent, resulting in several initiatives, such as the rightsizing of employee numbers, reducing the layers of management, reducing the bureaucracy of organizational structures, creating autonomous work teams, and outsourcing.

Firms today realize that innovative and creative employees who hold the key to organizational knowledge provide a sustainable competitive advantage because, unlike other resources, intellectual capital is difficult for competitors to imitate. Accordingly, the people management function has become strategic in its importance and outlook and is geared to attract, retain, and engage talent. These developments have led to the creation of the **HR balanced scorecard** (Becker, Huselid, & Ulrich, 2001; Huselid, Becker, & Beatty, 2005), as well as to added emphasis on the return on investment (ROI) of the HR function and its programs (Cascio, 2000; Fitz-enz, 2000, 2002).

The increased use of technology and the changed focus of the HRM function, which shifted to adding value to the organization's product or service, led to the emergence of the HR department as a strategic partner. With the growing importance and recognition of people and people management in contemporary organizations,

strategic human resource management (Strategic HRM) has become critically important in management thinking and practice. Strategic HRM derives its theoretical significance from the resources-based view of the firm that treats *human capital* as a strategic asset and a competitive advantage in improving organizational performance (Becker & Huselid, 2006).

Reflecting the resource-based view, Becker and Huselid (2006) stress the importance of HR systems and structure—that is, the "systems, practices, competencies, and employee performance behaviors that reflect the development and management of the firm's strategic human capital"—for organizational performance (p. 899). Context is a crucial element in Strategic HRM, and, therefore, researchers increasingly emphasize the **"best-fit" approach to Strategic HRM** as opposed to the **"best-practice" approach to Strategic HRM**. The success of Strategic HRM is contingent on several factors, such as national and organizational culture, size, industry type, occupational category, and business strategy. Accordingly, Becker and Huselid (2006) argue that "it is the fit between the HR architecture and the strategic capabilities and business processes that implement strategy that is the basis of HR's contribution to competitive advantage" (p. 899).

A good example of the importance of HR and the information provided by an HRIS can be found in the **human resources planning (HRP)** function, which will be covered in greater detail in Chapter 11. HRP is primarily concerned with forecasting the need for additional employees in the future and the availability of those employees either inside or external to the company. Imagine, for example, that a company is considering a strategic decision to expand by establishing a production facility in a new location. Using the information recorded and analyzed in the HRIS, HRP can provide estimates of whether or not there are enough people available with the necessary skills in the external labor market of the new location to staff the new facility. Determining the availability of potential employees in the labor market may be critical to the strategic decision to build the new facility, and this, of course, could involve millions or billons of dollars.

In tracing the evolution of strategic HRM (Strategic HRM), M. L. Lengnick-Hall, C. A. Lengnick-Hall, Andrade, and Drake (2009) identify seven key themes:

- **HR contingency perspective** and fit: HR strategies are dependent on business strategies (cost reduction, quality improvement, and innovation) and business settings (manufacturing, services, public sector, and not for profit, as well as firm size)
- Shift in focus from managing people to creating strategic contributions, signifying the resource-based view of the firm and social capital
- HR system components and structure, focusing on HR system architecture and bundles of high-performance work practices

- Expanding the scope of HRM beyond the focal organization to include customers, suppliers, and competitors, both locally and internationally
- Achieving HR implementation and execution by translating the rhetoric into practice
- Measuring the outcomes of Strategic HRM by various means, such as the HR balanced scorecard approach
- Research methodological issues that stress the importance of evidence-based management

Another critical characteristic of Strategic HRM is the adoption and use of **HR metrics** (Lawler & Mohrman, 2003; also see Chapter 6). The focus on cost effectiveness, discussed in the previous section and covered in detail in Chapter 7, not only has continued to the present time but has broadened and deepened further with increasing global competitiveness. Kaplan and Norton (1996) first popularized the concept of the *balanced scorecard* that goes beyond traditional financial measures to assess firm performance to include customer, internal process, and learning perspectives. Lawler, Levenson, and Boudreau (2004) emphasize that three types of metrics are important to evaluate the HR function—*efficiency* of administrative tasks, *effectiveness* of HR practices, and *impact* in terms of the overall objective of developing and optimizing workforce capabilities and competencies. Incorporating the principles of the balanced scorecard approach, Beatty, Huselid, and Schneier (2003) developed the "HR Balanced Scorecard" that seeks to achieve the key HR deliverables (workforce mindset, technical knowledge, and workforce behavior) by aligning, integrating, and differentiating the HR systems.

The most recent development related to the role of HRM in Strategic HRM has been the application of HRIS-enabled "**Six Sigma**" processes to HRM. Most professionals associate Six Sigma with General Electric, as the company was the first major user of the Six Sigma approach. In general, Six Sigma refers to streamlining operations through business process reengineering and has been structured around five key processes—define, measure, analyze, improve, and control (DMAIC). The DMAIC approach uses an assortment of statistical tools to reengineer business processes, improve decision making, and improve customer service. Six Sigma will be discussed in Chapter 8.

As we will see in the ensuing chapters, information technology is a key enabler of Strategic HRM (Haines & Lafleur, 2008). However, in determining the strategic fit between technology and HR, it is *not the strategy per se that leads to competitive advantage but rather how well it is "implemented,"* taking into account the environmental realities that can be unique to each organization and, indeed, between units and functions of the organization. A critical aspect of an HRIS in supporting the implementation of strategic plans is using it to make decisions about employees, human capital programs, and initiatives. All of these HRM decisions are aided by the ability of the HRIS to generate reports, for example, the number of new employees needed for a specific job. Thus, in the section entitled "A Primer on HRIS" later in this chapter, you will note the generation of reports to be a key benefit of an HRIS. HRM reports are central to decisions involving the human capital of an organization, and they enable the translation of strategic plans to operational decisions. As you go through the chapters in this book, you will see how reports are used in a variety of HRM programs and activities.

HR ACTIVITIES

Typical HR programs involve things such as record keeping, recruiting, selection, training, employee relations, and compensation. However, all these programs involve multiple activities, and these HR activities can be classified into three broad categories: transactional, traditional, and transformational (Wright, McMahan, Snell, & Gerhart, 1998). Transactional activities involve day-to-day transactions that have to deal mostly with record keeping—for example, entering payroll information, tracking employee status changes, and the administration of employee benefits. Traditional activities involve HR programs such as planning, recruiting, selection, training, compensation, and performance management. These activities can have strategic value for the organization if their results or outcomes are consistent with the strategic goals of the organization. Transformational activities are those activities that add value to the organization—for example, cultural or organizational change, structural realignment, strategic redirection, and increasing innovation.

Wright et al. (1998) estimate that most HR departments spend approximately 65% to 75% on transactional activities, 15% to 30% on traditional activities, and 5% to 15% on transformational activities. One of the major purposes of the design, development, and implementation of an HRIS is to reduce the amount of time HR employees have to spend on transactional activities, allowing the staff to spend more time on traditional and transformational activities. This notion of using technology to improve transactional activities and accomplish them more efficiently is the central theme of this book and provides one of the primary justifications for a computer-based system. In later chapters that discuss various HR programs such as selection and training, we will see how a computer-based system can aid in both traditional and transformational activities to make them consistent with the strategic goals of the organization.

In terms of the broad roles of HR, Ulrich (1998) identifies four main roles, namely, strategic business partner, administrative expert, employee champion, and change agent. Ulrich, Younger, and Brockbank (2008) stress that, in the 21st century, the HR organization should function as a business within a business, shifting its focus from activities to outcomes and capabilities and its structure so that it mirrors that of the business.

INTERFACE BETWEEN HR AND TECHNOLOGY

Technology-driven automation (IT) and the redesign of work processes certainly help reduce costs and cycle times as well as improve quality. Information systems (IS) can further help decision makers to make and implement strategic decisions. However, IT is only a tool and can only complement, not substitute for, the people who use it. Often, organizations mistake IT as a message and not the messenger, so they divert time, effort, and money away from a long-term investment in people to developing and deploying information technologies (Thite, 2004). In fact, the critical success factors in information systems project implementation are non-technical and are due more to social and managerial issues (Martinsons & Chong, 1999). This topic is covered in detail in Chapters 8 and 9.

With the increasing use of information technologies in HR planning and delivery, the way people in organizations look at the nature and role of HR itself may change (Roehling et al., 2005). With HR data and reports now readily available on their desktops, will managers interact less with the HR department and see it as being less important? If that is so, how will it affect the attitude of HR professionals toward their jobs and profession? Will they resist the adoption of technology if they perceive that this technology lessens their status?

In traditional organizations with silo mentalities, turf wars between operational departments and functions acting as independent entities are common. Therefore, top management needs to be mindful of organizational politics in managing change. This awareness can be particularly important when developing and implementing an HRIS. Through most of its evolution, HRM has had an administrative and caretaker focus in its delivery, and, even today, this administrative and caretaker focus is important. But, with technology significantly decreasing the time required for administrative tasks, HR departments will begin to allocate resources to more complex, strategic, and transformative activities. Through these changes, the role of HRM is redefined and transformed through value-added, strategic initiatives and interventions. This also means that HR professionals will need to learn new skills and rethink the way the HR department is organized and delivers its services. With the improved job skills of HR professionals, technology will be seen as HR's "partner in progress." While having an advanced, full-fledged system will not automatically make HR a strategic business partner, this system acts as a building block and an effective aid in the process (Lawler & Mohrman, 2003).

A PRIMER ON HRIS

What Is an HRIS?

After reviewing the many definitions of an HRIS, Kavanagh et al. (1990) define it as a

> system used to acquire, store, manipulate, analyze, retrieve, and distribute information regarding an organization's human resources. An HRIS is not simply computer hardware and associated HR-related software. Although an HRIS includes hardware and software, it also includes people, forms, policies and procedures, and data. (p. 29)

It is important to note that a company that does not have a computerized system still has an HRM system on paper. The paper systems that most companies used before the development of computer technology were still comparable with an HRIS, but the management of employee information was not done as quickly as in a computerized system. If these companies had not had paper systems, the development and implementation of computerized systems would have been extremely difficult. For the purpose of this book, however, we will use the term *HRIS* to refer to a computerized system designed to manage the company's HR.

The primary purpose of the HRIS is to provide service, in the form of *accurate and timely information,* to the "clients" of the system. There are a variety of potential clients, as HR information may be used for strategic, tactical, and operational decision making (e.g., planning for needed employees in a merger); to avoid litigation (e.g., identifying discrimination problems in hiring); to evaluate programs, policies, or practices (e.g., evaluating the effectiveness of a training program); and to support daily operations (e.g., helping managers monitor the work time and attendance of their employees). All these uses mean that there is a mandatory requirement that data and reports be accurate and timely and that the "client" can understand how to use the information.

Because of the complexity and data intensiveness of the HRM function, it is one of the last management functions to be targeted for automation (Bussler & Davis, 2001/2002). This fact does not mean that an HRIS is not important; it just indicates the difficulty of developing and implementing it compared with other business functions—for example, the billing and accounting systems. Powered by information systems and the Internet, almost every process in every function of HRM has been computerized today.

The systems and process focus helps organizations keep the customer perspective in mind, since quality is primarily defined and operationalized in terms of total customer satisfaction (Evans, 2005). Today's competitive environment requires organizations to integrate the activities of each functional department while keeping the customer in mind. An effective HRIS helps by providing the technology to generate accurate and timely employee information to fulfill this objective.

e-HRM and HRIS

Confusion can arise concerning the distinction between e-HRM and HRIS. Electronic human resource management, or e-HRM, reflects a philosophy for the delivery of HR; it uses information technology, particularly the Web, as the central component of delivering efficient and effective HR services. This philosophy can be best seen through the words of Gueutal and Stone (2005): "Things will look a bit different here. No longer will you deal with an HR professional. . . . The HR portal will take care of you" (p. xv). Essentially, technology becomes the nerve center for disseminating, connecting, and conducting human resources (Strohmeier, 2007). Organizations embracing an e-HRM approach don't simply utilize technology in the support of human resources but instead see technology as enabling the HR function to be done differently by modifying "information flows, social interaction patterns, and communication processes" (Stone & Lukaszewski, 2009, p. 136).

Conversely, as conceptualized in this book, an HRIS comprises the technology and processes underlying this new way of conducting human resource management. An HRIS can include technologies such as databases, small functional systems focused on a single HR application (e.g., performance management), or a large-scale, integrated **enterprise resource planning (ERP) architecture** and Web-based applications. In today's environment, it can even be devices such as smart phones and social networking sites that enable employees to access HR data remotely or to connect with others in the organization.

Another way of looking at the differences between e-HRM and HRIS is that e-HRM tends to be more application and HR-function focused (e.g., e-recruitment and e-training), and an HRIS is more focused on the systems and technology underlying the design and acquisition of systems supporting the move to e-HRM. Thus, issues such as needs analysis (Chapter 4), cost-benefit analysis (Chapter 7), and the entire cycle of HRIS implementation and post-implementation, including project management (Chapter 8) and change management (Chapter 9), should be addressed when implementing an HRIS.

Why Do We Need HRIS?

Using HRIS gives firms several advantages (Beckers & Bsat, 2002). They include the following:

- Providing a comprehensive information picture as a single, integrated database; this enables organizations to provide structural connectivity across units and activities and to increase the speed of information transactions (Lengnick-Hall & Lengnick-Hall, 2006)
- Increasing competitiveness by improving HR operations and management processes
- Collecting appropriate data and converting them to information and knowledge for improved timeliness and quality of decision making
- Producing a greater number and variety of accurate and real-time HR-related reports
- Streamlining and enhancing the efficiency and effectiveness of HR administrative functions
- Shifting the focus of HR from the processing of transactions to strategic HRM
- Reengineering HR processes and functions
- Improving employee satisfaction by delivering HR services more quickly and accurately

The ability of firms to harness the potential of HRIS depends on a variety of factors, such as

- the size of the organization, with large firms generally reaping greater benefits;
- the amount of top management support and commitment;
- the availability of resources (time, money, and personnel);
- the HR philosophy of the company as well as its vision, organizational culture, structure, and systems;
- managerial competence in cross-functional decision making, employee involvement, and coaching; and
- the ability and motivation of employees in adopting change, such as increased automation across and between functions (Ngai & Wat, 2004).

In assessing the benefits and impact of an HRIS to an organization, typical accounting methods do not work with the HRM function (Becker et al., 2001; Cascio, 2000; Fitz-enz, 2000, 2002; Huselid et al., 2005; Thite, 2004; Ulrich & Smallwood, 2005). While there are several tangible benefits in implementing an HRIS, such as payroll efficiencies and a reduction in labor costs due to automation, there are several intangible or hidden benefits as well (Roberts, 1999). They include employee satisfaction with streamlined and efficient HR processes and freeing up HR from routine, administrative matters to focus on strategic goals.

Furthermore, HR practices can help organizations untangle the rigidity and inertia associated with the mechanistic, routine nature of enterprise resource planning (ERP). ERP software applications are a set of integrated database applications or modules that carry out the most common business functions, including HR, general ledger, accounts payable, accounts receivable, order management, inventory control, and customer relationship management. Obviously, HRM's emphasis on knowledge management, human capital stewardship, and relationship building can provide considerable assistance in the implementation and use of ERPs (Lengnick-Hall & Lengnick-Hall, 2006). Therefore, active engagement of HR professionals in the introduction and ongoing functioning of an ERP is important so that organizations can realize the strategic benefits associated with these systems (Dery & Wailes, 2005).

Different Types of HRIS

Although there are multiple typologies for the classification of computer-based systems, we are going to define the most basic types of systems that are most readily applied to the HR context and for use within an HRIS. Although there are many ways of categorizing information systems, one of the most common ways of doing this is to focus on what level of organizational processing the system supports: daily operations, managerial functioning, executive level processes and strategies, and those that span organizational levels. Table 1.1 catalogs the major types of information systems, lists their major focus and goals, and provides examples of how they can be used to support human resources.

As seen in Table 1.1, specific computer-based systems have been created to support HRM at different organizational levels with applications for HRM. Although large, global organizations have likely implemented most, if not all, of these types of systems, it would be unusual for small to midsized organizations to have the resources to do so. Despite this, most organizations would have some of these systems in place and would depend on them to support operations and decision making. As you go through this book, these systems and their HR examples will be discussed, and you should refer back to this table as needed.

System Development Process for an HRIS

According to engineering and information processing literature, the formal design of any information processing system is supposed to follow a set of steps labeled the **system development life cycle (SDLC)**. However, as Sprague and Carlson (1982) and other writers (Aktas, 1987; Davis, 1983) have noted, the traditional SDLC is somewhat difficult to use as originally specified. But there is agreement

Table 1.1 Information Systems Providing Support for HRM

Organizational Level	*Type of System*	*Major Goals and Focus*	*HRM Examples*
Operational	Transaction Processing System	Improved transaction speed and accuracy Improved efficiency in the processing of daily business transactions Automation of routine transactions Reduced transaction costs	Payroll processing Time and attendance entry Online creation and dissemination of application forms
Managerial	Management Information System	Provides key data to managers Supports regular and ongoing decisions Provides defined and ad-hoc reporting	Producing EE03 reports Calculating yield ratios for recruiting Calculating per-capita merit increases
Executive	Executive Information System	Provides aggregate, high-level data Helps managers with long-range planning Supports strategic direction and decisions	Succession planning Aggregate data on balanced scorecard
Boundary Spanning	Decision Support System	Interactive and iterative managerial decision making Supports forecasting and "what-if" analysis Supports business simulations	Staffing needs assessment Labor market analysis Employee skills assessment
	Expert System	Embed human knowledge into information systems Automate decisions with technology	Resume keyword searches
	Office Automation Systems	Designing documents Scheduling shared resources Communication	E-mail training-room scheduling

(Continued)

(Continued)

Organizational Level	*Type of System*	*Major Goals and Focus*	*HRM Examples*
	Collaboration Technologies	Supports electronic communication and collaboration between employees Supports virtual teams	Communication support for e-learning Online meetings and shared documents HR departmental wikis
	Enterprise Resources Planning System	Integration and centralization of corporate data Share data across functional boundaries Single data source and common technology architecture	OrangeHRM Oracle/PeopleSoft Lawson HRM SAP

that the SDLC has five general phases: (1) planning, (2) analysis, (3) design, (4) implementation, and (5) maintenance. As will be seen, particularly in Parts I and II of this book, there are multiple references to the SDLC and its phases.

Kavanagh et al. (1990), applying the main concepts and phases of the traditional SDLC to the HRM function, recommend the following system development process for an HRIS: "The HRIS development process refers to the steps taken from the time a company considers computerizing its human resources functions through the analysis, design, development, implementation, maintenance, evaluation, and improvement of the system" (pp. 92–93). This system development process is quite similar to the one proposed by Walker (1982). He indicates that development of an effective HRIS should follow seven stages: "Proposal to Management, Needs Analysis, System Specifications, System Design, System Development, Installation and Conversion, and Evaluation" (p. 38).

Although this book will cover all the phases in the development and implementation of an HRIS, there are two *critical* points to be emphasized from these descriptions of the phases or stages of system development. One, the system development process *begins* when the company first begins to consider computerizing its HR functions. It is important to *document* this beginning of the process so that it can be considered when the system is being evaluated and maintained. The second critical point is the *importance of the evaluation* and, as needed, the improvement of the system. This evaluation must be continuous and occur not only after the system has been implemented but also at every stage of the development. The quality of these evaluations of the system will depend heavily on the documentation of the stages of the entire system development process. The documentation of the planning and development of a system is one of the most important determinants of successful system implementation, as well as of continued system improvement.

A MODEL OF ORGANIZATIONAL FUNCTIONING

As stated in the previous paragraph, the documentation and evaluation of HRIS development and implementation are critical since we envision the effective functioning of any organization as dependent on the effective management of its employees. The use of computer technology to improve the management of employees is centered on the creation and maintenance of an HRIS. Figure 1.2 depicts a model of an organizational system centered on an HRIS. This model shows the interrelatedness of the parts of an organization that can affect the functioning of the organization. It indicates the interrelatedness between the strategic management system, the strategic HRM system, and the performance, business, and HR goals that are generated during the strategic planning process. Note particularly how the business goals directly affect the HR goals; this relationship should be an ongoing process in an organization, with adjustments made to either set of goals as needed. The HR goals drive the HR programs that provide management the tools for the efficient and effective use of employees. As will be emphasized throughout this book, the *alignment* between the strategic management system, the strategic HR management system, the business goals, the HR goals, and the HR programs is critical to the organization's maintenance of its competitiveness in the market (Evans & Davis, 2005; Huselid, Jackson, & Schuler, 1997).

There are several aspects of this model that are critical. First, this model is a framework to use in reading, organizing, and understanding the information given in this book. Second, this is a systems model; that is, it is organic and can change over time, as represented by the feedback loops from goal achievement to other parts of the model. Third, the model is centered on the use of an HRIS as critical to the efficient operation of an organization. Note that, if the HRIS were removed, it would still be a model of organizational functioning. However, it is our contention that an organization operating in accordance with this model would run more slowly and less efficiently, and this could hurt its competitiveness in the marketplace. Fourth, the HRIS and the HR program evaluation results, in terms of HR metrics and cost-benefit results (value added and **return on investment**—ROI), are in continual interaction. This emphasis is consistent with current thinking in the HRM field (Cascio, 2000; Fitz-enz, 2000, 2002) and has generated the **HR workforce scorecard** (Becker et al., 2001; Huselid et al., 2005). Finally, it is important to note that the *successful* design, development, and implementation of

Figure 1.2 Model of an Organizational System Centered on HRIS

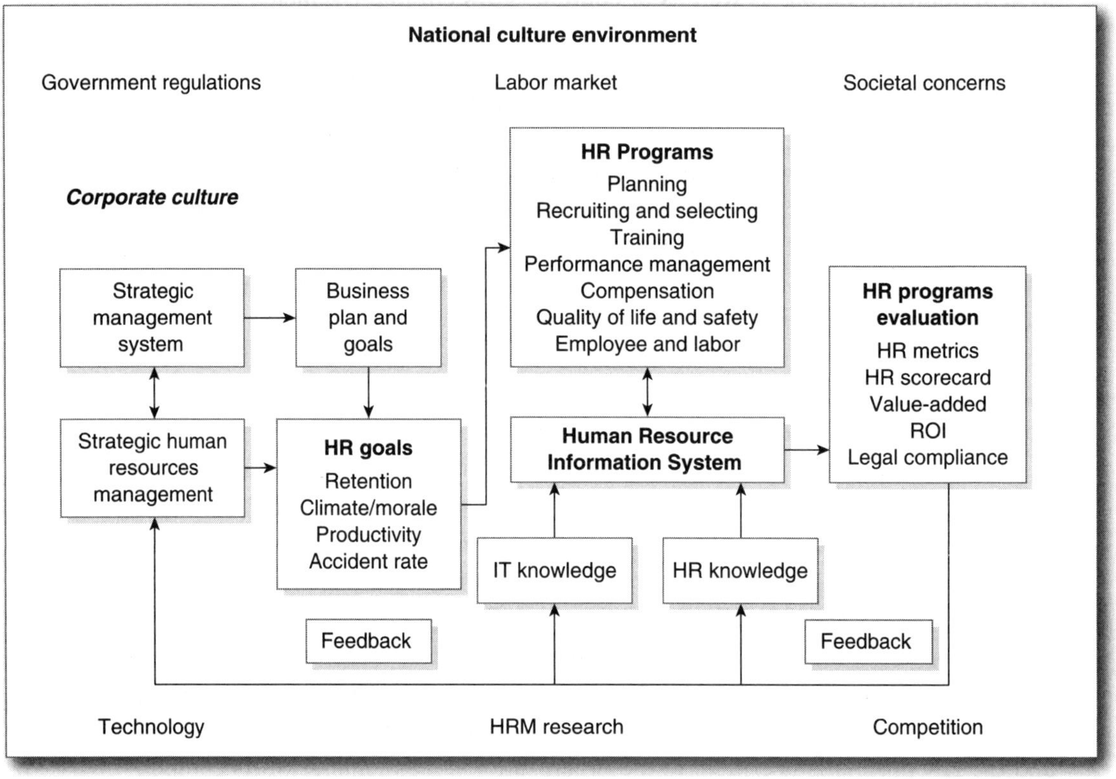

an HRIS *depend equally on IT and on HR knowledge,* which is the basic philosophy of this entire book.

Other aspects of this model are important. First, all the factors in the external environment will influence the internal functioning of the organization. The most important of these factors is national culture. National culture will affect all the factors in the external environment: government regulations, the labor market, societal concerns, technology, HRM research, and competition. These factors, in turn, will have an impact on the organization. Simple comparisons across various countries—for example, the United States, Australia, Europe, and China—on most of these six external factors would discover significant differences. We feel that these differences are important and have devoted a chapter to them (Chapter 15). Second, the two-way arrow between the strategic management system and strategic HRM indicates our understanding that this interaction will improve the functioning of the organization. Finally, note that corporate culture influences the entire internal operation of the organization. In the next section, the themes of this book that are central to the operation of this model are discussed.

THEMES OF THE BOOK

The *overall theme* of this book is that the HR and IT functions operate separately and together in an HRIS and are focused on providing accurate and timely information for managerial decisions, both strategic and operational. There are other themes that are emphasized in this book, which can also be seen in the model of organizational functioning presented in Figure 1.2. These themes are the major factors that influence the effective operation of the organization through their impact on managerial decisions. In addition, they directly affect the success of both the HRM programs and the use of the HRIS. These factors are as follows:

1. The effective alignment between the strategy of the firm, the HR strategy, and HR programs
2. The importance of legal considerations in all HR programs and functions
3. The need for a cooperative relationship between HR and IT professionals
4. The critical need for the creation and use of HR metrics to both guide decision making and evaluate the cost-effectiveness of the HR strategy and programs

All the chapters of this book will contain some reference to some or all of these factors, and their effects will be discussed in detail in the chapters.

OVERVIEW AND STRUCTURE OF THE BOOK

This book is divided into five main parts. Part I, "Introduction to Human Resource Management and Human Resource Information Systems," includes three chapters. In this first chapter, the evolution of human resource management (HRM) and its interface with information technology (IT) was covered to show how the field of human resource information systems (HRIS) emerged. In addition, a general introduction to the types of activities in which HRM engages was provided, as well as a brief introduction to the current interface between HRM and technology. Finally, a detailed description of an HRIS was provided, and the model of organizational functioning that incorporates an HRIS was discussed.

The second chapter, "Database Concepts and Applications in HRIS," by Janet Marler and Barry Floyd, is focused on understanding databases and the applications of IT on the HRIS. This is an introductory chapter, which provides a solid basis for later chapters in the book. The third chapter, "Systems Considerations in the Design of an HRIS: Planning for Implementation," by Michael Bedell, Michael Canniff, and Cheryl Wyrick, is focused on foundational knowledge that is critical for the design and subsequent implementation of an HRIS. The different types of information about the users or customers of the HRIS, the categorization of HRIS data into categories of human capital, and the main concepts of hardware and database security are covered. This chapter is also a good lead-in for the next part of the book—"Part II: Determining Human Resource Information Systems Needs."

Chapter 4, "HRIS Needs Analysis," by Bradley Alge and Karen Upright, covers the first formal analysis of the need for an HRIS in an organization. It should be noted that a needs analysis can be done for an organization that only has a paper system or for an organization that is planning to improve or update its current HRIS. In this chapter, the steps in an HRIS needs assessment are covered—namely, who is involved in the assessment and the deliverables from a comprehensive needs assessment. In Chapter 5, "System Design and Acquisition," by Richard Johnson and Jim Dulebohn, the fundamentals of system design based on the needs assessment are covered. Chapter 5 also investigates the process of acquiring a system once the design has been completed. It should be noted that the activities described in Chapters 4 and 5 always remain focused on the implementation of the HRIS since this is an important element in the success of the HRIS.

Chapters 6 and 7 deal with one of the most critical components of "determining HRIS needs," namely how to measure the effectiveness of the system after it has been implemented and how to justify the cost of developing and implementing an HRIS. Chapter 6, "HR Metrics and Workforce Analytics," by Kevin Carlson and Michael Kavanagh, covers the ways in which HRM measures its effectiveness. The emphasis in this chapter is on the main reason to engage in assessment and analytics—to improve organization effectiveness. The authors argue that HR professionals and managers like to use metrics and analytics derived from an HRIS if these result in payback, which is measured by managers making *different* and *better* decisions. Chapter 7, "Cost Justifying HRIS Investments," by Kevin Carlson and Michael Kavanagh, describes one of the most important aspects of the needs analysis, design, and development of the HRIS—cost justification of the HRIS. Without a careful analysis of the costs and benefits of an HRIS, there should not be any attempt to get approval for or implement the system. There are numerous stories and examples of failed systems that were implemented without a comprehensive needs assessment, one that includes a cost-benefit analysis. In addition, a comprehensive needs assessment will be very useful during the evaluation phase after the system has been fully implemented. The *needs assessment will define the evaluative criteria* by which to judge the success of the HRIS. Thus, this chapter is a convenient introduction to Part III of the book—"Human Resource Information Systems Implementation and Acceptance."

Chapter 8, "Project Management and HRM Advice for HRIS Implementation," by Sal Belardo and Michael Kavanagh, provides a comprehensive discussion of project management techniques and their importance to the implementation and acceptance of an HRIS. Project management provides excellent tools for ensuring that the implementation of the HRIS proceeds in an orderly fashion by establishing goals and timetables for the tasks and activities during implementation. Chapter 9, "Change Management: Implementation, Integration, and Maintenance of the HRIS," by Romuald Stone, emphasizes the people processes necessary for the successful implementation of an HRIS—a major organizational change. Although there typically will be some technical difficulties during the HRIS implementation, the major issues will be with the lack of employee and user acceptance and involvement in the implementation. Chapter 9 offers a variety of approaches to organizational change, both theoretical and practical, that can be used to focus on the behavioral aspects of the HRIS implementation.

Part IV of the book, "HRIS Applications," provides information and guidelines for the use of an HRIS in the programs involved in the operation of the HRM function. In Chapter 10, "HR Administration and HRIS," Linda Isenhour covers the administrative, transactional aspects of HRM. This chapter illustrates the fact that HRM is still a caretaker of employee records; however, the existence of an HRIS makes this information readily available and useful for managerial decision making. Most important, Isenhour discusses how the HRIS can cover legal compliance with government mandates much more easily than a paper system. In Chapter 11, "Talent Management," Kevin Johns and Michael Kavanagh discuss the use of an HRIS in the human resources planning (HRP) function that provides input to the talent management process. HRP is discussed in Chapter 11 with a focus on the speed of obtaining accurate employee information when discussing potential strategic plans for the company. In Chapter 12, "Recruitment and Selection in an Internet Context," Kimberly Lukaszewski, David Dickter, Brian Lyons, and Jerard Kehoe cover both HRIS and Internet applications within the context of a computer-based HRM function. Chapter 13, "Training and Development: Issues and HRIS Applications," by Ralf Burbach, provides information and ideas for how to use the power of an HRIS to address important issues in training and development programs. In Chapter 14, "Performance Management, Compensation, Benefits, Payroll, and the HRIS," Charles Fay and Ren Nardoni focus on one of the major motivational functions of the HRM system and how the existence of an HRIS can improve the operation of many aspects of the management and motivation of employees. Finally, Chapter 15, "HRIS and International Human Resource Management," by Michael Kavanagh and John Michel, covers the complexities that are created when a company enters the international marketplace.

The last part of this book, "Part V: Special Topics in HRIS," covers two additional topics of importance to the effective operation of an HRIS. In Chapter 16, "Information Security and Privacy in HRIS," Yuk Kuen Wong and Mohan Thite discuss the many legal, ethical, and moral issues that surround the use of an HRIS. In the final chapter (Chapter 17), "The Future of HRIS: Emerging Trends in HRM and IT," Michael Kavanagh, Mohan Thite, and Richard Johnson take a look at what new developments to expect given the continuing use of an HRIS in the operation of the HRM function of an organization.

SUMMARY

The primary purpose of this chapter was to introduce the academic and practitioner field of human resource information systems (HRIS), emphasizing that an HRIS is at the intersection of IT and HRM. The evolution of the field of HRIS, from its initial role of a record keeper concerned with only transactional HR activities, such as changing addresses on employee records, to one of becoming a strategic partner was covered in detail. This evolution demonstrated that, as IT improved over time, so did HRM, and these improvements made their marriage into HRIS that much easier. The advances in the field of HRIS also led to a reduction in the percentage of time that HR professionals spent on routine transactional and traditional activities and an increase in the percentage of time spent on transformational ones. The increase in time spent on transformational activities improves the "value added" by HRM programs to the strategic plan of an organization.

A basic primer on HRIS was presented, and the different types of human resource information systems were discussed, showing how the different types are needed for decision making at different levels in the organization. The distinction between HRIS and e-HRM was explained to help the reader avoid confusing these terms when they appear in the remainder of the book. In addition, the chapter discussed the development of HRIS and how it has helped enable HRM to become a strategic partner in organizations, which then led to the emergence of strategic HRM (Strategic HRM) as a field of study. Various strategic approaches were discussed, such as HR in a contingency model, the HR balanced scorecard, and the use of Six Sigma in HR.

A model of organizational functioning centered on an HRIS was discussed briefly, with the discussion focusing on how the feedback from results generated by an HRIS can influence the operation of the entire organization. The central themes of this book were emphasized, and the reader was alerted to the fact that these themes will occur throughout the chapters of the book. Finally, an overview of the structure of the book was provided to demonstrate the connections between the chapters of the book.

KEY TERMS

"best-fit" approach to Strategic HRM

"best-practice" approach to Strategic HRM

"caretaker" function

Comprehensive Occupational Data Analysis Program (CODAP)

cost-benefit ratio

enterprise resource planning (ERP) architecture

establishment of labor unions

HR balanced scorecard

HR contingency perspective

HR metrics

HR workforce scorecard

human capital

human resource management (HRM)

human resources planning (HRP)

Internet-enabled Web services

job analysis

job description

legislative compliance

management information system (MIS)

model of organizational functioning

return on investment (ROI)

scientific management

Six Sigma

Strategic HRM—strategic human resource management

system development life cycle (SDLC)

timely and accurate employee information

traditional HR activities

transactional HR activities

transformational HR activities

DISCUSSION QUESTIONS

1. What are the factors that changed the primary role of HRM from a caretaker of records to a strategic partner?
2. Describe the historical evolution of HRM and HRIS in terms of the changing role of HRM and the influence of computer technology on HRM.
3. What is required for the effective management of human resources in a firm to gain a competitive advantage in the marketplace?
4. Describe the emergence of strategic human resources management (Strategic HRM) and the influence of computer technology. What are some of the approaches used in HRM to facilitate the use of Strategic HRM in a firm's business strategy?
5. How does technology help deliver transactional, traditional, and transformational HR activities more efficiently and effectively?
6. Describe Six Sigma.
7. Justify the need for an HRIS.
8. Describe and differentiate the major types of information systems.
9. Using the organizational model presented in this chapter, explain why and how national culture and organizational culture influence the nature and importance of the IS function.

CASE STUDY: POSITION DESCRIPTION AND SPECIFICATION FOR AN HRIS ADMINISTRATOR

One way to assess the nature and importance of a particular function or position in an organization is to examine the job description and job specifications for this position, as they tell us what activities, duties, and tasks are involved in the job as well as what knowledge, skills, and abilities (KSA) are required to perform the job. The following is an actual advertisement for an HRIS administrator. A large corporation placed this ad in the "Job Central" section of the Internet site for the International Association for Human Resources Information Management[1] (http://ihrim.hrdpt.com/cgi-bin/a/searchjobs_quick.cgi, accessed July 10, 2010).

HRIS Administrator

Job Level: Senior (5+ Years), Full time
Reports to: Sr. Director of Human Resources Operations

Position Summary

MOMIRI, LLC is an Alabama Native Owned Corporation, providing shared services to the MOMIRI family of companies and planning and incubating the next generation of companies serving federal and commercial customers. MOMIRI companies offer core expertise in telecommunications, information technology, product development, major program management, open source software, construction management, facility operations, and operations support. MOMIRI companies realize that quality personnel are the key to our success. An excellent benefits package, professional working environment, and outstanding leaders are all keys to retaining top professionals.

Primary Function

The incumbent will serve as a key member of the HR Support Services department and provide professional human resources support in specific functions or disciplines to management and staff for the MOMIRI family of companies. This position is viewed as going to a midlevel professional who assists management and staff with HR programs at the tactical level and performs all essential duties and responsibilities at the direction of the Manager of HR Operations.

Essential Duties and Responsibilities

- Provides technical assistance to senior-level HR staff and management on several HR programs to include employee relations, compensation, EEO compliance, company policies and procedures, disability programs (STD, LTD, FMLA, ADA), federal and state employment laws, and personnel actions as needed.

- Supports and maintains the Human Resources Information System (HRIS) in addition to other systems supported by the management of enterprise applications.
- Serves as technical point-of-contact for assigned functional areas and assists subject matter experts with ensuring data integrity, testing of system changes, report writing and analyzing data flows for process improvement opportunities.
- Supports HRIS and other enterprise systems' upgrades, patches, testing and other technical projects as assigned.
- Recommends process/customer service improvements, innovative solutions, policy changes and/or major variations from established policy.
- Serves as key systems liaison with other departments and process stakeholders (e.g., Payroll).
- Writes, maintains, and supports a variety of reports or queries utilizing appropriate reporting tools. Assists in development of standard reports for ongoing customer needs.
- Maintains data integrity in ATS, HRIS, and other enterprise systems by running queries and analyzing and fully auditing data across all HR departments.
- Conducts new hire in-processing to include systems training for new employees and entering new employee information in Costpoint.
- Conducts termination out-processing to include entering employee separation information in Costpoint and reporting attrition data.
- Develops user procedures, guidelines, and documentation for HR-related systems. Trains system users on new processes/functionality.
- Provides HR tools and resources for management and staff to accomplish their goals and objectives.
- Processes personnel actions (hires, terminations, pay & title changes, promotions, employment status, etc.) to include entering data into HRIS.
- Assists with special HR-related projects and provides training to other staff members as required.
- Performs other duties as assigned.

Requirements

Specialized Knowledge and Skills

- Experience working with a multiple-site workforce.
- Working knowledge of federal and state employment laws and related acts.
- Advanced to expert level computer skills.
- Excellent verbal and written communication and presentation skills.
- Great interpersonal skills.
- Strong time-management and prioritization skills.

Qualifications

- Bachelor's degree in HR and/or equivalent professional experience.
- 3–5 years of technical HRIS experience in professional HR environment.
- Self-directed, highly responsive, and detail oriented.
- Ability to maintain absolute confidentiality in all business matters.
- Government contracting experience is a plus.

Case Study Questions

1. How does this position help the HR function become a strategic partner of the organization?
2. From the position description, identify the traditional, transactional, and transformational HR activities that this position is involved with.
3. Using the key responsibilities identified for this position, explain why and how the HRIS function plays a pivotal role in the organizational model as described in this chapter.

NOTE

1. The name of the company in the advertisement has been changed.

REFERENCES

Aktas, A. Z. (1987). *Structured analysis and design of information systems.* Englewood Cliffs, NJ: Prentice Hall.

Beatty, R. W., Huselid, M. A., & Schneier, C. E. (2003). New HR metrics: Scoring on the business scorecard. *Organizational Dynamics, 32*(2), 107–121.

Becker, B. E., & Huselid, M. A. (2006). Strategic human resource management: Where do we go from here? *Journal of Management, 32*(6), 898–925.

Becker, B. E., Huselid, M. A., & Ulrich, D. (2001). *The HR scorecard: Linking people, strategy, and performance.* Boston: Harvard Business School Press.

Beckers, A. M., & Bsat, M. Z. (2002). A DSS classification model for research in human resource information systems. *Information Systems Management, 19*(3), 41–50.

Bussler, L., & Davis, E. (2001/2002). Information systems: The quiet revolution in human resource management. *Journal of Computer Information Systems, 42*(2), 17–20.

Cascio, W. F. (1984). *Costing human resources: The financial impact of behavior in organizations.* Boston: PWS-Kent.

Cascio, W. F. (1991). *Costing human resources: The financial impact of behavior in organizations* (3rd ed.). Boston: PWS-Kent.

Cascio, W. F. (2000). *Costing human resources: The financial impact of behavior in organizations* (4th ed.). Cincinnati, OH: South-Western College.

Davis, W. S. (1983). *Systems analysis and design: A structured approach.* Reading, MA: Addison-Wesley.

Dery, K., & Wailes, N. (2005). Necessary but not sufficient: ERPs and strategic HRM. *Strategic Change, 14,* 265–272.

Drucker, P. F., Dyson, E., Handy, C., Saffo, P., & Senge, P. M. (1997). Looking ahead: Implications of the present. *Harvard Business Review, 75*(5), 18–24.

Evans, J. R. (2005). *Total quality.* Toronto, ON: Thomson.

Evans, W. R., & Davis, W. D. (2005). High-performance work systems and organizational performance: The mediating role of internal social structure. *Journal of Management, 31,* 758–775.

Fitz-enz, J. (1980). Quantifying the human resources function. *Personnel, 57*(3), 41–52.

Fitz-enz, J. (2000). *The ROI of human capital: Measuring the economic value of employee performance.* New York: AMACOM/American Management Association.

Fitz-enz, J. (2002). *How to measure human resource management* (3rd ed.). New York: McGraw-Hill.

Greer, C. (1995). *Strategy and human resources: A general managerial perspective.* Englewood Cliffs, NJ: Prentice Hall.

Gueutal, H. G., & Stone, D. L. (2005). *The brave new world of eHR: Human resources management in the digital age.* San Francisco: Jossey-Bass.

Haines, V. Y., & Lafleur, G. (2008). Information technology usage & human resource roles & effectiveness. *Human Resource Management, 47*(3), 525–540.

Huselid, M. A., Becker, B. E., & Beatty, R. W. (2005). *The workforce scorecard: Managing human capital to execute strategy.* Boston: Harvard Business School Press.

Huselid, M. A., Jackson, S. E., & Schuler, R. S. (1997). Technical and strategic human resource management effectiveness as determinants of firm performance. *Academy of Management Journal, 40,* 171–188.

Kaplan, R. S., & Norton, D. P. (1996). Linking the balanced scorecard to strategy. *California Management Review, 39*(1), 53–79.

Kavanagh, M. J., Gueutal, H. G., & Tannenbaum, S. I. (1990). *Human resource information systems.* Boston: PWS-Kent.

Lawler, E. E., Levenson, A., & Boudreau, J. W. (2004). HR metrics and analytics: Use and impact. *Human Resource Planning, 27*(4), 27–35.

Lawler, E. E., & Mohrman, S. A. (2003). HR as a strategic business partner: What does it take to make it happen? *Human Resource Planning, 26*(3), 15–29.

Lengnick-Hall, C. A., & Lengnick-Hall, M. L. (2006). HR, ERP, and knowledge for competitive advantage. *Human Resource Management, 45*(2), 179–194.

Lengnick-Hall, M. L., Lengnick-Hall, C. A., Andrade, L. S., & Drake, B. (2009) Strategic Human Resource Management: The evolution of the field. *Human Resource Management Review, 19,* 64–85.

Martinsons, M. G., & Chong, P. K. C. (1999). The influence of human factors and specialist involvement on information systems success. *Human Relations, 52*(1), 123–152.

Ngai, E. W. T., & Wat, F. K. T. (2004). Human resource information systems: A review and empirical analysis. *Personnel Review, 35*(3), 297–314.

Porter, M. E. (1990). *The competitive advantage of nations.* Boston: Free Press.

Roberts, B. (1999). Calculating return on investment for HRIS. *HR Magazine, 44*(13), 122–127.

Roehling, M. V., Boswell, W. R., Caligiuri, P., Feldman, D., Graham, M. E., Guthrie, J. P., et al. (2005). The future of HR management: Research needs and directions. *Human Resource Management, 44*(2), 207–216.

Smith, A. F., & Kelly, T. (1997). Human capital in the digital economy. In F. Hesselbein, M. Goldsmith, & R. Beckhard (Eds.), *The organization of the future* (pp. 199–212). San Francisco: Jossey-Bass.

Sprague, R. H., & Carlson, E. D. (1982). *Building effective decision support systems.* Englewood Cliffs, NJ: Prentice Hall.

Stone, D. L., & Lukaszewski, K. M. (2009). An expanded model of the factors affecting the acceptance and effectiveness of electronic human resource management systems. *Human Resource Management Review, 19*, 134–143.

Strohmeier, S. (2007). Research in e-HRM: Review and implications. *Human Resource Management Review, 17*(1), 19–37.

Thite, M. (2004). *Managing people in the new economy.* New Delhi, India: Sage.

Ulrich, D. (1998). A new mandate for human resources. *Harvard Business Review, 76*(1), 124–135.

Ulrich, D., & Smallwood, N. (2005). HR's new ROI: Return on intangibles. *Human Resources Management, 44*(2), 137–142.

Ulrich, D., Younger, J., & Brockbank, W. (2008). The twenty-first-century HR organization. *Human Resource Management, 47*(4), 829–850.

Walker, A. J. (1982). *HRIS development: A project team guide to building an effective personnel information system.* New York: Van Nostrand Reinhold.

Wright, P., McMahan, G., Snell, S., & Gerhart, B. (1998). *Strategic human resource management: Building human capital and organizational capacity* (Technical report). Ithaca, NY: Cornell University.

Chapter 2

DATABASE CONCEPTS AND APPLICATIONS IN HRIS

JANET H. MARLER AND BARRY D. FLOYD

EDITORS' NOTE

As mentioned in the book overview in Chapter 1, this chapter is focused on understanding databases and the applications of IT to the development and use of an HRIS. Although this chapter may be a review for some students, the material in it is critical to understanding the remaining chapters of the book. Therefore, students may want to refer to this chapter as they are studying subsequent chapters. This introductory chapter is also an excellent example of the contribution of IT to the field of HRM in building an HRIS.[1]

CHAPTER OBJECTIVES

After completing this chapter, you should be able to

- Discuss the differences between the terms *data, information,* and *knowledge*
- Identify problems with early database structures
- Understand what a relational database is and why it is better than older database structures
- Discuss three types of data sharing and why they are important
- Know the different ways in which data can be delivered to the end user
- Know what a query is and discuss three different types of queries
- Discuss how queries are used to support decision making

- Discuss the key steps involved in designing a simple database in Microsoft (MS) Access
- Identify key data fields in an HR database
- Discuss how business intelligence software can support HR decision making

INTRODUCTION

Data are produced, stored, updated, and used by HR employees and managers on a daily basis. In fact, this process is so pervasive that it often goes unnoticed. For example, an HR recruiter who reviews a job applicant's resume and then files it for later action is collecting, using, and storing business data about a potential hire. Indeed, effective collection, storage, and use of data are essential for any business, and the most successful organizations are masters of this process! Many believe that managing data and turning data into information is a competency necessary to succeed in today's marketplace.

Today's HRIS consist of **business applications** that work in conjunction with an electronic database. Together, these software programs transform data into information that is essential for business operations and for decision making. In this chapter, we will discuss how **database management systems (DBMS)** and business applications work together to process and share data that are the foundation of business information for workers, managers, and executives. We define key **relational database** terminology, describe how a database is structured, and show how to develop a simple database using **MS Access**, a basic DBMS, as an example. We close by providing examples of HRIS built on MS Access and on other larger commercial databases.

DATA, INFORMATION, AND KNOWLEDGE

Data are the lifeblood of an organization. The production and maintenance of data are critical to the smooth operation of every part of the organization. Data represent the "facts" of transactions that occur on a daily basis. A transaction can be thought of as an event of consequence, such as hiring a new employee for a particular position for a specified salary. The organization attempts to capture the data (facts) associated with each of these transactions, such as the date of the hire, the name of the person hired, the title of the position, the location where the new hire will work, and so on, and then store these data for future use.

Information, on the other hand, is the interpretation of these data. An interpretation of data always has some goal and context, such as making a hiring decision for a particular department or understanding the performance of an employee to make a promotion decision. Note that sometimes the data themselves can be informative without any additional transformation (e.g., the salary range of the job). But other times, we must do additional work (e.g., calculating totals or presenting the data in some order) to turn the data into information to answer important questions such as "What is our full-time employee head count in Corporate Sales?" or "Which employee should be promoted?"

Knowledge is information that has been given meaning (Whitehill, 1997). Knowledge is different from data and information. More than what and why, knowledge is about *how.* Knowledge, therefore, consists of the procedures one follows to use data and information *to make decisions and conduct business*, which is one of the main themes of this book. In many instances, such procedural knowledge is mostly hidden, residing in the minds of individuals and groups in the organization. For example, in HRIS, facts about age, gender, and education are the data. Information created from these data could include average age, gender ratio, and number and types of graduates at the business unit level. Such data and information help HR managers plan recruitment, schedule training programs to bridge skill gaps, and identify whether there may be employee discrimination. Knowledge represents how HR managers can execute the recruitment plan or decide which training programs are best to bridge skill gaps or what to do if employee discrimination exists. In the HR function, *data* about employees and jobs are the foundation of most of the *information* that is critical to analyzing and making HR decisions. *Knowledge,* on the other hand, constitutes knowing what information is needed from a database and how to use it to achieve HR objectives.

DATABASE MANAGEMENT SYSTEMS

A DBMS is a set of software applications (i.e., computer programs) combined with a database. These systems allow organizations to effectively manage data electronically. Managing data means

- identifying the data needed to create information that is necessary to make HR decisions,
- defining the characteristics of that data (e.g., number data vs. character data),
- organizing those data in a manner that promotes data quality and accessibility, and
- restricting access to the data to the right personnel.

By performing these functions effectively, a DBMS turns data into an organizational resource.

A database is a set of organized data. Significantly, it is a permanent, self-descriptive store of interrelated data items that can be processed by one or more business applications. *Self-descriptive* means that the database knows about the characteristics of the data; for example, the length of an employee's last name can be no greater than 30 characters or a paycheck can only be associated with one employee. *Interrelated* means that there are "links" between different sets of data in the database. For example, there can be a link between the data about employees and the jobs that they have. Because a database is a central repository of data, many different business applications and users can access the data, making an organization's database a very valuable organizational asset that, therefore, needs to be managed appropriately.

The main functions of a DBMS are to create the database; insert, read, update, and delete database data; maintain data integrity (i.e., making sure that the data are correct) and security (i.e., making sure that only the right people have access to the data); and prevent data from being lost by providing backup and recovery capabilities. Database management systems are also designed to have high performance, allowing data to be retrieved quickly by the many users in the organization.

DBMS and databases work in conjunction with business applications, such as **transaction processing systems**, to make organizations run smoothly. As shown in Figure 2.1, these business applications consist of a set of one or more computer programs that serve as an intermediary between the user and the DBMS while providing the "functions" or "tasks" that the user wants performed, such as storing data about the new hire (Kroenke, 2003). The business application must communicate in an easy-to-use manner with the user sitting at a computer terminal while maintaining efficient database processing. For example, a payroll business application involves collecting data from an employee's time card, storing these data in a database, and then retrieving and manipulating these data to produce a paycheck. Data from this transaction processing system can also be used to generate **reports** on monthly personnel expenses. These reports are the basis of **management reporting systems (MRS)**. We'll talk more about these later in the chapter.

There are thousands of commercially available business applications that work in conjunction with a DBMS to process business transactions. In a 2000 census of comprehensive HR software for the HR function, Richard Frantzreb cataloged more than 150 HR applications (Meade, 2003). In another census of specialized HR products under headings such as employment management, Equal Employment Opportunity (EEO), training management, career development, HR planning, performance management, personnel policy, survey processing, employee scheduling, attendance/timekeeping, payroll, and so on, Frantzreb counted 2,500 HR software products from about 1,700 vendors (Meade, 2003).

Figure 2.1 Database, Database Management System, and Business Applications

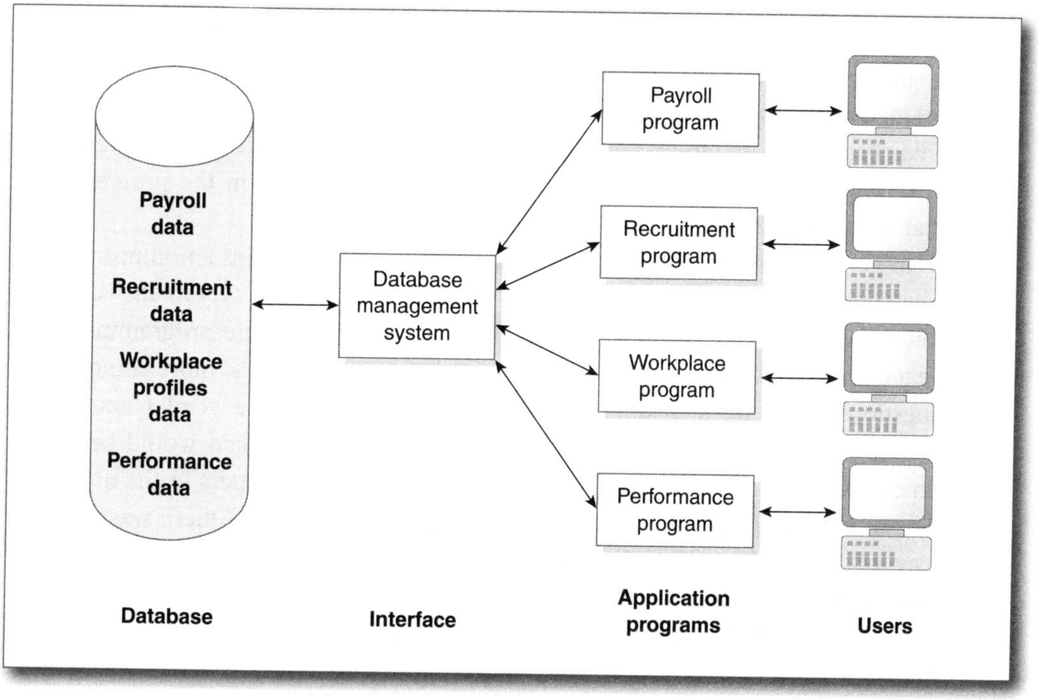

Early DBMS[2]

Early DBMS were simply data-processing systems that performed record-keeping functions that mimicked existing manual procedures. Thus, electronic data were stored in computers in much the same way that they were stored in paper filing systems. Paper filing systems typically consisted of a filing cabinet and a drawer for each type of business document (e.g., an employee personnel form). These documents were also called "records." Inside would be paper documents with each document being a "record" of a transaction (e.g., promoting Susan to senior manager). Computer systems mimicked this, creating individual computer files, typically one for each type of document. For example, there would be an "Employee File" with employee records, a "Time Card File" with time-card records, multiple "Employee Benefit Files" with their associated documents, and so on. The main objective of these file-processing systems was to process transactions, such as updates to payroll records and the production of payroll checks, as efficiently as possible. The goal was not data sharing among different business applications and users, only record keeping.

These traditional **file-oriented data structures** had a number of shortcomings. These shortcomings included (a) data redundancy—an employee's name and address could be stored in many different files; (b) poor data control—if you had access to the file, you had access to *all* the data in the file, which is not desirable if the organization wants to restrict the data viewed by a particular user; (c) inadequate data manipulation capabilities—it was very difficult to combine the data across files and to update and add new data; and (d) excessive programming effort—any change in the data required extensive changes in the programming that accessed the data.

In general, early file systems were good at specialized transaction processing. They were not designed to provide information easily and quickly to answer questions such as "What was the average hourly wage for female programmers last year compared with this year?" because the data to answer these more complicated questions came from different files; for example, employee gender and salary would be in the **master file on employees**, and hours worked would be in the time-card transaction file. Difficulties also arose when managers in the organization wanted to share data across applications. Fundamentally, there was no easy way to "link" information. For example, managers could not connect information about employee salaries and sales projections.

To overcome the shortcoming of file-oriented structures, **hierarchical and network database systems** evolved in the mid-1960s and early 1970s. The key to these systems was that **relationships** between different records were explicitly maintained. Although relationships among the data were created between sets of data, as illustrated in Figure 2.2, the relationships were created based on where the data were stored (e.g., the job records for Employee X are located in Sector 3 of Disk 4). Thus, only the very knowledgeable technical staff members were able to interact with the database effectively. These database systems also required an excessive programming effort and suffered from inadequate data manipulation capabilities if the program was poorly designed. The advent of relational database management systems addressed the many problems associated with these older DBMS and database structures.

Relational DBMS

In 1970, E. F. Codd introduced the notion that rather than programming relationships between data based on physical location, the information needed to integrate data should reside within the data (Hansen & Hansen, 1996). Included in Codd's proposal was that data be stored in tables, with each table representing one "entity" in the real world, and that the information associated with this "entity" be stored only in that table. For example, a company could have an employee table

Figure 2.2 Hierarchical and Network Database Structures

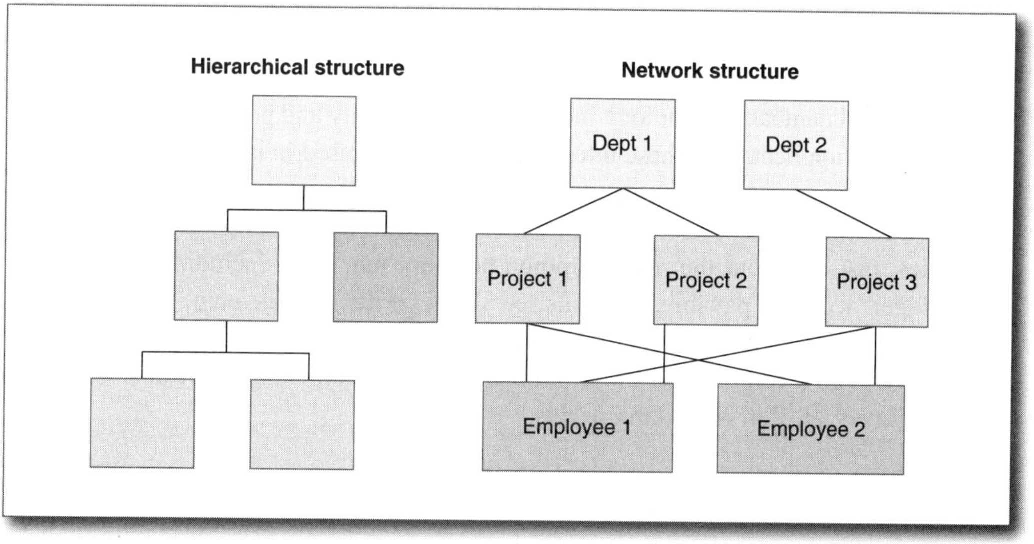

(i.e., each employee is an "entity"), and so information about the employee, such as name, address, and date of hire, would be stored only in that table and nowhere else. Such an idea removed problems with redundancies, such as storing an employee's address in many locations and then not knowing which address is the correct one if it is changed in one location and not in the other. These tables were called relations, and from this model came the name *relational database.*

In relational database systems, retrieval of data from different tables was based on logical relationships built into the table structures, which made feasible the creation of a query capability that was much more accessible to end users, who generally had limited programming experience. We'll talk more about this a bit later in the chapter.

Perhaps, the most significant difference between a file-based system and a relational database system is that data are easily shared. There are three types of *data sharing:* (1) data sharing between functional units, (2) data sharing between management levels, and (3) data sharing across geographically dispersed locations. Data sharing requires a major change in end-user thinking, particularly in those employees who are accustomed to owning their own data on their PCs. Fundamentally, sharing data means sharing power because both data and information are power. Sharing data also means being a good citizen and making certain that the data you enter are correct.

Data Sharing Between Different Functions

Relational DBMS facilitate data integration across different functions such that each function might have access not only to its own data but also to other data as well. Thus, the HR department is able to maintain its employee database but also access cost information from the accounting department's database. As a result, relational database technology increased the feasibility and popularity of integrated business applications. These integrated applications used in large organizations are referred to as **enterprise resource planning (ERP)** business applications.

ERP software applications are a set of integrated database applications, or modules, that carry out the most common business functions, including HR, general ledger, accounts payable, accounts receivable, order management, inventory control, and customer relationship management. ERP modules are integrated, primarily through a common set of definitions and a common database (Martin, Brown, DeHayes, Hoffer, & Perkins, 1999).

Data Sharing Between Different Levels

Operational employees, managers, and executives also share data but have different objectives and, thus, different information needs. Operational employees focus on data-processing transactions to ensure smooth operation of critical business transactions. A common business transaction is processing the information from an employee's time card. At this level, transaction-processing information systems help conduct business on a day-to-day basis to provide timely and accurate information to managers and executives. For example, transaction-processing systems update employee work history, attendance, and work hours. Operational employees are concerned with the accuracy and efficiency with which these data are processed.

Managers, on the other hand, are more interested in summary data that can be aggregated into daily, weekly, or monthly reports on hours worked by employee or absences by employee.

Executives rely on information produced at an even more aggregated level to evaluate trends and develop business strategies. For example, executives might ask for reports that compare turnover statistics across business groups and over time.

These three different levels of use correspond to three different types of software systems that have evolved over the past three decades: transaction processing systems (TPS), management reporting systems (MRS), and **decision support systems (DSS)** (Hansen & Hansen, 1996). TPS were first applied to lower operational levels of the organization to automate manual processes such as payroll. Their basic characteristics include (a) a focus on data storage, processing, and flows at the daily operational level; (b) efficient transaction processing; and (c) summary reports for management (Sprague & Watson, 1989). Early ERP applications were used primarily for their transaction-processing functionality.

Note the similarity between the categorization of software systems and the classification of information systems into electronic data processing (EDP), management information systems (MIS), and decision support systems (DSS), which was discussed in Chapter 1 (Sprague & Carlson, 1982). These terms correspond to TPS, MRS, and DSS in this chapter. As you may recall from Chapter 1, an additional information system was identified—the human resources decision support system (HRDSS). The HRDSS was described as consisting of the reports managers and HR professionals receive on a regular basis but that are actually used in their daily work, *particularly in their decision-making capacity.* The HRDSS could be classified as a special instance of an MRS or MIS system but focused specifically on information used in decision making—a central theme of this book.

In addition to TPS capabilities, relational databases can also provide MRS capability. Characteristics of an MRS include (1) information aimed at middle managers; (2) integration of TPS data by business functions such as manufacturing, marketing, and HR; and (3) inquiry and report generation from the database (Sprague & Watson, 1989). Management reporting systems can be designed to provide daily, monthly, quarterly, or annual summary reports of key transactions such as employee head counts by department or the distribution of employee performance reports to meet budgets and manage performance.

Decision support systems assist senior managers and business professionals in making business decisions. **Data mining**, data analytics, and **business intelligence (BI)** are examples of information derived from a DSS, which relies on data warehouses. **Data warehouses** represent aggregated data (e.g., the total salary information by department by month) collected from the various databases available to a business.

Data Sharing Across Locations

In today's global environment, access to data from any physical location in the world is increasingly important. Teams of employees may be stationed in Thailand, India, and the United States. Two issues arise when data are shared across wide geographic locations. These are (1) managing the day/time of a transaction and (2) determining where to store the various components of the business application, DBMS, and database.

To deal with the day/time issue, developers of DBMS such as Oracle, MS SQL Server, and IBM DB2 are building the capability to deal with recording dates and times according to the time zone in which the data originated. So, for example, if a database is stored in London and an employee records a transaction while sitting at a terminal in Los Angeles, in addition to the time (say 1 PM in Los Angeles), the time zone (–08:00 from Greenwich Mean Time) is also stored with the transaction.

As part of a global information system design, organizations have chosen to break their business application and DBMS into components, often called "tiers." More detail on tiers will also be covered in Chapter 3. Traditional client-server architectures broke an application into two tiers, typically with the **user interface** and some business logic on the user's computer, such as a PC (the client), and the database and mainstream parts of the application stored on a server. In today's global environment with high-speed data networks, **N-tier architectures** exist with databases and applications being distributed among many different computers around the world. So if, for example, you are in an Internet café in Bangkok trying to get information about your benefit election, the hosting computer may be in London and the data may be located on a computer in Chicago. In sum, computer networks are created that provide instant access to these operational data, allowing real-time managerial decision capability regardless of physical location.

A centralized database allows a company to confine its data to a single location and, therefore, more easily control data integrity, updating, backup, query, and control access to the database. A company with many locations and telecommuters, however, must develop a communications infrastructure to facilitate data sharing over a wide geographical area. The advent of the Internet and a standardized communication protocol made the centralized database structures and geographically dispersed data sharing feasible.

KEY RELATIONAL DATABASE TERMINOLOGY

As discussed earlier, relational DBMS are used to store data important to the organization. Key terms in relational database management include entities, attributes, tables, primary keys, foreign keys, and relationships, queries, forms, and reports. Below we define each term and describe its function in a database.

Entities and Attributes

Entities are things such as employees, jobs, promotion transactions, positions in a company, and so on. They include both physical things such as desks and conceptual things such as bank accounts. A company must analyze its business operations and identify all the entities that it believes are important.

Each of these entities is made up of "attributes." An attribute is a characteristic of the entity. For example, an employee has a name, address, and phone number, an education, and so on. **Attributes** also have properties, such as the type of data (e.g., date, number, or character) and size (e.g., number of characters or the largest number that can be stored), and these properties have implications for data storage.

In addition to identifying the entities and attributes, a database creator must define the relationships among the entities. For example, a company may have an employee entity and a department entity. Then the company must define the relationship between the employee entity and the department entity. Does an employee have to be assigned to a department, for example? Can an employee be assigned to more than one department?

Tables

How does this information fit into a relational DBMS? **Tables** are used to store information about entities. As illustrated in Figure 2.3, one table is created for each entity—in this example, driver table, car table, moving violation table, and

Figure 2.3 Relational Database Structure

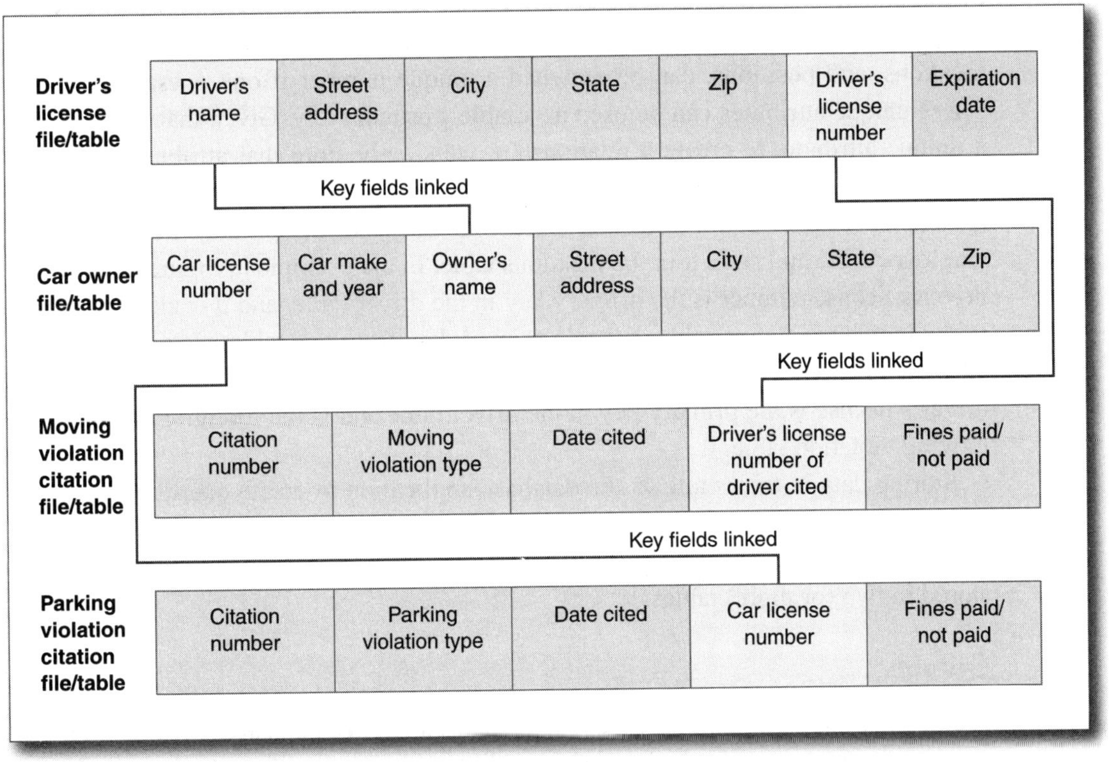

parking violation table. Attributes are stored as the columns (also called fields) in the table. As noted earlier, attributes represent a single data element or characteristic of the data table. For example, a table of driver data would have the following columns or characteristics: first name, last name, street address, city, state, driver's license number, expiration, and so on. Each of these characteristics represents an attribute or field of the table.

Each table in a database contains rows. Rows are also referred to as records and represent an "instance" of the entity. For example, in the driver table, each row contains data about a particular driver, and each column contains data that represent an attribute of that driver, such as name, phone number, and license number.

Relationships, Primary Keys, and Foreign Keys

To represent the relationships among the tables, we have to do a bit more work. In a relational DBMS, relationships are created by having the same attribute in each table with the value of the attribute being the same in each table. Most often, this is done by taking the **primary key** of one table and including it in the related table. What is a primary key?

Typically, each entity has an attribute that has unique values for each instance of the entity. For example, each employee has a social security number that is unique (i.e., only one person has a particular number). Other entities, such as jobs, locations, and positions, can be assigned a unique number if one doesn't exist. These unique attributes can be used as a table's primary key. Given that we have a unique attribute, to create a relationship, we simply store that attribute in the related table. So if an employee is associated with a position, we have two tables, an employee table and a positions table. We then take the primary key of the employee table and store it in the positions table. In the example in Figure 2.3, the driver's license number is the primary key in the driver table, and it is also stored in the moving violation table. When a primary key from one table is stored as an attribute of another table, that attribute is called a **foreign key**. Thus, in Figure 2.3, driver's license is the primary key in the driver table and is the foreign key in the moving violation table.

Storing data in tables allows the database application to create queries, forms, and reports that permit users to retrieve, update, or analyze these data. Creating relationships allows users to accurately combine data that "go together" but are stored in two (or more) tables.

Queries[3]

A query is a question that you ask about the data stored in a database. For example, you may want to know which employees live within a specific city. You could generate these results by scrolling through the relevant table or by sorting the table by city and then looking at the result, but this is time-consuming, and you would have to do this task each time you wished to find the answer to your question. A better approach is to create a query. A query is a structured way of posing your question to the DBMS in a language the DBMS understands. This definition (e.g., show all employees with city Albany) can be saved in the database and used again and again. Significantly, each time the query is executed, it searches through the *current* table records and lists the results. The results of a query on a table or tables are always displayed in something that looks just like another table. However, this results table is only temporary and is not stored in the database. It is important to note that queries do not store data! All data are stored in tables. **Queries** only report on data currently in the table.

There are three different kinds of queries: select queries, action queries, and cross-tab queries. A **select query** allows you to ask a question based on one or more tables in a database. This is the most commonly used query. These queries can be quite general or quite specific. For example, a general query might extract all employees from the database that have reached retirement age. A more specific query might retrieve employees who have reached retirement age and who live in New York and are engineers.

An **action query** performs an action on the table on which it is based. Actions include updating data in the table (e.g., increasing the base salary of all employees who were rated above average in the latest performance rating), deleting records from the table (e.g., removing employees from the employees table if they no longer work at the company), or inserting records (e.g., adding a new set of benefits to the benefits table). You can also use this type of query to create new tables.

A **cross-tab query** performs calculations on the values in a field and displays the results in a datasheet. The reason it is called *cross-tab* is that it tabulates the data for a set of descriptor attributes, contrasting them or crossing them in a table format. For example, we might want to see the total personnel count by gender by region. So we would see the gender on the left side of the table and the different regions listed across the top. A cross-tab query could display different aspects of the data, including sums or averages or minimum or maximum values. As another example, a cross-tab query could determine head count by department or determine pay range maximums and minimums in pay grades by department.

Select queries and cross-tab queries provide the information that managers and executives expect from IT. These queries can serve as the foundation for MRS and DSS information and decision making. Action queries, on the other hand, improve the operational efficiency of managing and maintaining a database and are most closely associated with TPS. These tasks are important to the operational staff but of less interest to HR managers and executives.

Queries are also used as the basis for forms and reports. In addition to retrieving data, they can add, update, and delete records in tables. You can define fields in a query that perform calculations, such as sums and averages. The following list summarizes the typical capabilities of queries (Bast, Cygman, Flynn, & Tidwell, 2006):

- Display selected fields and records from a table
- Sort records on one or multiple fields
- Perform calculations
- Generate data for forms, reports, and other queries
- Update data in the tables of a database
- Find and display data from two or more tables
- Create new tables
- Delete records in a table based on one or more criteria

Forms[4]

A form is an object in a database that you can use to maintain, view, and print records in a more structured manner. Although you can perform these same functions with tables and queries, forms can present data in many customized and useful ways. For example, you can design a form to look like the time sheet submitted by an employee. Well-designed forms can improve data input efficiency and accuracy. Consequently, **forms** represent the main mechanism for creating end-user interfaces. A form can be based on a table, multiple tables, or queries. A form can display one record at a time or many records. Often, we select only one record and then create a nice-looking, easy-to-use layout to work with the data in that one record. To view and maintain or add data using a form, you must know how to move from field to field and from record to record. Forms provide navigation buttons that facilitate doing this. Entering or changing data in a form will automatically change the values in the underlying table once you save the changes.

Reports

A report is a formatted presentation of data from a table, multiple tables, or queries that is created as a printout or to be viewed on screen. Data displayed in a report are dynamic, reflecting the latest data from the tables on which the report is based. Unlike with forms, however, you cannot change the data or add a new record in a report; you can only view the data in the report.

Although you can print data appearing in tables, queries, and forms, reports provide you with the greatest flexibility for formatting printed output. As with forms, you can design your own reports or use a "report wizard" to create reports automatically.[5]

INTRODUCTION TO MS ACCESS

MS Access differs from other commercial database management software such as Oracle, DB2, or MYSQL in that it integrates both database application and DBMS software into one. MS Access is a relational DBMS in which data are organized as a collection of tables. As in any relational database, the data in tables can be queried. MS Access also makes it easy to create forms and reports through the use of form or report wizards. A form or report wizard is a computer program or tool that guides you through the creation of a form by asking you a series of questions. For example, which table is the form to be created from and which attributes do you want to be displayed on the form? The form or report is created based on your answers.

MS Access is designed for relatively small databases and assumes limited knowledge of database programming. MS Access provides the following functions (Adamski & Finnegan, 2005):

- It allows you to create databases containing tables and table relationships.
- It lets you easily add new records, change table values in existing records, and delete records.
- It contains a built-in query language, which lets you obtain immediate answers to questions you ask about your data.
- It contains a built-in report generator and report wizard, which lets you produce professional-looking, formatted reports from your data.
- It provides protection of databases through security, control, and recovery facilities.

Data in an MS Access table or query can be exported to other database applications or to spreadsheet programs such as Excel or Lotus 123, which then can be used in decision-making situations. Once these records are in a spreadsheet program, further analyses may be conducted and graphs and charts constructed to enhance analytical HR metric reports. Data can be exported by simply opening the database that has the object—for example, the table or query—that you want to export. Then select *File*, and *Export* from the database menu. Select the type of file you want the object to be saved to—for example, *.xls*—and specify a name. Click *Save*. Now you can open the file in Excel. You may also "link" the data in the database to the spreadsheet. When the spreadsheet is opened, the most recent data from the database are retrieved and presented in the spreadsheet.

Unlike spreadsheet software programs, MS Access handles substantially more data and contains the ability to model relationships. Each MS Access database, for example, can be up to 2 GB in size and can contain up to 32,768 objects, including tables, queries, forms, reports, and so on.

Designing an MS Access Database

The design process begins with an analysis of the data and information that the users of the database will need to have stored and retrieved in order to accomplish their work. Typically, we think of work as consisting of tasks within a business process, and so we can think of the data that will be required to be stored in a database and of the information that will need to be extracted. We find out the data to be stored by interviewing the intended end users of the database. We ask about entities that they need to keep information on, the attributes of those entities, and also how the entities are related. In addition, we may watch users at work and look at the forms, reports, and other business documents that they use to be successful. Gathering copies of all existing forms and reports currently used may also help, as these can act as guidelines for creating forms and reports, though sometimes our intention is to change how they are doing business, so some of these documents may be significantly changed or even discarded.

In general, the database design process can be broken down into several steps that are somewhat sequential but oftentimes have to be repeated until the database meets the users' needs:

- Determine what the users want from the database: what questions need to be answered, what information needs to be tracked, what reports are produced, and what data are needed to provide the basis for those results?
- Identify the data fields needed to produce the required information; in doing so, we also identify rules that define the integrity of the data, including data type (number, character) and data limits (e.g., if we are storing days, we might only allow the numbers 1 to 31).
- Group related fields into tables (entities).
- Determine each table's primary key.
- Normalize the data: Make sure the data for an entity are really associated with only that entity.
- Determine how the tables are related to one another and include common keys.
- Create the relationships among the different entities and ensure referential integrity.
- Create queries to define data needs that are not handled by only looking at individual tables.

- Create reports to provide a structured view of the data.
- Create forms, and, in doing so, identify a common design for the forms: Typically, we create a form for each table along with a "main menu" form that allows the user to navigate to each form associated with a table and to view queries and reports.
- Enter test data to verify the quality and accuracy of the system design.
- Test the system: Do all the queries work correctly? Are the forms easy to use? Are the end users happy?
- Enter or populate the database.

HR Database Application Using MS Access

For small companies, generally with fewer than 1,000 employees, there are commercially available HR database applications based on MS Access. One such system, popular in the United States, is HRSource™ from Auxillium West (www.auxillium.com). This software package offers a wide breadth of functionality and flexibility to import and export data from and to Excel and to integrate with other database applications, particularly payroll. It also provides a centralized relational database with basic transaction processing and management reporting systems.

HRSource™ utilizes the familiar MS Access form as its user interface and allows users to create custom queries and reports. However, the database applications also come with preconfigured reports and queries. HRSource™ offers users 70 built-in reports. Customers also claim that, with a little expertise in MS Access, they are able to mine their HR information in a way that they never could before they centralized in one HRIS database (Meade, 2003).

Other HR Databases

A few decades ago, database application programs were often written by companies for their particular use; in today's business environment, customized application programs termed *legacy systems* are being replaced by commercially developed database application programs (e.g., PeopleSoft Enterprise HCM, SAP ERP HCM, Lawson HCM, UltiPro, Workday). Most top selling HR database applications use a variety of database applications such as Oracle, MySQL, DB2, and Microsoft SQL Server as their DBMS. These commercial database application programs can be licensed and installed onto computer hardware a company buys itself, or, now, given the ability to share database information regardless of geographic location, some vendors of HR database applications are leasing HR DBMS and business applications to business customers. This new way of acquiring an HRIS is called software as a service, or SaaS. UltiPro and Workday are HR software vendors selling HR database applications as a service. Some believe SaaS may be the way in which most small and medium-sized businesses will acquire an HRIS in the future, rather than buying or developing their own.

Regardless of how complex your HRIS DBMS is, you must ensure that you know what information can be derived from any database. To know this, you must have an idea of what tables and attributes (fields) are in the database. Software vendors should be able to provide this information to end users; however, for the large complex HR applications, these specifications may run into thousands of tables and fields! Auxillium West, makers of a low-priced HRIS, offer a document to prospective customers that lists the data items commonly tracked. The most commonly tracked HR fields by organizations are shown in Table 2.1 (Meade, 2003).

Although the list in Table 2.1 appears to be comprehensive, in fact, it is quite sparse when compared with listings of HR fields within more complex database

Table 2.1 Examples of Common Fields in an HR Database

Employee ID	Job Code/Title
First Name	Pay Rate Type
Last Name	Rate Effective Date
Address	Salary
City	Bonuses
State	Status
Zip Code	Category (full-time/part-time)
Home Phone Number	Contract Employee Status
Gender	Department
Ethnic Code	Office Information
Birth Date	Manager
Veteran Status	Division/Location
Visa Expiration Date	Company Property
Education	Emergency Contact
Past Employment	Time-Off Accruals
Skill Code	Benefits
Training/Certification	Work-Related Injuries
Performance Rating	Disability
Next Review Date	
Hire Date	
Termination Date	
Termination Reason	
Rehire Date as Applicable	

applications. More complex database applications will also have fields that relate to business processes other than HR, such as accounting and finance. Integrated databases allow sophisticated queries and analytical reports, such as hours spent on recruiting, recruiters' hourly pay, job board posting costs, number of positions filled, number of declined offers, number of open positions, number of voluntary terminations, and number of involuntary terminations.

DATA WAREHOUSES, BUSINESS INTELLIGENCE, AND DATA MINING

An organization's ability to generate meaningful information to make good decisions is only as good as its underlying database. As Dr. John Sullivan notes, "I have found that the largest single difference between a great HR department and an average one is the use of metrics" (Gur, 2006). **Metrics** are various measures of organizational performance that are derived from organizational data. A current goal and emphasis in HRM is functioning as a strategic business partner. A requisite to this is the use of methodologies or metrics to assess and monitor quantitative HRM data. The overarching objective of HR metrics is to improve organizational efficiency and effectiveness. The use of metrics in HRM will be discussed in greater detail in Chapter 6.

Much of the data now available to create HR metrics come from an organization's data warehouse. A data warehouse is a special type of database that is optimized for reporting and analysis and is the raw material for management's decision support system. **Business intelligence**, BI, is a broad category of business applications and technologies for creating data warehouses and for analyzing and providing access to these specialized data to help enterprise users make better business decisions. BI applications include the activities of decision support systems, query and reporting, statistical analysis, forecasting, and data mining.

BI systems allow organizations to improve business performance by leveraging information about customers, suppliers, and internal business operations from databases across functions and organizational boundaries. Essentially, BI systems retrieve specified data from multiple databases, including old legacy file database systems, and store these data in a new database, which becomes that data warehouse. The data in the data warehouse can then be accessed via queries and used to uncover patterns and diagnose problems.

Patterns in large data sets are identified through **data mining**, which involves statistically analyzing large data sets to identify recurring relationships. For example, data mining an employee database might reveal that most employees reside within a group of particular zip codes. This may help if the organization wants to supply transportation or encourage carpooling. Data mining is relatively new to business analytics and has not yet been widely used for HRM decisions.

BI systems also provide reporting tools and interfaces (e.g., forms) that distribute the information to Excel spreadsheets, Internet-based portals, pdf files, or hard copies. These results can also be distributed to key executives in specialized formats known as executive dashboards, which are becoming a popular executive decision support tool.

A major reason for a DBMS is to provide information from various parts of the organization in an ad hoc manner. *Ad hoc* means that a user can ask a question of the data that no one has thought about yet. The user can sign into the data and pose his or her question in the form of a query. The ability to access data in an ad hoc manner is a powerful tool that enables all levels of the organization to make better decisions. In addition, data warehousing and BI software enable managers to create information from an even greater store of data.

SUMMARY

In this chapter, we have described the key aspects of current DBMS technologies and how these systems work to create, store, and manage critical data about an organization. We covered the differences between data, information, and knowledge and discussed the problems with early database structures. Importantly, we covered relational databases and how they differ and are superior to earlier databases. We also explained the three types of *data sharing:* (1) data sharing between functional units, (2) data sharing between management levels, and (3) data sharing across geographically dispersed locations. The most common data fields for an HR database were illustrated in Table 2.1. Data are transformed into information by relational DBMS and business applications that work together. The underlying data in a database are collected from business transactions and stored in tables that are related to each other through shared fields called primary and foreign keys. Queries represent questions asked of the data and are used to access specific data stored in tables. The three types of queries were discussed in terms of their uses. The results of queries can be viewed in forms or reports that are customized so that the end user can better interpret the data that are retrieved from the database. In this manner, queries can be used to support decision making. More sophisticated data analyses and reports, such as executive dashboards, are produced from specialized databases called data warehouses and using business application software called BI software.

Most HRIS rely on an underlying database. Understanding how database systems work, therefore, is relevant to HR decision makers because knowledge about how to create, store, and access data can be a key differentiator in a competitive environment. Small

HR databases can be created using MS Access, or more sophisticated ones can be purchased from software vendors. The sequential steps in creating an MS Access database were covered, and where to find the data for this database was discussed. There are literally hundreds of HR database business applications that create, process, and analyze HR data. The challenge is to find one that can most cost-effectively collect and share data from which meaningful information can be extracted to support making good decisions.

KEY TERMS

action queries
attributes
business applications
business intelligence (BI)
cross-tab queries
data
data mining
data warehouse
database management systems (DBMS)
decision support systems (DSS)
enterprise resource planning (ERP)
entities
file-oriented data structures
foreign key
forms
hierarchical and network database systems
information
knowledge
management reporting systems (MRS)
master file on employees
metrics
MS Access
N-tier architectures
primary key
queries
relational database
relationships
reports
select queries
tables
transaction processing systems (TPS)
user interface

DISCUSSION QUESTIONS

1. Explain the differences between data, information, and knowledge.
2. What are the main functions of a database management system, and how is it different from a database?
3. What were the shortcomings of early file-oriented database structures?

4. What are the three types of data sharing?
5. Define the key terms in a relational database.
6. What is the difference between a primary key and a foreign key?
7. What are the three types of queries?
8. How are forms and reports similar, and how are they different?
9. Take the list of HR database common fields and group them into tables.
10. What are the differences between data warehouses, BI, and data mining?
11. Can knowledge be turned into a database?

CASE STUDY

You have been asked to create an applicant database for a small recruiting firm that specializes in recruiting HR professionals for small to medium-sized firms. Describe the process that you would use to design this database. Use MS Access to develop a prototype of the database that you could show your manager.

APPLICATIONS EXERCISE

As noted in this chapter, there are two commercially available HR database applications based on MS Access that are popular in the United States: (1) HRSource from Auxillium West (www.auxillium.com) and (2) Epicor Human Capital Management (www.epicor.com). Go to both of these Web sites for the HR database applications, and prepare a short report for the class. Your instructor will inform you of whether your report will be written or presented verbally in class.

NOTES

1. This chapter contains basic information about IT concepts. Therefore, the content does not lend itself to an "HRIS in Action" vignette.
2. For a more detailed discussion, see Hansen and Hansen (1996, pp. 52–56).
3. For a more detailed discussion, see Bast et al. (2006, chap. 3).
4. For a more detailed treatment, see Tutorials 4 and 5 in Adamski and Finnegan (2005).
5. For a more detailed treatment, see Tutorials 4 and 6 in Adamski and Finnegan (2005).

REFERENCES

Adamski, J., & Finnegan, K. (2005). *New perspectives on Microsoft Access 2003.* Boston: Course Technology Thomson Learning.

Bast, K., Cygman, L., Flynn, G., & Tidwell, R. (2006). *Succeeding in business with Microsoft Office Access 2003.* Boston: Course Technology Thomson Learning.

Gur, Z. (2006, June/July). Up.link. *IHRIM.link, 11*(3), 5.

Hansen, G. W., & Hansen, J. V. (1996). *Database management and design.* Upper Saddle River, NJ: Prentice Hall.

Kroenke, D. M. (2003). *Database concepts.* Upper Saddle River, NJ: Prentice Hall.

Martin, E., Brown, C., DeHayes, D., Hoffer, J., & Perkins, W. (1999). *Managing information technology.* Upper Saddle River, NJ: Prentice Hall.

Meade, J. (2003). *The human resources software handbook.* San Francisco: Jossey-Bass.

Sprague, R. H., & Carlson, E. D. (1982). *Building effective decision support systems.* Englewood Cliffs, NJ: Prentice Hall.

Sprague, R., & Watson, H. (1989). *Decision support systems* (2nd ed.). Englewood Cliffs, NJ: Prentice Hall.

Whitehill, M. (1997). Knowledge-based strategy to deliver sustained competitive advantage. *Long Range Planning, 30*(4), 621–627.

Chapter 3

Systems Considerations in the Design of a Human Resource Information System

Planning for Implementation

Michael D. Bedell, Michael L. Canniff, and Cheryl R. Wyrick

EDITORS' NOTE

This chapter covers the information necessary to understand the system development process for HRIS in more depth in order to improve the design of the HRIS. As mentioned in Chapter 1, the system development process involves multiple stages from initial design to implementation and evaluation. Failure to follow these steps or rushing through them will result in a poorly designed system that will ultimately fail when it is implemented. Thus, this chapter begins to identify some of the information that is critical for the eventual implementation and evaluation of an HRIS. The authors start with a focus on the users of the system to help the system development and design process in its beginning steps. The types of information about the users or customers of the HRIS, the sorting of HRIS data into categories of human capital, and the main concepts of hardware and database security are covered.

CHAPTER OBJECTIVES

After completing this chapter, you should be able to

- Understand the different types of users or customers of the implemented HRIS and their different data needs
- Discuss the differences between the five general hardware architectures that are presented, from "dinosaur" to "cloud computing"
- Discuss, very generally, the main concepts of hardware and database security
- Discuss the "best of breed" approach to HRIS acquisition and the various options available for each functional area of HR
- Develop an understanding of the general steps and factors that affect system implementation
- Understand the pros and cons of implementing a changeover from one software system to another

HRIS IN ACTION

A billion-dollar retailer with 4,000+ stores finds that it cannot move fast enough to beat out the competition. The organization's senior management arrives at the conclusion that it would be easier to achieve the strategic goals enumerated by the board of directors if the various organizational functions would share information. Shared information would enable them to develop and deploy new actions and tactics more quickly. The CEO and president have therefore ordered the major functions to update their information systems immediately so that data sharing is possible. The **senior vice presidents (SVPs)** of accounting and human resources immediately conclude that the only solution is to decide jointly on an **enterprise resource planning (ERP)** product. An ERP software application is a set of integrated database applications or modules that carry out the most common business functions, including human resources, general ledger, accounts payable, accounts receivable, order management, inventory control, and customer relationship management (see www.erpsupersite.com). To speed the installation along, the VPs decide on a rapid-implementation methodology that a company down the street used. The goal is to have the new systems operational in nine months.

Shortly after this decision has been made, the SVP of HR calls you into his office and tells you that you will be **management sponsor** for this project. You have to decide on everything. You sit back in your nice office and think:

What's the problem with this scenario? It shouldn't be difficult to select a vendor and then borrow the methodology from down the street. It worked for them; it should work for us! We'll call a few vendors in the morning and find out about cost, time frame, and implementation methods. In the meantime, I should find out a little more about how to do this and who will be using the ERP. I remember from my information systems class in college that this is a reasonable first step when it comes to buying software.

What do you think your response would be to this inquiry? As you go through this chapter's material, keep this vignette in mind, and see if your answer changes.

INTRODUCTION

Successful implementation is the central goal of every HRIS project, and it begins with a comprehensive design for the system. As the steps in the system development process are covered in this chapter, the foundation knowledge that is critical to the implementation process will be emphasized. Only by understanding the users or customers of the HRIS, the technical possibilities, the software solution parameters, and the systems implementation process can we increase the probability that the completed software installation will adequately meet the needs of the **human resources management (HRM)** function and the organization. The chapter will begin by identifying the potential users and the kind of information that the HRIS will be managing and storing to facilitate decision making. The chapter will next discuss the technical infrastructure, how the technical infrastructure has evolved, and the many choices that the organization must make. After the technology is discussed, the systems implementation process will be presented.

Those who have participated in a system implementation will tell you that success is the result of careful planning, a dedicated team, top-management support, and an awareness of potential pitfalls. These same people will also tell you that the implementation process provides a host of opportunities to reengineer and systematically improve non-software processes to reflect best practices in HRM. These opportunities should not be ignored, as they can benefit the organization as much as implementing the software will. Finally, the implementation team members will tell you that getting the system up and running was the most intense six months, year, or two years of their work life but that they learned a lot and every moment of the experience was worth the time.

There are four things that should be remembered throughout the chapter:

1. It is important to keep in mind the customer of the data, the process, and the decisions that will be made.
2. Everything about HRM is a process designed to support the achievement of strategic organizational goals. The HRIS, in turn, supports and helps manage these HR processes.

3. An HRIS implementation done poorly may result in an HRIS that fails to meet the needs of the organization or worse.
4. Successful implementation requires careful attention to every step in the system design process. However, done well, the implementation process is full of opportunities to improve the organization and processes. More consistent processes will contribute to enhanced organizational performance.

HRIS CUSTOMERS/USERS: DATA IMPORTANCE

Individuals who will be using the HRIS can be split into two general groups: employees and nonemployees. The employee category includes

- managers who rely on the HRIS and the data analyzed by the analyst or power user to make decisions;
- analysts or power users who use the HRIS to evaluate potential decision choices and opportunities;
- technical staff who are responsible for providing a system that is usable and up-to-date for each user, or clerical employees who largely engage in data entry; and
- employees who use the HRIS on a self-service basis to obtain personal information, for example, to look up paycheck information, to make choices about benefits during open enrollment, or to see how much vacation time they have available.

The nonemployee group includes potential employees, suppliers, and partners. Potential employees are those who might log in via a Web portal to search for and apply for a position. Suppliers and partners are organizations that interface with the HR function for a variety of purposes, from recruiting to benefits administration and payroll.

Employees

Managers

The **managers** referred to within this section may have a variety of titles: manager, director, vice president, and even CEO. What they all have in common is that their primary HRIS need is to have real-time access to accurate data that facilitate decision making with regard to their people (Miller, 1998). The HRIS provides the manager with data for performance management, recruiting and retention, team management, project management, and employee development (Fein, 2001). The

HRIS must also provide the information necessary to help the functional manager make decisions that will contribute to the achievement of the unit's strategic goals and objectives (Hendrickson, 2003). Easy access to accurate employee data enables the manager for each employee to view and engage in employee life cycle changes such as salary decisions, job requisitions, hiring, disciplinary action, promotions, and training program enrollment (Walker, 2001; Zampetti & Adamson, 2001).

Many HRIS products provide real-time reporting and even screen-based historical information that can provide managers with information about their employees or their functional units. There are also several third-party software products available that provide managers with almost continuous data about the status of their unit and the organization—much as a dashboard on a car provides immediate information. The analysis of more complex situations is beyond the capabilities of many of these reporting and query tools. To facilitate decision making on complex issues, the manager, before making a decision, usually relies on the analyst or power user to complete some type of analysis.

Analysts (Power Users)

The **analyst or power user** is perhaps the most demanding user of the HRIS. The primary role of the analyst is to acquire as much relevant data as possible, examine it, and provide reasonable alternatives with appropriate supporting information to facilitate the decision process of the manager. The analyst is referred to as a power user because this person accesses more areas of the HRIS than almost any other user. Analysts must be proficient with reporting and query tools. Analysts must also understand the process used to collect the data, how new data are verified, and how the HRIS and the employee life cycle interact. They also need to understand the data definitions in terms of what data exist, the structure of the data, and what data fields are up-to-date and complete. Some HRIS also provide tools that the analyst can use to model scenarios or perform "what-if" analyses on questions of interest.

As an example, a recruiting analyst might be asked to provide a short list of potential internal candidates for a position that opened in the marketing function of a large retailer. The potential candidates' characteristics of interest are queried and may include (1) when they were last promoted, (2) whether they have engaged in continuous personal-skills development, (3) what their undergraduate degrees were, and (4) whether they have ever expressed any interest in marketing. The analyst would query appropriate tables and develop a list of internal candidates.

Another example might have the HR analyst completing an analysis of corporate headquarters turnover to determine if a particular function or salary issue is the cause of the problem. This information would be drawn from existing reports, ad hoc queries, and available salary information. Data could be compiled into categories by salary, function, gender, or organizational level and examined to determine if the cause of the turnover can be pinpointed and then countered.

Technicians (HRIS Experts)

Technicians or **HRIS experts** straddle the boundary of two functions. Their role is to ensure that appropriate HR staff members have all the access, information, and tools necessary to do their jobs. HRIS experts do this by understanding what is needed from an HR-process standpoint and then translating that into technical language, so the technical employees—programmers, database administrators, and application administrators—know exactly what to do. When the technical staff is planning to install the latest update and one of the results will be a change in functionality, the HRIS expert must take what the technical staff provides and translate that into language HR users understand, so as to indicate how processes and activities might change. For example, if an HR professional required that a new report be generated every other Tuesday, the HRIS expert would learn what data the report requires—perhaps mock the report up with the user—and then explain to the technical people how to make sure that this report is automatically generated on the time schedule.

Clerical Employees

Much like power users, **clerical employees** also spend a significant portion of their day interacting with the HRIS. The difference is one of depth. The clerical employee must understand the process required to enter information into the HRIS and may also need to start the process or generate periodic reports. While clerical staff members in the HR employment department do not generally provide input about whether to hire an individual to a particular position, they bear considerable responsibility for seeing that the new employee gets paid properly. Hiring a new employee requires that someone, for example, a clerical employee, enter the appropriate information into the HRIS—such as the reporting relationship of the new employee as well as his or her benefits, salary, and direct deposit information.

Organizational Employees

Organizational employees are essentially all the other employees throughout the organization who interact with the HRIS. These employees serve in roles such as bank teller, nurse, machinist, salesperson, and accountant. These employees are not involved in human resources and are not likely to make decisions with

HR data, but they may utilize the HRIS to help manage their personal information. Typically, all the employees in the organization may interface with the HRIS through a self-service Web portal or secure employee kiosk, removing the necessity of an HR clerk or staff member assisting with many routine HR record modifications (Walker, 2001). Self-service capabilities encourage employees to manage their personal HR profiles with respect to a variety of functions, such as benefit and retirement plan monitoring or computerized training, in addition to using HRIS-based systems to complete numerous personnel forms (Adamson & Zampetti, 2001; Zampetti & Adamson, 2001). Typical self-service applications are accessible most of the day throughout the week. Employees log on to the system, where their identity is authenticated and verified. Then appropriate change options are offered to the employee based on certain parameters that control the areas where the employee is allowed to make valid alterations to the HRIS—such as personnel data updates, job postings, or desired training enrollments (Adamson & Zampetti, 2001; Zampetti & Adamson, 2001). One fairly large financial-services organization noted that self-service options significantly enabled them to reduce the annual benefits open-enrollment process by reducing the paper documents generated, reducing necessary mailings, and reducing the data that had to be read and entered into the HRIS. Data entry time alone was reduced from six to two weeks (Bedell, 2003b).

Nonemployees

Job Seekers

It is estimated that 70% to 90% of large organizations use online recruitment, and that number continues to increase (Stone, Lukaszewski, & Isenhour, 2005). Online recruiting tends to attract individuals who are well educated, Internet savvy, and searching for higher-level positions (McManus & Ferguson, 2003). Online recruitment also attracts people born since 1980, who have grown up with computers and are therefore comfortable with obtaining information on the Internet (Zusman & Landis, 2002). A successful recruitment Web site needs to be user-friendly and easy to navigate, while attracting candidates to apply to an organization by clearly communicating the benefits of joining it.

Typical **job seekers** have little or no prior information about how to interface with the HRIS and have had nearly zero training opportunities with it. Therefore, the recruiting portal needs to provide ease of use and ease of access to up-to-date job information. The Web form that is used to collect applicant data must also be reliably entered into the appropriate fields within the company's HRIS database. This online recruiting activity will facilitate searches for new employees to fill existing and future positions.

Sourcing Partner Organizations

The partner organizations to HR functions require certain information to complete their tasks. **Sourcing partner organizations** such as Monster.com, Adecco, and most executive recruiting firms require information about vacant positions, including a position description, job specifications, desired candidate competencies, potential salary range, and contact information. The information provided is limited to specific searches for open jobs and is updated as needed.

Business partners that are the recipients of decisions to outsource portions of the HR function (e.g., benefit management firms) or that facilitate process completion on behalf of the employee (e.g., banks) require information that is related to current employees. This requirement increases the need for accurate data, training, and specialized security assurances, as employee information is leaving the organization.

Important Data

As is evident in the previous sections, each customer or user of the HRIS has slightly different needs with regard to what information he or she will be using. Some users simply input data and information, a few simply look at data and information provided in the form of reports, while a few others analyze the data and information to make decisions. What these users all have in common is that all the information is about potential and current employees with a focus on managing the organization's human capital to achieve strategic organizational goals. Specific data from the HRIS database fit into three categories:

1. Information about people, such as biographical information and competencies (knowledge, skills, abilities, and other factors)
2. Information about the organization, such as jobs, positions, job specifications, organizational structure, compensation, employee/labor relations, and legally required data
3. Data that are created as a result of the interaction of the first two categories: for example, individual job history, performance appraisals, and compensation information

HRIS ARCHITECTURE

The HRIS "Dinosaur"

In the early days of HR applications (in the 1970s), large "dinosaurs" roamed the **information technology (IT)** landscape. These were called mainframe computers and were primarily built by IBM. These large systems hosted payroll applications for most enterprises. Users of the system, which mainly consisted of IT personnel and HRMS (human resource management systems) administrators, executed large batch processes while directly logged onto the mainframe computer. Although access to the mainframe was possible via a desktop monitor, no processing was done locally. This architecture is commonly called a single-tier computing system—user interface, application processing, and data storage resided on the mainframe.

Client-Server (Two-Tier) Architecture

During the 1980s, it was discovered that many typical HR functions (such as employee benefits and recruiting) did not require the high-powered and expensive processing available on the mainframe computers. With the advent of the **personal computer (PC)**, many of these functions could be reallocated to the local processing power of the PC. By the end of the decade, HRIS software vendors such as PeopleSoft began using this power of PCs and created the **two-tier (client-server) architecture** (see Figure 3.1).

The purpose of client-server architecture was to spread out low-powered processing capability to the dozens of PCs then being used across an organization. High-performance applications such as payroll would still be run in a batch process on the mainframe computer or outsourced to vendors such as **Automated Data Processing (ADP)**. But day-to-day processing could be implemented on the PC. In this case, an

Figure 3.1 Two-Tier (Client-Server) Architecture

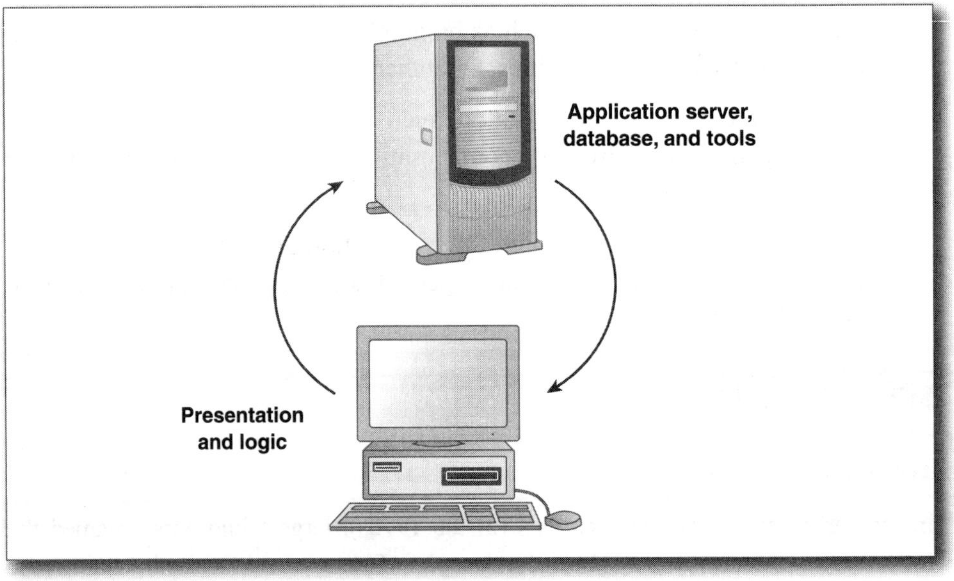

HR application's logic or set of business rules would run on the local machine. Issues such as having valid data entries for hiring dates, home addresses, and name formats could be checked instantly by the PC, that is, without looking up the business rule at the server on the mainframe. Even more complex checks, such as term of employment and salary deduction calculations, could be done on the local PC. In addition, software applications could apply the new **graphical user interface (GUI)** of the Windows environment. The ease of using the GUI compared with the traditional command-based interface was a major factor that enabled individuals with limited technology experience to use these PC-based applications.

This two-tiered architecture meant that the HR software application technology could be divorced from the database technology. This separation simplified the HR application and allowed enterprises to select the most appropriate **database management system (DBMS)** for their needs. (See Chapter 2 for an extended discussion of DBMS.) The most common database design is the relational model. This model standardizes how data are physically stored on the computer and provides standard data access via Structured Query Language (SQL). In fact, most software products are able to communicate to a variety of DBMS servers. This two-tier architecture was a huge leap forward in allowing HR professionals to serve many more employees—data were still located in a centralized database, but logic could be distributed to the PC that needed to run the specific application, and thus usability of the HRIS increased!

Three-Tier Architecture

Throughout the 1990s and into the current decade, this division of processing activity expanded from two-tier to three-tier and, finally, to **N-tier architectures**. With a **three-tier architecture**, the servers have two roles—as a database (DBMS) server and as an application server (see Figure 3.2).

With the development of the two-tier and three-tier systems, the HRIS professional still managed the user interface, but more demanding processing occurred in the middle, in the tier comprising the application server or servers. Software would implement transaction logic to maintain data reliability. For example, if two recruiters updated the same job position at the same time, a transaction processor would ensure that both updates were entered into the database. This functionality allowed several users to access the central database simultaneously. This type of software, which performed tasks between the client and the database server, became known as **middleware**—software that managed data and transactions before they were saved to the database. There are a couple of drawbacks with both two-tier and three-tier systems, however. First, a large amount of information has to move from the client computer across the network to the server to execute database transactions quickly, which necessitates the use of significant **bandwidth** or

Figure 3.2 Three-Tier Architecture

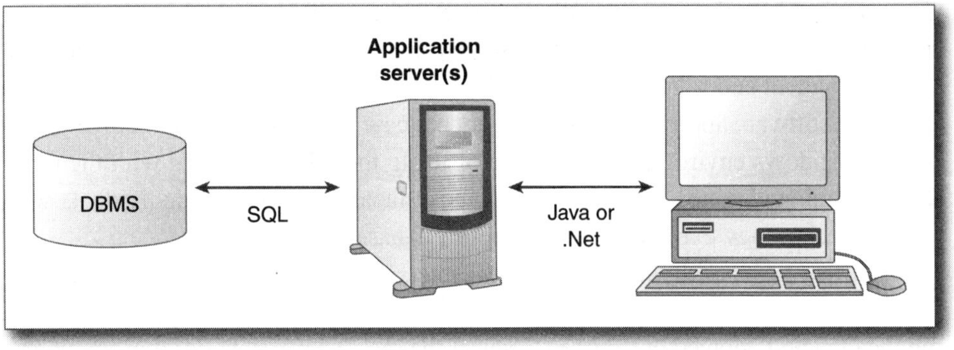

the ability to move lots of data quickly between computers. Second, the user interface client needs to be installed (along with database drivers) on every PC needing to access the HRIS. The corollary issue of this requirement is that employees need to be trained on this application. Therefore, HRIS access tended to be limited to employees within the "four walls" of the enterprise, that is, only to those residing within the local area network of the organization. Low-bandwidth access, such as Internet dial-up, was impractical.

To overcome some of these shortcomings and to support broader employee access to employee self-service applications, organizations utilized the Web browser. The browser provides a "thin client" and is a relatively small piece of software requiring fairly small client computing resources made possible by the three-tier computing model. A "thick client" would require a significant-sized software product and computing power at the client location (as necessitated by the two-tier model). An Internet Web browser comes installed on all major **operating systems** (Windows, Mac OS, Linux, and even Palm OS). The browser's user interface has become ubiquitous. Therefore, very little employee training is required to use a browser-based application. Finally, a browser works well in a low-bandwidth network environment. So, now, the typical HRIS application architecture looks like that depicted in Figure 3.3.

A standard Web server, such as Microsoft's Internet Information Server (IIS) or Apache's Web server, manages communication between the browser and the application server using the **Hypertext Markup Language (HTML)**, a software language used to create and display Web pages. The application server manages multiple user sessions logged onto the system at the same time as well as more complex business rule execution. And the application server also issues transactions to the centralized database server. Instead of just limiting ourselves to a four-tier label, this architecture has been labelled N-tier for the following reasons:

Figure 3.3 N-Tier Architecture

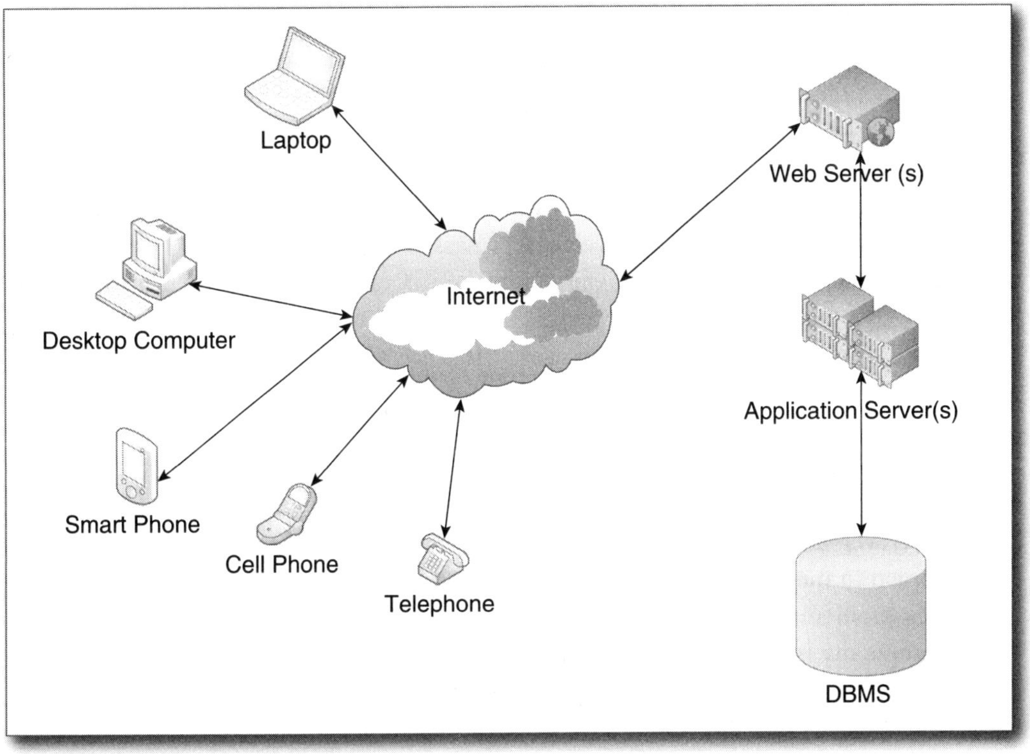

- It is expandable to multiple Web servers and application servers to handle **load balancing**, or distributing processing across multiple computers.
- Web servers can be geographically dispersed to provide worldwide access.
- Additional file servers can be added to save documents, reports, error logs, and so on, that are generated on a daily basis.
- Multiple print servers or specialized printers can be added as needed. For example, payroll check printing requires a security-enabled toner called magnetic ink character recognition (MICR) to print encoded checks for bank cashing. These check printers can be physically located in a secure environment but connected to the HRIS N-tier architecture like any other printer.
- Additional "process schedulers" can be added to handle large batch jobs such as payroll cycles. These servers offload "heavy" processing from the main application server so that user interaction is not affected.

N-Tier Architecture With Enterprise Resource Planning

The architecture diagram becomes even more complicated when other ERP components are added. HRIS do not exist in a vacuum. They interact with other business operations within the company. For example, when payroll is run, these financial-related transactions need to be registered in the company's general ledger (GL) application. Typically, GL exists within the financial/accounting component of large ERP systems from SAP, Oracle, and Microsoft. Therefore, GL transactions must be interfaced between Payroll and these systems. So additional application servers and databases enter the picture, as depicted in Figure 3.3. In this figure, the Internet browser communicates (using HTML) to one or more Web servers. The Web server manages various client sessions to accommodate many users at the same time. The Web server passes requests to the application server, where the business logic for the application is executed. Finally, information is stored in the DBMS as in the two- and three-tier models. There exist many variations of this diagram: In some cases, databases can be shared (in this situation, HRIS is subsumed within the ERP system); in other cases, Internet technologies such as the **eXtensible Markup Language (XML)**, which is similar to HTML, and Web services are used to integrate HRIS and ERP. The ultimate goal is to provide a single data truth so that all enterprise data can be accessed by all users wherever and whenever needed. Data should not be duplicated, re-entered, or copied to multiple systems. ERP applications provide the infrastructure to avoid this problem. So, even though the architecture may be more complicated, this complexity is hidden from the end user, and the logical view of the system remains relatively simple. For example, a consultant for a large IT services company can travel throughout the world, work with multiple clients, but still be able to record his or her time and prepare expense reports using a single browser application from any hotel room.

Cloud Computing—Back to the Future!?

In the latter half of this decade, a new architectural model has become prevalent called *cloud computing*. **Cloud computing** is a computing architecture that uses the Internet and central remote servers to maintain data and applications. To achieve this, a "server cloud," or group of computers, is operated off-site, and hosted services are then delivered over the Internet to the client organization. Cloud computing technology allows businesses to use applications without actually having to own the hardware and software. The underlying goal of cloud computing is to reduce software and equipment capital outlays, and this aim is achieved because the company does not need to keep purchasing new software or hardware to keep pace with technology changes. That investment becomes the responsibility of the vendor offering the cloud computing services.

Cloud computing can be sold on demand, by the minute or the hour, and is elastic—meaning that an enterprise can consume as much or as little of a service as it wants at any given time. From an accounting perspective, an enterprise leases a preset amount of computing power over an annual period. This cost can be budgeted for in a similar manner to budgeting for telephony or electrical expenses. Computing charges then become part of the operational budget expense as opposed to large capital investments. There exist three general service categories commonly recognized in cloud computing. These include

- **Infrastructure as a Service (IaaS)**—This type of service basically provides access to an operating system (such as Microsoft Windows or Linux) or to a cluster of connected systems. Amazon Elastic Compute Cloud (EC2) provides access to on-demand operating systems.
- **Platform as a Service (PaaS)**—The next level of services include application and Web server technology pre-built into the leased computer. Enterprises still build out custom applications on top of these servers. Microsoft Azure is an example of PaaS.
- **Software as a Service (SaaS)**—In this case, a complete application is delivered over the Internet. What is delivered can be as simple as an e-mail service (think Google Mail) or as complex as the entire HRIS application (e.g., see Workday, Inc. at www.workday.com).

In a sense, cloud computing is a return to the single-tier model of the 1980s. Instead of a single large mainframe running all of the applications, the various servers together act as the "super computer" providing the application runtime environment over the Internet. And instead of a dumb terminal accessing a single function over a mainframe, the browser now provides the interface to the entire suite of HR applications. In the ancient history of mainframe applications, human resources departments had to rely on corporate data centers (or IBM) to provide high-performing and up-to-date applications. With cloud computing, the burden lies with software vendors such as Workday or Taleo (www.taleo.com—hosted recruiting and talent management solution) to provide the updating. And, of course, leveraging the cloud requires solid high-performance Internet access all of the time. Finally, the cloud service providers now maintain sensitive corporate data. So when choosing a cloud solution, the evaluation process must include a thorough security analysis.

Security

Security in the HRIS context means protecting the hardware, software, and data in the HRIS from unauthorized access, use, disclosure, disruption, modification, or destruction. Security ranks as a top priority for any HRIS, and policies and practices need to be addressed to handle the following situations:

- Exposure of sensitive payroll and benefits data between employees
- Loss of sensitive personnel data outside the enterprise (such as Social Security numbers)
- Unauthorized updates of key data, such as salary amounts, stock options (both quantity and dates), or named beneficiaries
- Sharing of personnel or applicant review comments with unauthorized employees
- Sharing data with external organizations and service providers, such as temporary employment companies or Automated Data Processing, Inc.

Security needs to be maintained at a variety of levels. First, physical access to the DBMS and the application server needs to be limited so that machines cannot be destroyed or logged into directly. Network, operating system, and DBMS access must be limited so that tools outside of the HR application cannot be used to query sensitive data. This control should prohibit hackers directing probes at the systems or using a variety of phishing techniques to gain access. In the case of external users, special, "private" network access may need to be set up using a public network such as the Internet. A **virtual private network (VPN)** can be implemented so that users outside of the company can log into the computing resources as if they were within the **firewall** (specialized software that monitors data at the organizational boundary and blocks unauthorized data from entering or leaving the organization). Alternatively, many HRIS applications provide specially built "portals," which enable Internet browser access to specific components of the system. This design leads to the segregation of users into different categories.

All enterprise-level HRIS systems implement their own level of security on top of those of the operating system and DBMS. Access to the data by employees is typically administered via users and user roles. A user of the system is assigned a security role (such as recruiter, benefits administrator, manager, payroll administrator, or just base employee). Then, each role can be assigned to access certain parts of the system. Security can limit or allow access to each user role through column and row level security. Each is briefly discussed below.

1. What menu items, links, pages, or screens can the user access? For example, only the payroll administrator should be able to see links to the payroll setup and execution processes. The average employee would not realize these pages exist.

2. Once on a particular page or screen, a user in a specific role may be able to edit or change certain fields that a user in another role would not. This distinction

is called **column-level security**. For instance, an employee would be able to view his or her own job title and salary information but would not be able to change these values.

3. Also, within a particular page or screen, someone assigned to a specific user role would be able to retrieve only the data belonging to that user. This security feature is called **row-level security**. For example, an employee could view his or her own payment history but not those of other employees. Row-level security supports **hierarchical access**—the more people that report to an employee (such as a manager or supervisor), the more data become viewable to that user. In some cases, a manager may need to allocate bonuses across several departments. Each employee would be able to see only his or her bonus, while the managers would be able to edit the bonus records of all employees reporting to them (but not those of employees reporting to other departmental managers).

Within the typical corporation, the HR function exists primarily as administrative support for the operational components of the corporation (sales, marketing, procurement, and manufacturing). In the same way, human resource information systems support the general ERP system operations. Employee information must be shared between procurement and HR so that approval processes can be maintained. Employee data is also shared between the sales force automation (SFA) function and payroll to determine commissions. Many other examples also exist that demonstrate the need for HRIS to be integrated with ERP. This ever-tightening coupling of HR data with broader organizational data, which spans information silos and eliminates data redundancy, heightens the need for security in the HRIS. In many cases, these security issues have been addressed by subsuming the stand-alone HRIS into the broader organizational ERP, with shared security and functionality.

BEST OF BREED

An HRIS, as discussed in the previous section, often exists as one of the main parts of an overall ERP software solution for the company. Yet the HRIS is not a monolithic solution even within HR business processes. There exist alternative software applications that solve specific HR business problems. This section addresses these types of solutions, the pros and cons of using multiple applications, and technical infrastructure. In general, an architecture that combines products from multiple vendors is called "**best of breed**" (BOB).

The most well-known example of these BOB architectures comes from the audio industry—surround-sound receivers combined with CD players, DVD players, high-end speakers, and even the occasional retro turntable. All these components "plug and play" with each other to provide the best possible sound experience. This architecture works because of the standards that have been established for decades and that enable different devices to work together. We will see below that BOB software components for an HRIS still need to mature somewhat to reach the capability of the analog audio components. Yet the goal remains the same—deliver the best possible point solution to meet the business need.

For this synergy to work properly, three conditions need to be present for each software solution:

- First, there should be a perceived need for a specialized solution. For example, if a company expects to receive electronic job applications over the Internet 90% or more of the time, an **optical character recognition (OCR)** program, which scans handwritten or typewritten forms into an electronic format, would not be needed for resume scanning.

- Second, a universally agreed-on set of guidelines for interoperability must exist between applications. This exists at both the syntactical and the semantic levels. The **syntactical level** refers to the base "alphabet" used to describe an interface. For any two applications to communicate, they will need to share data. This data exchange can be done through databases, simple text files (such as Excel), or, increasingly, XML. Basically, XML is similar to HTML, which is used in all Internet browsers. XML files can be shared or transmitted between most software applications today. XML presents a structured syntax—an alphabet—to describe any data elements within an HRIS.

  An HR example would consist of selecting the most robust HR software applications—regardless of vendor—for each need and then using the XML language to move data efficiently among those applications. The HR department might select Resumix software for resume tracking, Oracle's PeopleSoft for most HR applications and data management, Chronos software for time and labor tracking, ADP software for payroll purposes, and a proprietary vendor product for outsourced HR benefits administration.

- Third, applications need to "speak the same language." Just as the Roman alphabet allows the spelling of words in multiple languages and formats, XML enables data to be described with many different tags. At the **semantic level**, the language needs to map between software applications. An employee's data description may consist of various tagged fields, such as Name, Address, Birth

Date, Phone, Title, Location, and so on. If one of the applications does not have most of the same set of XML tags, it will not be able to exchange employee data. As important as the shared data semantics between applications is having analogous business process semantics. For example, a time-keeping system may define a pay period differently from the payroll application that actually prints employee checks.

If the above conditions are met, HRIS applications should be able to interoperate with many point solutions. What are the typical solutions found in an HRIS implementation? The following sections will detail examples of solutions for some of the HR programs in an organization.

Recruitment

The business process to recruit new employees for a company has many BOB opportunities. Large HRIS applications tend to focus on the internal hiring processes of the company—creating and approving job requisitions, saving applicant data, scheduling interviews, capturing interview results, and, finally, hiring the new employee. Yet there exist other software applications to "fine-tune" the hiring process. OCR scanning applications can eliminate the rekeying of applicant data from paper-based resumes, and other applications can perform applicant database searches, post job requisitions directly to Internet job sites, and run applicant background checks. These examples of specific functionality are typically not provided in an HRIS.

Time Collection

Most companies require employees to submit time-keeping data each pay period. For hourly employees, this typically means using a punch card and time clock to track hours. Some solutions use employee badges with magnetic stripes, thereby enabling employees to clock in and out. Again, most HRIS vendors do not provide the hardware needed to track time. Time-keeping systems will capture the hourly data from various readers throughout a site. Employee scheduling for various shift coverages can be implemented with time collection or planning software. For example, transit districts schedule bus operators to cover a very complex route system throughout the week. Unionized rules force certain break periods and preferences for senior operators. Driver schedules are posted for future pay periods; and actual hours worked, reported sick, taken as vacation time, and so on, are collected for prior pay periods. Such data will be reviewed each pay period prior to being transmitted to the HRIS payroll application.

Payroll

In some cases, the entire payroll process may be outsourced to another vendor, such as ADP. ADP specializes in providing payroll services for companies of all sizes. For some enterprises, the cost of maintaining a payroll application and staff in-house may outweigh the benefits of controlling the process. In this case, employee time data, pay rate, and benefit information would be transmitted to ADP for processing. This choice of using an outside provider is conceptually the reverse of the typical BOB motivation. The enterprise is not looking for the *best* technical or functional solution but for a provider offering a commodity service at the *lowest* cost. In the case of a large multinational corporation with lots of employee levels, it would probably be prudent to purchase the HRIS payroll application.

Benefits

Each year, most employers present their employees with what is called the benefits open enrollment period during which signing up for benefits is similar to course enrollment for students each semester. Instead of enrolling in courses, though, employees enroll for major medical, dental, and insurance benefits. For example, employees choose between health care providers such as Kaiser or Blue Cross for their medical insurance. These providers support interfaces with the major HRIS applications so that, as employees log into the enrollment software, they can review offerings tailored to their company's plan. Thus, when employees select a particular insurance program, they can then transmit enrollment data to the provider through their organization's HRIS.

As one can see in Figure 3.4, BOB solutions introduce additional complexity into the software architecture. This complexity can add IT expense in the form of new software licensing and programming charges. The justification for the added functionality needs to compensate for these additional costs. So a cost-benefit analysis should be performed by the HR function to determine whether the BOB alternative is to be used. Detailed procedures to compute a cost-benefit analysis are covered in Chapter 7.

In summary, BOB options can create a much more powerful solution than a stand-alone HRIS. The BOB alternative also creates system flexibility, as each application can be managed and upgraded independently. Yet this power and flexibility may end up costing the IT department by giving rise to more complex systems administration issues.

Figure 3.4 Best-of-Breed Solutions Architecture

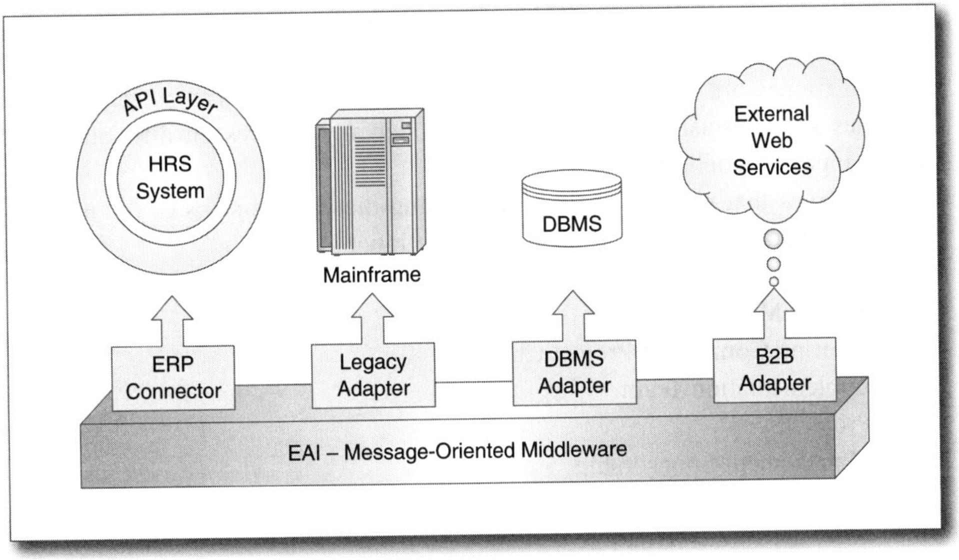

PLANNING FOR SYSTEM IMPLEMENTATION

A variety of authors, consultants, and others have discussed implementation methods for information systems. Rampton, Turnbull, and Doran (1999) discuss 13 steps in the implementation process. Jessup and Valacich (1999) divide the implementation of a system into 5 steps, with a focus on the systems side of the process. Regan and O'Conner (2002) provide 8 steps for implementing information systems. Some organizations have proprietary processes that they use for all implementations. Points to remember as this section is examined are as follows: (1) this is a process that will take a team of individuals anywhere from six weeks to three years to complete; (2) a variety of ways to manage this process may be attempted, so long as the key issues are examined and organizational goals for the implementation are achieved; and (3) there is no single definitive approach to be used in all situations.

The first key step is planning. This is an absolutely critical step in any business process and especially in the design of any large-scale software implementation involving multiple-process interfaces. Note that the planning process doesn't guarantee success—rather, it increases the probability that the implementation will be successful. The systematic examination of the following topics provides the organization with the opportunity to see how the implementation will work—to peer into the crystal ball—and identify some contingencies for implementation steps that might not go perfectly. In other words, a robust planning process provides a framework within which the implementation team can proceed, and it provides some decision-making parameters for any unforeseen difficulties that might appear (Bedell, 2003a).

The topics that need to be discussed during the various steps of the planning process include, but are not limited to, the following:

- Project Manager
- Steering Committee/Project Charter
- Implementation Team
- Project Scope
- Management Sponsorship
- Process Mapping
- Software Implementation
- Customization (Vanilla vs. Custom)
- Change Management
- "Go Live"
- Project Evaluation
- Potential Pitfalls

Project Manager

The choice of **project manager** deserves some serious thought. The project manager is the person responsible for managing all of the activities of the system implementation. There are really three good options for project manager. The first choice is to hire a consultant to be the project manager. This is the most expensive option and provides the best project management expertise but brings the least knowledge of your organization's mission, processes, and needs to the implementation.

The second option is to hire a full-time project manager who has presumably been certified by the project management institute. This option is more affordable, although you must have plenty of projects to justify this position. Anyone hired into this full-time position must have project management knowledge and certification, as well as personal knowledge of your organization's mission, goals, and, to a lesser extent, HR processes.

The third option is to select someone who is involved in the project and temporarily move him or her into a project management role. This person should bring excellent knowledge of the organization's mission, processes, and needs. However, unless the candidate has a project management certification, he or she may not be the strongest choice to keep a project on time. This decision is largely about the trade-off between cost and existing organizational knowledge.

Steering Committee/Project Charter

While project managers are responsible for the project, they are often assisted with the planning and implementation process by a team of individuals known as the **steering committee**. The steering committee is usually composed of the project manager, the senior-management member who is the project sponsor, and the lead employee from each involved area (e.g., lead systems analyst, lead database administrator). Also on the steering committee are HR functional experts, whose role is to provide expertise about what HR data are needed, how the HR process maps should be interpreted, and what data are required for decision making.

The steering committee has three key purposes. First, this group works under the direction of the project manager to establish the project scope, which is then often codified through the development of a **project charter** document. A second role of the steering committee is to develop a change management plan. The third major role of the steering committee is to assist the project manager in decision making.

Once a set of preliminary planning decisions are completed, the steering committee may develop a document known as the project charter, which will help maintain the guidelines on how the project should function. The charter is an all-encompassing document that

- makes the case for the implementation,
- shows the project's connection to organizational goals and strategies,
- provides identification of project scope,
- identifies implementation team members,
- identifies additional expertise that might be available,
- provides a training plan,
- explains the agreed-on decision-making process,
- discusses the process by which customization requests will be reviewed and acted on,
- covers the project management methods used,
- defines reporting,
- identifies deliverables, and
- defines political reporting relationships.

The project charter helps keep the entire team focused on the goals for the project by forcing the team to agree on what is critical. The project charter can also serve as a valuable political document within the organization, as some members of top management are usually asked to participate in developing the charter through an approval process or by helping draft the document. This approval process signifies to other, less involved management individuals that the implementation of this software is an expected organizational goal. Finally, the charter provides all the team members with key "talking points" about the project so that the scope, process, and goals can be clearly and consistently shared with those who might have questions. An example of a real steering committee's list of responsibilities is presented in Figure 3.5.

Implementation Team

The **implementation team** works with the project manager to complete the actual software implementation. A good configuration for the implementation team includes both functional and technical personnel. Functional personnel are usually drawn from the ranks of the HR department in the form of HR professionals with some technological proficiency. These functional experts are most often the power users, and they bring to the implementation team their extensive knowledge about HR processes as well as some technological skills. Technical personnel include HRIS specialists, systems analysts, database administrators, and hardware experts.

Figure 3.5 Example of a Steering Committee's List of Responsibilities

- Decides issues that involve policies and dollar amounts under the charge of the Executive Sponsor Committee
- Resolves issues where there is no consensus within the functional implementation team
- Reviews and approves plan, approach, and key decisions
- Reviews project budget, agreeing on necessary funds, and champions availability
- Manages expectations and guides communications
- Ensures that appropriate resources are available to the project
- Recommends policy and advocates needed change; ensures that policies are carried out
- Reviews progress as it relates to implementation timetable
- Provides periodic reports and advice to the executive management team

SOURCE: This is from an HRIS implementation that was early and under budget—a rarity (M. D. Bedell, personal communication, 2002).

Ideally, the technical personnel will have more than just a passing familiarity with HR processes; however, it is most likely that the HRIS specialist will be translating the functional references of the HR functional experts into the technical language of the technical personnel. The implementation team reports to the project manager while working on project-related activities; however, it is very likely that a matrix organizational structure will develop for the duration of the project. In this matrix structure, the implementation team members continue to be evaluated by the regular supervisors, yet they also report to the project manager for project-related issues. The lead implementation team members—both functional and technical—are usually also included on the steering committee, as described in the previous section.

As soon as the implementation team is chosen, two steps need to be taken quickly. First, the functional team experts should begin process mapping (see below). Second, implementation team training provided by the software vendor should be identified and scheduled by the project manager for the implementation team to attend.

Project Scope

Project scope is defined as those portions of the information system that need to be completely operational to satisfy the needs of the various customers, employees, and senior management. This definition of the scope of the project is absolutely critical to success. One difficulty that all steering committees face is project creep. Project creep occurs when decisions are made to implement additional functionality beyond what was defined in the project scope. The problem with project creep is that it may lead to huge cost overruns, a failure to complete the project on schedule, and then, in the rush to meet final deadlines, the delivery of a project that fails to meet the needs of the customers (see Sidebar 1).

Sidebar 1

One of the authors participated in an implementation during which a mid-sized oil company changed its HR system from PeopleSoft to SAP to match the financial product the company was using. Implementation team members used a methodology to define the project scope (and avoid project creep) by asking all the HR professionals to spend a few days with them over a couple of weeks discussing what HRIS capabilities would be implemented. Capabilities were divided into categories of "mission critical," would "make our lives easier," and "in our wildest dreams." The "mission critical" items were of course implemented. The "make our lives easier" items were prioritized into three categories: (1) those that were added, (2) those that would be implemented if the project were ahead of schedule, and (3) those that could be implemented during the second phase. The "wildest dreams" category items were given to the IT folks to work on in the future as time allowed (Bedell, 2002).

Management Sponsorship

Management sponsorship of the implementation project is crucial. Senior management has the ability to add or remove budget dollars and other resources as needed, move political hurdles out of the way, and facilitate the change management process through publicly demonstrated support for the project. Needless to say, the project manager and steering committee would be politically astute enough to develop and maintain an open, honest relationship with the management sponsor. A strong relationship with the senior management sponsor also reassures other senior managers that their employees are working. Remember, the implementation team usually consists of individuals from HR, IT, accounting, and potentially other functions. Their supervisors are not necessarily involved.

The senior management sponsor usually has a vested interest in the project. However, his or her formal acceptance as a project sponsor probably will not happen until the project charter is completed and the business case has also been made as to why the implementation should take place.

Process Mapping

The implementation of any new information system represents an immense change from the way processes and decisions were previously made. To facilitate that change, the team must understand an existing process before starting any implementation. On the surface, this appears to be a rather straightforward task—simply flowchart the process and identify (1) the data elements that go into the process at each step, (2) how those data elements are stored and modified, and (3) what output exists. In reality, additional information and structure are required to ensure that the essence of the entire organizational process is captured.

The first step is to generate one list of all the processes performed by each area of the HR function and a second list of processes that are touched by more than one area of the HR function. For example, three processes of interest in the recruiting department are (1) bringing candidates in for interviews, (2) checking references, and (3) extending offers. The functional team experts would ask questions such as the following: Are these three processes or three steps of one larger process? What data are required? Are there processes (or steps) that are completed by other departments that are critical? Does the compensation area do anything to help determine what an appropriate salary is? If it's a new position, does the organizational development group have to make a decision about how to place this position with regard to formal reporting and budgeting relationships?

The second step is to start generating a model of each process within the entire HR function. A successful model will incorporate both a flowchart picture and a data flow diagram (i.e., what data elements, processes, and outputs go with each step of the process). One of the authors helped develop a template for an implementation he was previously involved with. This template is presented in Figure 3.6 and is designed to be used by any subject matter expert as a guide to mapping processes. The example in question requires the subject matter expert or functional implementation team member to provide the name of the business process and a description of the process, as well as the procedure. In addition, the person mapping this process is asked to provide an inventory of the inputs needed as well as the outputs created by the process. In all cases, it is useful for the person completing the process to provide an example of each input and output.

The steering committee and implementation team concerned with obtaining the most benefit from a new or upgraded HRIS should understand the activities associated with the identification and mapping of business processes. The business processes described here are comparable with those used in many reengineering projects (Hammer & Champy, 1993). Much of the value of reengineering—as well as of this implementation process—comes from taking a systematic look at processes and removing duplication of effort and processes that are no longer necessary. Of the implementations in which one author was involved, one implementation "accidentally" found cost savings as a result of this mapping process, another intentionally set time aside to ask these questions and found considerable duplication and potential process-related cost savings, and a third did not care to take the time (M. D. Bedell, personal communication, 2002, 2004; Darter & Bedell, 1997).

The completed process maps are ideally compiled into a large chart that provides an overall view of the organization's processes. The details of the processes can be stored electronically in an easy-to-access central storage location, and it is useful to have copies in binders that can be distributed during the software implementation and configuration process. More information on creating process models can also be found in Chapter 5.

Software Implementation

Once the planning process is reasonably complete, the process-mapping process is nearly complete, and the implementation team has received most of its training, the actual software implementation can begin. Software implementation involves eight steps. Some of the steps go on concurrently while some work in sequence. For example, the first step—hardware verification—must precede any software installation. Hardware verification consists of examining the specifications of the various software components (e.g., database, file server, compiler) and ensuring that the hardware can meet the needs of the organization now and in the near future. After

Figure 3.6 Process-Mapping Template

Business Process/Function Description	*Procedure Description*
A. General description – Describe the business purpose – Provide a flowchart of the process B. Customers – Who are the customers of the process (who needs the process completed)? C. Group differences 1. Does this process apply to different subgroups? 2. Is the purpose different for different subgroups? 3. Is the timing different for different subgroups? D. Workload 1. Frequency of the process (daily/weekly/monthly/ad hoc) 2. Approximate elapsed time from start to finish of process 3. Estimated total work hours of process	A. Inputs 1. What kicks off the process? How do you know when to start? 2. What information do you need for the process? 3. What are the inputs to the process? What tools are used (forms, worksheets, electronic information, etc.)? 4. Are there any difficulties or complications getting the information? 5. Are the inputs different for different subgroups? B. Steps 1. How is the process performed (step-by-step)? 2. Are the steps different for different subgroups? C. Outputs

Input Inventory

What?			How?	Who?	When?
Form/input name	Form ID	Description	Paper/ electronic?	Who supplies the input?	How much and how often?

Output Inventory

What?			How?	Who?	When?
Report/output name	Report ID	Description	Paper or electronic?	Who supplies the input?	How much and how often?

SOURCE: From Darter and Bedell (1997).

the hardware is verified, the software installation process begins. Usually, an installer from the vendor works with the organization's technical professionals to install the ERP software and any related software tools. Note that this is also a training situation for the technical professionals as they work with the installer.

Data migration and configuration or fit-gap processes should also be ongoing. **Data migration** involves identifying which data should be migrated and how much historical data should be included, as well as the actual process of moving the data. The configuration or "**fit-gap**" process consists of systematically working through every HR process and matching each of those to each of the integral HRIS processes. The result is an understanding of where organizational processes and the software processes mesh (fit) and where they do not (gap). Any gaps that are identified need to be closed either through modification of organizational processes or by software customization.

The last step of the software implementation is system testing. In most cases, extensive testing is done while data are migrated, to verify data integrity. Data integrity means that the information is stored where it should be, that it can be queried, and that it is available to individuals with appropriate security clearance. The technical software team members test each module for proper functionality, and the functional HR team members verify that the module functions and maintains data integrity. For example, payroll modules have to be tested thoroughly to avoid double payments or missing payments and to make sure that checks print.

Throughout the entire implementation process, documentation of each action and decision must be recorded. This will provide the ongoing maintenance team with the roadmap to follow while they work on each new update, patch, security adjustment, or biannual legal change.

Customization

One of the most difficult decisions that many steering committees face is whether to customize the software to their specific needs—especially since modern HR software comes with ample opportunity and excellent tools for customization. This decision appears to be simple. **Customization** will enable the software to match the organization's process more closely. The organization will have to do less change management training since all the screens and reports will look just like the old ones. The main downside to customization is that there will be significant maintenance costs, as every tiny change has to be customized all over again with each software upgrade.

With no customization, the version of the software to be implemented is referred to as the "vanilla" version. The advantage of a **vanilla implementation** is that the software can be implemented as designed by the software vendor, and it provides a catalyst for the organization to engage in **process reengineering** in order to develop best practices that will match the industry best practices around which the software was developed. The downside is that the cost of change management efforts will increase. Most steering committees will decide that truly unique processes that are related to organizational competitive advantage are worth customizing. To customize simply so as to replicate old reports or screens is usually determined to be not worth the cost. A good method to determine which modifications need to be done is to have the steering committee request a complete business case, including a cost-benefit analysis, from the person requesting the customization. The goal of the business case is to determine whether the modification will help the software manage mission-critical decisions well enough to justify the cost.

Change Management

Change management focuses on the most difficult part of the implementation process—the interaction between the user and the software. The major obstacle is to get user acceptance of the new HRIS. The introduction of this new system will typically encounter strong resistance from the employees. Thus, it is important that the implementation team develop a change management plan consisting of communication, education, and training to prevent difficulties and solve problems. Failure to develop a change management plan may lead to morale issues, fear, and potential turnover among the workforce. Chapter 9 covers the issues associated with managing change and solutions to change management problems.

"Go Live!"

This is the moment of truth. It is time for the implementation to be put in place. There are two possible ways that the new software can be put to use. Option 1 is to do a **direct conversion**—the old software is turned off and the new software is turned on. As issues with the new software are identified, they are reported, and adjustments are made. The positive of a direct conversion is that it is done! The potential negative of deciding to do a direct conversion is that, regardless of training and the change management process, there is an organization-wide learning curve while the users adjust to the new software. There may be a period when customers are served at a level that is less than expected. And—as illustrated by Hershey's choice to use this "go-live" option in 1999 when implementing a new distribution system—if there are significant problems, significant profits may be destroyed as well. In Hershey's case, the company could not deliver $100 million of inventory to stores during the Halloween sales season (Koch, 2002).

The second option is a **parallel conversion**. This option turns the new software on some period of time before the old software is to be turned off, and it incorporates final system testing into the changeover process. The time period in question is usually a meaningful business cycle to the organization (e.g., a month or a quarter). During this time, both software systems are functioning, receiving input, running reports, and being queried. The positive of a parallel conversion is that there is enormous testing that goes on before the old software disappears. The negatives are that the users will hang on to the old software because it is comfortable and that there will have to be dual data entry performed for every task.

Regardless of which option is chosen, it is absolutely critical that appropriate support for training and software be in place. Many of the larger HRIS products employ context-sensitive help modules that rely on the end-user training materials to remind users of what they previously had learned. The user should also have access to help-desk staff members who are aware of the change and able to assist the user in getting through a variety of tasks.

Project Evaluation

A **project evaluation** focuses on the assessment of the project that was just completed. Every project provides an opportunity to learn something about what might have been done better. Any organization that plans to maintain a large information system should begin to collect regular data about what worked, what did not work, and where potential areas for improvement exist. A specific schedule of measurement or identification of milestones and related reporting should be created during the planning process and adhered to rigorously. Measurement milestones could be weekly, quarterly, or attached to each major step in the implementation process. In addition, a dollar value should be assigned to each critical step so that budgets can be assessed and evaluated. The emphasis here should be on measurement of important business metrics; this topic is covered in Chapter 6.

Potential Pitfalls

Even the most comprehensive list of what might go wrong during an HRIS implementation would be woefully incomplete. Instead, some of the most common pitfalls are reiterated here:

- Poor planning
- Incomplete steering committee or steering committee without top management support
- Implementation team problems or incomplete implementation team
- Failure to assess the politics of the organization adequately
- Insufficient process mapping
- Scope creep
- Poor implementation of or insufficient change management

SUMMARY

The implementation of an HRIS goes beyond simply placing a new technology into the organization. This chapter focuses on several of the many different organizational, people, and technical issues that must be addressed. The first section considers the important internal and external users or customers of the HRIS and organizational goals. In the second section, four different types of HRIS architectures are enumerated. The evolution of technology, from legacy "dinosaur" systems to contemporary N-tier architectures and cloud computing, has dramatically affected the scope and influence of HRIS in organizations. Therefore the strengths and weaknesses of each architecture are discussed. Next, a brief overview of hardware and database security is provided to make the reader aware of their importance in any HRIS adoption process. The third section of the chapter discusses the best of breed approach to HRIS adoption and the pros and cons of this approach in different functional areas. Finally, the chapter concludes with a general discussion of the steps that organizations might take to plan and implement an HRIS and of the factors that can affect these processes. A brief discussion of the conversion approaches to "going live" with the new HRIS illustrates the choices available to organizations when switching over to the new system. In summary, organizations that are able to manage the people, processes, and technology involved in an HRIS implementation should be more likely to find that the new HRIS is able to meet their goals more effectively in terms of budget, functionality, and usability.

KEY TERMS

analysts or power users
Automated Data Processing (ADP)
bandwidth
best of breed (BOB)
change management
clerical employees
cloud computing
column-level security
customization
data migration
database management systems (DBMS)
direct conversion
enterprise resource planning (ERP)
eXtensible Markup Language (XML)
firewall
fit-gap
graphical user interface (GUI)
hierarchical access
human resources management (HRM)
Hypertext Markup Language (HTML)
implementation team
information technology (IT)
infrastructure as a service (IaaS)
job seekers

load balancing

management sponsor; management sponsorship

managers

middleware

N-tier architecture

operating system (OS)

optical character recognition (OCR)

organizational employees

parallel conversion

personal computer (PC)

platform as a service (PaaS)

process reengineering

project charter

project evaluation

project manager

project scope

row-level security

security

semantic level

senior vice presidents (SVPs)

software as a service (SaaS)

sourcing partner organizations

steering committee

syntactical level

technicians (HRIS experts)

three-tier architecture

two-tier (client-server) architecture

vanilla implementation

virtual private network (VPN)

DISCUSSION QUESTIONS

1. Identify the various types of users or customers of an HRIS.
2. What are the three broad categories of data that an HRIS manages?
3. How does network bandwidth affect a two-tier (client-server) architecture?
4. How does an N-tier architecture simplify the IT department's task of maintaining client software?
5. Discuss row-level security. How does this work? Why may this be more valuable to an HRIS than a manufacturing software solution?
6. Research various middleware products from IBM, BEA, or Oracle, and discuss how these products can be leveraged in an HRIS.
7. Research hr-xml.org. How many transactions or interfaces do the standards support? How many software vendors are involved with the organization?
8. Take a specific industry, say the K–12 education industry. How might HireRight's integration with Oracle's PeopleSoft assist the process of hiring employees such as bus drivers, janitors, or campus security?

9. When might BOB not be "best"?
10. The systems development process has been discussed by many. Name five discussion topics that need to be completed during the planning process.
11. Discuss the different project manager options and explain the pros and cons of each.
12. What is a project charter? Why is it important?
13. Why is it absolutely critical to have the scope of the project identified?
14. Why is project creep not a good thing?
15. Complete a flowchart of the process you follow to enroll in classes and pay your tuition. Then apply the process template in the section "Planning for System Implementation."
16. Why do employees fear change? Give some examples of how you might eliminate the fear of change.

CASE STUDY: VIGNETTE REVISITED

This case is revisited with some additional information that involves the understanding of the material in this chapter. The additional information will be added to the situation described in the vignette at the beginning of this chapter.

A billion-dollar retailer with more than 4,000 stores finds that it cannot move fast enough to beat the competition. The organization's senior management arrives at the conclusion that it would be easier to achieve the strategic goals enumerated by the board of directors if the various organizational functions would share information. Shared information would enable them to develop and deploy new actions and tactics more quickly. The CEO and the president have therefore ordered the major functions to immediately update their information systems so that data sharing is possible. The **senior vice presidents (SVPs)** of accounting and human resources immediately decide that the only solution is to decide jointly on an ERP product. ERP software applications are a set of integrated database applications, or modules, that carry out the most common business functions, including human resources, general ledger, accounts payable, accounts receivable, order management, inventory control, and customer relationship management. To speed the installation along, they will install it using a rapid implementation methodology that a company down the street used. The goal is to have the new systems operational in nine months.

Shortly after this decision is made, the SVP of HR calls you into his office and tells you that you will be management sponsor for this project. You have to decide on everything. You sit back in your nice office and think:

> What's the problem with this scenario? It shouldn't be difficult to select a vendor and then borrow the methodology from down the street. It worked for them; it should work for us! We'll call a few vendors in the morning and find out about cost, time frame, and implementation methods. In the meantime, I should find out a little more about how to do this and who will be using it. I remember from my information systems class in college that this is a reasonable first step when it comes to buying software.

What do you think your response would be to this inquiry? Has your response changed now that you have read this chapter? If so, how?

New Information for the Case: Part 1

After some discussions with department heads from all the departments in the organization, you realize that there are a large number of people (stakeholders) who will be affected by the new systems. Furthermore, you come to realize how important HR data really are to these stakeholders. Based on this information, you think, Wow, there are far more people who could be potentially using this information system than I expected! The old textbook and the vendor information should provide a lot to think about.

Using the information from the section of this chapter titled "HRIS Customers/Users: Data Importance," please answer the following questions:

1. Identify some of the customers who would be logical members of the implementation team and explain why.

2. Think through an HR process and sketch out what data are necessary to complete your sample process well. How much history does the organization need to convert to continue functioning?

3. Pick one area of the HR function (e.g., recruiting), and make a list of processes that will need to be mapped and possibly reengineered during this implementation.

New Information for the Case: Part 2

Over the next month, as you continue to obtain information about the design and implementation of the new system, you are still somewhat confused about what to do. Once again, we find you in your office thinking:

> There are so many potential decisions to make with regard to hardware! I wonder what we need to schedule, if we need to buy hardware, and how we should configure the servers to ensure maximum security. It's time to make another list of questions!

Based on the information in the section of the chapter titled "HRIS Architecture," please respond to the following:

1. Make a list of questions for each of the following individuals: lead hardware technical expert, network manager, and chief software manager.

2. What configuration should the company use? Make a suggestion and support it!

New Information for the Case: Part 3

As part of your investigation, you have uncovered a system concept called "best of breed." You are in your office again trying to decide what to do, and you think, "Perhaps best of breed might be the easiest and best way to go."

1. Make a recommendation as to whether a BOB option should be chosen or a more standardized option with simpler interfaces between hardware and software should be selected.

2. Think about what the best answer should be when you have to connect your system with accounting and finance. Make a recommendation and support it!

New Information for the Case: Part 4

You have just sat down in your office feeling as if there is way too much to do! Your IS software professional has given you the information from one of the potential vendors about the various steps that need to be taken in implementation of the HRIS. Your immediate reaction is, "Man, am I going to be at work late for the next many months!"

Case Study Questions

Based on the information in this chapter, answer the following questions:

1. Develop the first few steps of the project plan.
2. Discuss the potential political necessities outlined in this section as they relate to this type of implementation.
3. Think about and create a list of steps that make sense for your organization.
4. Is the nine-month rapid-implementation time frame feasible? Or will it just lead to failure?

REFERENCES

Adamson, L., & Zampetti, R. (2001). Web-based manager self-service. In A. J. Walker (Ed.), *Web-based human resources* (pp. 24–35). New York: McGraw-Hill.

Bedell, M. (2002). *A PeopleSoft to SAP conversion/implementation.* Unpublished research notes.

Bedell, M. (2003a). Human resources information systems. In H. Bidgoli (Ed.), *The encyclopedia of information systems* (Vol. 2, pp. 537–549). Burlington, MA: Academic Press.

Bedell, M. (2003b). *An identification of the cost savings resulting from an HR information system implementation.* Paper presented at the meeting of the American Society of Business and Behavioral Sciences, Las Vegas, NV.

Darter, K., & Bedell, M. (1997). *Process mapping template.* Unpublished research notes on a PeopleSoft ver. 7.0 implementation.

Fein, S. (2001). Preface. In A. J. Walker (Ed.), *Web-based human resources* (pp. vii–x). New York: McGraw-Hill.

Hammer, M., & Champy, J. (1993). *Reengineering the corporation: A manifesto for business revolution.* New York: HarperCollins.

Hendrickson, A. R. (2003). Human resource information systems: Backbone technology of contemporary human resources. *Journal of Labor Research, 24*(3), 381–394.

Jessup, L., & Valacich, J. (1999). Information systems foundations. In L. Jessup & J. Valacich (Eds.), *Que education & training* (pp. 4–10). Indianapolis, IN: Macmillan.

Koch, C. (2002). Hershey's bittersweet lesson [Electronic version]. *CIO Magazine.* Retrieved June 18, 2008, from www.cio.com/article/31518

McManus, M. A., & Ferguson, M. W. (2003). Biodata, personality, and demographic differences of recruits from three sources. *International Journal of Selection and Assessment, 11,* 175–183.

Miller, M. S. (1998). Great expectations: Is your HRIS meeting them? *HR Focus, 75,* 1–2.

Rampton, G. M., Turnbull, J., & Doran, J. A. (1999). *Human resources management systems: A practical approach* (p. 142). Toronto, ON: Carswell.

Regan, E., & O'Conner, B. (2002). *End-user information systems: Implementing individual and work group technologies* (pp. 26–28, 368–369). Upper Saddle River, NJ: Prentice Hall.

Stone, D. L., Lukaszewski, K. M., & Isenhour, L. C. (2005). e-Recruiting: Online strategies for attracting talent. In H. B. Gueutal & D. L. Stone (Eds.), *The brave new world of eHR.* San Francisco: Jossey-Bass.

Walker, A. J. (2001). Best practices in HR technology. In A. J. Walker (Ed.). *Web-based human resources* (pp. 3–12). New York: McGraw-Hill.

Zampetti, R., & Adamson, L. (2001). Web-based employee self-service (pp. 15–23). In A. J. Walker (Ed.), *Web-based human resources.* New York: McGraw-Hill.

Zusman, R. R., & Landis, R. S. (2002). Applicant preferences for Web-based versus traditional job postings. *Computers in Human Behavior, 18,* 285–296.

PART II

DETERMINING HRIS NEEDS

Chapter 4

HRIS Needs Analysis

Bradley J. Alge and Karen Bruner Upright

EDITORS' NOTE

This chapter begins the section of the book focused on how to determine the needs for an HRIS and how that determination affects the design of the HRIS. The idea that there will be different users of the HRIS with differing data and information needs was introduced briefly in Chapter 3. In this chapter, you will see the importance of the initial needs analysis and how it is done. In keeping with the holistic nature of HRIS, the system development life cycle (SDLC) is introduced; however, this chapter deals only with the planning and analysis parts of the SDLC as the remaining parts, namely, design, implementation, and maintenance, are discussed in subsequent chapters. The authors emphasize that the needs analysis begins the process of HRIS design but that this analysis is also done continuously throughout the system design process. This notion of continuously updating the needs analysis recognizes the possibility of both organizational and technology changes during the development and implementation of the HRIS. In addition, it is important to complete an accurate and comprehensive needs analysis because this will provide the blueprint for the evaluation of the HRIS after it is implemented.

CHAPTER OBJECTIVES

The learning goals for this chapter are listed below. At the end of this chapter, you should be able to address the following questions:

- What is a needs analysis, and why is it important?
- What is a system development life cycle (SDLC), and how do the planning and analysis parts of an SDLC inform the needs analysis process?
- What is phase containment, and how does it relate to a needs analysis?

- Where does a needs analysis fit within the broader scope of an HRIS project?
- What are the "Big 3" questions?
- What is involved in an HRIS needs analysis? What types of activities are performed?
- Who is typically involved in an HRIS needs analysis?
- What are the key deliverables of an HRIS needs analysis?
- Related to this question, what is a gap analysis, and what might a gap analysis report look like?
- How would a gap analysis be used in the needs analysis?

HRIS IN ACTION

Failing to Plan Is Planning to Fail

A multimedia company planned to offer a special benefits package to a select group of employees. The purpose of the package was to encourage some employees to retire early, which would provide cost savings to the company as well as meet some of its other needs, such as providing promotional opportunities to help attract and retain younger employees. The special package included granting additional years of service for the purposes of calculating retirement and retiree medical benefits, granting additional age to employees to be used in the calculation of eligibility for early retirement incentives from the pension plan, and eliminating some portion of the normal reductions in pension plan benefits for those taking early retirement. The cost of implementing these changes in the existing system for the estimated eligible group of just over 500 employees was prohibitive due to the complex nature of the calculations involved.

The project was in danger of being canceled until a careful needs analysis was done. For 500 employees, did the solution need to be fully automated? Did employees need to be able to model their retirement benefits on the Internet? How much manual work could be relied on to handle the workload? Did the project need to be repeatable?

The answer for the multimedia company was to build a simple solution outside its HRIS using spreadsheet and word merge applications and to couple that simple solution with a high-touch customer service group that was able to respond to the needs of program participants, manage the increased manual paperwork requirements, and perform the interventions into the system to make the components that had to be automated, such as the payment of benefits, function properly. The program that had nearly been canceled was a success, so much so that it was repeated just the next year in another company division.

Implementing the changes in the existing HRIS would have been the obvious solution, but creating a one-time solution when it appeared there would be little future need for a complicated implementation was the right choice in this case. Careful, honest, and practical needs analysis made possible what had been impractical due to cost concerns. It should be noted, however, that the HRIS provider recognized the need the multimedia company had expressed and later made a decision to augment its software to include features that would provide greater flexibility for future offerings, meeting a need the provider hadn't recognized during its own original planning and needs analysis phases.

INTRODUCTION: HRIS NEEDS—PLANNING AND ANALYSIS

In this chapter, the focus is on a critical set of activities that take place early in the life cycle of an HRIS—namely, the planning and analysis of an organization's HRIS needs. **Needs analysis** refers to the process of thoroughly gathering, prioritizing, and documenting an organization's HR information requirements, and it serves as a necessary input for the subsequent design and implementation of an HRIS. An HRIS needs analysis usually takes on a particularly prominent role in the planning and analysis stages of an HRIS development project, prior to significant design and implementation activities. It is important to note, however, that the needs analysis for the HRIS continues through the entire system development process since each stage in the process could lead to the identification of new needs for the HRIS.

Successful HRIS implementations are critically dependent on planning. In turn, successful planning is critically dependent on a comprehensive needs analysis. Consider some of the potential costs of not planning and conducting a thorough needs analysis:

- Users reject an HRIS that fails to provide the functionality they need.
- Vendor software packages are selected based on incomplete, inaccurate, or irrelevant criteria.
- Costly custom systems are developed and built based on arbitrary data.
- Custom additions to the HRIS are required to fill needs after implementation, needs that were not properly identified during the needs analysis.
- Scope creep: New, but unneeded, functionality is erroneously added to the system, increasing the time and cost of implementation.

Consequently, planning and needs analysis are not something that HRIS project personnel choose to do; they are tasks they *must* do. The following sections in this chapter provide a road map for conducting a needs analysis. As a beginning, planning and needs analysis will be described as phases within the system development life cycle.

System Development Life Cycle (SDLC)

The following description of the **system development life cycle (SDLC)** is similar to the description of the system implementation process in Chapter 3. However, the focus in Chapter 3 was on the implementation phase of an HRIS project, whereas the focus here is on the completion of an accurate HRIS needs analysis within the SDLC. The overlap between these chapters is deliberate since the specific details on both needs analysis and implementation are complementary and represent two important parts of the development and design of an HRIS.

Scholars and practitioners may disagree on the number of steps and terminology used in describing the SDLC, but most would agree that the following activities take place at various stages throughout the conceptualization and ultimate implementation of any technological system: planning, analysis, design, implementation, and maintenance. These activities are formally codified as a set of five distinct yet related phases (see Figure 4.1).

Let us consider more closely the SDLC phases depicted in Figure 4.1:

1. *Planning:* The planning phase of the SDLC includes both long-range or strategic planning and short-range operational planning. Because of the integral nature of needs analysis to planning, we devote an entire section to planning below.
2. *Analysis:* It is in the analysis phase that an organization's current capabilities are documented, new needs are identified, and the scope of an HRIS is determined. Again, because needs analysis is such an integral part of the analysis phase, we devote an entire section to analysis below.

Figure 4.1 An Example of the Phases in a Typical System Development Life Cycle (SDLC)

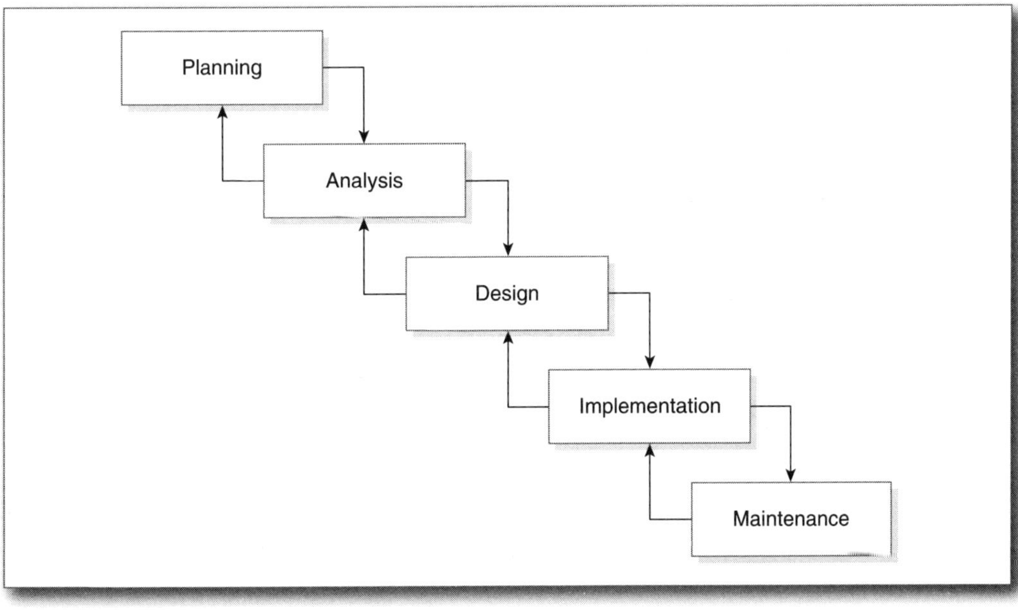

3. *Design:* In the design phase, the "blueprint" for the system is finalized. Whereas the analysis phase finalizes the needs or requirements for the HRIS, here, the detailed specifications for the final system are laid out. It is often during the design phase that the final vendor evaluation and selection occurs. (This topic is covered in detail in the next chapter.) **Business process reengineering (BPR),** or the redesign of HR work processes, also occurs during this phase, and the final specifications of the system and its HR functionality are defined. Design is covered more extensively in the next chapter.

4. *Implementation:* During implementation, the HRIS system is built, tested, and readied for actual rollout, or the "go live" stage—the point in the SDLC at which the old system is turned off and the new system is put into operation. Key steps in this process include coding or configuring modules, system testing, finalizing procedures, converting old data for use in the new system, and training end users.

5. *Maintenance:* The SDLC does not end once the "go live" date arrives. The maintenance phase, sometimes referred to as the "forgotten phase" (Smith, 2001), is that phase in the life of an HRIS during which the primary objective is to prolong the useful life of the HRIS, and it begins once the new system is put into operation. Consequently, a crucial part of maintenance is the evaluation of the HRIS. Does it meet the needs of all users as determined during the earlier phase of the SDLC? Has it been accepted by the users? Is the HRIS being used properly?

In addition, maintenance has four other important functions:

1. Maintenance is also corrective—to fix something that is broken or not functioning properly (e.g., computer bugs, misinterpreted designs, incorrectly specified designs, or identified needs ignored).

2. Maintenance can also be adaptive; that is, system modifications are implemented such that the HRIS changes to meet the changing demands of the environment within which it operates. For example, new government regulations affecting HR practices, such as legislation addressing racial and gender discrimination, can prompt new requirements or alter the old requirements of the system.

3. Maintenance can be perfective; that is, some maintenance is designed to tweak or improve on the existing system. For example, a more efficient

routine that speeds up processing times could be developed in the maintenance phase.

4. Finally, some maintenance is preventative. For example, a growing company may need to expand its hardware storage capacity to accommodate an increasing number of new employees and meet more extensive employee record-keeping requirements. Such a maintenance action will prevent future system crashes due to inadequate hardware. Regardless of the type of maintenance, a careful assessment of need is required to ensure an efficiently run maintenance function.

Having briefly reviewed the SDLC, we will focus the remaining discussion on needs analysis. Although needs analysis is important throughout the life of a project, it is particularly important early in the project—in the planning and analysis phases. Although the focus here is on planning and needs analysis in these two early phases of the SDLC, the feedback loops in Figure 4.1 are meant to depict the continuous and iterative nature of planning and needs reanalysis. Thus, the concepts discussed in the planning and analysis phases can be applied or revisited at any point in the SDLC.

PLANNING

As mentioned, planning can be divided into long-range or strategic planning and short-range, operational planning.

Needs: Long-Range Planning

Long-range (strategic) planning for an HRIS examines the "big picture" of an organization's HR function and its information needs in light of its overall business strategy. Consider Sony Corporation's strategic vision in the 1950s:

> Fifty years from now, our brand name will be as well known as any in the world . . . and will signify innovation and quality that rival the most innovative companies anywhere. . . . "Made in Japan" will mean something fine, not something shoddy. (as quoted in Collins & Porras, 1996, p. 76)

If this is a company's guiding vision, how does it translate into a directive for the HR function? That is, to achieve the above vision, HR must play a pivotal role, and the HRIS should be supportive in every way possible of HR's role.

A hypothetical extension of Sony's vision to HR might entail wording similar to the following: "We aspire to attract, develop, and retain the best and brightest human capital in the world by becoming an employer of choice." This statement of purpose provides a foundation on which all future HR decisions are based. When questions of need arise, the vision provides the barometer against which these needs can be assessed. For each "need" one can ask, will this particular functionality better enable our organization to attract, develop, or retain the best and brightest? Will it help us in our effort to be an employer of choice? If the answer is not a resounding yes, then that particular "need" becomes less of a priority. If the answer is yes, the need for that functionality carries strategic importance.

When considering long-range planning for HRIS needs, what time frame are we talking about? Typically, long-range planning looks beyond the present, usually focusing on needs in the future 1, 5, and 10 years from now. Rapid change in technology or market competition can make planning that far in advance difficult. Consequently, long-range planning is something that is revisited annually. That is, each year, the HRIS planning team meets to assess changes and new developments in the HRIS landscape (e.g., what new technologies have entered the market), as well as in the strategic environment (e.g., changes in industry, government regulations, competition), that might necessitate a change in course. Planners ask, "Has anything changed that would alter our long-term direction?"

Planners gather information on the environment and weigh that information against their organization's strategy. Based on this assessment, they may develop a comprehensive case for change in which they lay out the reasons that the organization must take action regarding its HRIS. In particular, planners will examine the immediate future needs of the organization by identifying projects that should be considered for possible execution in the upcoming year. At the same time, these planners will also examine the status of existing projects to determine whether such projects should continue. In essence, this planning team not only sets the future direction of a firm's HRIS but also serves as a quality control group for existing and future HRIS projects. That is, the team ensures that the projects are on time, on budget, within scope, and, importantly, fulfilling their intended goal in support of the organization's strategy.

One of the critical quality control functions the planning team must enforce is called **phase containment**. That is, organizations should identify problems as early as possible in the life cycle of a system and, as important, deal with those problems at that time rather than allowing them to continue, possibly leading to greater, more costly reworking and modification later. Phase containment is a quality control principle that should guide all HRIS projects.

Y2K: A Colossal Failure of Phase Containment

The phase containment concept can be summed up with the phrase, "Pay a little now, or a lot later." Back in the early days of computing, applications were coded in such a way that only a portion of the date was stored (the last two digits); so 1967 was coded as 67. The purpose of this coding procedure, at the time, was twofold: convenience (it was easier) and efficiency (it took up less valuable storage space). However, designers of the systems in the 1960s and 1970s knew that, eventually, systems using the truncated date function would have to be modified to reflect the year 2000 and beyond. If no changes were made to legacy systems built on the old date algorithms, it was predicted that there would be serious errors to any function that relied on a date calculation. In HR systems, for example, every existing employee hired prior to the year 2000 would have a negative tenure with their companies. A report on years working with the firm for an employee hired in 1990 would show –90 years (00 – 90 = –90)—a nonsensical output.

These problems facing software applications that utilized a two-digit year became known as the Y2K bug—a bug that the experts insisted needed a fix and that futurists and alarmist media predicted would occasion doom and gloom if not fixed properly (see, e.g., Peterson, Wheatley, & Kellner-Rogers, 1998). In response, organizations invested billions of dollars in the 1990s in an effort to assess the scope of their Y2K problem and develop a strategy for fixing it. In some cases, organizations saw the fixes as so expansive and so costly that they opted instead to implement an entirely new Y2K-compliant system—a multimillion-dollar proposition for large firms. Others opted to fix their legacy systems or pay others (i.e., consultants) to do it for them. Many consulting firms became richer by specializing in Y2K audits and consultations.

How could this costly problem have been avoided? The answer lies in the discipline of phase containment. The problem was not only a result of the design of initial legacy systems; many replacement custom systems simply replicated or converted the old programming logic without fixing it.

The key to phase containment, then, is to create a culture wherein "mistakes are okay." Importantly, however, mistakes need to be detected and dealt with immediately.

Discussion Questions

In light of the Y2K example above, answer the following:

1. Why is adherence to the principle of phase containment so difficult? Why is adherence so important?
2. Why do you suppose so many organizations were vulnerable to the Y2K bug?
3. What processes, procedures, and safeguards can you implement in your organization to ensure phase containment?

Needs: Short-Range Planning

Short-range (operational) planning typically involves a needs analysis of the organization, but one with a much more immediate focus—for example, over the next one to two years. Here, specific projects are evaluated and selected for commencement, continuation, or possible termination.

Typically, the long-range plan will identify a list of priorities or priority systems and projects for the future. The long-range plan sets budgets and allocates resources to those priorities by officially sanctioning projects. Short-term planning, therefore, refers to the planning of specific projects to be implemented in the near future following the guidelines established by the priorities in the long-range plan. In many instances, functional departments within an organization may compete for a limited pool of resources. For example, finance may wish to implement a new financial planning system; marketing may wish to implement a customer relationship management system; manufacturing may wish to implement an inventory, scheduling, and material requirements system; and HR may wish to implement an HRIS. In addition, there may be competing projects and priorities for the HRIS within the HR department. For example, there might be competition for limited dollars between a project to implement employee self-service functionality and a plan to purchase a computer-based, state-of-the-art performance management system.

What should guide such decisions? The answer lies in presenting a compelling case for the need for change and developing a solution that provides a strong return on investment (see Chapter 7 for a detailed discussion of this topic). When needs are identified to a point that a new or modified system is necessary, a planning process to investigate systems needs to begin. To accomplish this planning, a systems investigation team will need to be formed and develop a plan. This team is typically small, headed by a functional leader or owner (e.g., HR manager) and supplemented with other expertise in the organization (e.g., HRIS and IT professionals). The system investigation involving short-term planning culminates with a business case report or system investigation report.

Planning for investigating systems focuses on a specific system to be implemented in the short term. The steps involved include the following:

- Form a team—consider who specifically should be on the project.
- Identify at a high level the critical business needs that a system would have to satisfy.
- Complete scenario analysis: Identify potential solutions—the team is not selecting a system yet but rather gaining knowledge of the solutions that exist.

- Complete a feasibility analysis in terms of a cost-benefit analysis.
- Develop a tentative scope and schedule for viable scenarios.
- Estimate the return on investment (ROI) for viable scenarios.
- Complete a system investigation report with specific recommendations for action.

Eventually, the project steering committee, which typically includes top management or those individuals controlling the resources, will approve one or more projects. This committee will also have to make difficult decisions on whether current projects should continue (see phase containment above). For each project that is approved, a project team is formalized for the management of the project. Usually, this core team is the same team that was involved in the system investigation and in building the case for change. Some members may leave, and new members will join a project team, but this core team will ideally form the basis for the execution of the project through the remaining phases of the system development life cycle.

THE BIG 3: THE GLOBAL POSITIONING SYSTEM OF HRIS

A simplification of the complexity of the planning and needs analysis can be accomplished by reducing the entire process to three general questions that must be answered. These questions, referred to here as the **Big 3**, are as follows:

1. Where are we now?
2. Where are we going?
3. How are we going to get there?

Like a global positioning system (GPS) in your automobile, these questions provide the navigational direction for an HRIS project. Throughout an HRIS development process, these questions will be asked at varying levels of breadth and depth. First, to understand where you are going, you must know where you are now. That is, you must know the details of your current situation. For example, asking the question "Where are we now?" should spawn additional questions and answers regarding an organization's capabilities. Of course, simply knowing where "you are now" is not enough. However, knowing where you are will provide information to help you determine how far you need to go. In other words, you need to know where you wish to be—what future state you envision for your

HR function and how an HRIS will fit into that planned destination. Finally, the question of "How are we going to get there?" bridges the "gap" between where your organization currently is and where it desires to be.

As noted, each organization might have a different way of describing its SDLC, but, regardless, each specific SDLC will include planning, analysis, design, implementation, and maintenance. Answering the "Big 3" questions provides a road map throughout the life cycle of your HRIS—a mental map and physical description in a report that can be used to assess whether or not your system is on track.

Consider the recent implementation of SAP™ Business Suite for financials, human resources, and payroll at Purdue University—an institution with more than 19,000 employees spread across a main campus and several regional campuses. Coined as "OnePurdue," this project began with in-depth planning and analysis phases to document the existing systems and their limitations and, importantly, to identify the critical functional and technical needs of the organization moving forward. The question of "Where are we going?" was guided by the OnePurdue project's guiding vision: *To transform the University's way of doing business into a flexible and user-centric portfolio of applications that integrates all Purdue enterprise data, information, and processes.*

A number of guiding principles can be drawn from this vision. First, the status quo was problematic, as is evident by the felt need to "transform." The existing configuration was comprised of a hodgepodge of disparate systems, often developed within Purdue University using outdated hardware and software. Even getting access to data proved problematic. Second, future systems were required to be focused on users. This heavy emphasis on involving users, understanding their needs, and building usable technologies was paramount. Third, any new IT infrastructure needed technology and systems that were integrated. All information was to be unified into a central repository with real-time updates—that is, regardless of point of entry, information would be immediately updated and stored in a central repository and, thus, immediately available to all users. Users, in this future state, would be able to quickly and easily access information. Moreover, confusion over how to get the data or even where to go to get the data would be eliminated.

The above analysis of strategic vision ("Where are we going?") helped Purdue identify its needs in greater detail and select a system that best met its needs. This information served as critical input for the selection of an enterprise-wide resource planning system. Purdue chose SAP (www.sap.com/company/index.epx) as its primary software vendor for HR applications. The SDLC continued once SAP was selected following SAP's ASAP (Accelerated SAP) methodology—a road map that documents the "who, what, where, and when" for an ERP implementation (see the SAP Web site for details on ASAP). Figure 4.2 shows the ASAP process at OnePurdue and the steps that occurred.

Figure 4.2 ASAP Process at OnePurdue

- SAP Standard
- Single, Pragmatic, and Standardized Methodology
- Evolved out of 20 Years of Experience
- Manageable Scope, Costs, and Common Expectations
- Common Language
- Pre-configured Documentation and Tools

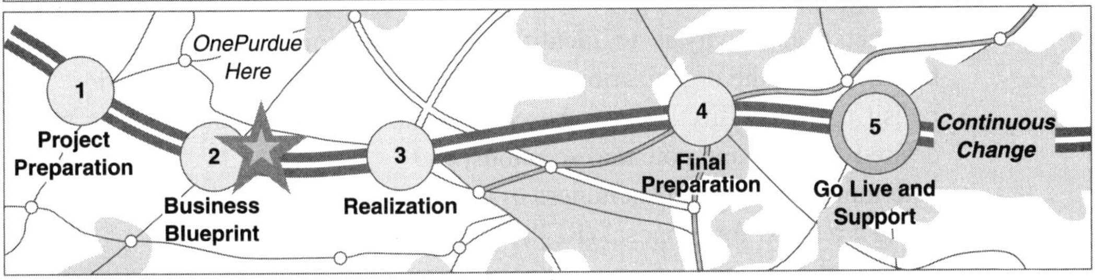

Organize Team	Identify Organization Structures	Configure Business Processes	Final Testing	Support Users
Initial Planning	Business Process Design	Design Validation	End-User Training	Verify System
SAP Training	Install SAP	RICE Design	System Cut Over	
Kickoff	SAP Training	Testing	Establish Help Desk	
		Develop End-User Training Materials		

Student Challenge

Compare and contrast the generic SDLC in Figure 4.1 with the ASAP process used in the OnePurdue project in Figure 4.2. What is similar? What is different?

The Big 3 questions are not asked only one time and then ignored. Rather, they should be revisited on a regular basis. Moreover, these questions can be applied at any level of analysis—be it long-range planning and needs analysis or short-range planning and investigating systems. The culmination of a systems investigation process is the approval or rejection of a system proposal. If approved, the project launches into the analysis, design, and implementation phases (see Figures 4.1 and 4.2). Like the planning phase, the analysis phase is a critical step in fleshing out the capabilities and needs of the organization going forward.

Analysis

The purpose of the analysis phase is to take a project that has been approved in the planning phase and

- meticulously dissect and document the organization's current capabilities, including existing data, information, systems, and work flows so as to gain a thorough and accurate understanding of the organization's current capabilities;
- thoroughly identify and prioritize needs—both current and future needs;
- conduct a gap analysis to identify critical functional and technical gaps between what the organization needs to do and what it can currently do;
- revisit the feasibility analysis based on what is known about existing and desired systems and potential solutions; and
- determine the potential usefulness of the results of the gap analysis in developing a request for proposal (RFP) for vendors.

Detailing Where We Are

Part of analysis involves a thorough **current analysis**—developing a detailed understanding of the organization's current capabilities and limitations and, thus, answering in precise detail the question "Where are we now?" This is difficult for a single person or a small team to do alone. Indeed, a great deal of effort must be put forth in this part of the analysis phase. To accomplish the current analysis, the project team will likely increase in size. Recall that, in the planning phase, a small core team is formed to conduct a systems investigation and develop a case for change. Once the project is approved and moves to the analysis phase, more personnel and resources will be needed. New people will be added to the core project team and may remain a part of the team beyond implementation. Other personnel may be brought onto the project on an as-needed basis. Figure 4.3 shows a reverse hourglass in terms of the amount of effort, and thus people, needed relative to the point in the HRIS project.

As can be seen, planning typically involves fewer resources as the project is in its infancy and may not yet have been officially sanctioned by the top management. As the project moves into analysis, design, and implementation, the amount of resources needed (e.g., employees, consultants) increases.

To conduct a proper analysis, an organization needs to identify methods of data collection and sources from which the data will be collected. Common methods of data collection include the following:

- Interviews
- Focus groups

Figure 4.3 Reverse Hourglass: Effort/Resources Required for HRIS Project

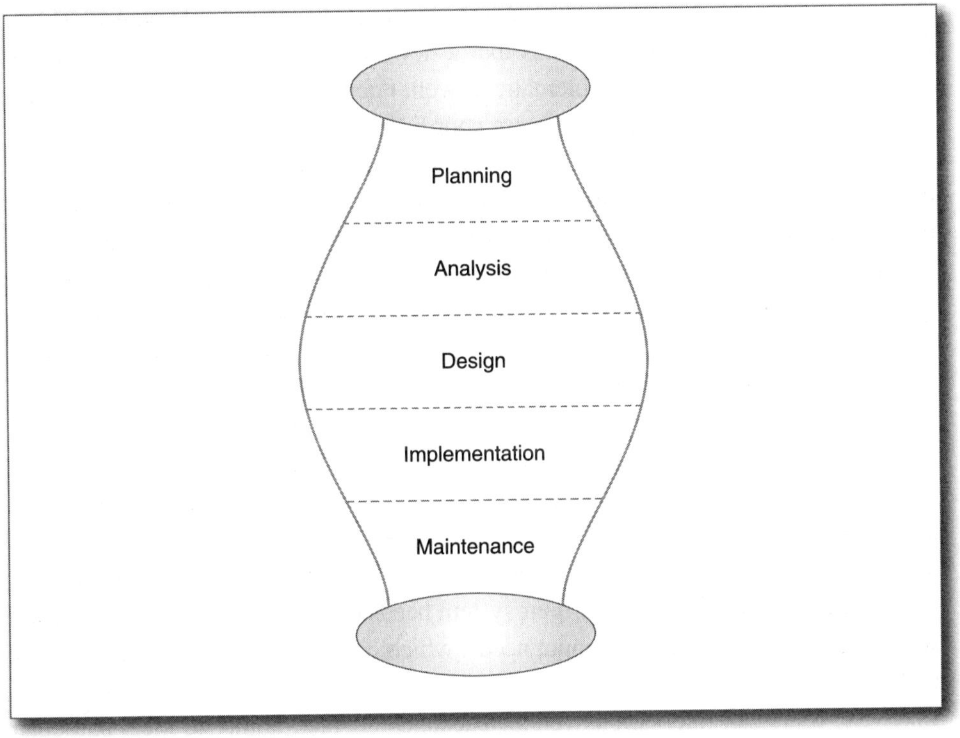

- Surveys and online tools
- Organizational archives

Interviews are particularly useful for getting at rich sources of information. That is, consistent with information richness theory (Daft & Lengel, 1984), when one wishes to develop a deep understanding of a situation, rich, two-way communication serves that purpose. Project leaders will need to develop a list of interviewees—people with expertise in functional or technical areas—and an interview schedule. A drawback of interviews is that they are time-consuming. For this reason, careful thought should be devoted to selection of interviewees, such that a large amount of valuable information can be obtained from a relatively small pool of experts. Interviews also enable project team members to develop relationships with key users and identify potential change agents or change champions—line-level employees who will serve as project liaisons to the wider organization.

In addition to interviews, focus groups provide another rich way to gather detailed information on current systems. An advantage of focus groups is that you can involve many more people in the data-gathering effort, increasing the likelihood of a more thorough analysis. Also, research shows that the more involved people are in a systems implementation project, the more they feel as though they own the system and, thus, the more willing they are to accept the system when it is implemented. Therefore, focus groups increase the odds that a new HR solution will be accepted. Of course, focus groups can be problematic as well. Focus groups require more time just for scheduling meetings and, thus, more coordination than individual interviews.

Surveys and online tools are an excellent way to assess the needs of an organization in a timely and efficient manner. Moreover, such methods can be applied to as many individuals in the organization as you want, with little additional cost. That is, surveys and online tools are cheap to administer and can reach many people quickly, thus enabling the project to receive input from a large percentage of the affected population. The downside of surveys is that they do not offer the opportunities of rich two-way exchanges that interviews and focus groups can provide. Moreover, surveys can be vulnerable to social desirability and other biases. Ensuring anonymity of responses can help alleviate some of these concerns.

A number of groupware systems are available that support online surveys as well as other decision-support diagnostics. For example, both Expert Choice and Advantiv are software vendors and application service providers that provide software and services to firms looking to evaluate their system needs (see www.expertchoice.com and www.advantiv.com). Users can input needs, which can then be organized, prioritized, and voted on; that is, the user community can rank the importance of particular needs. Likewise, users can rate various vendor packages for their ability to meet particular needs. Such a tool provides a centralized system for gathering user input.

Finally, analysts can use archival methods by examining existing documentation and records. Examples of documentation include current system screens, reports, and forms. Organizational charts, policy manuals, exit interviews, and performance data can also be useful in this analysis. By analyzing this information, the HRIS project team will have a better grasp on the overall business and the types of information it collects.

In addition to data-gathering methods, it is important to identify and enlist critical sources or targets of the data-gathering initiatives. These sources can provide information on the current system as well as participate in identifying current and future needs. Sources include the following:

- HR functional experts—managers of employment recruiting and selection
- Job experts—job analysts and compensation specialists
- Technical experts—HRIS and IT professionals
- End users—including employees and nonemployees, such as customers
- Top management—individuals and teams involved in business decisions
- Consultants and other business partners

In selecting sources for input, the development team must keep certain important things in mind. First, what is the level of expertise of the source? You would certainly want to have people with functional or technical expertise. People with specific knowledge of the firm who have been with it for a long period of time can contribute useful insights. Also, because employees with longer organizational tenure and experience with the old system can have a more difficult time adapting to a new HRIS, involving them in the analysis can go a long way toward getting their buy-in for the project. There may also be benefits in having a few new or inexperienced users involved in the process. Such sources often do not have any strong interest in or bias toward a particular system and, thus, are not protective of the current system. Moreover, having people from different jobs with a diversity of job knowledge and experience participate helps ensure that the system that is developed and implemented will serve everyone's needs. Finally, hiring consultants is often worthwhile as they can bring an objective, independent perspective on a firm's needs. In particular, consultants—because they work with many clients—have a good grasp of the HRIS market, including emerging trends and best practices.

The information that is gathered and documented includes, but is not limited to, an inventory of current HR modules comprising computer programs and applications (e.g., software used in recruiting new employees), current outputs (e.g., reports and screens), data flows (e.g., where data are generated, where they are processed, where they are stored), data structures and definitions (e.g., what data fields are stored, how they are organized and linked), technical architecture (e.g., hardware, systems software, application software), and work processes or work flows (e.g., business process maps of how work currently gets done).

Figure 4.4 provides an example of an inventory of modules in a hypothetical system. A detailed understanding of current work flows provides a mechanism through which one can assess the efficiency and effectiveness of how work is currently being performed. During the design phase, organizations will attempt to redesign inefficient work flows. Obsolete work flows or those that no longer add value to the organization can be eliminated. In Figure 4.5, for example, a current work flow for processing a payroll is illustrated. Although this is useful information in its own right (e.g., communicating to a new payroll clerk how things work), it provides an opportunity to reanalyze the process and look for inefficiencies. For example, in the current process outlined in Figure 4.5, there are multiple manual processes that are HR intensive and, consequently, prone to human error (e.g., data entry error). Indeed, the Hackett Best Practices Benchmark Study of Human Resources estimates that every HR transaction that occurs costs an organization $17 (as reported in Howes, 2002). Thus, data entry errors or unnecessary transaction steps that occur can greatly increase the cost of the HR module for processing payroll.

Figure 4.4 Hypothetical Example: Inventory of Current HR Applications/Modules

Inventory of Modules for Current HR Applications

Functional Area	*Module ID*	*Module Descriptions*	*Manual/ Computerized*	*Entry/ Interface*	*Sourcing*	*Platform*	*Vendor (If Purchased)*	*Owner*
Staffing – Applicant Management	ST000110	Applicant Resume Scan	Computerized	Auto-generated	Vendor Purchased	Sun Solaris Server	Appli-trac ®	Staffing Manager
	ST000120	Applicant Batch Entry	Computerized	Auto-generated	Vendor Purchased	Sun Solaris Server	Appli-trac ®	Staffing Manager
	ST000120	Applicant Tracking/ Update	Computerized	Ad hoc/ User	Vendor Purchased	Sun Solaris Server	Appli-trac ®	Staffing Manager
	ST000130	Person-Job Matching	Computerized	Ad hoc/User	Vendor Purchased	Sun Solaris Server	Appli-trac ®	Staffing Manager
	ST000140	Applicant Reporting Menu	Computerized	Ad hoc/User	Vendor Purchased	Sun Solaris Server	Appli-trac ®	Staffing Manager
	ST000150	Requisitioning/ Job Analysis	Computerized	Ad hoc/User	Vendor Purchased	Sun Solaris Server	Appli-trac ®	Staffing Manager
	ST000210	Selection Assessment Module	Computerized	Ad hoc/User	Vendor Purchased	Sun Solaris Server	Appli-trac ®	Staffing Manager
	ST000220	EE0/AA Compliance	Computerized	Ad hoc/User	Vendor Purchased	Sun Solaris Server	Appli-trac ®	Staffing Manager
	ST000310	On-Boarding Management	Computerized	Ad hoc/User	Vendor Purchased	Sun Solaris Server	Appli-trac ®	Staffing Manager

Employee Tracking	ET000110	Add New Employee On-Boarding	Computerized	Ad hoc/User	Made In-House	Sun Solaris Server/C#		HR Manager
	ET000120	Update/ Change Employee Info	Computerized	Ad hoc/User	Made In-House	Sun Solaris Server/C#		HR Manager
Performance Management	PM000110	Employee Performance/ History	Computerized	Ad hoc/User	Made In-House	PC/IBM (Excel Spreadsheet)		Line Manager
	PM000120	Employee Evaluation	Computerized (Word Processor)	Ad hoc/User	Made In-House	PC/IBM (MS Word)		Line Manager
Training & Development	TD000110	Course Management Maintenance	Computerized	Ad hoc/User	Made In-House	Sun Solaris Server/C#		Training Manager
	TD000120	Class Management Maintenance	Computerized	Ad hoc/User	Made In-House	Sun Solaris Server/C#		Training Manager
	TD000130	Training Program Maintenance	Computerized	Ad hoc/User	Made In-House	Sun Solaris Server/C#		Training Manager
Payroll	PY000100	Bi-Weekly Payroll API	Computerized ASCII File to Vendor	Auto-generated	Made In-House	Sun Solaris Server/C#		HRIS Manager
	PY000200	Bi-Weekly Payroll Batch Run	Computerized	Auto-generated	Outsourced	n/a	EasyPeople Pay ®	HRIS Manager

Figure 4.5 Sample Work Flow for a Legacy Payroll Process

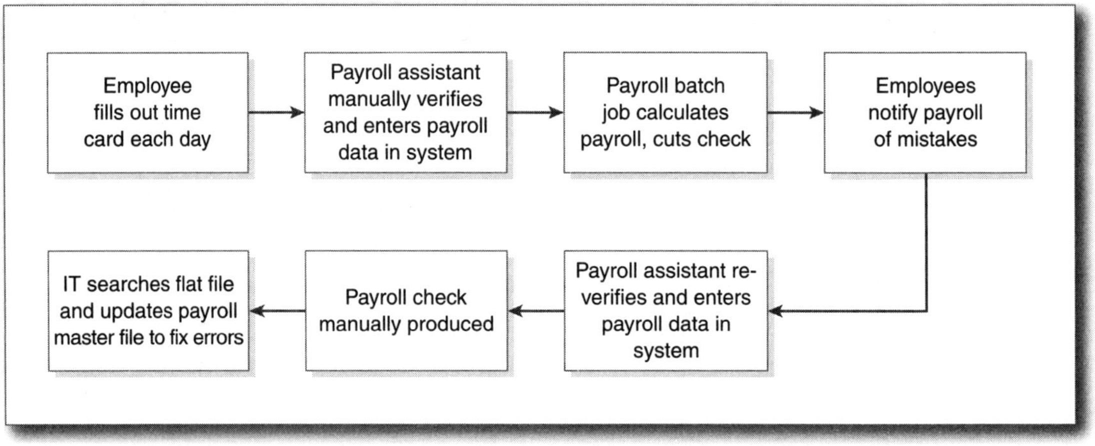

Student Exercise

Suppose an organization has 10,000 employees that must be paid every other week. Also, suppose that the process for paying employees currently follows that detailed in Figure 4.5.

1. What steps can be streamlined or eliminated? How (i.e., what might a new and improved process look like)?
2. Using the $17 per transaction estimated by the Hackett survey, how much can you expect to save your organization every payroll run, based on the improvements you've made to the payroll process? How much can you expect to save annually? (Assume that every step in the process equals a transaction; thus, every person paid entails multiple steps or transactions.)
3. Based on your analysis, would you recommend a new process?

In sum, documenting the current system provides a baseline against which needs, to include opportunities for savings, can be identified and assessed.

Detailing Where We Need to Go

Knowing how your organization currently operates and its capabilities and limitations is a good starting point for a needs analysis. However, assessing the needs for the future—that is, answering the question "where do we want to be" in detail—is the heart of a needs analysis. Some HRIS scholars draw a distinction between a needs analysis and a **business requirements definition**. Ceriello and Freeman (1991), for example, argue that needs analysis focuses on an organization's current needs, whereas a business requirements definition focuses not only on current needs but also on future needs. Here, we use the terms *needs analysis* and *business requirements definitions* interchangeably. They both refer to that point in the analysis at which an organization determines and documents its current and future needs. These needs become the targets or goals that the new system will attempt to satisfy.

One point of caution: Both *needs* and *requirements* are strong words in the sense that they imply something that the organization, and therefore the HRIS, *must have*. It is important to recognize that, as needs are being identified, a process should be put into place to prioritize them. This ranking will result in a list of needs that fall along a continuum from high-priority or critical needs, those that definitely will be built into the system, to medium-priority needs, which are likely to be included, to low-priority needs, which may be incorporated if time and resources allow.

Many of the same people who were involved in identifying the current system can also be used to identify future needs. However, it is always wise to bring in additional people who can bring a fresh, unencumbered perspective. In decision making, for example, using a stepladder technique that adds new people to provide fresh new insights at different phases in the project can prove useful for reaching better decisions (Rogelberg, Barnes-Farrell, & Lowe, 1992).

GAP ANALYSIS

The culmination of a needs analysis is the **gap analysis**, the process of documenting and comparing the current state of the HRIS with the desired future state based on needs that are not being met with the current system. In essence, gap analysis brings the two previous activities together (where we are now and where we are going) and provides a communication tool by which to see where the current system falls short for meeting future needs. Figure 4.6 provides an example of a hypothetical gap analysis for several capabilities within an HR training function. As can be seen, a list of functional requirements appears down the left column. For each requirement, the gap analysis identifies if the organization currently performs that function. Also, priorities are assigned to each requirement. Gaps occur where there is a requirement not currently being met, and the gap is classified (high, moderate, low) based on the priority of the requirement.

Figure 4.6 Hypothetical Gap Analysis Report for a Training Function

Function	*Currently Have*	*Requirement*	*Priority*	*Gap*
1. Manager access and enrollment online to courses, dates, and location		✓	**3**	**Mod**
2. Tracking of courses taken and production of training profile	✓	✓	**4**	
3. Fully online		✓	**4**	**High**
4. Ability to link with development module and core module to permit cross-comparisons with developmental plans and current job location, department, and EEO data		✓	**3**	**Mod**
5. Course content available (not just title)	✓	✓	**3**	
6. Ability to link participant evaluation data to internal course and external seminar tables		✓	**3**	**Mod**
7. Online registration facility with ability to maintain employee status		✓	**4**	**High**
8. Automatic linkage to facilities/classroom records for scheduling, allocating equipment, etc.		✓	**4**	**High**

A gap analysis tells us what important needs are not being met with the existing system as well as those that are being met. A gap analysis is an important decision tool for HRIS project leaders. For one thing, it helps answer these questions. Does our current system enable us to meet our critical needs? Are there significant gaps in our ability to meet our current needs? Assuming that there are significant gaps, the gap analysis becomes a critical document for selecting a new solution going forward. If an outside vendor will be used to help develop and implement the HRIS, a gap analysis will be included in an organization's request for proposal (RFP), which will be sent to competing vendors.[1] In this regard, the gap analysis serves as a communication device informing potential vendors of your firm's critical needs—needs that their vendor system must fill in order to be in contention for ultimate selection.

Importantly, the gap analysis may reveal needs that the current system does meet. However, that the current system can meet the current needs does not suggest it is the *best* system for meeting these needs. As organizations move forward in their designs (see Chapters 3 and 5), they will ascertain the best way to meet future needs and design their systems accordingly. Figure 4.7 depicts the Big 3 triangle generated by the Big 3 questions, and it summarizes the analysis process and links it to the design process. Specifically, in analysis we compare the current system (where we are) with the envisioned future (where we are going) and create a gap analysis that identifies discrepancies between the current state and the future desired state and prioritizes needs. This information becomes critical input into the design of the new system—that phase in the HRIS project that answers the question "How are we going to get there?"

As we conclude the needs analysis and move toward designing and implementing an HRIS, let's summarize some of the critical questions or challenges in the analysis phase that the HRIS project team will need to address:

- Who should determine what our needs are going forward? That is, who should be involved in the needs analysis, and what processes are in place for prioritization?
- How can we ensure that all of our needs are identified?
- How can we be sure to exclude "needs" that might unnecessarily expand our scope, thereby threatening the schedule and cost of the project? That is, how do we limit the scope to the things we truly need?
- Is it feasible at this point to implement a system that can meet our critical needs?

Figure 4.7 The Big 3 Needs Triangle Relating Analysis and Design

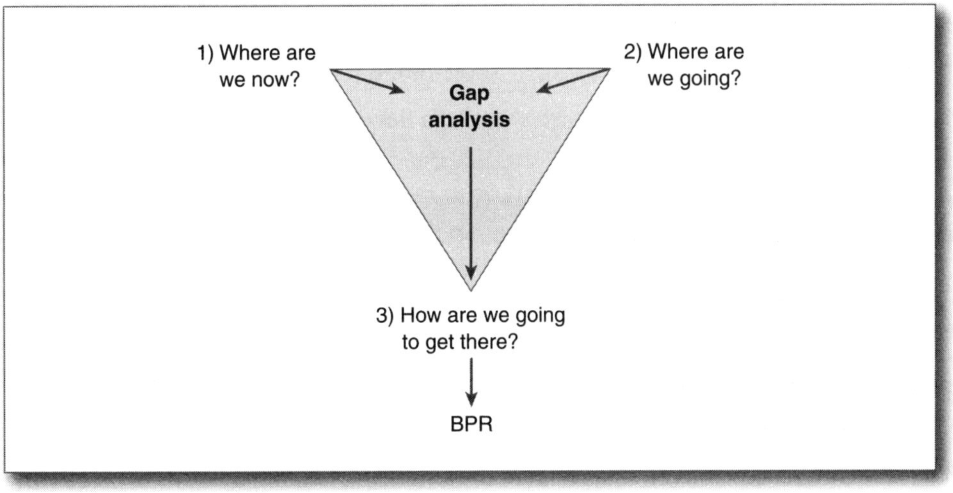

NOTE: BPR stands for **business process reengineering**.

SUMMARY

Needs analysis refers to the process of gathering, prioritizing, and documenting an organization's HR information requirements thoroughly, and it serves as a necessary input for the subsequent design and implementation of an HRIS as part of the system development life cycle (SDLC). HRIS planning can be divided into long-range or strategic planning and short-range or operational planning. Throughout an HRIS system development process, three big questions will be asked in the company, at varying levels of breadth and depth: (1) Where are we now, (2) where we are going, and (3) how are we going to get there? The purpose of this analysis phase is to identify and document the organization's current capabilities, prioritize needs (both current and future), conduct a gap analysis, revisit the feasibility analysis, and determine the potential usefulness of the results. Common methods of data collection during the analysis phase include conducting interviews and focus groups, using surveys and online tools, and consulting organizational archives. It is also important to enlist critical sources in these data-gathering initiatives, including HR functional experts, technical experts, end users, top management, and consultants. The needs analysis for the HRIS continues through the entire system development process since each stage in the process could lead to the identification of new needs for the HRIS. Planning and needs analysis are not things that HRIS project personnel choose to do; they are things they must do.

KEY TERMS

Big 3 questions
business process reengineering (BPR)
business requirements definition
current analysis
gap analysis
long-range (strategic) planning
needs analysis
phase containment
short-range (operational) planning
system development life cycle (SDLC)

DISCUSSION QUESTIONS

1. What are some critical success factors for effectively conducting an analysis of HRIS needs?
2. Explain how planning and analysis integrate and inform further steps in the system development life cycle (SDLC).
3. What is the difference between long-term and short-term planning in terms of an HRIS?
4. What is phase containment? Why is it so important? How can you ensure its adherence in an HRIS project?

CASE STUDY: "PLANNING THE NEEDS OF OTHER ORGANIZATIONS"

If you think a thorough, high-quality needs analysis is daunting on an internal project, imagine if you were an HRIS vendor with the job of providing a "best of breed" system (see Chapter 3) that meets most of your many different clients' needs. Such an approach makes planning and needs analysis more challenging because difficult choices must be made as to the functionality that is sufficiently broad to go into a general market package. It is costly to vendors, and indeed may be infeasible, to include functionality that is so specific that only a small portion of a vendor's client base benefits from the function.

On the other side of the coin is the difficulty firms face when shopping for a vendor, or the critical question they must ask: "Will this system meet my needs?" In general, it is wise to adhere to the 75% rule—that is, if a package can meet approximately 75% of your needs, it is pretty good. In this case, the advantages of a package begin to outweigh the disadvantages. When a package falls below the 75% rule, an organization is left with a system with significant functional gaps that will require costly custom patches or manual work-arounds, defeating the purpose of a vendor system in the first place. A needs analysis, therefore, is critical to addressing this question: Is there a vendor-packaged system available that can meet at least 75% of my business needs?

Consider the following hypothetical company, Benefast Partners, that provides a specific market niche HRIS product, benefits administration software. Its challenge: Provide comprehensive benefits administration software that meets the needs of a growing and complex benefits marketplace.

According to Davis Hunter, a former employee of Benefast, Benefast Partners (name changed to protect confidentiality) was only doing defined benefit pension plans for large employers (20,000+ employees). Here is how he explains the situation:

> When you focus your business opportunities on *Fortune* 100 companies, it limits your potential for growth to small and midsized markets. Given that there is competition in the market for small, medium, and large clients, there was no real way to expand. We were, however, doing 401(k) retirement plan administration both on our proprietary system, designed and marketed for large employers, and on a purchased platform for smaller companies. We had interest from existing 401(k) clients to take on administration of their defined benefit plans, and we felt we had lost 401(k) business in the past because we didn't offer total retirement outsourcing, just 401(k).
>
> It wasn't possible to charge small employers the kinds of fees necessary to implement their plans on our proprietary system, so our efforts centered on what could be done with the purchased system used for small to midsized 401(k) plans. We quickly determined that the purchased system's defined benefits platform wasn't sophisticated enough from a calculation standpoint to handle most of the complexity of defined

benefit plans, so we decided to use a combination of the purchased system with the calculation engine component for the proprietary system.

We had a lot of needs analysis conversations with our colleagues in another office who were running the project. Given the multiple platforms involved, processing time was a huge concern. We decided to segment the market and serve only those customers who met a fairly stringent set of requirements. Basically, we built a system to serve clients whose plans were easy to administer. In other words,

1. No multiplan clients
2. No retirement modeling
3. No coordination of benefits, for example, no combination of 401(k) and defined benefit plans
4. Limited Web interface

So, based on this segmentation, we launched our new product with one of our parent companies (a bank). By the time we had signed our third client, we had already begun to move towards a fairly complex multiplan environment. Our fourth and fifth clients were even more complex. We were over budget and off schedule on everything, and then we started trying to figure out how to do coordination of benefits. We built a system for plans that were easy to administer—but plans that are easy to administer are few and far between in the marketplace, and those that exist aren't typically managed by organizations shopping for external sources for benefits.

Case Study Questions

1. How would you evaluate Benefast Partners' strategy?
2. What changes (if any) would you make going forward?
3. What methods would you employ to ensure that an HRIS package meets the majority of your clients' needs?

NOTE

1. The RFP process is described in detail in Chapter 7.

REFERENCES

Ceriello, V. R., & Freeman, C. (1991). *Human resource management systems: Strategies, tactics, and techniques.* New York: Lexington Books.

Collins, J. C., & Porras, J. I. (1996, September/October). Building your company's vision. *Harvard Business Review,* 65–77.

Daft, R. L., & Lengel, R. H. (1984). Information richness: A new approach to managerial behavior and organization design. In B. Staw & L. L. Cummings (Eds.), *Research in organizational behavior* (pp. 191–234). Greenwich, CT: JAI Press.

Howes, P. (2002, February/March). ROI for an HRIS business plan. *IHRIM.link, 7,* 12–15.

Peterson, J. L., Wheatley, M., & Kellner-Rogers, M. (1998). The Y2K problem: Social chaos or social transformation? *The Futurist, 32*(7), 21–28.

Rogelberg, S. G., Barnes-Farrell, J. L., & Lowe, C. A. (1992). The stepladder technique: An alternative group structure facilitating effective group decision making. *Journal of Applied Psychology, 77,* 730–737.

Smith, J. (2001, February/March). Knowledge transfer: The forgotten phase. *IHRIM.link, 6*, 53.

Chapter 5

System Design and Acquisition

Richard D. Johnson and James H. Dulebohn

EDITORS' NOTE

Building on Chapters 3 and 4, this chapter focuses on the design and acquisition of an HRIS. Thus, the focus of this chapter is on the "design" phase of the systems development life cycle (SDLC), as illustrated in Figure 4.1. The authors differentiate between the logical and the physical design of an HRIS, as well as emphasizing the differences between the data and process views of a computer system. As will be discussed in this chapter, these differences are critical for the effective design of an HRIS that will meet the needs of the various stakeholders of the system, that is, HR and information technology (IT) professionals, managers, and employees. Data flow diagramming is discussed as a tool used to analyze the process design characteristics prior to the actual physical design of the HRIS. In addition, the three choices or options that organizations face when moving into physical design are examined. All the effort involved in completing an accurate and comprehensive logical and physical design of the HRIS helps ensure that the acquisition of the system will be done properly. The chapter concludes with a discussion of how to develop a request for proposal (RFP) and how to evaluate proposals received from outside vendors. This last section is a good lead-in to Chapters 6 and 7, which are focused on using HR metrics and analytics to calculate cost-benefit analysis for the acquisition of an HRIS.

CHAPTER OBJECTIVES

After completing this chapter, the reader should be able to

- Understand the difference between the data and process views of a system
- Understand the purpose and components of the data flow diagram (DFD)
- Understand the hierarchy of DFDs and the concept of DFD balancing
- Understand the three choices or options that organizations have when moving into physical design
- Understand the purpose of an RFP and what information should be included in it
- Understand the various criteria used to evaluate vendor proposals
- Describe the various types of feasibility and their purpose in evaluating potential solutions

HRIS IN ACTION

Larson Property Management Company is one of the largest property-management companies in California, with more than 1,000 employees. The company provides a full array of commercial management and development services. These activities include complete management services for commercial office and retail buildings and apartment complexes; the construction, repair, and maintenance of commercial properties; and financial management and billing services for commercial real-estate clients. The company has experienced significant expansion over the past five years in response to the growth in apartment and commercial construction in southern California, and this expansion has resulted in the need to hire a large number of employees on an ongoing basis to staff its operations.

Larson Property Management has depended on a legacy HRIS to manage its applicant and employee databases. The system runs on a client-server computer system. The system was implemented approximately 10 years ago, prior to the rapid growth of the company and when the organization had fewer than 100 employees. The system's functionality is limited to the storage and retrieval of employee and applicant data. For recruiting purposes, the system requires a clerk to manually enter basic applicant data, the results of the application test, and whether or not an offer of employment has been made. Prior to this, applicants' files were passed around to those who reviewed the materials and were sometimes misplaced, so trying to locate a particular applicant's file was often a problem. The current HRIS has limited file storage capability for applicant and employee records and currently has reached its storage capacity.

Larson Property Management has decided to replace its legacy HRIS. One application module in the new HRIS that the company wants is a sophisticated **applicant-tracking system (ATS)**. The primary objective of the ATS will be to provide a paperless hiring process. The basic functions of the new system will be managing the requisition and approval of job openings, storing resumes and job applications and retrieving through query functions the names of applicants who match job requirements, tracking a candidate's progress through the recruiting and selection process, and providing automated reporting functions. The company's managers also want an e-HR functionality that includes the Internet posting of job openings through the company's Web site and external job-posting services, application and resume submission through the Web and through kiosks at various office locations, staff ability to access and use the system remotely through a Web browser, and online resume- and application-scanning capabilities.

Part of the design phase is modeling the processes that will be used in the system for applicant tracking. For Larson Property Management, this modeling will allow the system analysts to design an efficient paperless hiring process.

Case note: As you read this chapter, keep the situation at Larson Property Management in mind. It will be the basis of the case analysis at the end of the chapter.

INTRODUCTION

Never tell people how *to do things.*

Tell them what *to do and they will surprise you with their ingenuity.*

—General George S. Patton (1947/1995)

The goal of this chapter is to provide a deeper understanding of the process through which an HRIS is designed and acquired. This design and acquisition of an HRIS comprises but one phase in a larger systems development process. As noted in previous chapters, the larger development process is called the **systems development life cycle (SDLC)**. As seen in Chapter 4 (Figure 4.1), the five generic phases of the SDLC are planning, analysis, design, implementation, and maintenance. This chapter focuses on the design phase by discussing briefly the role and features of the structuring of a system's requirements through process system modeling, during which analysts create data flow diagrams (DFDs) to model both the business processes that the system will use to capture, store, manipulate, and distribute data and the options facing the HR department as it moves into design. Next, the vendor-management relationship is covered, including the creation and use of a request for a proposal (RFP), the evaluation of vendor responses, and the choice of a vendor or vendors. Finally, the chapter ends with a discussion of the HRIS feasibility criteria.

DESIGN CONSIDERATIONS DURING THE SYSTEMS DEVELOPMENT LIFE CYCLE

As discussed in previous chapters, the SDLC is a structured set of phases focused on the analysis and design of information systems. The goal of the SDLC is to provide those organizations updating existing systems or designing new ones with a stronger, more structured process to follow. A report by the Standish Group (2004) provides evidence that, as the use of structured development techniques is increasingly practiced, system quality improves. At the same time, this report also found that less than 30% of systems projects are successful and more than 50% go live later than planned and are over budget. Given the wide variety of program needs in the HR department, such as recruiting, selection, training, performance management, and compensation, and the complexity of these needs, the importance of following a structured approach to the development of an HRIS cannot be overstated.

Although each phase in the life cycle is important, the goal of this chapter is to focus specifically on the activities associated with designing the HRIS. The design of the HRIS can occur in two phases: logical and physical design. The design phase is separated into two components because each has a different aim and perspective. The **logical design** of a system focuses on the translation of business requirements into improved business processes, irrespective of any technological implementation. For example, a business requirement for organizations such as Larson Property Management is the acquisition of new employees. HR business processes typically include (1) identifying jobs requiring new employees and approving those jobs, (2) analyzing the requirements of those jobs, (3) posting those positions and recruiting applicants from the labor market, (4) tracking applicants through the recruiting process, (5) selecting from the recruiting pool, through the use of selection tools such as interviews, applicants that best fit the job requirements, and (6) bringing new hires on board and placing them in their jobs. The HR programs associated with these processes are (1) HR planning, (2) job analysis, (3) recruiting, (4) applicant tracking, (5) selection, (6) placement, and (7) record keeping.

Conversely, the focus and goal of *physical design* is determining the most effective means of translating these business processes into a physical system that includes hardware and software. To merge the phases together can invite the temptation to focus heavily on the physical aspects of the new system (hardware and software) at the expense of improved business processes. In addition, focusing on the physical aspects of a system can lead to premature decisions and the selection of physical solutions that may not be the most effective ones for the business processes identified.

For example, a new and improved version of software may appear on the market. Imagine that this software is designed to automate and help manage compensation systems based on a combination of base pay administrative features along with merit modeling, reporting and analysis, and bonus pay plan tools. However, a company purchasing this software because of its elegance may have made a serious error if the company's top management is planning to drop the bonus program in two years as part of the company's new strategic plan. Another example would be the failure to acquire needed software features due to lack of attention on processes. Of course, adequate logical design enables effective physical design. Revisiting the example of Larson Property Management, we can imagine a design scenario related to staffing and the acquisition of new employees in which a thorough and careful analysis of the staffing process (logical design) would permit the company to determine that it needs a particular level of work-flow processing and Web enablement to track applicants and allow the posting of jobs online and online application to posted jobs (physical design).

Logical Design

As discussed in Chapter 4, once an organization has completed the analysis phase of the SDLC, which results in a comprehensive process analysis for the new HRIS, one of the key tasks facing the HR staff and development teams is to model the needs for the new system. There are two ways in which the system can be modeled: the physical model and the logical model. The physical model focuses on the computer technology for the HRIS, that is, on the hardware, software, networking plans, and technical manuals. The strength of this type of model is that it focuses on how the system will actually operate. In turn, this strength also becomes its weakness because, by focusing on the actual way the system will be implemented in terms of technology, analysts and HR staff may be constrained by the current, operational physical model. That is, HR staff members are familiar with the functioning of the current (i.e., legacy) HRIS they are using but, typically, not with the technological aspects of new systems or with the current technology available.

Therefore, system developers like to focus on the essence of the business processes independent of any technological implementation. To do this, logical models of the system are created. Logical models are HRIS models that could be operationalized in multiple ways in terms of the technology. For example, in the logical model, an organization might focus on receiving and processing applicant files. There are several physical ways in which an organization could implement this process. It could use a Web portal in an HRIS, a kiosk at a retail outlet, direct e-mail, or physical mail. The strength of using logical models is that the HR staff and developers can focus specifically on the business processes, policies, and procedures instead of on technology. Marakas (2006) refers to this as "separating the 'what' from the 'how'" (p. 116). By focusing on what the system does or needs to be able to do, the analyst and HR staff will be less likely to be distracted by or to focus on a single technology platform. In turn, they will be more likely to design a stronger solution.

Essentially, a **logical model** is similar to the blueprints for a home or an airplane. It provides the organization with an outline of the key business processes and goals for the system. Then, as the physical system is designed, these are translated into the hardware and software platforms that best fit the business's needs. For an HRIS, there are two types of models created for the system: those focused on the system processes and those focused on the data the system captures.

Two Ways to View an HRIS: Data Versus Process

For any HRIS, the organization must look at the total HR system from two different perspectives: the data perspective and the process perspective.

The **data perspective** focuses on an analysis of what data the organization captures and uses, and on the definitions and relationships of the data, while ignoring how or where the data are used by the organization. For example, a system whose aim is employee recruiting would need data about the applicants and their knowledge, skills, and abilities (e.g., name, address, degrees received, work experience). The data perspective would focus on the important data to be captured but would not be concerned with how the data are to be used within the organization. In addition, the data perspective focuses on the most efficient and effective way to capture the data to ensure accuracy.

The **process perspective**, conversely, focuses on the business processes and activities in which the organization engages and on how data flow through the HRIS. For example, a recruiting module from this perspective would consider business activities, such as receiving applications, sorting and scanning resumes to determine the interview pool, scheduling interviews, reporting candidate information for legal purposes, and so on, but not the data definitions and relationships. The designer would focus on the specific business processes, including the input of the data into the system, the flow of data through the system, and the storage of the data, but not on precisely what data are captured and how they are best organized or stored. Essentially, process modeling uses tools to describe the processes that are carried out by a system.

A key question that the reader might be asking is "Why should I care about these distinctions?" The reason the distinction between the process and data perspectives is important is that each represents a portion of the total HRIS but neither provides the complete picture. By modeling each separately, the organization is better able to understand and communicate its needs to the technical staff (e.g., the project management team responsible for designing and implementing the HRIS and any external consultants, vendors, or software developers). In addition, while processes may change in the future, data generally represent the most permanent and stable part of a system. For example, employee data from prior systems are often converted into the new HRIS data format and transferred into the new system. This data conversion and migration process is a critical step in the implementation phase, and it provides a bridge and continuity between the legacy system and the new HRIS. This permanency of data and the more dynamic aspect of processes suggest the importance of dealing with each separately.

Over the past three decades, a well-established procedure for modeling information systems has been developed. The procedure is based on a process perspective that uses data flow diagramming. A common aspect of all design methodologies is the use of diagrammatic modeling techniques. While the style of the charting symbols varies, the fundamentals are well established. Our focus in this chapter is on the creation and use of process models.

Logical Process Modeling With Data Flow Diagrams

A **process model** describes and represents the key business processes or activities conducted by the organization, such as applicant tracking. The specific type of process model typically used by organizations is a **data flow diagram (DFD)**. A DFD is a graphical representation of the key business activities and processes in the HR system, the boundaries of this system, the data that flow through the system, and any external individuals or departments that interact with the system.

The focus of a DFD is on the movement of data between external entities (such as a job applicant) and processes (the applicant-tracking process) and between processes and data stores. Kendall and Kendall (2008) argue that DFDs have four distinct advantages over narrative (e.g., written) descriptions:

1. There is freedom from committing to the technical implementation of the system too early.
2. They provide a deeper understanding of the interrelatedness of systems and subsystems.
3. They allow for stronger communication of system knowledge to the employees, since the diagrams are in pictorial form.
4. They ensure a deeper analysis of the proposed system to determine if all business processes have been identified.

A DFD consists of four symbols (see Figure 5.1). These include the entity, the data flow, the process, and the data store. The **entity** represents any external agent (e.g., an individual, department, business, system) that either receives or supplies data to the HR system. For example, in an applicant-tracking system (ATS), a manager could request that a job opening be posted, or an applicant could submit her resume online. In this scenario both the manager and applicant are entities. Other examples of an entity are a manager inputting merit pay raise information on an employee into the payroll system or the production/manufacturing system inputting piece-rate production data about the number of products produced by an employee into the payroll system. Similarly, the time-and-labor module, which provides time-card information on employees and their start and end times on workdays, represents an entity for payroll systems. Because entities represent a specific person, place, system, or department, they are labeled with a noun in the DFD.

The **data flow** represents the movement of a single piece of data from point to point through the system (e.g., from process to process, entity to process, or process to data store). As a data flow represents data about a person, place, or thing, it should also be labeled with a noun. The label of a data flow should describe exactly what data are contained in the flow. For example, a data flow labeled "Time Sheet" would represent an employee's time sheet, and the exact data contained in the flow would be precisely defined as part of the diagramming process. Because DFDs describe the key business processes and the flow of data between them, *an important rule to remember is that all data flows must begin or end at a process.*

The third component of a DFD is the **process**. A process represents a business activity. The goal of each process is to change or transform inputted data into a useful output (e.g., creating an applicant record, updating an employee record, creating a recruiting yield ratio report, reporting Equal Employment Opportunity Commission data on applicants). Since data are transformed as part of these processes, they should be labeled with action verbs, for example, *calculate, send, print,* or *verify.*

The final symbol represents the **data store**, in other words, the data at rest in the system or a repository of data. This repository could be a filing cabinet, a file on a desk, a computer file, or a database table. A data store contains data about a person, place, or department and should be labeled with a noun. Examples of data stores include employee files, applicant files, employee records, and customer or current benefits records. Data stores are typically identified with a "D*n*," where D identifies that what is labeled is a data store and *n* is a number reflecting the data store's unique identifier (D1, D2, etc.). The symbols and their use are illustrated in Figure 5.1.

Figure 5.1 Symbols of the DFD

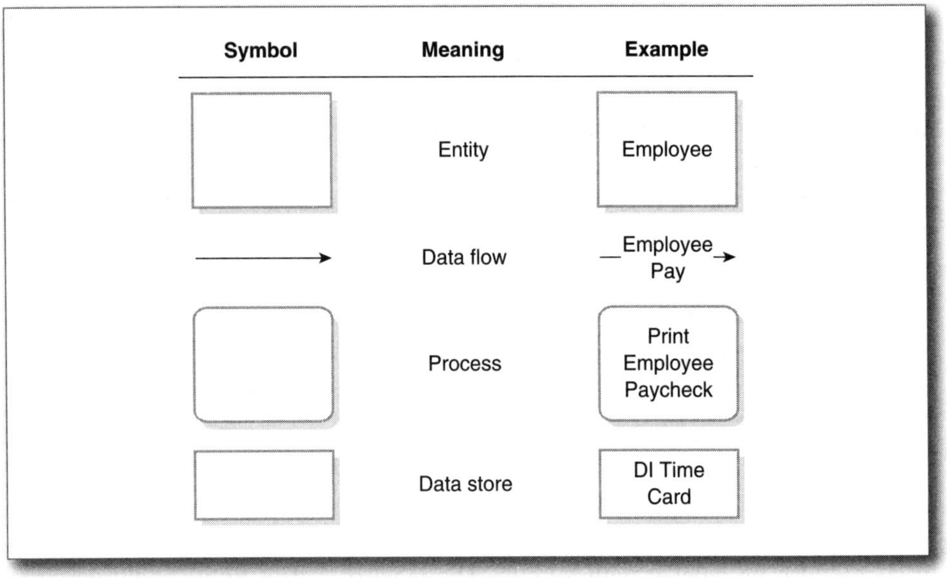

Creating and Using the DFD

Most DFDs for integrated business systems are very complex, consisting of hundreds to thousands of processes, data flows, and data stores. If all of these were included on a single diagram, it would make the task of developing and using the DFD too complex. Therefore, DFDs are organized by modeling the individual processes (such as the applicant-tracking process) and components (such as the recruiting module) of an information system. Furthermore, a series of DFDs are created to depict visually increasingly detailed views. The value of this approach is that all individuals involved in the logical design of the system can view the model at their own level of understanding and complexity. Viewing the model provides much better understanding than creating written documents to describe the model and all the processes.

The highest-level DFD developed is called the **context level diagram**. This diagram describes the full system, its boundaries, the external entities that interact with the system, and the primary data flows between the entities outside the system and the system itself. The context level diagram contains only one HR process, representing the system, data flows, and entities. This process is labeled with the system name and is identified as the context level diagram. A sample context level diagram for an ATS is shown in Figure 5.2.

Figure 5.2 Context Level Diagram

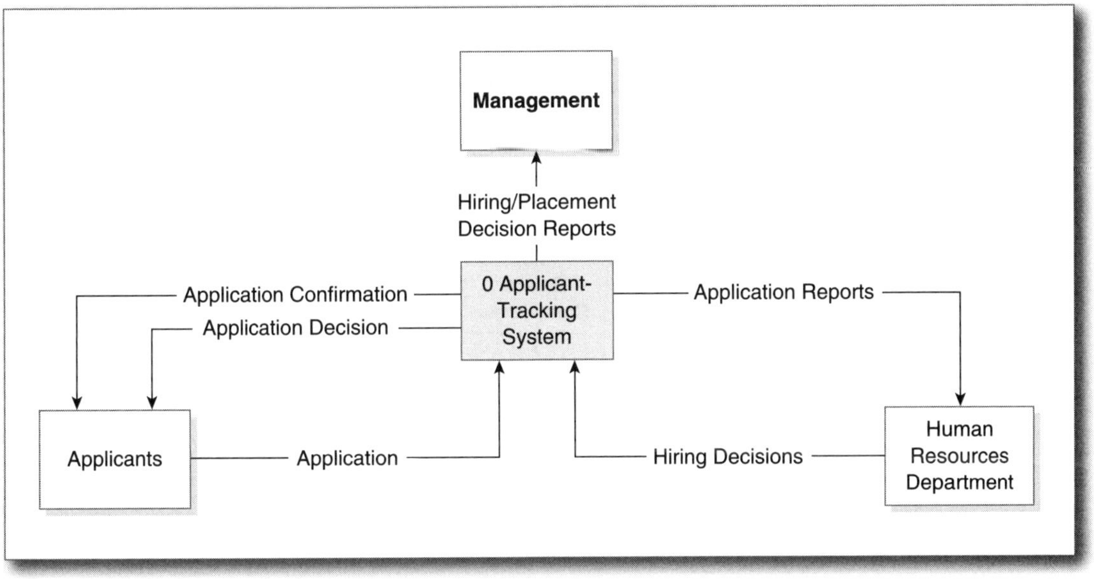

The single HR process in the context level diagram is then broken into greater detail on the **level 0 diagram** to provide a clearer picture of the HR business process. The level 0 diagram contains the major system processes and the data that flow between them. Each process should be labeled with a verb that reflects the action that the process conducts. In addition, each process is numbered consecutively starting with 1.0 (1.0, 2.0, 3.0, 4.0, etc.). It is important to note at this point that the context level diagram and the level 0 diagrams should reflect and communicate the same information (see Figure 5.3).

This concept is called the **balancing** of DFDs. Notice that, although the level 0 diagram shown in Figure 5.3 has more detail than the context level diagram, it contains the same inflows and outflows from management, applicants, and human resources. For example, on both levels, the three flows, "Application," "Application Confirmation," and "Application Decision," flow between the Applicant entity and the system in the same way. Balancing DFDs is important because we want to ensure that all individuals are viewing and using the same model of the system. Otherwise, there is the risk that the system will not be designed appropriately.

In the same manner that the context level can be decomposed into a level 0 diagram, the level 0 diagram can be decomposed into *additional-level diagrams*. As with the context level diagram, the level 0 diagram in Figure 5.3 also hides specific details about all the processing tasks within the HR system. Thus, the

Figure 5.3 Level 0 DFD

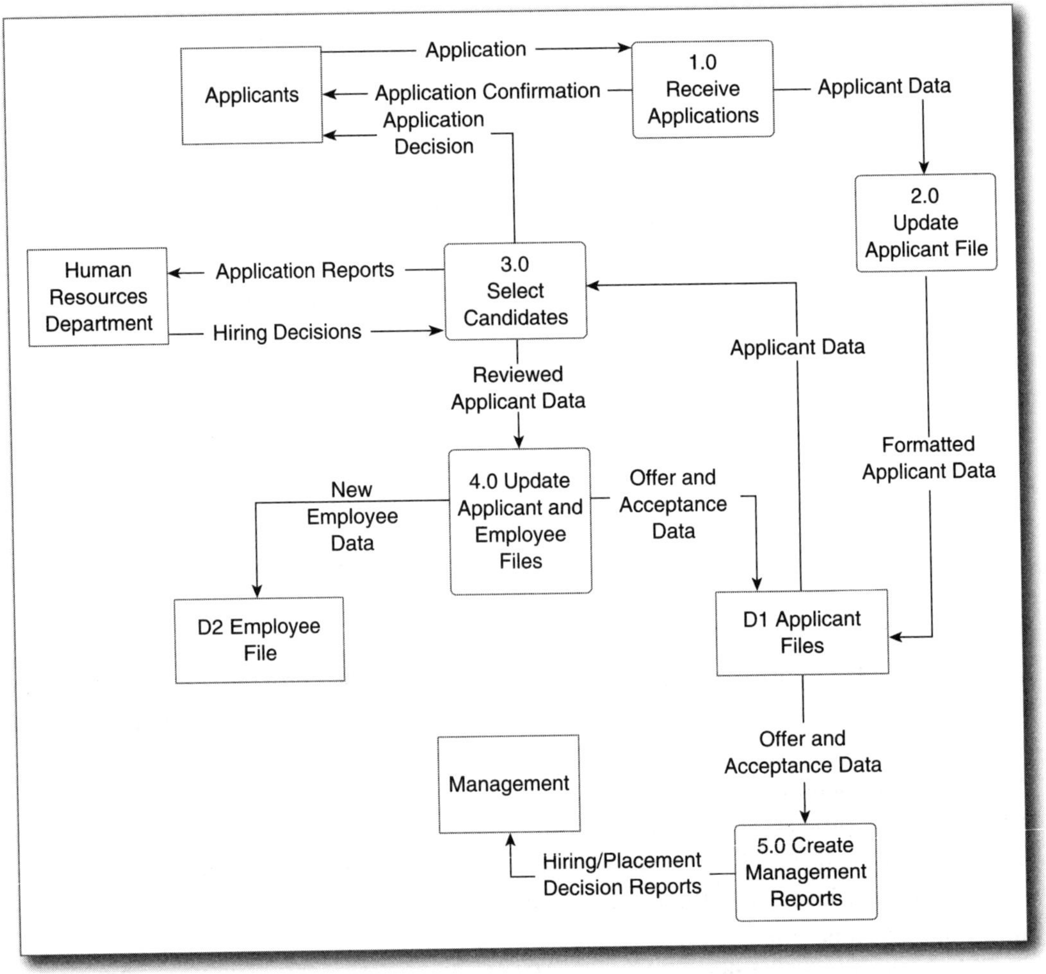

next-level diagram (the level 1 diagram) would break down the processes within the level 0 diagram to better portray and help staff to understand the HR processes in the system. This level of detail will, in turn, improve the accuracy of the logical design of the system. The same process of decomposition could occur at successive levels (level 2, level 3, etc.); however, this diagramming becomes a very complex task and is beyond the scope of this book.[1] The DFD is considered complete when it includes all the components necessary for the system being modeled.

The DFD can also be used as a tool for analyzing the current system versus the desired system. In addition, DFDs are often used for business process reengineering, in an effort to improve the system. For example, through the DFD, the analysts designing the ATS for Larson Property Management might discover that data (e.g., rating scores) from a lower-level manager's interview of job candidates currently flow back to the HR department for approval prior to allowing the applicant file to proceed to the next-level manager. Through this analysis, they could find that this step is unnecessary in the new HRIS because the system would use a decision rule, based on the minimum score needed to proceed, to forward the applicant data to the next manager automatically upon an applicant receiving a passing score.

Physical Design

As was discussed in earlier chapters of this book, the acquisition of a system is the culmination of a series of important steps. By this point, the organization should have a strong understanding of its current operations, a set of requirements for the new system, and a new logical model for how it wishes the system to operate. Once the new system has been designed and logical models of the new system have been tested against the business requirements, the organization will move to the **physical design** phase. The major goal of this phase of the SDLC is to translate the logical model and requirements into a physical system, including all hardware, software, and networking.

Major activities in this phase include (1) determining whether or not there is value in continuing the system design and actual implementation processes, (2) determining hardware and software options and requirements, (3) determining where to obtain the hardware and software (e.g., by in-house development or commercial software purchase), (4) developing an implementation schedule, and (5) working with potential vendors to assess and select software if system software is to be obtained externally. For most organizations, these activities will typically mean that the HR staff specialists (e.g., the recruiting manager) will work closely with HRIS specialists and the internal **information technology (IT)** staff, as well as with software vendors and any external consultants brought in to help with the physical design of the system. The extent of involvement of these various stakeholders depends on the size, scope, and type of HRIS developed.

During the physical design phase, the HRIS and IT staff will focus heavily on how any new software and hardware will fit within the current **IT architecture**. In addition, IT and HRIS staff will provide technical recommendations on the relative value and cost of building the system internally or purchasing an off-the-shelf package from a commercial vendor. The HR staff will also work with the external vendors to ensure that the focus of the system is on the business requirements and not the technology itself. It is also important at this point to remind the HR staff to be very careful of scope creep (which was discussed in detail in Chapter 4).

Three Choices in Physical Design

The first step in this design phase is to determine how to proceed with physical design. First, the organization has the option of doing nothing. Although this may seem to be counterintuitive because much time and money typically have been spent on the analysis and design process to date, there may be important organizational or environmental reasons for not proceeding. For example, on completion of a thorough analysis and logical redesign of the HR processes, a small organization in the southern United States was faced with a public lawsuit, and it was forced to delay the final design and implementation of the project until this was settled. In other instances, companies have postponed proceeding after learning that a target software vendor was in the process of a major revision of the software product.

The second option is to *make changes to only the HR business processes without implementing new or upgraded technology.* Before any time or money is spent on new technology, it is important that the organization address all proposed business process changes and determine if these processes can be handled using the current HRIS technology. In the book *Good to Great,* Collins (2001) suggests that one important difference between good companies and great companies is that good companies view technology as a solution, whereas great companies see technology as a tool to be used to support great business processes. Furthermore, Brynjolfsson and Hitt (1998) found that organizations were much more likely to increase productivity and performance when they coupled any technology changes with business process changes.

At this point in the process, it can be easy to forget that the goal for the development of the new system should be to use technology to support HR practices, making them more efficient and adding value to the organization; an organization should not get so caught up in the promise of a new technology with industry "best practices" that it ignores actual needs. In HR or IT, although using best practices is desirable, if these practices are not compatible with the specific needs of your organization as identified in the needs analysis, any business process and technical changes are likely to be less effective.

The final option that an organization can choose is to *implement the business process changes along with new or upgraded technology.* There are three basic ways that this can be done: build it, buy it, or outsource the development. Organizations that choose the first approach—to build the technology internally—will take responsibility for the development of the software and hardware. The advantage of this approach is that the organization will control all aspects of the development, including the look and feel and functionality. Using this approach, the organization will be able to write software to meet 100% of the business's requirements. Finally, internally building the software can also provide increased flexibility and creative solutions for the issues within the HR business processes.

There are several shortcomings in building the HR system internally from scratch. First, it can be much more expensive to implement than an off-the-shelf solution. In addition, since it is a unique application, the amount of software testing and the developmental risk are much higher with this approach than for an off-the-shelf system. Further, for this approach to work, the organization must already have or readily be able to obtain the technical, functional, and project management skills necessary to build the system effectively. For most organizations, obtaining what is needed to build the system is a daunting task because software development is generally not part of their **core competency**, and they likely do not have the staff and resources available to complete such an undertaking. Finally, since an HRIS is typically one of at least several core modules that are part of the overall **enterprise resource planning (ERP)** system, building the module in-house often leads to issues and challenges associated with integrating the HRIS with the other core modules, including the data warehouse component used to integrate data as a basis for business intelligence features.

For most organizations, the second approach of buying prepackaged, **commercial off-the-shelf (COTS) software** fits many needs. These systems can range from small single-function applications costing a few thousand dollars to large-scale, ERP software packages costing millions of dollars. The advantage of using this approach to acquiring software is that the systems are well tested and proven and can be purchased and implemented in a short period. For this reason, most of the HR software adopted and used today is COTS. The good news for organizations considering the adoption of a COTS solution is that most business operations are fairly generic, so there are applications available that should meet the majority of the needs of most organizations. The bad news is that even the best system will rarely meet all the specific needs of the organization, with most meeting about 70% of the organization's needs. Thus, organizations choosing to purchase a COTS solution should be prepared either to work with the vendor to customize the system to meet their unique needs or to change their processes to fit with the software (and thereby opt for what is referred to as the "vanilla" approach). As mentioned briefly before, the risk of adapting your business processes to the software is that the business processes supported by the software may be incompatible with the way your organization operates, which can result in increased costs or reduced competitive advantage. In addition, when an organization implements a vendor's upgrade in the future, it will likely be necessary to redo whatever customization was done during the initial implementation.

Alliance Programs

To assist organizations that wish to implement a customized solution, most of the major HRIS software vendors (e.g., Oracle, SAP, Lawson) supplement their mainline enterprise solutions by investing in alliances with other independent software vendors (ISVs). The primary goal of these **alliance programs** is to provide a total solution to make both vendors' products more attractive and effective for their customer base. A secondary goal for the HRIS vendors is to create an "ecosystem" of solutions that can compete more effectively with other HRIS applications. The larger the ecosystem or number of partners in a program, the bigger the footprint the HRIS application will have. A side effect is that the HRIS provider appears to be more "open" from a technical perspective. In fact, Oracle and SAP are actively selling their technical integration capabilities (middleware) alongside their HR applications.

The final approach to developing the software is to outsource the development to an external company or to obtain access to existing software through an **application service provider (ASP)**. The greatest advantage of outsourcing is that an external software development can bring vast resources, experiences, and technical skills to design a much more effective solution than would otherwise be possible. However, outsourcing the development can be risky. For example, by outsourcing, the firm may expose confidential internal information and business processes to an external organization. Second, outsourcing may not lead to reduced time and expense for the organization because many of the tasks that would need to be completed if the software were developed in-house would still need to be completed *with* the external software developer.

As can be seen from the previous discussion, there are advantages and disadvantages to each approach for software development. Thus, the decision as to which approach to use will be based on multiple factors and may differ from organization to organization and project to project. In addition, an organization need not rely on a single approach. For most organizations, the solution chosen is often a combination of in-house and external development. The decision regarding which approach to choose is based on a series of factors, including the nature of the business process; the size, technical skills, and project management skills of the software staff; and the development time frame. Table 5.1 contains a matrix of how these different factors may influence the approach chosen.

If the decision is made to purchase and customize COTS or to outsource development, the organization will need to work closely with external software vendors. Thus, vendor selection becomes a very important decision.

Table 5.1 Software Acquisition Strategies

	Development Strategy		
	In-House	*COTS*	*Outsource*
Business need	*Unique*	*Standard*	*Noncore function*
In-house skills	Functional and technical expertise exists	Functional expertise exists	Functional and technical expertise not in-house
Project management skills	Project has skilled and experienced project manager	Project has a manager with experience to coordinate and manage vendor relationship	Project has manager with experience to manage an outsourcing relationship
Time frame	Flexible	Short	Flexible or short

SOURCE: Adapted from Dennis, Wixom, and Roth (2006).

WORKING WITH VENDORS

Although building a new HRIS from scratch with internal resources may be a viable option for some organizations, by far the most common decision that the HR department will make is to work with an external vendor to develop or acquire the system. To do this, the HR staff will need to work closely with both the internal IT department and external vendors to ensure that the business process requirements and all technical requirements are presented to the vendor. The first step in this process is to develop a **request for proposal (RFP)**.

An RFP is a document that solicits proposals and bids for proposed work from potential consultants or vendors. An RFP defines the organization's goals and requirements for the new information system. It provides the details that define hardware, software, and services requirements. For the organization, it provides a structured approach that minimizes the chance of omitting important criteria. On return from vendors or consultants, it simplifies the vendor comparison process by providing a format to elicit consistent and complete responses.

The RFP provides an opportunity for the HR department to record systematically what its staff will need the system to do. As part of this process, any remaining implicit assumptions should be made explicit. Basically, the RFP will define what is needed and what is not needed in the system. In addition, the RFP begins the communication process and relationship building with vendors.[2]

Although there are many different factors that will determine precisely what should be included in the RFP, experts in the field have argued for the inclusion of a key set of components. Table 5.2 presents an example of these key factors, adapted from recommendations made by the Society for Human Resource Management and the work of Hinojos and Miller (1998).

Table 5.2 is an excellent starting point for developing an RFP, but it should not be taken to include all items that may be required. Those developing an RFP for an organization should keep in mind their unique situation and add or subtract what is included as appropriate for their needs. The information in this table is also very general in nature, and how it is developed will be different for each organization.

Table 5.2 Recommended Components of a Request for Proposal

- ♦ **Data about you**
  - Who you are as a business
    - o Company name, size, scope, industry, annual sales, locations, etc.
  - Business requirements
    - o Required business processes, functionality, and project scope
  - Technical requirements
    - o Does it need to work with a particular operating system, existing organization systems, etc.?
  - Delivery time frame needed
    - o Is there a desired target implementation date?
- ♦ **Requested data from vendor**
  - Vendor details
    - o Company name, size, scope, annual sales, experience, etc.
    - o Number of implemented applications
  - System pricing
    - o May include license fees, maintenance charges, training costs, implementation costs, and support costs
  - System details
    - o Functionality included in the system
  - If customization is necessary, how will this be addressed (timing, delivery, cost, support, etc.)?
    - o Supported technology now and in the near future
    - o Customer support options
    - o Training options
  - Customer references
    - o Find out user and organizational experiences with the system.
    - o Ask these references for other companies they know using the system to broaden your knowledge (after all, the vendor is likely to provide you with clients who have had positive experiences).
  - Sample contract terms

When developing the RFP, organizations should keep several things in mind. The first recommendation is to *focus on the business requirements.* Given that the system is being considered in association with business process changes, an excellent place to begin the development for the vendor is to review the requirements and logical redesign of the business processes. These should then be communicated to each vendor.

Associated with this requirement, the second recommendation is to *be specific.* After all the effort given to the needs analysis and the redesign of business processes, very specific requirements will be available and should be included in the RFP. It is important to be specific as to your organization's needs because, if you are not specific, you risk allowing the vendors to determine what is included in the final system. Although it is desirable to work with a vendor to develop the final system, it is important that the system be developed to meet your specific business needs, not just designed to match the system a vendor has available. Furthermore, an RFP that is too general may not be screened in sufficient detail by the vendor, leading to a product that has too much detail and is too complex and too expensive for the business's needs. The overall objective of the RFP is to have the vendors propose system hardware and software to meet the specific requirements you have identified for your new system.

The third recommendation is to *keep it simple.* One of the temptations in developing an RFP is to include all possible business and technical requirements in it. The problem with including many technical details in the plan is that vendors may review the RFP and screen themselves out because they think they cannot fill the needs outlined in the RFP. For example, it would be important to ask whether a benefits system allows for benefits reports, benefits administration, and so on. Conversely, the RFP would want to stay away from including requirements as to length of fields, types of passwords used, and so on, which do not focus on business needs but instead are focused on technical and physical design issues. Essentially, if something is not important to the HR department and reflective of the business processes modeled in the DFDs, it is best not to include it.

This point leads to the fourth recommendation, which is to *work closely with the HRIS and IT staff* as the RFP is developed. The professional staff will be responsible for working with the vendor to ensure the smooth installation and maintenance of the HRIS. Therefore, it is important for the HR staff to work closely with the information systems professional staff to make sure that any essential technical considerations are included. For example, if there are existing systems that need to provide information to or receive information from the system, then this should be included. In addition, if there is a certain platform (e.g., UNIX, Windows) that the organization has experience with and with which it would like the system to integrate, this too should be included.

Vendor Selection

After the RFPs are sent, the vendors will then evaluate them to determine if they have a product that would fit the company's needs. If the HR and IT staff have put together a strong RFP, then they should get a set of vendors who have a better understanding of the company's specific needs and who can provide a better-tailored response and proposal for the HRIS. After receiving the vendor responses, you will have the opportunity to evaluate the relative strengths and weaknesses of each vendor. To do this, you should consider several things and assess software options according to a number of criteria. These are described below.

Functionality

As you assess the different vendor responses, it is important to evaluate how fully the functionality of the HRIS meets the HR needs. For example, a software product that meets 70% of the organization's needs will be less desirable than one that meets 98% of its requirements. On the other hand, software that meets 98% of the organization's needs but has no additional functionality may not provide the organization with the opportunity to grow and expand its options in the future, so it may be less attractive than a product that meets 90% of your HR needs but allows for growth over time. It is important that the HRIS implemented today is able to change as the organization grows. Otherwise, within a few years, the organization will have to go through the entire systems development process and purchase or develop an entirely new solution. Finally, an HRIS that will meet your organization's needs with minimal customization for actual use would be more attractive than one requiring significant customization.

IT Architecture and IT Integration

The next issue focuses on the IT architecture for the HRIS. The organization will need to know whether the HRIS will be a stand-alone system or a networked system or a Web-based one, and so on. In addition, the organization will want to know with what technology or platform the HRIS has been developed (e.g., UNIX, Linux, Windows). Finally, as important as knowing the answers to these questions is understanding the extent to which the HRIS will integrate within the broader corporate IT architecture. An HRIS that can more readily interact and communicate with operations, manufacturing, and sales can provide a much stronger return for the company than one that stands as an isolated entity. The easier the integration with the broader IT architecture, the easier it will be to implement and use the system. In today's environment of employee self-service and Web portals, the ability to provide remote access to employees can also be a plus as different systems are considered. Finally, if functional HR systems are being considered from multiple vendors, the extent to which they can be integrated and communicate with each other also becomes important.

Price

Although price will ultimately play a very large role in the selection of an HRIS, price should be secondary to the goal of finding a system that meets your process needs. At the same time, price will ultimately determine which system is selected. The ultimate cost of the system will include the visible costs, such as the cost of hardware and software, as well as the less visible costs, such as customization costs, employee training costs, licensing fees (e.g., site licenses, per seat licenses), upgrade costs, and the cost of system operation and maintenance over time. HRIS costs and cost-benefit analyses are covered in more detail in Chapter 7.

Vendor Longevity and Viability

As with any purchase decision, it is important to evaluate the quality of the vendor itself. The good news is that many vendors have been in business for 10 to 20 years, so vendor longevity is usually not an issue. In today's environment, the viability of vendors can often be assessed through their responsiveness to existing clients and their history of providing timely upgrades and increasingly flexible systems. Furthermore, the HRIS vendor marketplace has been undergoing some consolidation as companies seek to better position themselves to provide value-added services across the HR functional spectrum, so the vendor you sign with today may end up merging with another company.

ASSESSING SYSTEM FEASIBILITY

At this point in the design process, it is very important that you stop and consider whether or not the system will work for you. Although the system may meet all the requirements as defined in the requirements document, it still may not be feasible to implement for several reasons. Therefore, it is important to conduct a thorough feasibility assessment of the project. A feasibility assessment should go beyond the traditional economic metrics and should include multiple dimensions, such as technical, operational, human factors, legal, political, and economic.

Technical Feasibility

Technical feasibility focuses on the current technological capabilities of the organization and the technological capabilities required for the implementation of the proposed system. As part of any assessment of technical feasibility, the HR staff must work closely with systems analysts and technical staff to determine whether or not the current technology can be upgraded to meet the needs of the organization or whether an entirely new technological architecture will be needed to implement the proposed system changes.

Typical questions an organization might ask as part of a technical feasibility assessment are as follows:

1. Do the hardware and software exist to implement this system? Are they practical to obtain?
2. Do we add on or patch the current software or start from scratch?
3. Does our organization have the ability to construct this system?
4. Can we integrate the new system with our current systems?

Operational Feasibility

Operational feasibility focuses on how well the proposed system fits in with the current and future organizational environment. For example, a system, despite meeting technical feasibility criteria, may make such a drastic change in how the organization operates that it may not have a strong chance of being successfully implemented. For example, a series of research studies in information systems has found that the more compatible a system is with an employee's current ways of working, the more likely the employee will be to use the system (Agarwal, 2000). Therefore, when a new system is highly incompatible with current practices, HR staff or designers might seek to change or decrease the scope of the project to reduce these incompatibilities.

In addition, operational feasibility assesses the extent to which the project fits within the overall strategic plans of the HR and IT departments as well as within the organization's overall strategy. Other areas addressed as part of the assessment of operational feasibility include the likelihood of meeting the proposed implementation schedule and delivery date. The HR staff and developers must work together to ensure that the schedule will meet any critical operational deadlines, that resources are sufficient to meet the schedule, and that the schedule takes into account key organization dates (e.g., annual budgeting). The techniques used in project management are very important and will be discussed in detail in Chapter 8.

A second area of operational feasibility focuses on human factors. An assessment of the human factors feasibility focuses on how the employee uses and works with the system, on the system's usability, and on the training the employees receive. The usability of the system reflects the effectiveness and efficiency of the system to the employee and is often characterized by the usefulness of the system to the employees and the ease with which they can use the system. It can reflect how intuitive the interface is to navigate, the effort an employee must put into learning to use the system, and how effective the system is in supporting the employees' work.

Do not underestimate the importance of human factors in determining the operational feasibility and ultimate success of a system. Over the past 20 years, hundreds of studies have found that the usefulness and ease of use of a system play a large role in system use and adoption.[3] In addition, recent research has found that usefulness estimations can be accurately assessed by employees early in the development process but that perceptions of ease of use may evolve as employees gain direct experience with the software (Davis & Venkatesh, 2004). These human factor considerations will be covered in Chapter 9 in more detail, along with suggestions as to how to solve the acceptability issue.

Typical questions asked as part of the assessment of operational feasibility would include the following:

1. How well does the system fit within our organizational context? Will this make us better?
2. How much will our organization change because of the new business and technical changes?
3. How long will this take to do, and does the schedule fit our business's needs?
4. If we have to squeeze, what might we be able to eliminate?
5. Do we have or can we get the personnel to do this?
6. Can people use the system?
7. What kind of training do we need?

Legal and Political Feasibility

Legal and political issues also play a very important role in assessing the feasibility of an HRIS. The best-designed and -implemented system can end up causing major headaches for the organization if it violates existing laws and regulations. This point is even truer for an HRIS than for many other types of information systems because existing laws and regulations play a larger role in HR than in other core business functions (as will be discussed in Chapter 10). For example, if the HRIS fails to maintain specific employee performance records correctly, legal challenges of wrongful discharges will be more difficult for the company to defend against.

Political feasibility focuses on the political environment of the organization in which the HRIS is being implemented. Issues such as power redistribution involving loss of individual or department control can have major political implications that can affect the effectiveness of the implementation. What is interesting is that political issues can undermine the implementation of a new HRIS more quickly and completely than any technical shortcomings. The challenge here is that, while political feasibility may be fairly easy to identify, it can be challenging to effectively address. Individuals who are negatively affected by the implementation of the system (or who perceive themselves to be negatively affected) are likely to undermine, resist, or disrupt its implementation, either overtly or covertly. Thus, it is important to understand and anticipate the political consequences of a system implementation at this point, before implementation is started. Again, these issues are discussed more fully in Chapter 9.

Typical questions asked as part of a **legal and political feasibility** analysis include the following:

1. Does the implementation of this system infringe on existing copyrights?
2. Are we violating any antitrust issues by implementing the system?
3. Do we have contracts with other companies that don't allow use of the new software?
4. Does the system violate any governmental policies?
5. Does the system violate any foreign laws? (This question would be significant for global companies who have operations in multiple countries where different laws require different practices supporting the capture and use of HR data, for example.)
6. Who is likely to resist the implementation of the system?
7. Who may "win" or "lose" as a result of this implementation?
8. What is the risk of system sabotage?

Economic Feasibility

The final aspect of a feasibility assessment is evaluating **economic feasibility**. The goal of an economic feasibility analysis is to determine whether the costs of developing, implementing, and running the system are worth the benefits derived from its use. To do this, an analyst would identify the appropriate costs and benefits of the HRIS and assign precise values to each. Then, these costs and benefits should be subjected to a thorough cost-benefit analysis. As mentioned earlier, Chapter 7 provides comprehensive coverage of how to assess the costs and benefits of an HRIS.

SUMMARY

The goal of this chapter was to discuss the factors that contribute to a more effective system design strategy. First, we discussed how the HR staff and consultants translate the requirements from previous phases of the SDLC into improved logical business processes. We then discussed how these new processes are modeled through logical modeling tools such as the DFD. DFDs are important because they allow the HR staff, consultants, and programmers to have a common model of the system from which to work and because they can be used to identify potential shortcomings not yet identified in the new system. In addition, because DFDs are hierarchical in approach, they allow for the system to be viewed at multiple levels of specificity. This makes them a useful tool for communicating with all relevant actors in the systems development process while also being technical enough to allow developers to best determine how to translate business requirements into the new HRIS. Given that the cost of making changes becomes significantly more expensive once the physical design of the system has been undertaken, it is important that these models be as effective and accurate as possible to avoid system rework.

Third, we discussed the options available for the firm when developing the final physical design for the new system. One option available to firms is not to change their existing practices. Other options include building the software internally or sourcing the software through external vendors. The chapter also briefly outlined the steps of working with a vendor, from the RFP through the selection of the vendor, and it provided several suggestions for getting the most out of the RFP and the vendor selection process. Finally, whatever approach is chosen for the final design, any selected physical system must be assessed as to its feasibility. Although budgeting committees will pay especially close attention to the profitability of the system, we also explained the importance of considering different types of system feasibility. Although this phase of the SDLC can be complex and challenging to manage, we believe that following a structured and disciplined approach such as the one outlined will result in the development or acquisition of a system that is a stronger fit for the organization.

KEY TERMS

alliance programs
applicant-tracking system (ATS)
application service provider (ASP)
balancing
commercial off-the-shelf (COTS) software
context level diagram
core competency
data flow
data flow diagram (DFD)
data perspective

data store
economic feasibility
enterprise resource planning (ERP)
entity
information technology (IT)
IT architecture
legal and political feasibility
level 0 diagram
logical design
logical model
operational feasibility
physical design
process
process model
process perspective
request for proposal (RFP)
systems development life cycle (SDLC)
technical feasibility

DISCUSSION QUESTIONS

1. What is the difference between the data view of a system and the process view of a system? Why is this distinction important when designing a new system?
2. Discuss four reasons that a DFD is a stronger tool than a written narrative of the business processes.
3. How do companies use an RFP when sourcing software? What are the key items that should be included in the RFP?
4. If you were advising a firm on developing an RFP, what would be some key suggestions you would make for improving the effectiveness of the RFP?
5. When evaluating vendor offerings, what are the key factors that will help your firm determine the best software product to acquire?
6. Even if a system pays for itself financially, an organization must conduct a thorough feasibility study. What types of feasibility should be assessed, and what information does each type of feasibility assessment provide the organization?

CASE STUDY[4]

Larson Property Management Company is one of the largest property management companies in California, with more than 1,000 employees. The company provides a full array of commercial management and development services. These activities include complete management services for commercial office and retail buildings and apartment complexes; construction, repair, and maintenance of commercial properties; and financial management and billing services for commercial real-estate clients. The company has experienced significant expansion over the past five years in response to the growth in apartment and commercial construction in southern California, and this expansion has resulted in the need to hire a large number of employees on an ongoing basis to staff its operations.

Larson Property Management has depended on a legacy HRIS to manage its applicant and employee databases. The system runs on a client-server computer system. The system was implemented approximately 10 years ago, prior to the company's rapid growth and when it employed fewer than 100 employees. The system's functionality is limited to the storage and retrieval of employee and applicant data. For recruiting purposes, the system requires a clerk to manually enter basic applicant data, the results of the application test, and whether or not an offer of employment has been made. Prior to this, applicants' files were passed around to those who reviewed the materials and were sometimes misplaced, so trying to locate a particular applicant's file was often a problem. The current HRIS has limited file storage capability for applicant and employee records and currently has reached its storage capacity.

Larson Property Management has decided to replace its legacy HRIS. One application module in the new HRIS that the company wants is a sophisticated applicant-tracking system (ATS). The primary objective of the ATS will be to provide a paperless hiring process. The basic functions of the new system will be managing the requisition and approval of job openings, storing resumes and job applications and retrieving through query functions the names of applicants who match job requirements, tracking a candidate's progress through the recruiting and selection process, and providing automated reporting functions. The company's managers also want an e-HR functionality that includes the Internet posting of job openings through the company's Web site and external job-posting services, application and resume submission through the Web and through kiosks at various office locations, staff ability to access and use the system remotely through a Web browser, and online resume- and application-scanning capabilities.

Part of the design phase is modeling the processes that will be used in the system for applicant tracking. For Larson Property Management, this modeling will allow the system analysts to design an efficient paperless hiring process.

Larson Property management is well aware that the *design stage* of the SDLC is critical for the successful implementation of the new ATS. However, there is considerable confusion about how to proceed with this phase. The HR and IT professionals assigned to the ATS committee have been meeting to plan the new system. From their planning and needs analysis, it is clear that a new HRIS application is needed, can save considerable time, and can result in more accurate storage and retrieval of applicant data for cost-benefit and other management reports.

The company has had several vendors provide presentations, with each vendor outlining its particular approach to the design of an ATS. But these presentations were primarily focused on the physical design of the new ATS. The HR and IT committees must now begin the design process, which must be completed in three months.

Case Study Questions

1. Based on the material in this chapter, design a three-month operational plan for the ATS.
   a. In your plan, make certain you differentiate between the logical and physical design of the ATS. Which one should be done first? Which one is more important?
   b. Describe the importance of the data view versus the process view for the design of the new ATS.
   c. Who are the important stakeholders to be considered in the design of the ATS?
   d. How will you determine whether these stakeholders need the information that the new ATS will deliver?
   e. Based on your personal knowledge of recruiting by companies, develop a DFD with at least two levels.
2. Based on the work you have completed for Question 1, provide a brief outline of the RFP that is to be sent to the HRIS vendors.

NOTES

1. The interested reader seeking more information on developing DFDs, including the rules for their completion as well as the decomposition process, can check out the following resources: *The Structured Analysis Wiki*, written by Ed Yourdon (http://yourdon.com/strucanalysis/wiki/index.php?title=Introduction), or any of the systems analysis and design textbooks listed in the reference sections of this book.

2. The interested reader is encouraged to visit http://www.albany.edu/its/iasproject/rfp/software.pdf for an example of an RFP from a large state university developing an HRIS for faculty and students.

3. Interested readers are encouraged to read Ma and Liu (2004) for a thorough review of this research.

4. Note that this is the case from the vignette, plus added material.

REFERENCES

Agarwal, R. (2000). Individual acceptance of information technologies. In R. W. Zmud (Ed.), *Framing the domains of IT management* (pp. 85–104). Cincinnati, OH: Pinnaflex Educational Resources.

Brynjolfsson, E., & Hitt, L. M. (1998). Beyond the productivity paradox. *Communications of the ACM, 41*(8), 49–55.

Collins, J. (2001). *Good to great: Why some companies make the leap . . . and others don't.* New York: HarperCollins.

Davis, F. D., & Venkatesh, V. (2004). Toward preprototype user acceptance testing of new information systems: Implications for software project management. *IEEE Transactions on Engineering Management, 51*(1), 31–46.

Dennis, A. R., Wixom, B. H., & Roth, R. M. (2006). *Systems analysis and design* (3rd ed.). Hoboken, NJ: John Wiley & Sons.

Hinojos, J. A., & Miller, M. (1998, July/August). Methodologies for selecting the right vendor. *Benefits & Compensation Solutions,* 38–42.

Kendall, K. E., & Kendall, J. E. (2008). *Systems analysis and design* (7th ed.). Upper Saddle River, NJ: Pearson.

Ma, Q., & Liu, L. (2004). The technology acceptance model: A meta-analysis of empirical findings. *Journal of End User Computing, 16*(1), 59–72.

Marakas, G. M. (2006). *Systems analysis and design: An active approach* (2nd ed.). New York: McGraw-Hill.

Patton, G. S. (1995). *War as I knew it.* Boston: Houghton Mifflin. (Original work published 1947)

Standish Group. (2004). *The chaos report.* Boston: Author.

Chapter 6

HR Metrics and Workforce Analytics

Kevin D. Carlson and Michael J. Kavanagh

EDITORS' NOTE

The capacity to manage is limited by the accessible information in our possession. Research on goal setting confirms that being able to articulate the specific goal for a task and the level of the goal we want to achieve enhances performance of that task. Better information about the expectations of customers, the actions of competitors, and the state of the economy provides strong support for the strategic direction of organizations. Information about levels of output, for example, numbers of defects and efficiency of processes, positions line managers to produce high-quality products in the right amounts at the right time to meet customer needs. The same is true for the effective management of human capital in organizations. As discussed in this chapter, effective approaches to the measurement of human capital and the impact of people on organization processes, for example, HR programs such as recruiting, will enable both HRM professionals and line managers to utilize the human capital in organizations effectively. This measurement is accomplished by focusing on the development of systems of workforce analytics and supporting HR metrics that meet the needs of organization decision makers. This chapter offers a brief history of the efforts involved in the development of HR metrics and workforce analytics and of how these efforts have been enhanced by the advent of integrated human resource information systems.[1] From benchmarking to operational experiments, the HRIS field is rapidly evolving on many fronts. These advances are changing how HR metrics and analytics are used in organizations and their impact on organization effectiveness. The use of HR metrics and workforce analytics will help managers and organizations balance the costs and benefits consequences of decisions. These cost-benefit analyses are covered in Chapter 7.

CHAPTER OBJECTIVES

After completing this chapter, you should be able to

- Discuss the factors that have led to increased organizational interest in HR metrics and workforce analytics
- Discuss why the information from numeric systems like HR metrics and workforce analytics[2] do not generate any return on investment (ROI) unless they lead to different and better decision making
- Discuss the difference between metrics and analytics
- Describe the limitations of the traditional HR metrics
- Discuss the historical role of benchmarking and its strengths and weakness today
- Discuss the roles that activities such as data mining, predictive analytics, and operational experiments play in increasing organizational effectiveness
- Discuss the differences between metrics and analytics for HR efficiency, operational effectiveness, and organizational realignment, and offer examples of each
- Describe which characteristics of HR metrics and workforce analytics are most likely to have an organizational impact

HRIS IN ACTION

When Dan Hilbert arrived as Manager of Employment Services at Valero Energy in December 2002, he wasn't quite sure what he wanted or needed to do. Coming from a background in operations, he was used to having information about the effectiveness of all current operations; yet, as he quickly learned, these data were not available for HR operations and programs, nor were there systems in place to generate them. He recognized the potential value of having even simple descriptive statistics about the HR organization, its people, and its operations—to highlight potential opportunities and how changes in these values could signal potential problems. However, since these data were not currently available or easily developed, he created a small team, consisting of one HR staff member who could help get access to data from the organization's current systems and a graduate student with a statistical background, who was hired as a part-time employee. The team's assignment was to collect data about the human capital in the organization in an effort to learn more about the organization and its people, which Dan was now charged with supporting.

The team's analysis highlighted a unique characteristic of the Valero workforce—all of its refinery managers were all at least 55 years old. This meant that these managers, each with long tenure in one of the most critical positions for assuring operating success, would be eligible to retire in fewer than ten years. Further, given that these managers had all joined the company at roughly the same time and had held these refinery manager positions for many years, the promotion pipeline for succession to this position was limited. In other words, promising managers who had joined the organization at lower managerial positions decided to leave the company when it was clear that upward opportunities were limited.

When Hilbert presented the results of this analysis and his conclusions to senior managers, they were shocked. No one had considered this issue of the aging of refinery managers, and, likely, management would not have become aware of the situation until the refinery managers began to retire. By then, it would have been too late to act to get immediate replacements. Interestingly, as Valero success increased and the stock price increased, the retirement age lowered, compounding the problem. The pipeline of trained managers capable of filling these positions internally would not have been sufficient to meet the demand created by the mass retirements, and the time to train them as refinery managers was lengthy. As a result, the computation of relatively simple metrics and analytics provided new insights on the current retirement status of employees. This data allowed management to engage in the training and development needed to build internal bench strength for this critical position prior to these managers retiring, likely saving the refiner millions in salary expense and reduced refinery performance.

INTRODUCTION

Human resources (HR) metrics and **workforce analytics** have become a hot topic in organizations of all sizes. Interest is rising, and organizations are reaching out to learn more about metrics and analytics and how they can use them to improve organizational effectiveness. Although the use of HR metrics and workforce analytics is not new, various factors have driven increased interest during the previous decade. The most important driver has been the implementation of integrated HRIS in response to the "millennium problem" of Y2K (Year 2000). The adoption of these systems shifted what had been primarily paper and pencil processes to electronic processes and, as a result, greatly increased the capacity of organizations to access and examine transaction-level data.

These new HRIS featured faster and more capable computers, improved connectivity through organizational networks and the Internet, and the earliest versions of user-friendly analytics software. These changes fundamentally altered the dynamics of human capital assessment in organizations, driving the marginal cost of assessment lower while providing the potential for near real-time analysis and distribution of information.

In addition, the quality revolution that swept through U.S. manufacturing and service firms in the 1980s and 1990s, including Total Quality Management (TQM), Six Sigma, and lean manufacturing, increased managers' expectations about the availability of organizational data and the capability of using this data to generate analytics that could support managerial decisions. These factors, combined with recent and growing interest in evidence-based management, have produced a rapidly growing interest in HR metrics and workforce analytics.

A BRIEF HISTORY OF HR METRICS AND ANALYTICS

Interest in HR metrics and workforce analysis is not new. Systematic work on the development of measures to capture the effectiveness of an organization's employees can be traced as far back as the days of scientific management (Taylor, 1911) and industrial and organizational psychology (Munsterberg, 1913). Methods of quantitative analysis and its use in decision making were developed during the build-up of both men and materiel occasioned by World War II. Further study and development occurred during the great post-war industrial expansion in the United States that continued into the 1970s. In fact, many of the most common HR metrics in existence today were first considered and developed during this period (e.g., Hawk, 1967).

Many of the HR metrics most frequently used in organizations can be traced to the pioneering work of Dr. Jac Fitz-enz and the early benchmarking work he conducted through the Saratoga Institute. In 1984, Fitz-enz published *How to Measure Human Resources Management,* currently in its third edition (Fitz-enz & Davidson, 2002), which is still a highly valued overview of many HR metrics and the formulas used to calculate them. These metrics were developed through the joint efforts of the Saratoga Institute and the American Society for Personnel Administration (ASPA), the forerunner of the current Society for Human Resource Management (SHRM). This effort produced the set of 30 metrics listed in Table 6.1, which have formed the foundation for the HRM benchmarking program conducted by the Saratoga Institute.

Kaplan and Norton's (1996) introduction of the **balanced scorecard** (see Chapter 10) further refined managers' thinking about metrics. The balanced scorecard recognizes the limitations of organizations' heavy reliance on financial indicators of performance. Such measures focus on what has already happened rather than providing managers information about what *will* happen. Balanced scorecards focus on developing leading indicators of performance from several important perspectives, including customer satisfaction, process effectiveness, and employee development, as well as financial performance.

Table 6.1 Measures in the Saratoga Institute/SHRM Human Resources Effectiveness Report

Revenue per Employee
Expense per Employee
Compensation as a Percentage of Revenue
Compensation as a Percentage of Expense
Benefit Cost as a Percentage of Revenue
Benefit Cost as a Percentage of Expense
Benefit Cost as a Percentage of Compensation
Retiree Benefit Cost per Retiree
Retiree Benefit Cost as a Percentage of Expense
Hires as a Percentage of Total Employees
Cost of Hire
Time to Fill Jobs
Time to Start Jobs
HR Department Expense as a Percentage of Company Expense
HR Headcount Ratio—HR Employees: Company Employees
HR Department Expense per Company Employee
Supervisory Compensation Percentage
Workers' Compensation Cost as a Percentage of Expense
Workers' Compensation Cost per Employee
Workers' Compensation Cost per Claim
Absence Rate
Involuntary Separation
Voluntary Separation
Voluntary Separation by Length of Service
Ratio of Offers Made to Acceptances

SOURCE: Adapted from Fitz-enz, J. (1995). *How to Measure Human Resources Management*, 2nd Edition. New York, NY: McGraw-Hill, Inc.

About the same time, Huselid's (1995) work on high performance work systems demonstrated that the systematic management of human resources was associated with significant differences in organizational effectiveness. This work provided evidence that human resource management did indeed have strategic potential. Becker, Huselid, and Ulrich (2001) helped bring these ideas together in the HR scorecard, which highlights how the alignment of HR activities with both corporate strategy and activity improve organizational outcomes.

CONTEMPORARY HR METRICS AND WORKFORCE ANALYTICS

The field of **HR metrics** and **workforce analytics** is currently in transition. During the previous 30 years, most medium to large organizations did engage in some HR assessment and analytics. But these efforts were not systematic. Due in part to the expense involved, they were conducted on only a sample of activities, and often for only a limited set of metrics. More recently, because of the development of strong computer-based communications infrastructures and greater access to data through the adoption of integrated human resource information systems, organizations are engaging in more consistent and systematic reporting of HR metrics.

Increased interest in human capital metrics and analytics work has resulted in more organizations reporting a larger number of metrics more consistently. It is important to recognize that many organizations use metrics to measure or audit their HR programs and activities. Historically, the use of such audit metrics to measure the effectiveness of HR was identified by Cascio (1987) and Fitz-enz and Davidson (2002). The Society for Human Resource Management has identified a number of metrics that organizations can use to measure their HR effectiveness (SHRM, 2010). For example, absence rate can be calculated as follows: [(# days absent in month) divided by (Avg. # of employees during mo.) × (# of workdays)] × 100 (Hollmann, 2002; Kuzmits, 1979). Another useful metric from SHRM (2011) is cost per hire, which can be calculated as Cost Per Hire (CPH) = the sum of external costs (recruiting) and internal costs (training new employees) divided by the total number of starts in a time period.

There are also more detailed approaches for the measuring and benchmarking of employees' behaviors, such as absenteeism (Hollmann, 2002) and turnover (Cascio, 2000), as well as for creating HR metrics for programs such as employee assistance and work-life programs (Cascio, 2000).

Unfortunately, while the infrastructure supporting HR metrics and analytics has undergone dramatic change in the last 20 years, the metrics themselves have not. Current computing operations are capable of capturing data on a wide range of electronically supported HR processes, extracting, analyzing, and then distributing that information in real time to managers throughout the organization. Current popular HR metrics, however, were not developed with our current computing infrastructure in mind. The Saratoga Institute's early efforts in benchmarking were primarily conducted using paper-and-pencil processes. As a consequence, recognizing what data most organizations could easily and inexpensively gather played an important role in identifying which metrics could reasonably be included in benchmark studies. The emphasis on available data can be seen in the original **Saratoga metrics** listed in Table 6.1. They focus on readily available data, most of which came from accounting systems.

Consequently, these metrics emphasize costs or easily calculated counts (e.g., head count, turnover) that often serve as proxies for costs. Every managerial decision has **cost and benefit consequences**, whether we recognize them or not. As a result, if our information systems only provide information about costs, they are of limited value to managers. Managers will try to use the information they are provided; if we offer them only cost information but little information on benefits, costs are likely to become the primary driver of managerial decisions.

Further, it is also common for metrics to be aggregated to the level of the organization. As such, they offer limited information that could be used to identify and diagnose within-organization differences. Organizational turnover rates will be heavily influenced by the turnover rate in the organization's dominant job category, masking any differences in turnover rates for jobs with fewer incumbents. Because the turnover data were extracted from the end of a specific time period, the reports provide feedback about previous activity. They only offer insights after the fact. This situation results in extended periods of time between potential problems and the opportunity for remedial responses by the organization. Change in both the analyses conducted and the metrics utilized allow organizations to take advantage of today's more capable infrastructure.

THE MAIN OBJECTIVE OF HR METRICS AND WORKFORCE ANALYTICS

Despite reporting more metrics with greater frequency to a wider group of managers, many HR professionals tasked with this reporting question whether these efforts have had a significant impact on organization effectiveness. Often, these individuals report frustration with their inability to get managers to (a) tell them what information they need, (b) use the HR metrics information included in existing reports, or (c) even acknowledge receipt of the reports. These perceptions represent a fundamental problem in the approach organizations take toward the utilization of metrics and analytics.

Many managers perceive the increased interest in metrics and analytics as simply a mandate to compute and report more metrics. The assumption behind assessing and reporting HR metrics is that it results in better organizational performance. But it is not clear that generating and reporting more HR metrics will necessarily result in better individual, unit, or organizational performance.

HR metrics and analytics comprise an information system, and information systems can only have an impact on organizations if, as a result of the information they receive, managers make different and better decisions than they would have without that information. No information system, including HR metrics and analytics, generates any return on the investment unless managers change their decision behavior for the better. If managers do not make different and better decisions as a result of the information reported to them, the time and effort expended in conducting and reporting HR metrics and analytics is wasted.

The emphasis on improving managerial decisions changes the dynamics driving metrics and analytics assessment efforts; that is, it raises the bar. It is not simply good enough to "do" metrics and analytics. These activities need to be approached in a way that increases the possibility that access to the information from these efforts will change managerial decisions, making them more effective. A fundamental problem is that many of the currently popular HR metrics do not provide a clear impact on important managerial decisions. The challenge, therefore, is to identify metrics and analytics that provide managers with the information they need to make better decisions regarding the acquisition and deployment of an organization's human capital.

USING HR METRICS AND WORKFORCE ANALYTICS

Human capital metrics has become an umbrella term that encompasses a wide range of activities and processes. There is a fundamental distinction between HR metrics and workforce analytics. Metrics are data (numbers) that reflect some descriptive detail about given processes or outcomes, for example, success in recruiting new employees. In the domain of human capital, these reflect characteristics of the organization's HR programs and activities. Analytics refer to strategies for combining data elements into metrics and for examining relationships or changes in metrics. Understanding these combinations is done to inform managers about the current or changing state of human capital in an organization in a way that can impact managerial decision making. The importance of this view is that the analytics an organization needs depend on the problems and opportunities that currently face its managers. This path leads to the metrics that the organization needs in order to compute these analyses. A number of important HR activities fall within HR metrics and workforce analytics. Several of the most common are described briefly below.

Reporting

A substantial amount of effort in the study and practice of metrics and analytics has focused on reporting. **Reporting** incorporates decisions about (a) what metrics will be reported; (b) how these metrics will be packaged; and (c) how, (d) when, and (e) to whom they should be reported. Effort has focused on attempting to identify what metrics an organization should use. However, trying to identifying what metrics should be reported without considering an organization's problems and opportunities misses the reasons for the metrics. How metrics should be reported focuses on depicting metrics for decision makers so that the "message" relevant to them has a greater probability of being understood. *How* questions deal with choosing between distributing metrics to decision makers using e-mail or creating opportunities for decision makers to extract metrics as needed. This latter approach can be done by posting the metrics on company Web sites.

When questions deal with the timing and frequency of metrics reports. In some cases, reporting is currently done annually, quarterly, or monthly. Some organizations are also considering the possibility of real-time updating for some metrics. *To whom* questions address who receives metrics data. To date, it is most common for metrics and analytics to be reported first to senior executives. However, there is a growing recognition that managers at lower levels of the organization may be able to make more immediate use of the information contained in these data in order to assist in tactical, operational decisions.

Dashboards

Dashboards are an enriched component of reporting. **Dashboards** reflect efforts to align real-time analysis of organizational and HR processes as well as an increased capacity to aggregate organizational data. Dashboards also contain business unit analyses to permit managers to drill down to examine metrics on several levels within the organization. The dashboard allows users to maintain a current snapshot of key HR metrics.

Benchmarking

The Saratoga Institute's **benchmarking** efforts were the first to develop information on standard HR metrics regarding the use and management of human capital. Benchmarking data is useful in that it provides insights into what is possible. However, a challenge in using HR metrics as benchmark data is that an organization's human resource practices and the use of its HR staff reflect current challenges facing that organization. As a result, most organizations have an HR department, but the specific functions performed by these departments vary widely across organizations. Consequently, direct comparisons of HR benchmarking data from one's own organization to data from other organizations may not provide realistic guidelines for either goal setting or forecasting the potential effectiveness of remedial actions an organization might undertake.

Data Mining

Interest in data mining human capital information has been on the rise since the implementation of integrated HRIS and digitized HRM processes. **Data mining** refers to efforts to identify patterns that exist within data and that may identify unrecognized causal mechanisms that can be used to enhance decision making. To identify these causal mechanisms, data mining uses correlation and multiple regression methods to identify patterns of relationships in extremely large datasets. An example would be the identification of a correlation between employee job satisfaction and employee turnover. Data mining has a number of important applications, but the caveat with its use is that it can also uncover spurious and nonsensical relationships (e.g., taller employees make better leaders; older employees have longer tenures).

Predictive Analyses

Predictive analysis is the goal of many metrics and analytics efforts. **Predictive analysis** involves attempts to develop models of organizational systems that can be used to predict future outcomes and understand the consequences of hypothetical changes in organizations, for example, a change in existing organizational systems. To continue the simple example above, if the organization discovered a correlation between employee job satisfaction and turnover, HR could use this data to suggest modifications to the employees' work situation or their benefits. Efforts to develop balanced scorecards are examples of elementary predictive systems. They involve identifying leading indicators of important organizational outcomes and the nature of the relationships expected to lead to them. Engaging in efforts to test the assumptions in these models over time can lead to enhancements in the quality of the models' underlying predictive analyses, either by identifying additional leading indicators or better specifying the nature of the relationships between predictors and outcomes.

Operational Experiments

The evidence-based management movement argues that managers should base their decisions on data drawn from the organization and evidence about the actual functioning of its systems rather than using personal philosophies or untested personal models or assumptions about "how things work." One of the most effective methods for developing the evidence on which to base decisions is through **operational experiments** conducted within the organization. Ayres (2007) describes how Google uses operational experiments to test the effectiveness of the ad words used on its Web site. Rather than simply relying on intuition or "expert judgment" about which ad wording is more effective, it creates an experiment. It configures its site to alternate the presentation of competing ad text to visitors to its site and then tracks the number of click-throughs on the ad for a period of time. Given the large number of daily hits, Google can get objective data on the effectiveness of the various ads in a relatively short time and then adopt the ad wording demonstrated to be most effective.

Workforce Modeling

Workforce modeling attempts to understand how an organization's human capital needs would change as a function of some expected change in the organization's environment. This change may be a shift in the demand for the organization's product, entry into a new market, divestiture of one of the organization's businesses, or a pending acquisition of or merger with another organization. This process involves establishing a human resources planning (HRP) program, which is covered in more detail in Chapter 11.

BETTER PROBLEM SOLVING AND DECISION MAKING

In organizations, decisions result in tactical choices. These choices may be among alternative tactics to achieve specific outcomes or in response to specific problems. The choices could also involve a specific tactic to adopt a standard response, as compared trying something new, or to take no action at all. Making these decisions requires three things: (1) understanding the outcomes that one is attempting to achieve, (2) understanding the factors that influence those outcomes and their current states, and (3) knowing available tactical options and their costs. For any information system, including an HRIS that can produce metrics and analytics, improving decision making requires that these sources of information influence decision makers to choose to make different and better decisions.

A Common and Troublesome View

A common perspective adopted in many organizations is that data elements lead to metrics. These metrics can then be combined in various analyses that can then be reported to managers who use the information in these analyses to drive decision making. This view was dominant in the development of many metrics and analytics over the last decade. However, the problem with this approach is that it is not clear which data elements are relevant, and there is no basis for guiding how they should be combined into metrics, or how those metrics should contribute to analytics. These types of approaches to metrics have two common and predictable outcomes. First, individuals tasked with developing and reporting HR metrics in organizations struggle to determine what metrics to report and how those metrics should be calculated. Second, as a result of the first outcome, these organizations subsequently report large numbers of metrics, which ultimately have little or no impact on decision making and, therefore, offer no return to the organization.

A more effective approach is to start with the problems or opportunities faced by the organization and develop an understanding of what information is likely to be useful to managerial decisions. An understanding of these problems permits organizations to determine effectively the analytics that are most likely to be useful in improving organizational effectiveness. These analytics then determine which metrics are relevant to the analysis and which data elements need to be incorporated into the analysis. The difference in these two approaches is dramatic. The latter one is targeted at specific managerial decision situations while the first one does not have this focus.

Opportunity Domains of HR Expertise

Excellence in human resources functioning requires three sets of expertise. These are depicted in Figure 6.1. *First,* an organization must have access to the knowledge in "**centers of excellence**" to potentially change the activities of HRM. This access to knowledge does not refer to information systems, but rather to the "know-how" required to deploy available human resource programs and tactics in recruitment, selection, job design, development, motivation, compensation, performance management, retention, safety, benefits, and regulatory compliance to accomplish the objectives of the organization and to improve organizational effectiveness. This knowledge exists in HR experts who understand new advancements in these programs and activities, as well as how and when they might be employed to improve effectiveness. This HR expertise might exist within an organization's full-time staff, or it might be found in consultants hired on a contract basis to assist the organization or in third party vendors who take on responsibility for improving outsourced organization processes.

A *second* set of expertise exists in HR's business partners. Whereas the "centers of excellence" represent the technical expertise of internal HRM professionals, these external **business partners** can work with managers from other

Figure 6.1 Components of HR Functionality

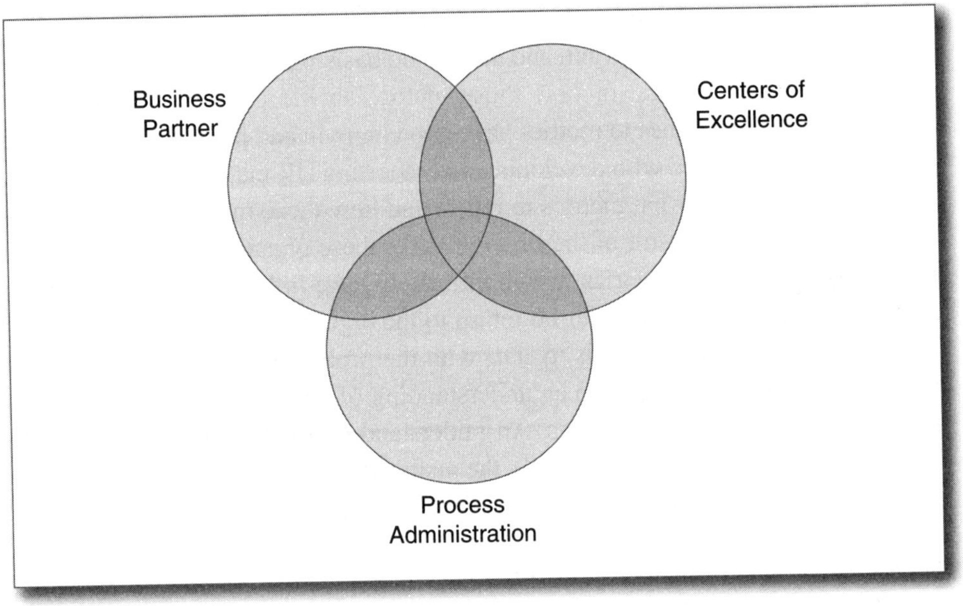

functional departments (e.g., production, marketing) to examine the organization's business and processes to understand how HR programs can support these processes. This understanding allows them to identify opportunities to change HR programs and processes in ways that overcome problems affecting the operational functioning of their departments or that capture new opportunities. HR business partners can translate the activities of HRM to their situations in order to meet the specific needs of the organization. They work to identify when and how changes to HRM programs and processes can enhance organizational effectiveness.

The *third* set of expertise is **administrative process efficiency**. This sort of **HR efficiency** refers to the capacity to conduct existing HRM processes accurately and on time while minimizing costs. Centralizing certain HRM processes, for example, recruiting new employees, offers process efficiency benefits. Only a limited number of individuals need to be trained on how to complete complex or detailed processes. This centralization is particularly valuable when a process is subject to dynamic legislative or administrative guidelines determined outside the organization. Centralizing processes can result in greater emphasis on continuous quality process improvement. The increased repetition of specific processes also fosters learning that can result in faster and more error-free execution.

HR PROCESS EFFICIENCY

Each of these three areas of expertise represents a separate domain in which organizations can conduct both metrics and analytics work. Currently, most metrics focus on the third set of expertise—administrative process efficiency. These metrics focus on how well the HR department accomplishes its critical processes to support organizational effectiveness. Metrics in this area might include cost per hire, days to fill positions, percentage of performance reviews completed on time, and HR department costs as a percentage of total costs or sales. However, process administration is only desired when the organizational processes are those that best support the company's operating departments in pursuit of their goals.

Organizational Effectiveness

HR metrics and workforce analytics focused on organizational process improvement are primarily focused outside the HR department. Here, the objective is to utilize the technical competence of the HR professionals in HRM regarding their understanding of how best to recruit, select, deploy, train, design jobs for, motivate, develop, evaluate, and retain employees in order to help organizational units more effectively accomplish their objectives. The outcomes are the business units' operational metrics, that is, percentage of on-time deliveries, operational downtime, lost time accidents, units sold, or cost per unit. Analyses will attempt to identify what changes in HRM practices can help organizations or specific business units improve their **operational effectiveness**. HR managers need to first identify what processes most effectively accomplish organizational objectives at multiple unit levels and then find ways to maximize the efficiency and effectiveness of the implementation of those processes in the organization. This task requires close coordination with the HR business partners in the company.

Strategic Realignment

Strategic realignment involves the set of activities most commonly known today as human resources planning (HRP; for more detail, see Chapter 11). These planning efforts focus on both long-term plans to assure replacement of the labor power needed to operate as an organization as well as planning for needed strategic changes in the organization. Boeing, for example, engages in a number of efforts to assure that it will have sufficient numbers of engineers available to staff operations in future years, as the company faces the approaching retirement of a large portion of its engineering workforce. Strategic realignment also extends the use of HRM analytics to planning for new situations and circumstances. New situations and circumstances occur when an organization undergoes a strategic change in direction, such as through merger, acquisition, divestiture, or entry into new geographic or product markets. The ability of the HR department to estimate the future demand and supply of needed human capital is largely driven by changes in organizational strategy, and this ability to forecast these future needs is crucial to the survival of the organization.

In sum, all three areas of expertise are important. HR managers must to be able to demonstrate their capacity to use metrics and analytics to manage their own operations well, and then others will be more likely to listen to their recommendations. HR managers and professionals must also work closely with their business partners in operational departments to help improve their capability to achieve their desired outcomes. Finally, using HR metrics and workforce analytics to improve decision making related to organizational effectiveness and strategic realignment can affect the organization's bottom line.

MEASUREMENT, METRICS, AND ANALYTICS BASICS

Getting Started

When undertaking a metrics and analytics effort, the first question the organization needs to answer is, What problems in the organization are worth solving or what opportunities for enhancing organizational effectiveness exist? Organizations are awash in opportunities for increased effectiveness. Due to current improvements in computing and communications infrastructures, the effort and costs required to develop metrics for different opportunities may not differ dramatically. Thus, choosing to spend your time on projects with a greater potential return for the company makes good business sense. Given that most organizations' capabilities in HR metrics and analytics may not be well developed at this point, focusing on a limited number of potentially high-payback opportunities may be the best strategy associated with developing any new capability.

Once a problem and an opportunity are identified, the first step is to determine the organizational outcome that is associated with the problem. For instance, if the organization is struggling with getting orders shipped to its customers on time, an appropriate outcome metric will measure the extent to which the organization ships its orders on time. If an organization is concerned with the amount of time positions remain vacant before a new employee is hired, a measure of the amount of time positions remain vacant or the total time required to fill positions may be the appropriate outcome measure.

Outcome measures capture the extent to which a problem exists and should provide an indication of the extent to which actions taken by the organization are successful. Organizations are also interested in factors that cause these outcomes, and we will turn our attention to these shortly. Our first focus, though, is identifying the outcomes that matter.

The Role of "Why?"

Management scholars have theories of how organizations work. Most organizational members have their own personal theories regarding how their companies work. These theories provide a framework for identifying potentially important information, focusing attention on environmental stimuli, and strengthening the capacity to identify the tactics that can be used to solve problems. A common problem in identifying outcomes is that choices for outcome measures are often based on personal theories about how things work in the organization, theories that may not reflect reality. For example, company employees often identify intermediate outcomes, such as implementation of flexible work hours (flextime) or changes in supervisors, as outcomes of interest. Intermediate outcomes are those that are more immediate indicators of things that employees believe lead to more important outcomes, for example, changes in the two previous intermediate outcomes leading to a "much happier" workplace. However, in some cases, the intermediate outcomes may not be the best ones on which to focus. This situation occurs when changes in decisions impact intermediate outcomes but do not have the expected impact on the ultimate or distal outcomes.

An important test of the appropriateness of outcome metrics is the "why" test. When one considers a potential outcome variable, it is useful to ask why the organization is interested in that particular outcome. If the answer is because it impacts some other variable that influences an important outcome, for example, profitability, then care must be taken to assure that changing the intermediate (or proximal) outcome also impacts the distal outcome. Organizational factors such as pay and working conditions that have influence through their effects on intermediate variables are reasonable targets for assessment, particularly if we understand the subsequent impact these factors have on ultimate, distal, and more important outcomes. Often, changing factors such as pay and working conditions will impact intermediate outcomes but may not produce any effect on the ultimate outcome of company profitability.

Employee turnover of valued employees, for example, is often identified as an important organizational outcome due to the costs associated with it (Cascio, 2000). It is among the most frequently assessed and reported HR metrics in organizations. Most managers agree that excessive turnover is a significant problem. High levels of turnover are disruptive to operations and can cause organizations to lose the critical expertise and capabilities of employees that leave. The answer to "why" turnover is important is that it disrupts operations and leads to potential loss of knowledge and important skill sets. But, in many cases, it is not clear whether the departure of specific employees actually results in decreasing profits. In some cases, a departing employee is replaced by a stronger performer, which will enhance profits. At a minimum, asking "why" helps highlight the potential causal sequence through which these intermediate variable effects are expected to have their influence. These analyses can highlight which metrics are likely to be more critical and provide a framework for understanding how change in these metrics should be interpreted.

Putting HR Metrics and Analytics Data in Context

Reporting HR metrics data alone is ineffective in leading to improvement in managerial decision making. Data points representing important organizational outcomes become useful when the decision maker can attach some meaning to them. Often data will need to be placed in context. For example, that an organization's turnover level for newly hired management trainees is 13% is more meaningful when it can be placed in the context of the organization's previous turnover history for this position. Is turnover rising or falling for this position, and, if so, how quickly? Reporting trend information for metrics is one way to provide the context that gives meaning to the data, thus creating useful information.

Benchmarking is a second method for adding context to an organization's metrics. Data on metrics from other organizations in the same industry can provide information that offers insight into an organization's performance relative to its peers. However, not all companies are organized in the same way. As a result, and particularly for HR metrics, how the HRM function is structured in an organization can have a significant impact on the value of HR efficiency metrics. A department with a more centralized structure of HR functions typically has lower efficiency metrics than HR departments structured such that more of the responsibility for HR processes and activities exists in operating units. As a result, HR benchmarking data need to be considered in the context of how the organization has structured the HR function. Senior management needs to ensure that the HRM function is supporting organizational effectiveness. Then, the HR organization can be structured in order to maximize HRM effectiveness in supporting organizational objectives. HR effectiveness measures can then be maximized within the context of that structure.

For these reasons, internal rather than external benchmarking will often provide more appropriate data for establishing operational objectives for the HR efficiency benchmarks. Although external data is useful, care needs to be taken to understand how HR functions and activities are structured in the organizations providing this data.

Reporting What We Find

In discussions with individuals who construct metrics and analytics reports, we hear a common concern: These individuals wonder *whether anyone pays any attention* to the reports they produce. Often, they send reports to managers and professionals and receive no feedback. Among those who do get positive feedback from the benchmark information are HR professionals who embed this data in an interpretation of what they mean for the organization. Reporting data in context is a key component of their success stories.

For individuals conducting metrics and analytics work, paying attention to the capabilities and needs of the targeted audience is critically important. The information reported must be relevant to the issues facing the managers who receive it. Further, simply providing numbers to managers is unlikely to be of much use to them until they can understand the meaning of the information for their decision situations. Consequently, the HR analyst must report the numbers but also provide an interpretation of what the data means for the manager's decision situation. Some HR analysts argue that the interpretation of metrics results is the central message that speaks to managers, which, in turn, is then supported by the numbers. When packaging a metrics analysis, then, we must understand the needs of the recipients and fit the data to the information needs of the decision maker.

HR metrics and analytics information can be reported in a number of ways. Generally, a combination of "push" and "pull" means of communication will work for most organizations. Push communications channels, such as e-mail, actively push information and analyses to the attention of managers. These channels are used for information that is time critical or that the manager is unaware of. **Push systems** are excellent for getting information to decision makers. However, sending irrelevant or poorly timed information through push systems can contribute to information overload and reduce managers' sensitivity to messages. As a result, they may only skim the information sent through push systems or, even worse, not attend to it at all.

Pull systems are ways of making information available to managers so that they can access any of it at a point in time when it will be most useful for their decision making. Examples include (1) posting HR metrics and analytics analyses and reports on internal company Web sites, (2) offering access to searchable information repositories, or (3) providing access to analytics tools as examples. These "pull" methods avoid the e-mail clutter associated with push systems, but pull systems can be ineffective because managers may not know what information is available or when or where to look for the information.

How frequently data are analyzed and reported is also an important consideration. The existence of an integrated HRIS, faster computing capabilities, more effective software, and advanced internal communication systems creates the capability to analyze and report information in real time for managers. How frequently data are reported and how narrowly data are packaged are also critical to supporting effective decision making. Creating reporting cycles that are too long risks losing opportunities to make changes in operations on the basis of the reported information. Aggregating too much data from subunits to higher-level units can result in the problem of causing differences between operating units, departments, or functions to be buried in the aggregated averages for the higher unit. This information for managers' work units must be available to support decision making.

USEFUL THINGS TO REMEMBER ABOUT HR METRICS AND ANALYTICS

Don't "Do Metrics"

The *primary objective* of developing capabilities in HR metrics and workforce analytics is *to increase organizational effectiveness.* It is not simply to generate a static menu of HR metrics reports. Simply conducting the analysis and developing reports are activities, and activities raise costs. Developing HR metrics and workforce analytics to be used by managers and professionals must involve a return on the organization's investment. The real test of the value of HR metrics and workforce analytics is whether managers who have access to the information provided by these analyses make different and better decisions.

Bigger Is Not Always Better

The success of any metrics and analytics project is not measured by how many people are involved, how many metrics the project tracks, or how many people receive reports. It is gauged by the impact that the project's results have on managerial decisions. Many successful efforts have been focused on small, narrowly targeted metrics and analyses that have addressed organizationally important questions.

Small metrics and analytics projects have several advantages over the multimillion-dollar implementation projects that include integrated prepackaged analytics systems. First, they cost less and require fewer resources in terms of time and materials. Second, they are less visible during the initial start-up while the project team is learning through trial and error. These two aspects provide the project team with opportunities to focus on critical HR metrics while giving them the flexibility to work through the necessary trials and errors.

HR Metrics and Analytics Is a Journey—Not a Destination

Because the focus is on identifying and responding to opportunities and problems, useful and effective HR metrics and workforce analytics projects change over time. Markets for both products and labor will change, as will organizational processes. These changes will require adjustments in the ideal size, skill requirements, and deployment of an organization's human capital. If organizations are successful in solving operational problems or capturing opportunities, the focus for managers naturally shifts to other problems or new opportunities. These problems are unlikely to require the same analytics and therefore may depend on identifying new metrics.

Be Willing to Learn

Organizations that have an HR metrics and analytics function will develop a bias for experimentation to try out new HR activities, programs, or processes. One consequence of organizational life is the ongoing opportunity to recognize that there may be a better way to do things than your current approach. This point is true not only for the organization's operational processes but also for its metrics and analytics efforts. The organization should develop a metrics and analytics "laboratory" where the HRM professionals can experiment with new analyses and test existing assumptions about the requirements of the organization's current systems. This examination can foster new approaches and allow new metrics and analytics to be created.

Avoid the Temptation to Measure Everything Aggressively

Not every HR function, process, or metric that can be analyzed should be. Successful efforts will focus on those things, at a given point in time, that are most likely to have the greatest impact on managerial decision making. The intensity of an assessment project should be matched to how much opportunity it offers for improvements, and the project itself should be focused on factors, processes, and functions related to those things that are likely to have the greatest impact on organization effectiveness.

HR Metrics and the Future

The development of useful and effective HR metrics and workforce analytics is likely to be viewed in the future as a very significant source of competitive advantage. We now have the tools and the computing infrastructure to handle these projects that can help us understand organizations and support effective organizational functioning. By using HR metrics and workforce analytics, decision makers will acquire the ability to more effectively manage and improve HR programs and processes as well as to improve the effectiveness of HRIS use. Using this acquired ability, managerial decision makers may be able to modify entire employment systems to manage the company's human capital more effectively.

As a result, organizations that make investments in internal human capital assessment resulting in useful HR metrics and workforce analytics will become less willing to share their knowledge with other organizations in their industry. Benchmarking, which has been a staple of HR metrics and workforce analytics for almost three decades, will become more difficult to access and develop as organizations recognize the competitive value of these capabilities.

SUMMARY

The central focus of this chapter was to define the domain of HR metrics and workforce analytics and discuss how they can contribute to improving organizational effectiveness. HR metrics are data elements that contribute to analyses that provide information to help decision makers in organizations make better decisions. HR metrics and analytics activities provide no return on the organization's investment unless managers make different and more effective decisions as a result of the information provided by metrics and analytics reports. Therefore, focusing the development of HR metrics and workforce analytics around organizationally important problems and opportunities is likely to increase the possibility of significant returns for the organization.

This chapter also highlights the wide range of activities that fall within the domain of HR metrics and workforce analytics. Although classic metrics offered some value in the past, new **computing infrastructures** offer tremendous opportunities to change both the metrics and types of analyses organizations undertake. We can expect the types of metrics organizations use in the future to change as the needs of decision makers change, and as these analyses continue to work toward effectively balancing the cost and benefit consequences of decisions (see Chapter 7). Components of this continued evolution of metrics and analytics capabilities are driven by increased use of both push and pull reporting systems, more extensive use of predictive analytics and operational experiments, and the development of organizational expertise in metrics and analytics capabilities. As these skills mature, organizations will be able to move beyond simple analyses of HR efficiency metrics to a greater emphasis on operational effectiveness and organizational realignment analyses, which will further enhance the value of HR metrics and workforce analysis systems.

KEY TERMS

administrative process efficiency
balanced scorecard
benchmarking
computing infrastructures
cost and benefit consequences
dashboards
data mining
HR business partners
HR centers of excellence
HR efficiency
HR metrics
operational effectiveness
operational experiments
predictive analysis
pull systems
push systems
reporting
Saratoga metrics
strategic realignment
workforce analytics
workforce modeling

DISCUSSION QUESTIONS

1. What factors have led to increased organizational interest in HR metrics and workforce analytics?
2. When might the information from numeric information systems such as HR metrics and workforce analytics *not* generate any return on investment (ROI)?
3. What relationships should exist between the metrics an organization chooses to calculate and report and the types of analyses it conducts?
4. What are some of the limitations of the traditional HR metrics?
5. Discuss the historical role of HR benchmarking and its strengths and weaknesses as part of a metrics and analytics program in organizations today.
6. What roles might more recent analysis activities, such as data mining, predictive statistical analyses, and operational experiments, play in increasing organizational effectiveness?
7. What differences exist between metrics and analytics that focus on HR efficiency, operational effectiveness, and organizational realignment? Offer examples of each.
8. Describe which characteristics of HR metrics and workforce analytics are likely to result in greater organizational impact.

CASE STUDY

Regional Hospital is a 500-bed hospital and several associated clinics in a major East Coast metropolitan area. It has been an aggressive adopter of computing technologies in efforts to decrease costs and improve operational efficiencies. A critical challenge facing the hospital is meeting its ongoing challenges to staff the hospital and allied clinics effectively, given the ongoing shortage of nurses; uncertainty in health care legislation; emphasis on shortening hospital stays to reduce costs, which causes the daily census (numbers of patients in various departments) to vary dramatically from day to day and shift to shift; the continued aging of the population in its primary care area; and the unending competition for employees with key skill sets. Employee expenses represent more than 80% of the overall costs of operation for the hospital, so identifying ways to match optimal skills and numbers of employees to the appropriate shifts is critical to achieving consistent success. However, individual shift managers struggle to make effective staffing decisions, resulting in consistent overstaffing or understaffing of shifts and departments. These staffing problems potentially increase the high costs of varied levels of patient care and satisfaction and potentially increase the risk that staff turnover may escalate because of dissatisfaction with the continuing inability of managers to match staffing needs to demand.

Company managers recognize the potential that HR metrics and analytics might have for their organization, and they have come to you for help. They are hearing from their peers in other hospitals that metrics can help in this area but are not quite sure where to start. They are looking for you to offer guidance on how to do HR metrics and workforce analytics.

Case Study Questions

1. Do you believe that a program of HR metrics and workforce analytics might be useful in Regional Hospital? If so, why?
2. What opportunities do you see regarding "where" and "how" metrics and analytics might be applied in this organization?
3. Identify three analyses and associated metrics you think might be useful for Regional Hospital to consider.
4. How might Regional Hospital utilize benchmarking as a part of its metrics and analytics effort, if at all?
5. What advice would you offer to the managers at Regional Hospital about developing a program of HR metrics and workforce analytics?

6. What potential problems might occur in the establishment of an HR metrics and workforce analytics program for Regional Hospital managers about which you would want to alert them prior to beginning this project?

NOTES

1. The content of this chapter was based in part on two articles published in the *IHRIM Journal* (Carlson, 2004a, 2004b).
2. Throughout this chapter we will often refer to HR metrics and workforce analytics in a shorter form, as metrics and analytics. The meaning is the same.

REFERENCES

Ayres, I. (2007). *Super crunchers: Why thinking-by-numbers is the new way to be smart.* New York: Bantam.

Becker, B. E., Huselid, M. A., & Ulrich, D. (2001). *The HR scorecard: Linking people, strategy and performance.* Boston: Harvard Business School Press.

Bureau of Labor Statistics. (1997, Summer). Measuring trends in the structure and levels of employer costs for employee compensation. *Compensation and Working Conditions,* pp. 3–14. Retrieved March 3, 2011, from http://www.bls.gov/opub/cwc/archive/summer-1997art1.pdf

Bureau of Labor Statistics. (2010). *Employer costs for employee compensation.* Retrieved March 3, 2011, from http://www.bls.gov/news.release/ecec.toc.htm

Carlson, K. D. (2004a). Estimating the value of the indirect benefits of new HR technology. *IHRIM Journal, 8*(4), 22–28.

Carlson, K. D. (2004b). Justifying HRIS investments post Y2K: Identifying sources of value. *IHRIM Journal, 8*(1), 21–27.

Cascio, W. F. (1987). *Costing human resources: The financial impact of behavior in organizations* (2nd ed.). Boston: Kent.

Cascio, W. F. (2000). *Costing human resources: The financial impact of behavior in organizations* (4th ed.). Boston: Kent.

Drake, N., & Robb, I. (2002). *Exit interviews* (SHRM White Paper). Alexandria, VA: Society for Human Resource Management.

Fitz-enz, J. (1995). *How to measure human resources management* (2nd ed.). New York: McGraw-Hill.

Fitz-enz, J., & Davidson, B. (2002). *How to measure human resources management* (3rd ed.). New York: McGraw-Hill.

Galbreath, R. (2000). *Employee turnover hurts small and large company profitability* (SHRM White Paper). Alexandria, VA: Society for Human Resource Management.

Hawk, R. H. (1967). *The recruitment function.* New York: The American Management Association.

Hollmann, R. W. (2002). *Absenteeism: Analyzing work absences* (SHRM White Paper). Alexandria, VA: Society for Human Resource Management.

Huselid, M. A. (1995). The impact of human resource management on turnover, productivity, and corporate performance. *Academy of Management Journal, 38,* 635–672.

Kaplan, R. S., & Norton, D. P. (1996). *The balancedscore card: Translating strategy into action.* Boston: Harvard Business School Press.

Kuzmits, F. E. (1979). How much is absenteeism costing your organization? *Personnel Administrator*, *24*(6), 29–33.

Lilly, F. (2001). *Four steps to computing training ROI* (SHRM White Paper). Alexandria, VA: Society for Human Resource Management.

Munsterberg, H. (1913). *Psychology and industrial efficiency.* Boston: Houghton Mifflin.

SHRM. (2010). *HR metrics toolkit.* Retrieved October 15, 2010, from www.shrm.org/hrtools/hrmetrics_published/cms_002620.asp

SHRM. (2011, January 31). *Cost per hire standard* [Draft American National Standard]. Retrieved March 3, 2011, from http://hrstandardsworkspace.shrm.org/apps/group_public/download.php/3055/ANSI-SHRM2006001-201X-Cost_Per_Hire_Standard-draft-01-31-2011.pdf

Taylor, F. (1911). *The principles of scientific management.* London: Harper Brothers.

Wiley, C. (1993). *Employee turnover: Analyzing employee movement out of the organization* (SHRM White Paper). Alexandria, VA: Society for Human Resource Management.

Chapter 7

COST JUSTIFYING HRIS INVESTMENTS

KEVIN D. CARLSON AND MICHAEL J. KAVANAGH

EDITORS' NOTE

Central to the decision to develop and implement a new or improved HRIS will be the costs and benefits of the investment. Like most consumers, HR professionals and managers are frequently awed by the new computer-based HR applications or the entire HRIS and make a purchase decision on this basis. However, as discussed in this chapter,[1] without a comprehensive cost-benefit analysis (CBA), this purchase could be disastrous. As emphasized by several authors (Cascio, 1987, 2000; Fitz-enz, 2001; Kavanagh, Gueutal, & Tannenbaum, 1990), the language of business is dollars,[2] not just good feelings about an HRIS investment. The CBA for an HRIS investment needs to be made prior to purchase, early in the system's development life cycle. In fact, a preliminary, estimated CBA of an HRIS investment should be presented to senior management before any detailed work on the project is begun. This preliminary estimate should assist senior management in deciding whether or not the HRIS project should continue. A more detailed analysis can then be made as part of the needs analysis. The information in this chapter provides guidance for making CBA estimates as well as practical advice on how to make the CBA palatable to managerial decision makers. Finally, there is an emphasis on the value of the CBA and its documentation for the management of the project and its implementation, which will be covered in Chapters 8 and 9.

CHAPTER OBJECTIVES

After completing this chapter, you should be able to

- Explain why a CBA is critical for a successful HRIS project
- Explain the differences between cost reduction and organizational enhancement as strategies for HRIS investments
- Explain how using guidelines for approaches to investment analysis will lead to a better HRIS project
- Identify the various costs and benefits in a CBA of an HRIS investment
- Explain the differences between direct and indirect benefits and costs
- Describe how to estimate costs and benefits, both direct and indirect
- Explain the difference between average employee contribution (AEC) and variance estimates for estimating values in a CBA, and understand why the difference between these indices is important for investment analysis
- Discuss three common problems that can occur in an HRIS CBA

HRIS IN ACTION

An HRIS development and implementation project was being done by FarmforMore,[3] a U.S. manufacturer of farm machinery. FarmforMore has manufacturing operations in the major geographic regions of the United States, although a larger number of plants are situated in the Midwest. Its sales staff is also regionalized with sales offices in all major U.S. cities. FarmforMore currently has approximately 28,000 employees. The HRIS project was designed to have computer applications for 90% of the HR functionality, excluding payroll, which was outsourced to a vendor. The proposal emphasized the benefits of the new HRIS in terms of time saved for HR professionals as well as the timely reports designed for supervisors and managers. According to the project team, the costs, totalling 1.5 million dollars, seemed reasonable considering the potential benefits.

The HRIS project began two years ago with a needs analysis and basic design, approval from the CEO, and the selection of the project team and steering committee. The project team was led by the vice president of HRM, and steering groups had representatives from all regions of the country as well as from all major departments—finance, IT, HR, production, marketing, and research and development. A cost-benefit analysis was done. The major costs in the proposal were software, implementation costs, and the salaries of the project team's members. However, the project team indicated that time saved by computer-based transactions was the main cost-reduction benefit, estimated to save 14.3 full-time equivalent (FTE) budget lines, which would easily cover the costs of the new HRIS.

About eight months ago, there was information in a project team interim report that indicated the HRIS project was behind schedule and had some minor cost overruns. There did not seem to be much concern at the time since, even though the project was behind schedule, the project team was certain that the delay was due to developing better working relationships among team members. Plus, it had taken more time to transfer the basic employee information from the old system to the new one.

Two weeks later, the CEO sent a memo to the project team leader, the VP of HRM, to meet with her to determine whether the HRIS project was back on schedule and the cost overruns had been resolved. Unfortunately, the HRM VP reported that the project was now running about nine months behind schedule and so would need more funding to complete its tasks. This delay meant that the costs of the project had increased by 147%. The HRM VP could not really explain what had happened since the project team felt it had done a careful cost-benefit analysis. When the CEO looked at the cost-benefit analysis, however, she stated that her college-age son could have done a better job. Since there had been a downturn in national sales as well as profits, the CEO put the HRIS project on "hold."

INTRODUCTION

In most organizations today, an HRIS provides the primary infrastructure used to deliver HR programs, ensure HR regulatory compliance, and produce the metrics that are used to evaluate not only the HR function but also the contribution of the organizations' human resources to the accomplishment of firm-level strategic objectives. **HRIS functionality** continues to evolve and to expand—we no longer see the simple shifting of paper-and-pencil processes to their electronic equivalents but rather new capabilities that leverage the advantages of **integrated information systems** and faster and more capable computing technologies. As a result, organizations are faced with new opportunities to extend their investments in HRIS functionality. HRIS functionality refers to the number of programs or functions—such as recruiting, compensation, and job analysis—that are operational using the specific HRIS configuration, as well as to the features of these programs that enhance their usability and capacity to affect outcomes. Thus, HRIS functionality could include all HR programs in a fully integrated system or only a number of the more important programs, for example, compensation and benefits. HRIS functionality typically varies with organizational size, with larger companies having a greater number of programs or functions in their HRIS configurations than smaller companies.

However, as will be discussed in Chapter 8, statistics measuring the success of HRIS projects are not very encouraging. The failures of the implementation of systems have been well documented (Browne & Rogich, 2001). Delays in projects and budget overruns as well as user dissatisfaction are some of the most common reasons for the failure of HRIS projects. Systems that are completed generally exceed cost estimates by more than 55% and time estimates by a factor of 2. In addition, only 13% of the systems projects that are completed are considered successful by the executives who sponsor them (Lemon, Bowitz, Burn, & Hackney, 2002). Further, there have been significant failure rates for the implementation of human resource information systems in major corporations that indicate HRIS projects need better planning and cost estimates (Bondarouk & Meijerink, 2010; Dery, Hall, & Wiblen, 2010; Dulebohn, 2010; Grant, Newell, & Kavanagh, 2010; Tansley, 2010). Many of these failures occurred because a **cost-benefit analysis (CBA)** was not done as part of the business case for the justification of the HRIS project. Historically, HRIS were justified because of their primary benefit of improving employee transactions, plus their potential to save HR time.

In the 1990s, CBA played only a limited role in HRIS investment decisions. The pending obsolescence of noncompliant systems in Y2K (Year 2000) fueled widespread implementation of new HRIS technology. The result was one of the most concentrated and dramatic shifts in HR practice ever. During this period, purchase decisions were driven by two primary criteria: Did new systems offer the **baseline functionality** required by the organization in a Y2K-compliant form, and could the systems be delivered and implemented on time? It was apparent that something had to be done to meet the potential problems of Y2K, and more fine-grained investment analyses would not have affected purchase decisions. Thus, many organizations chose not to invest the time and effort to complete an investment analysis. However, the business landscape has changed today. Many decision makers, some of whom are still waiting to see returns from past IT purchases in terms of successes and failures, are wary of new HRIS investments. Without an event like Y2K driving change, justifying new investments in HRIS will require strong business cases, that is, cost-benefit analyses (CBAs).

Justification Strategies for HRIS Investments

Strategies for justifying HRIS investments fall into two categories—**risk avoidance** and **organizational enhancement. Risk avoidance strategies** are used when investments are believed to eliminate or mitigate significant future risks faced by the organization, for example, generating reports of the gender and racial diversity of employees. The potential obsolescence of **legacy computing systems** was a prototypical risk avoidance scenario. The old system simply needed to be changed to avoid Y2K problems and also because it was out of date. The need to comply with laws and regulations (e.g., the Equal Employment Opportunity Act) and changes to these laws provide other circumstances in which justification based on risk avoidance is popular. Risk avoidance justifications focus on the magnitude and probability of risks and often are not supported by the extensive investment analyses required by a CBA.

Organizational enhancement strategies, on the other hand, highlight how the effectiveness of the firm will be improved by the addition of a new or improved HRIS—as measured by increases in revenues or reductions in costs such as employee turnover. Organizational enhancement justifications are often more challenging to "sell" to decision makers than risk avoidance ones because enhancements do not carry the threat of real loss if no action is taken. Hence, there is often a reduced sense of urgency. This situation is supported by research on decision making under risk that consistently demonstrates that, when faced with potential losses, decision makers are willing to accept much greater risk; in other words, they become more risk seeking to avoid the loss than when alternatives are framed as gains (Kahneman & Tversky, 1979). Investments justified by organizational enhancements typically require more rigorous support and are subjected to more intense scrutiny by decision makers.

Evolution of HRIS Justification

Several factors suggest that the next generation of HRIS functionality will be more difficult to justify. Much of the "low-hanging cost reduction fruit" has already been picked due to the Y2K implementation "scare." HRIS implementations in the past decade have shifted many organizations from administratively intense paper-and-pencil HR processes to electronic transaction processing supported by integrated computer systems. Employee and applicant self-service, online recruitment, electronic payroll processing, and work flow software have dramatically reduced transaction costs. Employee self-service alone is reported to reduce the cost of many HR transactions by 50% or more. These changes were the "low-hanging cost reduction fruit" mentioned previously. The next wave of HRIS functionality is unlikely to generate comparable reductions in costs, making investment decisions based on further cost reductions more difficult to justify.

Of course, there will be small and medium-size organizations that still have paper-and-pencil systems or HRIS legacy systems that need to be updated. For many of these organizations, the value of reducing costs, such as transactions costs, will still serve as legitimate justification for adopting or upgrading an HRIS. In addition, these firms may also use a risk avoidance approach to justify the new HRIS—for example, the need for accurate and timely employee records in litigation. However, as will be argued in this chapter, the use of an organizational enhancement approach, which incorporates a **cost reduction strategy**, may provide a powerful means of determining the cost-benefit analysis (CBA) for investment in a new HRIS.

It is therefore less certain that organizations with an operational HRIS will continue to pursue investments in new HRIS functionality aggressively. In fact, underinvestment in HRIS—that is, failing to approve many worthwhile investments—is likely. This underinvestment will not occur because the benefits of new investments in HRIS functionality are too small—in absolute terms, they are still substantial. Rather, it is more likely to result from the use of outdated CBA methodologies that emphasize cost reduction and do not adequately recognize the value of organizational enhancements attributable to important new HRIS functionality. HRIS managers will need tools so they can identify the sources of value to the organization that will result from HRIS investments. The field is maturing, and investment analysis tools must mature with it. This chapter examines HRIS cost-benefit dynamics and provides tools and techniques that can be used to conduct and evaluate HRIS CBAs that incorporate organizational enhancement.

Approaches to Investment Analyses Make a Difference: Some Guidelines

As indicated previously, one *must* conduct an **investment analysis**, frequently referred to as "making the business case" (Mayberry, 2008), for the acquisition of a new or improved HRIS. Usually, there is an HR or HRIS professional with selected team members who form the **HRIS project team**, as described in Chapter 3. This project team, or usually a subset of it, conducts the analyses and can be referred to as the CBA team. The members of this team include senior professionals from the HR and IT departments as well as representatives from other departments who will be affected by the HRIS project. The CBA is one of the first steps in seeking initial approval from senior management for an HRIS project. It is important to recognize that a proper perspective has as much to do with conducting an effective HRIS investment analysis as do the tools and techniques used. Understanding why the analysis is being conducted and understanding the expectations of what is going to be done with the results will influence the judgments made by both the CBA and the entire HRIS project team during the analysis, as well as increase the value of the results produced. It is important that the CBA team be representative of the project management (PM) team to ensure the complete involvement of all operational departments and maintain communications between the two teams. In addition, here are several considerations or guidelines that can help the CBA team approach the analysis with an improved likelihood of making the best decision for the organization. These guidelines are contained in Table 7.1.We will briefly cover each of these **CBA guidelines**.

The objective for conducting a CBA is to improve organizational effectiveness. The primary purpose of each analysis is to make the best decision for the organization. In some instances, the best decision may be not to proceed with an investment. Making an investment should never be the ultimate objective—investments are a means

Table 7.1 Guidelines for Successful HRIS Cost-Benefit Analysis (CBA)

Key	*Description*
The objective is improving organizational effectiveness.	The objective of any HRIS CBA is not to purchase specific hardware or software. The objective is to improve organizational performance.
Be honest with yourself.	Start each analysis with an open mind, not an investment to justify.
Focus on functionality, not products.	The analysis should focus on the improvement in organizational functionality that is to be achieved. Start with that functionality, and let it lead to the product. Don't start with the product and attempt to identify ways to justify its purchase.
Estimate benefits first.	Examine costs only after you have completed the analysis of benefits.
Know your business.	This means really understanding what your business is and how your current processes allow your organization to accomplish its objectives. Understand the dynamics of your current processes and where potential for improvement can be found. Understand organizational politics.
Develop the best estimate possible.	Don't be overly optimistic or conservative. Develop the best estimate you can with the data available to you. This is the core of making the business case.
Separate the CBA from questions of how best to justify a final decision.	The questions involved in developing an accurate CBA and attempting to determine how best to justify a choice are two separate processes. The latter involves choices about which sources of value should be included in the business case to be presented to decision makers. These are determined by the relative comparisons of costs with the magnitudes and types of revenue sources. The latter should be pursued only after a complete analysis has been accomplished.

to achieving some other organizationally meaningful outcome. The desired outcome is to become a more effective organization, not simply *to justify a purchase.*

Be honest with yourselves. The CBA team should enter each analysis with an open mind—not with a solution to justify. It is best to think of the analysis as an investigation devoid of any personal biases. The team needs to come into the decision process without preconceived notions, willing to approach the analysis objectively and willing to accept whatever results the analysis produces. If members of the team have a vested interest in a particular solution, for example, cloud computing or employee self-service portals, it will cause difficulties in the analysis. CBA techniques can be used to identify investment opportunities and important contingencies that can influence the success of eventual implementations. Developing a reputation as an impartial evaluator will increase management decision makers' confidence in analyses done by the CBA team.

Focus on key functionality rather than on specific hardware or software solutions. Many proposals for a new HRIS have erroneously started by identifying a new software application and then trying to justify how its features and capabilities could benefit the organization. However, it is whether your organization performs more effectively after an HRIS implementation that will determine the success of any HRIS investment. The CBA team must focus on the organization and its process and outcomes (i.e., reduced costs or increased revenues), identify opportunities in order to improve effectiveness, and only then look to identify software solutions that provide the desired capabilities. Centering the analysis on a specific software solution shifts the focus of the analysis to the capabilities that solution offers, not necessarily the capabilities that are most needed by the organization. Thus, the question to be answered is not just whether the system will increase HR functionality but whether the new HRIS will improve organizational effectiveness and fit with the business strategy of the firm.

Examine benefits before you examine costs. This is often difficult to do, but training the CBA team to examine the benefits of a change in HRIS functionality before estimating costs will produce better analyses. Knowing before you conduct the analysis of benefits how much would need to be spent to acquire new functionality can easily lead to an inaccurate CBA. This "backward" approach makes it almost impossible not to consider what level of benefits will be necessary to justify the investment. This approach can cause the team to abort prematurely the process of identifying and analyzing benefits, especially if a single source of benefits appears to be sufficient to guarantee adoption of the HRIS project. It can also encourage "fishing" for questionable benefits when the initially identified benefits may not be enough to justify the HRIS investment.

Know your business. As stated in Table 7.1, this means really understanding the organization's business and how the current processes in all departments allow the organization to accomplish its objectives. Furthermore, it means that the CBA team must understand the dynamics of the current business processes and where potential for improvement exists. Since the CBA team consists of senior representatives from all staff departments affected by the HRIS project, this business knowledge should exist within the team. Obviously, then, the CBA team must have cooperative relationships among its members. Further, it is important that the CBA and PM teams understand the internal politics of the firm.

Develop the best estimate possible. Various methods to achieve this goal are discussed in this chapter. It is also critically important, as mentioned in the previous paragraph, that cooperative relationships exist among members of the CBA team as well as within the PM team. The project team leader must try to reduce or eliminate interdepartmental politics, particularly between the HR and IT departments. Chapters 7 and 8 provide more details on this topic. Finally, note the advice in Table 7.1 not to be overly optimistic or conservative but to develop the best estimate possible with the available data.

Distinguish between the analysis and the packaging of that analysis for decision makers. The primary purpose of analyzing an HRIS investment is to determine whether and to what extent it will improve your organization. The objective of the analysis should be to provide the "best" estimate of the impact of an HRIS investment as is possible. Developing the estimate should be seen as separate and distinct from the process of presenting and "selling" the investment opportunity to management decision makers. Decision makers may choose to rely on specific forms of benefit evidence or to adopt conservative assumptions in order to gain approval for the investment. Inappropriate investment decisions may result if overly conservative assumptions in the HRIS investment analysis conducted by the CBA team are compounded by the conservative bias common among decision makers.

HRIS COST-BENEFIT ANALYSIS

A CBA is simply what its name indicates—a comparison of the projected costs and benefits associated with an HRIS investment, a cost-benefit ratio. **A cost-benefit ratio** can be expressed mathematically, with the benefits of the project as the numerator and the costs as the denominator. Therefore, values greater than one indicate a positive ratio. A cost is any new outlay of cash required for the initial purchase, implementation, or ongoing maintenance of the investment. A benefit is any financial gain resulting from the investment that occurs at any time during the investment's useful life. Benefits include both revenue enhancements and cost reductions. At its core, the CBA is an analysis of change in the cost-benefit ratio—a comparison of current existing circumstances with new conditions that are projected to exist after the HRIS investment. This comparison means the cost-benefit ratio for the current HRIS must be calculated first. Then the cost-benefit ratio is estimated for the projected HRIS. The *size of the gap between these two cost-benefit ratios* is what will have an effect on the decision to implement a new HRIS or new HR functionality.

A common misconception is that conducting a meaningful CBA requires financial expertise. Knowing some financial basics, such as discounting, cost of capital, cash flow, **return on investment (ROI)**, **payback period**, net present value, and **internal rate of return (IRR)**, is useful but not required. Organizations differ in the specific financial measures they use to evaluate investments. Organizations may use ROI, IRR, payback period, or other measures alone or in combination. Therefore, it can be useful to seek out an internal adviser to help you package your analysis for the managerial decision-making process used in the organization. Typically, this internal adviser will be someone in the finance or accounting department. However, regardless of the specific financial measures used in the organization, investment analyses, that is, CBAs, are based on **three basic pieces of information**: (1) sources of costs and benefits, (2) an estimated dollar value for each cost and benefit item, and (3) the time when the organization will incur each cost and receive each benefit. These are the core data on which any investment analysis is based, including one for a new HRIS. Developing these data requires a thorough understanding of your business—which includes finance and other business considerations. The remainder of this chapter will cover how these three basic pieces of information are obtained and used in a CBA.

Identifying Sources of Value for Benefits and Costs

Investments in HRIS functionality differ from more traditional investments because HR is commonly perceived as a source of costs rather than a direct source of revenue (Cascio, 2000). Any impact that HR department activities have on revenues occurs *indirectly* through the effect of HR programs and practices on other units of the organization. For example, a program focused on training retail employees to provide quality customer service is typically a cost ascribed to the HR department; however, its indirect effect of increased sales is classified as revenue for the operations department. Thus, the effects of many HR programs or practices are often described as "soft" or, more appropriately, indirect. As a result, managerial decision makers are justifiably concerned about using "soft" benefits to justify spending "hard" dollars, particularly when considering large investments such as a new HRIS. Approving an investment only to find that the expected benefits never materialize is something all decision makers fear. In the absence of obvious risk avoidance justifications and significant reductions in costs from previous HRIS investments, developing expertise in identifying and valuing the direct and indirect benefits derived from HRIS investments is one of the critical challenges that HRIS managers face.

Failing to recognize important sources of costs or benefits is a common problem in HRIS CBA. The HRIS CBA matrix shown in Figure 7.1 can be used to help

Figure 7.1 HRIS Cost-Benefit Analysis Matrix

		Direct (Hard)	*Indirect (Soft)*
Benefits	Revenue enhancement	1 New revenue (new sales)	2 Improvement potential (better decision making)
	Cost reduction	3 Direct costs (canceled vendor contracts)	4 Potential costs (saved staff time)
Costs	New implementation costs	5 Out-of-pocket costs (software, service agreements)	6 Indirect costs (increased technical support needs)

uncover all reasonable benefit and cost components in HRIS investment analyses. The HRIS CBA matrix consists of six cells.

The four upper cells (1–4) represent sources of benefits (i.e., direct revenue enhancements, indirect revenue enhancements, direct cost reductions, and indirect cost reductions). The two cells of the bottom row capture costs of implementation (i.e., direct and indirect costs). A simple evaluation of each cell of the HRIS CBA matrix can ensure that important sources of benefits or costs are not overlooked.

Direct Benefits

The four "benefit" cells of the HRIS CBA matrix (Figure 7.1) represent the crossing of two dimensions. The first dimension is the type of benefit—revenue enhancements versus cost reductions. Organizations can enhance revenues by changing employees' job performance. These changes could result in *new revenue* in terms of new sales due to more efficient procedures, for example, those instituted because of a better training program for new employees. Organizations can also reduce costs by changing the locations of HR functions to make them more effective. For example, an organization with a new HRIS could decide to outsource programs (such as employee recruiting) to vendors, thus giving the HR staff more time to handle other functions. HRIS investments often involve both types of effects. HRIS investments can also permit the offering of new products and services that can increase revenues and enhance profit margins. Thinking about opportunities for cost reductions and revenue enhancements separately allows each to be explored more fully.

The terms *direct* and *indirect* are used here to refer to benefits and costs that might be described elsewhere as "hard" and "soft," respectively. Hard or direct outcomes generally refer to benefits (and costs) (a) that are very likely to occur and (b) whose values are easily estimated. Some examples of **direct benefits** can be seen in Table 7.2, which shows an example of a CBA for an e-learning investment. As can be seen, the organization is considering having e-learning modules created by an external vendor to replace in-house training programs. The direct revenue enhancements include additional revenue the organization can earn by selling the e-learning modules, outsourcing the development of the e-learning, and training sales employees on customer service and managerial leadership via e-learning modules. The direct cost reductions include all the typical costs involved in training programs, as seen in Table 7.2, for example, reduced travel expenses and reduced facilities costs.

Indirect Benefits

Soft or **indirect benefits**, on the other hand, are often less easily quantified because their occurrence may be less certain or because their value is more difficult to establish. After the HRIS functionality is introduced, indirect revenue enhancements result from improvements in intermediate outcomes that could position the organization to be able to increase revenues. For example, in Table 7.2, using e-learning training modules to improve customer service by improving the skills of sales employees and managerial leadership could impact the indirect benefits at the top of Table 7.2. Thus, in this example, the intermediate outcomes are the e-learning training modules, and the revenue increases, as listed in Table 7.2, are "Better customer service leading to increase in repeat sales" and "A more agile organization able to respond rapidly to market changes." The intermediate outcomes (the e-learning training modules) may also affect revenue increase outcomes, by, for example, improving the organization's capacity to attract and retain high-quality employees, achieving a reduction in turnover and absenteeism (see Table 7.2), improving employees' capacity to make decisions, or freeing up time for employees to engage in activities that more directly support the strategic objectives of the organization (see Figure 7.1). Often, indirect revenue enhancements represent intermediate outcomes that require that some additional activity or condition exist before an increase in revenues is realized. For example, before managers can work on leadership responsibilities and activities that are directly related to strategic company goals, it may be necessary to restructure several departments and provide some in-service training.

Since these benefits are not reported in a dollar metric, current CBAs typically do not include these items in the numeric analysis but will often address them in

Table 7.2 Example of an e-Learning CBA Matrix

	Direct (Hard)	*Indirect/Contingent (Soft)*
Revenue enhancements	Outsourcing e-learning training module development Sales of locally developed learning modules or programs	Better customer service leading to increase in repeat sales A more agile organization able to respond rapidly to market changes
Cost reductions	Reduced travel expenses Reduced facilities costs (e.g., for room and equipment rentals and refreshments) Reduced requirements for paper-based training materials and teaching aids Reduced expenses for instructor fees or salary and benefits costs (if internal) Reduced costs for replacement workers if trainees are required to be away from their work	Improved training effectiveness through customization and just-in-time delivery = faster learning curve, less lost productivity while waiting for training, and right amount and type of content More agility, able to disseminate new cost-reducing best practices more quickly Reduction in turnover (41% of employees will look for another job within 12 months due to poor training and education; with good training and education, this percentage drops to 12%) and in absenteeism Improved safety (fewer injuries, less lost time, fewer insurance claims, lower workers' compensation costs)
Costs of implementation	Installation support Software fee/license Software support Analyst/administrator Training administrator Courseware development Courseware purchase Bandwidth fees	Increased use of end-user help desk Courseware redevelopment Lost productivity during conversion to new system

the narrative discussion supporting the investment. In the e-learning example, better customer service (i.e., service that can lead to increased customer retention and repeat sales) and a more agile organization (i.e., one that can retrain or retool its employees more quickly to respond to rapidly changing markets) are examples of indirect or contingent sources of revenues.

Indirect cost reductions involve those changes that are expected to lead to reduced costs. If we reexamine Figure 7.1, these benefits would fall in box number 4, potential cost reductions through saved staff time, and would include (a) reductions in the time required to perform activities, but not those reductions that lead to direct reductions in payroll (i.e., not ones tied directly to reductions in overtime or **employee head count**); (b) expected reductions in the amount of or requirements for technical support; (c) expected reductions in absenteeism and turnover; and (d) expected reductions in the time required to bring trainees up to the status of fully functioning employees.

In many instances, time-saving applications are incorrectly projected to result in reductions in employee head count or FTEs—a direct savings in payroll expenses. More often, though, the deployment of new HRIS functionality results in a new structuring of work that enables the elimination of parts of jobs rather than whole jobs. As a result, the benefit is indirect—a saving of time that can be deployed in other activities rather than a saving of the costs of employing staff. In the e-learning example, enhancements in training effectiveness are expected to lead to faster learning curves and less time to proficiency. This benefit is expected to result in fewer errors and less rework. Reductions in turnover costs are also anticipated because better-trained employees are expected to have higher satisfaction and remain in their jobs longer. Lower turnover rates for valued employees would have a strong positive effect, allowing the firm to reduce the costs of hiring new employees (see Cascio, 2000). Furthermore, improved access to safety training is also expected to result in less time lost as a result of injuries and reduced insurance claims and worker compensation costs.

Consequently, analyses of indirect benefits can be challenging, but, in many instances, these indirect effects are the real source of benefits for new HRIS functionality. Being able to identify the indirect effects and understand how they are expected to affect costs and revenues is critical to understanding how to justify HRIS investments. An important advantage of understanding how and where indirect benefits are expected to occur is that it allows the organization to plan and manage HRIS implementations specifically, in ways that make it more likely for indirect benefits to actually occur. Because these benefits are often contingent on other events, knowing what those events are and managing them as a part of the implementation will likely result in greater organizational impact.

Implementation Costs

Once benefits have been estimated, the analysis can proceed to estimating the costs of implementation (Table 7.2). In contrast to estimating benefits, cost estimation is often easier to complete because cost information is readily available and already offered in a dollar metric. In most cases, many sources of **implementation costs** will be direct. **Direct costs** will include but are not limited to (a) costs for the initial purchase and updates of software and any additional hardware and

(b) ongoing costs for internal or external systems support. In the e-learning example (Table 7.2), direct costs include the purchase of any new software, hardware, and licenses required to implement the system as well as the cost of the expertise necessary to develop and manage training on this new HRIS platform.

Indirect costs comprise those areas of cost that cannot be known specifically up front but may arise in the process of implementing the system. These include the impact of the implementation on the organization, such as lost productivity while the organization completes implementation. This impact includes lost productivity for rank-and-file employees as well as for the HR staff involved in implementation. The e-learning example includes increased use of end-user help desks or other support functions, costs necessary to revamp existing courseware while the organization learns how to use the new system most effectively, and the lost productivity that will occur for any current employees who will be required to take on additional responsibilities associated with the adoption of the new system.

It is important to be thorough in attempting to identify all the sources of cost. If your analysis recognizes some benefit without incorporating an offsetting change in cost, you likely have missed a source of cost in your analysis. For example, organizations that projected significant reductions in employee head counts due to converting paper-and-pencil transactions to electronic systems, as was erroneously done in the opening vignette, often failed to recognize the full additional costs that would be required in technical support, training on the new system, or transitioning large numbers of employees out of the organization.

Also, the total costs of implementation will depend on the current state of information system development in the organization. The components of organizational information systems evolve at different speeds across organizations. Knowing the current level of technological evolution of the organization's total information architecture and systems is quite important. These components would include those that are operational within departments concerned with finance, operations, marketing, and information systems, as well as HR. Assessment of these departments' systems should include evaluations of (a) the current state of their computer hardware, software, data, and processes; (b) user sophistication and networking; and (c) telecommunications technology. New HRIS investments may affect all these information systems (IS) components. In any one of these areas, the greater the change required to support the implementation of the new HR functionality, the more expensive the implementation will be. Total cost will be driven by (a) the scope or size of the HRIS implementation; (b) the amount of customization required; (c) the maturity of the HRIS functionality being considered—the less mature the functionality, the greater the costs of implementation and upgrades are likely to be; and (d) the experience levels of the implementers.

Although early attempts at CBA often grossly underestimated or ignored significant sources of costs, the experiences of organizations over the past decade have provided insights that can be used to do a much better job of recognizing what cost items need to be included in cost analyses. Several sources for determining cost of implementation are available, including organizations that have previously implemented specific packages or functionality, vendors in the HRIS field, and implementation consultants.

ESTIMATING THE TIMING OF BENEFITS AND COSTS

Once you have identified and valued the benefits and costs associated with an investment in HRIS functionality, the next step of the analysis is to determine when in time each benefit and cost will be incurred during the entire HRIS project. Organizations use this information to estimate the cash outflows and inflows associated with investments. The **timing of cash flows** is particularly important when costs and revenues occur in different time periods and when the organization's cost of capital is relatively high. This information will also be critically important in the management of the entire HRIS project, which will be discussed in Chapter 8.

The task of assigning the benefits and costs to time periods can be accomplished by constructing a simple grid that lists benefit or cost items along one axis and future time periods on the other axis. The number of time periods required will depend on the expected useful life of the investment and the relevant length of time periods (usually years, but months or quarters may be used in some instances). The critical period for most HRIS investments is the first five years. Few organizations are likely to approve HRIS investments with longer payback periods. Furthermore, current rates of development of HRIS functionality and computing systems suggest that most HRIS investments may be functionally obsolete after five years.

ESTIMATING THE VALUE OF INDIRECT BENEFITS

Most HRIS cost-benefit analyses will include some indirect benefits. One of the more difficult tasks in producing an HRIS CBA is estimating the value of these indirect benefits. The difficulty of converting indirect benefit estimates to a dollar metric has limited their role in HR technology investment decisions. To this point, it has not been uncommon for soft benefits to be relegated to the narrative supporting an investment analysis that is otherwise based solely on estimates of direct cost reductions. For good reason, many managers consider these indirect savings cautiously. That does not mean, though, that these benefits are any less important than direct benefits to the organization. In fact, as noted earlier, ignoring them in HRIS investment analysis could result in incorrect or misleading analyses. As a result, we need to adapt the general techniques used to analyze HR technology investments to meet these new requirements. The challenge is to provide an estimate of the value of soft or indirect benefits and to do so in a way that can be justified to skeptical decision makers.

Estimating Indirect Benefit Magnitude

Constructing dollar estimates of indirect benefits is challenging, but it can be done. To simplify estimation of the dollar value of indirect benefits and provide a basis for justification, one should break this task into the following three steps: (1) estimating benefit magnitude, (2) mapping benefits to cost or revenue changes, and (3) converting magnitude estimates to dollar values. By separating these steps, we can begin to understand better the factors that influence the value of indirect benefits and, perhaps more important, when these benefits are likely to occur during the HRIS project. Also, since magnitude and value are often driven by different factors, separating these decisions provides a better framework for post-implementation evaluations. Both benefit and value estimates are then open to objective review.

An objective of HRIS CBA is to develop the best possible estimates of the likely effect of the new HRIS functionality. Therefore, using a metric that is familiar or comfortable to those developing the estimate of this impact is likely to improve accuracy and, ultimately, make the project easier to manage. For instance, if the new functionality is predicted to reduce turnover (see Figure 7.2), the magnitude of the expected change in "turnover rates" would be estimated first. Then, the determination of the dollar value of the differences between the current rate and the expected rate is likely to produce better estimates than if decision makers attempted to estimate the dollar impact of the expected reductions in turnover in a single step. The objective is to choose the metric and measurement procedure that will result in the most accurate estimate possible of the size of the benefit.

Once that metric has been chosen, there are three approaches for estimating **benefit magnitude**: (1) direct estimation, (2) benchmarking, and (3) internal assessment. Which method is the most appropriate depends on the amount of specific information that is available to the organization and the CBA team.

Direct Estimation

Direct estimation is the simplest of the three methods. It is quick and easy to perform. It relies solely on the expertise of analysts or subject matter experts in the CBA team to "estimate" the expected magnitude of the benefit. **Direct estimation** is most appropriate when the scope of the project is small, compliance or risk avoidance is a primary investment justification, other substantial sources of direct cost reduction or direct revenue enhancement exist, or no other method for estimating benefit magnitude is available. The primary limitation of direct estimation is that the accuracy of the analysis depends on the expertise of the estimator.

When several equally qualified subject matter experts are available, collecting independent estimates from each expert and using the average of these estimates is recommended. In addition, it can be useful to require that experts articulate the rationale for their estimates. Requiring this step not only ensures that experts are thoughtful in the preparation of their estimates but also provides the organization with an analysis of the assumptions or expectations contained in these rationales, which can be used to help improve the accuracy of future estimates.

Benchmarking

Benchmark data on the magnitude of indirect benefits achieved in other firms can be used. The advantage of **benchmarking** is that it allows an organization to build on the experiences of others. These data can provide evidence that a specific outcome can occur as well as evidence of its potential magnitude. Howes (2002) offers an insightful example of how benchmarking data can be used to estimate how much reduction in turnover an organization might expect. In this example, benchmark data about industry-wide levels of turnover are used to construct estimates of the potential for improvement in turnover that might be possible for a given organization. If an organization has high turnover relative to industry standards, it has the potential for greater improvement than might be expected for other firms in that industry.

Benchmarking information of various types is becoming more widely available from a number of sources (e.g., Gartner, Inc., The Hackett Group, the Saratoga Institute, the Society of Human Resource Management, and Harris Associates—see the Web sites provided in the Appendix). Chapter 6 contains a reference to HR metrics that can be used in benchmarking (SHRM, 2010). Organizations can also conduct their own benchmarking studies to gather specific data from targeted firms, data that may not be readily available from third-party sources. Benchmarking is preferred over direct estimation for larger, more costly projects for which investment risks are greater. Benchmarking is also useful when organizations have limited experience with the targeted functionality of the HRIS project or when there is no access to local data. The primary disadvantage of benchmark data is that the experiences of other organizations may not completely generalize to your firm or business unit. A good recent source of information on benchmarking is the *SHRM Human Capital Benchmarking Study: 2009 Executive Summary* (Dooney, Blackmon, & Williams, 2009).

Internal Assessment

Internal assessment involves the use of a firm's own internal metrics (see Table 7.1) or other forms of the firm's specific data as the basis for estimates. Use of this method requires that the organization has maintained historic records on previous information system projects. Internal assessment is best done when investment scopes are large and direct estimation or benchmarking suggests that benefits may not be dramatically higher or lower than costs (e.g., less than ± 30%). Internal assessment requires that the organization possesses the capability of gathering data about its own processes, as these data are necessary to support this kind of analysis. An advantage of integrated information systems—systems built on common platforms that permit single instances of data to be used in several applications and the seamless transfer of data between applications—is that the marginal costs of assessments are greatly reduced, permitting cost-effective assessments of a wide range of organizational outcomes. Internal assessments offer the most precise estimates of the costs and performance of existing or newly implemented processes. Internal assessments, though, may be able to provide only a portion of the needed data. That is, an organization may be able to gather accurate data about the outcomes of current processes, but, in order to complete the analysis, it may need to rely on benchmark data from other organizations or obtain direct estimates of the outcomes for new processes.

Even though possessing integrated information systems can reduce the marginal costs of assessments, conducting internal assessments and evaluating the data they produce are not costless activities. As described in Table 7.3, internal assessment provides the most precise estimates of the baseline costs and current performance of existing processes against which to compare potential improvements. However, internal assessments will result in higher costs than direct estimation and, depending on the nature of the assessment, could result in higher decision-support costs than benchmarking. As noted, internal assessment is only possible when the organization has experience with a given form of functionality. It is not possible to assess the effects of new functionality that has not been previously implemented anywhere in the organization.

Each of these three approaches is recapped in Table 7.3. The ideal method for estimating the magnitudes of indirect benefits in most HRIS analyses is to use a combination of these three approaches. This permits each benefit to be estimated using the method that is most appropriate given the availability of data and the investment's cost, risk, and opportunity characteristics. For high-stakes investment decisions, using multiple methods to develop estimates can provide additional insight and increased confidence in the final decision.

Table 7.3 Different Approaches to Estimating Benefit Magnitude

Approach	*Description*	*When to Use It*	*Advantages/Limitations*
Direct estimation	Direct ("gut level") estimates of the relationship of the potential benefits to the estimated costs of engaging in an investment	Best when costs are not large Appropriate when attempting to gain compliance or mitigating extreme risks When substantial direct cost reduction or revenue enhancements exist	Quick and low cost to perform May not provide data that contain sufficient detail for use in monitoring implementation effectiveness or to perform follow-up analyses Highly dependent on the expertise of the decision maker
Benchmarking	Using benchmark data from other firms to estimate the potential benefits and costs that are likely to result from the purchase of HRIS functionality	Superior to direct estimation when costs are large When the organization either has limited experience or no data concerning the area of functionality	Allows the organization to develop more precise estimates than direct estimation based on the collective experience of other organizations Average estimates of outcomes may not generalize to the target organization
Internal assessment	Analysis based on specific internal assessments of actual costs and likely benefits (e.g., activity-based costing)	When costs are high and benefits are not obviously dramatically larger than costs When the organization has the assessment capabilities in place to gather the appropriate data	Provides the most precise estimates of the baseline costs and current performance of existing processes against which to compare potential improvements May increase both costs and time required to make decisions
Mix and match	Using combinations of these approaches	When different amounts or sources of information are available for different types of costs and benefits (e.g., most likely scenario)	Permits the organization to use the best methods available

Mapping Indirect Benefits to Revenues and Costs

In some instances, the metric of choice may not be one that is easily or unambiguously tied to reductions in costs or increases in revenues. That is, estimating the value of indirect benefits requires that the analyst first be able to articulate how the indirect benefit is linked to an actual reduction in costs or increase in revenues. To examine this idea further, let's assume that an indirect benefit of a proposed investment is reduced turnover; and we predict that implementing a new HRIS functionality will result in a reduction in voluntary turnover from 10% to 5% for

Figure 7.2 Conceptualizing the Effects of Turnover

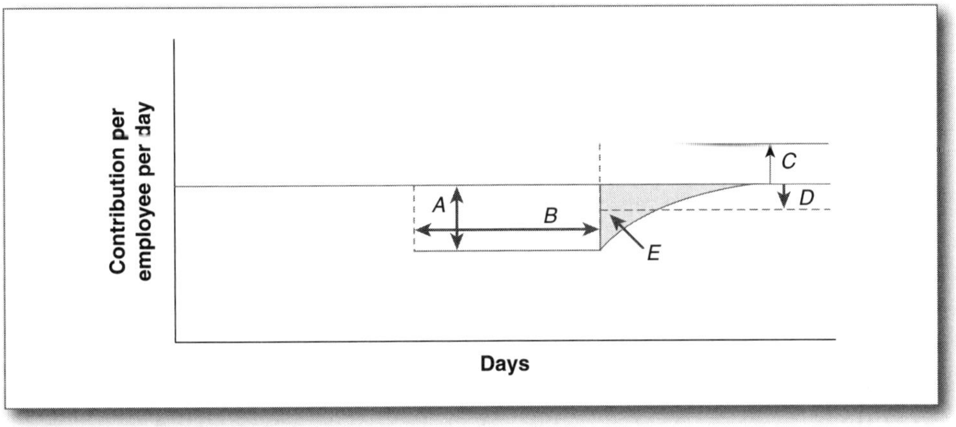

NOTE: A is the average value (contribution) that is lost per day that a given position is left unfilled. *B* is the number of days that a position remains unfilled. *C* and *D* represent the increase or decrease in contribution that occurs if a new hire is more or less effective, respectively, than the employee who left. The grey area noted as E represents the loss of contribution that occurs during the time when a new employee is learning the job.

a targeted group of jobs. Since the effect of turnover on costs and benefits is indirect, we need to understand how reducing turnover is expected to affect an organization's revenues or costs in order to translate our 5% reduction in turnover to other metrics that are more closely associated with changes in costs and revenues.

Employee turnover is a good example because it affects costs and revenues in several ways, some of which are depicted graphically in Figure 7.2. The departure of an employee can increase costs because it may require the organization to engage in a new recruitment and hiring cycle, and the new employee is likely to require training. But there are other effects as well. For instance, the loss of an employee in a position critical to the day-to-day functioning of the organization will require that efforts be made to cover the work responsibilities in that employee's absence. How an organization chooses to cover those responsibilities will influence the magnitude of the net loss of contribution that results from the vacancy. There will be salary savings for the vacant position, but the cost of temporary hires or of shifting other employees off their primary assignments, not to mention the opportunity costs that result from using less than fully effective temporary or overextended employees, also must be considered. The total loss added by this vacancy is represented in Figure 7.2 by the region *A* * *B*—the value of the daily loss of contribution multiplied by the number of days the position remains vacant. Also, as noted in Table 7.2, turnover affects the contribution the organization derives from a position. Perhaps the departing employee was a poor performer and replacing him or her will actually result in a net gain in average long-term effectiveness for that position (i.e., *C* in Figure 7.2). Even with training, new hires will most likely require some time on the job before they can become fully effective; their effectiveness will increase as they gain expertise. But, during this time, contribution will be less than would have been experienced had there been no turnover in the position (i.e., *E* in Figure 7.2). Each of these intermediate outcomes can be tied to a specific cost or revenue effect through one or more links.

In this example, a comprehensive estimate of the impact of the expected reduction in turnover is represented by the sum of the estimates of each of these components in Figure 7.2. In some cases, and for specific types of benefits, these relationships may seem quite complex. Do not be discouraged or dissuaded from being thorough. Understanding exactly how these changes are projected to affect the organization may yield important new insights about intermediate outcomes and contingent factors, insights that may put managers in a position to ensure the success of HRIS investments. Understanding which factors are affected by the investment can also aid in further refining magnitude estimates and is essential for estimating value. Cascio (2000) provides a complete list of the costs of voluntary turnover. In addition, there are several metrics important for measuring the effects of turnover, such as "time to fill," "turnover costs," "vacancy costs," and "vacancy rate."

Methods for Estimating the Value of Indirect Benefits

Direct revenue enhancements or direct cost reductions are typically estimated in dollars, so their value is provided by the total estimate. Estimates that are developed in other metrics, such as total absenteeism in days lost, must also be converted to dollars. For indirect benefits that can be tied more directly to cost reductions or revenue enhancements (i.e., new products developed or market share increased), the task is somewhat more difficult, but it can be done. It requires estimating the strength of the relationship between the change in intermediate outcomes and changes in revenue or cost (e.g., each new account will generate $50,000 in gross profit annually; reducing scrap by 5% will save $10,000 per month). For other outcomes, such as employee time saved, these conversions are somewhat more difficult to conduct.

For this last category, employee time saved, there are two methods for estimating the value of employee time—average employee contribution (AEC) and utility analysis and each method has slightly different purposes. These methods are alternatives to a third practice that is *not recommended*—estimating an employee's value as equal to his or her cost to the organization. In nearly all cases, employee cost dramatically underestimates the average employee's contribution. We know that this is true because most organizations are profit-making concerns. For an organization to be profitable, each individual in that organization, on average, should contribute enough value to compensate for the cost of his or her wages and benefits and for the outlay on the equipment and facilities employed on the job, in addition to covering taxes and accounting for profit. This scenario helps explain why downsizing does not always improve financial results. Downsizing only makes sense when the contribution of the employees eliminated is less than their cost in salary and benefits to the organization.

Average Employee Contribution

In the turnover example discussed earlier, estimating the value lost while a position remains open (i.e., the region represented by the area $A * B$ in Figure 7.2) requires an estimate of the value of the average daily contribution made by an employee. The average contribution approach argues that the **average employee contribution (AEC)** in an organization is equal to total gross profit divided by the number of employees or full-time equivalents (FTEs). FTEs are the budgeted number of positions for each job in an organization. AEC is not a metric that most organizations track, although a measure of average daily gross margin (i.e., revenue – cost of goods sold) generated per salesperson would be an example of this type of measure. This is one of the simplest metrics that captures AEC as accurately as is needed for estimating the value of indirect benefits.

$$\text{AEC} = (\text{Net revenues} - \text{Cost of goods sold})/\text{No. of employees}$$

By definition, in a profitable organization, this number will be substantially higher than labor costs, which is the sum of total employee pay and benefits. Dividing this number by the number of workdays in a year (i.e., 252) produces an estimate of average daily contribution. Note that this method, as indicated in the previous equation, does not reduce contributions attributable to employees by the amount of capital expenditures and other nonemployee-related expenses—the equipment and tools that aid employees in doing their jobs. The reason is that these tools are used to enhance employee contribution. The tools enhance what employees can do, but they do not generate contribution on their own. That is, if you take away the employees who use the tools and equipment, the contribution goes with them. The tools provide no independent and unique contribution to the organization in the absence of the employee.

AEC can be used to estimate the average annual contribution of an organization's employees. Obviously, average contribution can and does differ across jobs. Thus, organizations may want to adjust this number up or down for specific jobs to recognize differences in contribution potential. Jobs that more closely support the organization's mission and offer jobholders broader authority to influence the work of others, and greater autonomy for choosing how and when work will be accomplished, are likely to offer above-average levels of contribution. The advantage of this method is that it establishes a baseline contribution value for each of the different jobs, one that is consistent with the actual financial performance of the organization.

Average contribution estimates, though, provide little guidance in estimating differences in contribution between employees holding the same or similar jobs. This calculation is represented in the turnover example in Figure 7.2 by the difference between the values *C* and *D*—the differences in contribution for two different employees who might hold the same position. Differences in contribution can be developed using internal assessment by examining directly the individual employee differences (variance) in the work outcomes produced by a large number of individuals holding equivalent positions. This assessment can be accomplished more readily for jobs when individual production rates can be monitored (i.e., sales, transaction processing, and some manufacturing settings). It is important to understand the difference between AEC and the variance of work outcomes by employees. AEC is the average contribution of work outcomes, and it can be estimated for entire organizations or for individual jobs. So it would be fairly easy to calculate the AEC for sales representatives by week by adding the sales for all representatives and dividing by the number of representatives. However, this does not tell us the range or variance in the weekly sales for the representatives. Some individuals could have done poorly in terms of weekly sales whereas others could have done quite well. This variance in productivity is very important in the calculation of utility analysis (Boudreau, 1991; Cascio, 1987, 2000; Schmidt & Hunter, 1983), which is beyond the scope of this book.

AVOIDING COMMON PROBLEMS

It is not uncommon for HRIS CBA to include an extensive analysis of costs matched with a single source of benefits—typically, an estimate of direct cost reductions. Recognizing only direct cost reductions is problematic for two reasons. First, it ignores HR's more strategic role in improving organizational effectiveness. Online recruitment that results in hiring employees with higher potential and in developing and administering training programs through online tools, for example, is designed to enhance employee job performance and organizational effectiveness—not necessarily to reduce employee head count. Ignoring these benefits can lead people to dramatically understate the actual value of HRIS investments.

A second problem is that, in many instances, items listed as direct cost reductions are actually indirect cost reductions. Time saved is a prime example. An HRIS will reduce the amount of time required to complete typical HR transactions, but these time savings do not result in actual reductions in overtime or head count. In these instances, time saved is actually an indirect benefit. Its value depends on how individuals spend the extra time made available to them. As noted in Chapter 1, transactional activities deal mostly with day-to-day record keeping—for example, entering payroll information or employee status changes—and the administration of employee benefits. An HRIS that reduces the time on transactional activities would allow the HR employee to spend more time on traditional or transformational activities (see Chapter 1), both of which can assist the organization in meeting its strategic goals.

Incorrectly recognizing time saved as a direct cost reduction creates the wrong expectation among decision makers. This false expectation can lead to the incorrect perception that an investment did not succeed—no reduction in payroll expenses occurred—when, in fact, the benefits to the organization actually occurred in other forms. This point is illustrated in a CBA completed by the National Institute for Health's Center for Information Technology. This analysis, which does an exceptional job of cost analysis, includes only one source of benefit—employee time saved. In this example, investing in the new system was projected to reduce staff time required by 75%, resulting in a 53% ROI.

Admirably, this organization was required to conduct a post-implementation review within 18 months to examine actual versus estimated costs and benefits and to determine whether use of the new system should be continued. The post-implementation analysis revealed that time saved was only 50%, not 75%. As a result, instead of the expected 53% ROI, the revised ROI was only 6%. One can only wonder what might have happened if the post-implementation review indicated the amount of time saved had been only 45%. In that case the CBA formulas would have shown a negative ROI. Would this organization have been forced to abandon this new system? Interestingly, in the post-implementation analysis, the evaluators pointed to other benefits to justify the continued use of the new system. However, since they were not included in the original analysis, bringing them into the post-implementation review may have been seen by some as inappropriate. Nevertheless, an indirect benefit, such as the improved employee morale that analysts found in the post-implementation evaluation, would be a powerful indication that the HRIS investment was worthwhile. In addition, employee morale has been directly linked to voluntary turnover, for which costs can be measured.

Third, be sure that value estimates assigned to time saved are reasonable. Many HRIS investments purport to save employee time, making it a common component of HR technology CBA. When new HRIS functionality will save enough time to make it feasible to reduce the number of employees or reduce overtime expenses, time saved is a source of direct cost reduction. However, more often HR technology saves time in smaller increments that do not permit direct savings. That is, the amount of time saved does not permit whole positions to be eliminated. In these circumstances, time saved is an indirect benefit. The value of the time saved actually depends on what value-generating activities employees engage in during the time made available to them. For example, if the implementation of self-service functionality reduces workload but does not lead to head count reductions, the new functionality might still have tremendous organizational value if those saved hours are used to improve the effectiveness of recruitment efforts or some other value-generating activity, such as the development of a team-training program.

Time saved, though, may not always have value. Consider a situation in which an individual engages in an activity that requires five minutes every day, but the application of new HRIS functionality is estimated to cut this time from five minutes to 1 minute. What is the value of the four minutes saved each day? Generally, larger blocks of time are more easily employed in value-enhancing activities. Consider your own use of time during the day. Could you constructively employ an additional minute of time each day? In most cases, we already have several of these minutes in our schedule that, because of the ebb and flow of daily events, are difficult to use productively. Therefore, it is questionable whether most employees can consistently use short periods of time (i.e., blocks of less than five minutes, for instance) productively. Thus, it may be very difficult to generate value for HR technology that is expected to save time but does so in many small increments.

Obviously, knowledge of your organization's business, as noted earlier in this chapter, will be important in identifying potential benefits. Use your own knowledge, but enlist other knowledgeable professionals and managers in this process as well. Individuals in your organization who are currently responsible for HR functionality prior to implementation of the HRIS (i.e., staff engaged in recruiting) or who are downstream customers of these HR products or services are good resources to enlist to identify benefits. They can help fill in the gaps and highlight other sources of benefits that might not be readily apparent to others. Vendors are a second resource. A review of the features and benefits cited by vendors in the relevant HRIS product space can also be used to identify potential sources of benefits. Vendors may also provide case studies that describe the experiences of companies that have implemented their products and the outcomes that were effected in those organizations. Using a combination of these sources can ensure a comprehensive list of the benefits to be gained when new HRIS functionality is developed.

PACKAGING THE ANALYSIS FOR DECISION MAKERS

When you have completed your analysis, you should have (1) data that identify each benefit and cost component examined; (2) estimates of the dollar magnitude of each, including upper and lower bounds; (3) estimates of when the organization will incur each cost and receive each benefit; and (4) documentation justifying each decision you made in developing these values. The importance of documentation has been emphasized in all previous chapters and will be reemphasized in Chapters 8 and 9. After steps 1 to 4 are completed, the next step is to package the analysis for decision makers in your organization. Obviously, this process involves "selling" the analysis to senior management so that it will not be overlooked or minimized. Managerial decision makers prefer well-organized and clear CBAs to help them make their investment decisions.

Packaging the analysis for consideration by decision makers includes deciding what data to include and how the data should be organized. This process should be done with the entire project management (PM) team since the report must cover the entire HRIS project, not just the investment analysis. A table outlining the value and timing of costs and revenues is likely to be the central focus of the analysis. Some experts encourage limiting the number of sources of benefits presented to decision makers to simplify the presentation and the required justifications. This approach is satisfactory for small projects, that is, for a stand-alone HRIS application such as applicant tracking, but would be inappropriate for a complex HRIS project.

Although being able to make your case on a single page is beneficial, there are several advantages in including all the cost and benefit components that influence the likely outcomes of the investment decision. First, this offers the most complete, best estimate of the value of the investment, thereby giving decision makers the best information to make an appropriate investment decision. Second, it provides the decision maker with a fuller understanding of the investment and of the impact of the investment on the organization. Particularly with respect to indirect benefits, contingent actions taken by managers are likely to influence the extent to which the estimated benefits will be achieved. Making decision makers aware of these contingencies can help enlist their assistance in ensuring each investment's future success.

The Role of Variance in Estimates

Since the estimates produced for cost-benefit analyses are necessarily based on forecasting future events and may also depend on events outside the control of management, actual outcomes are likely to deviate from those estimated. For example, one may expect an average reduction of 2 hours in transaction processing time. However, the actual amount of reduction will vary depending on the mix of transaction types, operator expertise, and other job requirements, and could range from 105 to 135 minutes. *The primary estimate of interest is the overall average expectation.* However, particularly for indirect benefits, it is useful to develop expectations about the range and potential distribution of possible outcomes. Lower- and upper-bound estimates as well as deviations from the average (variance) for magnitude and value estimates are useful auxiliary information that can help convey expectations about potential variability in outcomes.

Variance estimates can be developed by each of the estimation methods described in Table 7.3. For direct estimation, HR and IT professionals could produce estimates of the range and likelihood of various outcome levels. In addition, multiple estimators could be used if two or more equally knowledgeable individuals exist. Each could be instructed to estimate a target value and upper and lower bounds for the estimated expectations, and these could then be averaged to develop overall estimates. Variance estimates for benchmark data from other organizations in the same industry are more difficult to acquire, since most sources only report averages and do not report variance data. In some instances, it may be possible to request the standard deviations associated with each benchmark value from other organizations. However, with internal analysis, variance estimates can be calculated from the archival records of existing HR or IT processes before and after implementation. In all instances, an estimate of the variance of outcomes could then be used to provide a range of the most likely outcomes. However, remember that, in the absence of compelling evidence to the contrary, the best estimate is the one you developed, and that should be the focus of your analysis.

CONCLUSION

Accurately identifying and estimating the value of the benefits and costs of new HRIS functionality will play a critical role in HRIS investment decisions in the foreseeable future. A renewed interest in detailed investment analysis is healthy and should be embraced by analysts and decision makers. In addition to supporting improved investment decisions, detailed CBAs of HRIS investments are also likely to identify implementation contingencies and opportunities that can increase the chances for successful implementations. These analyses also provide the desired organizational targets against which to judge the effectiveness of an investment after implementation.

SUMMARY

The central focus of this chapter has been estimating and understanding the cost effectiveness dynamics of new investments in HRIS, which are assessed by the completion of a cost-benefit analysis (CBA). The calculation of a CBA has become critical for any new investment by an organization, as CBAs are closely linked with strategic goals such as profitability and the survival of the organization. Without a well-done CBA, managerial decision makers will be much less likely to approve expenditures for new HRIS investments, especially today. In the past, investments in an HRIS were primarily driven by a risk avoidance strategy or by cost reductions made possible by replacing paper-and-pencil or out-of-date systems. Since Y2K, organizations have had to rely on organizational enhancement strategies to justify the investment in new HRIS functionality. Organizational enhancement strategies highlight how a firm's effectiveness will be improved by the addition of a new or improved HRIS, as measured in a formal CBA by estimated increases in benefits (e.g., revenues) compared with estimated costs. This requires that we change our approach of cost justifying HRIS to account for these new types of benefits.

This chapter also addressed the importance of adopting an appropriate perspective on the CBA before any numbers are analyzed, and it provided guidelines for successful HRIS CBA (Table 7.1). An organizational enhancement strategy was shown to be the appropriate approach for conducting a CBA to justify an HRIS investment in today's organizations. Instructions on how to estimate direct and indirect costs and benefits were covered in detail, with a focus on creating a palatable CBA report for managerial decision makers. The various direct and indirect costs and benefits of an HRIS that go into the CBA have been discussed throughout the chapter, and several are listed in Table 7.2. Identifying the direct and indirect costs and benefits for a CBA must be extensive and complete. Without a comprehensive listing of direct and indirect costs and benefits, it will be impossible to calculate a correct CBA. After this comprehensive list is complete, the final step is to estimate the value of direct and indirect costs and benefits. This estimating task is done by the HRIS project team, and therefore it is critical that the project team have individuals who can provide significant input to the estimates. This chapter has provided examples of how to enumerate and then define the value of these estimates (Table 7.2 and Figure 7.1).

Both AEC and variance analysis were covered as methods to assess the indirect benefits of an HRIS investment. It was argued that, when possible, both AEC and variance estimates should be used in developing a CBA. Also, both approaches to the estimation of indirect benefits, as well as the other methods discussed in this chapter for estimating costs and benefits, should be used for the post-implementation evaluation of the HRIS. The three common problems that can occur in a CBA were covered: (1) an extensive analysis of costs matched with a single source of benefits, which typically, is an estimate of direct cost reductions; (2) the listing of items as direct cost reductions that are actually indirect cost reductions (which is a very frequent occurrence); and (3) an unreasonable estimate of the value assigned to time saved or of the effects of time saved on the organization, probably the most common error in developing a CBA. In addition, as recommended in the earlier chapters, the CBA should be documented carefully and completely, as it will be useful in both HRIS project management and HRIS implementation.

KEY TERMS

average employee contribution (AEC)
baseline functionality
benchmarking
benefit magnitude
CBA guidelines
cost-benefit analysis (CBA)
cost-benefit ratio
cost reduction strategy
direct benefits
direct costs
direct estimation [of benefits]
employee head count
HRIS functionality
HRIS project team
implementation costs
indirect benefits
indirect costs
integrated information systems
internal assessment
internal rate of return (IRR)
investment analysis
legacy computing systems
organizational enhancement strategy
payback period
return on investment (ROI)
risk avoidance strategy
three basic pieces of information [for CBA]
timing of cash flows [in HRIS project]

DISCUSSION QUESTIONS

1. How has the use of HRIS evolved over the past 10 years in organizations, and how might this influence an organization's evaluations of additional investments in new or updated HRIS functionality?
2. Why is it important to estimate the benefits to be derived from new HRIS functionality before you estimate the costs? If costs were estimated first, how might this change the analysis?
3. Organizations have traditionally used "employee time saved" as the primary source of benefits to justify HRIS and other types of information system investments. Why can this be problematic? Give several reasons and relate them to conducting a CBA.

4. What are the direct and indirect benefits of a new HRIS that decreases the transactions of the HR department by creating employee portals (see Chapter 10) and allows HR employees to work on other projects such as talent management or online recruiting?
5. What makes indirect benefits so difficult to include in a CBA? What techniques might be used?
6. When should benchmarking be preferred to direct estimates of the magnitudes of benefits? When should direct estimates be preferred? Is it appropriate to use both?
7. Why does average employee contribution offer a better estimate of the contribution of individuals to an organization than total compensation (wages, incentives, and benefits)?
8. What are the factors you would have to use in calculating a cost-benefit ratio to support a decision to purchase a new HRIS when the organization already has an HRIS that was acquired 10 years ago? Be sure to mention the factors that would comprise the costs, direct and indirect, and the benefits, direct and indirect, of the current system versus the proposed system.
9. Develop an argument for the implementation of an HRIS using a risk reduction strategy and an organizational enhancement strategy.

CASE STUDY

Investment Associates, Inc. (IA)[4] started as a small firm in 2001 with four employees plus its owner, Jim Tower. The company specialized in providing financial investment and tax advice to its clients. Jim had brought a substantial number of clients from his private practice, which had become too large for him to handle by himself. His four employees included three colleagues who had some experience in financial investment advice and a secretary/administrative assistant. Jim and his three colleagues were all certified public accountants (CPAs), and a considerable portion of the company's business was in tax consultation and the completion of individual and corporate tax returns.

IA was quite successful and, by 2007, had added 42 new employees—financial and tax advisers and additional administrative staff, including an office manager, Marian Sweet. In addition to the office manager's supervisory tasks, Marian had to complete federal and state reports on the employees as required by law.[5] However, Marian was not trained in HRM, and she suggested to Jim that the company needed to hire someone with a background in HRM before they "got into trouble" with the government. Marian was particularly concerned about gender and racial discrimination but did not understand how to apply the provisions of the appropriate laws and guidelines.

In November 2007, IA hired Sylvia Wong, who had an undergraduate degree in psychology and four years' experience in HR. In addition, in December 2007, Jim was negotiating to purchase the financial consulting business of an old friend who was retiring. This purchase would mean the addition of 17 new employees in February or March 2008. Sylvia met with Jim in mid-January 2008 to discuss the growing burden of employee reports and payroll processing, all of which were currently being done using a paper-based HR system. She advised Jim that the company needed an HRIS to process employee records and complete the required government reports. As an example, she stated that, because she had to search through paper copies of all employee files, it took her a full week to complete the Equal Employment Opportunity Report (EEO-1)[6] required by the federal government. Furthermore, based on this report, it appeared that the company could have problems in terms of compliance with several federal laws. She suggested that the company purchase an HRIS to assist with company record keeping and the production of required reports.

Since the company had been using computer-based applications for financial analysis and tax reporting, Jim thought that Sylvia's suggestion to computerize employee records was a good one. However, given his financial background, he wanted Sylvia to develop a business case, including a cost-benefit analysis, for the purchase of an HRIS.

Your task is to help Sylvia justify the purchase of an HRIS.

Case Study Questions

1. What approaches to justifying this investment might Sylvia consider?
2. What are some of the ways you can use the HR metrics that would be available after the implementation of an HRIS to justify its purchase?
3. What are some of the costs and benefits involved in this investment in an HRIS? Which would you be sure to include in your CBA of this project and why?
4. Explain how to estimate costs and benefits, both direct and indirect, in terms that Jim will understand. (Remember, Jim always has his eye on the "bottom line.")
5. Explain how to calculate a CBA to justify the HRIS project. Would you use cost reduction or organizational enhancement (or both) as a strategy for justifying the purchase?
6. What are the three common problems that could occur in your CBA for an HRIS? How would you avoid them?
7. Finally, and most important, explain how variance estimates that can be generated for a CBA would be useful to Jim in the management of his company.

NOTES

1. The content of this chapter was based in part on two articles published in the *IHRIM Journal* (Carlson, 2004a, 2004b).
2. Dollars will be used as an example of currency throughout this chapter. When used so, it implies that other currencies such as the euro, yen, or peso could be substituted for it.
3. The company name is fictitious to protect the confidentiality of the actual company.
4. The names of the company and employees are fictional to protect confidentiality.
5. See Chapter 10 for a discussion of some of these reports.
6. See Chapter 10.

REFERENCES

Bondarouk, T., & Meijerink, J. (2010, August). *Implementation of an HR portal: Results of a qualitative study from a public sector organization.* Paper presented at the annual meeting of the Academy of Management, Montreal.

Boudreau, J. (1991). Utility analysis for decisions in human resource management. In M. D. Dunnette & L. M. Hough (Eds.), *Handbook of industrial and organizational psychology* (Vol. 2, pp. 621–752). Palo Alto, CA: Consulting Psychologists Press.

Browne, G. J., & Rogich, M. B. (2001). An empirical investigation of user requirements elicitation: Comparing the effectiveness of prompting techniques. *Journal of Management Information Systems, 17*(4), 223–249.

Carlson, K. D. (2004a). Estimating the value of the indirect benefits of new HR technology. *IHRIM Journal, 8*(4), 22–28.

Carlson, K. D. (2004b). Justifying HRIS investments post Y2K: Identifying sources of value. *IHRIM Journal, 8*(1), 21–27.

Cascio, W. F. (1987). *Costing human resources: The financial impact of behavior in organizations* (2nd ed.). Boston: Kent.

Cascio, W. F. (2000). *Costing human resources: The financial impact of behavior in organizations* (4th ed.). Boston: Kent.

Dery, K., Hall, R., & Wiblen, S. (2010, August). *HRISs and the constraint of human agency: The implications for HR skills.* Paper presented at the annual meeting of the Academy of Management, Montreal.

Dooney, J., Blackmon, O., & Williams, S. (2009). *SHRM® Human capital benchmarking study: 2009 executive summary.* Washington, DC: Society of Human Resource Management.

Dulebohn, J. (2010, August). *Assessing cross-functional teams in ERP/eHR implementation projects.* Paper presented at the annual meeting of the Academy of Management, Montreal.

Fitz-enz, J. (2001). *How to measure human resources management* (3rd ed.). New York: McGraw-Hill.

Grant, D., Newell, S., & Kavanagh, M. J. (2010, August). *Realizing the potential of an HRIS: Unintended consequences, human agency, and the HR function.* Symposium presented at the annual meeting of the Academy of Management, Montreal.

Howes, P. (2002, February/March). Calculating the ROI for an HRIS business plan. *IHRIM.link,* 12–15.

Kahneman, D., & Tversky, A. (1979). Prospect theory: An analysis of decisions under risk. *Econometrica, 47,* 313–327.

Kavanagh, M. J., Gueutal, H. G., & Tannenbaum, S. I. (1990). *Human resource information systems.* Boston: PWS-Kent.

Lemon, W. F., Bowitz, J., Burn, J., & Hackney, R. (2002). Information systems project failures: A comparative study of two countries. *Journal of Global Management, 10*(2), 28–39.

Mayberry, E. (2008). *How to build an HR business case* (SHRM White Paper). Alexandria, VA: Society for Human Resource Management.

Schmidt, F. L., & Hunter, J. E. (1983). Individual differences in productivity: An empirical test of estimates derived from studies of selection procedure utility. *Journal of Applied Psychology, 68,* 407–414.

SHRM. (2010). *HR metrics toolkit.* Retrieved October 15, 2010, from http://www.shrm.org/hrtools/hrmetrics_published/cms_002620.asp

Tansley, C. (2010, August). *Project team branding on global human resources information systems projects.* Paper presented at the annual meeting of the Academy of Management, Montreal.

Part III

HRIS Implementation and Acceptance

Chapter 8

Project Management and HRM Advice for HRIS Implementation

Salvatore M. Belardo and Michael J. Kavanagh

EDITORS' NOTE

This chapter focuses on the implementation and maintenance of the HRIS, the final two stages of the system development life cycle (SDLC). Although these topics have been discussed in Chapters 3, 4, and 5, the use of the **project management (PM)** tools and processes covered in this chapter will ensure that the implementation of the HRIS will be more orderly and completed on time. Chapter 9 will extend the information technology (IT) approaches outlined in this chapter's discussion of PM and examine critical issues involved in the implementation, acceptance, and maintenance of an HRIS from a behavioral view. Project management involves a planned set of procedures to accomplish a specific (and usually) one-time effort—for example, changing a maternity leave policy or implementing a new HRIS. PM includes the following components: (1) develop a project plan, (2) determine project goals and objectives, (3) define tasks to achieve goals, (4) identify the resources (people and money) needed, and (5) estimate a budget and timeline for completion. The use of PM in the development of an HRIS project involves combining knowledge from both HRM and IT[1] to ensure successful implementation. IT provides us with PM technical approaches, techniques, and tools, while HRM provides behavioral knowledge, team management, leadership advice, and change management techniques. Following formal PM procedures and recommendations is important for the successful development and implementation of the HRIS. More important, the use of PM techniques and tools should begin in the early stages of the development of the HRIS, that is, prior to senior management's approval of the initial proposal. The interrelatedness of the content of this chapter with that of Chapters 3, 4, and 5 is important to acknowledge because it illustrates how effective management of an HRIS project requires the cooperation and skills of both IT and HR professionals. In addition, HR metrics and workforce analytics (Chapter 6) and the cost-benefit analysis (CBA, Chapter 7) are critical elements of a PM development and implementation plan for an HRIS. **Critical success factors** in the management, implementation, and acceptance of the HRIS project are also covered at the end of this chapter.

CHAPTER OBJECTIVES

After completing this chapter, you should be able to

- Understand how the use of PM approaches, techniques, and tools helps throughout the entire SDLC
- Be able to describe and define the factors that are used to develop the program evaluation and review technique (PERT), the critical path method (CPM), and Gantt charts
- Understand how monitoring the project activities carefully on a Gantt chart will ensure project completion on time
- Be able to construct a Gantt chart
- Understand how Six Sigma can be used in HR and project management
- Understand how the combination of knowledge from the IT and HRM fields makes the development and implementation of the HRIS successful
- Be able to describe how IT factors can affect HRIS project success
- Understand how knowledge from the HRM literature provides guidance for handling the behavioral problems and issues that arise in HRIS development
- Understand the different roles of the steering committee, the CBA team, and the PM team in the HRIS project
- Be able to describe how training and documentation are crucial to both the development and the implementation of an HRIS
- Be able to describe how critical success factors affect the success or failure of an HRIS project

HRIS IN ACTION

In a national organization with 24 plant locations within the United States, a new software package for use in recruiting and selecting new employees, that is, for applicant tracking, was being developed and implemented as an add-on to the firm's current HRIS.

The software was created by an external vendor; however, the implementation was being done by the internal HR and IT staff. As part of the contract, the vendor agreed to make modifications to the software as needed, until the management of the organization felt the software was operating properly. (This feature of an external vendor contract is typically required in the **request for proposal [RFP]**.)

The project team had used one project management technique, PERT, and a specific visual device—the **Gantt chart**. These PM tools will be described later in this chapter. Their plan included (1) a project plan, (2) project goals and objectives, (3) tasks or activities to achieve goals, (4) an outline of people and dollar resources needed, and (5) a budget and a timeline for completion. As a critical part of the PM plan for this firm, a steering committee and a project team were established at the corporate level; and each company location was to form parallel steering committees and project teams at their location, teams that included IT and HR professionals.

The initial phase of the implementation involved a small-scale pilot test of the first version of the new software in two plant locations in order to make changes to the software if there were any problems. This initial phase took three months to complete, and the necessary modifications to the software were made. The next phase, to be accomplished over the next three months, was to field-test the revised version of the software in all company locations. It was decided to have the corporate-level leader of the HRIS project teams visit each location to meet with the HR and IT staff on the local project team to answer questions and generally assist with any problems during the field test. The feedback from this field test was to be sent to the vendor, so any necessary additional modifications of the software could be made.

In most of the firm's locations, the meetings with the HR and IT staff went fairly well, and the managers at these locations were pleased with their progress in implementing the new software. In 11 of the company locations, however, no formal meetings on the field test had been held. In these locations, the HR and the IT departments have had many difficulties cooperating, and each blamed the other for the lack of action on the current project. In addition, there were very few meetings in these 11 plant locations, and the project manager did not really understand the PERT analysis and the Gantt chart. Local project teams had been appointed that had both HR and IT professionals as members, but, unfortunately, the teams had only a few meetings. The corporate project team leader conducted interviews at the local plants to determine the source of these problems.

The results of these interviews revealed several problems. Even though the local staff meetings in the 11 plant locations had been scheduled by the local project leader, there were always key personnel, IT or HR, missing at each meeting, and this situation led to a cancellation of the meetings. Unfortunately, which key personnel were missing changed from meeting to meeting, making the accomplishment of the field test near impossible. Thus, it appeared obvious that the project charter and the **steering committee** (see Chapter 3 and later in this chapter) were poorly done, which, in this case, resulted in poor coordination between the corporate team leader and local team managers. There was also very little preparation or training in the use of PM tools or techniques for the PM team. In addition, there was no project or team training done for this project.

After intervention by senior management and ten months of struggling with this problem in the 11 company locations, the field test was finally completed. This set the timetable for the total software implementation to ten months longer than anticipated. The project was completed ten months late, which led to a major cost overrun of 153%. As a further negative result, it appeared that there were going to be layoffs to counter the additional costs for this project.

What was the central problem in this situation? Even though the corporate project team had used well-tested IT approaches and techniques from the PM field, the lack of a clear project charter and the poor selection of local steering committees in the 11 "problem" locations led to project failure. The information in this chapter will focus on the *necessity* of having well-tested PM techniques, good HRM programs, and team leadership training to enhance the effective management of the project team, as well as on recognizing the needs of all stakeholders in the organization, in order to ensure that the project is implemented properly and within the defined timeline.

INTRODUCTION

Statistics measuring the success of systems development efforts are not very encouraging. The failures of systems implementation have been well documented in the past. Browne and Rogich (2001) assert that "despite good faith efforts by organizations, analysts, and users, a majority of systems are either abandoned before completion or fail to meet user requirements." Inordinate delays and excessive budget overruns as well as user dissatisfaction, late deliveries, and customer dissatisfaction are some of the most cited reasons for the failure of HRIS projects. It has been estimated that this problem costs organizations in the United States alone at least $100 billion a year (Ewusi-Mensah, 1997). Of those systems that are completed, more than 55% will exceed cost and time estimates by a factor of 2. Even more troubling is the fact that only 13% of the IS projects that are completed are considered successful by the executives who sponsor them (Lemon, Bowitz, Burn, & Hackney, 2002).

Recent reports of the failures of HRIS implementation in major corporations indicate that these projects need to be more closely monitored due to the significant failure rates (Bondarouk & Meijerink, 2010; Dery, Hall, & Wiblen, 2010; Dulebohn, 2010; Grant, Newell, & Kavanagh, 2010; Tansley, 2010). The failure to deliver successful systems poses risks not only to those whose operations depend on these systems but also to those responsible for delivery. The inability to employ "quality" systems can prevent the firm from performing critical operations satisfactorily. In most cases of these failures to implement systems, the use of project management (PM) tools, techniques, and management procedures, as well as advice from the HRM "organizational change" literature, was largely ignored.

A classic example is the well-documented failure of Hershey Foods' $112 million computer system (Nelson & Ramstad, 1999). Due to the poor design and implementation of this new system, Hershey was unable to fill an order for 20,000 pounds of candy placed by a regional distributor in mid-September in anticipation of Halloween demand. The distributor, in turn, could not satisfy 100 of his 700 retail customers. The journal article describing the debacle further quoted a candy buyer for Lowes Foods, a chain of supermarkets, who advised stores to stop reordering Hershey candies and switch to a competitor. Although Hershey claimed that it lost only a small percentage of its market share, others contended that the shelf space the company lost would be difficult to win back. Many of these problems could have been avoided if an effective PM methodology had been utilized.

Project management is a systematic and structured approach to planning and properly executing a specific, and usually one-time, objective. The objective of any project can range from planning a social event like a college-wide picnic to the implementation of a complex, multimillion-dollar computer-based system like an HRIS. In both of these examples, the IT and HRM tools are absolutely necessary to ensure the project objective is achieved.

This need for effective management of an HRIS development project was extensively discussed by Walker (1982) when he identified the 10 most common mistakes in developing an HRIS. One of the major issues that he identified was **loose project control**, which was a central problem in the situation described in the vignette at the beginning of this chapter. Likewise, Kavanagh, Gueutal, and Tannenbaum (1990) provided a list of 14 recommendations based on an extensive review of the HRIS literature. Prominent among these recommendations was the "need to make a detailed plan" and to "develop a checklist to monitor implementation"; as well, they noted that "documentation . . . is critical for successful implementing and maintaining of the HRIS" and that HR and IT managers should "audit the new system periodically for maintenance" (p. 191). This chapter focuses on describing the approaches and techniques you can use to meet these recommendations and successfully develop and implement an HRIS.

PROJECT MANAGEMENT COOPERATION

Effective PM for the HRIS depends completely on a positive relationship between the IT and HR departments. As seen in the vignette, a poor relationship between these departments caused the project to fail in 11 company locations. Without this necessary cooperation, the HRIS development and implementation will fail. In the next several sections of this chapter, the contributions from the fields of IT and HR will be described along with a prescribed approach to combine them to make the HRIS fulfill the needs of all end users.

THE IT PERSPECTIVE

Project Management Processes

An examination of the project management literature reveals a number of methodologies for managing an HRIS project. Information on PM in general and PM techniques and tools can be found at the Web sites of the State of Kansas (www.da.ks.gov/kito/ITPMM.htm) and the Project Management Institute (www.pmi.org). Although there are a number of PM approaches and methods described in these Web sites, detailed coverage of each is beyond the scope of this book. However, Josler and Burger (2005) provide an excellent description of the use of PM methodology in the successful implementation of an HRIS in a university setting.

Regardless of the methodology employed, each approach has four general **project management process phases** in common. These phases are quite similar to the stages of the system development life cycle (SDLC) for an HRIS project and, basically, parallel the various steps and requirements in the development and implementation of an HRIS as covered in Chapters 3 to 5. However, it is important to examine project phases from the perspective of the IT discipline since this examination can uncover additional issues regarding the success of an HRIS project.

The PM methodologies all begin with the **project initiation phase**. In this phase, a **project concept** and a **project proposal** are developed. The project concept describes the key stakeholders and seeks to ensure that the right questions are asked so that the right problem is solved. In the initial stages of an HRIS, this information is critical. The project proposal, also called a **project charter**, contains objectives and performance targets (e.g., cost, time, scope). The project concept and charter must be approved by top management to fulfill the requirements of this initial phase and begin the development of an HRIS. Without a firm and continuing commitment from top management on the project timeline and budget, the HRIS project will likely fail.

The second phase of project planning identifies the tasks that must be performed. A **work breakdown structure (WBS)** is created along with **work packages** (i.e., what must be done, by whom, using what resources, in what time, and at what cost). During this phase, the time order in which activities, tasks, and jobs are to be performed is planned, and specific checks or monitoring points are established. These monitoring points could have important effects on the direction, scope, or requirements of the HRIS project, and, thus, designating monitoring points on the timeline is critical.

As discussed in the IT field, the third phase is called **project execution**. In this phase, the HRIS project is tracked, and periodic progress reports are prepared for management and the project team. During this phase, five key factors are assessed: schedule, budget, open issues, risks, and communication. PM approaches such as the PERT (performance evaluation and review) and the CPM (critical path method) are used in conjunction with visual tools such as Gantt and bar charts during project execution. A description of the use of these approaches and tools is available on the Internet (http://en.wikipedia.org/wiki/Project_management_software).

The final phase is **project closeout**, which involves the implementation, evaluation, documentation, and maintenance of the HRIS. This phase includes the following goals and activities:

1. Accepting the project's products (indicated by user sign-off)
2. Completing the **post-implementation evaluation report (PIER)**
3. Disbursing resources (staff, facilities, and automated systems)
4. Conducting a "lessons learned" session
5. Completing and archiving project records
6. Recognizing outstanding achievement
7. Celebrating project completion

The celebration of the project's completion is as important as the initial proposal since it will help employees feel more committed to making the new HRIS operate properly.

Quality considerations are also important in the design of any new business process or information system, and an HRIS is no exception. In pursuit of quality processes, many organizations are adopting a "Six Sigma" approach to assessing the effectiveness of HR processes. Although originally developed by Motorola, USA in 1981, and famously applied by General Electric to improve the quality of its manufacturing processes, Six Sigma is now being applied to a wide variety of production and service processes. It has become one of the most widely recognized quality improvement methods used in businesses today.

Six Sigma focuses on business process reengineering with the goal of improving the quality of process outputs by identifying and removing the causes of defects (errors) and minimizing variability in business processes. Six Sigma is a structured approach for improving business processes through a step-by-step method labeled DMAIC, which stands for define, measure, analyze, improve, and control. The **DMAIC approach** uses an assortment of statistical tools to reengineer business processes, and HRM processes such as recruiting, training, and compensating employees, can be examined using this approach. "The DMAIC project methodology has [the following] five phases":

- *Define* the problem, the voice of the customer, and the project goals, specifically.
- *Measure* key aspects of the current process and collect relevant data.
- *Analyze* the data to investigate and verify cause-and-effect relationships. Determine what the relationships are, and attempt to ensure that all factors have been considered. Seek out the root cause of the defect under investigation.
- *Improve* or optimize the current process based upon data analysis using techniques, such as design of experiments . . . or mistake proofing, and standardize work to create a new, future state process. Set up pilot runs to establish process capability.
- *Control* the future state process to ensure that any deviations from target are corrected before they result in defects. Implement control systems . . . and continuously monitor the process. ("Six Sigma," 2010)

As can be seen, the IT field offers a number of techniques and approaches to PM developed by professionals. Using these techniques, one can develop an **overall work plan** based on the work breakdown structure and work packages described previously. This overall work plan is a written time schedule of tasks and responsibilities with deadlines so that the HRIS project will be done in the total time allotted. Note, however, that the orientation of this plan is toward the management of the project itself, not the people who are responsible for the development and implementation of the HRIS.

The management of the people involved—the project team, end users, and organizational managers—is contained in advice from the HRM and HRIS fields. This distinction between the IT and HR fields is sometimes referred to as the *gap* between the IT capabilities of the organization and the use of these capabilities by HR professionals. Frequently, there is a mismatch—positive or negative—between what the HR department wants and the capabilities available through the IT department. This fact, as seen in the opening vignette, underscores the need for cooperation between these departments in staffing the project team. The next section discusses some of these issues regarding the formation and operation of the project team.

Project Management Approaches and Tools

The IT field has provided some powerful approaches and tools to be used in managing any project. **Performance evaluation and review technique (PERT)** is a method for analyzing the tasks involved in completing a given project, the time needed to complete each task, and the minimum time needed to complete the total project. It was invented in 1958 by the U.S. Department of Defense's U.S. Navy Special Projects Office and was intended for complex, one-of-a-kind projects such as its first application—developing the Polaris mobile submarine-launched ballistic missile.

The **critical path method (CPM)**, meanwhile, uses a mathematically based algorithm for scheduling a set of project activities and was developed by DuPont and the Remington Rand Corporation for managing plant maintenance projects. CPM is used to construct a project model that includes the following:

1. A list of all activities required to complete the project
2. The time (duration) that each activity will take to complete
3. The dependencies among the activities

Using these values, CPM calculates the starting and ending times for each activity and determines which activities are critical to the completion of a project (called the critical path) and which activities have "float time" (are less critical). In PM, a **critical path** is the sequence or project network that determines the shortest time possible to complete the project. Any delay in activity on the critical path directly affects the planned project completion date (i.e., there is no float on the critical path). A project can have several, parallel critical paths. An additional parallel path through the network with a total duration shorter than the critical path is called a subcritical or noncritical path.

Finally, one can develop a Gantt chart, which is a graphical representation of the duration of tasks against the progression of time in a project. *Wikipedia* defines a Gantt chart as follows:

> A Gantt chart is a type of bar chart that illustrates a project schedule. Gantt charts illustrate the start and finish dates of the terminal elements and summary elements of a project. Terminal elements and summary elements comprise the work breakdown structure of the project. ("Gantt Chart," 2011)

For a more detailed and technical explanation of PERT, CPM, and Gantt charts, consult one of the several good texts available (O'Brien, Crnkovic, & Belardo, 2006; Wiest & Levy, 1969). In addition, Jon Peltier (2008) has developed a method using EXCEL to build Gantt charts.

Of all the PM tools available, the Gantt chart is the simplest to construct and use. Most people have probably constructed a Gantt chart informally, without realizing they have done so. You might have constructed one when planning a party at your home. As an example, let's imagine this scenario to investigate more fully the elements of a Gantt chart. There are several tasks that need to be done: shopping for groceries, ordering any special items such as a birthday cake, shopping for invitations or sending e-mail invitations, and, of course, making sure there are ample beverages purchased. To plan the party, you would probably develop a list of these tasks and when they must be done. In addition, if you were planning a big event, you would probably have identified specific individuals to execute the tasks. Although you haven't yet constructed a formal Gantt chart, you have the basic information available for doing so. Instructions for how to develop a Gantt chart and then covert it to a PERT chart are available from *Gantt Project* (http://ganttproject.biz/). This Web site is designed as an educational tool, and, thus, you can view tutorials and download the open source software to construct a Gantt chart. Here are the steps to follow to view the tutorial and download the software:[2]

1. After you open the Web site, click on "Learn more" (at the right side of the introductory page).
2. Find the listing "Tutorial," and click on "on Teacher Tube." You will get a video explaining the use of the software. There is an ad at the beginning of the video, which you can ignore.
3. The video goes quite quickly, so you may have to rerun it. However, the video demonstrates how to develop a Gantt chart and derive a PERT chart from it.
4. To download the software, go back to the introductory page (http://www.ganttproject.biz/), and click on "Download GanttProject."
5. From the new page, download the Gantt chart software, making sure you select the appropriate operating system and follow the download instructions. You should save the software, and then go to that location and run and install it.
6. If you want to try to develop a Gantt chart, why not use the party planning example from above. Perhaps it can be a class or small group project.

There are multiple advantages in using these PM approaches and tools; the major one is a tighter control over the process to ensure successful implementation of the HRIS. This tighter control is attained by the following means:

1. Definition of all activities to be accomplished to complete the project
2. Establishment of a specific schedule for activities that includes an estimate of when each activity will start and end

3. Project milestones that are used to monitor specific activities set by this schedule
4. Assignment of resources in terms of equipment, people, and, thus, costs for all activities
5. Computation of the total budget and allocation of the budget needed to accomplish each activity
6. A graphical picture of the entire project showing all activities, their costs, and their milestones

Extending these IT ideas and providing more detail for the management of an HRIS project, Rampton, Turnbull, and Doran (1999) indicate that every project has resource limits and specifications in the following categories:

- Time—start and end dates
- People—identification, specific skills they bring to project, availability, costs
- Tools—equipment, software
- Money—budget (p. 76)

In addition, they note that PM also brings a critical capability to the HRIS project—namely, evaluation of the project's performance by monitoring progress against the planned timetable. This monitoring allows for periodic adjustments as well as ensuring that project creep is not occurring.

Software has been developed for all the PM approaches and tools—CPM, PERT, and Gantt charts. The interested reader can consult *Wikipedia: The Free Encyclopedia* (http://en.wikipedia.org/wiki/Project_management_software) for a fairly comprehensive listing of different types of software. Software applications *will not be recommended* in this book since each organization's situation will vary, and choosing software and hardware for HRIS decisions is a complicated matter. The International Association for Human Resource Information Management (IHRIM) has a buyers' guide for HRIS software that is available to members, and, if any outside consultants are used, they usually have information on the most current and effective PM software for the HRIS project.

General IT Factors Affecting PM Success

Rather than presenting a detailed discussion of the various stages and templates found on the Project Management Institute and State of Kansas Web sites, this chapter will consider three general issues that must be addressed and that are critical to the success of any of these PM methodologies. The *first issue* is the importance of *solving the right problem*. All too often, IT developers create systems that they *think* end users want. The end users are frequently dissatisfied with the results, which accounts for the dismal statistics cited previously. The *second issue* involves having people with *the right knowledge to solve the right problem*. Frequently, IT system developers do not understand the HRM domain and its problems and constraints adequately. It is necessary to have systems developers who are sensitive to HR issues and willing to learn about the constraints in HR functionality. With such systems developers, the information requirements phase can be completed within the timeframe and budget constraints specified by the project plan. In most organizations, this problem can be solved by having both IT and HR professionals on the project team. Obviously, if the organization has an HRIS professional, this problem will be greatly reduced. The *third issue* involves having project managers, from either an IT or an HR department, who *understand the dynamic nature of any HRIS project* and how the interrelations among various factors might render decisions ineffective or even counterproductive. For example, studies have shown that assigning more people to an overdue project might actually delay project completion.

In addition to these three issues, the three general factors that affect successful PM are time, cost, and scope. The cost of project development depends on a number of variables, including labor rates, material, plant resources (e.g., buildings, machines), equipment, and profit. In addition to the total fixed and variable costs are contingency costs and time to completion, which can be broken down into the units of time required to complete each task. Scope refers to what the project is supposed to accomplish and what the end result should be (i.e., what the end user wants). Time and cost are process measures of performance and, therefore, measures of efficiency. Scope, on the other hand, is about effectiveness and is measured by whether the right questions have been asked and whether the right problem is being addressed. Staying within the project costs, time, and scope depends highly on the ability of the project team to gather the correct information requirements for the HRIS project during the needs analysis, which was described in Chapter 4.

THE HUMAN RESOURCE MANAGEMENT PERSPECTIVE

The techniques of PM from the IT literature will ensure the development of an overall written work plan for the HRIS project. However, there are still a number of organizational requirements involved in the successful completion of the HRIS project. Grossman (2009) has a number of recommendations regarding how to manage the people who manage the projects. In addition, the HRM literature provides guidance on how to handle the behavioral and management issues that arise in fulfilling these requirements during the HRIS project. The organizational and management requirements include the following:

1. Identification of steering committee and project charter
2. Configuring the PM team
3. Identification of available resources and constraints
4. Controlling project creep
5. Selection of the implementation team
6. Training and documentation

Each of these requirements and their use in PM will be described in the following sections.

Identification of the Steering Committee and Project Charter

During the initial considerations for the development of an HRIS, typically, there are strategic goals set for the project. Often this process is referred to as "making the business case" for the HRIS project, which would include estimating both the costs and the benefits of the new system—that is, estimating its cost-effectiveness (see Chapter 7). Consequently, a subset of members from the project team must be selected to develop an investment analysis, as described in Chapter 7, that is a cost-benefit analysis (CBA). However, the central focus before project initiation would be on both strategic and operational goals. For example, some possible goals could be (1) reducing the transaction costs in HR processing; (2) improving the quality of HR information for managerial decisions; or (3) improving the HR processes of talent management, which includes the recruiting and selecting of new employees as well as the retention of valued ones. Regardless of the specific strategic and operational goals for the new system, the project will still have constraints in terms of resources available.

Because of these goals and constraints, the steering committee must include representatives of senior management from HR, finance, IT systems, marketing, research and development, and operations. The steering committee members must be selected on the basis of their competence in project management as well as their availability (Grossman, 2009). A crucial player is the senior management member who is selected as the **project sponsor**, since this person typically has overall fiscal responsibility for the project. The primary responsibility of the steering committee is the *oversight of the project* in terms of progress toward meeting strategic goals and staying within the project budget. Thus, the steering committee does not get involved in the day-to-day activities and operations associated with the development of the HRIS. This is the role of the project team, which will be covered later.

One important task for the steering committee is the development of the **project charter**. The project charter was discussed in Chapter 3, and it does the following:

- It makes the case for the implementation.
- It shows connection to organizational goals and strategies.
- It has a plan for end users' involvement and participation.
- It provides identification of **project scope**.
- It identifies implementation team members.
- It identifies additional expertise that might be available.
- It provides a training plan.
- It explains the agreed-on decision-making process.
- It discusses the process by which customization requests will be reviewed and acted on.
- It covers the PM methods used.
- It defines reporting requirements.
- It identifies deliverables.
- It defines political relationships of importance to project success.

The development of the project charter and the coordination of the members of the steering committee involve a great deal of communication and interpersonal skills on the part of the project sponsor, who serves as the chair. As Rampton et al. (1999) note, the communication of project planning and project status in the steering committee and throughout the organization involves an inordinate amount of time. Thus, when it comes to the project sponsor and the steering committee, being patient while keeping an eye on meeting project deadlines is an art. Having well-done PM tools such as CPM, PERT, or Gantt charts is an absolute necessity for the HR project. However, it is people, not the existence of the charts, that make the project successful (Dulebohn, 2010; Grant et al., 2010). Merely sending a memorandum indicating progress on a Gantt chart will not ensure cooperation from either the steering committee or the project team members. It is necessary to both train project managers and, more specifically, provide team training in communications and interpersonal relationships for the steering committee members. Steering committees often will hire outside "process consultants" to help develop and maintain good working relationships within the steering committee, with the **project team**, and with the end users in the organization.

Configuring the PM Team

A central idea that has been discussed through the first seven chapters of this book is that **end-user involvement** and participation is crucial if the HRIS project is to be successful. In systems development, getting the end users to tell a system developer what they know about their domain (e.g., HR programs and processes) and their information and decision requirements largely depends on the developer's ability to ask the right questions. If the systems developer knows how to ask the right questions, knowledge of the users' domain and their unique problems and needs will be easier to obtain. Thus, Belardo, Ballou, and Pazer (2004) contend that it is necessary to educate developers regarding how to ask the right questions and to teach them how to develop the interpersonal skills necessary to gain the cooperation of the users.

Whereas the steering committee oversees the entire HRIS project, the PM team is involved in the day-to-day activities necessary to develop and implement the new HRIS. Its members have the job of completing the activities specified by the CPM, PERT, or Gantt chart according to the defined timetable. The team must be capable of estimating the actual resources, both personnel and monetary, needed to complete the project. A major responsibility of the team is to communicate—by way of written reports on a regular (weekly or monthly) basis—with both the steering committee and the important stakeholders, for example, the vice president of HR, regarding progress on the HRIS project. If the organization has a newsletter or a company bulletin board, these should be used to keep all members of the organization apprised of the progress of the HRIS project.

The PM team should be comprised of representatives from the functional units affected, most notably the HR and IT departments. There may be other units affected, for example, operations, marketing, or finance, and a judgment must be made whether to include representatives from these functional units or simply supply regular update reports on the project to them. The HR professionals chosen for the team should have significant functional knowledge, some technical proficiency, and a positive status within their department and the organization. An example might be the manager of employment or compensation. Likewise, IT professionals could include systems analysts, hardware and software specialists, and HRIS professionals, all of whom should be respected members of the organization.

One of the critical issues faced by the PM team is the selection of the team **project manager**. This person should have strong communication skills, including the ability to speak, listen, and write effectively. The project manager must ensure that the team members understand the importance of regular communication with their supervisors. Team training is an absolute necessity for the project team. Many of the failed HRIS projects were the result of poor team cooperation and interpersonal difficulties (Grant et al., 2010). Furthermore, to be successful in implementing the new HRIS, all potential users must be made aware of the project's progress and how it will affect them. Feedback loops should be developed so that users can provide valuable information to the project team during development and implementation. Kavanagh (2001) used surveys to assess users' attitudes regarding the implementation of a new system. The results of these surveys were then used to guide the development and implementation of the new system as well as to provide feedback to members of the organization.

Identification of Available Resources and Constraints

The steering committee, by way of the project charter, will have established preliminary estimates of available resources for the project and constraints on its scope. Except in unusual situations, the constraints established by the steering committee cannot be altered. However, sometimes it may be necessary to change the initial identification of needed resources, that is, personnel time and other costs. One of the major tasks of the PM team is to identify the need for more resources in the early phases of the project, particularly if legitimate project creep occurs because the initial plans for the HRIS project missed some important aspects of the project. As a result, the project manager must be in constant communication with team members regarding any unforeseen difficulties—for example, if a project team member leaves the organization. In situations where project resources change, the project manager has the responsibility to inform the steering committee chair immediately.

Controlling Project Creep

Project creep is defined as the enlargement of the original boundaries of the project as defined in the project charter. As noted previously, project creep may be legitimate if a major aspect of the project was omitted at the early planning stage. However, other forms of project creep can easily occur as end users see the potential usefulness of computerization. If effective communications have been established within the project team as well as with the entire organization, project creep can be contained by frequent updates on the project's progress, updates that include a definition of the project charter. In addition, using PM tools such as a Gantt chart ensures that the project is meeting its goals and not being extended into activities not contained on the Gantt chart. Surveys of users, as noted, are also useful to ascertain if system users' perceptions of the project have started to creep. In other words, continuous and regular communication is the key to avoiding project creep.

Selection of the Implementation Team

In some cases, the entire PM team, plus the steering committee, will serve as the implementation team. A more common configuration is that a subset of individuals from the PM team is tasked with focusing on implementation issues, such as employee cooperation and training, as well as on change management techniques. It is not unusual to have an external consultant provide technical assistance on implementation using change management techniques such as survey-guided feedback and focus groups. The implementation team also has primary responsibility for communication with the entire organization and, as noted in Chapter 3, begins this communication with the initial planning for new system development. The implementation team should include professionals from both HR and IT, as well as representatives of all functional departments in the organization. It is also important to have a senior manager serve as the leader of the implementation team. Note that these additional people can be added as the project enters its actual implementation phase; however, these individuals must be in the communication loop throughout the entire project.

Training and Documentation

There are a variety of activities involved in training for the new system and its documentation. However, without the necessary training, usually provided by the external vendor who supplies the software, the system will either fail to be developed properly or fail during its implementation. Likewise complete, accurate, and **up-to-date documentation** of the system is critical for the implementation of a successful HRIS. Documentation in terms of notes, diaries, memorandums, and reports created during the development and implementation of the HRIS will be invaluable when updates to the system are needed.

There are several different training programs that are necessary for the development and use of the new HRIS. As discussed earlier, one of the first considerations when beginning the HRIS project is to develop a project plan using CPM, PERT, or Gantt charts. It is desirable to use an employee (from IT or HR) who is certified by the Project Management Institute (www.pmi.org/) or who has taken seminars on PM from the American Management Association (www.amanet.org/). Obviously, without a carefully developed project plan using PM techniques, no amount of communication or employee involvement will suffice to make the HRIS a success. When they have no internal employees with PM skills, companies frequently use outside consultants to develop the project plan.

It is also recommended that the PM team receive training in group processes such as decision making and in communication skills. Furthermore, it is necessary that the project team leader and the implementation team members be trained in the use of planned change or "change management" methods. **Change management** is a structured approach to changing individuals, groups, and organizations to accept new ideas and processes, that is, a new HRIS. Lewin (1951) described change management as involving three phases—unfreezing current attitudes and behaviors, changing to new attitudes and behaviors, and refreezing these new attitudes and behaviors. There are other change management approaches in the literature (Kotter, 1996; Luecke, 2003). The important point is that these approaches work and are absolutely critical for the successful implementation and use of the HRIS. These approaches will be covered in detail in Chapter 9.

The final training that needs to be done is training on the new system. Most vendors of new software will provide training on the new system and more extensive training at an additional cost. The additional cost depends on the level of training needed for the users. To determine the amount and type of training needed for users, the organization should complete an analysis of the training needs and follow the recommended phases for effective training (Wexley & Latham, 2002). In most organizations, the HR department will have training professionals who should be used to complete the training phases. It is important that this training effort be included in the project plan in terms of time needed for the training and the costs. Premature introduction of a new HRIS or introducing it without appropriate training will lead to failure (Kavanagh et al., 1990).

Critical Success Factors for IT and HRM Issues

Several authors have discussed "critical success factors" in HRIS development and implementation (Ceriello & Freeman, 1991; Kavanagh et al., 1990; Rampton et al., 1999; Walker, 1982). These lists of success factors and mistakes serve as both cautions and recommendations for a successful HRIS project. Some of these mistakes and success factors have been mentioned in previous chapters as well as earlier in this chapter. However, for your convenience, we present here a compilation of critical success factors:

1. *Top management support:* Simply stated, the project must have **top management support** at the beginning and throughout implementation and evaluation. The top management, that is, the CEO and department or unit heads, must be willing to provide the necessary resources and authority for project success.

2. *Provision of adequate and timely resources:* These resources include technology, money, time, and personnel. Without a carefully constructed PM plan, organizations will typically have inadequate resources to develop and implement the HRIS. The development of a "business plan" for the HRIS project is an absolute necessity for success. Chapter 7 provides excellent approaches to the development of a business plan for the HRIS, one that includes a cost-benefit analysis (CBA).

3. *Ongoing communication:* Everybody involved in and affected by the HRIS project needs to be informed regularly about the goals, progress or lack of it, issues, and challenges throughout the life of the project, so there is less room for organizational politics, rumor mongering, and misapprehensions. Constant monitoring and frequent feedback are integral parts of the communication process.

4. *Conducive organizational culture:* The culture of the organization will be strongly affected by the history of changes in the organization and how they were accomplished. Contrast an organization in which change was dictated by management versus one in which there was extensive participation by employees in the change effort. You will discover that the organization with the more participatory culture accepted change more readily. When it comes to change, then, this organization has a more **conducive organizational culture**. In addition, the training on the new system will not transfer to the users of the new HRIS unless there is a supportive organizational culture for learning (Lance, Kavanagh, & Brink, 2002; Tracey, Tannenbaum, & Kavanagh, 1995; Velada, Caetano, Michel, Lyons, & Kavanagh, 2007).

5. *User involvement:* As indicated in Chapters 3 and 4, user involvement is critical to the effective development and implementation of the HRIS. This ensures that the project is designed and implemented in accordance with user requirements and, therefore, will have a better chance of being accepted. User involvement will be discussed in more detail in Chapter 9.

6. *Project champions:* The best possible situation would be to have two **project champions** for the HRIS project—the steering committee chair and the project team manager. Obviously, this means that the selection of these individuals must be done carefully, and the persons selected should enjoy a good reputation and status in the organization.

7. *Organizational structure:* Typically, the implementation of a new HRIS will require changes in reporting lines of authority as well as changing responsibilities for HR and IT. If the departments are not used to cooperation and

collaboration, they will develop a "silo mentality" and will compete against each other to the detriment of the organization.

8. *Change management methodology:* The assumption that employees will "love" the new system because of its sophisticated features is naive. Communication and user involvement throughout the development and implementation phases of the project, as well as good training on the new HRIS, are critical to success.

9. *Project control and monitoring:* Trying to execute an HRIS project without a written project plan—for example, the Gantt chart—will lead to failure. Likewise, the project team's failure to communicate project milestones and progress will severely damage the project effort. This loose project control could also be the result of a weak project team or steering committee. The necessary communication from both of these groups will ensure strong project control.

10. *Cross integration between business systems:* Poor integration between systems is usually the result of poor communication across functional departments during the development of the HRIS. Without effective communication, the HRIS will be unable to interface with other business systems, such as the financial, operations, or marketing systems.

SUMMARY

This chapter has been concerned with understanding the value and use of project management (PM) and HR change practices throughout the entire SDLC as a new or upgraded HRIS is developed and implemented. The use of PM tools and techniques such as CPM, PERT, and Gantt charts was covered in detail. The factors involved in developing these PM tools were discussed. Software for the development of a Gantt chart based on the human resources, tasks, and timelines was identified as well. Finally, the IT factors that can affect project success negatively or positively were identified, and their effects on an HRIS project were discussed.

A dynamic perspective of HRIS project management has been presented that uses the joint contribution of IT and HRM approaches, and the chapter argues strongly that organizations cannot rely only on IT approaches such as CPM, PERT, and Gantt charts, thereby excluding the useful behavioral approaches found in the HRM literature. Likewise, using only the behavioral, group, and organizational approaches from the HRM literature without a written plan provided by a bar or Gantt chart will result in either a poorly designed HRIS, expensive cost overruns, or the abandonment of the project. The importance of a project charter and scope management were discussed. Further, the importance of carefully selecting the project team and steering committee was covered in light of how these planners affect project completion.

In general, this chapter has not only focused on PM tools from IT but also identified how HRM knowledge and practices can help handle the behavioral problems and issues that can arise during the development and implementation of an HRIS. Team training of the project team and steering committee was described as crucial to HRIS project success. In addition, the use of continuous documentation through the four PM stages was covered, and behavioral techniques were discussed that address the challenges faced by all project managers—namely, how to improve project effectiveness and efficiency.

Finally, ten critical success factors for overall HRIS project management have been identified from both the IT and the HRM literature. In discussing these ten factors, we explained how each should be used in the development and implementation of an HRIS. Throughout, the chapter has emphasized the importance of documentation by and communications from and to the steering committee and the PM team. Also, documentation and communication were linked to the implementation processes for the HRIS; however, a complete discussion of implementation processes will be provided in Chapter 9.

KEY TERMS

change management
conducive organizational culture
critical path
critical path method (CPM)
critical success factors
DMAIC approach [define, measure, analyze, improve, and control]
end-user involvement
Gantt chart
loose project control
overall work plan
performance evaluation and review technique (PERT)
post-implementation evaluation report (PIER)
project champions
project charter
project closeout
project concept
project creep
project execution
project initiation phase
project management process phases
project managers
project proposal
project scope
project sponsor
project team
request for proposal (RFP)
Six Sigma
steering committee
top management support
up-to-date documentation
work breakdown structure (WBS)
work packages

DISCUSSION QUESTIONS

1. What are the advantages of using a PM approach from the IT literature for the management of an HRIS project?
2. How does the behavioral advice from the HRM literature complement the formal IT tools, such as a Gantt chart?
3. What is the information needed to construct a CPM, PERT, or Gantt chart?
4. Construct a Gantt chart for planning a surprise birthday party for your mother or father.
5. In which phases of the SDLC is documentation important? Why?
6. Do the critical success factors from the IT and HRM literature complement each other? Or is there disagreement between the recommendations from these two fields? Explain your answer.
7. Discuss the organizational factors that might affect the quality of the HRIS being developed. For example, how does a change in organizational structure or in project leadership influence the outcome of an HRIS development project?

CASE STUDY: IMPLEMENTING AN HRIS

ABC Finance provides financial services to customers and employs around 2,500 staff. The organization is currently facing major changes in its environment, both internally and externally. Externally, factors such as increasing globalization, new and innovative technologies, changing demographics and demands of customers, increasing deregulation, and competition in the industry have forced the firm to be more competitive by reducing costs and offering innovative services—by doing more with less. Internally, there has been a shift over the past few years to a client focus from a product focus, continued growth in the organization resulting in geographical dispersion across the country, and a move toward the delivery of online services. Historically, different functional departments within the firm have rarely collaborated with each other to solve organizational issues. The organization is cautious and consultative in its decision making and could best be described as bureaucratic.

The organization has made a decision to implement a new HRIS along with a new finance system and a new customer relationship management (CRM) system. The existing systems are all more than 10 years old and do not support the current or future environments in which the organization sees itself operating. The existing HRIS will be unsupported by the current vendor in the next six months, and there is an urgent need to implement the new system as soon as possible. The implementation has the support of key senior people in the organization. The HR, finance, and customer relations business units see this implementation as a business project with the software and IT resources as the enabler of better and more effective services.

The organization has two support units—corporate services (HR, finance, operations, CRM) and information services—and three business lines: retail services, commercial services, and investment products. A major organizational restructuring took place only two years ago. The introduction of this structure was largely successful, particularly in the corporate services units. However, there was little emphasis on managing the change issues during restructuring, and, as a result, some of the areas in the business lines are still coming to terms with the change and have become highly suspicious of new programs and initiatives that emanate from corporate services and information services. There is a perception that the "head office" is too concerned with itself and does not take into account the needs of other areas and locations. In the past, employees and managers from various geographic locations have complained that the central administration has done a poor job of including or consulting them when decisions are being considered.

The organization includes an HR function and a separate payroll function that reports through to the finance function. HR and payroll currently use the same HRIS. The HR function was, until two years ago, a decentralized function, with many HR services staff reporting through to different business lines. Following the company-wide restructuring, the HR function was predominantly centralized so that the majority of staff now report through to the HR director. Some areas were not centralized and continue reporting to the relevant head of a business unit. After implementation, a new business model may be required to assist with a more complex and integrated system, particularly as the HRIS and the CRM system will share some aspects of the same database.

A major factor affecting the CRM system implementation is that the firm currently does not have staff sufficiently skilled in project management or in implementing a system of this size and complexity. It has looked to external organizations to assist it in implementing the new systems. ABC Finance expects to gain a transfer of skills, knowledge, and methodologies to its own staff for the ongoing maintenance of the production system, so it may manage future upgrades and implementations.

The existing HRIS was poorly documented when it was implemented, and the vendor provided limited documentation. Because of the decentralized history of HR, data were input with various codes and into various fields; that is, there was no consistency in the way data were recorded. It is a well-known fact that the data in the current IS are neither up-to-date nor correct. The HR data in the current system carry little credibility in the company.

Furthermore, the software vendor has advised of an upgrade to its product that is nearing completion. This upgrade will provide for additional functionality that will support the objectives of process efficiency, cost reduction, and the use of the Web and work flow management tools at no extra cost. It is known that the software provider has a history of not delivering new versions on time and that these can sometimes be shipped with "bugs."

The project has a fixed budget. Although there are some contingency funds, it is expected that these will be for emergency issues only, such as unforeseen costs within the existing scope. Although the HRIS/CRM implementation is still some time off, the PM team needs to make a decision soon on the postproduction support model. Previously, each system had its own support team. The team is considering an integrated support model in which staff members are multiskilled in each of the major areas—HR/payroll, finance, and CRM. This model would necessitate another round of company-wide restructuring.

Obviously, ABC Finance has undergone significant change in the past few years, and all staff are feeling some change fatigue. However, there is a significant commitment to managing the change process as part of this project. A change management team has been appointed comprising training and communication staff.

Case Study Questions

1. What PM approaches, techniques, and tools that have been discussed in this chapter can be applied to aid this organization in successfully managing the HRIS project?
2. It is often said that people factors are more important in technical project success than technology. From this perspective, explain the contribution that the HRM department can make to the management of this project.
3. Prepare a list of critical success factors that you think are most important for this project and compare them with the list presented in this chapter.

NOTES

1. For ease of reading, the information technology/information systems (IT/IS) field will be referred to as the IT field in this chapter.

2. Your instructor will be able to help you through the download and use of the software.

REFERENCES

Belardo, S., Ballou, D. P., & Pazer, H. L. (2004). Analysis and design of information systems: A knowledge quality perspective. In K. V. Anderson & M. T. Vendelo (Eds.), *The past and future of information systems* (pp. 43–60). New York: Elsevier.

Bondarouk, T., & Meijerink, J. (2010, August). *Implementation of an HR portal: Results of a qualitative study from a public sector organization.* Paper presented at the annual meeting of the Academy of Management, Montreal.

Browne, G. J., & Rogich, M. B. (2001). An empirical investigation of user requirements elicitation: Comparing the effectiveness of prompting techniques. *Journal of Management Information Systems, 17*(4), 223–249.

Ceriello, V. R., & Freeman, C. (1991). *Human resource management systems: Strategies, tactics, and techniques.* New York: Lexington Books.

Dery, K., Hall, R., & Wiblen, S. (2010, August). *Human resource information systems: Constraining human agency and implications for HR skills.* Paper presented at the annual meeting of the Academy of Management, Montreal.

Dulebohn, J. (2010, August). *Assessing cross-functional teams in ERP/eHR implementation projects.* Paper presented at the annual meeting of the Academy of Management, Montreal.

Ewusi-Mensah, K. (1997). Critical issues in abandoned information systems projects. *Communications of the ACM, 40*(9), 74–80.

Gantt chart. (2011). *Wikipedia: The free encyclopedia.* Retrieved March 7, 2011, from http://en.wikipedia.org/wiki/Gantt_chart

Grant, D., Newell, S., & Kavanagh, M. J. (2010, August). *Realizing the potential of an HRIS: Unintended consequences, human agency, and the HR function.* Symposium presented at the annual meeting of the Academy of Management, Montreal.

Grossman, R. J. (2009). Managing the people who manage the projects. *HR Magazine, 54*(8), 12–16.

Josler, C., & Burger, J. (2005). Project management methodology in human resources management. *College and University Professionals HR Journal, 56*(2), 25–30.

Kavanagh, M. J. (Chair & Presenter). (2001, August). *Planned change of information technology in the NYS probation department.* Professional Development Workshop presented at the annual meeting of the Academy of Management, Washington, DC.

Kavanagh, M. J., Gueutal, H. G., & Tannenbaum, S. I. (1990). *Human resource information systems.* Boston: PWS-Kent.

Kotter, J. P. (1996). *Leading change.* Boston: Harvard Business School Press.

Lance, C. E., Kavanagh, M. J., & Brink, K. E. (2002). Retraining climate as a predictor of retraining success and as a moderator of the relationship between cross-job retraining time estimates and time to proficiency in the new job. *Group & Organization Management, 27,* 294–316.

Lemon, W. F., Bowitz, J., Burn, J., & Hackney, R. (2002). Information systems project failures: A comparative study of two countries. *Journal of Global Management, 10*(2), 28.

Lewin, K. (1951). *Field theory in social science.* New York: Harper & Row.

Luecke, R. (2003). *Managing change and transition.* Boston: Harvard Business School Press.

Nelson, E., & Ramstad, E. (1999, October 29). Trick or treat: Hershey's biggest dud has turned out to be its new technology—at the worst possible time, it can't fill its orders, even as inventory grows—kisses in the air for Kmart. *Wall Street Journal,* p. A1.

O'Brien, J. A., Crnkovic, J., & Belardo, S. (2006). *Management information systems.* New York: McGraw-Hill.

Peltier, J. (2008). Gantt charts in Microsoft EXCEL. *TechTrax, 3*(4), Article 3. Retrieved January 18, 2008, from http://pubs.logicalexpressions.com/Pub0009/LPMArticle.asp?ID=343

Rampton, G. M., Turnbull, I. J., & Doran, J. A. (1999). *Human resources management systems: A practical approach.* Scarborough, ON: Carswell.

Six Sigma. (2010). *Wikipedia: The free encyclopedia.* Retrieved October 26, 2010, from http://en.wikipedia.org/wiki/Six_sigma

Tansley, C. (2010, August). *Project team branding on global human resources information systems projects.* Paper presented at the annual meeting of the Academy of Management, Montreal.

Tracey, B., Tannenbaum, S. I., & Kavanagh, M. J. (1995). Applying trained skills on the job: The importance of the work environment. *Journal of Applied Psychology, 80*, 239–252.

Velada, R., Caetano, A., Michel, J. W., Lyons, B. D., & Kavanagh, M. J. (2007). The effects of training design, individual characteristics, and work environment on transfer of training. *International Journal of Training and Development, 11*(4), 282–295.

Walker, A. J. (1982). *HRIS development: A project team guide to building an effective personnel information system.* New York: Van Nostrand Reinhold.

Wexley, K. N., & Latham, G. P. (2002). *Developing and training human resources in organizations* (3rd ed.). Upper Saddle River, NJ: Prentice Hall.

Wiest, D., & Levy, J. (1969). *A management guide to PERT/CPM.* Englewood Cliffs, NJ: Prentice Hall.

Chapter 9

CHANGE MANAGEMENT

IMPLEMENTATION, INTEGRATION, AND MAINTENANCE OF THE HUMAN RESOURCE INFORMATION SYSTEM

ROMUALD A. STONE

EDITORS' NOTE

Perhaps one of the major obstacles in the use of an HRIS is its implementation. The IT as well as the HR literature is filled with stories about the failure to implement well-designed and well-developed computer technology. This failure has occurred not only in HRIS implementation but also in operations, marketing, and financial computer-based systems. Although technical challenges will always remain in implementing complex human resource information systems, the major challenge to successful implementation is more behavioral than technical. Lack of employee and user involvement has been one of the central problems, causing many of the reported failures. In this chapter, we will examine various theoretical and practical approaches to organizational change and apply them to the problem of implementing a new or re-automated HRIS.

CHAPTER OBJECTIVES

After completing this chapter, you should be able to

- Understand the management of change through the perspectives of various change models
- Understand why HRIS implementation can fail

- Discuss the elements important to successful HRIS implementation
- Discuss the importance of a post-implementation review of the HRIS within the organization
- Discuss the importance of the continual maintenance of the HRIS

HRIS IN ACTION

The Arizona Department of Administration, Human Resources Division manages the largest HR system in Arizona.[1] The division has a customer base that includes more than 9,000 retirees and more than 62,000 active employees from 100 state agencies, boards, and commissions and three state universities. The department administers the state's HR information solution system.

The Human Resources Division initiated a program in 2002 to update its HRIS. The implementation of the new system would proceed in phases. Phase 1 was completed in December 2003, and Phase 2 was to be completed in 2004. According to department estimates, the new system would "produce more than $100 million in cost savings over the next 10 years by automating functions previously performed by administrative staff and [by] reducing turnover due to increased employee satisfaction" (Office of the Auditor General, 2005, p. ii).

The implementation plan failed to meet planned milestones by a wide margin and, in fact, exhausted most of the project budget early into Phase 2. With the loss of funding, the HRIS project staff was reduced from 60 to 18 positions. As a result, some state agencies have had to rely on in-house systems or manual processes to ensure that they have the necessary personnel information-processing capabilities. Compounding this situation was the fact that the implementation team had been slow to address some of the user requests for Phase 1 modifications, some of which were needed to correct programs that did not function properly. The net result of this poor management of the HRIS implementation project was that state agencies had not realized the anticipated efficiency savings from the new system (Office of the Auditor General, 2005).

In 2005, the Human Resources Division was rethinking a new plan to restart the project. Some of the questions that the members of the change leadership team were thinking about included the following: Did they have the right change management competencies to manage this project? What were the likely obstacles that they would face during this next phase of the project—and could they prepare for them in advance? Could they deal with the resistance from some agency managers and users? What mistakes made in the earlier effort could they avoid going forward? And finally, would the division be ready for this new implementation project? What other steps were needed to ensure that the HRIS project was successful?

We hope to answer many of these questions in this chapter.

INTRODUCTION TO THE MANAGEMENT OF CHANGE

It's not the progress I mind, it's the change I don't like.

—Mark Twain

Most mangers face change management issues every day; managing change is now a permanent part of every manager's job. It's clear that HR departments and leaders are in the middle of this climate of seemingly endless change, change that involves not only the functioning of the HR department but also its role within the enterprise and the HR technology used to provide strategic value to the business (Fletcher, 2005).

The evidence is clear that successfully introducing major HRIS into organizations requires an effective blend of good technical and good organizational skills. As Lorenzi and Riley (2000) remind us,

> A "technically best" system can be brought to its knees by people who have low psychological ownership in the system and who vigorously resist its implementation. The leader who knows how to manage the organizational impact of information systems can sharply reduce the behavioral resistance to change, including to new technology, to achieve a more rapid and productive introduction of information technology. (p. 116)

Effective management of change represents a critical core competence that all organizations and HR leaders must master. By better understanding the field of knowledge and competencies related to managing change, HR professionals can better manage change in organizations and reap the rewards that accrue to successful change initiatives. However, as the HRIS literature suggests, the track record of most change initiatives—be they restructuring, introduction of new technology, mergers, **process improvement**, or **reengineering**—is poor. One expert in the field noted that at best only one third of these kinds of initiatives achieve any success at all (Beer & Nohria, 2000). Clearly, learning to manage change effectively is an important managerial competency and competitive advantage.

What Is Change Management?

We define change management as a systematic process of applying the knowledge, tools, and resources needed to effect change in transforming an organization from its current state to some future desired state as defined by its vision (Potts & LaMarsh, 2004, p. 16). And because what happens in an organization is driven by the attitudes and behaviors of the individuals in that organization, change management must also consider altering the behavior patterns of the people within that organization. If the change is planned, the process typically involves the use of a systematic approach that includes both a vision and a plan to ensure that the change activities are on course and on target with respect to cost, time, and expected results. One of the ways in which this process is controlled is by the use of project management, as discussed in Chapter 8.

Consider this example. When the catalog retailer Lillian Vernon Corporation undertook a major transformation of its IT infrastructure, the initial results proved dismal. What happened was that the change management team—which included the president and the chief information officer (CIO)—failed to take change management seriously. In particular, they overlooked the importance of assessing and managing readiness for change. "Employees resisted mightily, avoiding training and blaming new applications for their frustration. . . . The employees had already made up their minds that the system was not going to work, and they didn't want any part of it" (Paul, 2004, p. 80). The net result was that the company fell short of its ambitious timeline for implementation and missed an opportunity to leverage the new information system to improve overall performance. The lesson here is that implementing change goes beyond just installing the physical equipment and system. What Lillian Vernon failed to do was help the employees understand how the new IT system would be better than the current system. Effective communication is critical to the change process, as discussed later in this chapter. Successful change requires a "critical mass of people who are committed, are willing to change and will sustain their new behavior to align with the needs of the change" (Miller, 2004, p. 10).

The Change Management Process: Some Terminology

Organizations are in a constant state of change, which enables them to remain competitive in the marketplace. Some of the forces for change are external, such as the appearance of new technology, while others are internal, for example, downsizing the workforce. Regardless of the reason for change, it must be effectively managed or chaos will exist. The person who is in charge of the change is referred to as a **change agent** or a **change leader**. This change agent can be internal to the organization, for example, the director of HR, or external to the organization, for example, a consultant. The process of managing change typically begins with a gap analysis. A **gap analysis** indicates the differences between the current state of affairs in the organization and the desired future state. Sometimes this analysis is done by senior management or the HRIS project team, in terms of strategy forecasts, and sometimes it is done through questionnaires distributed to employees. After the gap analysis has been completed and plans for the change process have been made, the next stage is to begin the implementation of the change. At this point, a major consideration is the resistance to change from members of the organization. Overcoming this resistance to change is one of the primary aspects of this chapter.

There is a discipline to managing change. Consequently, we know that managing change can be applied to any change initiative with a reasonable expectation of success. We begin by discussing several models of change in the following section.

MODELS OF THE CHANGE PROCESS

In this section, we introduce and describe a general model of the change process and then four specific models of organizational change that have received considerable attention in the change management literature: Lewin's change model, Gleicher's change formula, Nadler's congruence model, and **Kotter's eight-stage change model**. Some of these models are focused at the individual employee or group level, what is referred to as the micro level, while others are focused at the organizational or macro level. These models help draw our attention to the elements important in the successful management of any HRIS implementation project.

Action-Research Model

We begin this section of the chapter with an introduction to a process model of the management of change in organizations. The **action-research model** can best be seen as a general perspective to use in any planned change effort. Examination of the use of any successful change effort approaches will reveal some, if not all, of the components of the action-research model. Thus, although we use the term *model* to describe the prescriptions of action research, it is better viewed as an approach to the management of change. Careful reading of the change management literature reveals that the action-research model appears in, or is part of, most change management projects.

The term *action research* is not new. It can be traced to the work of Collier (1945), of Lewin (1946), and of Lewin's student (Lippitt, 1950), while others (Corey, 1953; French & Bell, 1973) have provided excellent descriptions of the action-research model. Frohman, Sashkin, and Kavanagh (1976) provided the following definition:

> Action-research describes a particular process-model whereby behavioral science knowledge is applied to help a client (usually a group or social system) solve real problems and not incidentally learn the processes involved in problem-solving, while generating further knowledge with respect to the field of applied behavioral science. (p. 130)

The basis of the action-research model is the interaction of managerial or organizational action and research that both evaluates the action taken and provides data for future planning of the change effort. Thus, using this model involves the interlocking of the research processes of data collection, analysis, and evaluation and the management action processes of planning, directing, and implementing change. As seen in Figure 9.1, a cycle in the action-research model would include the following: (1) initial data collection and gap analysis, (2) feedback of results to the HRIS project team, (3) action planning for the next phase of the HRIS project, (4) directing and implementing changes during the next phase, (5) data collection and analysis to evaluate the changes, and (6) feedback of results to the project team and action planning for the HRIS project.

Lewin's Change Model

One of the earliest and key contributions to organizational change is Kurt **Lewin's three-step change model** (see Figure 9.2). Lewin's (1946) framework serves as a general model for understanding planned change. The model has been used to

Figure 9.1 The Action-Research Cycle

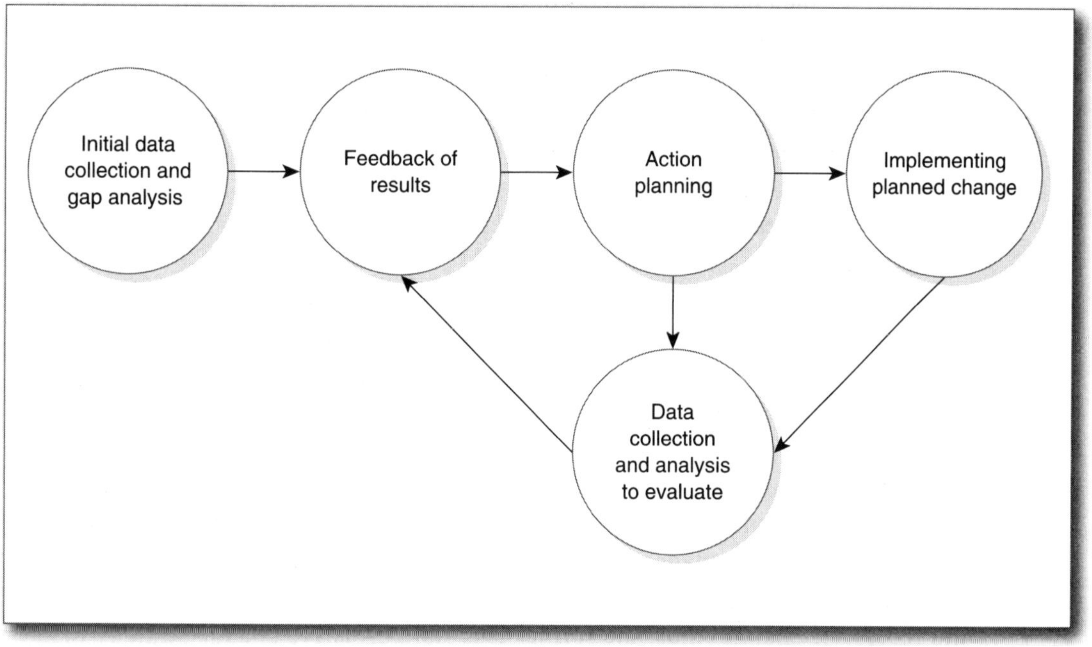

SOURCE: Reprinted with permission from Kavanagh, Gueutal, and Tannenbaum (1990).

Figure 9.2 Lewin's Three-Step Change Model

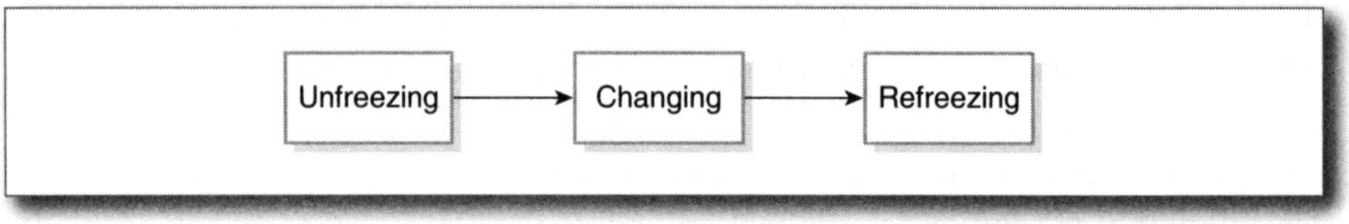

explain how information systems can be implemented more effectively (Benjamin & Levinson, 1993).

Lewin's (1946) change model evolved from his interest in resolving social conflict and in improving the human condition through behavioral change. In his study of group behavior, Lewin argued that behavior was a complex interaction of what the individual brought to the situation and the environment (or *field*, as he called it). We can express this relationship as $B = f(P, E)$, where behavior is defined as a function of the person and the environment. In the main, Lewin believed that the existing condition (or status quo) was maintained by a set of forces affecting the situation. So only by identifying and plotting the potency of these forces could we bring about change.

Lewin's (1946) change model conceived of change in terms of a modification of the forces that stabilize a system's behavior. In particular, he envisioned a dynamic in which there are two sets of opposing forces—those that are focused on maintaining stability and the status quo and those driving change. When we have a balance between these two opposing forces, we have what Lewin called a state of "quasi-stationary equilibrium." To alter that state to enhance the probability of change, we must decrease the forces that oppose the change while simultaneously increasing the forces for change. Conversely, increases in the forces to oppose change and decreases in the forces for change would reduce the probability of change occurring.

To better understand these forces, we can use a change tool called force-field analysis. To develop a force-field analysis, create two columns on a sheet of paper. In one column, list the forces that drive or support a change in an HRIS, for example, and, in the other column, list the forces that will inhibit the change. It is helpful to also assign a relative potency or strength to each force listed. By plotting the forces, we can better understand which forces need to be strengthened or diminished to bring about change. Lewin (1946) suggested that the path of least resistance—that is, modifying those forces maintaining the status quo—would produce less tension and resistance than would increasing the forces for change; thus, the former is a more effective change strategy than the latter.

The key to understanding this approach, at the individual level, is to see change as a profound, dynamic psychological process (Schein, 1996). This psychological process involves painful unlearning and difficult relearning as one cognitively attempts to restructure one's thoughts, perceptions, feelings, and attitudes. Lewin (1946) viewed these three steps as follows.

Unfreezing

At the outset, every change project requires getting people to change their minds and behavior regarding the old way of doing things and to embrace the new state. This means that people need to "see the purpose of the change, agree with it, be supported by rewards and recognition, have the skills to perform the new activities, and see key people modelling the new behavior" (Warhaftig, 2005). To use Lewin's terms, the quasi-stationary equilibrium supported by the complex set of driving and restraining forces needs to be destabilized (unfrozen) before the old way of doing things can be discarded (unlearned) and the new behavior successfully adopted (Burnes, 2004, p. 985). **Unfreezing** is sometimes accomplished through a process of "psychological disconfirmation." By introducing information that shows discrepancies between the behavior desired by organization members and those behaviors currently exhibited, managers can motivate individuals to engage in change activities.

However, the unfreezing process is not that easy to accomplish. Edgar Schein (1996), in his excellent reflection on Lewin's (1946) impact on his own thinking and work, argues that three processes are necessary to ready people for and motivate them to change: (1) disconfirmation of the validity of the status quo, (2) the induction of guilt or survival anxiety, and (3) creating psychological safety (Schein, 1996). Schein suggests that, for any change to occur, some form of dissatisfaction or frustration with the status quo must be presented. People need to know what drives the need for change, why they should change, and where they are headed. What is and is not going to change? What is the business case or rationale? The emotional and motivational needs of those affected by the change also need to be addressed. For example, managers should help people understand what's in it for them if they change. What are the rewards or consequences of changing? Of not changing?

Here, Schein's "survival anxiety" comes into play. Providing a reason for change is not always enough. We also need to convince people that, if they do not change, individual and organizational goals will be frustrated. This process is what Kotter (1996) calls creating a **sense of urgency**. Without a sense of urgency, "people won't give that extra effort . . . they won't make needed sacrifices. Instead they will cling to the status quo and resist initiatives from above" (p. 5).

Psychological safety refers to mitigating the anxiety that people feel whenever they are asked to do something different or new. People are concerned about losing their identities, looking dumb, and losing their effectiveness or self-esteem. This anxiety can be a significant restraining force to change. Without sufficient psychological safety present, change leaders will find the road to change filled with more obstacles than they planned on. We can address psychological safety by addressing employee needs: What must I do differently? What are the new ways I will have to work? How do I learn the new things that I'm going to have to do? Who's going to teach me? Am I capable of making the changes that I will need to make?

Changing/Transition

Whereas unfreezing creates the motivation to change, the changing or transition stage focuses on helping change the behavior of organization members to the new state of affairs. William Bridges (2003) defines this stage as "psychological; it is a three-phase process that people go through as they internalize and come to terms with the details of the new situation that the change brings about" (p. 3). Not getting everyone through the **transition** phase puts the outcome of the change project in jeopardy. The transition phase consists of three key stages: ending → neutral zone → new beginnings (pp. 4–5):

1. *Ending*: "Before you can begin something new, you have to end what used to be. You need to identify who is losing what, expect a reaction, and acknowledge the losses openly. Repeat information about what is changing—it will take time to sink in" (Cameron & Green, 2004, p. 108).
2. *Neutral zone*: The step between the old and new way of doing things is a "neutral zone" where people need to make the psychological adjustments necessary to say goodbye to the old and begin to welcome the new. In the neutral zone, people feel disoriented, motivation falls, and anxiety rises. Consensus may break down as attitudes become polarized.
3. *New beginnings*: This final step is about coming out of the transition and making a new beginning. In this stage, people develop new identities, experience new energy, and discover a new sense of purpose that makes the change begin to work.

As Bridges (2003) reminds us, if change agents

> don't help people through these three steps in the transition process, even the most wonderful training programs often fall flat. The leaders forget endings and neutral zones (Steps 1 and 2); they try to start with the final stage of the transition. And they can't see what went wrong! (p. 6)

Refreezing

This final step seeks to stabilize the organization at a new state of equilibrium and to ensure that the new behaviors are relatively safe from regression (Burnes, 2004, p. 986). **Refreezing** often requires changes in the organization's culture and norms, policies, and practices. We address culture in a later section.

Change Equation Formula

When we initiate an organizational change project, it's important early on to determine how ready people are to accept and implement the change (Burke, 2002, p. 150). Gleicher's **change equation formula**, as modified by Dannemiller and Jacobs (1992), helps us assess this degree of readiness as follows (Beckhard, 1969; Beckhard & Harris, 1987):

$$C = (D \times V \times F) > R,$$

where C is the change, D the dissatisfaction with the status quo, V the vision, F the first steps (feasibility), and R the resistance to change (costs).

If we refer to Lewin's (1946) **force-field analysis** discussed earlier, D, V, and F are all "forces for change," while R represents the "forces against change." Gleicher's change equation formula provides a simple and straightforward perspective that reveals the possibilities and conditions at work in organizational change. Note that all three forces for change must be active to offset the forces against the change, which are usually manifested as resistance to change from organizational members. The change program must address *dissatisfaction* with the present situation, present a clear *vision* of the future and what is possible, and demonstrate knowledge of the *first steps* necessary to reach the vision. If any one of the three is missing, the product of the equation will tend toward zero and *resistance to change* will dominate.

> In sum, this change formula is deceptively simple but extremely useful. It can be brought into play at any point in a change process to analyze how things are going. When the formula is shared with all parties involved in the change, it helps to illuminate what various parties need to do to make progress. (Beckhard & Harris, 1987, p. 104)

Nadler's Congruence Model

According to David Nadler (1998), one of the key steps in understanding and managing change is first to fully understand the dynamics and performance of the organization. Without this understanding of the varied issues affecting performance, successful change may be misdirected by focusing on the symptoms rather than the true causes of a problem. A useful tool that helps change leaders understand the interplay of forces that shape the performance of each organization is **Nadler's congruence model** (p. 41). The model is based on many years of academic research and practical application in a wide range of companies and industries (see Figure 9.3).

There are several benefits in using the congruence model (Mercer Delta Consulting, 2003, pp. 10–12):

1. If we use a computer metaphor, at its core, the model depicts both the "hardware" and the "software" dimensions of an organization. The hardware represents the strategy, work, and formal organization—how the firm is organized to coordinate, communicate, and motivate the workforce in accomplishing its vision and goals. The software side of the model makes up the social dimension of the organization—its people and the informal processes (e.g., shared values) that shape the behavior and performance of an organization's employees.

2. The model helps us understand the dynamics of change by allowing us to predict the impact of change throughout the organizational system. When

Figure 9.3 The Congruence Model: Managing Change

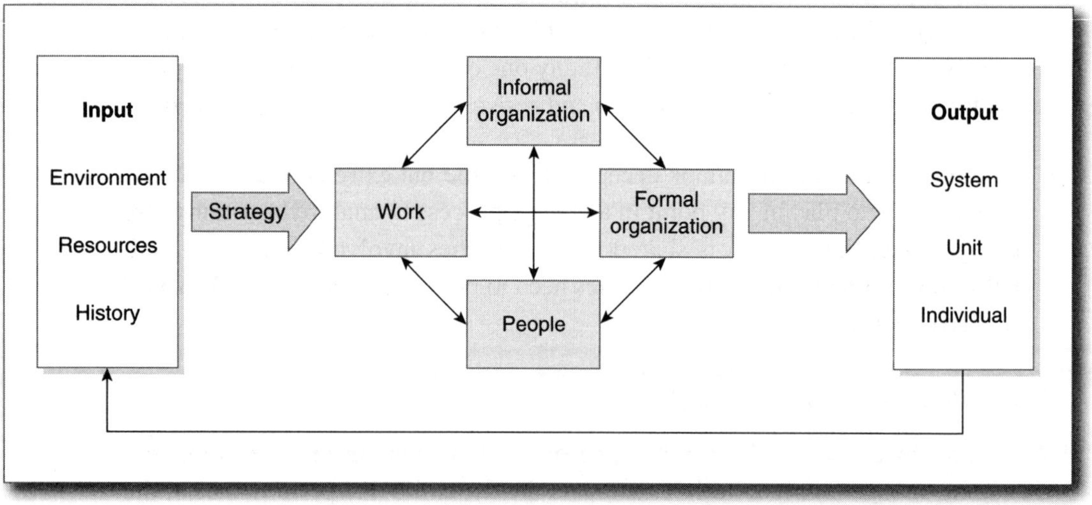

leaders conduct a gap analysis to compare results with expectations, it may trigger a review of strategy and a reassessment of what change is needed to achieve stated goals and objectives. This reevaluation may lead to changes in work and formal organization, after which too many change leaders stop without undertaking the difficult but critical task of reshaping the firm's culture to align it with the new strategy.

3. Finally, the model helps change leaders see organizations not as inflexible, static structures that produce outputs but as organic, dynamic sets of people and processes that are interdependent. It helps us recognize that managing real change is a function of several complex dimensions. It provides a useful "mental model" for understanding organizational problems and for enhancing our ability to pinpoint a solution.

Nadler's congruence model is an organizational performance model that is built on the view that organizations are systems and that only if there is congruence ("fit") between the various organizational subsystems can we expect optimal performance. As reflected in the model, the basic components of any organizational system include the following elements (Nadler, 1998):

- The *input* is taken from both internal and external sources. These include the organization's macro environment, resources, and history.
- The *strategy* of the firm translates management's vision into a set of decisions about how to deploy its resources given the demands, opportunities, and constraints within its operating environment and moderated by its history.
- The *output* reflects the products and services that the organization creates to fulfill its financial and strategic objectives.
- The *operating organization* is at the core of the congruence model. This is the transformation mechanism that takes the strategy, in the context of history, resources, and environment, and converts input into output.

The transformation process of any organization is composed of four components, or subsystems, which all depend on each other (Nadler, 1998, p. 32):

- *The work* is comprised of the actual day-to-day activities carried on by the organization, its departments, and its people. Any change effort must consider the characteristics of the work to be performed, the knowledge and skills required, and the stress and uncertainty that the work involves.

- *The people* who work in an organization and their skills and characteristics form a significant component in organizational transformation. It's important to identify their needs and preferences in terms of the rewards (both intrinsic and extrinsic) that they expect to receive from their work.
- *The formal organization* refers to the structure, systems, and processes in place to organize and coordinate the work in ways to achieve the strategic objectives.
- *The informal organization* consists of all the informal, unwritten guidelines that exert a powerful influence on people's collective and individual behavior. It encompasses the beliefs, values, and norms of the organization (its culture).

This model proposes that effective management of change means paying attention to the alignment of all four components, not just one or two. You can't assume that changing one element will cause the other elements to fall into place (Nadler, 1998, p. 42). Cameron and Green (2004) use an apt metaphor to highlight this important point:

> Imagine tugging only one part of a child's mobile. The whole mobile wobbles and oscillates for a bit, but eventually all the different components settle down to where they were originally. So it is with organizations. They easily revert to the original mode of operation unless you attend to all four components. (p. 104)

If alignment of each of the components—work, people, structure, and culture—with the others is deficient, then performance will suffer. The greater the fit or congruence, the greater will be the organization's ability to manage a change process.

The Nadler model is helpful because it provides a useful framework for understanding the organization as a social and technical system.

> The model is particularly good for pointing out in retrospect why changes did not work, which although psychologically satisfying is not always a productive exercise. It is important to note that this model is problem-focused rather than solution-focused, and lacks any reference to the powerful effects of a guiding vision, or to the need for setting and achieving goals. (Cameron & Green, 2004, p. 107)

Kotter's Process of Leading Change

Kotter's (1996) eight-stage model was developed after studying more than 100 organizations undergoing change. The model offers a process to manage change successfully and avoid the common pitfalls that have beset failed change programs (see Figure 9.4). We can view his approach as a vision for the change process, one that calls attention to its key phases.

The model provides two key lessons, first that the change process goes through a series of phases, *each lasting a considerable period of time,* and, second, that critical mistakes in any of the phases can have a devastating impact on the momentum of the change process.

The Eight-Stage Change Process (Kotter, 1996)

The first four stages focus on the practices associated with "unfreezing" the organization:

1. Establishing a greater sense of urgency
   a. Getting people to examine seriously the competitive realities
   b. Identifying crises, potential crises, or major opportunities
2. Creating the guiding coalition
   a. Putting together a group with enough power to lead the change
   b. Getting the group to work together like a team

Figure 9.4 Kotter's Eight-Stage Change Process

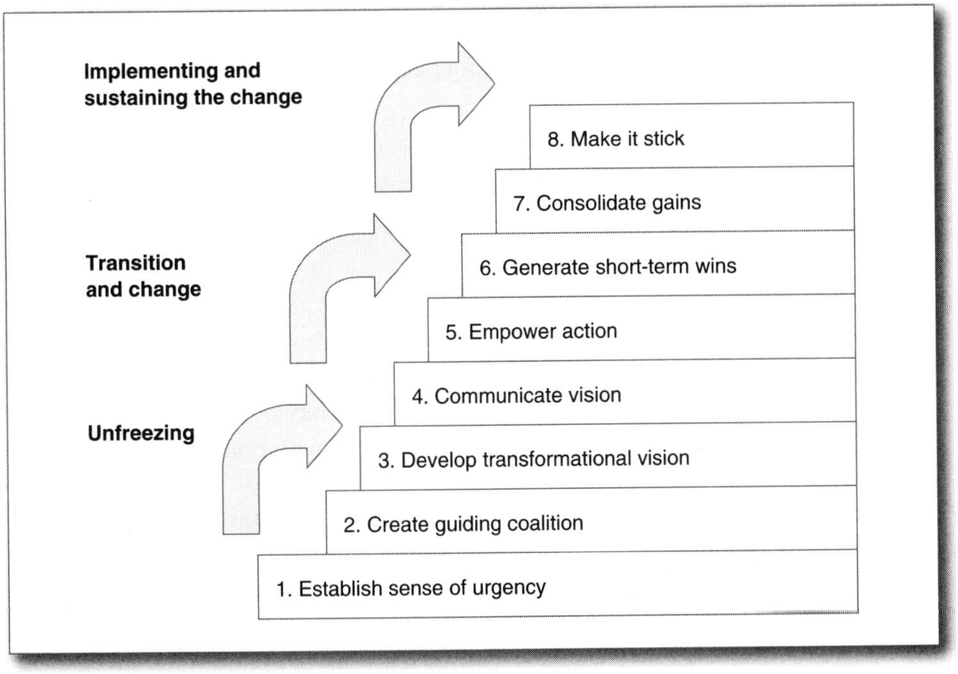

3. Developing a transformational vision and strategy
   a. Creating a vision to help direct the change effort
   b. Developing strategies for achieving that vision
4. Communicating the change vision
   a. Using every vehicle possible to communicate continually the new vision and strategies
   b. Modeling needed behavior by the guiding coalition

The next three stages introduce many new practices ("change/transition"):

5. Empowering a broad base of people to take action
   a. Getting rid of blockers
   b. Changing the systems or structures that seriously undermine the change vision
   c. Encouraging risk taking and nontraditional ideas, activities, and actions
6. Generating short-term wins
   a. Planning for some visible performance improvements
   b. Creating those wins
   c. Visibly recognizing and rewarding people who made the wins possible
7. Consolidating gains and producing even more change
   a. Using increased credibility to change all systems, structures, and policies that don't fit together and don't fit the transformation vision
   b. Hiring, promoting, and developing people who can implement the change vision
   c. Reinvigorating the process with new projects, themes, and change agents

Finally, the last stage is required to ground the changes in the corporate culture ("refreezing") and make them stick:

8. Institutionalizing new approaches in the culture
   a. Creating better performance through customer- and productivity-oriented behavior, more and better leadership, and more effective management
   b. Articulating the connections between new behaviors and firm success
   c. Developing the means to ensure leadership development and succession

The model requires that all the stages must be worked through in order, and completely, to effect change successfully. Skipping even a single step or getting too far ahead without a solid base almost always creates problems. People under pressure to show results will often skip the unfreezing activities (the first four steps). In this case, you rarely establish a solid enough base on which to proceed. Failure to reinforce earlier stages as you move on results in the urgency dissipating or the guiding coalition breaking up. Without the follow-through that takes place in the final step, you may never get to the finish line and make changes stick. It is also important to view the change process as a continuous cycle rather than as a step-by-step progression. More than one step may be activated at any one time.

Next, we turn our attention to the factors that contribute to HRIS implementation failures.

WHY DO SYSTEM FAILURES OCCUR?

Increasingly, the failure to implement information systems successfully has less to do with the hardware or software aspects of the new system and more to do with the skills of the change leader and the people and organizational issues related to the change. Research has identified a number of key factors that contribute to IT system implementation failures (see Figure 9.5). Although no one single factor is the culprit, Lorenzi and Riley (2000) suggest that "a snowball effect is often seen, with a shortcoming in one area leading to subsequent shortcomings in other areas" (p. 117). We have grouped the key causal factors related to HRIS implementation failures into five main categories: leadership, planning, change management, communication, and training (Blanchard, 2007, pp. 203–204; Kandel, 2007; Lorenzi & Riley, 2000).

Leadership

Major change is almost impossible without top leadership support. "Leadership must set the direction, pace, and tone and provide a clear consistent rationale that brings everyone together behind a single mission" (U.S. Government Accountability Office, 2003, p. 2).

Lack of executive support is one of the main reasons that HRIS implementations fail. Without this support, organizations lack the funding, approvals, and leadership necessary to implement, integrate, and maintain the system properly.

Project managers lacking in leadership skills have also contributed to project failure. Those individuals given the responsibility to manage the HRIS project are often very knowledgeable in HR or IT. However, they cannot lead a major change project effectively unless they possess strong **leadership** and communication skills. They must be able to communicate clearly, prioritize projects, make tough decisions, manage people effectively, and navigate the political environment (Kandel, 2007).

Figure 9.5 Reasons for IT System Failure

Leadership	• Lack of executive support • Lack of strong leadership and change management skills in project manager • Lack of recognition for team's efforts • Lack of accountability for implementing the change
Planning	• No clear vision for the change • Failure to define a clear and comprehensive project scope • Lack of a comprehensive project plan • Failure to define fully the functionality of the system • Insufficient project staffing; staff turnover and complacency • Insufficient project funding • Roles and responsibilities not clearly defined or understood by everyone • Failure to meet budget and deadlines • The change leadership team doesn't include early adopters, resisters, or informal leader • Inadequate testing of the system
Change management	• Culture and level of readiness for change are not assessed prior to the start of the project • Change leaders fail to respect the power of the culture to kill the change • No strategies to nurture or grow a new culture • The change isn't piloted, so the organization doesn't learn what's needed to support the change • Organizational systems and other initiatives aren't aligned with the change • End users are not involved in the process • Lack of a plan for user resistance/rejection • Processes are not reengineered
Communication	• Lack of a comprehensive communication plan • Ineffective ongoing communication with all affected stakeholders • Failure to customize communications to different audiences • People leading the change think that announcing the change is the same as implementing it
Training	• Inadequate or poor-quality training • Poor timing of training—too early or too late • People are not enabled or encouraged to build new skills • Lack of ongoing training

Any successful major change initiative must also be driven by a strong and stable project management team. It would take a superhuman individual to lead a successful change initiative by himself or herself. What is needed for successful change is a team of individuals: key executives, department heads, managers, and frontline employees who are committed to the change and who can work together as a team.

Planning

Effective **planning** is essential to change management. Each successful project has a clearly identified project scope and strategy that outline key business requirements and project goals. It is important to keep team members on the same page and working toward the same outcome. Additionally, a clearly defined project scope will prevent "project creep" from occurring—an enlargement of the project as it progresses.

Often, organizations begin HRIS implementation projects without a clear definition of the scope of the project. The project scope must be defined in advance and should identify the project objectives, priorities, goals, and tasks—these serve as the guiding principles for the team throughout the project's life cycle (Kandel, 2007).

Inadequate funding and staffing further contribute to project failure. Organizations often consider the initial start-up costs for an HRIS project but fail to consider fully the costs of the change management process, of ongoing training, and of the support and **maintenance** of new systems. Change leaders must look at the big picture and the resources that will be required to implement and maintain the system successfully.

One key resource relates to adequate staffing to manage the project. Change leaders make the mistake of thinking that employees can implement a new system by working on this implementation part time, while continuing to perform all their regular duties. The time requirements needed to manage a project are often severely underestimated. Although, in smaller organizations, individuals may need to continue with their regular duties, all efforts should be made to have at least some team members dedicated full time to the project. If team members are not fully dedicated, their regular responsibilities will almost always take priority over the project, causing delays and lack of focus.

Change Management

Without question, change management is an ongoing challenge for HR leaders and organizations. Prager and Overholt (1994) argue that a failed effort to implement new technology is always a failure to understand and manage the change process adequately. They indicate that projects often fail not because of technical flaws but because the people in the organization reject them (p. 64). In fact, research shows that the critical factor in achieving rapid and complete adoption of new technology is effective change management (Correll, 2005, p. 12). Unfortunately, too many change initiatives fail to deliver their promised value.

Likewise, a review of the research literature on change suggests that a large percentage of change efforts end in discouraging results. Experts suggest that the figure may be as high as 70% (Mourier & Smith, 2001; Pascale & Millemann, 1997). If only 30% of change efforts are successful, consider then the cost in terms of economic and human resources: "In too many situations the improvements have been disappointing and the carnage has been appalling, with wasted resources and burned-out, scared, or frustrated employees" (Kotter, 1996, p. 4). In a world where the only constant is change, this poor track record is disappointing to say the least, and it suggests that there is considerable room for improvement in successfully managing change.

Eric Abrahamson offers an excellent suggestion to help mitigate the twin problems of forgetting about and perpetuating the failures of past change initiatives. He says that we should not ignore the memory of employees who have been involved in change programs in the past. To this end, we can learn about "whether a proposed change was attempted previously and what its outcome was and why" (Abrahamson, 2004b, p. 4).

Margaret Wheatley (1997) offers an equally compelling insight, which is applicable when organizations consider whether a change effort has been successful. She suggests that change leaders need to ask the following questions:

1. Are people in the organization more committed to being here now than at the beginning of this effort?
2. Do people feel more prepared for the next wave of change?
3. Did we develop capacity [for change] or just stage an event?
4. Do people feel that their creativity and expertise contributed to the changes? (p. 28)

When we pay attention to these kinds of questions as indicators, Wheatley (1997) argues, "we can create organizations [cultures] that know how to respond continuously" to the driving forces in their operating environment. Why? Because we tap what she calls "the intelligence that lives everywhere" in organizations and, in the process, we succeed in engaging people and their capacity to deal with change (p. 28).

In a world where the only constant is change, this poor track record is disappointing to say the least and suggests that there is a lot of room for improvement in managing change successfully.

Given its high potential for failure, we next review some of the key change management issues affecting HRIS implementation.

Communication

Effective change **communication** can make the difference between success and failure of an HRIS implementation project. Employee communication is especially critical when we're "trying to get others to see and do things differently" (Duck, 2001, p. 27).

Armenakis and Harris (2002, p. 169) suggest that change leaders who overlook the importance of communicating a consistent change message and vision fuel some of the negative responses (resistance) encountered in managing change. It is the communication process that starts to unfreeze and predispose people to change (Eccles, 1994, p. 158). As Duck (2001) reminds us,

> If leaders want to change the thinking and actions of others, they must be transparent about their own. If people within the organization don't understand the new thinking or don't agree with it, they will not change their beliefs or make decisions that are aligned with what is desired. (p. 28)

No matter what kind of change initiative an organization's leadership may desire, the change won't be successful without the support and commitment of a majority of its managers and employees. Getting people "unstuck"—that is, getting them to not only embrace the vision but also change their beliefs and thinking to move in the new direction—is a huge communication challenge.

For example, the catalog retailer Lillian Vernon encountered huge problems with its IT transformation project when change leaders failed to communicate effectively to employees why the project was necessary and how it would affect each employee specifically. In discussing the end-user training for the new system, the CIO's comments are particularly poignant:

> Before the classes began, "we should have put everyone in a room and said, Here is how you fit into this new picture." . . . Instead, the project team fell back on blanket statements that everyone's job would be "better." Once rollout began, however, they were angry when their jobs were harder instead. Since most had not taken the training seriously, they did not know how to use the application. And many were uncertain as to how their jobs had changed. "People were blaming the system for everything." (Paul, 2004, p. 84)

Figure 9.6 Common Reasons Change Leaders Don't Communicate

1. ***They don't need to know yet. We'll tell them when the time comes. It'll just upset them now.*** For every week of upset that you avoid by hiding the truth, you gain a month of bitterness and mistrust. Besides, the grapevine already has the news, so don't imagine that your information is a secret.
2. ***They already know. We announced it.*** **OK, you told them, but it didn't sink in.** Threatening information is absorbed remarkably slowly. Say it again. And find different ways to say it and different media (large meetings, one-on-ones, memos, a story in the company paper) to say it.
3. ***I told the supervisors. It's their job to tell the rank and file.*** The supervisors are likely to be in transition themselves, and they may not even sufficiently understand the information to convey it accurately. Maybe they're still in denial. Information is poor, so they may not want to share it yet. Don't assume that information trickles down through the organizational strata reliably or in a timely fashion.
4. ***We don't know the details ourselves, so there's no point in saying anything until everything has been decided.*** In the meantime, people can get more and more frightened and resentful. Much better to say what you do know, say that you don't know more, and tell what kind of schedule exists.

We should recognize too that there are many rationalizations for not communicating. Figure 9.6 highlights some common reasons that change leaders do not communicate (Bridges, 1991, pp. 27–28).

In the Lillian Vernon example, when the CIO began work on the IT transformation project, he expressed his rationalization for not communicating this way:

> We're bringing in vendors who will bring change management expertise to the table. We have capable, gung-ho teams. Giddyap, let's go. . . . In other words, launch the projects and fix problems later. [The CIO] learned that far from being a frill, basic communication creates the underpinning for a successful implementation. The essence of change management . . . is a few well-placed, well-delivered conversations to the right audience. And then you follow up, again and again. (Paul, 2004, p. 86)

The lesson the CIO learned from this experience is that it is crucial for leaders to develop and widely communicate a compelling case for change. Mercer Delta Consulting (2000) suggests that five key elements (see Figure 9.7) make up a persuasive case for change:

Figure 9.7 Defining the Case for Change

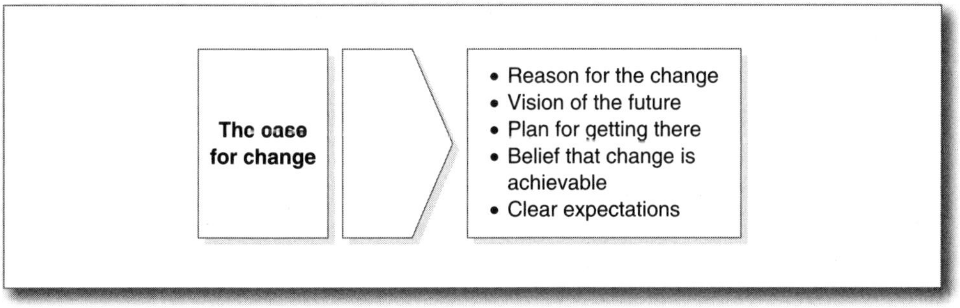

Reason for the change: Answers the question "Why change?" and creates motivation for change. Simply saying that one's job will be better is not sufficient. Employees need to know the business case for the change and how change affects the bottom line.

Vision of the future: Serves as a starting point and anchor for what we do; answers the question "Change to what?" by providing leadership's vision of the new organization; and creates energy and excitement about the future. We address this factor more deeply later in the chapter.

Plan for getting there: Answers the question "How are we going to change?" and mobilizes people in a common direction. Here, we want to provide the big picture—the agenda, key strategies, and implementation plans.

Believe change is achievable: Answers the question "Is this really possible?" and encourages interest, engagement, and optimism.

Clear expectations: Answers the question "What can I expect of you and what is expected of me?" and helps people prepare for the change while reducing their uncertainty.

In sum, communication plays a vital role in the success of change programs. It is difficult to engage everyone based on communication alone, however. Ideally, people must participate in the process from beginning to end. If the sentiment is that the change is imposed from the top, then gaining commitment will be tough.

Training

Ongoing, effective **training** is essential in any change management initiative, particularly when new technology and work processes are involved. Successful companies typically offer training in the early stages of the project to reduce uncertainty about the new technology by providing information about its characteristics and to generate user acceptance (Ruta, 2005, p. 38).

The value of training cannot be underestimated:

> At E&P, the budget for training was cut in the midst of an implementation project. One site was able to do more training with their staff because they had some additional resources they could use. Even though it wasn't much more, there was a difference in how much better the users were able to take advantage of the new system than those from other locations. (Jones & Price, 2004, p. 32)

At the beginning of the project, a training plan should be developed. This plan should include a complete assessment of the current skills and future requirements for all who will be affected by the change. The plan must also include the following:

- What training will be provided
- When training will be provided for implementation team members and user groups
- Who will provide the training—vendors, consultants, staff, or others
- A plan for training new users and addressing turnover issues
- A plan for ongoing training, including advanced skills and refresher training
- A plan for training users in the event of system upgrades or procedural changes
- The resources needed—financial and human—to provide the training

Although some training early in the process is recommended, full training should not be offered until just before the system will be used. One common error is providing too detailed training too early in the learning process. If training is provided too early, users will not retain the material. A person may learn how to perform 10 new tasks on the system. Of those, the user may encounter only 5 in a normal workday, 3 over the next year, and 2 in exceptional circumstances, by which time the training will have been forgotten. Additionally, advanced training should be provided in phases, as users become accustomed to performing routine tasks. On-the-job training, coupled with self-paced e-learning and personalized assistance as required, is a more effective way of ensuring that staff get training that is relevant to their jobs (Dawson & Jones, 2003).

We should not overlook training for employee self-service applications. If training is not provided, employees will be less likely to use and accept the system. Training should also be provided in new employee orientation programs.

> At Chevron, training in self-service is backed up with supplementary material, including online guides and laminated cards to guide employees through the process of scheduling a vacation or changing their address. Employees can refer to them if they run into problems, and in most cases, they find them useful as memory aids in the first weeks following formal training. (Twentyman, 2006, p. 24)

Involving "**power users**" can be an effective training technique. Organizations may use individuals who adapt to the new technology quickly to provide one-on-one on-the-job training to those who do not learn the system as rapidly.

> USWhole used a power user concept for changing users. They identified users in each of the business units that were influential in their units and interested in the new technology and trained them extensively to do transaction processing as well as in how processes were changing and being integrated. As power users shared their knowledge with other users, knowledge about how to use the system began to permeate the organization. (Jones & Price, 2004, p. 29)

ORGANIZATIONAL AND INDIVIDUAL ISSUES IN HRIS IMPLEMENTATION

Cultural Issues

One of the challenges of implementing any new or updated HRIS is getting people to use the technology. Simply introducing the new system does not automatically lead to successful implementation. Successful implementation is more than putting in new technology; it often requires a change in the organization's culture. A wide variety of people and cultural issues play a huge role in any change effort or transformation.

Culture can "not only stop a change effort dead in its tracks, it can also propel it to great heights. Wisdom during organizational change is understanding the power of culture and how to get it to work for you instead of against you" (Senn & Childress, 2000, p. 1). How do you get employees suddenly to change their most basic assumptions about their company? This is the challenge for change leaders—often the need is to create a new organizational culture that is congruent with the realities of its changing environment and that supports the implementation of the new system.

We define **organizational culture** as a complex set of shared beliefs, guiding values, behavioral norms, and basic assumptions acquired over time that shape our thinking and behavior; they are part of the social fabric of the organization—its genetic code. As such, culture drives the organization and guides the behavior of everyone in that organization—how they think, feel, and act. In other words, the culture forms a behavior template.

Not understanding a firm's culture in implementing an HRIS project can be fatal. The change literature is clear: Any change initiative is unlikely to be successful—that is, implemented and sustained—unless there is an appropriate organizational culture in place to support the plan. So it's critical that change leaders fully understand the organization's cultural profile before undertaking the change. How then can we go about getting an accurate picture of an organization's culture so that leaders can transition its current value set to a new value set?

An assessment of a firm's culture (sometimes called a gap analysis) is a useful tool in ensuring that the correct cultural elements are in place and aligned to support the strategy or vision, resources, and systems required to follow the road map to change. For each change initiative, change leaders must align all four elements to ensure lasting transformation. This alignment is conveyed by the arrows in Figure 9.8. All the arrows should be pointing in the same direction—that is, aligned with one another.

Figure 9.8 Elements of Change Aligned

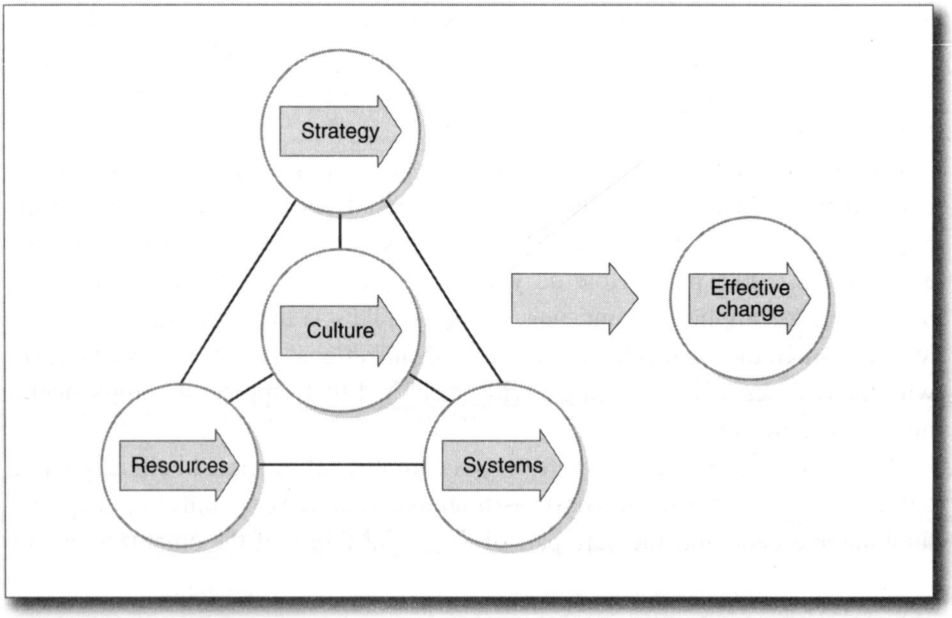

Whenever there is an incongruity between the current culture and the goals of the change initiative, the culture always wins (Conner, 1998, p. 207). For this reason, many change initiatives are ultimately unsuccessful due to lack of the appropriate cultural support needed to get people to embrace and implement the change. So, in effect, what is done to assess the cultural infrastructure is to define the existing organizational culture (i.e., what is the shared mindset of the people within the organization), characterize the target culture needed to support the change, define what gaps exist between the current culture and the desired culture, and then devise a way to bridge that gap.

Perhaps Lou Gerstner (2005), former CEO of IBM, puts this all in perspective with his apposite observation:

> Leading cultural change is not just one of the things you do when you change an enterprise—it's a totality of what you have to work on if you are going to do a true, transformational change. At the end of the day, you do not change an institution, fundamentally altering how it thinks and behaves, without a deep understanding of the cultural bearings that exist. (p. 18)

As we discussed previously, many organizational change initiatives fail to meet planned expectations. When the elements of change are not in alignment, the picture looks more like the one shown in Figure 9.9. This figure portrays an organization with nonaligned elements of change, with its arrows pointing in all sorts of directions. That the arrows are pointing in different directions may reflect the impacts of previous leadership on these dimensions or failure to consider the implication of these factors on executing change. For example, although the strategy for change may reflect the change vision and steps for reaching that vision, the organization's resources could remain inadequate, the organization's systems unchanged, and the organization's behavioral norms fixed, as has been the situation for years. These kinds of misalignments put an HRIS change effort in jeopardy of not achieving the desired outcome. What is required is alignment, getting all the arrows to point in the same direction as the strategy for change.

The elements of change can become misaligned for many reasons, but at least two stand out. The change leaders either don't recognize the need to align the four dimensions, or they do so "only perfunctorily because they don't understand the implication of the required alignment" (Higgins, 2005, p. 7). We should note that not all four elements need to be misaligned to reduce the effectiveness of the change. The misalignment of the culture, for example, is enough in itself to lead to difficulties in successfully executing the transformation.

Culture, although difficult to measure precisely, is a real and very powerful force in organizations. Change leaders can use the information gained through the

Figure 9.9 Nonaligned Elements of Change

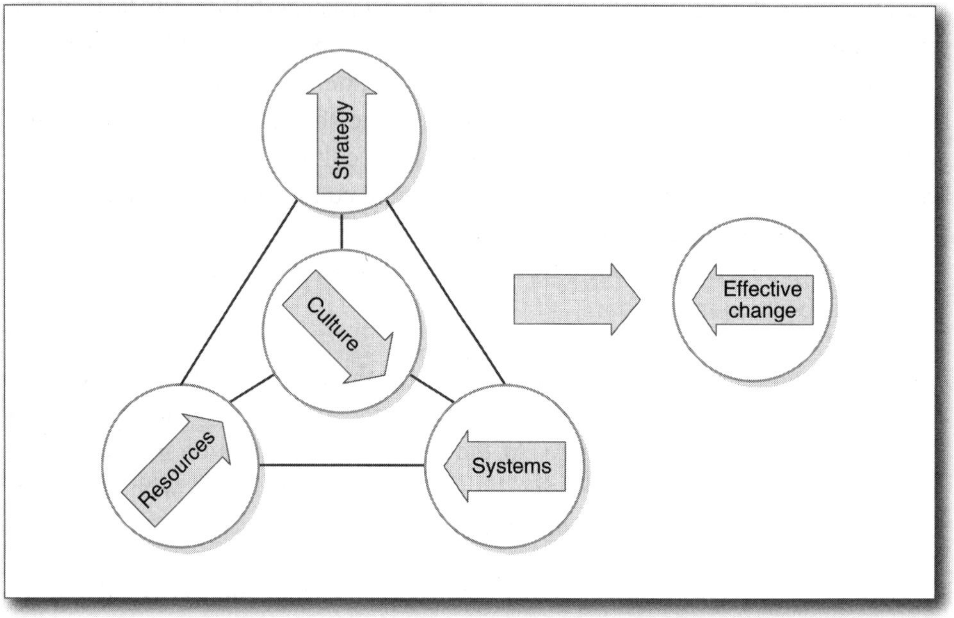

assessment of a firm's culture to help guide each phase of the change process, from the unfreezing phase and determining readiness for change to implementing the transformation and then consolidating and institutionalizing the new state. Through careful planning and using effective change techniques and processes, change leaders can shape and develop organizational cultures that are in alignment with, and supportive of, the desired changes.

Process Reengineering

Implementing the right technology infrastructure and streamlining the business processes that flow through it are essential ingredients for effective organizational change (Dawson & Jones, 2003). One of the reasons organizations do not realize their full return on investment (ROI) from new technology is that they simply automate existing processes rather than using the implementation as an opportunity to reengineer them.

Reengineering business processes is often one of the greatest drivers—but also the greatest challenge—involved in new HR software implementations. Each process, from how payroll staff members enter data to how employees file their expenses, has to be redesigned in order to obtain the full advantages offered by the new technology (Twentyman, 2006, p. 24).

Resistance to Change

At a basic level, when we ask employees to change totally the way they have been working, it's like asking a basketball team to switch to playing golf. People cannot change their behaviors overnight, "get smarter over the weekend, or 'grow' skills they do not have" (Williams, 2003).

Lou Gerstner (2002), former CEO of IBM, aptly noted why organizational change can be so difficult: "Nobody likes change. Whether you are a senior executive or an entry-level employee, change represents uncertainly and, potentially, pain" (p. 77). It's natural for individuals to resist change because they are comfortable with the status quo. Gerstner's observation suggests that it's much easier to hang onto what made you great than to change, which can be costly.

Both groups and individuals resist change. As Mark Twain (1896/2007) wrote, "Habit is habit, and not to be flung out of the window by any man, but coaxed downstairs a step at a time" (p. 31). Indeed, people's habits are hard to change. Michael Beer (1987) captured the essence of why people resist changing old habits:

> Changes usually mean losses of power as responsibility and accountability are shifted; losses in relationships as new patterns of interaction are demanded by new approaches to management; losses in rewards, particularly status, money, and perquisites as power shifts; and losses in identity as the meaning people make of their work lives is threatened by changes in the firm's strategy and allocation of responsibility. (p. 52)
>
> In the end, what people resist is the loss of control over their lives that they fought so long and hard to create. This sense of loss of control often leads to a lot of uncertainty about the future. One way to help people regain control of their work lives is effective two-way communication. People need to understand what is happening, that change is essential. It is through change we learn and grow, although not always without pain. (Handy, 1989, p. 28)

Another barrier to organizational change related to maintaining the status quo is the tendency for many organizations to develop a comfort level based on their current performance. John D. Rockefeller (1973) described the conservatism of large organizations:

> An organization is a system, with a logic of its own, and all the weight of tradition and inertia. The deck is stacked in favor of the tried and proven way of doing things and against the taking of risks and striking out in new directions. (p. 72)

What happens is that management becomes overconfident, complacent, and even a bit arrogant about the organization's success. Managers develop a myopic view of their company as the center of the competitive universe. They rationalize: "Why should we rock the boat or change the formula that has led to our success?" And, in the process of making better widgets, they fail to notice that the competitive landscape and customer preferences are changing. "That very reluctance to change ultimately turns success into failure" (Handy, 2002).

In addition, Kotter (1996) suggests that change initiatives can encounter challenges because of "inwardly focused cultures, a paralyzing bureaucracy, parochial politics, low levels of trust, lack of teamwork, arrogant attitudes, lack of leadership in middle management, and the general fear of the unknown" (p. 20). To manage change effectively, change agents and managers must learn to address these barriers to change—and do it well.

We also know that, if an organization accumulates a series of failed change initiatives, big or small, expensive or relatively inexpensive, employees can become burned out and cynical. When this happens, it's hard to create a feeling of enthusiasm and zeal for the next change. People are no longer motivated, nor do they exhibit the level of commitment and buy-in necessary for any change program to be a success.

The same outcome can result with what Eric Abrahamson (2004a) calls "repetitive-change syndrome," whose symptoms include initiative overload, change-related chaos, and employee anxiety, cynicism, and burnout (pp. 2–3). Initiative overload is like huge waves rolling in off the ocean—people are hit with one change initiative after another. Before one change program can be brought to fruition and institutionalized, there comes another wave. Soon people become so overwhelmed that they lose track of which change initiative they are working on and why. So people can cope with this dilemma, Abrahamson suggests that leaders nurture an organizational culture that is capable of ongoing adaption. Establishing this culture may require what Abrahamson calls "pacing": "alternating periods of change . . . with periods of stability during which a business can recover" (Abrahamson, 2004b, p. 4).

If we go beyond the inertia to change or to preserve the status quo, there are indeed powerful lessons to be taken from understanding why change programs fail. Unfortunately, not many organizations bother to assess why change programs don't succeed. Instead, they try some other change initiative. To paraphrase Samuel Johnson, they regard each new change project as one might a second marriage—the triumph of hope over experience. By recognizing the mistakes to avoid in managing change, we can better focus on the key success factors necessary to increase the probability of success while trying to avoid some of the key pitfalls—one of which is **employee resistance to change**.

The barriers and pitfalls to change notwithstanding, change leaders need to anticipate and take on these challenges and manage them accordingly. It's important to remain sensitive to the fact that every individual may have concerns that can lead him or her to act in a way that undermines the change effort (Baum, 2000, p. 13).

Despite the fact that the new system is being implemented to improve the efficiency and effectiveness of the HR function, fear and resistance to the new system from HR staff will be common and must be anticipated and addressed. HR employees may be concerned about job loss due to the more efficient processes, or they may fear the new roles, responsibilities, and uncertainty that will result from the change. It should be noted that, in general, HR technology doesn't cause a reduction in staff. But it certainly can change the skills that are needed from the people in the HR department (Gunsauley, 1999, p. 23).

When employees outside the HR department are affected by new technology, as is the case with the introduction of manager or employee self-service components, resistance to the change is also a common source of problems in an implementation. These systems represent a change in the relationship between HR and the rest of the organization. Employees may view this change with suspicion—they may feel that HR is eliminating customer service to cut costs. They may feel as though they are being left to fend for themselves. Employees and managers alike may fear the new technology or the responsibility of taking on new roles.

All these issues can be prevented or addressed with proactive, regular communication and effective, ongoing training.

User Acceptance

Mourier and Smith (2001) remind us that, for any change initiative to be successful, the management must cultivate the soil (culture) and provide the nourishment (motivation) needed for the change to grow and develop to fruition. One expert suggests that 20% of employees buy in and tend to support and drive a change from the beginning, another 50% are fence sitters and don't commit, and the remaining 30% tend to take a hard-core stand and oppose the change (Kirschner, 1997). One approach to improving the odds of convincing people that the change is necessary is to help them understand that the vision for the change is headed in the right direction.

For example, people's response to change depends on whether they understand the basic purpose of the change. Why is it necessary? What is the big *picture* of how the end result will look and feel; people need to visualize the change project before they can commit to it in their hearts. What is the step-by-step *plan* for carrying out the change? And what *part* do the employees play in the change? What must they do to support the change? (Bridges, 2003, p. 52). It's important that people understand both emotionally and intellectually why they need to change. Along with addressing the needs of employees, we also need to mobilize the support of key players—both inside and outside the organization—who will be affected by the change.

Ultimately, acceptance of the new technology and new processes represents project success. Although the technical challenges of implementing any system can be great, it is the people "challenges that cannot be overlooked (although often are) during the implementation phase" of an HRIS (Ruta, 2005, p. 36). Organizations cannot simply rely on the strategy of "if you build it, they will come." Change leaders must use appropriate change management techniques to create **user acceptance**—otherwise, they risk failure.

Research on the user acceptance of IT is well developed. The basic framework that underlies this research is depicted in Figure 9.10.

Venkatesh, Morris, Davis, and Davis (2003, p. 427) reviewed the user acceptance literature and, from their study, defined a unified theory of the acceptance and use of technology. Their model contains four main elements, which are considered the prerequisites of user acceptance: effort expectancy, performance expectancy, social norms, and facilitating conditions.

To help us achieve the successful acceptance of an HRIS, we should understand how users will develop and experience the information system (Ruta, 2005, p. 40). User perception related to the ease of use of the HRIS (effort expectancy) is an important determinant of user acceptance. The extent to which a user perceives that the HRIS will enhance his or her job performance (performance expectancy) is considered the strongest predictor of intention. These expectancies are obviously important to consider in the early stages of the implementation of the project. Social influence (subjective norms) is defined as the degree to which users perceive others in the organization to feel that the system is important and, consequently, how they think their behavior as users will be viewed by others. In other

Figure 9.10 Basic HRIS User Acceptance Model

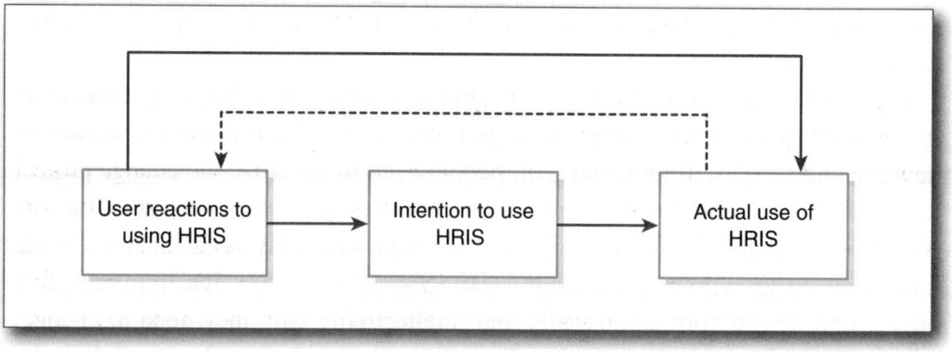

words, users are more likely to accept the HRIS if they think doing so will help them fit in and conform to the behavior of others (Ruta, 2005). Facilitating conditions relate to the extent to which users believe that the organization is committed and resources are in place to support implementation and use of the system.

End users must be involved and feel ownership of the new system. When future users participate in the planning and acceptance testing of a new HRIS, as well as in the process of converting to a new system, their commitment to the project increases. The project team can actively engage others who are not directly involved by inviting them to attend occasional meetings, keeping them informed, asking for feedback, and telling them why decisions were made (Keener, Heard, & Morgan, 2000).

Informal ambassadors or change agents can help influence the rest of the organization and can make or break the acceptance of a new system. Implementation teams should identify influential individuals and those who have shown an interest in the project and engage them in becoming informal ambassadors for the change (Prager & Overholt, 1994, p. 67; Ruta, 2005, p. 46).

It may also be a good idea to identify the most resistant users and involve them right from the beginning to gain their buy-in (Keener & Fletcher, 2004). Otherwise, they may influence others negatively toward the change.

Individuals or departments may use the new technology but not to its full capacity. Research indicates that up to 70% of the functions of new HR systems go untapped because users make the new system do only what the old system did (Roberts, 1998, p. 40). A strong focus on communication, ongoing training, and process reengineering will help prevent this underuse.

Instituting a **phased implementation** plan or an initial pilot program can provide a higher comfort level, allowing some users to "try out" the new system and to share outcomes (hopefully positive) with the remaining users. In more complex or highly challenging implementations, Morgan (2000) recommends starting with small steps to increase user acceptance. Having users start with less critical tasks, such as completing online surveys, viewing HR policies or organizational newsletters, responding to holiday party invitations, or enrolling in United Way campaigns online, can increase their level of comfort before requiring them to perform complex or critical tasks, such as enrolling in benefit plans (Morgan, 2000, p. 22).

One of the major obstacles to gaining user acceptance is user reluctance to try out the new system. This obstacle can be especially challenging when the users are not required to use the system to perform their jobs.

Offering rewards to encourage user participation in new systems can be very effective. By including the use of new technology and revised procedures in performance goals and linking those goals to compensation, we can reinforce the importance of the change. Of course, this tactic is only applicable when the new technology is required for an individual's job. However, when system usage is not required for an individual's job, incentives can still be used. Some examples follow:

- The State of Kentucky offered those who completed an online survey providing feedback on the new system a chance to win a weekend stay at a Kentucky state park (Anheier & Doherty, 2001).
- One organization awarded gift certificates to the first 50 employees who used the system to update their personal information.
- One organization gave employees a $100 bonus for completing their annual benefits enrollment online.

A small investment in rewards such as these can be returned with increased user comfort and acceptance.

Research clearly shows that acceptance is improved if information is clearly communicated, if users are involved in the process, and if ongoing training is provided. Not everyone will accept the changes at the same time. User acceptance can be influenced by culture and demographics. Younger employees may accept the new technology more quickly because of their higher comfort level with technology and personal computers (Morgan, 2000, p. 20). Those who have been working in the same capacity or who have been using the former system and processes for an extended period of time may take more time to accept the change than someone who has only recently joined the company.

The Importance of HRIS Integration

HRIS should be integrated with other systems within HR and the rest of the organization when appropriate to obtain maximum benefits and efficiencies. Systems should certainly be integrated with payroll and automated time systems. Benefits enrollment systems and other similar vendor software can also be integrated to avoid duplicate entries and prevent errors. Ideally, other corporate functions, such as financial systems, should be integrated for an efficient flow of information.

Practical Approaches to Implementation

Implementation can be completed all at once or in phases. The advantage of implementing all at once is that everyone is moved at one time. The disadvantage is that there is no test period, and resources are more strained. Phased implementations or pilot programs allow for testing of the system with smaller groups so that unforeseen problems can be fixed and success can be communicated and celebrated.

Nestlé USA, the California-based food company, opted for a gradual, phased-in implementation rather than going live all at once. The company started by implementing a new payroll system—first to a small group of 600 employees, then to other business units over time. "'By focusing on a small group first, we were able to address many of our interface and reporting needs upfront with a small population of employees. . . . Demonstrating successes and celebrating them along the way reinforced senior management's decision to fund the project, and motivated our team to keep going,' says [Mike] Benson [director of HRIS]" (Henson, 1996, p. 5).

When new systems are introduced, running the old system in parallel for a period of time allows you to test the capabilities of the new system and compare the results achieved by each system. It also allows for a backup in the event of problems with the new system—which, it is hoped, would not occur at this point. The downside of this tactic is that there will be duplicate work performed during this phase. A potential problem to watch out for in this scenario is user resistance causing users to remain with the old system and resist using the new one as long as the old system remains available.

Post-implementation

The HRIS implementation process does not end when the system goes live, as there will be ongoing revisions and improvements to the system. Some of these revisions may include enhancements (upgrades or add-ons), system abandonments, and vendor switches, both at an early or late stage of the **post-implementation review** phase. Further, as Nicolaou and Bhattacharya (2006) contend, "ERP [enterprise resource planning] implementations are often modular in nature and thus may yield productivity gains or losses as a result of discrete changes that might be initiated after the initial system implementation" (p. 18).

Research shows that the immediate aftereffects of ERP implementations often lead to severe systems integration problems; misalignment between people, processes, and technology; and overall change management issues during and shortly after the implementation process. However, these performance and productivity problems may be short-lived (Nicolaou, 2004b). In the long run, performance gains can be obtained through subsequent changes, such as job redefinition, the establishment of new procedures, the fine-tuning of the software, and harnessing the new streams of information created by the ERP system. Therefore, the full effects of the ERP adoptions do not surface until after a considerable time lag.

When we review the performance of a system that has been recently implemented, some of the critical dimensions to be considered are overall project scope and planning, the driving principles for project development, the effectiveness of misfit resolution strategies, attained benefits, and user and organizational learning (Nicolaou, 2004a).

Maintenance of the HRIS

The ongoing task of operating and maintaining the new system is often forgotten. Turnbull (2005) reminds us that revised business practices and processes require new organizational structures with new roles and budgets. HR should have a process in place to audit, review, and reconsider business processes (p. 13).

Organizations must determine who will be responsible for the ongoing maintenance of the system. This task includes performing system updates and upgrades and adjusting for legislative changes and changes in organizational procedures. Although in some smaller organizations, HR professionals take on HRIS responsibilities along with their other tasks, larger organizations will have one or more dedicated HRIS professionals to manage the system. Typically, this function will report to the HR department.

Organizations should establish a help desk to assist end users with system questions, problems, and report-writing issues. A best practice is to have the project team provide support for a period of time, allowing team members to track issues. Project team support is often followed by the creation of an HR system help desk that coordinates with the IT technical help desk as required. Generally, most issues that arise are functional rather than technical, and these are best handled by the HR staff (Anheier & Doherty, 2001; Turnbull, 2005).

Turnbull (2005) reminds us that we need to ensure that the system is being used correctly and to validate the integrity of the new data. The issue of data security and privacy must be addressed also, and policies and procedures regarding electronic data should be established and maintained, along with scheduled audits.

User satisfaction and acceptance must be measured to evaluate the effectiveness of the project and identify any areas for correction. Although user feedback can help us get a picture of satisfaction levels, actual usage has been shown to be a more precise measure of both satisfaction and acceptance (Ruta, 2005, p. 38). Organizations can use these results to diagnose problem areas and provide additional information or training to users. If there is a trend of light usage in one department compared with other departments, the reasons can be identified and addressed (Anheier & Doherty, 2001).

Finally, ongoing refresher training and advanced user training must be planned to reinforce the new system and processes as well as expand the knowledge of the users. User group meetings can be a good informal way of providing training support and information sharing.

SUMMARY

Perhaps one of the major obstacles in the use of an HRIS is its implementation. While technical challenges will always remain in implementing complex human resource information systems, the major challenge to successful implementation is more behavioral than technical.

The evidence is clear that successfully introducing a major HRIS into an organization requires the effective blend of good technical and good organizational skills. Effective management of change represents a critical core competence that all organizations and HR leaders must master. By better understanding the field of knowledge and competencies related to managing change, HR professionals can better manage change in organizations and reap the rewards that accrue to successful change initiatives.

Change management is a process by which an organization moves from its current state to some future desired state as defined by its vision. In this chapter, we introduced and described a general model of the change process and then four specific models of organizational change that have received considerable attention in the change management literature: Lewin's change model, Gleicher's change equation formula, Nadler's congruence model, and Kotter's eight-stage change model. Some of these models are focused at the individual employee or group level, which is referred to as the micro level, while others are focused at the organizational or macro level. These models help draw our attention to the elements important in successful managing of any HRIS implementation project.

Increasingly, the failure to implement information systems successfully has less to do with the hardware or software aspects of the new system and more to do with the skills of the change leader and with the people and organizational issues related to the change. Research has identified a number of key factors that contribute to IT system implementation failures, including lack of leadership, communication, planning, change management, and training.

Process reengineering is a critical component in HRIS implementation. One of the reasons organizations do not realize their full ROI from new technology is that they simply automate existing processes rather than using the implementation as an opportunity to reengineer them.

Finally, change leaders must prepare for the inevitable resistance to change and plan to gain user acceptance. A plan must also be created for ongoing post-implementation review and maintenance of the new system.

KEY TERMS

action-research model

change agent

change equation formula

change leader

communication
employee resistance to change
force-field analysis
gap analysis
Kotter's eight-stage change model
leadership
Lewin's three-step change model
maintenance
Nadler's congruence model
organizational culture
phased implementation
planning
post-implementation review
power users
process improvement
psychological safety
reengineering
refreezing [third step in Lewin's change model]
sense of urgency
training
transition [second step in Lewin's change model]
unfreezing [first step in Lewin's change model]
user acceptance

DISCUSSION QUESTIONS

1. Discuss each of the theoretical change models introduced in this chapter. How can we use them when planning an HRIS implementation to increase our chances of success?
2. Analyze the main reasons for HRIS implementation failure. How can we prevent these from affecting us?
3. Discuss the importance of communication in managing a technology change. What roadblocks might an organization face if it fails to create a good communication plan?
4. If you were asked to develop a training plan for an HRIS implementation, what kinds of things would you include? Why?
5. Discuss the role of culture in HRIS implementation. How might two different organizations with very different cultures approach the same HRIS implementation differently?
6. Create recommendations for an organization that is facing resistance to change from its own HR department. What are some of the likely causes of this resistance? How can they be overcome?
7. Discuss how informal leaders within the organization might be used to increase user acceptance.

CASE STUDY: THE GRANT CORPORATION

The Grant Corporation is a financial services firm based in Chicago, Illinois. Its revenue exceeded $1 billion last year, producing a net income of $530 million. It has just over 1,000 employees. Although the organization has been in business for almost 10 years, it has experienced rapid expansion in the past 2 years due to tremendous business growth and a merger with the Enelrad Group, another local firm. Managers have had difficulty keeping up with this growth, especially in the HR department, which has been stretched thin to keep up with staffing needs and other, mainly administrative, duties.

Six months ago, the CEO, Todd Jackson, recognized the need to expand the size and functionality of the HR department and hired Julia Woodland to be its director, reporting directly to him. This was a newly created position, and its incumbent would replace the HR administrator, who had previously reported to the VP of Finance and who decided to retire when the new HR position was announced.

When Woodland was hired, Jackson told her that she would have "full reign" to create a more strategically focused HR department that would be better equipped to handle the organization's needs. She had had quite a bit of experience at her previous company and was eager to take on the task.

Although the organization used advanced technology for its business applications, HR was still using a basic payroll processing software program and Excel spreadsheets to track various categories of employee information, including personal data, benefits enrollments, performance evaluation schedules, and compensation. All payroll and benefit information was manually entered into these respective systems, and much of the information had to be entered into multiple spreadsheets when there was a change. The department could not keep up with the information needs—new hires were getting paid incorrectly, or not at all. Benefits enrollments were delayed or contained mistakes, and performance evaluations and pay raises were late. The printed employee handbook, benefits binder, and orientation materials were in serious need of updating. In addition, the company had 16 open positions and stacks of resumes everywhere. It was no wonder that the HR administrator had decided to retire!

Julia Woodland spent long hours trying to determine what she could do to address the immediate and long-term concerns of her new department. She brought in a temporary employee to help her staff file, process paperwork, and enter data. She focused on hiring two higher-level HR representatives and a payroll clerk. She turned to a staffing agency to help the firm identify candidates for open positions, including those in HR. Finally, she proposed the purchase of an integrated payroll/HRIS that was capable of integrating with the finance department's system as well as with the organization's benefit and 401(k) providers' systems. The proposed software solution also offered the option of a Web-based employee portal, which would allow employees to view information online and change their personal data. Jackson responded favorably and told her to "go ahead and do whatever she needed to do to fix the mess." The next day, Woodland contracted with the HRIS provider.

Woodland spent the next week meeting with her new HRIS vendor representative to discuss the installation and implementation of the system. Because she was so overwhelmed and wanted to get the new system in as quickly as possible, she didn't have time to discuss the project with her staff right away, but she knew that employees would be excited about the new system and the opportunities it would open up for them as the burden of administrative tasks eased. She closed her door during the meetings, so participants could concentrate. She wanted to be able to implement the system by January 1, so that the company's year-end payroll data were accurate and managers could track other data on an annual basis with a full year of data. Since she had been through the process in the past and was familiar with such systems, she figured that she could manage the implementation with the help of IT and her staff as needed. She would make all key decisions to move the project along and meet her deadline.

The current HR staff consisted of an HR assistant and two generalists who seemed to function as clerks and recruiters. They had all been hired at the same time more than 5 years ago, when the HR administrator was the sole member of the department. They were very proud of how they had worked so hard together to build HR and keep up with the increasing demand. They were just getting used to working with Woodland but thought that she was very nice and had high hopes for the improvements and new strategic focus that she would help them implement.

Day by day, the staff watched the vendor representative come and go, along with a parade of candidates sent over by the staffing agency to apply for the new HR positions. They soon began to wonder about all the changes that their new boss was making and what these changes would mean for them. They started making assumptions that had them very concerned.

Woodland contacted the IT director to tell him about the project. He expressed concern over the ability of the server to handle the new system and wondered how they would address firewall issues with the portal. Furthermore, all his staff members were tied up with a critical upgrade to the customer service system, which had caused more than its share of problems. He demanded to know why he and his staff had not been involved sooner and told her that it would be unlikely that they would be able to participate in the implementation or help her meet her deadline. Upset, she called Todd Jackson, who advised her not to worry about it—he would tell them to get it done.

When she contacted Finance to obtain information that the HRIS vendor needed to link the HRIS to that department's system, the finance manager was more than willing to help—but she did not know where to get the system information from and did not understand how the information would flow from one system to another. She asked why they couldn't just keep the systems separate and enter the necessary data into the finance system from reports provided by HR. "That's the way we've always done it," she said. "It doesn't take long, and it will be much simpler that way."

In the meantime, morale was declining in HR. Whenever Woodland asked HR employees for information about payroll or their Excel spreadsheets, they seemed uneasy and never provided her with exactly what she was looking for. She didn't understand their antiquated forms or their backward processes but decided she could fix those after the new system was in. Also, it felt like the rest of the company was suddenly treating her differently. They had all made her feel so welcome six months ago when she came on board. Now, employees approached her with caution, and managers always seemed abrupt.

Julia Woodland began to wonder if this was the right role for her. Why were things so difficult? She thought that everyone would be thrilled about the new system and its efficiencies and would be eager to help. Was it her problem or theirs?

She thought that perhaps people didn't realize the impact she was making in the organization. She decided to make an announcement about the exciting new system that would help make things more effective and efficient in HR and help the employees simplify their lives as well. She sent out a company-wide e-mail announcing the new payroll/HRIS and outlining its ability to interface with other systems and its Web-portal capabilities. To her disappointment, no one seemed to understand the significance or even pay attention. A few employees asked her if their paychecks would be delayed as a result.

She wondered how she would ever get through this project and what she needed to do to get everyone on board.

Case Study Questions

1. Overall, what did Julia Woodland do right? What could she have done differently?
2. Were the correct people involved in the process? Whom would you have included and why?
3. What errors did Woodland make with her own staff? What impact might these errors have had on the success of the implementation? What should have been done?
4. Discuss the cultural issues involved in this case. Are there things Julia Woodland should have taken into consideration prior to starting the implementation? Why are they important?
5. If you were in Julia Woodland's position, what would you include in your communication plan for the implementation?

6. How can training be used in this case to make the implementation more successful?
7. How can the Grant Corporation increase user acceptance of the system?
8. Discuss the potential benefits of process reengineering in this implementation. What impact might it have had?
9. After the implementation, what steps should the HR department take to ensure proper maintenance and support of the system?
10. What can Julia Woodland do now to "get everyone on board" and increase the likelihood that this implementation will be successful?

NOTE

1. See Arizona Department of Administration, Human Resources Division Web site, www.hr.state.az.us.

REFERENCES

Abrahamson, E. (2004a). *Change without pain.* Boston: Harvard Business School Press.

Abrahamson, E. (2004b, February). The road to better recombination. *Harvard Management Update, 9*(2), 1–4.

Anheier, N., & Doherty, S. (2001, October). *Employee self-service: Tips to ensure a successful implementation* (SHRM HRTX Forum Library). Retrieved March 3, 2007, from www.shrm.org/hrtx/library_published/IC/CMS_000210.asp

Armenakis, A. A., & Harris, S. G. (2002). Crafting a change message to create transformational readiness. *Journal of Organizational Change Management, 15*(2), 169–183.

Baum, D. (2000). *Lightning in a bottle.* Chicago: Dearborn.

Beckhard, R. (1969). *Organization development: Strategies and models.* Reading, MA: Addison-Wesley.

Beckhard, R., & Harris, R. (1987). *Organizational transitions: Managing complex change* (2nd ed.). Reading, MA: Addison-Wesley.

Beer, M. (1987). Revitalizing organizations: Change process and emergent model. *Academy of Management Executive, 1*(1), 51–55.

Beer, M., & Nohria, N. (2000). Resolving the tension between theories E and O of change. In M. Beer & N. Nohria (Eds.), *Breaking the code of change* (pp. 1–33). Boston: Harvard Business School Press.

Benjamin, R., & Levinson, E. (1993, Summer). A framework for managing IT-enabled change. *Sloan Management Review, 34*(4), 23–33.

Blanchard, K. (2007). *Leading at a higher level.* Upper Saddle River, NJ: Prentice Hall.

Bridges, W. (1991). *Managing transitions: Making the most of change.* Reading, MA: Addison-Wesley.

Bridges, W. (2003). *Managing transitions* (2nd ed.). Cambridge, MA: Perseus Books.

Burke, W. W. (2002). *Organizational change.* Thousand Oaks, CA: Sage.

Burnes, B. (2004). Kurt Lewin and the planned approach to change: A re-appraisal. *Journal of Management Studies, 41*(6), 977–1002.

Cameron, E., & Green, M. (2004). *Making sense of change.* London: Kogan Page.

Collier, J. (1945). United States Indian administration as a laboratory of ethnic relations. *Social Research, 12,* 275–276.

Conner, D. R. (1998). *Leading at the edge of chaos: How to create the nimble organization.* New York: Wiley.

Corey, S. M. (1953). *Action research to improve school practices.* New York: Columbia University, Teachers College, Bureau of Publications.

Correll, B. (2005, February/March). Change management: Using the right techniques and technologies to ensure success. *IHRIM.link, 10*(1), 12.

Dannemiller, K. D., & Jacobs, R. W. (1992). Changing the way organizations change: A revolution of common sense. *The Journal of Applied Behavioral Science, 28*(4), 480–498.

Dawson, M. J., & Jones, M. L. (2003). Human change management: Herding cats. In PriceWaterhouseCoopers (Ed.), *Risky business: The art and science of risk management* (pp. 21–25). New York: Author.

Duck, J. D. (2001). *The change monster.* New York: Crown Business.

Eccles, T. (1994). *Succeeding with change.* London: McGraw-Hill.

Fletcher, P. A. K. (2005). Personnel administration to business-driven human capital management. In H. G. Gueutal & D. L. Stone (Eds.), *The brave new world of eHR* (pp. 1–21). San Francisco: Jossey-Bass.

French, W. L., & Bell, C. H., Jr. (1973). *Organization development.* Englewood Cliffs, NJ: Prentice Hall.

Frohman, M. A., Sashkin, M., & Kavanagh, M. J. (1976). Action-research as an organization development approach. *Organization and Administrative Sciences, 7,* 129–161.

Gerstner, L. V. (2002). *Who says elephants can't dance? Inside IBM's historic turnaround.* New York: HarperCollins.

Gerstner, L. V. (2005). Lou Gerstner on change. *Leadership Excellence, 22*(6), 18.

Gunsauley, C. (1999). Losing sight of human mission can trigger new systems failure. *Employee Benefit News, 13*(8).

Handy, C. (1989). *The age of unreason.* Boston: Harvard Business School Press.

Handy, C. (2002, Spring). Elephants and fleas: Is your organization prepared for change? *Leader to Leader, 24.* Retrieved November 9, 2004, from www.leadertoleader.org/knowledgecenter/journal.aspx?ArticleID=119

Henson, R. (1996, November). HRIMS for dummies: A practical guide to technology implementation in human resource information management system. *HR Focus, 73*(11), 3–5.

Higgins, J. M. (2005, March). The eight S's of successful strategy execution. *Journal of Change Management, 5*(1), 3–13.

Jones, M., & Price, R. L. (2004). Organizational knowledge sharing in ERP implementation: Lessons from industry. *Journal of Organizational and End User Computing, 16*(1), 21–40.

Kandel, A. (2007). *The eight fatal flaws of HR system implementations and how to avoid them* (SHRM HRTX Forum Library). Retrieved March 14, 2007, from www.shrm.org/hrtx/library_published/nonIC/CMS_006586.asp

Kavanagh, M. J., Gueutal, H. G., & Tannenbaum, S. I. (1990). *Human resource information systems.* Boston: PWS-Kent.

Keener, D., & Fletcher, R. (2004, January). *Good planning, realistic scope and executive sponsorship important in HRIS projects* (HRTX Library). Retrieved from www.shrm.org/hrtx/library_published/nonIC/CMS_006631.asp

Keener, D., Heard, D., & Morgan, M. (2000, February). *Implementing human resources system: Lessons learned* (SHRM White Paper). Alexandria, VA: Society for Human Resource Management.

Kirschner, E. M. (1997, November 3). Managers for the millennium: In times of change, managers should forget noisemakers and focus on fence-sitters [Sidebar]. *Chemical and Engineering News, 75*(44), 44–48. Retrieved October 30, 2004, from http://pubs.acs.org/hotartcl/cenear/971103/change.html.

Kotter, J. P. (1996). *Leading change.* Boston: Harvard Business School Press.

Lewin, K. (1946). Action research and minority problems. *Journal of Social Issues, 2,* 34–46.

Lippitt, R. (1950, September). *Value-judgment problems of the social scientist participating in action-research.* Paper presented at the annual meeting of the American Psychological Association.

Lorenzi, N. M., & Riley, R. T. (2000). Managing change: An overview. *Journal of the American Medical Informatics Association, 7*(2), 116–124.

Mercer Delta Consulting. (2000). *Transition leadership: A guide to leading change initiatives.* Retrieved October 6, 2005, from www.biasca.com/archivos/for_downloading/management_surveys/Mgmt_Change_and_TransitionLeadership.pdf

Mercer Delta Consulting. (2003). *The congruence model.* Retrieved February 26, 2007, from www.mercerdelta.com/organizational_consulting/help_change_metrics.html

Miller, D. (2004). Building sustainable change capability. *Industrial and Commercial Training, 36*(1), 9–12.

Morgan, L. (2000). Technology changing the role of human resources. *Workspan, 43*(3), 16–22.

Mourier, P., & Smith, M. (2001). *Conquering organizational change.* Atlanta, GA: CEP Press.

Nadler, D. A. (1998). *Champions of change: How CEOs and their companies are mastering the skills of radical change.* San Francisco: Jossey-Bass.

Nicolaou, A. I. (2004a). ERP systems implementation: Drivers of post-implementation success. In R. Meredith, G. Shanks, D. Arnott, & S. Carlsson (Eds.), *Decision support in an uncertain and complex world: The IFIP TC8/WG8.3 International Conference* (pp. 589–597). Melbourne: Monash University.

Nicolaou, A. I. (2004b). Firm performance effects in relation to the implementation and use of enterprise resource planning systems. *Journal of Information Systems, 18,* 79–105.

Nicolaou, A. I., & Bhattacharya, S. (2006). Organizational performance effects of ERP systems usage: The impact of post-implementation changes. *International Journal of Accounting Information Systems, 7,* 18–35.

Office of the Auditor General. (2005). *Performance audit* (Department of Administration, Report No. 05-02). Retrieved February 28, 2007, from www.auditorgen.state.az.us/Reports/State_Agencies/Agencies/Administration_Department_of/Performance/05–02/ 05–02.pdf

Pascale, R., & Millemann, M. (1997, December). Changing the way we change. *Harvard Business Review, 75*(6), 126–139.

Paul, L. G. (2004, December 1). Time to change. *CIO Magazine, 18*(5), 78–86. Retrieved December 16, 2004, from www.cio.com/archive/120104/change.html

Potts, R., & LaMarsh, J. (2004). *Master change, maximize success.* San Francisco: Chronicle Books.

Prager, K. P., & Overholt, M. H. (1994). How to create a changed organization. *Information Systems Management, 11*(3), 64–70.
Roberts, B. (1998, February). The new HRIS: Good deal or $6 million paperweight? *HR Magazine, 43,* 40–48.
Rockefeller, J. D., III. (1973). *The second American revolution.* New York: HarperCollins.
Ruta, C. (2005). The application of change management theory to HR portal implementation in subsidiaries of multinational corporations. *Human Resource Management, 44*(1), 35–53.
Schein, E. H. (1996). Kurt Lewin's change theory in the field and in the classroom: Notes toward a model of managed learning. *Systems Practice, 9*(1), 27–47.
Senn, L. E., & Childress, J. R. (2000). *Why change initiatives fail: It's the culture dummy!* London: Senn-Delaney Leadership Consulting Group.
Turnbull, I. (2005). After the implementation: Maintenance of your new HR system. *Canadian HR Reporter, 18*(19), 13.
Twain, Mark. (2007). *Personal recollections of Joan of Arc.* Stilwell, KS: Digireads. (Original work published 1896)
Twentyman, J. (2006, May 30). Teams before technology. *Personnel Today,* pp. 24–25.
U.S. Government Accountability Office. (2003, July). *Results-oriented cultures: Implementation steps to assist mergers and organizational transformations* (Publication No. GAO-03-669). Washington, DC: Author. Retrieved January 16, 2007, from http://www.gao.gov/new.items/d03669.pdf
Venkatesh, V., Morris, M. G., Davis, G. B., & Davis, F. D. (2003). User acceptance of information technology: Toward a unified view. *MIS Quarterly, 27*(3), 425–478.
Warhaftig, W. (2005). Flight to the future: Managing change in financial services for sustainable growth. *LIMRA International.* Retrieved March 11, 2007, from www.limra.com/abstracts/abstract.aspx?fid=5184
Wheatley, M. (1997, Summer). Goodbye, command and control. *Leader to Leader, 5.* Retrieved February 2, 2007, from http://www.leadertoleader.org/knowledgecenter/journal.aspx?ArticleID=147
Williams, W. (2003). Why almost all organizational change efforts fail. *CEO Refresher.* Retrieved October 19, 2004, from www.refresher.com/!wwfail.html

Part IV

HRIS Applications

Chapter 10

HR Administration and HRIS

Linda C. Isenhour

EDITORS' NOTE

This chapter begins the examination and discussion of the HRM applications enabled by the successful development and implementation of an HRIS. It is appropriate to begin the applications chapters with an introduction to HR administration. The first nine chapters of this book explained how to build an HRIS, so, in a sense, these chapters were the building blocks for the HRIS "house." Now the filling of the "house" begins. One of the crucial outcomes of following the advice from the first nine chapters is that the employee database, frequently referred to as the basic employee information module (BEIM),[1] will be accurate and up-to-date. This characteristic of the module allows HR professionals to use the software in the HRIS to develop HR programs, such as recruitment and compensation, with confidence. The use of human resource information systems for compliance with government laws and guidelines, which is discussed in this chapter, absolutely requires an accurate and timely database. In addition, benchmark data for use in cost-benefit analyses of HR programs demand accuracy in the BEIM or serious and costly mistakes could be made in decisions to continue or expand an HR program such as e-learning. Finally, as explained in this chapter, the accuracy of the BEIM is doubly important because of the use of the data and results to build the HR balanced scorecard, which is used in assessing strategic alignment with organizational goals.

CHAPTER OBJECTIVES

After completing this chapter, you should be able to

- Understand the basic role of job analysis in human resources, and explain the role of HRIS in supporting job analysis
- Discuss the complexity of HR administration and the advantages of an HRIS over a "paper-and-pencil" HR operation
- Discuss the advantages of having a service-oriented architecture (SOA) for the HRIS
- Differentiate among the four structural approaches to HR administration service delivery (e.g., self-service portals, shared-service centers, human resource outsourcing, and offshoring)
- Discuss the advantages and disadvantages of each of the four structural approaches to HR administration
- Understand how legal compliance with government mandates is an important part of HRIS functionality and how these mandates add to the complexity of an HRIS in both domestic and multinational organizations
- Discuss the various privacy laws, particularly as they relate to an HRIS
- Discuss the elements important to successful measurement of the strategic alignment of the HR balanced scorecard and how this alignment is related to the strategic alignment of an organization

HRIS IN ACTION

At the end of 2009, Procter & Gamble (P&G) had more than 135,000 employees in 80 countries. Identifying common measures, improving employee service, and reducing HR administrative costs continue to be strategic imperatives for this global consumer products company committed to ensuring its principles: "Everyone Valued, Everyone Included, Everyone Performing at Their Peak" (Procter & Gamble, 2011).

The human resource managers at P&G continue to consider a variety of solutions to meet their strategic goals. Should they maintain their decentralized global operation in HRM and use technology such as Internet service portals to improve efficiency, join the burgeoning trend toward shared-services centers (SSCs) to centralize their operations, or investigate outsourcing for selected human resource functions? With so many countries and governmental regulations involved, how can P&G achieve sufficient standardization through HRIS to gain increased savings and still meet its varied responsibilities to those multiple entities? Would its internal customers view the move from decentralized to centralized shared services as meeting their needs? How would such changes be measured from an internal customer satisfaction perspective? Which measures for the various administrative approaches would best align the HR functions with the P&G balanced scorecard strategic goals and objectives?

These are common HRM problems faced by businesses today. This chapter provides a framework to help answer such questions.

INTRODUCTION

Human resource management (HRM) administration deals with the efficient performance of the transactional activities introduced in Chapter 1. Record keeping, updating policy and informational materials for a self-service portal, generating and disseminating internal reports, complying with governmentally mandated external reporting, and administering labor contracts are all examples of HRM administration associated with managing an organization's workforce. Research has shown that approximately 65% to 75% of all HR activities are transactional (Wright, McMahan, Snell, & Gerhart, 1998). Human resource information systems (HRIS) are vital tools in managing these increasingly complex transactional requirements. For this reason, it is absolutely crucial that the employee database, frequently referred to as the **basic employee information module (BEIM)** (Kavanagh, Gueutal, & Tannenbaum, 1990), be carefully constructed so that the information is *accurate and timely* (Kavanagh et al., 1990; Walker, 1982). The BEIM is a record and repository for all relevant employee information and must be created prior to any other modules for programs, such as recruiting and applicant tracking. The approaches and technological techniques described in this chapter ensure that the BEIM, once initially built, remains accurate and up-to-date. Before this module can be developed, though, an analysis of the jobs in the firm must be conducted and specific job descriptions for each position in the organization must be developed.

JOB ANALYSIS

The aim of an effective HR department is to ensure that the organization has the best available people working in the proper jobs at the appropriate time to maximize the organization's productive capacity. To do this, however, the organization must know not only what each job entails but also what **knowledge, skills, and abilities (KSA)** are necessary to perform the job successfully. Job analysis provides the organization with both sorts of information. Specifically, **job analysis** is the process of systematically obtaining information about jobs by determining the duties, tasks, or activities of jobs, from which KSA can be estimated. From this analysis, job descriptions can be developed. **Job descriptions** define the working contract between the employee and the organization. In the United States and other industrialized countries, job descriptions are always entered into evidence for any litigation involving unfair discrimination in hiring, promoting, or terminating employees. Job descriptions are also used for the development of all the HRM programs in organizations, for example, recruitment, selection, training, and performance appraisal programs. Job descriptions are also used in developing compensation structures as well as in employee disciplinary programs and union grievances. In fact, job descriptions are often termed the "heart" of the HRM system. Given the importance of job descriptions, it is *critically important that they be accurate and timely.* In addition, to ensure that the above processes are effectively managed, the HR department should capture and store the results of the job analysis and job descriptions within the HRIS.

Approaches and Techniques

There are a variety of approaches to job analysis that are covered in detail in other sources (Ghorpade,1988); thus, only a general approach to conducting job analyses will be discussed in this chapter. Job analysis involves the following phases or considerations:

1. Identify the sources of information about the job. The best sources are usually job incumbents and their supervisors; however, professional job analysts can be used for newly created or complex jobs. Company records and the Internet, specifically the U.S. Department of Labor's **O*Net database**, are also good sources of information about jobs.

2. Identify the type of job information needed. This information can include tasks, duties, responsibilities, the knowledge required, performance standards, job context, and the equipment used. A determination of what specific information will be used for the analysis of all jobs must be made to maintain consistency across the final job descriptions.

3. Determine the appropriate methods of collecting the job data. Again, there are several techniques, including interviews, questionnaires, observation, and focus groups. The choice of technique or of techniques depends on the number of jobs to be analyzed and the funding available.

4. Finally, consider using one or more of the standardized techniques for conducting job analysis, such as functional job analysis, the **position analysis questionnaire (PAQ)**, task inventory analysis, or the critical incident method (see Ghorpade, 1988).

Regardless of the approach or technique used to analyze the jobs in an organization, it should be emphasized that the outcome must be to obtain accurate and timely job descriptions. Thus, a key question facing HR professionals is, How can technology or an HRIS assist in establishing and maintaining the accuracy of job descriptions?

HRIS Applications

The utilization of technology, especially Web-based job analysis tools, has dramatically increased the availability of information supporting job analysis and the convenience of conducting job analysis. For example, the O*Net database is an online repository of information on 1,000 broad occupations (http://online.onet center.org/), which can be used to help guide in the development of job descriptions. Consider, for example, the occupation of professor. O*Net contains generic descriptions for professors of physics, architecture, sociology, forestry, business—the list goes on (e.g., see http://www.onetonline.org/link/summary/25-1011.00 for the summary description of the position "business teacher, postsecondary"). To ensure that the KSA list is accurate for a specific position in a specific discipline (e.g., human resources) at a specific university, additional information and reviews of this job description would need to be conducted. As another example, HR-Guide.com (http://www.hr-guide.com) provides a simple, free job analysis tool for HR professionals (http://www.hr-software.net/cgi/JobEvaluation.cgi). Finally, there are many different vendors who offer these tools as stand-alone products or components of a larger product offering.

Completing job analysis and deriving job descriptions can be accomplished through online survey techniques. Job analysis questionnaires can be administered online to job incumbents and supervisors, and the resulting job descriptions can be obtained through statistical analyses. This online questionnaire capability can be part of an integrated HRM software package, that is, a package that contains HRM software for a large number of HR programs, or it can be stand-alone software. The position analysis questionnaire, for example, has its own software package (see www.paq.com/?FuseAction=home.main), and the Economic Research Institute (ERI) has **Occupational Assessor® software** (www.erieri.com/index.cfm?fuseaction=EDOT.Main) to aid in completing job analysis.

Maintaining accurate job descriptions can also be aided by an HRIS. Later in this chapter, service-oriented architecture (SOA) with self-service portals for employees (ESS) and managers (MSS) will be discussed. These portals can be used to make sure that job descriptions remain accurate and timely. For example, if a work procedure or new equipment is introduced, it would be easy to request that the persons affected by the change, both employees and supervisors, access their current job descriptions via portals to make any necessary changes to the job descriptions. In addition, it is a good idea to establish an annual review of all job descriptions to maintain their timeliness. If a company requires annual reviews of employee performance and these forms are generated by the HRIS, it would be quite easy to generate a copy of the current job description to accompany each request for a job performance evaluation. The employees and the supervisors could then review the accuracy of the job descriptions and submit any changes necessary through portals. With accurate and timely job descriptions, human resources planning (HRP) is now possible.

THE HRIS ENVIRONMENT AND OTHER ASPECTS OF HR ADMINISTRATION

HRIS can assist managers charged with improving the efficiency of HR administration by reducing costs, enhancing the reliability of reporting, and improving service to internal customers. Information technology facilitates administration in multiple ways. First, an HRIS can help improve data accuracy by reducing the need for multiple inputs, eliminating redundancies in data, and reducing the opportunity for human input errors and associated corrections. In addition, an HRIS, through *relational databases* (see Chapter 2), speeds the process of building reports with simple query capabilities. Moreover, an HRIS, if properly designed for flexibility, can support differences in reporting mandated by global governmental jurisdictions. Finally, a properly designed HRIS permits secure global distribution of data while providing the desired privacy for employee data, facilitating consideration of alternative methods of consolidating and improving services to internal customers (Ceriello, 1991; Gueutal & Stone, 2005; Kavanagh et al., 1990; Osle & Cooper, 2003; Walker, 1982, 1993, 2001).

Administrative issues associated with specific HRM functions as part of the development and implementation of an HRIS have been briefly mentioned in earlier chapters (e.g., recruiting, training, compensating) and will be discussed in more detail in later chapters. However, HR managers face a variety of other administrative requirements in the rapidly evolving HRIS era. The HRM administrative issues highlighted in this chapter include (1) organizational approaches for providing HR in a global economy (i.e., self-service portals, SSCs, outsourcing, offshoring); (2) compliance mandates for record maintenance and report requirements (e.g., **Employer Information Report EEO-1**), which are associated both with government laws in the United States (e.g., **Occupational Safety and Health Act [OSHA]**) and with the labor laws of other countries; and (3) the measurement of HRM contributions to an organization's strategic goals via a balanced scorecard.

HRM ADMINISTRATION AND ORGANIZING APPROACHES

Historically, HR managers operated as adjunct staff to organizations, overseeing the daily transactions associated with hiring, paying, or training employees and reporting on employee issues as required by managers in organizations. As organizations grew more complex, administering these daily transactions also grew more complex. The introduction of mechanization to handle payroll signaled the changing future of HR administration; technology would play an increasingly important role in managing daily employee transactions. Walker (1982, 1993, 2001) detailed chronologically the technological innovations (e.g., transistors, the Internet) and the social changes (e.g., employment regulations and laws, the rise of multinational corporations) that "pushed and pulled" HR administration into the modern era.

Today, computer hardware and the accompanying software packages offer considerable support for daily HR transactions and make it possible to move beyond the limited administrative approaches available to the HR managers of the 1950s (PricewaterhouseCoopers, 2006). HR professionals of that era, whose work involved managing numerous employees charged with collecting, recording, and maintaining thousands of handwritten records, fought annual budget battles to hire more employees to perform the rapidly increasing functions and to secure more filing cabinets to store the increasing numbers of paper records. In contrast, modern HR professionals use technology to more effectively support administrative activities that seek to reduce organizational costs while improving data accuracy, employee productivity, and customer service (Bender, 2001; Ulrich, 1997). Indeed, 92% of the companies worldwide included in the 2009 CedarCrestone HR technology survey indicated the use of some type of HR administrative technology. Moreover, global companies reported that, even with challenging economic conditions, they anticipated growing their technology commitment for strategic human capital talent management, as well as for workforce management, service delivery, and business intelligence. The next section briefly describes the enabling architecture that allows HR administrators to leverage technology.

Service-Oriented Architecture and eXtensible Markup Language

Service-oriented architecture (SOA) "is a paradigm for organizing and utilizing distributed [computing] capabilities that may be under the control of different ownership domains . . . providing a uniform means to offer, discover, interact with, and use capabilities to produce desired [business] effects" (Organization for the

Advancement of Structured Information Systems [OASIS], 2006, p. 8). It is focused on providing overall service that is well defined, self-contained, and context and platform independent; in other words, it is focused on adding value to the organization's business purpose rather than simply adding technological value. In effect, SOA is a collection of internal and external services that can communicate with each other by point-to-point data exchange or through coordination among different services to achieve a business purpose. Figure 10.1 demonstrates the business-driven SOA process (Marks & Bell, 2006).

For example, an HR administration manager in the United States who needs to generate the government-mandated, annual EEO-1 cares little about where the information is stored or which applications, servers, communications technologies, or programming languages are used. Rather, the manager wants easy access to the myriad data necessary to complete the report in a timely manner. SOA focuses on fulfilling that need, moving away from a point-to-point perspective (e.g., HR linked to a single EEO database) to a market perspective of services, reusing data and applications from multiple sources as long as the required service is provided. The

Figure 10.1 SOA Business-Modeling Process

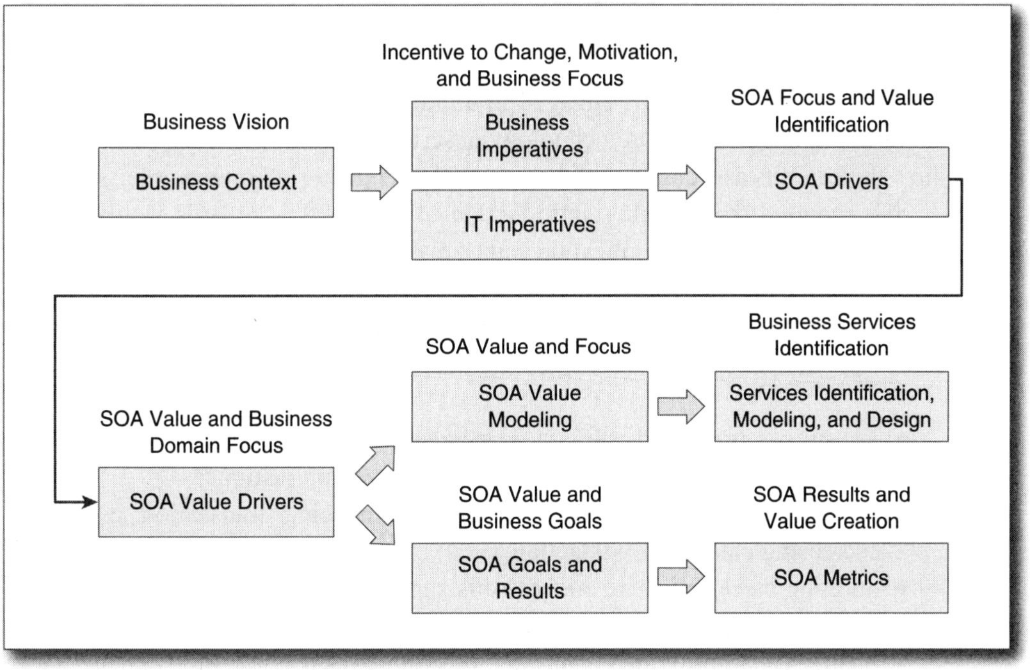

SOURCE: Marks and Bell (2006, chap. 3).

principles of SOA include loose coupling, flexibility, autonomy, standards-based computing, reusability, modularity, and services discoverability and optimization. The architectural benefits of SOA include (Campbell & Mohun, 2007)

- IT consolidation opportunities and standards-based integration, using a standards-based approach to integration for IT systems that are very complex and heterogeneous to reduce both cost and complexity over time;
- faster implementation and change management through reuse, modeling, and composite development; and
- improved alignment of business processes and IT implementation.

SOA is enhanced by eXtensible Markup Language (XML), described in Chapter 3. XML combines text and other information about the text, such as its structure, allowing data sharing across different information systems via the Internet. XML underpins SOA such that SOA is ineffective without it. Specifically, XML improves interface technology through platform independence and protocols, such as security and transactions, previously unavailable in interfaces (Erl, 2005). Platform independence refers to software that does not rely on any special features of any single platform (e.g., Windows, UNIX) or, if it does, handles those special features such that it can deal with multiple platforms.

Advantages of XML-Enhanced SOA

Although HR professionals engaged in administration may not make final decisions about the information technology described previously, they need to recognize the benefits associated with having such architecture. For example, Schwartz (2003) reported that Oracle's introduction of HR-XML standards would reduce the requirement to input applicant resumes manually. Therefore, today's use of HR portals for job application receipt and processing, including resume submission, is related directly to this technology. Thus, HRIS capabilities are leveraged dramatically by SOA and XML such that (Lublinsky, 2007; Walker, 2001)

- security is improved—this is especially important because of the privacy protection issues associated with HR data and applications;
- performance is enhanced—this aids in reducing transaction costs and increasing customer satisfaction;
- auditing capabilities are added—this supports the growing demand to demonstrate compliance with corporate quality and policy mandates;
- change capabilities are enhanced—this improves reaction time to better meet business-driven change requirements; and

- alternative HR administration structures (e.g., self-service portals, SSCs, outsourcing) are facilitated—this encourages HR managers to consider multiple approaches to meeting the HR administration goals of cost reduction and service improvement.

The remainder of this section will focus on the four structural approaches to HR administration facilitated by technology. Each has opened paths to increased efficiency and effectiveness, improved service, and cost controls, possibilities unimagined by HR professionals a decade ago. The four HR administrative approaches—**self-service portals**, **shared-service centers**, **outsourcing**, and **offshoring**—presented in this chapter are shown in Figure 10.2.

- The **self-service portal** is an electronic access point to an organization's HRM information, such as company policies, benefits schedules, an individual's payroll data, or other records; access may be via the organization's computers and intranet or remotely from other locations via the Internet.
- A **shared-service center (SSC)** is a technology-enabled HRM group focused on value creation by providing excellent service to internal customers while reducing costs through increased efficiency and continuous improvement.
- **Human resources outsourcing (HRO)** is the practice of contracting with vendors to perform HR services and activities.
- **Offshoring** is an extension of outsourcing that involves contracting with vendors outside a nation's boundaries to effect additional cost savings or gain other benefits over domestic outsourcing alone.

Figure 10.2 Typical HRM Administration Service Delivery Alternatives

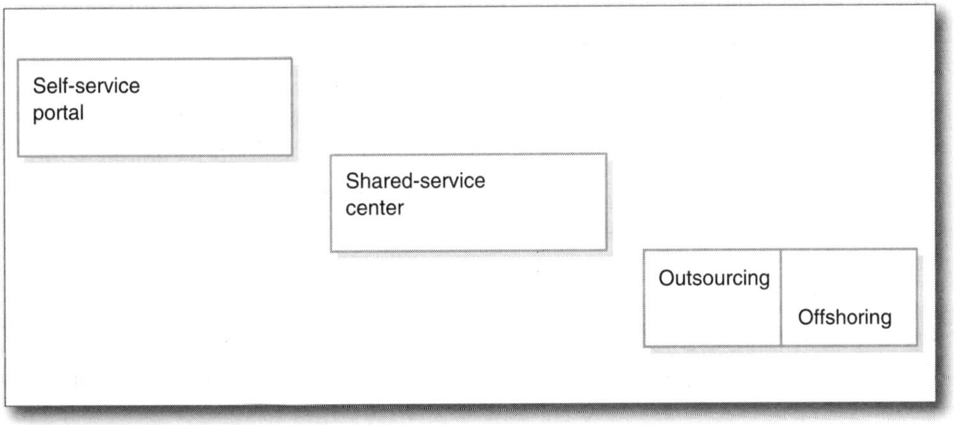

Following a discussion of the theories underpinning these approaches to HR administration, the purpose, advantages, and disadvantages of each will be highlighted. Next, the chapter will examine the different ways in which each alternative approach facilitates the HR administrative reporting mandated by government entities. The chapter concludes with a discussion of how each administrative alternative can be measured to demonstrate the value-added nature of efficient, effective HR administrative functioning in support of an organization's strategic goals.

Theory and HR Administration

The first theory that explains alternative approaches to HR administration is the **resource-based view** of the firm (Barney, 1991, 2001). Barney, in delineating the resource-based view of organizations, argued that organizations are bundles of resources, identified as physical capital, organizational capital, and human capital. Physical capital includes an organization's technology, geographic locations, physical assets (e.g., plants, money), and access to raw material. Organizational capital includes its formal reporting structure; its coordinating, planning, and organizing systems; and its internal and external group relationships. Human capital includes the experience, capabilities, relationships, and insights of individual employees. Taken together, these resources are combined and managed to determine an organization's *opportunity* to win sustainable competitive advantage in the marketplace.

To achieve sustainable competitive advantage, a firm's resources, when compared with those of its competitors, must be valuable, rare, difficult to imitate, and invulnerable to substitutes. Based on this theory, then, it is likely that innovative combinations of technology (physical capital), organizing systems (organizational capital), and strategic individual knowledge, skills, and abilities may serve to give an organization a strategic position in its marketplace. Thus, alternative HR administrative approaches seek to combine HR technology (e.g., HRIS and Internet) with organizing systems (e.g., self-service portals) and strategic HR knowledge, skills, and abilities (e.g., compensation expertise) to leverage a specific firm's competitive position. It is important to note that this theory suggests that *each* firm in an industry is likely to acquire resources such as human talent to support its *unique* combinations based on its strategic choices; it is this unique combination that leads to *sustainable* competitive advantage. *Merely benchmarking or following trends is unlikely to lead to sustainable competitive positioning for a firm!*

An example of the application of this theory can be seen in Wal-Mart. In the 1990s, Wal-Mart gained a substantial competitive advantage with its innovative combination of "just-in-time" supply chain management and proprietary technology. This approach linked each Wal-Mart store directly to its suppliers such that, when an item was sold, the supplier was notified electronically; when a store's predetermined inventory level was reached, the supplier shipped replacement items without any interaction with store managers. This resulted in significant cost savings and improved service with fewer individuals involved. For a time, it appeared that this innovation might lead to a sustainable competitive advantage. However, competitors were able to imitate the management supply chain techniques and even improve on the technology to negate the advantage. Wal-Mart's innovation did lead to an advance for the entire industry but did not provide a sustainable advantage for the firm because the innovation could be imitated. Thus, organizations looking to achieve sustainable competitive advantage are more likely to reach that goal through *strategic and unique* combinations of physical, organizational, and human capital than by relying on any one resource.

A second theory that explains alternative approaches to HR administration is **transaction cost theory** (Coase, 1937; Williamson, 1975). Transaction cost theory suggests that organizations can choose to purchase the goods and services they need in the competitive marketplace or make those goods and services internally. Transaction costs are the expenses associated with an economic transaction, whether internal or external. Managers can compare the "transaction costs" required to purchase products or services, such as contract administration, licenses, and delivery services, from external providers with those incurred in providing the same product or service internally by, for example, using additional personnel, retraining employees, or purchasing hardware and software. Thus, managers can make optimum economic decisions for their organizations. This decision is the classic "make or buy" economic choice facing rational economic actors. Behaving rationally, organizations would make such decisions based on total costs, choosing to "buy" from external providers when total costs were lower and products or services were readily available and choosing to "make" what was needed internally when total costs from external sources were higher or products or services were not readily available. Of course, this example assumes that the "make or buy" benefits of either choice are straightforward and equal. Typically, however, such decisions are more complex; thus, a cost-benefit analysis (CBA; described in Chapter 7) should be completed to determine if the organization should "make or buy." For example, a small business might elect to "buy" HR compensation and payroll services from an external provider rather than decide to "make" its own HR compensation program, which would require purchasing hardware and HRIS software and adding compensation specialists.

An example of the application of this theory can be seen at General Motors (GM). In the 1990s, amid market pressure to reduce costs as competitors increased their market share at GM's expense, GM elected to divest itself of its fully integrated parts manufacturing functions. GM managers found that "transaction costs" would be reduced if the company standardized automobile parts and purchased them from multiple external providers rather than continuing to manufacture them internally. Transaction costs associated with internal parts production were increasing rapidly in terms of employees' wages, salaries, and benefits and the ongoing maintenance of aging production plants. Thus, GM spun off its Delphi unit as an independent company in 1999. Although Delphi continued to sell to GM, GM no longer relied exclusively on the now independent company for parts, helping reduce GM's overall corporate costs. Increasing internal transaction costs coupled with a robust external parts production market determined GM's strategic "make or buy" choice.

Both resource-based and transaction cost theories can explain the different choices organizations make in their preferences for HR administration approaches. For example, the increasing internal transaction costs of recruiting and hiring employees may lead to the search for an external vendor who specializes in the recruitment and selection of new employees. Organizations may then decide to compare those internal transaction costs and benefits with external transaction costs and benefits from the specialized recruitment and selection providers, leading to outsourcing. Alternatively, strategic concerns about the security of having external providers inadvertently "share" crucial talent-positioning information with competitors, coupled with the decreasing costs of technology, might lead an organization to focus on internal innovation involving physical and organizational resources (e.g., self-service portals coupled with SSCs) to reduce transaction costs, while increasing spending on strategic talent management issues (e.g., hiring, development) to achieve a sustainable competitive position in its industry. Keep these theoretical perspectives in mind as we examine each of the HR administration approaches.

Self-Service Portals and HRIS

The first structural approach to HR administration (Figure 10.2), **employee self-service (ESS)** HR portals, provides an electronic means for a company's employees to access its HR services and information. Such portals provide a single sign-on capability for employees, who can complete transactions based on data previously established in records and knowledge bases, without HR's assistance. ESS portals can range from simple intranet Web sites that allow employees to access static HR policies, such as safety requirements, to sophisticated Internet Web sites that allow employees to access and change their individual records. For example, adding a new child to an employee's medical benefits, from any computer location on a 24-hour, 7-days-a-week basis, would be possible with ESS portals. A sample screenshot of an ESS screen is found in Figure 10.3 and a partial list of information and services commonly available via ESS portals is given in Table 10.1.

In addition to providing an interface for current employees, ESS portals are also available to prospective employees. For example, individuals who have applied for jobs online through an employer's Internet Web site have accessed the HR portal to complete the application and forward their resumes (Anheier & Doherty, 2001; Gueutal & Falbe, 2005; Walker, 2001). CedarCrestone (2010) reported that 67% of the responding global companies used ESS portals, with 23% planning to add the capability within 36 months. Chapter 12 discusses Web recruiting in more detail.

Manager self-service (MSS) portals are becoming more prevalent in organizations as well. CedarCrestone (2010) reported that 49% of responding companies used MSS portals, with an additional 18% planning to add the capability within

Figure 10.3 Sample Employee Self-Service Screen

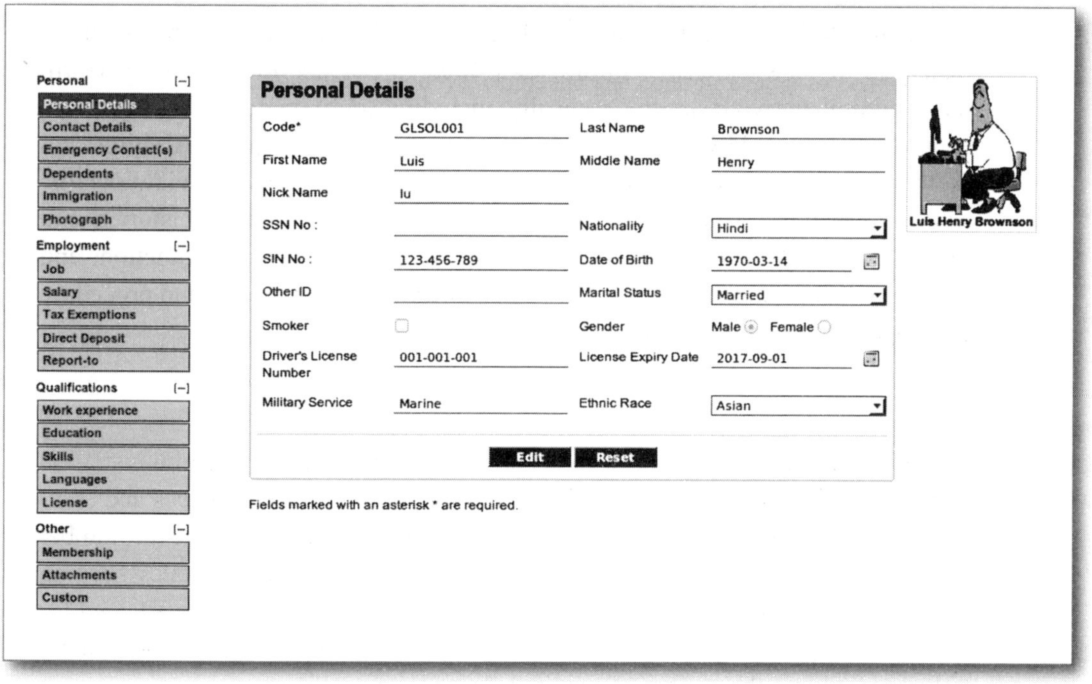

SOURCE: OrangeHRM (www.orangehrm.com). Reproduced with permission.

Table 10.1 Sample Employee Self-Service (ESS) Functionality

Communications	*Benefits Services*	*Personal Data*	*Development*
Review company communications	Research and view plan rules and requirements	Update emergency contact, address, telephone information	Enroll in training courses
Access company policies or procedures	Enroll in cafeteria-style programs (medical, dental, insurance)	Correct errors in personal data (degree, graduation date)	View completed training
Access HR policy manuals and e-mail inquiry or help request	Add or delete dependents	Change W-4 withholding forms	Access internal or external e-learning courses
Complete employee surveys or 360-degree feedback data	Model retirement or access 401(k) savings investment records	View previous or current pay and performance information	View or apply for internal job vacancies
View/respond to personal information requests from HR	Model health plan alternatives' costs (e.g., HMO, PPO)	Enter time reports, vacation or sick days, and travel expense reports	Complete employment tests for new jobs

36 months. MSS portals are specialized versions of ESS portals designed to allow managers to view extensive information about their subordinates and perform many administrative tasks electronically, including traditional HR functions. For example, in typical MSS applications, managers can complete job requisitions and view resumes of prospective applicants. In addition, managers can view **performance appraisals**, subordinate salaries, productivity, and training histories, and model annual salary increases. However, MSS is not limited to HR functions and may also include budgeting and tracking, reporting, and staff policy and procedure development (Gueutal & Falbe, 2005; Walker, 2001).

Advantages of Self-Service Portals for HR Administration

Self-service portals provide several advantages for achieving HR administration goals. First, they improve the speed and quality of service to employees and managers, simplifying routine inquiries and changes in particular. Reducing the number of inquiry transactions requiring direct HR staff involvement facilitates keeping information current. For example, changes in the doctors and hospitals allowed for each medical plan or status reports on the hiring of a new employee are more likely to be entered into the system as required. In addition, self-service portals enhance employee satisfaction by permitting employees to control when and where such access activities occur. This accessibility empowers employees, increases their productivity, especially for those who travel frequently, and offers privacy for those who prefer to handle such matters without the presence of coworkers. In addition, self-service portals facilitate easy, increased access to HR information, helping employees ensure that important personal data (such as individual job performance appraisals used by managers in making decisions about salary increases, promotions, or other employment rewards) are accurate and current.

Moreover, executives believe that having managers use this more accurate, timely information contributes to improved managerial decision making (Gueutal & Falbe, 2005; Walker, 2001). Finally, self-service portals help reduce the number of transactions for HR employees and, correspondingly, overall HR costs. For example, CedarCrestone's (2010) survey showed that companies with 500 to 10,000 + employees reported that those firms with minimal HR technology served an average of 93 employees per HR staff member. By comparison, organizations with ESS portals served an average of 99 employees per HR staff member, whereas those with MSS portals served an average of 118 employees per HR staff member. In addition, research has shown that organizations can realize cost savings of 67% to 99% on tasks such as changing employee information, providing current pay and benefit statements, and the posting of jobs (Gueutal & Falbe, 2005). Such savings relieve HR specialists of routine transactional work and allow them to focus more on both the traditional and transformational strategic activities described in Chapter 1.

Disadvantages of Self-Service Portals for HR Administration

Although HR administrators can gain advantages from deploying self-service portals, they are also faced with multiple disadvantages. First, permitting employees to access company data through self-service portals may increase the possibility of security breaches and the associated negative outcomes for affected employees, including identity theft. For example, more than 52 million customer and business records were stolen in 2005 because of poor security, and losses from identity fraud rose to $54.4 billion in 2005 (CMO Council, 2006). In the United States, the CMO Council reported that individuals are increasingly concerned about identity theft (80%), guarding financial information (70%), and Internet transaction security (65%). Moreover, employees are concerned that even having their data in a company's HRIS can lead to misuse of such information by others in the organization. Phillips, Isenhour, and Stone (2008) suggest that employees may feel that their privacy is being invaded when organizations fail to limit access to an employee's personal data in HRIS. For example, managers may learn negative information (e.g., that employees have medical disabilities) through MSS portal access that would have been unavailable in a paper record system. Even the inadvertent use or sharing of such information may preclude training or promotional opportunities for employees. Misuse of this personal information in this manner can constitute a violation of labor laws such as the **Americans with Disabilities Act (ADA)** in the United States. Privacy and security issues will be discussed in more detail later in this chapter, as well as in Chapter 16.

In addition to security issues, HR administrators may find that unions and managers resist using the self-service portals. In particular, unions may argue that employees are "doing HR work" when they enter data and make changes online via an ESS portal. Union members who perform such transactions on their own time may request overtime pay for completing such functions, which are not part of their job duties, or they may choose to do such functions at work, thus reducing productivity. Managers may also resent having to do work that previously was handled completely by HR staff, particularly when such work involved calling the staff members rather than completing forms. For example, managers may have had relationships with HR staff that permitted the managers to bypass established procedures for requesting a new hire. Thus, using MSS portals would not only require more actual work for the managers but also enforce standardized interfaces that might lead managers to perceive a reduction in their status and power in the organization. Accordingly, HR managers should recognize and take action to ameliorate such perceptions and concerns as part of the project management planning and implementation process for an HRIS.

Shared-Service Centers and HRIS

The second structural approach to HR administration, SSCs, generally appeared in response to the increasing globalization of competitive markets occasioned by the proliferation of multinational enterprises (MNEs). To compete successfully, organizations were pressured to reduce costs through the consolidation of administrative transactions while still providing excellent service. Such a challenge involved balancing the desire for control inherent in centralized administrative structures and the desire for flexibility inherent in decentralized administrative structures—a constant organizational conflict within large and expanding corporations (Lucenko, 1998; Quinn, Cooke, & Kris, 2000; von Simson, 1990). Over time, many organizations have chosen SSCs as the structural solution to that pressure.

> Shared services is a collaborative strategy whereby [one or more] staff functions of a firm are concentrated in a semi-autonomous organization and managed like a business unit . . . to promote greater efficiency, value generation and improved service for internal customers. (Goh, Prakash, & Yeo, 2007, p. 252)

To emphasize this aspect of SSCs, some organizations have described them as "centers of excellence" (Bender, 2001). Figure 10.4 illustrates that SSCs include HR in 66% of manufacturing and 53% of service companies (Powell, 2004).

Powell (2004, p. 6) identified the following common elements of SSCs:

- Centralizing or decentralizing of business processes
- Using economies of scale to reduce unit costs
- Developing customer relationship models (CRMs) to better meet the needs of customers
- Concentrating on cost reduction to enhance competitive positioning
- Deploying quality tools to ensure continuous process improvement

To be successful, a shared-service center involving HR, for example, must view itself as an independent business unit offering products (e.g., HR reports), which

Figure 10.4 Functions in Shared Services

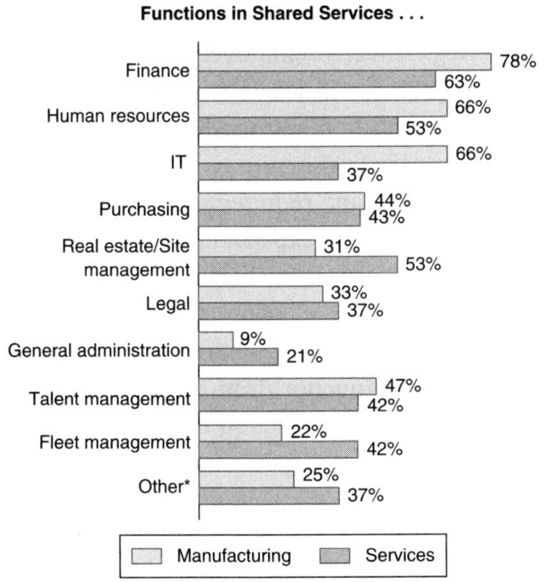

*Other functions included: communications, customer service, sales, engineering, environmental health and safety, regulatory affairs, and analytical sciences

. . . and the Percentage Covered*

	<25%	26–50%	51–75%	>75%
Finance	25%	25%	19%	31%
HR	31	27	12	30
IT	7	18	11	64
Purchasing	18	14	11	54
Real estate/Site management	10	14	5	71
Legal	–	–	13	67
General administration	–	–	17	83
Talent management	4	18	3	75
Fleet management	–	–	7	93
Other**	15	15	–	70

*Percentages refer only to companies whose shared services cover the functions

**Other functions included: communications, customer service, sales, engineering, environmental health and safety, regulatory affairs, and analytical sciences

SOURCE: Powell (2004).

it must "sell" to its customers at a price (internal transaction cost) they are willing to pay. These internal customers are managers in different business units such as operations and marketing. If the HR function is unsuccessful in reducing costs, providing desirable services, and adding value, it may find itself "outsourced" by business unit managers who perceive that they can get better service and value from an external provider. To demonstrate added value to the organization, the SSC should establish measures that demonstrate customer satisfaction levels, productivity, cost controls, and quality. Such measures are necessary to allow internal customers to assess the value of the consolidated unit and to facilitate continuous improvement by SSC managers.

Accenture (2007) outlined several principles to embrace when considering the use of SSCs:

- Establish a "global good" vision for the SSC that includes its definition and benefits to ensure that business units "losing" functions are willing to make the commitment to transfer their work.
- Identify leaders, in all the affected groups, to sponsor the SSC vision, promote the center's value to the organization, and serve as responsible change agents.
- Support transparency regarding who (e.g., affected employees), what (e.g., which functions), when (e.g., transition plans), and where (e.g., location of the new center). This openness is essential to building the trust needed to initiate and maintain the center's effectiveness.
- Conduct initial and ongoing customer "values and requirements" meetings to build trust, establish performance and service expectations, and solve problems. Implementing jointly acceptable measures facilitates SSC success and internal customer satisfaction.
- Focus on viewing the SSC's processes in the context of the overall business functions. Examine the process behind each function from "end to end." Understanding the context of all processes in each function encourages the recognition of the interdependencies inherent in the SSC concept and bolsters the value-creating goal of SSCs.

Advantages of Shared-Service Centers for HR Administration

There are a number of advantages of SSCs for HR administration (Robinson & Robinson, 2005; Ulrich, 1997; Walker, 2001). First, SSCs permit HR administration managers to focus on delivering the timely, high-quality transactions necessary to fulfill corporate requirements, such as mandated governmental reporting. This advantage is particularly important for multinationals, which have to respond to the labor laws of multiple countries. Also, Ulrich (1997) suggests that one way SSCs improve transaction delivery is by removing the artificial barriers inherent in the generalist-specialist continuum common in HR organizations, smoothing work and communication processes.

In addition, by combining such transactional responsibilities in a single business unit, organizations can encourage the unit to focus on customer satisfaction with specific user interactions, such as responses to employee questions or requests for assistance. This frees specialists to focus on more strategic activities. Moreover, SSCs encourage the efficiency and standardization necessary to support strategic cost-control goals by consolidating individuals responsible for transactions. This provides organizations with greater motivation to redesign procedures and create more effective ones. Finally, such centers facilitate development of the measures of efficiency, quality, and customer responsiveness that are necessary to demonstrate appropriate contributions to strategic goals. However, there are several potential pitfalls associated with SSCs.

Disadvantages of Shared-Service Centers for HR Managers

Frequently, organizations combine multiple, unrelated shared services into a combined business unit. Depending on the nature of such functions, the synergies needed to consolidate and improve processes may be less prevalent. For example, combining vehicle fleet management and HR transactions may offer few synergies. Moreover, leaders of such units may be stretched as they seek to unify and manage diverse functions. However, careful development of the mission and appropriate selection of the leaders of such units can overcome this problem by establishing a shared mindset among those involved (Walker, 2001).

In addition, creating SSCs may lead to unanticipated power shifts in organizations. For example, combining financial and HR transactions in a single center may lead to reduced emphasis on HR transactions since business managers are especially concerned with the budget reporting associated with financial transactions. Again, establishing an effective mission and overarching goals for the center can forestall such power shifts (Ulrich, 1997).

Finally, SSCs can lead to depersonalization. For example, line managers, accustomed to personal contact with HR professionals, may feel isolated when handling transactions through self-service portals. Similarly, they may feel abandoned when traditional communication patterns are disrupted because specialists have been consolidated in SSCs. Moreover, because such units are concerned with efficiency and cost controls, individuals working in them can become more involved with the technology with which they work and less involved with others who are engaged in the day-to-day aspects of the business (Ulrich, 1997).

Outsourcing and HRIS

The third approach to HR administration, outsourcing, is the practice of contracting with vendors to perform HR services and activities. Outsourcing is not new in HR administration. For example, Automatic Data Processing, Inc. (ADP) moved quickly in 1945 to offer its expertise in payroll and tax calculations to businesses facing increasingly complex employee income tax and withholding calculations (Dominguez, 2006). Nonetheless, few would have predicted the recent explosion in specialized organizations capable of providing a few or all of an organization's HR functions (Hewitt, 2005). Figure 10.5 shows the percentage of processes outsourced by respondents to the 2007 EquaTerra HRO (human resources outsourcing) survey. Apparently, ADP had it right! Even today, payroll and benefits are the most frequently outsourced processes. Esen (2004) reported that 60% of businesses engage in one or more forms of outsourcing. More recently, EquaTerra (2010) has reported

Figure 10.5 Percentages of HR Processes Outsourced

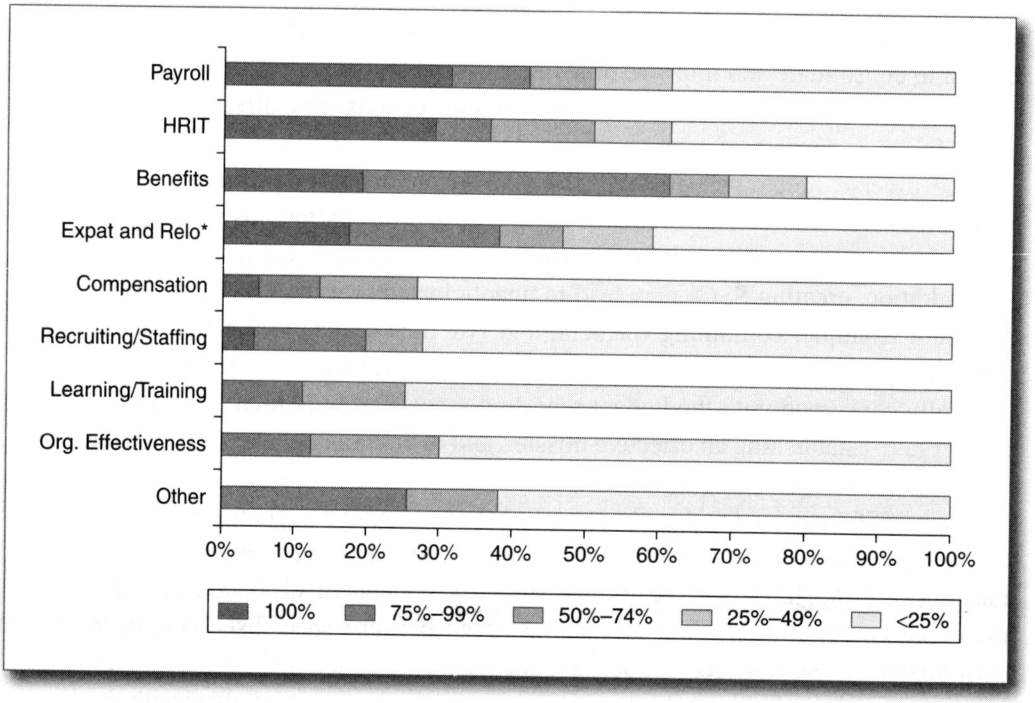

SOURCE: EquaTerra (2007, p. 4).

*Expat and Relo means Expatriation and Relocation.

on a robust outsourcing trend: firms are contracting for "pre-configured, hosted, multi-client platforms on which the service provider delivers standardised . . . payroll, basic HR administration, and employee call handling" (para. 3).

HR outsourcing firms are hardly uniform. There are many different types of providers, reflecting the diverse needs of organizations.

In 2006, HRO firms provided HR services for 3.3 million employees in North America (Everest Research Institute, 2007). Moreover, for firms that had more than 1,000 employees and revenues of greater than $100 million and that participated in comprehensive outsourcing (defined as more than five human resource functions outsourced), satisfaction with HRO levels increased over time. Of the 310 firms surveyed, HRO satisfaction (on a scale of 1 [*not at all satisfied*] to 5 [*very satisfied*]) improved from an average of 2.9 in the first two years to 3.4 after two or more years (EquaTerra, 2007).

Outsourcing contracts should include specific pricing agreements (e.g., flat or fixed fee per process or per employee served, unit prices per transaction levels, hourly and overtime rates, revenue sharing, risk-reward sharing, failure penalties), expected performance and associated measures (e.g., transaction quality standards, error rates, system availability and downtime, customer satisfaction levels, hours of operation), and terms and conditions (e.g., start and end dates, extensions permitted, termination agreements, dispute resolution procedures, audit procedures). Obviously, HR administration managers would require significant assistance from multiple groups such as the legal, operations, and information systems departments within the organization to establish and monitor the contract, ensuring that the organization is adequately protected from incompetent or unethical outsourcing providers.

Reasons to Pursue HR Outsourcing

HR administration managers elect to pursue HRO for multiple reasons (Keebler, 2001). Weatherly (2005) suggests that managers may pursue discrete, multiprocess, or total-process HRO. Figure 10.6 compares discrete or selective outsourcing with multiprocess or comprehensive outsourcing.

Some organizations outsource only discrete or selected functions, pursuing **discrete HRO** through niche third-party providers. This outsourcing involves having specialized external firms deal only with a particular HR function. External HR recruiting firms, for example, fall into this category. Such an approach is common in smaller organizations with limited numbers of HR professionals or in larger organizations with few, sporadic recruiting requirements. Also included in this category is the outsourcing of parts of various HR functions. For example, even organizations with large, effective recruiting staffs may elect to outsource executive or specialty recruitment functions (e.g., recruiting for multilingual positions) to external search firms that have unique expertise. Similarly, organizations may outsource only annual benefits enrollment, flexible spending accounts (FSA) administration, or payroll administration.

Generally, the outsourcing of discrete HR functions is attractive for two reasons. First, discrete HRO can achieve cost savings by eliminating the company's need to hire highly specialized HR professionals (e.g., executive recruiters) or those with the HRIS expertise necessary to perform infrequent functions (e.g., FSA administration). In addition, discrete HRO can reduce the HR administration costs associated with frequent, high-volume transactions such as payroll. In both cases, discrete HRO serves to reduce HRIS expenses and the number of HR employees while ensuring the desired strategic outcome of hiring the right executive or paying employees correctly on schedule. Although discrete tactical HRO has existed for many years, it still remains a popular HR administration approach for achieving strategic goals (Figure 10.6).

Figure 10.6 Selective Versus Comprehensive HR Function Outsourcing

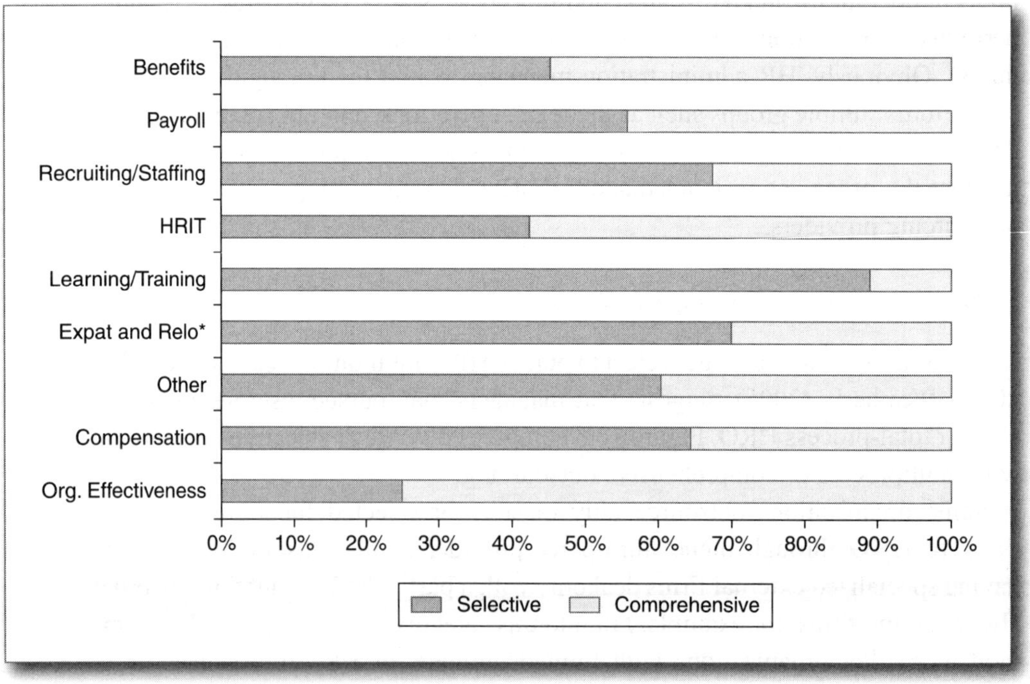

SOURCE: EquaTerra (2007, p. 4).

*Expat and Relo means Expatriation and Relocation.

HR administration managers may also pursue **multiprocess HRO**, also known as *comprehensive* or *blended services outsourcing*. This approach involves outsourcing to niche, third-party providers all of one or more related HR functions, for example, recruitment and selection or defined and 401(k) retirement plan administration. Multiprocess outsourcing has become more popular with the increase in the number of specialized vendors providing such services and the spread of enabling Internet portal capabilities. For example, organizations were less likely to outsource pension administration when employees needing information had to meet with in-house HR experts. With an HR portal and HRIS, however, employees can model their pension decisions independently (to determine pension amounts associated with different retirement dates, for example) and then change 401(k) investment directions by speaking to pension specialists at the third-party vendor when questions arise. This outsourcing of sets of functions reduces the number of specialized HR employees, improves service levels to employees, and reduces HRIS hardware and software upgrades and ongoing maintenance costs. Overall, such an HR administration approach can provide significant cost reductions and simultaneously maintain or enhance service levels.

Total HRO is the third type of outsourcing approach and involves having all, or nearly all, HR functions handled by one or more external vendors. All traditional HR administrative and functional activities would be managed through third-party vendors. For example, Johnson & Johnson Inc. contracted with Convergys to provide full HR administrative and transactional services for its global workforce for $1 billion (CBR, 2007). Under such arrangements, employees would contact the vendor for assistance or inquiries directly, without any company HR employee involvement or knowledge. Certainly, such a plan would reduce internal HR employee expenses, HRIS expenditures, and administration costs dramatically; however, such savings would be offset by costs for vendor contract administration, quality controls, and oversight. In addition, the HR strategic functions, such as long-term force planning and strategic business unit support, should not be outsourced because third-party vendors frequently deal with multiple clients, one or more of whom might be competitors. It is not hard to imagine how even the most sincere vendor efforts to secure strategic HR plans might be inadvertently compromised, leading to disclosure of these plans and severe strategic disadvantages. Although this HR administration approach is not as prevalent as either discrete or multiprocess outsourcing, it is gaining in popularity. Organizations might opt for such a total HRO solution to deal with the myriad HR requirements associated with the global workforce of an MNE, to focus on HR strategic issues, or to reduce costs. That this strategy is gaining support is demonstrated in Hewitt's HRO survey (2010): 82% of surveyed companies rated their outsourcing as effective or highly effective in meeting strategic goals.

Advantages of HR Outsourcing

The advantages of HR administration outsourcing can be both financial and strategic (Keebler, 2001; Weatherly, 2005). For example, organizations seeking to increase financial profitability and enhance shareowner value might employ HRO to reduce ongoing expenses for employees and software, forestalling capital expenditures for new buildings and equipment. This decision would entail a careful "make-buy" assessment of the total costs and benefits of continuing internal operations versus contracting for them in the external market. Benefits of such an approach might include redesigned processes, improved quality, centralized or consolidated operations, access to technology, and enhanced employee satisfaction. The cost-benefit analysis (CBA) approach covered in Chapter 7 would be essential in this situation.

The strategic advantages of HRO might include the ability of the organization to better focus on its core business by transforming the HR function. By outsourcing the simpler, transaction-based function, the HR department can move from its historical focus on administrative activities to a new position as strategic business partner. Organizations recognize that, more than ever, effective talent management may be the source of sustainable strategic advantage in a knowledge-based, global economy. However, many HR professionals are mired in day-to-day transactional administrative tasks that preclude the value-added consulting, planning, and visioning activities required from them to achieve strategic goals (Fletcher, 2005; Lawler, 2005). HRO could free HR professionals to focus on strategic issues, such as talent management, while providing the firm with skilled transactional and professional services in HR functional areas such as compensation and in administrative areas such as governmental compliance and regulations. Moreover, these services would be powered by the up-to-date technology provided by the external vendor.

Disadvantages of HR Outsourcing

Although there are a number of financial and strategic reasons for considering HR administration outsourcing, there are also serious potential problems for firms that use the approach without fully understanding how to manage it to achieve desired goals. For example, firms that used HRO to achieve HR transformation and cost savings rated their success at an average of 3 on a 5-point scale, (1 equaling *benefits not at all achieved* and 5 equaling *benefits fully achieved*) (EquaTerra, 2007). Thus, one big disadvantage of HRO is the likelihood that the organization will not achieve its strategic goals. Such a failure could have a significant, negative impact on the organization's ability to survive. Steps to minimize such a failure include realistic cost-benefit analyses (see Chapter 7), successful project planning and implementation (see Chapter 8), unambiguous goals and measures of HRO success, rigorous vendor assessment and selection processes, and skilled vendor contract negotiation, management, and auditing (Weatherly, 2005). Indeed, one of the primary responsibilities of HR administration managers in an outsourcing environment is to ensure that the contract terms are fulfilled on a daily basis and that corrective actions are immediately taken when failures occur.

Another disadvantage of HRO includes the loss of institutional expertise in the outsourced functions, making an HRO decision reversal difficult or impossible. Frequently, when outsourcing is undertaken, HR subject matter experts are reassigned or released. This restructuring can be a serious strategic error if the vendor is unable to fulfill its contractual obligations. As noted above, an organization would be unwise to outsource core or strategic HR planning functions because of the possibility that competitors might learn its plans from vendors. In addition, loss of internal strategic HR expertise may be devastating to an organization over time. Moreover, these outsourcing organizations may lack the contract management expertise to oversee the vendor and hold it accountable for contract terms. Other potential problems include security risks in multivendor outsourcing, internal employee and manager resistance, compliance failures, and cultural clashes between the organization and its vendors.

As outsourcing arrangements continue to increase, evidence from information technology (IT) outsourcing can provide a cautionary tale for those considering HRO. For example, in a recent study, approximately one-third of organizations reported that they had canceled an IT outsourcing contract (Lacity & Willcocks, 2001). In addition, when these contracts are canceled, the functionality is often brought back in-house instead of shifted to a new outsourcing partner (Lacity & Willcocks, 2000). The effort to bring functionality back in-house, also known as **backsourcing**, can be expensive, as firms pay to reorganize twice: first when outsourcing a function and again when backsourcing it.

In summary, HRO is another approach to HR administration that offers potential for cost reduction, process improvement, and employee satisfaction. However, managers of HR administrative functions must be highly skilled at using HRO strategically to achieve organizational goals.

Offshoring and HRIS

The final approach to HR administration, offshoring, is an expansion of HR outsourcing that includes sending work outside the United States to vendors located in other countries. Technological capabilities and global competition have combined to make HRO a global business, and offshoring for MNEs is quite complex. For example, if an Australian airline has call centers in India to obtain improved cost performance, why not have its SSC for HR there as well? Based on responses from 5,231 executives in North America and Europe, Hatch (2004) reported that 19% of all companies and 95% of the *Fortune* 1000 companies are considering offshore outsourcing. Moreover, there are now more than 10,000 offshore vendors in 175 countries competing for the business. However, only 65 of these vendors can offer full-service HRO worldwide (EquaTerra, 2005). Figure 10.7 shows the various reasons organizations consider offshoring.

Esen's (2004) survey of HR managers reported that organizations consider offshoring primarily for financial reasons, including lower labor costs (76%), increased profits (50%), and reduced health care costs (23%). For example, researchers found that labor costs for a software developer in India were $6 per hour as opposed to the $60 per hour earned for doing the same job in the United States (Chiamsiri, Bulusu, & Agarwal, 2005). In addition, some firms were seeking skilled employees (16%) or productivity (10%) and service improvement

Figure 10.7 Company Reasons for Considering Offshoring

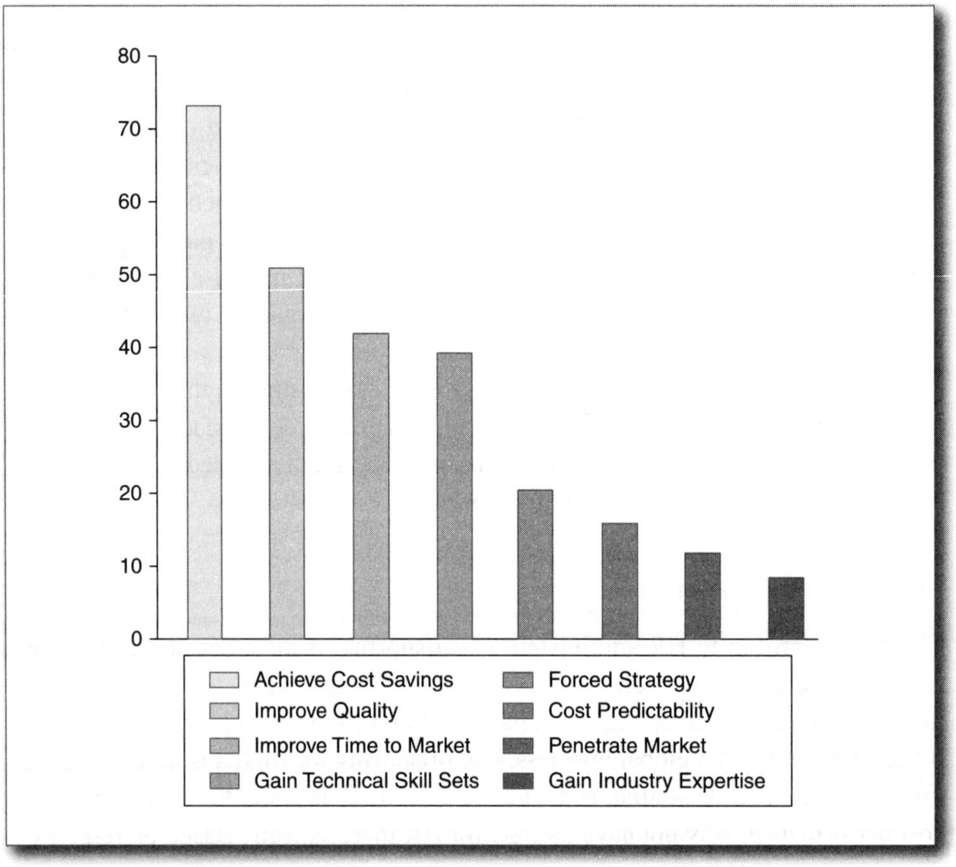

(7%). Only 7% considered offshoring for strategic reasons. In fact, 40% of HR managers reported that their organizations would not consider offshoring because it was inconsistent with strategic direction (Esen, 2004).

Types of HR Offshoring

When their organizations pursued offshoring, HR managers reported that manufacturing functions were most common (43%), followed by IT (29%) and computer programming (22%), customer call centers (29%), and HR functions (16%). Such organizations used both offshore ownership and offshore outsourcing (Esen, 2004). **Offshore ownership** may include opening a new subsidiary in the foreign country, entering into a joint venture with an existing firm in that country, or purchasing an existing firm. By comparison, offshore outsourcing is a traditional contractual relationship with an existing firm.

Offshore ownership is riskier than simple offshore outsourcing. In addition to appropriate strategic and financial due diligence, organizations considering offshore ownership must pay particular attention to

- ready availability of necessary employee knowledge, skills, and abilities such as language;
- information and communication systems compatibility with HRIS;
- governmental regulations and legal employment requirements such as wage laws;
- political stability of the country for facility and employee security; and
- cultural differences such as expectations about participative versus directive supervision.

Although an offshore outsourcing strategy is less risky than offshore ownership, organizations would still face more risk than they would had they outsourced domestically. HR managers should always perform due diligence in assessing the reputation and business capabilities of an outsourcing partner. However, such processes are more complex when dealing with organizations located halfway across the globe. For example, concerns about electrical power availability, which might determine whether HRIS processing can occur as scheduled, are rarely discussed with outsourcing firms in the United States but might be a significant issue in parts of Indonesia. In addition, worker availability to meet a 24/7 service center requirement is less of a problem in the United States than in countries where overtime is limited to a few hours per month, as it is in the European Union (EU). Finally, oversight and audit functions may be less onerous and expensive when U.S. companies establish offshore outsourcing agreements in nearby countries such as Canada or Mexico rather than in more distant nations such as India or China.

Summary of HR Administration Approaches

Based on the previous discussion, it is clear that HR administration managers have a number of approaches that can contribute to the goals of reducing costs, improving efficiency, and increasing service levels for internal customers. It is also important that such alternatives be pursued consistent with each organization's strategic plan to achieve sustainable competitive advantage in its industry. Moreover, multiple approaches may be appropriate based on those strategic goals. For example, HR portals may be combined with SSCs and selective outsourcing or offshoring to achieve the optimum solution for a particular firm.

In assessing whether one or more approaches is best, HR administration managers must understand the impact of their decisions on the specific administrative functions to be accomplished. Therefore, the next section describes two specific U.S. governmental reporting mandates (i.e., to the Equal Employment Opportunity Commission [EEOC] and OSHA) that are included among the many HR transactions for which HR administration is responsible. Following a discussion of the governmental mandates, their legal underpinnings, and the actual reports and records maintenance required, we explore how HR administration approaches can facilitate improved accuracy, reduced costs, and increased organizational value during the process of successfully completing such HR transactions.

LEGAL COMPLIANCE AND HR ADMINISTRATION

As noted in Chapter 1 (Figure 1.2), the country and its general environment constitute a major effect on HRM and on the development and implementation of HRIS (Beaman, 2002). Whether the organization pursues a "domestic only" strategy (i.e., doing business in only one country) or an MNE approach, countries' government and labor laws are important external forces in establishing the context for business (Hersch, 1991). In particular, the labor laws provide the foundation of employee protections in the workplace. For example, in the United States, the Constitution and its Amendments establish the rights of citizens in general. In addition, multiple employment laws have been passed by the U.S. Congress to complement those rights. Some of the more important of these U.S. employment laws are identified in the glossary provided at the end of the book. For a more detailed discussion of the employment laws in the United States, see Ledvinka (1982).

It is important to recognize that U.S. employment laws underpin the *general principles* used in the practice of HRM. There are a number of laws in the United States prohibiting unfair discrimination on the basis of employee sex, race, age, and disability. There are similar laws and regulations in other industrialized nations that prohibit unfair discrimination (Brisco & Schuler, 2004). The general principle underlying these unfair discrimination laws and regulations is that job performance should be the primary basis for employment decisions that change the employment status of an individual. When hiring new employees, for example, a company should base its hiring decision primarily on expected job performance, which might be assessed through employment tests and interviews. Whether applicants are male or female is irrelevant in all but a few cases (e.g., restroom attendant). Similarly, decisions to award a pay raise, or to promote or terminate an employee, should be based on the employee's job performance. As noted, the general principles underlying employment laws in the United States bear significant similarities to the general principles underlying employment laws or regulations in other countries, such as those specified in the EU directives (Briscoe & Schuler, 2004; Dowling & Welch, 2005; Paskoff, 2003). Since compliance with employment laws and regulations is a critical part of HR administration, provisions for handling the employment laws of multiple countries need to be considered in the development of an HRIS for a multinational firm.

What complicates U.S. employment laws for HR professionals is that the 50 states frequently expand on, adopt rules and regulations that differ from, or add additional protections not covered by federal law. For example, a partial comparison of elements of the **Family and Medical Leave Act (FMLA)** with the federal and state legislation of California and Oregon demonstrates these variations. Both California and Oregon deviate from the federal FMLA statute, but do so in different ways. The federal law specifies that its provisions apply to private employers with 50 or more employees in at least 20 weeks of the current or preceding year (U.S. Department of Labor, 2007). California law applies the provisions of the FMLA to *all* employers with 50 or more employees. In contrast, Oregon applies the provisions of the FMLA to employers with 25 or more employees in at least 20 weeks of the year. In this case, HR managers operating in both California and Oregon would be required to provide annual reports demonstrating that they have complied with both the federal and the state laws that are applicable. Since country-level and local laws can differ for all nations, administrative expenses to comply with employment laws can mushroom for firms with national and international exposure, even when an HRIS is used to support such compliance requirements. Indeed, this example reinforces the need for flexibility in HRIS software to accommodate such reporting differences.

This is, of course, just one example among many that demonstrates how governments affect HR administration. There are many laws and regulations in the United States that require organizations to report to government agencies (Ledvinka, 1982). All these reports are tedious and time-consuming, and they account for a significant amount of the transactional activity of the HR department. The processing for these activities was affected significantly by the introduction of computer technology and has always been a part of any integrated HR software package. The next sections take an in-depth look at two U.S. governmental mandates associated with equal employment opportunity (EEO) and employee safety. Specifically, HR administration and related concerns associated with EEO records and reporting (EEO-1 report) and OSHA record keeping and reporting will be highlighted. As you read about the reporting requirements of these laws, just imagine the tremendous amount of time it would take to complete an EEO-1 report manually for a medium-sized company of 1,000 employees; that is a considerable amount of "paper shuffling." Again, it is important to recognize that the following discussion is illustrative of HR administration, employment laws, and the use of an HRIS and, thus, could be applied to any country in the world.

HR ADMINISTRATION AND EQUAL EMPLOYMENT OPPORTUNITY

U.S. Civil Rights Act of 1964, Title VII, and the EEO-1 Report

Figure 10.8 displays the broad categories of HRM administration associated with governmental mandates for meeting the requirements of **equal employment opportunity (EEO)** and affirmative action laws and guidelines. That all individuals should be considered for employment based on knowledge, skills, and abilities rather than irrelevant factors (e.g., sex, race, religion) is the *general principle* of EEO. Title VII of the Civil Rights Act of 1964 provides the requirements for such EEO. Under Section 703 of Title VII (42 U.S.C. §2000e-2), it is illegal for employers with 15 or more employees working 20 or more weeks per year

> (1) to fail or refuse to hire or discharge any individual with respect to his compensation, terms, conditions, or privileges of employment because of such individual's race, color, religion, sex, or national origin, or
>
> (2) to limit, segregate, or classify his employees or applicants for employment in any way that would deprive or tend to deprive any individual of employment opportunities or otherwise adversely affect his status as an employee because of such individual's race, color, religion, sex, or national origin. (U.S. EEOC, 1964)

In addition, employers who engage in business with the federal government and have contracts valued at $50,000 or more must comply with additional

Figure 10.8 EEO/Affirmative Action Plan (AAP) Administrative Functions

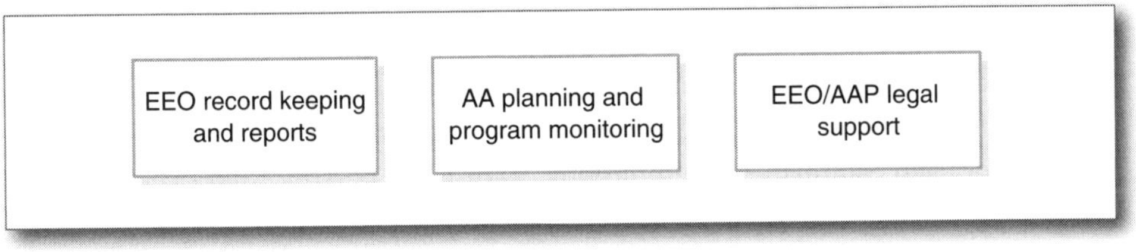

requirements that include providing a written **affirmative action plan (AAP)** to the Office of Federal Contract Compliance Procedures (OFCCP). This report details how the employer is actively seeking to hire and promote individuals in protected classes. Specifically, the AAP must (1) provide a detailed comparison of the available labor force with the employer's workforce by race, color, religion, national origin, and sex; (2) specify goals and timetables for achieving workforce balance if underutilization exists; and (3) indicate the specific steps to be taken to attain the goals in order to erase underutilization. In 1967, Congress expanded protection against illegal discrimination in employment by including the age criterion (i.e., persons aged 40 or older) with the passage of the **Age Discrimination in Employment Act (ADEA)**, and, in 1990, it provided protection to individuals with disabilities with its passage of the Americans with Disabilities Act (ADA). One example of the many mandated government reports is the EEO-1 report.

EEO-1 Report (Standard Form 100)

To monitor and assess equal employment opportunity practices, the EEOC was charged with gathering data, investigating alleged violations, and bringing legal charges against employers who failed to comply with Title VII requirements. Accordingly, all employers with 15 or more employees must keep records regarding their compliance with the law based on occupational category (i.e., professional, technical, managerial, craft) and sex and race/ethnicity. Although the records historically included six EEO categories (i.e., white, black, Hispanic, Asian or Pacific Islander, Native American), changes in the number and designation of categories were made based on the 2000 U.S. Census, with reporting by the revised categories beginning in 2007.

A sample of the "Employment Data" section of the EEO-1 report (Standard Form 100) with its revised categories is shown in Figure 10.9. Substantial changes in the report include expanding occupational categories from 4 to 10 and, more important, allowing individuals to specify more than one race/ethnicity category.

Previously, individuals were limited to a single designation. The EEO-1 report must be prepared each September 30 by

> all private employers . . . with 100 or more employees. . . . [M]ulti-establishment employers doing business at more than one establishment, must complete online: (1) a report covering the principal or headquarters office; (2) a separate report for each establishment employing 50 or more persons; and (3) a separate report . . . for each establishment employing fewer than 50 employees . . . showing the name, address and total employment for each establishment employing fewer than 50 persons . . . by race, sex, and job category. (U.S. EEOC, 2006)

Revised reporting instructions include definitions of the revised designated racial/ethnic categories shown below, columns for reporting individuals who specify more than one race/ethnicity, and strong encouragement to have employees "self-identify" rather than relying on the employer's visual categorization. The race and ethnic designations used by the EEOC are as follows:

- *Hispanic or Latino*—A person of Cuban, Mexican, Puerto Rican, South or Central American, or other Spanish culture or origin regardless of race.
- *White (not Hispanic or Latino)*—A person having origins in any of the original peoples of Europe, the Middle East, or North Africa.
- *Black or African American (not Hispanic or Latino)*—A person having origins in any of the black racial groups of Africa.
- *Native Hawaiian or Other Pacific Islander (not Hispanic or Latino)*—A person having origins in any of the peoples of Hawaii, Guam, Samoa, or other Pacific Islands.
- *Asian (not Hispanic or Latino)*—A person having origins in any of the original peoples of the Far East, Southeast Asia, or the Indian subcontinent, including, for example, Cambodia, China, India, Japan, Korea, Malaysia, Pakistan, the Philippine Islands, Thailand, and Vietnam.
- *American Indian or Alaska Native (not Hispanic or Latino)*—A person having origins in any of the original peoples of North and South America (including Central America) and who maintain tribal affiliation or community attachment. (U.S. EEOC, 2006, Appendix 4)

EEO-1 and HRIS

Smith (2006) suggests that the recent changes to the EEOC guidelines will be the most sweeping change in the history of the EEOC, as workers reclassify themselves based on the new EEO designations and organizations pore through job descriptions to classify individuals into the new work categories. For example,

Section D – EMPLOYMENT DATA

Employment at this establishment—Report all permanent full- and part-time employees including apprentices and on-the-job trainees unless specifically excluded as set forth in the instructions. Enter the appropriate figures on all lines and in all columns. Blank spaces will be considered as zeros.

Job Categories	Number of Employees (Report employees in only one category)														
	Race/Ethnicity														
	Hispanic or Latino		Not-Hispanic or Latino												
			Male						Female						
	Male	Female	White	Black or African American	Native Hawaiian or Other Pacific Islander	Asian	American Indian or Alaska Native	Two or more races	White	Black or African American	Native Hawaiian or Other Pacific Islander	Asian	American Indian or Alaska Native	Two or more races	Total Col A–N
	A	B	C	D	E	F	G	H	I	J	K	L	M	N	O
Executive/Senior Level Officials and Managers 1.1															
First/Mid-Level Officials and Managers 1.2															
Professionals 2															
Technicians 3															
Sales Workers 4															
Administrative Support Workers 5															
Craft Workers 6															
Operatives 7															
Laborers and Helpers 8															
Service Workers 9															
TOTAL 10															
PREVIOUS YEAR TOTAL 11															

1. Date(s) of payroll period used: ______________ (Omit on the Consolidated Report.)

O.M.B. No. 3046-0007
Revised 00/2006
Approval Expires 1/2009

SOURCE: U.S. EEOC (2006).

individuals who classify themselves as white could also classify themselves as Asian under the new plan. Even small firms without HRIS have a large amount of work to do. However, HRIS changes will be significant as well (Jossi, 2004). For example, human resource information systems and enterprise resource planning (ERP) systems have generally used a single field letter or number to represent race/ethnicity categories. Potential system changes required by the updated EEO-1 report include the following:

- Track race separately from ethnicity (e.g., Hispanic or not Hispanic).
- Provide separate codes for Asian and Native Hawaiian or Other Pacific Islander.
- Modify limitations on reporting only one race (e.g., individual may be black and Asian).
- Ensure that queries can identify all individuals in a particular category (e.g., American Indian), even when individuals self-identify as two or more race categories.

Moreover, the EEOC is encouraging online reporting of the EEO-1 and, simultaneously, discouraging manual reporting (U.S. EEOC, 2006). Thus, in addition to generating direct costs associated with software modification, employee self-designation, and job reclassification, these policy changes also affect, albeit in a more subtle way, HRM administration. For example, if firms choose to use electronic reporting, they may also find that the costs associated with complying with legislation will be reduced. This detailed description of EEO-1 reporting is provided to facilitate an understanding of how complex HR administration can be. The point is that the amount of paperwork required for compliance with all federal and local employment laws and regulations would be overwhelming without HRIS. The HRIS applications software helps greatly reduce this complexity. Nevertheless, no matter how sophisticated the HRIS and its reporting software, the employee and organizational data must *be entered accurately* into the system. To understand the complexity of governmental reporting requirements, let us examine a second example of how these affect HRM administration. Specifically, consider the necessity of reporting data to show compliance with the Occupational Safety and Health Act (OSHA).

Occupational Safety and Health Act Record Keeping

Figure 10.10 displays the broad categories of HRM administration associated with governmental mandates for safety requirements in OSHA. In 1970, with work-related fatalities reaching 15,000 annually, Congress charged the

U.S. Department of Labor with responsibility for establishing, monitoring, and enforcing occupational safety and health standards and practices for firms engaged in interstate commerce. OSHA primarily established, in the general duty clause of the law, that employers must provide a workplace free of known hazards likely to cause death or serious injury. The National Institute for Occupational Safety and Health (NIOSH) researches and publishes safety and health standards under the law. To ensure that all businesses with 11 or more employees fulfill their occupational safety and health obligations, OSHA compliance officers typically arrive unannounced for an OSHA inspection. The inspector then proceeds to

- review employer records of workplace deaths, injuries, and illnesses;
- conduct on-site inspections of the work premise and note observed violations;
- conduct employee interviews to elicit any safety concerns; and
- discuss findings and violations or issue citations to the employer (Noe, Hollenbeck, Gerhart, & Wright, 2004).

Failing to correct violations or maintain required records could result in substantial fines and jail sentences for employers.

OSHA Form 300 (Log of Work-Related Injuries and Illnesses) and HRIS

All covered employers are required to notify OSHA within eight hours of any accident involving either a fatality or an in-patient hospitalization of three or more employees. In addition, all covered employers must complete an annual **OSHA Form 300** recording all reportable work-related injuries and illnesses. **OSHA Form 301** (Injury and Illness Incidence Report) is used to record supplementary information about reportable cases. Finally, **OSHA Form 300A** (Summary of Work-Related Injuries and Illnesses), which displays total injuries and illnesses for the year, must be posted for all employees to view. A sample of the Form 300 is shown in Figure 10.11.

Figure 10.10 Occupational Health and Safety Administrative Functions

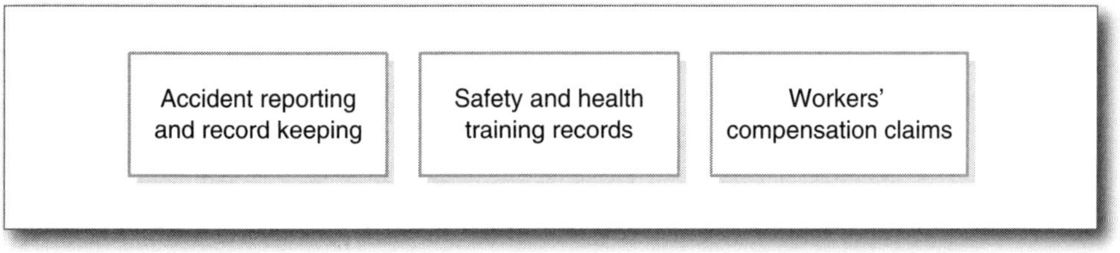

Figure 10.11 OSHA Form 300

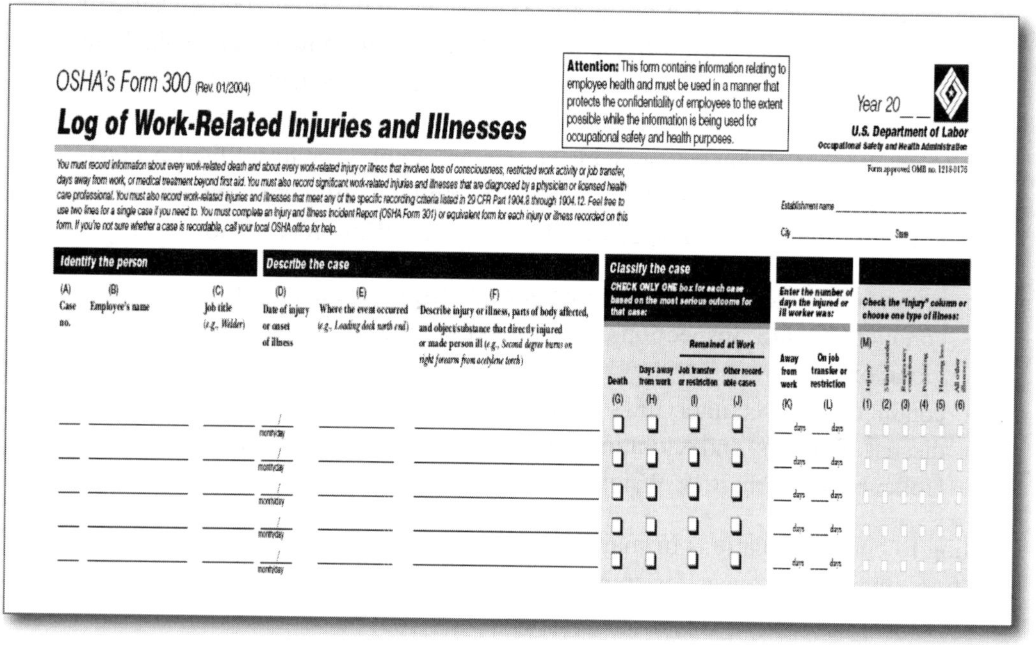

OSHA's Form 300 (Rev. 01/2004)

Log of Work-Related Injuries and Illnesses

Attention: This form contains information relating to employee health and must be used in a manner that protects the confidentiality of employees to the extent possible while the information is being used for occupational safety and health purposes.

Year 20__

U.S. Department of Labor
Occupational Safety and Health Administration

Form approved OMB no. 1218-0176

You must record information about every work-related death and about every work-related injury or illness that involves loss of consciousness, restricted work activity or job transfer, days away from work, or medical treatment beyond first aid. You must also record significant work-related injuries and illnesses that are diagnosed by a physician or licensed health care professional. You must also record work-related injuries and illnesses that meet any of the specific recording criteria listed in 29 CFR Part 1904.8 through 1904.12. Feel free to use two lines for a single case if you need to. You must complete an Injury and Illness Incident Report (OSHA Form 301) or equivalent form for each injury or illness recorded on this form. If you're not sure whether a case is recordable, call your local OSHA office for help.

Establishment name ______

City ______ State ______

Identify the person			Describe the case			Classify the case: CHECK ONLY ONE box for each case based on the most serious outcome for that case:				Enter the number of days the injured or ill worker was:		Check the "Injury" column or choose one type of illness: (M)					
(A) Case no.	(B) Employee's name	(C) Job title (e.g., Welder)	(D) Date of injury or onset of illness	(E) Where the event occurred (e.g., Loading dock north end)	(F) Describe injury or illness, parts of body affected, and object/substance that directly injured or made person ill (e.g., Second degree burns on right forearm from acetylene torch)	Death (G)	Days away from work (H)	Remained at Work: Job transfer or restriction (I)	Remained at Work: Other record-able cases (J)	Away from work (K)	On job transfer or restriction (L)	(1)	(2)	(3)	(4)	(5)	(6)
___	___	___	___/___ month/day	___	___	❑	❑	❑	❑	___ days	___ days						
___	___	___	___/___ month/day	___	___	❑	❑	❑	❑	___ days	___ days						
___	___	___	___/___ month/day	___	___	❑	❑	❑	❑	___ days	___ days						
___	___	___	___/___ month/day	___	___	❑	❑	❑	❑	___ days	___ days						
___	___	___	___/___ month/day	___	___	❑	❑	❑	❑	___ days	___ days						

SOURCE: U.S. Department of Labor (2004).

HR administration managers must be aware daily of any safety problems in order to meet OSHA Form 300 regulations and ensure that up-to-date records are available for OSHA inspections. Generally, details for the report must be obtained from the reporting supervisor involved in the reportable accident/illness investigation and recorded on OSHA Form 301. However, in smaller organizations, HR managers may be directly involved in accident/illness investigations. Reportable incidents are defined as work-related injuries and illnesses resulting in "death, days away from work, restricted work, transfer to another job, medical treatment beyond first aid, loss of consciousness, or diagnosis of a significant injury or illness" (U.S. Department of Labor, 2004). Because safety issues differ for different types of businesses, the HRIS may not have a standard safety module. More likely, limited fields are added to permit tracking and facilitate federal and state reporting (Ceriello, 1991). However, including safety modules in HRIS can be beneficial. Desirable functions would include HR portal access at remote locations so that supervisors could enter accident/illness data, linkages to safety training and equipment records, and interfaces with required workers' compensation claims, in addition to record keeping and report generation. Such functionality can be an important part of an overall safety program as well as a means of increasing HRM administrative efficiency (O'Connell, 1995).

Technology, HR Administration, and Mandated Governmental Reporting

Within the context of these complex legal requirements, what role can technology-enabled HR administration approaches have in increasing efficiency, quality, and cost reduction while enabling the fulfillment of mandated reporting? The answer to this question is especially important in the area of equal employment opportunities and safety and health. Certainly, the increasing use of HRIS is essential for the accurate, timely record keeping and reporting that facilitates the performance of both EEO and OSHA mandates. For example, accurate, timely completion of the EEO-1 reports presupposes ready access to employee records, where such information is maintained. For a smaller employer, paper records may suffice. For larger national or international employers with multiple locations, however, paper records are inadequate. Paper record keeping would require that each location search the records of each employee, manually record the appropriate information, and forward it to a centralized location for consolidation into the company report. For organizations with centralized HRM, either operations employees or managers would be required to do the report at each remote location. However, this waste of productive time is substantially reduced by the presence of an HRIS in the following ways:

- HRIS records can be established coincident with the employee application, including optional self-reporting of EEO race/ethnicity and sex data. No separate input functions are required unless corrections are needed. Self-reported data are likely to be more accurate and are preferred for compliance reporting.
- Simple queries of the HRIS database can secure required data, categorized by employee job classification, sex, and race/ethnicity in the EEO-1 format if desired.
- Required information for either EEO or OSHA reporting can be secured in minutes, with minimal HR employee involvement, rather than having staff take days or weeks to manually review records, compile the information, and forward it to a centralized location for further compilation.
- HR employees can handle the complete reporting function without interrupting productive time in operational units.
- Changes in mandated reporting requirements (e.g., an increase in the number of job classifications) can be handled mechanically by HR, without the involvement of field employees.
- Electronic reporting (i.e., computer to computer) can ensure timely receipt of reports.

If an ESS portal is available, government-mandated changes can be accomplished more easily, even when individual employees must be involved. For example, HR administration managers can communicate directly with employees, explaining the changes in EEO categories and requesting that each employee update his or her information directly via the ESS portal. Moreover, supervisors can be notified via the MSS portal of individual employees who have not updated their information, precluding meetings with all employees to introduce and monitor this type of change. Finally, if the employee refuses to update the information, the supervisor can use the MSS portal to enter the updated data directly.

If an SSC is added to the HR portal capabilities, individual employees with questions about the reporting requirements can contact the center directly for assistance. The supervisor need not be involved, and employees will receive rapid responses, which will allow them to complete the update more quickly and accurately. Thus, an HRIS, augmented by HR portals (i.e., ESS and MSS portals) and SSCs, can substantially improve the accuracy and timeliness of mandated governmental reporting while reducing the hours wasted on routine administrative work, hours that could be spent more productively.

Similarly, HR portals, SSCs, and even outsourcing can facilitate OSHA record keeping and reporting, reducing costs and enhancing timely reporting. For example, HRIS records and MSS portals permit supervisors to complete the required record of a reportable accident electronically, filling out the 300A Form via computer terminal immediately after an accident occurs. In addition, updates can be handled with minimal effort. With appropriate linkages, workers' compensation reporting to state agencies can be generated by the system. If an employee files a workers' compensation claim and the company disagrees, HR administration managers can access the data and provide the rationale for disallowing the claim. Moreover, if an organization outsources either workers' compensation reporting or accident investigation to third-party vendors, electronic linkages can notify those groups immediately so that appropriate procedures can be instituted. Finally, HR administration managers, without involving productive employees, can generate an accurate, up-to-date Form 300 whenever one is required for inspection, posting, or safety performance analysis.

Privacy and Security in an HRIS

It is important to differentiate between privacy and database security in an HRIS environment. The latter involves the protection of proprietary, company-owned information about human resources. **Privacy**, however, involves data in an HRIS database that should not be made known universally and is protected by U.S. federal and state laws. Of course, database security and personal privacy are related since a breach of data security may well involve releasing personal information about employees. However, we will focus only on privacy issues in this chapter since security is covered in Chapters 3 and 16. Privacy has become a very important topic with the advent of identity theft and laws establishing the confidentiality of health records (i.e., **Health Insurance Portability and Accountability Act** of 1996 [**HIPAA**]) as well as of any medical or disability information that is protected under the **Family and Medical Leave Act (FMLA)** of 1993 or the Americans with Disabilities Act of 1990.

The laws safeguarding personal privacy have added more requirements to the HRIS software, and often updates are needed due to court decisions or modifications to legal requirements. The initial federal privacy law was the **Privacy Act** of 1974, which allowed employees to review their personnel records, but the law applied only to federal agencies. Most states have extended this law to apply to all public and private organizations. The **Fair Credit Reporting Act** of 1970 permits applicants and employees to know of the existence and content of any credit files maintained on them. The 1974 **Family Education Rights and Privacy Act (FERPA)**, also known as the Buckley Amendment, prohibits educational organizations from supplying information about students without their consent and gives students the right to inspect their educational records.

All the aforementioned laws protect records on individuals from disclosure; however, the **Electronic Communications Privacy Act** of 1986 was enacted to protect private information from being communicated via electronic means. The law specifically prohibits the interception, recording, or disclosure of wire, electronic, and oral communications through any electronic, mechanical, or other device. An interception would take place when an employer monitors a telephone call or e-mail while it is occurring. However, the law permits employers to monitor this information for legitimate business reasons. The existence of e-mail, the Internet, and voice mail (to include text messages) can lead to very positive uses that enhance both employee and organizational productivity. However, some people may misuse these communication tools provided by their employer in unauthorized and unscrupulous ways, which could lead to legal problems for the organization. As a result, many organizations monitor Internet, e-mail, and phone use by employees to avoid litigation.

Actually, employers have considerable latitude to monitor the equipment they own. Court cases have supported the right of companies to monitor any information created, received, or sent by electronic means for business-related reasons. Many employees *incorrectly* assume that their right to privacy extends to all electronic media, whether personal or company owned; however, it does not. In fact, employees can be disciplined or terminated for inappropriate use of company e-mail, Internet, or telephones. It is highly recommended that employers create and disseminate policies indicating the circumstances under which employees can be monitored when using the employers' electronic media. It is wise to have employees sign a form indicating that they have read and understand the policy.

All this need for security and privacy directly affects HR administration within the context of an HRIS. It is most important that the employee database be secure, and this means limiting access to individuals through the use of passwords. In an ESS system, each employee needs to have a password, and the type of information the employee is permitted to access must be clearly indicated. Likewise, password security for immediate supervisors and upper-level managers, as well as professionals from HR, IT, marketing, finance, and operations, should be provided. The underlying principle for database security and individual employee privacy is the "need to know" rule; only persons with a "need to know" can access specific personnel records and reports. Adding these requirements to the HRIS makes it more complex; however, the gain in operating efficiency for HR administration compensates for the difficulties related to building and maintaining these HRIS functions. Of course, the United States is not the only country that has privacy and data security laws. In fact, these laws may differ significantly from country to country, which would add more complexity to an HRIS for an MNE.

Summary of Government-Mandated Reports and Privacy Requirements

The EEO-1 report and the OSHA Form 300 are only two of the many required administrative transactions for which HR managers are responsible. In addition, privacy laws add more complexity to the administration of the HR function via an HRIS. As noted, HRIS capabilities can be enhanced by the use of one or more HR administration approaches to improve accurate and timely reporting while reducing costs and increasing productivity. These examples demonstrate how effective HR administration can help organizations comply with government mandates while supporting strategic goals. The final HR administration issue included in this chapter is how, by using a balanced scorecard approach, HR managers can measure their activities in ways that demonstrate their contribution to an organization's strategic goals. Following a brief introduction of the use of a balanced scorecard in strategic management, we will examine which HR measures that are part of an HR administration can contribute to the balanced scorecard for an organization.

HR STRATEGIC GOAL ACHIEVEMENT AND THE BALANCED SCORECARD

As should be obvious from the topics covered thus far in this chapter, HR administration is crucial to effective HRM functioning. As discussed in Chapter 1, the HR department has historically been seen as performing a "paper-pusher" function in organizations and has been thought of as a cost-only operation. One of the major reasons for this situation was that the HR department could not easily or accurately generate metrics describing its operations and programs. The paper system existed, but it was exceedingly difficult to extract HR metrics (especially the metrics described in Chapter 6). Advances in computer technology, particularly those applicable to the HR function and its programs, made the calculation of these metrics possible. As a result, CBAs could also be calculated to evaluate the effectiveness of the HR department and its programs. The next step for HR was to become a part of the strategic management system in the organization.

The historic sequence and outcomes described in the previous paragraph depend on building an accurate, up-to-date database that is easy to access and manipulate. This is critical for all HR programs, and it all begins with a correctly designed HRIS that supports HR administration. The data from HR administration, particularly HR metrics (Chapter 6), are also used to support strategic goals, and one of the best examples of their use is in the balanced scorecard. Kaplan and Norton (1992, 1996, 2006), recognizing that an organization can no longer rely solely on a simple financial measure to assess its ability to achieve sustainable competitive advantage, devised the balanced scorecard to facilitate the organization's efforts to measure its success in achieving the strategic goals required to meet the needs of its stakeholder groups. A **balanced scorecard** is both a management and a measurement system that "enables organizations to clarify their vision and strategy and translate them into action, . . . [providing] feedback around both the internal business processes and external outcomes to continuously improve strategic performance and results" (Arveson, 1998).

Kaplan and Norton (1996) define the four components of the balanced scorecard as financial, customer, internal business processes, and learning and growth. Inclusion of these components represents an organization's commitment to balancing its strategic goals and reflects the expectations of its multiple stakeholders. An overview of all four components can be seen in Figure 10.12 along with the key question associated with each of the four.

HRM and the Balanced Scorecard

HRM is often not viewed as a strategic function in organizations primarily because its managers fail to develop measures demonstrating its strategic business value (Lawler, 2005; Ulrich, 1997). For example, successful HR administration efforts that ensure compliance with governmental mandates (e.g., EEO and OSHA reporting) are often viewed as simple administrative transactions rather than as strategic imperatives. However, failing to hire and retain the diverse workforce documented in EEO compliance reports can result in expensive lawsuits and reduced stock prices (Hersch, 1991), as well as in diminished firm credibility (Pomerenke, 1998) and decreased long-term innovation (Florida, 2002, 2005; Page, 2007). Each of these items is

Figure 10.12 Balanced Scorecard Components

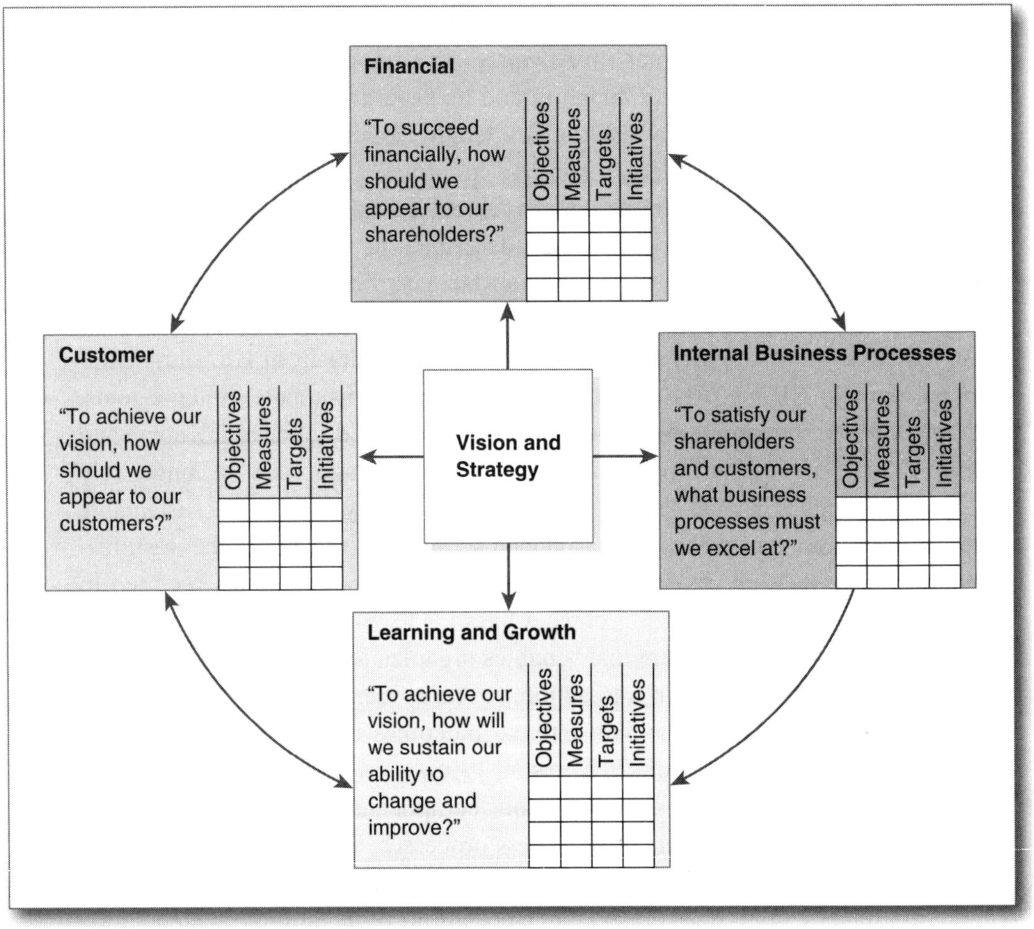

SOURCE: Arveson (1998).

directly related to the balanced scorecard categories. Specifically, lawsuits and stock price are associated with financial success, reputation is associated with the customer category, and innovation is part of the learning and growth category. Certainly, HR professionals understand the impact effective human capital management has on an organization. However, unless measures to reflect the value-added nature of HRM in leveraging human capital are developed and linked to the strategic goals reflected in a firm's balanced scorecard, it is unlikely that organizations will view such HRM-linked activities as strategic.

Figure 10.13 provides a simple example of the linkage between HR functions and an organization's balanced scorecard. The next section will highlight the development of an HR scorecard.

Figure 10.13 Sample HR–Balanced Scorecard Linkages

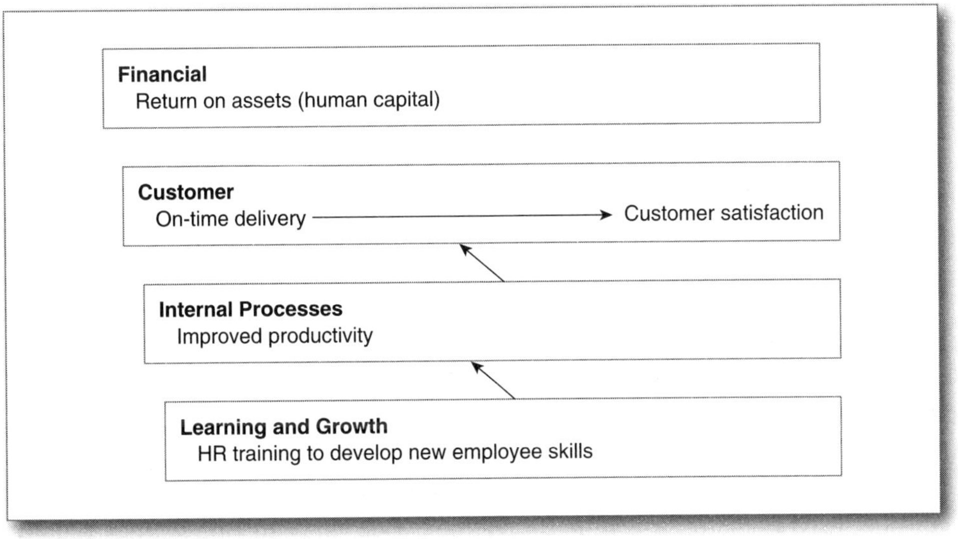

HR Scorecard, Its Measures, and Its Alignment With the Organization's Balanced Scorecard

Suppose that the company is losing some customers, and analysis indicates that customer complaints spiked and on-time product delivery and new orders declined just before these losses. HR professionals want to identify the processes and measures that support the strategic goal of customer retention. The steps they might take are as follows:

1. Specify the business strategy to be supported (e.g., customer retention).
2. Identify leading (e.g., on-time order delivery) and lagging (e.g., customer satisfaction level) indicators.
3. Identify associated internal processes (e.g., worker productivity, product quality).
4. Identify HR linkages (e.g., training, rewards).
5. Specify the HR strategy (e.g., offer enhanced productivity training for workers to reduce product time to market and ensure on-time order delivery).
6. Measure worker productivity increase, on-time deliveries, and reduction in customer complaints to demonstrate the strategic value of HR training in the "Customer" and "Learning and Growth" balanced scorecard categories.

A leading indicator is a predictor of future outcomes (e.g., on-time order delivery), whereas a lagging indicator shows what has already occurred (e.g., customer satisfaction level). Thus, to ensure the on-time order delivery required to retain customers, HR professionals must understand the internal business processes involved in this retention and identify the HR function (training) that can be employed to improve these processes (i.e., to improve productivity) and increase the probability of the desired strategic outcome (customer retention).

HR Scorecard and Balanced Scorecard Alignment

Researchers have long recognized the need to ensure goal alignment in organizations (Beatty, Huselid, & Schneider, 2003; Becker & Gerhart, 1996; Becker, Huselid, & Ulrich, 2001; Lawler, 2005). For example, Boswell (2006) reported that employees who did not have "line of sight" between their work and the strategic goals of the organization were more likely to have poor work attitudes and consider leaving the organization. In addition, Decoene and Bruggerman (2006) reported that failure to implement the business scorecard properly (i.e., by neglecting to cascade strategic goals to all levels in the organization) reduced middle managers' motivation to support strategic goals such that the organization failed to achieve its strategic financial objectives.

In recognition of the importance of alignment between the organization's balanced scorecard and HRM strategic initiatives, researchers (Becker et al., 2001) have suggested that HR professionals develop an HR scorecard as a means of establishing measures for HR that reflect this alignment. HR measures should reflect a balance of cost controls (e.g., improved productivity) and value creation (e.g., increased innovation) consistent with the business's balanced scorecard and strategic goals. Figure 10.14 identifies sample HR measures that might be included in an HR scorecard (Becker et al., 2001).

From the previous discussion, we can see multiple opportunities for HR administration managers to align with the strategic goals covered by the balanced scorecard. For example, deploying HR portals (i.e., ESS and MSS portals) can provide simultaneous support for financial goals (e.g., cost control through reduced employee expense) and learning and growth (e.g., e-learning courses). Similarly, strategic use of outsourcing can support financial goals (e.g., cost reductions) and internal processes (e.g., improved time from vacancy request to hiring). Thus, HR administration managers can make decisions that support the strategic goals contained in the balanced scorecard.

Figure 10.14 Sample HR Scorecard Measures Linked to a Firm's Balanced Scorecard

HR Functions to support Learning and Growth category (e.g., employee development)	• Backup talent ratio—Value Creation • Competency development expense per employee—Cost Control • No. of "special projects" for employee development—Value Creation • No. of employees with development plans—Cost Control
HR Internal Efficiency measures to support Financial category	• HR departmental expense/$ of sales revenue—Cost Control • HR sales training expense/$ of sales revenue—Value Creation • HR recruitment expense/R&D hires—Cost Control • No. of patents per R&D hire—Value Creation

SUMMARY

One of the most basic features within an HRIS is the HR administration module. HR administration allows organizations to streamline processes, increase service levels, and reduce costs. This chapter discussed the relative value of the HR administration module versus a traditional, "paper-and-pencil" approach to HR administration. In addition, the chapter discussed the various options available in the implementation of an HR administration module, including HR portals, shared services, outsourcing, and offshoring. Each of these approaches was considered in detail, and its advantages and disadvantages were outlined. The chapter also briefly discussed the flexibility that organizations have in implementing the HRIS. For example, HR portals may be combined with SSCs and selective outsourcing or offshoring to achieve the optimum solution for a particular firm.

Before developing and implementing the HR administration module, the organization must have conducted a basic job analysis to determine the appropriate knowledge, skills, and abilities for each job. In addition, basic job descriptions for each job should be developed. The data from this analysis form the basis for the data that are eventually entered into the HRIS. The chapter further discussed how human resource information systems can support organizations as they conduct a job analysis.

One of the key issues in implementing the HR administration module is to ensure that it meets legal and compliance requirements. This chapter discussed two specific U.S. governmental reporting mandates (i.e., EEO and OSHA reporting) as well as how an HRIS can facilitate improved accuracy, reduced costs, and increased organizational value by successfully completing such HR transactions. Even though the topic was a theme throughout the chapter, privacy, as this requirement relates to legislation and data security, was discussed in a separate section, which also presented a discussion of privacy laws and their consideration when one develops an HRIS. Finally, the chapter closed with a brief investigation of the elements important to the successful measurement of the strategic alignment of the HR balanced scorecard.

KEY TERMS

affirmative action plan (AAP)
Age Discrimination in Employment Act (ADEA)
Americans with Disabilities Act (ADA)
backsourcing
balanced scorecard
basic employee information module (BEIM)
discrete HRO
Electronic Communications Privacy Act
employee self-service (ESS)
Employer Information Report EEO-1 (EEO-1 report)
equal employment opportunity (EEO)
Fair Credit Reporting Act
Family and Medical Leave Act (FMLA)
Family Education Rights and Privacy Act (FERPA)
Health Insurance Portability and Accountability Act (HIPAA)
human resources outsourcing (HRO)
job analysis
job description
knowledge, skills, and abilities (KSA)
manager self-service (MSS)
multiprocess HRO
Occupational Assessor® software
Occupational Safety and Health Act (OSHA)
offshore ownership
offshoring
O*Net database
OSHA Form 300
OSHA Form 300A
OSHA Form 301
outsourcing
performance appraisals
position analysis questionnaire (PAQ)
privacy
Privacy Act
resource-based view
self-service portal
service-oriented architecture (SOA)
shared-service center (SSC)
total HRO
transaction cost theory

DISCUSSION QUESTIONS

1. Discuss the theoretical bases for the four HR administrative approaches introduced in this chapter. Are such theories useful to HR professionals in their efforts to improve transactional performance? Why or why not?

2. Why is service-oriented architecture enhanced by XML important to HR administration? Choose two HR administrative approaches, and discuss how each is facilitated by this architecture.
3. What are the primary advantages of HR portals and shared-services centers? Give examples of how HR professionals might use each to better achieve cost controls and service enhancement.
4. What are the primary purposes of ESS and MSS? What are the advantages and disadvantages of each?
5. Define outsourcing and offshoring. Compare and contrast the two as HR administrative tools. Give examples of the decision factors to consider when choosing one over the other.
6. Using the EEO-1 report as an example, discuss the purpose of government mandates. Give examples of penalties that organizations incur when they fail to comply with government mandates such as EEO and OSHA reporting.
7. Based on information in this chapter, recommend the most effective HR administrative approach or approaches for the owner of a small business with fewer than 50 employees and infrequent staffing needs. Would what you recommend work for a business with 5,000 employees and high turnover? Why or why not? Defend your position with information from the chapter.
8. Identify and explain the purpose of each of the four perspectives included in the balanced scorecard. Give two examples of HR measures for each of the four areas that would demonstrate the value of HR in achieving the strategic goals of organizations.
9. Return to the vignette that opened this chapter and answer the questions posed there.

CASE STUDY: THE CALLEETA CORPORATION

Jan Samson, CEO at CalleetaCO, sat staring at the now empty boardroom. Her board of directors had reacted negatively to Jan's growth proposals for expanding CalleetaCO globally, leaving Jan with a big problem. Shareholders, who had bought its stock as the radio frequency identification (RFID) manufacturer led the boom in new uses for its products, were restless as financial returns slowed. In addition, board members expressed concern that CalleetaCO plants in Mexico and Vietnam were becoming the targets of activists who advocated that organizations ensure that the humane working conditions common in the United States be established in American-owned offshore facilities. Finally, board members demanded that Jan move immediately to rein in the employee costs of the U.S. operation. Those costs were growing at a rate of 12% annually, compared with an industry average of 4%. HR Vice President John Nosmas defended his practice of hiring the best, paying them well, and providing them with expensive benefit programs to keep them developing the innovative products the market demanded. However, board members were adamant and demanded a plan at the next meeting, only six weeks away.

CalleetaCO, with its current 1,900 employees spread across three countries (i.e., the United States—1,000, Mexico—200, Vietnam—700), had grown rapidly over its eight-year existence. Although it started as a small entrepreneurial company, CalleetaCO was now challenging the top providers in its industry as it pursued its goal—to become the global leader in RFID products. RFID use exploded after the introduction of memory for passive radio transponders, which led to the production of RFID tags, microchip field radios embedded in products and used for electronic inventory. These tags were replacing traditional bar codes and manual scanning.

Electronic product coding associated with RFID has been embraced by retailers and consumers alike. Retailers such as Gillette, Hewlett-Packard, and Wal-Mart benefit through more rapid restocking, less likelihood of out-of-stock items, and the electronic identification of product expiration dates. In addition, consumers can more easily return purchases. Applications seem unending. Members of Congress have introduced legislation to track sales of tobacco products using RFID technology, for example. New U.S. passports contain RFID tags. "Swipe-less" checkouts, RFID medical alert bracelets, and security identification wristbands are on the horizon. In addition, California is likely to use RFID to comply with the 2005 Real ID Act mandated by Congress (Billingsley, 2007). However, some groups are concerned that RFID proliferation could lead to the surreptitious tracking of an individual's purchases and other privacy violations, especially since individuals may be unaware that their purchases include RFID devices. In addition, hackers may be able to steal identity information by remotely scanning an individual's passport, credit card, or driver's license.

Jan's company had grown rapidly by perfecting several of these products. To keep the innovations coming, Jan and John Nosmas devised a human capital talent acquisition and retention plan to attract the most highly skilled individuals in the industry. The company had 25 HR recruiters focused solely on identifying potential employees, 17 selection specialists to test and interview them, and above-market compensation and benefits at its U.S. location to retain them: health, dental, and life insurance at no cost to the employee; six weeks of paid vacation annually; elder care; child care; onsite pet boarding; liberal performance bonuses; 401(k) matching at 10%; stock options; and onsite spa and exercise facilities. The programs had been incredibly successful in finding the right people to fuel the company's innovative products.

With the company's success had come an even larger HR department. For example, employees regularly stopped by the HR office to chat with their designated HR support representatives (there was one HR support representative for every 10 employees). The employees were thrilled with the personal service and responsiveness to inquiries on everything from health questions to veterinary referrals. Managers had access to their own HR support specialists, who handled everything from performance appraisals and salary increases to filling vacancy requests and overseeing employee discipline. When the company had formed an SSC for information technology and financial services, the HR department had balked at participating because employees were so satisfied with service levels, even though departmental costs were 20% higher than those of counterparts at competitor firms. The firm's HRIS remained under the control of HR information technology specialists in the department, and there seemed few reasons to pursue portals. However, employees who traveled to Mexico and Vietnam had begun to complain about their inability to access HR support specialists for needed information because of time differences. U.S. expatriate managers from CalleetaCO controlled employees from Mexico and Vietnam at the offshore locations. HRO firms had recently approached John about the possibility of purchasing or managing those locations, but John had not yet explored such a possibility.

Jan picked up the telephone to call John. She explained the problem and asked him to prepare a list of ideas that could help them both demonstrate how successful CalleetaCO's talent programs had been and meet the board's requirements for cost controls. Jan knew that she would need to get John to work miracles to help meet the board's demands. She didn't want to stop talent searches or above-average total compensation, but board members were unyielding. Unless Jan could develop a successful plan to slow employee expense growth, control the activist stakeholder groups, and ultimately improve earnings, she could easily become the ex-CEO.

Case Study Questions

1. What are the key business issues facing Jan?
2. In what ways are CalleetaCO's HR operations contributing to the company's success? How do these contributions support the company's strategic goals? What changes can John make in his HR operations to meet the board's demands?
3. Describe whether each of John's proposed changes will hinder or help CalleetaCO achieve sustainable competitive advantage? Which ones would you choose if you were in John's position? Defend your choices.
4. How would a balanced scorecard help Jan explain the value of her HR talent approach? Provide sample measures for each of the four categories that would support Jan in her presentation to the board.

NOTE

1. This electronic record has also been called the master file for compensation or, simply, the employee master file, in general usage.

REFERENCES

Accenture. (2007). *Managing shared services change: Beyond communications and training.* New York: Author. Retrieved March 11, 2011, from http://www.accenture.com/us-en/Pages/insight-managing-shared-services-change-beyond-communications-training-summary.aspx

Anheier, N., & Doherty, S. (2001, October). *Employee self-service: Tips to ensure a successful implementation* (SHRM White Paper). Alexandria, VA: Society for Human Resource Management. Retrieved March 3, 2007, from www.shrm.org/hrtx/library_published/IC/CMS_000210.aspx

Arveson, P. (1998). What is the balanced scorecard? *Balanced Scorecard Institute*. Retrieved March 11, 2011, from http://www.balancedscorecard.org/BSCResources/AbouttheBalanced-Scorecard/tabid/55/Default.aspx

Barney, J. (1991). Firm resources and sustained competitive advantage. *Journal of Management, 17*, 99–120.

Barney, J. (2001). Resource-based theories of competitive advantage: A 10-year retrospective on the resource-based view. *Journal of Management, 27*, 643–650.

Beaman, K. (Ed.). (2002). *Boundaryless HR: Human capital management in the global economy.* Austin, TX: IHRIM Press Book.

Beatty, R., Huselid, M., & Schneider, C. (2003). New HR metrics: Scoring on the business scorecard. *Organizational Dynamics, 32*, 107–121.

Becker, B., & Gerhart, B. (1996). The impact of human resource management on organizational performance: Progress and prospects. *Academy of Management Journal, 39*, 779–801.

Becker, B., Huselid, M., & Ulrich, D. (2001). *The HR scorecard: Linking people, strategy, and performance.* Boston: Harvard Business School Press.

Bender, J. (2001). HR service centers: The human element behind the technology. In A. J. Walker (Ed.), *Web-based human resources* (pp. 212–225). New York: McGraw-Hill.

Billingsley, K. (2007). *Playing tag: An RFID primer.* San Francisco: Pacific Research Institute. Retrieved August 21, 2007, from http://www.pacificresearch.org/docLib/20070706_RFID.pdf

Boswell, W. (2006). Aligning employees with the organization's strategic objective: Out of "line of sight," out of mind. *International Journal of Human Resource Management, 17*, 1489–1511.

Brisco, D. R., & Schuler, R. S. (2004). *International human resource management* (2nd ed.). New York: Routledge.

Campbell, S., & Mohun, V. (2007). *Mastering enterprise SOA with SAP Netweaver and my SAP.* Indianapolis, IN: Wiley & Sons.

CBR. (2007, May 29). Convergys wins $1bn Johnson & Johnson HR deal. *Computer Business Review*. Retrieved May 22, 2010, from http://www.cbronline.com/news/convergys_wins_1bn_johnson_johnson_hr_deal

CedarCrestone. (2010). *CedarCrestone 2009–2010 HR systems survey: HR technologies, deployment approaches, value, and metrics* (12th ed.). Alpharetta, GA: Author. Retrieved May 22, 2010, from http://www.cedarcrestone.com/research.php

Ceriello, V. (1991). *Human resource management systems.* San Francisco: Jossey-Bass.

Chiamsiri, S., Bulusu, S., & Agarwal, M. (2005). Information technology offshore outsourcing in India: A human resource management perspective. *Research and Practice in Human Resource Management, 13*, 105–114.

CMO Council. (2006). *Secure the trust of your brand.* Palo Alto, CA: Author. Retrieved April 14, 2007, from http://wp.bitpipe.com/resource/org_1087482373_918/10139_CMO_TTsyndication.pdf

Coase, R. (1937). The nature of the firm. *Economica, 4*, 386–405.

Decoene, V., & Bruggerman, W. (2006). Strategic alignment and middle-level managers' motivation in a balanced scorecard setting. *International Journal of Operations & Production Management, 26*, 429–449.

Dominguez, L. (2006). *The manager's step-by-step guide to outsourcing.* New York: McGraw-Hill.

Dowling, P. J., & Welch, D. E. (2005). *International human resource management: Managing people in a multinational context* (4th ed.). Mason, OH: Thomson/South-Western.

EquaTerra. (2005). *EquaTerra research brief: Human resources outsourcing.* Retrieved October 14, 2006, from www.equaterra.com/KR/research/eq-research-brief-all.aspx

EquaTerra. (2007). *Taking the pulse of today's human resources outsourcing market.* Retrieved May 18, 2007, from www.equaterra.com/KR/download.aspx?fn=EquaTerra-HRO-Buyer-Pulse-Results-April-2007.pdf

EquaTerra. (2010). *"Generation 3 Outsourcing" deals have arrived.* Retrieved May 22, 2010, from http://blog.equaterra.com/2010/01/generation-3-hr-outsourcing-deals-have-arrived/

Erl, T. (2005). *Service-oriented architecture (SOA): Concepts, technology, and design.* New York: Prentice Hall PTR.

Esen, E. (2004). *SHRM human resource management outsourcing survey report.* Alexandria, VA: Society for Human Resource Management.

Everest Research Institute. (2007). *Human resources outsourcing (HRO) market update: May 2007.* Retrieved May 28, 2007, from www.outsourcing-requests.com/common/sponsors/60629/Human_Resources_Outsourcing_HRO_Market_Update.pdf

Fletcher, P. (2005). Personnel administration to business-driven human capital management. In H. Gueutal & D. Stone (Eds.), *The brave new world of eHR* (pp. 1–21). San Francisco: Jossey-Bass.

Florida, R. (2002). *The rise of the creative class: And how it's transforming work, leisure, community and everyday life.* New York: Basic Books.

Florida, R. (2005). *The flight of the creative class: The new global competition for talent.* New York: HarperCollins.

Ghorpade, J.V. (1988). *Job analysis.* Englewood Cliffs, NJ: Prentice Hall.

Goh, M., Prakash, S., & Yeo, R. (2007). Resource-based approach to IT in a shared services manufacturing firm. *Industrial Management & Data Systems, 107*, 251–270.

Gueutal, H., & Falbe, C. (2005). eHR trends in delivery methods. In H. Gueutal & D. Stone (Eds.), *The brave new world of eHR* (pp. 190–225). San Francisco: Jossey-Bass.

Gueutal, H., & Stone, D. (Eds.). (2005). *The brave new world of eHR.* San Francisco: Jossey-Bass.

Hatch, P. (2004). *Offshore outsourcing 2005 research: Preliminary findings and conclusions* (Ventoro Report, January 22, 2005, version). Retrieved February 7, 2007, from www.ventoro.com/Offshore2005ResearchFindings.pdf

Hersch, J. (1991). Equal employment opportunity law and firm profitability. *Journal of Human Resources, 26*, 139–153.

Hewitt. (2005). *A fresh look at the logic of HR outsourcing.* Lincolnshire, IL: Hewitt Associates LLC. Retrieved February 8, 2007, from www.outsourcing-requests.com/common/sponsors/54934/A_Fresh_ Look_at_the_Logic_of_HR_Outsourcing.pdf

Hewitt. (2010). *HR outsourcing trends and insights 2009.* Lincolnshire, IL: Hewitt Associates LLC. Retrieved March 11, 2011, from http://www.hewittassociates.com/Lib/MBUtil/AssetRetrieval.aspx?guid=1772D160-274B-43B9-9D0A-D30CEED38DFF

Jossi, F. (2004). Reporting race. *SHRM.* Retrieved January 7, 2007, from www.shrm.org/hrtx/library_ published/nonIC/CMS_006477.asp

Kaplan, R., & Norton, D. (1992). The balanced scorecard: Measures that drive performance. *Harvard Business Review, 70*, 71–80.

Kaplan, R., & Norton, D. (1996). *The balanced scorecard: Translating strategy into action.* Boston: Harvard Business School Press.

Kaplan, R., & Norton, D. (2006). *Alignment: Using the balanced scorecard to create corporate synergies.* Boston: Harvard Business School Press.

Kavanagh, M., Gueutal, H., & Tannenbaum, S. (1990). *Human resource information systems: Development and application.* Boston: PWS.

Keebler, T. (2001). HR outsourcing in the Internet era. In A. Walker (Ed.), *Web-based human resources* (pp. 259–276). New York: McGraw-Hill.

Lacity, M., & Willcocks, L. (2000). Relationships in IT outsourcing: A stakeholder perspective. In R. Zmud (Ed.), *Framing the domains of IT management: Projecting the future through the past* (pp. 355–384). Cincinnati, OH: Pinnaflex.

Lacity, M., & Willcocks, L. (2001). *Global information technology outsourcing: In search of business advantage* (1st ed.). West Sussex, England: Wiley.

Lawler, E. (2005). Making strategic partnership a reality. *Strategic HR Review, 4*, 3.

Ledvinka, J. (1982). *Federal regulation of personnel and human resource management.* Boston: Kent.

Lublinsky, B. (2007, May). Versioning in SOA. *Architecture Journal,* 11. Retrieved May 18, 2007, from http://msdn2.microsoft.com/en-us/arcjournal/bb491124.aspx

Lucenko, K. (1998, March). *Shared services: Achieving higher levels of performance* (The Conference Board Report R-1210-98-CH). New York: The Conference Board. Retrieved February 7, 2007, from http://www.conference-board.org/publications/publicationdetail.cfm?publicationid=396

Marks, E., & Bell, M. (2006). *Service-oriented architecture: A business planning and implementation guide for business and technology.* Indianapolis, IN: Wiley.

Noe, R., Hollenbeck, J., Gerhart, B., & Wright, P. (2004). *Fundamentals of human resource management.* New York: McGraw-Hill.

O'Connell, S. (1995, June). Safety first: computers to the rescue. *HR Magazine, 40*(6). Retrieved February 22, 2007, from http://findarticles.com/p/articles/mi_m3495/is_n6_v40/ai_17191250

Organization for the Advancement of Structured Information Systems. (2006). *OASIS reference model for service oriented architecture 1.0.* Burlington, MA: Author. Retrieved April 7, 2007, from www.oasis-open.org/committees/download.php/18486/pr-2changes.pdf

Osle, H., & Cooper, J. (2003). Structuring HR for maximum value. *IHRIM.link, 8,* 4.

Page, S. (2007). *The difference: How the power of diversity creates better groups, firms, schools, and societies.* Princeton, NJ: Princeton University Press.

Paskoff, S. M. (2003, September). *Around the world without the daze: Communicating international codes of conduct.* Paper presented at the fourth annual program on International Labor and Employment Law, Dallas, TX.

Phillips, T., Isenhour, L., & Stone, D. (2008). The potential for privacy violations in electronic human resource practices. In G. Martin, M. Reddington, & H. Alexander (Eds.), *Technology, outsourcing, and transforming HR* (pp. 193–230). Oxford: Butterworth Heinemann.

Pomerenke, P. (1998). Class action sexual harassment lawsuit: A study in crisis communication. *Human Resource Management, 37*, 207–219.

Powell, A. (2004). *Shared services and CRM* (Conference Board Technical Report E-0005-004RR). New York: The Conference Board. Retrieved March 11, 2011, from http://www.conference-board.org/publications/publicationdetail.cfm?publicationid=786

PricewaterhouseCoopers. (2006). *Key trends in human capital: A global perspective—2006.* London, UK: Author. Retrieved March 11, 2001, from http://www.pwc.co.uk/pdf/pwc_key trends_mar06.pdf

Procter & Gamble. (2011). Diversity and inclusion: Fulfilling our potential. *P&G.* Retrieved March 11, 2011, from http://www.pg.com/en_US/company/purpose_people/diversity_inclusion.shtml

Quinn, B., Cooke, R., & Kris, A. (2000). *Shared services: Mining for corporate gold.* London: Pearson Education.

Robinson, D., & Robinson, J. (2005). *Strategic business partner: Aligning people strategies with business goals.* New York: Berrett-Hoehler.

Schwartz, E. (2003, December 8). Oracle launches HR-XML product; Will Microsoft WORD follow? *InfoWorld.com.* Retrieved March 11, 2001, from http://www.infoworld.com/t/platforms/oracle-launches-hr-xml-product-390

Smith, A. (2006). New EEO-1 report kicks in for 2007 survey. *HR News*. Retrieved June 1, 2007, from www.shrm.org/hrnews_published/archives/CMS_015698.asp

Ulrich, D. (1997). *Human resource champions.* Boston: Harvard Business School Press.

U.S. Department of Labor. (2004). *OSHA instruction* (Directive No. CPL 02-00-135). Washington, DC: Author. Retrieved March 11, 2001, from http://www.osha.gov/pls/oshaweb/owadisp.show_document?p_table=DIRECTIVES&p_id=3205

U.S. Department of Labor. (2007). *Federal vs. state family and medical leave laws.* Washington, DC: Author. Retrieved June 12, 2007, from http://www.dol.gov/whd/state/fmla/index.htm

U.S. Equal Employment Opportunity Commission. (1964). *Title VII of the Civil Rights Act of 1964.* Washington, DC: Author. Retrieved March 11, 2011, from http://www.eeoc.gov/laws/statutes/titlevii.cfm

U.S. Equal Employment Opportunity Commission. (2006). *EEOC instruction booklet.* Washington, DC: Author. Retrieved March 11, 2011, from http://www.eeoc.gov/employers/eeo1survey/2007instructions.cfm

von Simson, E. (1990). The "centrally" decentralized IS organization. *Harvard Business Review, 68*(4), 158–162.

Walker, A. (1982). *HRIS development: A project team approach to building an effective personnel information system.* New York: Van Nostrand Reinhold.

Walker, A. (1993). *Handbook of human resource information systems.* New York: McGraw-Hill.

Walker, A. (Ed.). (2001). *Web-based human resources.* New York: McGraw-Hill.

Weatherly, L. (2005). HR outsourcing: Reaping strategic value for your organization. *SHRM Research Quarterly.* Retrieved January 4, 2007, from www.shrm.org/research/quarterly/2005/0805RQuart_essay.asp

Williamson, O. (1975). *Markets and hierarchies.* New York: Free Press.

Wright, P., McMahan, G., Snell, S., & Gerhart, B. (1998). *Strategic HRM: Building human capital and organizational capability* (Technical report). Ithaca, NY: Cornell University.

Chapter 11

Talent Management

Kevin M. Johns and Michael J. Kavanagh

EDITORS' NOTE

This chapter is the first of four on topics that are related to talent management (TM). Talent management has become an extremely important strategic goal for organizations, both domestic and global ones. Talent management has also been called human capital management (HCM), which recognizes that TM involves the effective management of the human capital of any organization. Talent management has multiple meanings. However, all of these definitions recognize that, to gain competitive advantage in the marketplace, an organization's talent (i.e., its people) must be managed effectively. This management of people includes attracting, selecting, training, compensating, and retaining employees. However, the underlying requirement for talent management is forecasting the need for talented employees in terms of both numbers and skills, particularly the need for employees in leadership positions. In order to forecast these needs, the organization must have accurate information about the knowledge, skills, and abilities (KSA) necessary for effective job performance, and these are identified through job analysis, as discussed thoroughly in Chapter 10. Thus, this chapter is focused on (1) managing talent, (2) forecasting future demand and supply of employees through human resource planning (HRP), and (3) understanding how an HRIS can assist both talent management and HRP. Chapter 12 will focus on recruiting and selecting employees with desired talent, Chapter 13 is concerned with improving talent through training and developing employees, Chapter 14 deals with managing employees' talent through performance management and compensation practices, and Chapter 15 covers the management of employees in international organizations.

CHAPTER OBJECTIVES

After completing this chapter, you should be able to

- Understand the origin of talent management and how it fits within human resources planning (HRP), human capital management, Strategic HRM, and corporate strategy
- Discuss the evidence for the importance of TM in general and, specifically, in terms of the talent management life cycle
- Discuss the common attributes of talented individuals
- Discuss the steps in the development and use of an HRP program
- Explain the use of HRP in forecasting supply and demand of new employees
- Explain the importance of job analysis and job descriptions to talent management programs
- Identify and discuss the important HR metrics for the HRP program of a company
- Explain the difference between a long and short strategy for TM and why it is important
- Explain the contribution of a TM program to corporate strategy as well as the importance of an adaptable workforce
- Discuss the effects of corporate culture on the talent management program
- Discuss how the use of computer applications in an HRIS support the components of talent management as well as their use in setting performance goals and evaluating job performance
- Discuss how companies are using social networks to recruit talented individuals
- Explain the relationship between talent management and performance management and the need to show measurable results on a balanced scorecard
- Explain how workforce analytics are used in a TM program
- Explain how to measure the success of a TM program

HRIS IN ACTION

Rudiger is sitting at his desk in his seventh-floor corner office in the City, gazing out over London and reflecting on life. At 43 he is at the top of his game. He has everything he could wish for—a lovely partner, a four-year-old in a private nursery, a new executive house in the suburbs, a holiday home in southern Italy, and a remuneration package that's the envy of his peers and beyond anything his German immigrant parents could have imagined. But it hasn't been easy, oh no! Hard work, long hours, geographical moves every two or three years, and sacrifices in terms of his personal life.

But now he has a problem. Rudiger has just been appointed Global Head of People and Talent responsible for the future of 35,000 people worldwide, the bulk of whom are based in the United States, the United Kingdom, and Europe, and manufacturing is likely to relocate to China in the next two years, adding to his responsibilities. In his previous role, he was responsible for the United Kingdom and Northern Europe and had operational oversight for 11,000 people. An initial consideration of his responsibilities has identified a number of people issues for the next five years:

- recruiting and placing new employees in appropriate jobs as vacancies occur,
- developing the skills of current and new employees in training programs, and
- retaining unique specialists in highly skilled roles.

In addition, several other issues have been brought to his attention by the outgoing Global Head of People and Talent:

- some of the brightest high performers and the most experienced midlevel managers appear to be leaving the company;
- the general employee population is aging, and there will be a significant number of retirements over the next decade, which will require extensive replacements; and
- there is an aging senior directorship, most of whom are looking toward early retirement.

Although he knows he has a problem, the main problem is that he does not have enough detailed information about the employees to know the scale of the problem. He wishes he could find a general framework in which to address these problems and issues, and he wants to be able to show how the framework and programs he implements will impact on the "bottom line" of the organization.

INTRODUCTION

Assume you recently have been looking to change jobs and move to a new company. Your phone rings, and on the other end of the line is Sarah, who, after saying hello, identifies herself as the executive director of people talent from the firm interested in hiring you. Not only is Sarah, a representative of the company, calling you directly, but her title appears to be different from what you are used to hearing. You smile as you say to yourself that someone has taken an interest not just in your skills but also in the current and potential talents you can bring to the company.

Talent management (TM) is not just a new title for the HR professional who is the manager of new hiring at a company. The field of TM brings with it a new perspective that unifies recruiting, hiring, training, promoting, and retaining talented individuals who can contribute to the overall growth and competitive advantage of a company. Historically, the management of a company's talent was primarily focused on hiring individuals who had good experience along with appropriate educational credentials—and then hoping they would fit. The concept of TM has transformed this approach. Just matching individual skills to specific job requirements is insufficient; TM requires an HRM plan that is a comprehensive program of using and developing the person's knowledge, skills, and abilities. The outcome of a TM program nested within the HRM function is that individuals can become high performing employees who can contribute to the effectiveness and profitability of the company.

Defining Talent Management

For the past 15 or 20 years, talent management has been defined in a number of ways. In general, TM refers to the process of hiring, socializing, developing, and retaining employees, while at the same time attracting highly skilled individuals from the labor market. A detailed approach to defining talent management comes from an article by Lockwood (2006) that appeared in *HR Magazine*: "Talent management is the implementation of integrated strategies or systems designed to increase workplace productivity by developing improved processes for attracting, developing, retaining and utilizing people with the required skills and aptitude to meet current and future business needs" (p. 17). More recently, Larry Dunivan (2010) notes that "talent management has become the call to action for a more consultative, knowledge-based role for Human Resources in overall business management. . . . In other words, talent management from a technological perspective provides companies the opportunity to collect and leverage rich data about people to respond to business needs" (p. 14).

Importance of Talent Management

In a poll conducted by the **Society for Human Resource Management (SHRM)** and entitled "Challenges Facing Organizations and HR in the Next Ten Years," the responses of HR professionals to a series of questions regarding specific challenges they expected over the next 10 years were received and tabulated (SHRM, 2010). There were 449 HR professionals who responded to questions asking them to describe the "top challenges that their organization and the HR profession will face during the next decade." Of these survey respondents, 72% were from U.S.-based companies and 28% from multinational organizations.

Responses to this question yielded the following results: "Nearly half the respondents (47 percent) said that obtaining human capital and optimizing on human capital investments was the top investment challenge for businesses over the next 10 years. Slightly less than a third (29 percent) of the respondents listed 'obtaining financial capital and optimizing capital investments' and 12 percent answered 'obtaining intellectual capital and optimizing intellectual capital investments' as the top challenges" (p. 1).

Another question on the poll asked the respondents to list the tactics that they thought would be effective in meeting the HR challenges they would face over the next ten years: "58 percent of the respondents listed providing flexibility to balance life and work as the top tactic to meet the challenge of attracting, retaining and rewarding the best people" (p. 1).

In another survey conducted by CedarCrestone (2010), respondents were asked what HR computer-based application categories would have increased adoption and usage in the near future. The results indicate that "three application categories will grow 90% or more: talent management, social media, and workforce optimization, the latter of which includes workforce planning and workforce analytics [see Chapter 6]" (p. 9). In addition, respondents thought that more talent management automation was related to net income growth, sales growth, and more sales per employee for organizations with talent management applications.

The Talent Management Life Cycle

Organizations recognize that an important workforce issue today is the lack of leadership capability in many companies. An example of a lack of leadership can be seen in the financial markets and the associated economic crises caused by "junk" subprime mortgages, as well as the lure of making easy money. Even more recent was the May 6, 2010, 1,000-point drop in the stock market. Blaming someone with fast fingers is a very poor explanation for an overall lack of leadership in our financial institutions.

But lack of leadership in companies today is not just tied to lack of experience or training. It also comes from (1) expanding too quickly into new markets or geographies, (2) the changing needs of the employees, and (3) the ongoing retirement of the "baby boomers." A report by McKinsey and Company (2001) stated that the United States was facing a long-term talent shortage as a result of retiring baby boomers. Since this report appeared, little has been done to solve this mass retirement problem. It is interesting to note that the McKinsey report could not predict what would happen if there were a severe economic downturn. The economic downturn of 2008–2009 kept many baby boomers in the workforce. However, it is still inevitable: baby boomers will eventually leave.

Criticisms have come from unions and former employees who have lost their jobs; they claim that companies are replacing an aging workforce with less expensive overseas workers, that is, through outsourcing. As opposed to the claim made by critics of outsourcing, it is not a new idea, but questions must arise as to whether leadership skills are being substituted for something that costs less but may be producing questionable results. Attracting less talented and less expensive employees to replace departing employees who have leadership skills can erode an organization's future revenues. So it is very important to ensure that key leadership skills are being replaced either from within the company or from outside sources. Acquiring and growing a talented human capital workforce that adapts to the new challenges occasioned by changes in the marketplace is key to the **talent management life cycle** and, subsequently, to finding the leadership capabilities necessary to compete in the global economy.

Attributes for Talent

The McKinsey report stated that talented employees who were "high performers" were 50–100% more productive than employees who were "average performers" (McKinsey and Company, 2001). During the downturn in the economy when forced layoffs have occurred, it is the talented performer that needs to be retained in the company. Job performance evaluations are a good method to determine employees' efforts to be effective in their jobs, but evaluations are sometimes narrow and do not measure the employees' potential for long-term success in an organization. The real measure for the long-term success of a talented individual is to evaluate the underlying attributes necessary for achievements.

There are many attributes from which to choose, and we will not try to identify and evaluate them for all employees in all job situations. Identifying the specific set of attributes that can lead to success in a job or business is difficult because no two individuals are alike, and attributes associated with the success of one individual may not apply to another. The best anyone can do is to choose the most likely attributes to measure people's potential for future success, but, again, there are no guarantees. However, there are some core attributes that organizations should evaluate in regard to current employees or potential hires, such as honesty and integrity. Unfortunately, there are executives in business today whose honesty and integrity are questionable.

One effective method to measure what it takes to succeed in a particular job is to look at the job performance of past individuals who have succeeded in that position and identify the attributes possessed by those individuals. This methodology has been used for many years by HR recruiters and line managers to find the "right" person for the "right" job. An organization needs to ensure that the higher performers are retained to help maintain the company's operations in case there are employee layoffs. Thus, it is important for the HR professionals and the executive management team to assess both employees' potential individual job performance and their overall contribution to the whole company.

However, the question still remains as to what an organization should try to determine beyond core values or particular job skills for current employees or new hires. Although a complete list of the characteristics that make for success is impossible, the following appear to be the **common attributes of talented individuals**:

- **Ability to communicate with others using multiple media**; for example, communication could be by phone, presentation, or e-mail. An individual's ideas may be the best, but if she or he cannot communicate those ideas with clarity, then those ideas have no impact.
- **Drive**; motivation plays a big role in determining who succeeds in any venture in life. Look at examples of people who constantly "reinvent" themselves, such as Governor Schwarzenegger—bodybuilder to Hollywood actor to California governor.
- **Ability and willingness to listen to the ideas of others**; listening is one of the most important ways of establishing good personal and business relationships.
- **Problem solving skills**; many tasks today in business deal with solving problems, whether that involves handling a small request by a client over the phone or closing the biggest acquisition deal in a company's history.
- **Imagination**; the closest version of the word "imagination" from a business perspective is when we are asked to think "outside the box."

The usefulness of the above attributes can be seen in numerous examples. If you have the ability to communicate and listen to others, you may be more likely to be a better team player and work effectively within teams. One reason to hire potentially talented employees may be based on their experience, for example, of running their own business—a venture for which initiative and drive are key success attributes. Being able to solve problems also relates to being willing to learn new things.

Imagination is an important attribute for people in business today. Albert Einstein once stated that the true sign of intelligence is not knowledge but imagination. How many companies today, in developing their talent, allow for a sabbatical from work, so an employee can just take a break and think? Use of one's imagination is the mechanism for building a vision for a business. Imagination is a key attribute for differentiating between talented individuals who can become future business leaders and those who will have difficulty succeeding.

JOB ANALYSIS AND HUMAN RESOURCE PLANNING: PART OF TM

Job Analysis

The introduction to this chapter discussed acquiring the most talented employees, such as skilled professionals and experienced managers; however, talent management comprises more than recruiting and so will be built on a program of **human resource planning (HRP)**.[1] Thus, the HRP program is closely related to **Strategic HRM** (Chapman, 2009). The aim of an effective HRP program is to have the best available people working in the proper jobs at the appropriate time so that the organization maximizes its productive capacity. Fulfilling this goal means that future employee needs are forecasted accurately based on annual employee turnover and expected strategic directions. For example, if a strategic goal for a company is to increase market share by 3% over the next two years, this will affect the number of needed new employees in multiple job categories. With accurate estimates of employee turnover in those job categories added to the forecasted employee needs based on the strategic goal, the company can begin planning to recruit new employees as well as train current ones. In order to make these forecasts accurate, however, it is *crucial* that the **knowledge, skills, and abilities (KSA)** required in the forecasted jobs be known. As was covered in Chapter 10, job analysis provides this information by producing **job descriptions. Job analysis** is the process of systematically obtaining information about jobs by determining the duties, tasks, or activities of jobs from which KSA requirements can be estimated.

Human Resource Planning (HRP)

HRP begins with the identification of the strategic goals of the company and of how an HRP program can assist in achieving the effective use of the human capital of the company. Organizations know that change is a constant in their business. It could be a change in competition, new markets, environmental concerns, or economic conditions. For example, a company may want to succeed under new competitive conditions by expanding its business into new geographic markets. A company may need to change its strategic vision, organizational values and structure, or corporate culture. When these types of changes occur, there must be corresponding changes in HRM programs, and one of the most important ones is the HRP program.

Changes in organizational strategy and business objectives focus attention on the use of the HRP program to estimate three factors related to an organization's employees:

- number of employees needed for growth or decline,
- required competencies and behaviors of these employees, and
- required levels of productivity expected from these employees.

This information is the primary input that starts the process of an HRP program. An HRP program involves three major processes and a number of actions within each process.

HRP Process Model

There have been a number of conceptual and descriptive models of the stages and processes involved in an HRP program. However, because of its simplicity, we favor the general three-phase model developed by Dyer (1982). In addition to being simple, this model can be used to implement the HRP program for all employees, sales associates to senior managers. In this model, the HRP program involves three major phases: (1) **setting HRP objectives**, (2) **planning personnel programs**, and (3) **evaluation and control** (Dyer, 1982). Figure 11.1 depicts an expansion and modification of Dyer's model, and it provides greater specificity in terms of the activities that occur within the three phases. These phase-specific activities will be discussed in the following sections.

Phase 1: Setting HRP Objectives

Estimating Demand. As can be seen in Figure 11.1, one of the first activities in phase 1 of the HRP process involves estimating demand for the total number of employees in a future business scenario. As an example, we will use a fictitious company that manufactures brake assemblies. The company has just had a very profitable year and currently has approximately 21% of the market for its products. The company's strategic planning committee has decided that a 2.5% increase in market share for the next fiscal year seems reasonable. This strategic statement comprises the "Strategic Future Business Plan," as seen in the lower left box in Figure 11.1, and is the first element in "estimating the human capital demand" for this company. The estimation of demand involves an examination of the history of the changes in numbers of employees by job when the company changed production levels in the past. This forecasted demand, then, is an estimate of the number of employees, by job category, needed to handle the 2.5% increase in market share, and it must be calculated by the HR department based on these

Figure 11.1 Model of the HRP Process With Use of an HRIS (as Modified From Dyer, 1982)

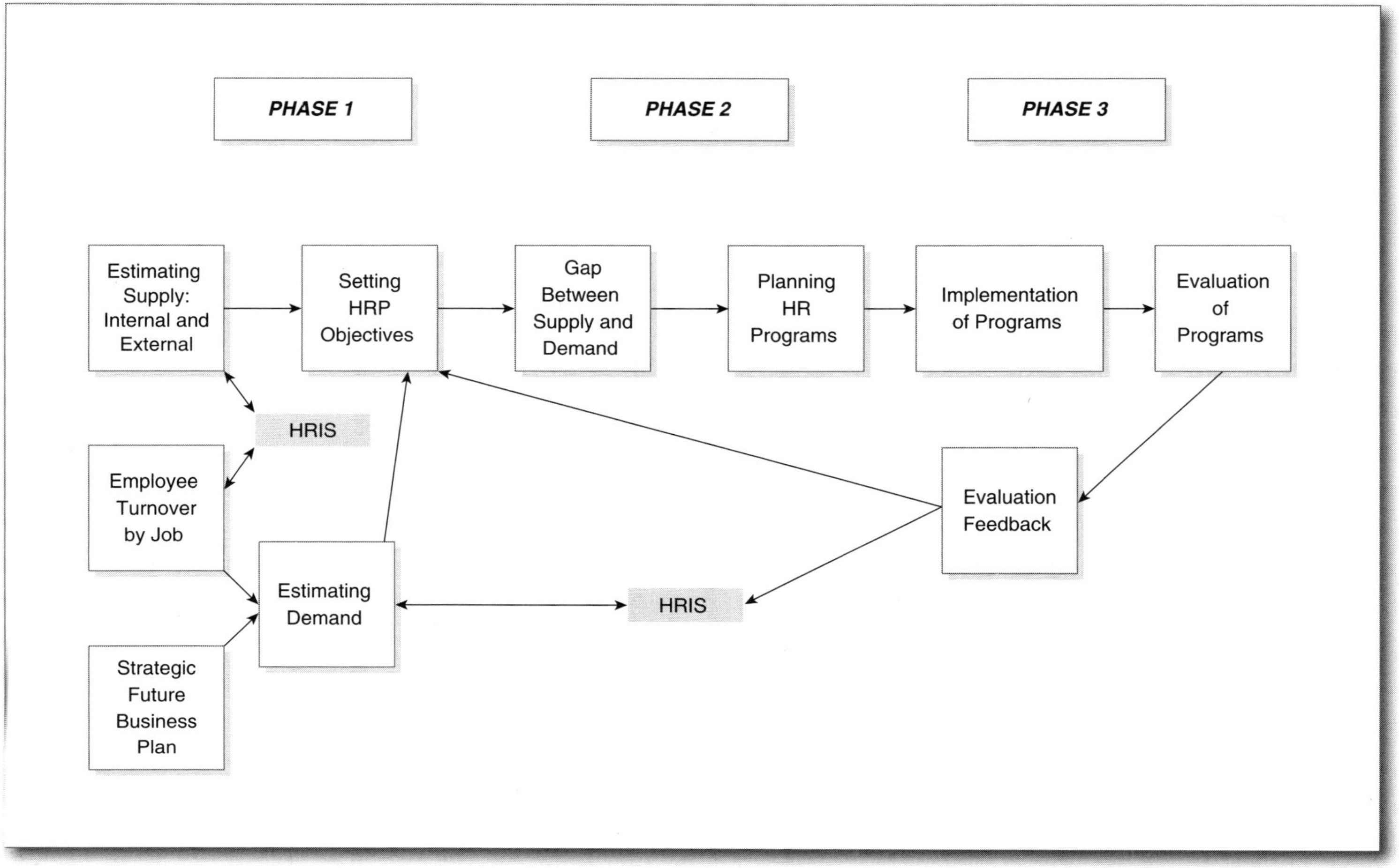

historical records. Note the two-headed arrow from "Estimating Demand" to the HRIS box. With the data from the historical records available in the HRIS, the company, using simple statistical tools, should be able to calculate the needed number of new employees.

In addition to using historical records, HR professionals can use a number of forecasting techniques, both statistical and judgmental, that are available in the literature (see Noe, Hollenbeck, Gerhart, & Wright, 2010). These techniques will all produce a list of the estimated number of *employees by job* needed to accomplish the increased workload necessary to meet production changes based on a projected 2.5% market share increase. However, note from Figure 11.1 that these estimates comprise only one part of the estimated demand. The other part of this demand estimate comes from the annual average employee turnover, again, *by job*. Adding the forecasted need for employees based on the strategic objective, a 2.5% market share gain, to the average employee turnover rate by job provides an estimate of the total demand for human capital.

Estimating Supply. As indicated in the box in Figure 11.1, estimation of the supply of available labor involves two components, external and internal. The external component is obtained from recent estimates of the potential availability of new employees by experience and skills in the company's geographic labor market. These estimates are available from state and national labor departments, local unemployment agencies, and employee referral agencies. These availability figures can be categorized by company jobs in terms of potential new employees with the necessary KSA sets to fill jobs. The second source of data for the supply estimate is internal and concerns the historic movement of employees within the company by job, for example, the number of promotions and lateral transfers of employees between jobs. Again, there are both sophisticated mathematical and judgmental techniques to estimate the internal supply of employees. Note again that most of the data necessary for estimating internal supply will be available in an HRIS. These two estimates of supply are combined to provide an estimate of the total supply.

Phase 2: Planning HR Programs

Phase 2 in Figure 11.1 involves calculating the gap between the estimated *demand for employees* and the estimated *supply* of current and potential employees. Subtracting the supply from the demand figures can result in a negative or positive gap. Returning to our case of the brake assembly manufacturing company, we would expect the gap to be positive, thus indicating a need to add new employees and promote some current employees to open job positions. Of course, the gap could be negative (more supply than demand), indicating a decrease in the need for future employees. This situation could occur, for example, in a company downsizing its workforce due to weak annual sales.

The important point is that there will be a gap, and, as a result, planning for HR programs to close the gap must be done. In the case of the company estimating a 2.5% market share increase, a variety of programs tied to the HRM functions could be initiated. For example, recruiting for new employees could be expanded beyond the current method of using only newspaper ads to include the use of television and radio advertising. The company might also want to start recruiting on college campuses or to develop Internet recruiting, which will be discussed in Chapter 12. Internally, the company could begin training programs to facilitate the promotion of current employees For example, it might offer a first-level supervisory training program for line workers that could have both formal classroom and on-the-job aspects (to be discussed in Chapter 13). Such programs would be expected to produce employees to fill the jobs that the HR department has predicted will become available.

Phase 3: Evaluation and Control

As indicated in Figure 11.1, this final phase involves the implementation of the planned HRM programs from phase 2. There are some choices to be made at this point regarding HRM programs, for example whether they will involve Internet recruiting and training. Will these programs be implemented by internal HR staff or by an outside vendor? Another aspect to consider is the expected cost-benefit ratio estimated for the new programs. Regardless of the programs that are implemented, one of the most important aspects of the HRP program is the evaluation of these new programs to determine if they have actually closed the gap between supply and demand. For the HRP program to be complete, the HR department must send the results of this evaluation to the HRIS, so they can be used in "Setting HRP Objectives" in future HRP programs. Particularly important is the evaluation of how useful the new HRM programs were in closing the demand-supply gap. This section covered the basics of HRP programs, which can be applied to planning the utilization of human capital, whether entry level or senior management. Having established the "nuts and bolts" of HRP, we will now examine the relationship between talent management and corporate strategy.

Long- and Short-Term Strategic Importance of Talent Management

There needs to be both a **long-term talent management strategy** and a **short-term tactical strategy** since the dynamics in the marketplace can change easily.

In the long term, organizations need to invest now in employee talent to sustain a competitive advantage over time. When a new competitor enters the market with a substitute product or when the economy goes sour, investment in human capital may be suspended for a short period of time. Then, short-term tactics must be put in place to get past the economic downturn and keep employees motivated until the market improves. When conditions do improve, then the short-term talent management (TM) strategy—the *tactical strategy*—is halted, and the long-term investment in talented individuals—the *management strategy*—returns.

Population characteristics and labor market diversity will also have an effect on the deployment of a talent management strategy in both domestic and multinational enterprises. Regional differences in work ethic, age, gender, education, and culture will affect how talent management will be implemented and tied to the business model deployed for a particular geographic area within a country. More important, organizations need to consider sources of potential labor when building new plants in other countries. Figure 1.2 in Chapter 1 illustrates the effect of national culture on the external environment of companies.

Long-term talent management strategies also need to be linked to corporate strategy. One very important strategy that must be maintained despite the state of the marketplace is **corporate brand management**. It has been confirmed repeatedly that the best labor talent is linked to highly regarded corporations that have excellent brand images (Burmann, Schaefer, & Maloney, 2008). Google, for example, is considered the number one brand in the world—over $100 billion worth in value. As a result of this brand image, the company receives over 1,000 resumes each day.

Maintaining the brand image, whether its excellence is derived from the company's products, services, or corporate leadership, is a key factor in attracting and keeping the best and the brightest employees in the workforce. Customer satisfaction, quality control, and promoting good corporate citizenship and a culture of learning and innovation help build a company-wide brand image. A good talent management strategy needs to be tied to that brand image.

TALENT MANAGEMENT AND CORPORATE STRATEGY

There is little question today that our world is linked together in a global economy. One of the primary reasons for that link is the amount of information available almost instantaneously to everyone. Information about industries, stock markets, and governments can be analyzed quickly and acted upon, resulting in more investments being made in assets and resources by companies in multiple countries. The best example of how tightly our global economy is integrated comes from the 2008 financial meltdown of the housing market, which caused defaults in subprime and adjusted-rate mortgages, tighter credit policy, and falling house prices. These "junk" securities, which had been seen as a lucrative investment by financial institutions not only in the United States but also in China, the United Kingdom, and Europe, triggered a global economic meltdown.

The financial crises led to layoffs, corporate bailouts, and a sense that our global economy can be affected easily by shifts in economic conditions. Corporations had to make fundamental changes, not only to their business strategies, which became focused on the ways to compete in targeted markets and industries, but also to their talent management programs, which rapidly had to determine how to manage a reduction in their workforce. As noted in the previous section, the long-term strategy of growing talent in an organization has to be suspended when there is a significant economic downturn, and a tactical plan must be introduced to reduce the workforce while retaining the most talented and skilled employees in the company. The fundamental requirement to connect business and corporate strategy to HRP and talent management is based on the capability to be able to adapt to changes in the global economy.

The literature on corporate and business strategy is vast and beyond the scope of this chapter, but multiple books on corporate strategy are available (Porter, 1998). However, an organization's strategic direction does have a significant impact on human resource planning and subsequently on its talent management strategy. There are a variety of definitions of corporate versus business strategy, but, simply put, corporate strategy answers the question of what businesses to pursue to maximize the long-term profitability and growth of an organization or of how to enter particular markets. Once the decision is made concerning which market or industries to enter, a business-level strategy defines how to compete effectively against other companies in that same market. In order to compete effectively, an organization needs its executive leadership to motivate its employees to execute the business strategy, and HR must play a key role by ensuring that employees have the right skills and tools to guarantee the success of that strategy.

But how can HR make a substantial contribution to executing a firm's business strategy when many executives at corporations still treat HR as a line of business focused on transactions and compliance? According to Becker, Huselid, and Ulrich (2001), for decades, HR professionals have struggled for credibility while achieving little or no impact on company strategy and only limited recognition of their contributions to corporate success. CEOs and top executives understand the importance of human resources—the number one asset within their companies.

But how can human capital be linked to the success of the corporation? HR departments need to take on a **value creation role** to support corporate and business unit strategy. Becker et al. (2001) argue that the HR function has to become a **high-performance system**, "where every element of the HR system (selection, rewards, performance management, development etc.) is designed to maximize the quality of human capital in the organization" (p. 3). The research reported in their paper suggests that firms that have aligned HR systems with company strategy have seen an increase in dollar market value per employee.

Despite the suggestion that HR should be a source of value creation for an organization, immediately investing heavily in new HRP systems is not recommended. The key is to understand what areas of an HRP program will make the most impact on a firm's strategy. Even more important is the notion that corporate and business strategies are not things to be kept inside an executive boardroom. Every aspect of a business operation, including marketing, sales, manufacturing, and HR, must be aligned to support the overall goals and strategies of the business.

An example of aligning HR with corporate strategy was the decision by Wal-Mart to enter the overseas market in China in the mid-1990s. Wal-Mart's success occurred primarily because the company took a successful infrastructure, including an HRP best practices program and information systems used in the United States, and implemented it overseas. Trunick (2006) noted that Wal-Mart brought its internal Walton Educational Institute to China when managers discovered that many of the Chinese employees were not fluent enough in English to come to the United States. Today, in comparison with its U.S. counterpart, Wal-Mart China has a higher percentage of employees with university degrees and a much lower turnover rate, 16% as compared with 40% (Trunick, 2006).

Another key to Wal-Mart's success in China was hiring qualified managers locally who knew the culture and buying habits of the local customers. Walking into a Wal-Mart is a different experience in China than it is in the United States. Not only can you buy fresh produce in China, but items such as fish, turtles, clams, and eels are cleaned at the store and handed to the shopper in a plastic bag. The Chinese tend to shop at Wal-Mart more often for fresh items because of their small-sized refrigerators and smaller living spaces, so the company fills a different need in China than it does in the U.S. market (Naughton, 2006).

This example illustrates how HR departments must make changes in their programs based on future corporate and business strategy. The marketplace for companies is changing constantly, and a sound business strategy that works today may not work tomorrow. Companies entering the consumer market compete for the same human resources available in the labor market. The only axiom with merit about the future business of a company is that things change, and any business that is successful today may not be successful tomorrow. If the HR function is going to be aligned closely with changing corporate and business strategy, then it must be able to anticipate change and develop new HRP programs and talent management practices based on forecasted future corporate strategy. Using business intelligence systems that model competitors' business processes is a good start to anticipating the future direction of a company.

ANTICIPATING CHANGE AND CREATING AN ADAPTABLE WORKFORCE

Change is given as a constant within any business, so companies need a workforce that can adapt to changes. In a study done by IBM (2008), three key capabilities were found to influence a workforce's ability to adapt to change. "*First,* organizations must be capable of predicting their future skill requirements. *Second,* they need to effectively identify and locate experts, and *lastly* they must be able to collaborate across their organizations, connecting individuals and groups that are separated by organizations' boundaries, time zones and cultures" (p. 2). Boundaries that exist today between the lines of business, geographies, and cultures of merged or acquired companies put a tremendous strain on an organization. If executive leadership is not involved to meld the workforce together under a unified vision, goal, or strategy, this strain will have negative consequences for the effective operation of the company.

The HR department needs to establish programs to assess the existing skills of employees, to develop new skills through training, and to create job conditions that help retain valued employees. Talent can be nurtured from within an organization by training. When the necessary skills are still not available from a workforce adaptable to change, then an organization must look to hire from the outside. It is interesting to note that, according to the IBM study (2008), almost 60% of the 400 executives interviewed believed they did a better job of attracting and retaining talent than their competitors. But, as seen in Figure 11.2, attracting employees or retaining them was still considered a high priority when the same executives were asked about the primary workforce-related issues facing their organizations. The inability to develop skills rapidly to address current and future business needs and the lack of leadership capability were, respectively, the number one and two workforce-related issues reported in this study.

In planning for the future needs of a company, traditional HR managers need to recommend changes in their programs to attract, hire, train, and retain employees effectively. Developing an employee's talent is a driving force that enables a

Figure 11.2 Some Primary Workforce Challenges Facing Human Resource Managers

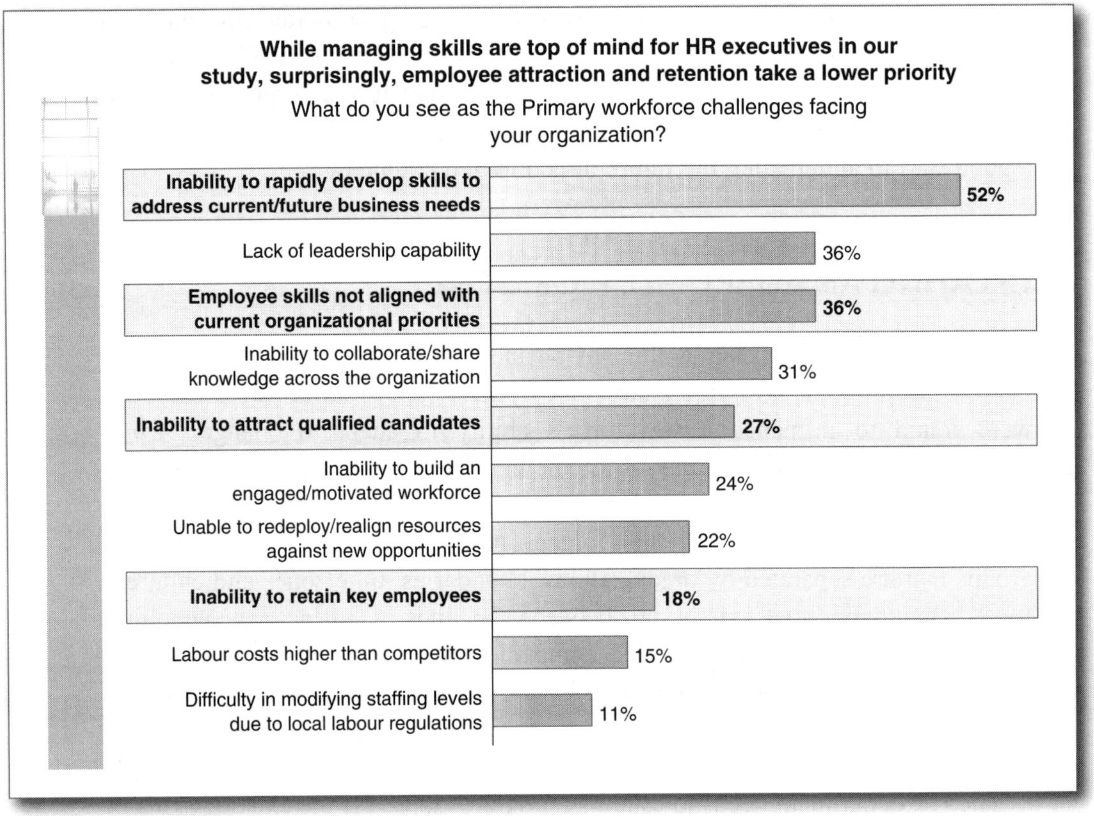

SOURCE: Adapted from the *IBM Global Human Capital Study 2008* (IBM, 2008, p. 20).

company to enhance employees' skills to adapt to future business needs. If HR executives are aligning HRM programs with corporate and business strategy, then unlocking and assessing employees' talent will give the employees the capability to adapt to change more easily. Some companies develop these capabilities by ensuring key individuals are rotated in job assignments every two years so that they learn multiple aspects of the company's business. Other companies use mentoring programs that partner long-term, experienced employees with newly hired employees. Still other companies have formal education programs for employees at various career development stages.

Just as the marketplace for doing business is in constant change, so too are the HRM programs to develop talent within an organization and create an **adaptable workforce**. Mentoring, formal education, and job rotation have been available for years and have been used effectively by many companies. When the business climate changes, some HR programs specifically used for talent management may get shelved. It may be cheaper to acquire existing talented professionals from outside the company rather than to hire university graduates and spend time and money on extensive training programs. However, it may also be more difficult for newly hired and talented individuals to assimilate to the organization's culture, which might clash with the values and culture they experienced at their previous jobs.

TALENT MANAGEMENT AND CORPORATE CULTURE

Choosing the right knowledge, skills, and abilities (KSA) to require of job applicants is important for an organization looking to hire talented individuals. But what are the organizational factors that a prospective applicant seeks when choosing an employer? Personal factors such as the applicant's age, family status, health, and financial condition can have a significant impact on what the applicant is seeking when he or she is considering joining an organization. For example, a young applicant who has a spouse with a good job at a *Fortune* 500 corporation may feel it would be more important to have a high income and forgo having the potential for promotion. There are a myriad of situations that could change what applicants are seeking in their next job; thus, there is not one set of organizational attributes that apply in all situations. But there seems to be one attribute of an organization that is considered important and valued by almost all applicants—the culture of the organization. As was discussed in Chapter 1 (Figure 1.2), the internal culture of an organization determines the manner in which HR programs and an HRIS are adopted.

Corporate culture is an interesting phenomenon. Corporate culture is based on the values that are seen as important to all members of a company. Corporate culture is developed as part of social networking and the creation of social norms when individuals work together as a group. Schein (1985), in an early definition of corporate culture, describes it as involving an understanding of what constitutes correct attitudes and perceptions, one that is shared by coworkers. Specifically, this culture is a

> pattern of basic assumptions—invented, discovered, or developed [by a firm's members] to cope with problems of external adaptation and internal integration—that has worked well enough to be considered valid and, therefore, to be taught to new members as the correct way to perceive, think, and feel in relation to those problems. (Schein, 1985, p. 9)

Corporate culture has a strong effect on employees' beliefs and actions since it is based on a set of fundamental norms and values. Thus, there are many attributes of corporate culture, including ethics, dress codes, working at home or in the office, planned or unplanned vacation schedules, brand image, goals, and vision for the future. Corporate culture is not just defined but rather described to a potential applicant. The role of company executives and HR professionals is to foster culture and cultivate it to support the vision of how to conduct business within the organization. In addition, potential applicants need to know if the culture of the company matches their own attitudes and values about appropriate behavior in an organizational setting. High-potential employees need to understand the fit between their work patterns and the way an organization goes about doing business; they need to be able to envision themselves as being a part of the way in which the organization operates.

It is important for the organization to project a positive and accurate image to the applicant. As with its creation of a positive brand image, the corporation has to create a positive employment image, and recruiters should include a description of this image when introducing the company's culture to potential applicants. A study done by the Aberdeen Group (Saba, 2009) indicated that *organizational fit*, also known as *cultural fit*, surpassed other organizational attributes for first-time applicants. If the company culture does not match the values, interests, work habits, and personality of the applicant, then that applicant either will not take the job or will only stay for a short while.

Keep in mind that cultural fit between the company and applicant is an important consideration, but it is not the only one. There is no guarantee that, if the applicant fits well with the company's culture, high performance will be the end result. Current skills, past experience, previous job references, and educational history are all important ways to determine if there is a good employee-organization fit. Cultural fit is an additional factor that is of high importance for both the employer and the potential applicant. Determining whether or not there is employee-organization fit is a critical component of a talent management program.

TALENT MANAGEMENT AND INFORMATION SYSTEMS

The Link Between Talent Management and Human Resource Information Systems

Investing in human capital is one of the most significant expenditures for corporations. Measuring the return on investment (ROI) for human capital, as described in Chapter 7, has to be reflected in the HR **balanced scorecard** program to justify its acquisition and use (see Chapter 10). Talent management (TM) is just one of many components involving the investment in human capital. The importance of using an HRIS is to ensure that the HR programs of attracting, hiring, educating, and nurturing employees are executed well and consistently over time because this is the heart of the talent management program. The numeric results of the components of the HRM program that comprise the criteria for the TM program are (1) the number of talented individuals hired, (2) the job performance of these talented individuals, and (3) the retention of these individuals. The HRIS can capture these results based on performance criteria, so it is possible to measure how well HR programs, as part of the overall talent management program, are meeting the expectations of HR executives and senior management. As discussed in Chapter 7, these numeric results can also be used to calculate cost-benefit ratios to determine the contribution of these HR programs to the profitability of the organization. Details on the criteria measures needed as well as on the calculation of the cost-benefit ratios can also be found in Cascio (2000).

Not only can an HRIS assist in the implementation of best of breed programs and processes, but it can also be used to help ensure adoption of these processes by the user community. Building consistency and setting standards are the key drivers for an HRIS—every process implemented should be done in a similar manner. An HRIS can also assist in developing those processes (see Chapter 5) and help to establish the best talent management programs. For example, an HRIS can also be used to help develop and administer education programs for all employees, regardless of job level.

Since talent management is only one component of **human capital management (HCM)**, there are many questions that need to be answered when one initiates a general HRP program that includes TM and considers how to best use the HRIS to support this program. Is there an existing HRIS system in use today that has software that can support talent management? If not, should you build the new system in-house, buy an out-of-the-box application, or outsource all of the processes to a vendor who specializes in TM? How will critical, secure data be protected for prospective applicants across multiple systems and, for MNEs, across multiple geographic regions?

Information systems can be found in every aspect of talent management, from conducting job analysis to focusing on the human capital demand and supply for current and future jobs, attracting the right talent in a specific location, hiring based on desired attributes, and retaining high-performing employees. Ultimately, the HR department of an organization would use an HRIS to monitor and measure the overall contributions of talented employees with other results on a balanced scorecard, and these results could affect the design of other HRM programs.

As noted in Chapter 10, Kaplan and Norton (1992, 1996, 2006) recognized that an organization cannot use only financial measures such as ROI on a balanced scorecard as an indication of its ability to survive and maintain a competitive advantage. Kaplan and Norton (2006) further identified the four components of the balanced scorecard as financial, customer, internal business processes, and learning and growth. As discussed in Chapter 10 and depicted in Figure 10.12, these components reflect a commitment to balance the organization's strategic goals, which are important to the expectations of its multiple stakeholders. An overview of all four components can be seen in Figure 10.12 along with the key question associated with each of the four. Particularly relevant to the results from a talent management program is the "Learning and Growth" box in Figure 10.12. Note the requirement in this box for **objectives** to be set, **measures** to be developed, **targets** to be achieved, and **initiatives** to be implemented. These categories represent the results that would be entered into the balanced scorecard for an organization.

However, no matter how an HRIS is used to support talent management or other functional business areas, accurate and timely data are the key to successful program operations. An organization needs not only to collect data about potential job applicants but also to know the skills of the current employee resource pool. Before planning new HR programs to resolve the gap between forecasted demand and supply of human capital, a company needs to know what skills exist in the current workforce and what skills are needed based on the future strategy, and it needs a systematic approach to acquiring this information. As depicted in Figure 1.1 in Chapter 1, an HRIS can be of great assistance in providing this information.

If the organization does not have the capability to develop the necessary HR business programs and processes, this is probably the time to use outside HRIS consulting companies as detailed in Chapter 10. HRIS consulting and management consulting companies are able to define future business strategies, and they can also help the organization implement those strategies. IT consulting companies, in particular, specialize in improvements to business processes in areas such as enterprise resource planning, supply chain management, and product life cycle management. HRIS consulting firms can also make recommendations to use business process management systems, and they can support the implementation and integration of those systems.

The key starting point for any consulting group is performing a business strategy assessment for an organization, and the organization should not proceed with a vendor until this project is finished. No information system, whether it is an application package recommended by a consulting firm or homegrown software, will fix, enhance, or salvage a poorly defined business strategy plan. For example, in the mid-1990s, Kodak was trying to transition from film-based to digital photography and then to focus its business on digital sharing. Kodak's business strategy shifted from the need to have employees skilled in the manufacturing of film to a need for employees skilled in the manufacture of digital cameras (Nossbaum, 2006). The age of digital equipment advanced so quickly that Kodak almost missed the revenue growth area of writing the software to support the sharing of digital photos across the Internet. But the company did finally shift its business strategy to offer digital sharing services.

The talent management functional areas offered by application software products include many of the topics that we have already covered in this chapter, such as skills assessment, succession planning, recruiting management, career development, and employee life cycle. There are also a number of consulting firms that can help tailor an application package for a company and help to implement it. The International Association for Human Resource Information Management (IHRIM) has a list of consulting companies and routinely evaluates HRIS software applications. Additionally, IHRIM is a good source for finding HRIS vendors.

Many of the applications covering the above topics are usually categorized as cross-industry packages. This label means that the application functionality and the processes are similar and can be applicable for all industries. Many of the functions and processes within HR tend to be the same and can be handled by the same application. Thus, the application companies can keep software development and ongoing maintenance costs low by supporting the concept of one version fits all. Today, HR processes supporting talent management are becoming more intricate, and application software vendors are now offering solutions by specific industry. An HR recruiter seeking to hire former doctors and nurses for a biotech or large pharmaceutical firm will get a different industry view of the recruiting software package than someone hiring drivers or dispatchers for a trucking company.

Application packages are also divided into offerings for small, medium, or large firms. There is a tendency today to offer scaled-down applications for small companies, which may not need all the features of a large-enterprise version. Software companies will also offer a hosted, subscription-based version of the application to various customers as part of a **software as a service (SaaS)** product. By using the hosted software, clients save on investing in licensing and maintenance fees; instead, they pay a low monthly rate to use the software. A hosted offering allows a customer to try the software using Web access without making a large investment in hardware and other computer infrastructure.

Recruiting Top Talent Using Social Networks

Social networking using the Web has become popular with recruiters and potential applicants. Print ads in newspapers are still being used but at a considerably lower rate than 10 years ago. These **social networks**, such as Facebook, LinkedIn, and Plaxo, are just media to increase the flow of information for making social connections. It is accurate to remember that many employees hired by a given company were referred to the HR department by a friend already working in the company. Contacting the people you know is sometimes the quickest way to get an interview. There are no guarantees that you will be hired, but personal referrals generally give you an advantage over those applicants just submitting a resume to a company. On the flip side, HR professionals network in support of talent recruitment. So social networking to support both HR and career development is not new—only the tools have changed.

Using social networks to recruit top talent can be effective, but there are some limitations. Social network demography indicates that social networks are primarily used by a younger audience. Therefore, recruiters have to be aware of the difficulty of matching potential applicants to the required skills. If recent college graduates comprise the target audience for your recruiting effort, then social networks can usually provide a direct link to potential applicants. But if a company is looking to hire individuals to work in IT jobs, then the age of the audience and the way you reach it may change due to the necessity of hiring experienced IT professionals.

Recruiters searching for top talent also must be aware of their own company's Web site and ask themselves if it has enough information for applicants to be interested in envisioning working for the company. A company Web site needs to target not only potential customers but also high-potential applicants. Here are some questions to keep in mind when you are looking to recruit top talent:

Does the Web site make it difficult to find the link to career paths?

Does the link use the word "careers" or the phrase "job opportunities"?

Are there employee testimonial videos or videos from senior level executives discussing the company's culture and mission?

Is it easy to use the search engine to find specific jobs?

Are there too many steps for an applicant trying to submit a resume and apply for a job?

What is the process to contact the applicant after he or she has applied for a job?

Is there any follow-up contact over a period of time?

See Chapter 12 for more information related to these questions and for a broader discussion of Internet recruiting.

Using Information Systems to Set Goals and Evaluate Performance

Tying measurable goals to company strategy is important. Studies have found that overall employee productivity increases along with company morale when employee goals are aligned with company strategy. Before employee goals can be set, the company strategy needs to be well defined, outlined, and communicated throughout the company. Large multinational enterprises (MNEs) are typically in global businesses and have to ensure that the strategy is passed down from the CEO to first-line managers and all employees—and then to all subsidiaries of the parent company. If goal setting at any level in the organization is done poorly, it can hurt overall employee morale and cause confusion in the company's operations. In order to develop and retain highly motivated employees, the company must link employees' job responsibilities to the overall company strategy, and this link must be visible to other employees.

There are many packaged goal alignment software tools available in the market to help show the value of an employee's contribution to an organization. SuccessFactors (2010) is a company that specializes in business alignment and performance management software that assists in managing the employee's life cycle in an organization. This package and integrated offering automates the creation of goals that are reviewed and agreed to by both the manager and the employee. This process allows the employee to develop a career path within the organization, and the manager can help by cooperatively aligning the employee's measurable goals to the company strategy. The software package speeds up the task of setting goals, and it helps define how to measure results and provide feedback to the employee.

Subjectivity, however, will never be removed from any manager-employee relationship or from any performance review, but HRIS package tools provide a basis from which to monitor performance results that are recorded throughout the course of the performance measurement cycle. Many performance tools utilize the S.M.A.R.T. acronym for goal setting. S.M.A.R.T. has gone through various interpretations over the years since it was first introduced by Doran (1981). In the article, Doran established the acronym S.M.A.R.T. to describe how to write performance goals. The acronym S.M.A.R.T. stands for (1) *s*pecific, (2) *m*easurable, (3) *a*ttainable or *a*cceptable, (4) *r*easonable or *r*esults oriented, and (5) *t*imely.

Using Analytics for Talent Management

Much has been said about **workforce analytics** and **business intelligence** in this book, specifically in Chapters 3 and 6. Analytics is a part of the business intelligence

(BI) tool set, and workforce analytics is specific to BI as it relates to HRM. Although the focus of this section is using analytics for talent management, it may be good to first dispel some of the assumptions about using analytics in general. Analytics is an interesting area within information systems and the HRIS literature. It is one of the most frequently discussed topics between IT professionals and line managers. Analytics have a tendency to be seen as a panacea for many problems associated with the inability of getting the correct information to the end users, managers, and HR professionals—the information they need so they can make better decisions. Whether it is in the HR, IT, or another department, most people know enough about analytics to use it to solve problems or make forecasts, for example, predicting future workforce needs or trying to discover why their organization has a high employee turnover rate. Unfortunately, analytics does not solve the problem of inaccurate data entry since garbage in garbage out (GIGO) will prevail. They also cannot predict the future with 100% accuracy. Instead, analytics can build a model of what the future may hold, but businesses cannot rely solely on strategic decision making based solely on the results of predictive analysis. Other factors must be taken into consideration, such as the competition, government compliance, or the current state of the economy. That is, analytics, by themselves, cannot solve everything, but they constitute a very powerful tool to analyze data and to provide the fuel for intelligent decision making—good information. In short, analytics can be used to gain a competitive advantage in the marketplace.

Today, there are software packages from HRIS and IT solution vendors that can build front-end dashboards and queries that anyone can use. These packages have taken the complicated world of business intelligence and its components, which were quite difficult to use in the past, and made it easier for business professionals to leverage BI tools more quickly. Deploying an analytic software package, however, does not tell you what specific kind of data you should be analyzing or what questions need to be asked. The skill of knowing the right questions still has to come from the business professional. When questions become complicated and linked to other areas of the business or the amount of data that needs to be analyzed is huge, then a skilled BI person is a necessary resource; you need someone able to get the most out of the software package.

Workforce Analytics and Talent Management

Using workforce analytics to manage talent can involve asking many questions about an individual person or a group of employees. Typically, a simple question about an individual employee's history is answered by using a query program against the **employee data warehouse**. This is not a really complicated environment as long as your organization has the query tools that can get the answer from a data warehouse. The real purpose of analytics for talent management is to use the analytics to model characteristics of success, in terms of the skills and abilities of employees who were successful in the company versus employees who were not successful. This empirical analytics model could then be used for a pool of existing employees or new potential hires to determine their possibility of success in the organization.

For new hires, an employer may like to know the demographics of existing, successful employees to see if the company image and recruiting programs are attracting the right individuals to the company. This is an important use of analytics because recruiting programs vary from Internet-based recruitment using social networking to programs focused on local media advertising through newspapers or television or participation in recruiting fairs. All of these recruiting programs cost money, and it is important to know where to spend the money to attract the best talent. By successfully using analytics, a company can also better train its managers on hiring tactics, and resources can be better funneled to the right recruitment channel.

For existing employees, analytics can be used to understand the personal characteristics of successful employees. Data such as previous work experiences and education and training both within and outside the company can be collected and analyzed to determine what helps prepare these employees for success. Also, data about performance objectives can be compared with actual business results. This information can be collected and stored in an employee's electronic career jacket, which also contains a record of current job responsibilities, previous promotions, and the length of time between promotions. Analyzing all of this data is the reason that models need to be designed and the right data must to be loaded into the data warehouse. It is better to understand the type of information that you need for decisions prior to building a data warehouse. Without this, data warehouses have a tendency to multiply across organizations until there are too many to manage. Generating reports and answering simple queries is the primary baseline for analytics within business intelligence systems. Being able to turn data into intelligent information and draw conclusions about the employee population is where sophisticated analytics come to the forefront of business intelligence systems. The newer generation of BI systems with HR-specific algorithms can now give what senior executives have desired for many years—an accurate description of the employee population and the means to make intelligent decisions regarding the company's human capital.

Mapping employee success to business results is not an easy task. The dilemma is that, although employees are the largest capital cost of any organization, not enough information is known about this most expensive asset. This problem leads one back to the HR balanced scorecard and the importance of using analytics to draw the right conclusions about the demographics of successful employees. This information on the HR balanced scorecard offers so much more than a simple monitoring of performance results. It helps to answer an important question: What characteristics make a talented employee successful?

Measuring the Success of Talent Management

As baby boomers retire and leave the workforce, both the competition to attract and the costs of acquiring new, highly talented individuals are only going to increase. Many boomers may delay retirement due to the 2008 economic crisis and the lack of stability associated with pensions, but, at some point, there will be a labor shortage that needs to be addressed by HR executives (Kavanagh, 2008). The HR organization will also be under heavy pressure to provide a succession plan for key executive roles, as well as a succession plan for the company's board of directors. All of the costs associated with acquiring the best applicants will have to be justified and approved by financial management no matter if the job is for a senior executive or a new sales representative. So given that the costs of developing succession plans and acquiring talented workers will increase in the future, it is important to measure the success of these programs over a period of time. Performance management and its use within the balanced scorecard (discussed in Chapter 10) will be critical in justifying the extra expenditures needed to acquire the most talented individuals in the market.

Performance management is not simply evaluating an employee at the end of a given business cycle; it is not just a year-to-year appraisal. There are critical success factors that are evaluated by management: for example, leadership, skill development, creativity, and knowledge about the industry and sales results. The key to performance management is to ensure there are measurable performance criteria that an employee can realistically achieve over a period of time.

Measuring performance results is critical in today's workplace. This results-oriented perspective is not just limited to the sales department, where results can be measured against quota objectives. It now exists in all departments from marketing, which measures campaign results by tracking new customers, to procurement, which accepts a new purchase order application that saves double the cost. This results-oriented perspective is also expected in the HR department (see Chapters 6 and 7). That is, the HR organization needs to compare the costs of current or proposed programs to the financial benefits produced. Then, the overall result can be expressed as a cost-benefit ratio, and this information can be reflected on the balanced scorecard.

SUMMARY

The primary purpose of this chapter on talent management (TM) was to investigate how an HRIS and other information systems can be used to support a talent management program. The importance of talent management was illustrated by examining the results of two comprehensive surveys. The origin of talent management and its fit with human resources planning (HRP) and human capital management (HCM) were discussed in detail. In addition, Strategic HRM was covered, and its relation to corporate strategy was discussed.

The relationship between TM and performance management was explained as being critical to the effectiveness of the entire TM program. In addition, the chapter emphasized that the metrics from both the performance management and the TM programs could be entered on the balanced scorecard, which, in turn, contributes to the Strategic HRM function. In order to understand a TM program, it is necessary to realize that the program reacts to labor and consumer market changes, producing a life cycle for TM. In developing and implementing a TM program, HR specialists must identify talented individuals by assessing the important personal attributes of employees and new hires.

A talent management program is part of the human resources planning (HRP) function of an organization. One of the important ingredients for an effective HR plan is to have *accurate and timely* job descriptions based on job analysis. An HRP program consists of three phases, (1) estimation of the demand and supply of human capital to set HRP objectives, (2) planning HR programs, and (3) evaluation of HR programs and control through feedback on program outcomes. The HRP program will generate HR metrics that are useful for the organization in going through these three phases.

Long- and short-term strategies for TM were covered. When an external event occurs unexpectedly, such as the recent recession, a short-term strategy should be available. Conversely, the company should have a long-term strategy for TM, usually one looking 5 to 10 years into the future; this long-term talent management strategy is part of the overall corporate strategy. In this way, the TM program can make a major contribution to the immediate and future strategic positions of the corporation. A major aspect of a successful TM strategy, short or long, is to have an adaptable workforce. For example, cross-training employees on jobs is a way to increase the adaptability of the workforce. Finally, the value of a positive corporate culture in attracting talented individuals was discussed.

The link between TM and HRIS was also covered in this chapter. There are quite a few quality TM computer applications available to companies, and most have been used successfully. Recruiting talented individuals by using social networks has been increasing too, but companies should be aware of the limitations of this approach. Some questions were posed that people should keep in mind when using social networks for recruiting talent. The use of analytics in TM was described, particularly the use of business intelligence to produce TM analytics. Finally, the last section of this chapter discussed the success of TM and emphasized the use of metrics generated by the performance management program and entered on the HR balanced scorecard.

KEY TERMS

adaptable workforce
balanced scorecard
business intelligence
common attributes of talented individuals
corporate brand management
corporate culture
employee data warehouse
estimating demand
estimating supply
evaluation and control
high-performance system
human capital management (HCM)
human resource planning (HRP)
job analysis
job descriptions
knowledge, skills, and abilities (KSA)
long-term talent management strategy
planning personnel programs
setting HRP objectives
short-term tactical strategy
social networks
Society for Human Resource Management (SHRM)
software as a service (SaaS)
Strategic HRM
talent management (TM)
talent management life cycle
value creation role [of HR]
workforce analytics

DISCUSSION QUESTIONS

1. Why is it important to establish the meaning of talent and talent management in a particular organizational setting?
2. How does the strategic direction of the organization influence human resource planning activities?
3. Given the different needs of the HRP process discussed in this chapter, what types of data would you expect the HRIS data warehouse to contain?
4. What would be the most effective "bundles" of metrics for talent management?
5. How would one justify the purchase of software for an HRP program?
6. Discuss the pros and cons of using social networks to recruit top talent.

7. What are some potential disadvantages of using a packaged application to help automate the employee goal-setting process?
8. How would you use workforce analytics to support talent programs such as recruiting, retention, and employee development?
9. Why is it important to have an adaptable workforce in a global economy?
10. Discuss the underlying attributes necessary to support high achievers.
11. How might the attributes of a highly motivated employee change for different job descriptions?
12. Discuss corporate tactics that can be used in a down economy to keep top talent.
13. Discuss how you would use information systems (IS) to support succession planning.

CASE STUDY: VIGNETTE CASE CONTINUED

18 months later . . .

Once again Rudiger is sitting at his desk in his seventh-floor office in central London reflecting on life. The move from Barcelona to England went smoothly with the last crate arriving only two months later than the rest. He is still working hard, but the hours are slightly better since the introduction of the work-life balance policy last year, and his family has settled well into the idyllic English countryside.

As the Global Head of People and Talent, he still has problems though—just different ones. The talent strategy "Our People—Our Talent—Our Future," which he presented to the board in his third month, identified the need for robust HRP information and analyses that required a new version of HRP software. It is in its early stages, but the intensive data-cleansing and updating activity has been straightforward so far. More concerning are the metrics responsible for producing the information needed to develop far-reaching HRP policies and practices for the future. The metrics are relatively easy to construct, but it is proving tricky to find the right "bundles" of predictive metrics—this is holding up progress with the analysis application package. In addition, there have been cost overruns in the implementation of the HRP software, and some senior managers are wondering if the new software should be abandoned.

At least 3 of the 12 board members will retire in the next two years, and they are looking to groom their successors. At least one will have to be hired from outside the organization, and the HR department is not sure what the CEO wants for this position. In addition, employee turnover and an aggressive growth strategy mean hiring new employees as well as training transferring current employees. The work that is involved in defining competences (KSA sets) at skill levels within jobs is progressing well, with hard-won support from the unions. However, job descriptions that can be found are at least three to five years old, and some jobs have no descriptions. The new apprenticeship scheme is about to be launched, and the international graduate student package and development program has been completely revised. Overall things are progressing OK, but there is much to be done.

Case Study Questions

1. How would you recommend that Rudiger begin to develop an HRP program? What are the steps that he needs to take?
2. How should the problem with the job descriptions be handled? Should the unions be involved?
3. What are some of the problems in the past that have led this current situation to occur?
4. Why do you think there are cost overruns? How could this have been avoided?
5. Why are there problems with implementation of the new software?
6. How will job descriptions be developed for the positions of board member and international student intern?

NOTE

1. Human resource planning (HRP) is also referred to as workforce planning. The two terms are synonymous.

REFERENCES

Becker, B., Huselid, M., & Ulrich, D. (2001). *The HR scorecard: Linking people, strategy, and performance.* Boston: Harvard Business School Press.

Burmann, C., Schaefer, K., & Maloney, P. (2008). Industry image: Its impact on the brand image of potential employees. *Journal of Brand Management, 15*, 157–176.

Cascio, W. F. (2000). *Costing human resources: The financial impact of behavior in organizations* (4th ed.). Boston: Kent.

CedarCrestone. (2010). *CedarCrestone 2010–2011 HR systems survey* (13th ed.). Alpharetta, GA: CedarCrest Corporation.

Chapman, S. (2009). Strategic workforce planning—the foundation of talent management. *IHRIM.link, 14*(5), 9–12.

Doran, G. T. (1981). There's a S.M.A.R.T. way to write management goals and objectives. *Management Review, 70*(11), 35–36.

Dunivan, L. (2010). Talent management: Changing demands, changing technology. *Workforce Solutions Review, 1*(3), 14–17.

Dyer, L. (1982). Human resource planning. In K. M. Rowland & G. R. Ferris (Eds.), *Personnel management* (pp. 31–47). Boston: Allyn & Bacon.

IBM Global Business Services. (2008). *Unlocking the DNA of the adaptable workforce: The Global Human Capital Study*. Somers, NY: Author.

Kaplan, R., & Norton, D. (1992). The balanced scorecard: Measures that drive performance. *Harvard Business Review, 70*, 71–80.

Kaplan, R., & Norton, D. (1996). *The balanced scorecard: Translating strategy into action.* Boston: Harvard Business School Press.

Kaplan, R., & Norton, D. (2006). *Alignment: Using the balanced scorecard to create corporate synergies.* Boston: Harvard Business School Press.

Kavanagh, M. J. (2008, February). *Global challenge: Managing the exodus of older workers.* Paper presented at the 17th Annual Zurich MBA Forum, Zurich, Switzerland.

Lockwood, N. (2006, June). Talent management: Driver for organizational success. *HR Magazine.* Retrieved March 14, 2001, from http://findarticles.com/p/articles/mi_m3495/is_6_51/ai_n26909340/

McKinsey and Company. (2001). *The war for talent.* New York: Author.

Naughton, K. (2006, October 30). The great Wal-Mart of China. *Newsweek, 148*, 1.

Noe, R., Hollenbeck, J., Gerhart, B., & Wright, P. (2010). *Fundamentals of human resource management.* New York: McGraw-Hill.

Nossbaum, B. (2006, August 1). Kodak struggles with innovating its business model. *Bloomberg Business Week,* 1.

Porter, M. (1998). *Competitive strategy: Techniques for analyzing industries and competitors.* New York: The Free Press.

Saba, J. (2009). *Assessments in talent management: Strategies to improve pre- and post-hire performance.* Boston: Aberdeen Group. Retrieved March 11, 2001, from http://www.aberdeen.com/aberdeen-library/5790/RA-assessment-talent-management.aspx

Schein, E. H. (1985). *Organizational culture and leadership.* San Francisco: Jossey-Bass.

Society for Human Resource Management (SHRM). (2010, September 21). SHRM poll identifies top HR challenges for next 10 years. *HR News.* Retrieved October 10, 2010, from http://www.shrm.org/Publications/HRNews/Pages/Challenges10years.aspx

SuccessFactors. (2010). *Driving success: The incredible power of company-wide goal management.* San Mateo, CA: Author.

Trunick, P. (2006, January 1). Wal-Mart reinvents itself in China. *Logistics Today,* 1.

Chapter 12

Recruitment and Selection in an Internet Context

Kimberly M. Lukaszewski, David N. Dickter, Brian D. Lyons, and Jerard F. Kehoe

EDITORS' NOTE

This chapter is the second one that is concerned with the talent management of employees. As noted in previous chapters, talent management is an extremely important strategic goal for organizations, both domestic and global, and relates directly to the HR balanced scorecard discussed in Chapter 10. After the need for external hiring of new employees has been identified via HR planning (Chapter 11), the next step is to design recruitment and selection programs that will result in the successful hiring of needed talent. Successful recruiting and hiring of new talent is the first step in the talent management process, which concludes with the retention of high-performance and committed employees. This chapter will cover the concepts of recruitment and selection and the use of the Internet and an HRIS to improve the operation of these HR programs.

CHAPTER OBJECTIVES

After completing this chapter, you should be able to

- Understand the relationship between the Internet and organizational recruiting objectives
- Discuss the potential advantages and disadvantages of online recruitment in the framework of recruiting objectives

- Understand the relationship between selection and assessment with HRIS
- Discuss the technological issues that influence selection and the solutions that have been reached
- Understand the value of HRIS selection applications through the use of utility analysis

HRIS IN ACTION

Bank of America looked for a computer-based solution for its problem of merging selection tests with the firm's applicant-tracking software application and found that this could be done. The company wanted to improve the quality of the applicant pool it obtained through Internet recruiting by adding selection tests to the process. It was thought that adding valid selection tests would improve the quality of candidates such that those assessed by tests would be much more likely to be successful on the job than those who simply applied through the Internet. Also, the company, by increasing applicant quality through testing, could reduce applicant-processing time.

Bank of America contracted with a test vendor to improve its selection system first. The vendor created competency profiles for jobs by interviewing about 50 current job incumbents and managers to ascertain that the competency profile for each job had the correct skills listed for the job. A "set of inventories was then identified to map onto the confirmed competencies and serve to identify the candidates who had the greatest potential for success in the job and would be the right candidates scheduled for final interviews" (Society for Human Resource Management [SHRM], 2004, p. 1). The next aspect of the project was to change the interface on the Web page for Bank of America so that recruiters could get the applicant information they needed to manage applicant information for 100 hiring sites.

Next, the promising applicants were asked to visit a Bank of America staffing facility, where they completed three tests and inventories on a computer terminal. Once there, candidates watched a job preview video and then were directed to a computer terminal to key in basic contact information and complete three more tests. Candidates who were not comfortable with computers were able to access a built-in tutorial. After candidates had completed this procedure on the computer, the site administrator had just-in-time access to the test results. This enabled the administrator to conduct on-the-spot interviews with the candidates or schedule just-in-time interviews for a later time. Thus, Bank of America was able to introduce technology in one area of the selection process rather than trying to automate the entire process. In addition, this procedure allowed human contact with the candidates and maintained system security, particularly for the selection tests.

By combining online testing with its applicant-tracking system, Bank of America netted some significant results:

Improved ability to identify successful performers. Of those who passed the test phase and were hired, 84 percent were rated as successful performers by their supervisors. In fact, passing candidates were five times more likely to be successful on the job.

Significant return on investment. The estimated annual return on investment from using the system in selecting for the Operations job family was more than 2,000 percent.

Favorable reactions from candidates. Ninety-seven percent of respondents expressed overall satisfaction with the selection process and agreed that the answers they were asked to provide represented their abilities.

Valid and fair assessment of candidates. The inventories included in the system were able to distinguish between high and low performers and increase the probability of selecting the best candidates. In addition, analyses broken out by race, gender, and age showed that the inventories treated all groups fairly. (SHRM, 2004, p. 2)

INTRODUCTION

To remain competitive in today's global environment, organizations are searching for more efficient and effective means of acquiring and maintaining a highly qualified workforce. One popular and highly productive strategy for meeting this goal has been the use of technology, especially the Internet. Thus, the focus of this chapter is to consider the impact of technology on the recruitment and selection processes in organizations. In the paragraphs that follow, we will discuss the effects of technology on these two key processes. In the recruitment section, we address the objectives of the recruitment process and whether or not online recruitment is helping to achieve these objectives. The recruitment objectives, which are based on the model of Breaugh and Starke (2000), include cost of filling a job opening, speed of filling a job opening, psychological contract fulfillment, employee satisfaction, retention rates, quality of applicants, quantity of applicants, and diversity of applicants. In addition, the impact of the attributes of the organizational Web site on applications is discussed. In the selection section, we address the importance of assessment and its role in HRIS. Technology issues surrounding selection, such as validity, computerized assessment, security, and proctoring, are also discussed. We then present the ways in which the HRIS has been integrated with the function of selection and assessment to address the issues mentioned previously. Finally, we demonstrate the value of selection with HRIS selection applications through the use of utility analysis.

RECRUITMENT AND TECHNOLOGY

The goal of the recruitment function is to identify, attract, and hire the most qualified people (Cascio, 2006). However, this task has become quite challenging because there is a growing competition for talent in the labor market. Companies are increasingly being required to expand their search for applicants beyond local and domestic borders in order to find qualified talent. As a result, they have begun using the Internet as a means of attracting job applicants. In the United States, over 90% of large companies use the Internet to recruit applicants for job openings (Cappelli, 2001). With more than 46 million people looking for job openings online (PewInternet, 2006), it is no surprise that many organizations, both large and small, are jumping onto the online recruitment bandwagon. Organizations are utilizing the Web as a way of attracting candidates, and they are also using Web-based HRIS to support the recruiting process (Figure 12.1).

Although there are certainly a number of benefits associated with using online recruitment, there are also several issues that need to be considered before organizations adopt this strategy. For instance, is online recruitment a win-win situation for both job applicants and organizations? A good way to answer this question is to step back and examine the degree to which online recruitment (a) enables organizations to meet their recruiting objectives and (b) provides applicants with the means of obtaining jobs. We discuss these issues in the following sections.

Figure 12.1 Screen Shot of Current Applicants Form

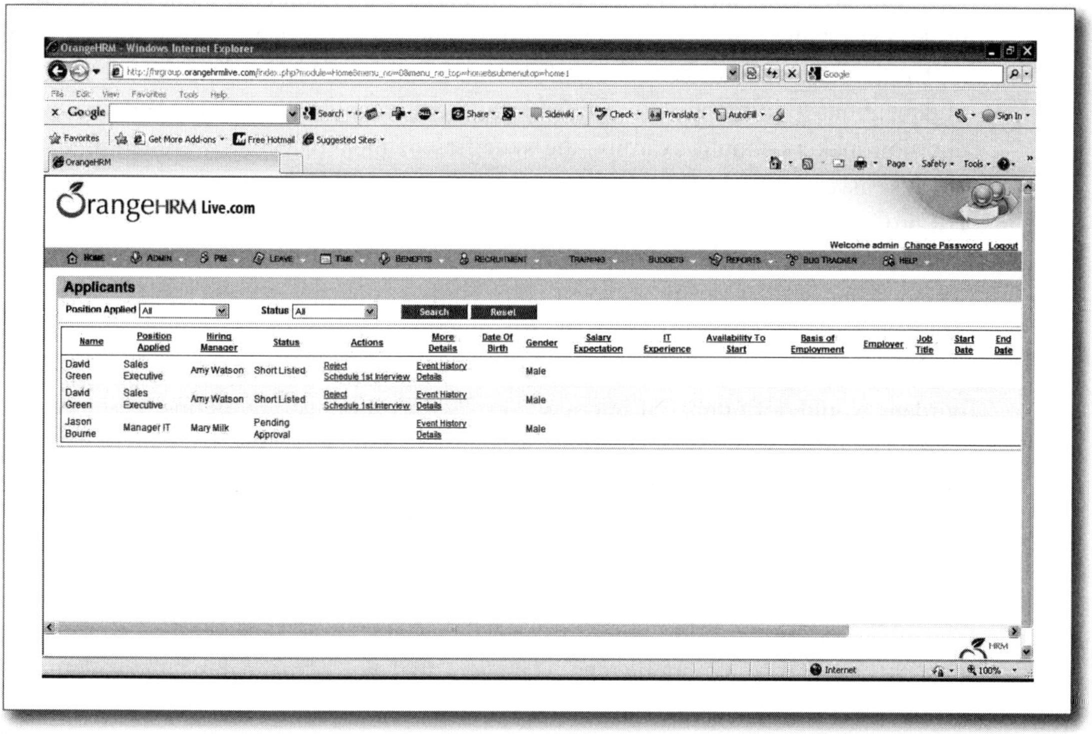

SOURCE: OrangeHRM (www.orangehrm.com). Reproduced with permission.

The Impact of Online Recruitment on Recruitment Objectives

Research by Breaugh and Starke (2000) has identified a number of objectives for the recruitment process, including (a) cost, (b) speed of filling job vacancies, (c) psychological contract fulfillment, (d) satisfaction and retention rates, (e) quality and quantity of applicants, and (f) diversity of applicants. To what extent does online recruitment help organizations meet each of these objectives?

Recruitment Objective: Cost of Filling the Job Opening

One important recruitment objective that organizations constantly strive for is to minimize the cost of filling job openings (Breaugh & Starke, 2000). Research has consistently shown that online recruitment does reduce costs (Cappelli, 2001; Chapman & Webster, 2003; Galanaki, 2002). For example, one study shows that organizations saved 95% of recruitment costs when they used online recruitment as opposed to more traditional methods (e.g., newspaper ads). Other estimates reveal that the cost of traditional systems of recruitment was $8,000 to $10,000 per position compared with $900 for online recruitment (Cober, Brown, Blumental, Doverspike, & Levy, 2000). This cost difference has prompted many organizations to replace more traditional systems with online recruitment. So it appears that online recruitment can save companies money when compared with traditional methods, but do these cost savings apply to all organizations? The answer is, not necessarily.

The evidence just presented is quite enticing and would probably persuade most organizations to jump into the online recruitment arena; however, before doing so, decision makers should examine the specifics of their recruitment situation and not just assume that online recruitment saves money for all organizations. First, HR professionals need to consider whether or not online recruitment is appropriate for their company. More specifically, organizations need to plan how to process resumes and screen out those applicants who do not possess the qualifications needed. Failure to think through the entire process may generate greater administrative burdens for the HR department or departmental managers. These burdens would definitely cut into any cost savings produced by online recruiting. A good example is found in an article written by Seminerio (2001), which profiles the **online recruiting** efforts of Sutter Health, a nonprofit health care network. Sutter Health decided to post jobs online to facilitate its recruitment process. The use of online recruitment generated an enormous number of resumes—more than 300,000—for fewer than 10,000 open positions. In most situations, this is something an organization would desire; however, Sutter Health failed to think past the generation of applicants. Managers had not planned how they would accommodate such a large volume of resumes in terms of processing and screening of applicants. Although, in this case, resumes were received quickly, they often sat for weeks on end before processing and selection occurred. Sutter Health quickly realized its error in planning and that the organization needed to revamp the use of online recruitment to serve its needs better.

In addition, organizations also need to track the effectiveness of the online recruitment method through the assessment of yield ratios and placements made. When dealing with a Web site for recruiting, you may find it useful to monitor the numbers of hits your company's Web sites are receiving on career pages. However, the number of hits on a Web site is only one small component in measuring effectiveness (Cober et al., 2000). In one study conducted in the United Kingdom, large organizations with 5,000 employees or more were surveyed about the effectiveness of online recruitment (Reed Company, 2003). The results of the study show that about 40% of the organizations consider online recruitment to be a more effective means than any other traditional method of recruitment. These results imply that organizations need to track the outcomes (e.g., successful placements) of using online recruitment and compare these outcomes with those achieved by other recruiting methods.

Thus, although some research shows that online recruiting may result in cost savings, other research shows that the use of online recruiting may generate a large number of applications, which may result in quite an administrative burden for organizations. As a result, organizations need to consider the overall costs associated with the entire recruitment process before implementing these new systems.

Recruitment Objective: Speed of Filling Job Vacancies

Another recruitment objective for assessing the effectiveness of recruitment is the speed of filling the job vacancy (Breaugh & Starke, 2000). Research has shown that online recruitment can decrease cycle time and increase the efficiency of the process by allowing organizations to spend less time gathering and sorting data (Cardy & Miller, 2003; Chapman & Webster, 2003; Cober, Brown, Levy, Keeping, & Cober, 2003; Web Recruiting Advantages, 2001, as cited in Braddy, Thompson, Wuensch, & Grossnickle, 2003). One estimate indicated that online recruitment can decrease hiring cycle time by 25% (Cober et al., 2000). Another study using data from 50 *Fortune* 500 companies showed that the use of online recruitment reduced their average hiring cycle time of 43 days by 6 days and allowed them to cut 4 days off the application process (Recruitsoft/iLogos, cited in Cappelli, 2001). Another study at Cisco Systems found that online recruitment allowed the company to fill job openings quickly. When Cisco Systems adopted online recruitment, the company attracted more than 500,000 individuals in one month, which enabled them to hire 1,200 people in just three months (Cober et al., 2000).

It is evident from this brief review that online recruiting can decrease the cycle time and enhance the speed with which vacancies are filled, but this leads to other questions that need to be answered. Does this speediness enable organizations to hire the most qualified employees? Do these hires remain with the organizations? What is the diversity of these new hires? These questions and others need to be examined further to determine whether certain disadvantages of online recruiting may offset the benefits of the shortened hiring cycle.

Recruitment Objective: Psychological Contract Fulfillment, Employee Satisfaction, and Retention Rates

Psychological contract fulfillment, employee satisfaction, and retention rates are three other important goals of the recruitment process. These three goals have a close relationship. The psychological contract refers to the employees' beliefs about the reciprocal obligations and promises between them and their organizations (Morrison & Robinson, 1997). Not surprisingly, when employees believe that their psychological contracts with the organization have been breached, they are more dissatisfied and more likely to leave the organization (Rousseau, 1990). Thus, it is important to explore the extent to which online recruitment can help ensure that employees' psychological contracts are fulfilled.

The information gathered and disseminated during the recruitment process shapes the expectations that lead to psychological contract fulfillment, which directly affects employee satisfaction and retention rates (Breaugh & Starke, 2000). There are numerous types of expectations that shape the psychological contract. These expectations include the work role (skills use, job performance), social relations (coworker and customer interactions), economic rewards (raises, monetary incentives), and company culture (Baker, 1985). It is critical during the recruitment phase that both the potential employee and the employer communicate what these expectations are and recognize whether this employment relationship will be able to meet the expectations of both parties (Baker, 1985).

Information that is provided by the applicant and by the recruiting company is a crucial part of the recruitment process. Oftentimes, the recruitment process is rushed by the recruiters, who want to complete the task of filling job openings. When a process is rushed, job seekers may find incomplete or vague information regarding job openings and company expectations. Furthermore, when job seekers receive sugarcoated information from recruiters that exaggerates the opportunities and provides unrealistic expectations about the company, then the expectations of employees are incongruent with those of the organization. Inaccurate, overly optimistic, or vague information is something organizations need to minimize or avoid. The use of such information can often lead to unrealistic expectations about the psychological contract between the organization and the individual. This circumstance is problematic for organizations because the new hires may begin to see the inconsistencies between their actual experiences and their expectations, which were formed throughout the recruitment process, and feel that their psychological contracts have been breached by their employer. Violations of the psychological contract can often result in negative attitudes and behaviors and higher levels of employee dissatisfaction and, eventually, will lead to greater turnover (Morrison & Robinson, 1997). Therefore, organizations really need to monitor and distribute accurate and timely information to potential job seekers to avoid such problems in the workplace.

Given that numerous companies now have their own Web sites, which contain a job page and endless space to provide information, more realistic information can be offered to job seekers. In addition, since the information is posted in real time, changes in content can be made at a moment's notice so that information is up-to-date and accurate. Therefore, it is no surprise that applicants rely more on posted information to form their expectations about the job and the company. Thus, employers can use Web sites to help provide realistic expectations about their companies and form psychological contracts. Companies really need to make sure that the message being conveyed on their Web sites is producing the psychological contract that can be fulfilled for both the employees and the employer. Once again, because the fulfillment of the psychological contract affects satisfaction and turnover levels, it is worthwhile for companies to convey realistic information about what new hires should expect and what will be expected of them—these expectations form the basis of the psychological contract. The use of a realistic recruitment message and the employment brand message should be the focus.

Realistic Recruitment Message

A realistic recruitment message is one that describes the organization and the job as they truly are without sugarcoating (Heneman & Judge, 2006). One important tool many organizations use is the realistic job preview. A **realistic job preview** shows applicants the positive and negative attributes of a job they are applying for to see if this job is truly what they desire or thought it was (Wanous, 1992). Realistic job previews can be communicated through written information that is posted on the employers' Web sites, but more and more companies are using video clips or Webcams that allow candidates to view what it is like to work for the organization in real time. One example is found at Target, a large retail organization, which posts video clips on its Web site, so you can see what working there is like (http://sites.target.com/site/en/company/page.jsp?ref=nav_footer_careers&contentId=WCMP04-030796). Some companies are taking this a step further by allowing some kind of interaction with current employees so applicants can gain realistic information about what it is like to work for the company. One example of a company that uses this feature is Cisco Systems, which offers online applicants a chance to "Make a Friend at Cisco." This allows the applicant to communicate with someone inside Cisco, who can describe what it is like to work for the organization (Cascio, 1998).

In addition to realistic job previews, organizations are also using the unlimited space on their company Web sites to provide a **realistic culture preview** (Cober et al., 2003; McCourt-Mooney, 2000). A realistic culture preview allows an organization to expand beyond the traditional job information and provide information about the company philosophy, value systems, history, diversity, salary structure, and benefits. This information could be vital for constructing realistic expectations in forming the psychological contract.

Research has shown that the availability of particular information (i.e., advancement opportunities, salary) can have a positive impact on applicants' attraction to an organization (Cober et al., 2003; Mohamed, Orife, & Wibowo, 2002). The use of a realistic culture preview is also helpful since often applicants seek out jobs and organizations that best fit their own personal values and beliefs (Dineen, Ash, & Noe, 2002). Providing this information about corporate culture could help develop a better relationship between the organization and the applicant and could lead to the building of trust between the applicant and the organization, which is key in the psychological contract. In addition, if the company fits the applicants' values and beliefs, they may experience higher satisfaction and stay with the company longer. Since research has shown that applicants feel that they have a better chance of collecting realistic information from Web sites than from traditional sources (Rozelle & Landis, 2002), online recruitment is a critical recruitment tool.

Overall, the use of realistic recruitment messages in online recruitment should enable organizations to increase the degree to which employees perceive that their psychological contracts are fulfilled and should also enhance satisfaction and retention levels. Realistic recruitment messages should not only help organizations attract applicants who possess the skills and values that are aligned with those of the company but also communicate what employers are looking for in candidates applying for job openings. This communication could potentially help applicants construct realistic expectations, which could lead to a well-developed psychological contract that could be fulfilled in the future on the job if candidates are selected for positions. The fulfillment of the psychological contract could lead to a long and productive relationship for both the employee and the employer, so satisfaction and retention rates could be increased.

Employment Brand Messages

A company's **employment brand** can be a powerful tool to attract applicants to its Web site. A company's employment brand is often based on the organization's well-known values or distinctive image and culture (think Southwest Airlines or Microsoft). A company often sets itself apart from competitors by means of its employment brand (Stone, Stone-Romero, & Lukaszewski, 2003; Ulrich, 2001) or uses the brand to help create a particular image in hopes of attracting job applicants (Galanaki, 2002). For example, Cisco Systems uses its image of being technologically advanced and, therefore, relies only on recruitment through the Internet to fill openings (Cascio, 1998).

Research shows that the use of online recruitment can help some organizations create a specific brand identity in the labor market (Chapman & Webster, 2003; Ulrich, 2001). One unique example is found on the Johnson & Johnson Web site (http://careers.jnj.com/home). The firm brands itself as having a "small-company environment, big-company impact philosophy"—to attract individuals who are familiar with the Johnson & Johnson brand but don't want to get lost among numerous employees. In addition, the current brand or reputation is another way that companies can lure applicants to their job pages, by simply linking employment opportunities to their products and services. Doing this is quite helpful in attracting applicants who are familiar with the company's products but possibly never thought about the company's employment opportunities.

Overall, the employment brand may be an important determinant of applicants' attraction to organizations and of subsequent satisfaction and retention rates. If a person believes in and identifies with a particular company, he or she may find fulfillment and satisfaction and stay there if extended a job opportunity. However, more research is needed in this area to examine the direct impact of this type of message.

Recruitment Objective: Quantity, Quality, and Diversity of Applicants

The quantity, quality, and diversity of applicants are three other important recruitment objectives (Breaugh & Starke, 2000). Each topic will be discussed in greater detail.

Quantity of Applicants

Online recruitment is extremely convenient for applicants and is available to them 24 hours per day and seven days a week. It also allows them to fill out an online application or upload a resume for various positions in a matter of seconds.

Although this convenience can be very beneficial, it may encourage applicants to apply for jobs without assessing their own qualifications for each job, which can result in a large number of applicants for every job opening. To offset this volume, organizations need to put into place methods to screen out applicants who are not qualified. Many organizations are using resume management systems that allow for keyword searches (i.e., of specific degrees or skills) to scale down the large volume of applications. However, some caution needs to be taken when using keyword searches. Applicants may tailor the content of their resumes to the words in the job descriptions to enhance their chances of passing through the resume-screening systems (Mohamed et al., 2002), which may result in the selection of those who use the right words but are not necessarily the most qualified for the job. Therefore, organizations using online recruiting need to be concerned with the quality of the numerous applications received.

Quality and Diversity of Applicants

Two other important goals of the recruitment process are to generate highly qualified applicants with diverse backgrounds. The quality and **diversity of the applicant pool** are determined by the users of online recruitment. Some research indicates that online recruitment systems place artificial limits on the applicant pool. Most applicants who typically use online recruitment are computer-literate, well-educated, driven individuals with a high need for achievement, seeking relatively high-level jobs (McManus & Ferguson, 2003). However, research also shows that these applicants are more likely to be job hoppers than those who do not use online recruitment (McManus & Ferguson, 2003). In addition, online recruitment users often have low levels of computer anxiety or high levels of computer self-efficacy (Marakas, Yi, & Johnson, 1998). Research has also found that college students preferred online recruitment methods as compared with other recruitment methods such as newspapers or television (Zusman & Landis, 2002).

Although online recruitment appeals to fairly well-educated applicants, research shows that there are also ethnic differences in the use of online recruiting, with these initiatives attracting 7% of Hispanics, 9% of blacks, and 16% of whites (Kuhn & Skuterud, 2000). However, the research findings on ethnicity and online recruitment usage have been somewhat contradictory. For example, one study found that African Americans often react quite favorably to online recruiting and use it to self-select themselves out of the application process for a poor fit job or organization (McManus & Ferguson, 2003). Some possible explanations for the low Internet usage of various groups include lack of access to computers, lack of computer skills, and poverty (Kuhn & Skuterud, 2000). Others have argued that cultural differences in relationship orientation may affect Hispanics' use of online recruiting systems (Stone, Lukaszewski, & Isenhour, 2005).

There are also gender and age differences in responses to online recruitment. Employed men are more likely to search for jobs on the Internet than employed women (Kuhn & Skuterud, 2000). The reason for this may be that females generally have more computer anxiety and lower computer self-efficacy than males (Jackson, Ervin, Gardner, & Schmitt, 2001). Research has also shown that older individuals (55 or above) tend to have lower computer self-efficacy (Reed, Doty, & May, 2005) than younger adults, which may inhibit older applicants' ability and perceived ability to use online recruiting. Given these findings, it is clear that the use of online recruitment may limit the extent to which an organization attracts qualified women, Hispanic Americans, and older workers.

Thus, if an organization relies only on Web-based recruitment, the system will indirectly influence the overall composition of the workforce and decrease the level of diversity within the organization (Stone et al., 2005). Therefore, online recruiting may facilitate workforce homogeneity and, as a result, hinder innovative and creative decision making (Schneider, Goldstein, & Smith, 1995). Organizations must be aware of the potential biases created by their recruiting practices and align their recruiting strategies with their overall business strategies to create competitive advantage (Becker & Gerhart, 1996; Wright & Snell, 1998). For example, if an organization wants to hire an individual for an HRIS-related job, the organization may find Web recruiting to be a cost-efficient and effective source of recruitment because members of the applicant pool are technologically proficient and would most likely use the Web in their job searches. Conversely, if the organization is looking for a person in a nontechnical position (e.g., staff writer, creative consultant), then the use of traditional recruitment sources may be more effective than the use of online recruitment alone.

Overall, it is apparent that online recruitment may help organizations meet the objective of increasing the number of job applicants (Chapman & Webster, 2003; Galanaki, 2002). However, it is not clear whether the use of online recruitment will help organizations attract high-quality applicants. If an organization is looking for job applicants with particular skills (e.g., computer skills), then it may be able to find and attract such applicants with online recruitment. However, the use of online recruitment may also result in some dysfunctional consequences. For instance, online recruiting may attract job hoppers and may be less likely to attract those with low levels of computer self-efficacy. Furthermore, online recruitment may have a negative impact on the extent to which organizations are able to attract women, older workers, and some minorities (e.g., Hispanic Americans). However, research is not clear about the extent to which online recruitment helps organizations attract African Americans. Further research is needed on this topic.

Organizations need to be very cautious about using only online recruitment, especially since this recruitment method may not help organizations meet their diversity-related goals. There is clearly potential for an adverse impact on the number of applications received from women, minorities, and older workers, which may pose potential legal problems for organizations (Hogler, Henle, & Bemus, 1998). Therefore, it is important that organizations consider the potential legal issues associated with the use of online recruitment and ensure that all qualified applicants are given the opportunity to apply for jobs (Stone et al., 2003). Furthermore, organizations may want to use online recruitment in conjunction with other recruitment sources (e.g., newspaper ads, job fairs) to ensure that their recruitment processes are fair.

Attributes of the Recruiting Web Site

Another factor that may affect the acceptance and effectiveness of online recruiting is the design of the Web site. In general, the best Web site design is user-friendly in that users can easily navigate and browse through multiple Web pages to find information. The extent to which the Web site is usable or not has been referred to as "Web site usability" in the empirical literature (Cober et al., 2003; Karat, 1997; Nielsen, 2000). The construct of Web site usability has been conceptualized as encompassing a number of dimensions, including navigability, content information, and aesthetic features. Each dimension and its use in recruitment are further discussed in this section.

First, **navigability** can be defined as the overall ease with which a user can browse through multiple Web pages to locate topics of interest. Hosting a Web site that displays current information and includes active hyperlinks to retrieve information is essential in maintaining user interest within the site. To achieve this goal, organizations should follow the "three-click" rule for users to locate information of interest. For instance, users who wish to browse job opportunities on the organization's Web site should be able to reach the desired Web page by the third hyperlink from the home Web page. Accordingly, research has shown that applicants have more favorable impressions of an organization when its Web site is easy to navigate as opposed to being difficult to navigate (Braddy, Meade, & Kroustalis, 2008). Such favorable impressions are important to elicit within applicants because they may lead to greater organizational attraction (e.g., Allen, Mahto, & Otondo, 2007; Lyons & Marler, 2011).

Next, **content** information refers to the degree to which the Web site hosts relevant information that the user deems valuable and informative in nature. Providing information that the user desires is another mechanism by which organizations can sustain user interest and satisfaction with the Web site. The **media richness** theory (Daft & Lengel, 1986) has been frequently applied to explain why hosting relevant content information is beneficial to applicants. Specifically, this theory contends that communication effectiveness is a function of the degree to which media sources reduce user uncertainty and equivocality (Daft & Lengel, 1986). Rich media sources (a Web site) contain enough relevant and accessible information to reduce user uncertainty and subsequent anxiety toward the target source (an organization). Conversely, when a source has a low degree of richness, inadequate information fails to reduce users' uncertainty about the organization, which may then lead to ambivalence and anxiety toward the target source. The result of this process may stimulate positive or negative attitudes toward the organization, such as more favorable impressions of an organization's image (Cable & Yu, 2006). Thus, an organization would be advised to host a Web site that includes information about the organization and its products, available job opportunities, developmental opportunities, compensation, and culture (Barber & Roehling, 1993; Cable, Aiman-Smith, Mulvey, & Edwards, 2000; Cable & Graham, 2000; Judge & Cable, 1997). For example, Walker and colleagues (2009) found that, when organizations posted employee testimonials on their employment Web pages, their sites generated greater organizational attraction than other Web sites that did not have such testimonials. Consequently, hosting information that applicants value will most likely facilitate person-job (P-J) and person-organization (P-O) "fit"-related decisions. Specifically, when applicants perceive similarity between their qualifications and the job description (P-J) and between their personality and the organization's values (P-O), it is more likely that they will pursue employment with the organization (e.g., Kristof-Brown, Zimmerman, & Johnson, 2005).

Overall, these applicant-evaluative processes cannot be formed if the organization does not include useful information on its Web site. For example, many organizations (e.g., Texas Instruments) provide a list of cultural values on their employment Web pages. It is important to note, however, that the more customizable information an organization provides on its Web page, the more likely an applicant will engage in appropriate **self-selection** behavior (to apply or not apply for a job within the organization). In other words, if the Web site provides direct feedback to applicants regarding their P-O or P-J fit, the online recruiting effort will likely attract a more qualified applicant pool (Dineen et al., 2002; Dineen, Ling, Ash, & DelVecchio, 2007; Dineen & Noe, 2009). Therefore, in order to avoid the "dark side" of Web recruitment, an organization must first determine and maximize the information that is most likely going to influence fit perceptions and then engage the user to seek and understand this information. Finally, companies should consider how the **aesthetic features** of their Web sites engage user interest and attention. These features encompass the overall stylistic or innovative aspects of a

Web site, such as contrasting colors, pictures, animation, and playfulness, which keep the user engaged while he or she navigates through multiple Web pages (Cober, Brown, Keeping, & Levy, 2004). When a user is engaged, it is more likely that he or she will maintain interest in the organization and browse for more information about the organization (Cober et al., 2003). Similarly, the aesthetic features of a Web site may affect applicant perceptions and behavior. Ultimately, an applicant may perceive these innovative features of a Web site as "signals" about broader organizational attributes, such as the organization's culture and image (Lyons & Marler, 2011). For example, if a Web site has attractive stylistic features (e.g., the Goldman Sachs Web site), it may stimulate more favorable perceptions of organizational image, which has been found to be positively related to organizational attraction (Lyons & Marler, 2011). These results are especially important for entrepreneurial or smaller firms that wish to attract qualified applicants to their organizations. That is, when an organization invests in the latest Web design, a user or applicant will be more likely to perceive that organization as reputable. Similarly, an information technology (IT) firm would be wise to invest in the latest Web design software to generate applicant or even customer perceptions that the organization values innovation and creativity. This investment is especially prudent from the perspective that this firm's potential applicants will most likely be attracted to an organization that values innovation and creativity.

Integrating these attributes together, a Web site's **usability** has been found to affect applicant perceptions and attitudes toward the organization. In a study by Cober et al. (2003), Web sites that contained valuable information about the organization and engaged the user when browsing such information resulted in a higher degree of attraction toward the organization as a potential employer. Similarly, Williamson, Lepak, and King (2003) found that higher perceptions of Web site usability produced higher perceptions of organizational attraction. A more recent study by Allen et al. (2007) found that Web site **attributes** were positively related to applicants' intentions to pursue employment, which is the immediate precursor to the actual behavior of applying for a job within an organization. All these studies converge on the finding that Web site usability perceptions influence applicant attitudes toward an organization. As a result, organizations should be attuned to how their Web sites influence applicant perceptions and be prepared to update their Web design to embody high navigability, content fidelity, and engaging aesthetic features. HR and IT employees should monitor the usability of their firm's Web site by surveying applicant perceptions of and reactions to the Web recruiting process, especially in situations where the Web recruiting function entails gathering applicant data and preliminary online ability testing.

The decision to host job openings on organizational Web sites and to have the capability of screening job applicants for positions should be based on the firm's resources and strategy. With this statement in mind, we can see that the purpose of an organization's recruitment Web site can be classified as either recruiting and screening oriented or as just recruitment oriented (Williamson et al., 2003). A **recruiting- and screening-oriented Web site** has the capability to list job openings and accept applications through a secure server. Conversely, a Web site that focuses only on recruiting just hosts a list of job openings with the option of submitting an application via mail, e-mail, or fax to an organizational representative. Williamson et al. (2003) articulated that both recruitment orientations can be effective in attracting applicants; however, it could be contended that applicants may prefer submitting personal information through Web sites that they perceive to be secure and trustworthy (Stone et al., 2003). Therefore, if an organization does not have the financial resources to invest in building a secure server to accept applications, an alternative would be to still offer information about the organization and its culture on the Web site's employment Web page and then have a hyperlink that connects interested applicants to jobs that are hosted by a third-party vendor, such as Monster.com. A more logical alternative would be to host an organization's job opportunities on a third-party vendor's Web site (e.g., Monster .com, Careerbuilder.com) and include a hyperlink on each announcement that connects the applicant to the organization's home Web page. These alternatives would allow the organization to achieve the benefits associated with Web recruiting and provide the applicant an opportunity to learn more about the organization by browsing the firm's home Web page. Also, from the applicant's perspective, these options would reduce any anxiety or adverse perceptions about lack of privacy or about Web security concerning those organizations that the applicant does not know well or does not entirely trust.

Recruitment Strategies and Social Networking

Organizations have always used social relationships and networking, including employee referrals, to attract talent. Increasingly, social networking sites such as Facebook, MySpace, and LinkedIn are gaining in use and popularity, and they now provide a unique method of allowing recruitment professionals to source, contact, and screen both active and passive job candidates. The Society for Human Resource Management (SHRM) conducted a survey about the use of **social networking Web sites** and recruitment (SHRM, 2008). The salient findings of this research are as follows:

- Social networking sites and online search engines are being used more frequently now as an HR tool than they were two years ago. However, most organizations do not have a formal policy on this use.

- They are primarily used to search for passive applicants, particularly at the middle-management levels, who might not otherwise apply or be contacted by an organization.

- They are, however, not used to screen applicants because of the legal issues associated with using social networking sites in this way and because of organizations not being able to verify with confidence the information on these sites.

- Negative information provided on the social networking sites, such as revealing confidential information about former or current employers; slanderous discussions of the applicant's friends, peers, or coworkers; and information on the applicant's profile page that contradicts that provided on the applicant's resume, has a greater influence on hiring decisions than positive information.

ONLINE RECRUITMENT GUIDELINES

Stone et al. (2005) offer the following research-based guidelines on the effective design and use of online recruitment strategies:

- Online recruiting is more suitable for well-known firms with excellent employer branding.
- It should be used as one of many sources of recruitment.
- It is more suitable when many candidates are needed for high-level jobs requiring high levels of education.
- Organizations should be aware of the limitations of this method, such as its limited ability to attract highly qualified candidates and minority candidates. It may in fact attract job hoppers.
- The Web sites should be easy to use and navigate and designed to attract, not screen, candidates.
- Online screening systems should be based on job analyses.
- E-recruiting systems should provide realistic previews of jobs and of the firm.
- Effectiveness should be regularly reviewed and continuously improved based on feedback from job applicants.
- Online recruiting should be culturally sensitive and suit people from diverse backgrounds, including those with low education levels and low computer self-efficacy.
- Online recruiting must incorporate privacy protection policies, including those limiting the collection of information to only employment specific data and those restricting access to and distribution of such data.

In summary, organizations should consider the extent to which online recruitment enables them to meet their recruitment objectives. Our previous discussion provides evidence that online recruitment can help organizations reduce the costs of recruiting, decrease the cycle time of filling job vacancies, and generate large quantities of applicants. However, organizations must remember that these are not the only recruitment objectives and must focus on finding the impact of online recruitment on the other recruitment objectives (quality and diversity of applicants, psychological contract fulfillment, employee satisfaction, retention rates). In addition, the attributes of the Web site can affect the acceptance and effectiveness of online recruiting. The best Web site design is user-friendly in that users can easily navigate and browse through multiple Web pages to find information that is valuable and conveys whether or not the applicants fit not only the job requirements but also the organization's value system. Last, the aesthetic features of a Web site, combined with the content presented, may shape the attributions of job seekers toward the organization in a positive manner. However, the attraction of applicants to job openings is only the beginning—organizations now have to focus on assessing the applicants who constitute their applicant pools. Therefore, we now need to switch our focus to a discussion of selection.

SELECTION AND TECHNOLOGY

This section focuses on tests and assessments of individual employees and candidates, which are at the heart of the evaluation processes that enable organizations to manage their talent. These tools are used for selecting employees, placing them in positions in the organization, training and developing them, promoting them, and evaluating them. Tests and assessments are important for HRIS because they provide data that are used for making organizational decisions. To explore the data-based decision-making process in further detail, we focus our discussion on the use of tests and assessments to make a critical decision—whether or not to hire a particular candidate.

What Are Selection Tests and Assessments, and Why Are They Used?

Most organizations that seek HRIS expertise on selection will likely consider the term *test* to refer to traditional multiple-choice examinations that can be used to measure ability, personality, or knowledge, as well as to skills tests, such as typing tests. Organizations seeking assessments may be referring to these same tests, or, alternatively, they may be thinking of different types of **selection procedures** and tools, such as reference checks or work samples. Whatever the label, tests and assessments are job-related decision-making tools that provide information about candidates, information that organizations can use in selection. Figure 12.2 contains examples of the major tests and assessment instruments. For this section of the chapter, we use the terms *test, assessment, selection tool,* and *selection procedure* interchangeably to refer to any tool designed to measure attributes of individuals for the purpose of selecting employees.

Here is a more comprehensive list of assessments, as provided by the Society for Industrial and Organizational Psychology (SIOP):

> Selection procedures refer to any procedure used singly or in combination to make a personnel decision, including, but not limited to, paper-and-pencil tests, computer-administered tests, performance tests, work samples, inventories (e.g., personality, interest), projective techniques [ambiguous stimuli such as inkblots or pictures, often used for personality assessment], polygraph [lie

Figure 12.2 Specific Examples of Tests and Assessments

Knowledge test: A multiple-choice training posttest of knowledge of the tools, machines, and equipment used in a factory and designed to measure how well the new hire has learned essential job information taught in classroom training.
Skill test: A practical exercise or simulation that tests the candidate's effectiveness in using Microsoft Word software.
Ability test: The Watson-Glaser Critical Thinking Appraisal, a multiple-choice reasoning test, in which the examinee reads a short or medium-length passage and draws logical conclusions about the statements, choosing the answer that makes the best logical sense. Many other ability tests are similar in appearance and format to educational tests that are familiar to students (e.g., the Scholastic Aptitude Test [SAT], the Miller Analogies Test [MAT], and the Graduate Record Examination [GRE]).
Personal attributes test: A multiple-choice personality assessment in which the examinee reads statements such as "I enjoy making presentations in front of large groups of people" and indicates the extent to which she or he agrees or disagrees with these statements. Results are scored on several scales or dimensions.
Work simulation: An in-basket exercise in which the examinee must examine the variety of types of information (correspondence, reports, and other information) and also interact with simulated coworkers, employees, or other business associates (whether computer simulated or role-played by actors over the telephone or in person). The examinee is evaluated on a variety of dimensions, from accuracy and the quality of decisions to work-related competencies, interpersonal skills, and other personal attributes.

detector] examinations, individual assessments, assessment center evaluations [summaries of multiple assessments, as evaluated by multiple raters], biographical data forms or scored application blanks, interviews, educational requirements, experience requirements, reference checks, background investigations, physical requirements (e.g., height or weight), physical ability tests, appraisals of job performance, computer-based test interpretations, and estimates of advancement potential. (SIOP, 2003, p. 3)

While this chapter will address a variety of important concepts about selection and assessment for personnel decision making, a full discussion is beyond the chapter's scope. Interested readers are encouraged to consult additional sources, including the SIOP document. We also recommend the text by Guion (1998), one of the essential references on the topic. The U.S. Department of Labor (1999) offers a less technical summary white paper, and the SIOP Web site (www.siop.org) provides links to many useful Web sites and papers.

Why Is Assessment Important for HRIS?

When used for employee selection, assessments have value because they assist organizations in identifying those individuals who are more likely to succeed on the job and prevent the hire of those who are less likely to succeed. The following paragraphs provide several reasons that it is important for HR managers to understand the purpose and use of assessments.

All Organizations Use Assessments

Resumes are assessment tools, and so are interviews. Every company that has ever had more than one candidate for a job opening has assessed in some way, whether or not it used structured, professionally developed assessments to make hiring decisions. Increasingly, human resource information systems are supporting organizations' selection processes: how firms identify the most qualified candidates and determine whom to choose for internal positions and promotions. The reason is that many organizations are using some type of selection instrument or tool in addition to the employment interview, and, in most cases, the tools involve HRIS. In 40% of the *Fortune* 100 companies, for example, there is some form of individual assessment of job candidates (Shaffer & Schmidt, 2006). In 2005, *Newsweek* estimated that the business of testing and assessing job candidates, including both the development and administration of tests, was a $400 million industry, growing at 8% per year.

Organization Leaders Know That Employees' Abilities, Skills, and Personal Attributes Are Critical for Success

To see the evidence, pick up a book by a business leader, such as former General Electric CEO Jack Welch, or a popular-press book on successful businesses, such as *Good to Great* (Collins, 2001). If, as leaders often say, an organization's greatest asset is its people, then selection determines the value of the company's most important advantage.

Some Selection Systems Work Better Than Others

Better-designed selection systems are more likely than poorly designed systems to select successful employees. In fact, many company-grown and commercially available assessments are of little value. The most frequent problems that occur include the following: (a) they assess attributes that are not relevant to job performance, (b) they are not used consistently or as intended, and (c) they are unreliable indicators of job-relevant attributes. HR departments must learn how to distinguish between effective and ineffective selection systems and how to choose or improve selection systems.

To be effective, assessments must be valid, they must provide information that is clearly related to their intended use, and the information must be related to the job's requirements in a manner that can be demonstrated by research. For instance, the research might show that the assessment mirrors the content of the job, such as a typing test or work sample that duplicates or simulates the actual job duties that are essential for employees to perform. Another aspect of validity involves the ability to predict important criteria: measures of work performance or behavior such as productivity, accident rate, absenteeism, tenure, reject rate, training score, and supervisory ratings of job-relevant behaviors, tasks, or activities (SIOP, 2003). For instance, an **ability test** can be shown to be valid if scores on the test are statistically correlated with scores on a post-hire training evaluation that measures the knowledge individuals have acquired that is critical for successful job performance. Unfortunately, many commercially available assessments are poorly designed and researched, and their creators make unjustifiable claims about their effectiveness. When deciding whether to purchase assessment tools and systems from vendors, the organization should always obtain validation documentation that follows professional and legal guidelines, including the federal government's *Uniform Guidelines on Employee Selection Procedures* (U.S. Equal Employment Opportunity Commission, 1978; see also www.uniformguidelines.com) and the SIOP *Principles* publication (2003).

Importantly, validity involves not only research but also proper use. It would be irresponsible to use a test for a purpose other than that for which it was validated, such as installing a typing test to predict training success if there is no reason to believe the two would be related. Thus, the selection system and the methods, procedures, and policies concerning the use of selection tools matter as much as the tools themselves.

Employee Selection Is Regulated by Antidiscrimination Laws

Many laws, such as the Civil Rights Act of 1991 and the Americans with Disabilities Act, regulate companies' employee selection decisions. HRIS experts can contribute to their organizations by being aware of these **antidiscrimination laws**. The primary intent of these laws is to prohibit employment practices that unfairly discriminate against people in various protected groups, such as racial/ethnic minorities, women, and older candidates. In general, these federal, state, and local laws require that selection decisions must be valid and fair if they differentially affect protected group members. Selection decisions that differentially affect protected group members must provide equal treatment and be equally predictive of success for minorities and other protected groups in order to be fair and legal. The most commonly used term, but only part of the story, in an evaluation of fairness is *adverse impact*, which describes the circumstance of candidates from a protected group, A (e.g., women and minorities), being proportionately less likely to be hired than candidates in group B, which has the highest selection rate (for good discussions on the topic, see Guion, 1998; SIOP, 2003). Often, but not always, the group with the highest selection rate is the nonminority group. A guideline that federal and state enforcement agencies and courts use is the 80% rule. By this rule of thumb, adverse impact may be judged to exist if protected group A's selection rate is less than .80 of group B's selection rate. Importantly, having adverse impact does not, by itself, make a selection system illegal. A selection system that causes adverse impact may be legal if it can be shown to be job relevant (i.e., valid) and consistent with business necessity (i.e., important for business success). Interested readers should consult the U.S. Equal Employment Opportunity Commission (1978) and SIOP (2003) for more details.

The Value of Selection Is Quantifiable

HR departments and HRIS experts, in particular, should understand how to use selection-related data in order to (a) provide strategic information to the company and (b) demonstrate the return on the company's investment in assessments.

Being able to provide important strategic information about the company, such as the expected skill levels of new employees who have been tested and the implications of these skills for business unit performance, can help transform the

HRIS manager's role from a supporting, transactional one to that of valued partner with key insight into the company's strategic directions. And, of course, being able to show a return on investment is essential for the survival of HRIS projects. A good system improves the quality of hires in a way that can be measured and verified. Although no selection system is perfect (not all individuals who are selected can be guaranteed to succeed and not necessarily all who are rejected would have been unsuccessful on the job), HRIS can measure the dollar value of selection to demonstrate its economic value as a company investment. This topic is discussed in more detail later in this chapter.

Technology Issues in Selection

The most common use of technology for selection systems is the use of computers to administer and score tests. HRIS experts need to be aware of several general concerns about the computer administration of selection procedures. First, if traditional **paper-and-pencil assessments** are computerized, does the computer version have different measurement properties? Second, as the capabilities of microprocessors increase, it is possible to make assessments that more closely simulate the job, that is, ones that closely approximate the work that would be done once the candidate is hired. What are the benefits and risks of high fidelity work simulations? Third, how does online testing affect the validity of selection systems? Does the technology that allows candidates to take tests anywhere, and organizations' increasing interest in using that technology, compromise the test security that is present in traditional settings with proctored examinations?

Equivalence Between Conventional and Computerized Assessments

Most of the first **computerized assessments** were meant to look like their paper-and-pencil, low-tech counterparts, except that they were delivered on a computer and required candidates to answer questions (generally multiple choice) via a keyboard or a mouse or to take a computerized skill test (e.g., a typing test). Interestingly, although today there are also simulations that mirror the job, traditional multiple-choice tests still abound, in part because the format is easy to administer and score and in part because there are many good multiple-choice tests in use that predate the availability of inexpensive stand-alone computers and online testing.

Organizations tend to think that the paper-and-pencil and computerized forms (versions) of a test are interchangeable, assuming that the test items and instructions are the same. (Often, particularly in large organizations, both types are used, depending on the availability of computer facilities at different offices and whether or not large test sessions are conducted at recruiting events and at other locations where there are not enough computers available at once.) However, the assumption of equivalence may not be justified, and the HRIS expert must know when the assumption is warranted. The primary concern is that the mode of administration (paper or computer) will affect the measurement properties of the test. For assessments that do not include ability, such as **personality tests** and career interest inventories, most researchers have little concern that giving the test on paper will result in a different measure than would occur with a computerized test. However, there is clear evidence that the mode of administration matters for ability tests that are speeded, those for which there is time pressure and the possibility that candidates will not finish all the items in the allotted time (e.g., see Mead & Drasgow, 1993; Potosky & Bobko, 2004). For such tests, the physical or virtual materials and test administration methods affect the time (in seconds) it takes to complete a test item and, thus, the results. For instance, think of a paper test form that requires a candidate to match questions printed in booklets to an answer sheet; now imagine a computer screen on which the examinee sees one item at a time and uses a mouse to click on the answers. Total scores, average scores, and performance on individual test items are affected. The more speeded a test is, the more likely that there will be differences between the paper and computer results. In contrast, **power tests**, tests in which there is no designated time limit to create time pressure or in which the time limit is set such that most candidates will complete the test without working hastily, typically do not show differences between paper and computerized testing modes. To understand the differences, an industrial/organizational psychologist or some other expert in tests and measurements will conduct a study of the equivalence between the two. The study entails administering both types of tests, ideally to the same individuals, with the order of administration counterbalanced across participants, and examining and comparing the overall results and the statistical results for each item. Then, when necessary, a formula equating the two can be developed to adjust for differences. The result is a method of ensuring that, irrespective of whether the candidate takes the paper test or the computerized test, he or she will have the same opportunity to perform well.

Bandwidth Versus Fidelity: How Closely Should We Simulate the Job?

Technology has enabled organizations to create work sample simulations that represent the job with high fidelity. Company leaders may want this because they believe that no assessment could be nearly as good as a simulation that closely matches the work that will be performed on the job. However, as Figure 12.3 illustrates, an analysis of decades of assessment research has found that general cognitive ability tests can, on average, predict success virtually as well as simulations, and, when combined with other types of assessments, they can exceed the predictive ability of simulations. The bar chart in Figure 12.3 displays statistical correlations between assessment scores and job performance data. Schmidt and Hunter (1998) provided these data in a comprehensive meta-analysis, research that quantitatively summarizes the data from many studies on a particular topic—in this case, the personnel selection research literature. The research is most supportive of **work simulations**, ability tests, structured interviews, and personality testing. Higher scores on these types of assessments are predictive of higher job performance. For comparison, less valid assessments are also shown, such as education and training ratings and graphology (handwriting analysis), which has been shown to have little or no validity.

It is also important to be aware of the trade-off between **fidelity** and **bandwidth**, the range of settings to which the simulation might apply. For example, suppose

Figure 12.3 Correlations Between Assessment Scores and Job Performance

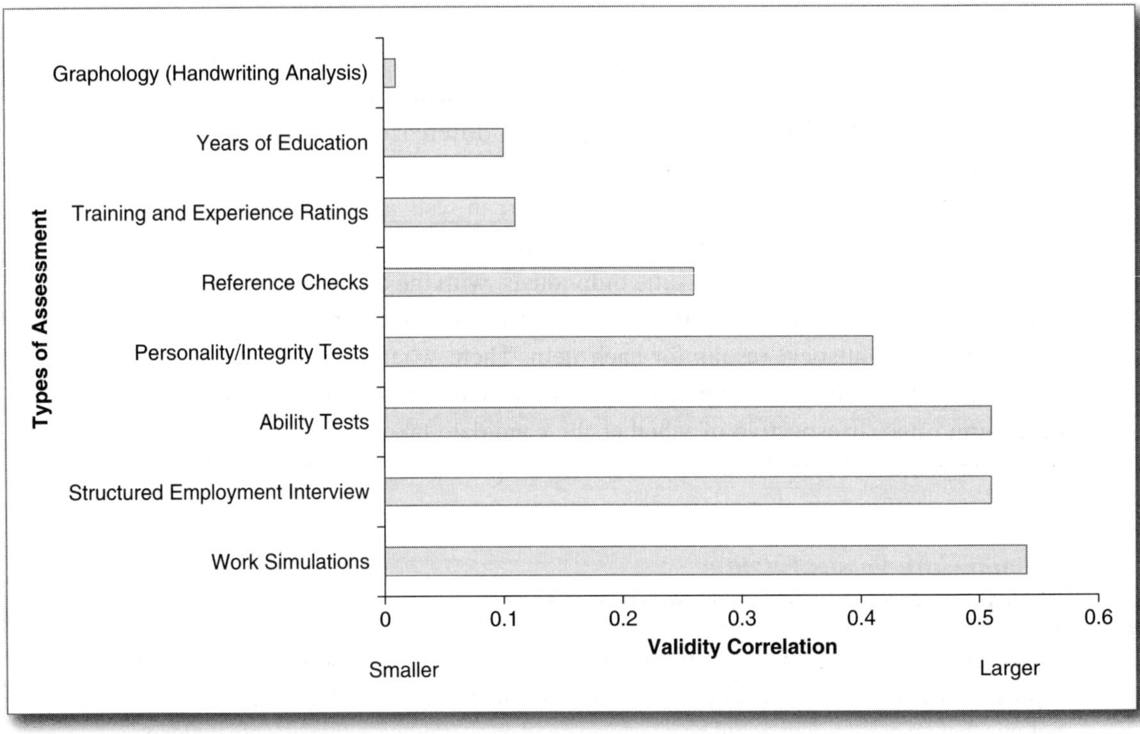

SOURCE: Schmidt and Hunter (1998).

that a management simulation is designed to closely represent a particular line of business in the actual organization chart and reporting structure, as well as the unique subject matter that is addressed in the management job from day to day. If the company then wants to use the simulation for a different business unit or job, the details that made the simulation highly appropriate in the first setting may interfere with its use in the other setting. The same problem applies to jobs and settings that change over time, as most do. Therefore, although as the HRIS expert you may be adept at creating an assessment that looks just like the job, such a tool might have a narrow range of uses. Also, simulations generally require that the job candidate already knows how to do the job, at least at some basic level, or that the job is simple enough that the candidate can learn the job tasks quickly to perform the simulation. In general, HRIS managers should keep in mind that, depending on the effort and expense one is willing to expend on assessment development and installation, lower-fidelity simulations or combinations of other types of assessments might be preferable to a simulation that is highly job specific. For example, Schmidt and Hunter (1998) argue that an ability test might be the most efficient general assessment method:

> Of all procedures that can be used for all jobs, whether entry level or advanced, it has the highest validity and lowest application cost. Work sample measures are slightly more valid, but they are much more costly and can be used only with applicants who already know the job or have been trained for the occupation or job. (p. 264)

Validity and Security Issues Created by Unproctored Online Testing

Numerous consulting companies offer online tests. These tests may be administered in the same way as paper-and-pencil or stand-alone computer tests, that is, they may be conducted in an office by a proctor who gives instructions, checks identification, and monitors the test session. **Online testing** also allows for the possibility of unproctored (unsupervised) administration, with tests taken anywhere at any time. (Note that this could also be said for other types of technology-enabled tests that are available, such as those administered by telephone keypad or telephone-based interactive voice response systems. Others that involve fixed facilities, in-store kiosks in particular, are similarly unproctored and convenient.) Such testing can be attractive to organizations because of its convenience for both the candidate and the hiring organization.

However, this convenience may come at a cost. A panel of industrial/organizational psychologists convened at the annual SIOP conference in 2006 and published an article that summarizes the issues well and describes the opinions of the various members of the panel. These individuals are employed by a range of different types of organizations: a university, several test-publishing firms, the U.S. government, and a publicly held company in the finance industry (Tippins et al., 2006). The issues they identified include candidate identity, test security and cheating, and fair access to testing for minorities.

Establishing candidate identity is a straightforward problem, currently without a straightforward solution. There is no failsafe method to verify who the test taker is. In contrast to in-office testing requiring identification, when testing is unproctored, anyone might be taking the test in the candidate's place. Perhaps a live video feed or a biometric method of verifying the candidate's identity would provide more assurance. Alternatively, the organization might choose to retest all the candidates who qualify, using a proctored setting. However, there are technical problems with evaluating and acting on score differences, and retesting diminishes the convenience and cost savings that were the original reasons for **unproctored testing** (Tippins et al., 2006).

A related issue is **test security**. One facet of this is keeping the test content under lock and key for future use. The HRIS manager must take precautions to prevent the test content from being copied and compromised. Another facet is preventing cheating. In addition to having someone else take the test or assist the candidate, the candidate might use resources that are not permitted (e.g., Internet search engines, offline dictionaries, calculators). Cheating is of particular concern when the tests have right answers (e.g., ability tests) or require skills that the candidate can have others perform (e.g., typing tests). Common sense tells us that the higher the stakes in a testing situation, the higher the likelihood of cheating.

HRIS experts also must be aware of a third issue, equal and fair access. In particular, tests must be fair to legally protected groups, yet unproctored testing and, indeed, Internet recruitment and candidate processing in general run the risk of having a chilling effect on minorities, who, because of the so-called "digital divide," might have greater difficulty accessing the Internet to apply for jobs. Organizations must provide for multiple ways to gain entry.

These problems do not have easy solutions for organizations that wish to rely on unproctored Internet testing. Tippins et al. (2006) discussed the pros and cons of unproctored Internet testing but did not come to a consensus about the ethics of administering unproctored tests and keeping the process fair.

Applying HRIS to Selection and Assessment

Selection systems are information management systems for organizational decision making and administration. Therefore, human resource information systems play an important part in their development and use. One uniquely HRIS-centered role is database design. Selection systems require the careful design of databases to store and keep track of selection data, both before and after individuals are hired, and the ability to link information in interrelated systems, such as candidate test data and demographics, employment data for those who are hired, and job movement and position histories within the company. Increasingly, HRIS experts will be called on to assist in integrating the organization's various HR systems. At a minimum, integration involves linking data in two or more systems, such as the candidate and employee identification data, so that one may conduct database queries and follow individuals as their information passes through the different systems. Integration often also involves linking transactional operations in a system such that, after the first system has conducted a transaction that requires follow-up in the next system, the first system contacts the next system to launch the required transaction. For instance, once a candidate has completed an online application, he or she may be automatically sent to another Web-based application to complete an assessment. The HRIS manager must have a conceptual understanding of what it means to link a test delivery system with other systems, such as applicant-tracking systems. In addition, organizations frequently wish to integrate a homegrown system with a vendor system or to integrate multiple systems, many or most of which are Internet based. Therefore, HRIS experts must have a technical knowledge of protocols and programming languages for sharing data between Web-based systems, such as eXtensible Markup Language (XML).

Another general HRIS role in selection systems is the development of **scoring and decision rules** and of the administrative functions of the system. Whether the output of the completed assessment is simple to interpret (e.g., pass/fail) or complicated (e.g., multiple sources of information, levels of performance, and data from various screening events that could follow), the HRIS expert who participates in the creation of scoring or decision rules must be sure that they are easy for the HR department and others to understand and apply consistently throughout the organization. Another key HRIS role is helping to design and apply the administrative functions of the system, the features permitting access to assessments results and the right to distribute candidate information. Below are some more specific considerations for designing a computerized or Web-based selection system (Kehoe, Dickter, Russell, & Sacco, 2005):

- *Test access and security:* The HR department must decide how candidates will gain access to the test (By permission? Will there be prescreening? Is testing open to anyone?) and how the test content will be kept secure.

- *Test inventory and administrative privileges:* The HRIS expert must consider how the computerized tests will be purchased and inventoried (if accessed from a vendor) and the **administrative privileges** that determine

   1. who should be assigned the right to work with particular types of test data,
   2. whether there will be multiple levels of access, and
   3. whether individuals will be able to delegate record-viewing rights to others.

- *Options for scoring:* Will there be multiple ways to score an assessment, with a variety of possible scoring rules? How might examinees' scores be compared with those of reference groups to make these scores more meaningful?
- *Accessing results:* In what data format and by what methods will test results be stored, transmitted, and interpreted?
- *Applying test policies:* What organizational requirements will affect the testing methods (e.g., systems that allow accommodations for disabilities) and the data that are kept and used (e.g., mandatory waiting periods before retests)?

For additional discussion on psychological testing on the Internet, the interested reader may wish to consult an article published by the American Psychological Association (Naglieri et al., 2004).

Demonstrating the HRM's Value With HRIS Selection Applications

As mentioned earlier, the HRIS manager plays a key role in proving the value of a selection system, through knowledge of how to obtain and use the right data on individual and organizational outcomes, data that will demonstrate a return on investment in the system. This expertise is also critical for defending the selection system, which is generally a high-stakes event: The use of the selection information determines individual careers and the company's ultimate success.

Demonstrating the value of selection requires that we know how well the employees who were assessed eventually perform on the job. For instance, if we measure their productivity (e.g., more products assembled or repaired, customers served, or products sold), we may find that people who score higher on the tests also are more productive. As another example, suppose the assessed individuals are supervisors. Among this group, we may find that the higher the supervisors' assessment scores, the better they supervise their subordinates, who have higher skill levels (perhaps as measured with a **knowledge test**) and lower turnover than the subordinates of people whose assessment results were not as high. Testing experts refer to this value or return on investment as utility: the extent to which a selection system results in the selection of better candidates than would have been possible if the system had not been used (Blum & Naylor, 1968). The quality of the candidates may be defined in terms of one or more of the following (Cascio, 1991):

1. The proportion of candidates who are successful on the job
2. The average numeric value of an outcome of interest (such as number of products sold or customers served)
3. The dollar amount of benefit resulting to the organization (such as the annual increase in revenue)

If a selection system produces a higher proportion of successful candidates (e.g., a 10% increase in the number of new financial advisers who, once hired, can pass a government-mandated licensure exam), then that system has clear value to the company. The same can be said of a selection system that results in an increase in some **performance criterion** (e.g., cable service technicians who are able to complete an average of 20% more installations per day as a result of testing). And the same can be said for a benefit that can be measured in dollars (e.g., for every 10 points higher a salesperson scored on a sales skill assessment, annual sales increased by $1,000).

There are many approaches to estimating utility. Apart from an anecdotal approach (Does it seem like more people are successful on the job now?), perhaps one of the simplest approaches is to conduct pre- and post-comparisons of measurable performance to see if the selection system has coincided with a change in performance. As a more precise alternative, industrial/organizational psychologists frequently use a **utility formula** that takes several factors into account: the **selection ratio**; the **validity coefficient**, expressed as the correlation between assessment scores and criteria (outcomes); and information about the dollar value of performance. The utility formula and related concepts are described here in some detail.

The selection ratio is the number of candidates who, based on the assessment, are chosen for the job, divided by the number of candidates who are assessed. The validity coefficient is a statistical correlation that indicates the correspondence between test scores and job performance or some other important work outcomes. When validity is high, there is a close correspondence between assessment performance and work results. In general, a high-validity, low-selection-ratio system produces the greatest benefit of selection but also incurs the highest cost of selection, all else being the same. When the selection ratio is low, the bar is set high on the assessment, and more rarified, higher-performing candidates will be chosen. (This generalization works as long as the selection ratio is not so high or so low that nearly everyone is hired or no one is hired, respectively; in those cases, the assessment has little value as a decision-making tool.) Information about the process used to estimate the dollar value of job performance follows. The value can be obtained from job experts at the organization. Alternatively, published research may be used to estimate this value, and, in many cases, the published value is used for utility estimates.

The result of the **utility calculation** is the dollar value of the selection system per individual, or group of individuals, hired. (Note that here utility refers to the dollar benefit of selection, without consideration of the cost. Certainly, it is important to compare this benefit with its corresponding cost to make good business decisions about selection systems.) The formula for utility is $\Delta U = r_{xy} * SD_y * N * \Phi/\rho$, and the elements of the calculation are as follows:

1. ΔU is the utility or annual change in the dollar value of productivity. Items 2 through 5 will be multiplied to calculate this number.

2. r_{xy} is the validity coefficient of the assessment, quantified as a correlation that falls between −1 and +1 and notated as a correlation between x (the assessment score) and y (the performance criterion score). Positive values indicate that the assessment (also called the predictor) and the criterion (work outcome) increase together; for instance, looking at the range of candidate data, as ability test scores increase, so might evaluations of ability to learn on the job. Negative values indicate that as one increases, the other decreases. For instance, as scores on an assessment of conscientiousness and work ethic increase, the frequency of absence and tardiness might decrease.

3. SD_y is the standard deviation (*SD*) of performance (y), that is, the difference, in dollar terms, between an average and a superior performer, which on a normal curve would be estimated as a 1 standard deviation difference. Estimated at 40% of salary based on published research across the spectrum of jobs in the U.S. economy, this value has consistently been shown to approximate the difference in the value of productivity between average and above-average employees (Hunter & Schmidt, 1982).

4. N is the number of employees hired.

5. Φ/ρ refers to the test score of applicants who are selected by the organization and is expressed in a statistically standardized form (the standard deviation units in this value and the standard deviation of performance in Item 3 cancel out, leaving a dollar value for the utility estimate).

For example, suppose an employer tests 2,500 clerical job candidates on an assessment with a validity of 0.43 and hires the top 1,000 scorers at an annual salary of $20,000. Therefore, $r_{xy} = 0.43$. The standard deviation of job performance (SD_y or 40% of salary) is estimated to be $8,000. One thousand employees are hired (N =1,000). The selection ratio is 40% (4 out of 10 qualify); for this ratio, Φ/ρ can be determined from statistical tables of the normal curve; this value is 0.64. Therefore, ΔU = (0.43) * (8000) * (1000) * (0.64)= $2,201,600, meaning that the average increase in utility per person hired is $2,202 per year. If all 1,000 employees were to stay three years, we would estimate the utility over that period at approximately $6.6 million. Supposing that the testing program expenses were $300,000 per year, the return on investment for a three-year period would still be about $5.7 million. This example serves to illustrate a method of estimating utility and also shows that, when many people are hired, the total value of the assessment quickly yields high numbers. Although organizational stakeholders occasionally are skeptical because of the extremely high utility values that are possible, the principles behind the numbers are sound.

After reading this section, you should reasonably conclude that there are a variety of technical concepts related to selection and assessment with which HRIS experts should familiarize themselves. Our intent has been to provide an overview of these topics and of the trends that are currently taking place in organizations, in the testing industry, and in research programs. By becoming familiar with this work, the HRIS student will gain awareness of the major issues he or she is likely to face when implementing database-based decision-making systems.

SUMMARY

In summary, this chapter explained the intersection between the use of technology in the recruitment and selection process and the use of HRIS in organizations. This highlighted the need for HRIS experts to understand how to use the Internet for recruitment as well as selection-related data in order to provide strategic information to the company and demonstrate the return on the company's investment in assessments. In addition, technology issues surrounding the selection process were addressed. Measurement properties of paper-and-pencil assessments and their computer versions were discussed. The mode of assessments that do not include measurements of ability is of little concern for researchers since giving these tests on paper will not result in a different measure from that obtained with a computerized test. However, there is clear evidence that the mode of administration (paper vs. computer) matters for ability tests that are speeded. The more speeded a test is, the more likely that there will be differences between the paper and computer test results. A second issue focused on in this chapter is the trade-off between fidelity and bandwidth. Technology has enabled organizations to create work sample simulations that represent the job with high fidelity. However, if the company then wants to use the simulation for a different business unit or job, the details that made the simulation highly appropriate in the first setting may interfere with its use in the other setting. In general, HRIS managers should keep in mind that, depending on the effort and expense one is willing to expend on assessment development and installation, lower-fidelity simulations or combinations of other types of assessments might be preferable. One of the final issues dealt with was unproctored testing, which can be convenient to both the applicant and the organization. Unfortunately, this means of delivering assessment gives way to a floodgate of concerns such as how to verify candidate identity, provide test security and eliminate cheating, and ensure fair access to testing for minorities. The chapter further examined the role that HRIS experts have to play in solving these problems through the use of technology and the decision to develop and use an HRIS.

KEY TERMS

ability test
administrative privileges
aesthetic features [of a Web site]
antidiscrimination laws
attributes [of a Web site]
bandwidth
computerized assessments
content [of a Web site]
diversity of the applicant pool
employment brand
fidelity
knowledge test
media richness
navigability [of a Web site]
online recruiting
online testing
paper-and-pencil assessments
performance criterion
personality tests
power tests
psychological contract
realistic culture preview
realistic job preview
recruiting
recruiting- and screening-oriented Web site
reliability
scoring and decision rules
selection procedures
selection ratio
self-selection
social networking Web sites
test security
unproctored testing
usability [of a Web site]
utility formula; utility calculation
validity coefficient
work simulation

DISCUSSION QUESTIONS

1. What recruiting objectives are being met through the use of online recruitment?
2. What are some of the advantages and disadvantages of using online recruitment?
3. Should organizations rely solely on recruiting through the Internet? Why or why not?
4. What are some of the technological issues that arise through the use of technology in the function of selection?
5. Describe how the use of technology in the selection process is adding value to organizations.

CASE STUDY

The case from Chapter 11 will be used here, since recruitment and selection are the next step in the operationalization of a talent management strategy. The background for this chapter case is the case material from Chapter 11; at the end of this background material, more details relevant to the recruitment and selection of new employees will be presented.

Rudiger is sitting at his desk in his seventh-floor corner office in the City, gazing out over London and reflecting on life. At 43 he is at the top of his game. He has everything he could wish for—a lovely partner, a four-year-old in a private nursery, a new executive house in the suburbs, a holiday home in southern Italy, and a remuneration package that's the envy of his peers and beyond anything his German immigrant parents could have imagined. But it hasn't been easy, oh no! Hard work, long hours, geographical moves every two or three years, and sacrifices in terms of his personal life.

But now he has a problem. Rudiger has just been appointed Global Head of People and Talent responsible for the future of 35,000 people worldwide, the bulk of whom are based in the United States, the United Kingdom, and Europe, and manufacturing is likely to relocate to China in the next two years, adding to his responsibilities. In his previous role, he was responsible for the United Kingdom and Northern Europe and had operational oversight for 11,000 people. An initial consideration of his responsibilities has identified a number of people issues for the next five years: the company needs to recruit and retain particular specialist and skilled personnel; some of the brightest and most experienced midlevel managers are leaving; an aging senior directorship is looking toward early retirement. But the main difficulty is that, although he knows he has a problem, he doesn't have enough detailed information to know the scale of the problem.

18 months later . . .

Once again Rudiger is sitting at his desk in his seventh-floor office in central London reflecting on life. The move from Barcelona to England went smoothly with the last crate arriving only two months later than the rest. He is still working hard, but the hours are slightly better since the introduction of the work-life balance policy last year, and his family has settled well into the idyllic English countryside.

As the Global Head of People and Talent, he still has problems though—just different ones. The talent strategy "Our People—Our Talent—Our Future," which he presented to the board in his third month, identified the need for robust HRP information and analyses that required a new version of HRP software. It is in its early stages, but the intensive data-cleansing and updating activity has been straightforward so far. More concerning are the metrics responsible for producing the information needed to develop far-reaching HRP policies and practices for the future. The metrics are relatively easy to construct, but it is proving tricky to find the right "bundles" of predictive metrics—this is holding up progress with the analysis application package. In addition, there have been cost overruns in the implementation of the HRP software, and some senior managers are wondering if the new software should be abandoned.

At least 3 of the 12 board members will retire in the next two years, and they are looking to groom their successors. At least one will have to be hired from outside the organization, and the HR department is not sure what the CEO wants for this position. In addition, employee turnover and an aggressive growth strategy mean hiring new employees as well as training transferring current employees. The work that is involved in defining competences (KSA sets) at skill levels within jobs is progressing well, with hard-won support from the unions. However, job descriptions that can be found are at least three to five years old, and some jobs have no descriptions. The new apprenticeship scheme is about to be launched, and the international graduate student package and development program has been completely revised. Overall things are progressing reasonably well, but there is much to be done.

Case Supplemental Material

On the basis of your analyses and answers completed for Chapter 11, assume that Rudiger has completed an acceptable HRP program and his staff members have completed current and accurate job descriptions for all positions in the talent management project. These job descriptions all contain the specific duties, tasks, and responsibilities as well as the KSA sets needed for each job.

Rudiger's next task is to recruit and select individuals for jobs. He wants to use the new HRIS software applications that the company has purchased and implemented for recruiting and selecting new employees. Fortunately, he can get assistance on this task from the IT department, which has built and maintains the company's Web site. In addition, he has several staff members with doctorates in industrial/organizational psychology who can work with the IT professionals to develop recruitment and selection materials. However, Rudiger must provide the guidelines for the selection and recruitment of individuals who can fit into the talent management project.

Case Study Questions

1. What guidelines would you establish as part of Rudiger's plan that emphasized the use of the Internet via the company's Web site to communicate the recruiting objectives of the talent management project?
   a. What are the potential advantages and disadvantages of online recruitment to communicate recruiting objectives?
2. What guidelines would you establish for the use of an HRIS for the selection and assessment of potential employees?
   a. What selection and assessment tools could be used on the Internet, and which ones would need to be done on a face-to-face basis?
   b. What are the technological problems that affect selection via the Internet and the solutions that have been suggested?
   c. What guidelines would you develop to make sure that a utility analysis was done for all HRIS selection applications?

REFERENCES

Allen, D. G., Mahto, R. V., & Otondo, R. F. (2007). Web-based recruitment: Effects of information, organizational brand, and attitudes toward a Web site on applicant attraction. *Journal of Applied Psychology, 92*, 1696–1708.

Baker, H. G. (1985). The unwritten contract: Job perceptions. *Personnel Journal, 64*, 36–41.

Barber, A. E., & Roehling, M. V. (1993). Job postings and the decision to interview: A verbal protocol analysis. *Journal of Applied Psychology, 78*, 845–856.

Becker, B., & Gerhart, B. (1996). The impact of human resource management on organizational performance: Progress and prospects. *Academy of Management Journal, 39*, 779–801.

Blum, M. L., & Naylor, J. C. (1968). *Industrial psychology: Its theoretical and social foundations* (Rev. ed.). New York: Harper & Row.

Braddy, P. W., Meade, A. W., & Kroustalis, C. M. (2008). Online recruiting: The effects of organizational familiarity, website usability, and website attractiveness on viewers' impressions of organizations. *Computers in Human Behavior, 24*, 2992–3001.

Braddy, P. W., Meade, A. W., Michael, J. J., & Fleenor, J. W. (2009). Internet recruiting: Effects of website content features on viewers' perceptions of organizational culture. *International Journal of Selection and Assessment, 17*, 19–34.

Braddy, P. W., Thompson, L. F., Wuensch, K. L., & Grossnickle, W. F. (2003). Internet recruiting: The effects of Web page design features. *Social Science Computer Review, 21*, 374–385.

Breaugh, J. A., & Starke, M. (2000). Research on employee recruitment: So many studies, so many remaining questions. *Journal of Management, 26*, 405–434.

Cable, D. M., Aiman-Smith, L., Mulvey, P. W., & Edwards, J. R. (2000). The sources of accuracy and job applicants' beliefs about organizational culture. *Academy of Management Journal, 43*, 1076–1085.

Cable, D. M., & Graham, M. E. (2000). The determinants of job seekers' reputation perceptions. *Journal of Organizational Behavior, 21*, 929–947.

Cable, D. M., & Judge, T. A. (1996). Person-organization fit, job choice decisions, and organizational entry. *Organizational Behavior and Human Decision Processes, 67*, 294–311.

Cable, D. M., & Yu, K. Y. T. (2006). Managing job seekers' organizational image beliefs: The role of media richness and media credibility. *Journal of Applied Psychology, 91*, 828–840.

Cappelli, P. (2001). Making the most of on-line recruiting. *Harvard Business Review, 79,* 139–146.

Cardy, R. L., & Miller, J. S. (2003). Technology: Implications for HRM. In D. Stone (Ed.), *Advances in human performance and cognitive engineering research* (pp. 99–118). Greenwich, CT: JAI Press.

Carless, S. A. (2005). Person-job fit versus person-organization fit as predictors of organizational attraction and job acceptance intentions: A longitudinal study. *Journal of Occupational and Organizational Psychology, 78*, 411–429.

Cascio, W. F. (1991). *Applied psychology in personnel management* (4th ed.). Englewood Cliffs, NJ: Prentice Hall.

Cascio, W. F. (1998). *Managing human resources: Productivity, quality of work life, and profits* (5th ed.). New York: Irwin/McGraw-Hill.

Cascio, W. F. (2006). *Managing human resources: Productivity, quality of work life, and profits* (7th ed.). New York: Irwin/McGraw-Hill.

Chapman, D. S., & Webster, J. (2003). The use of technologies in the recruiting, screening, and selection processes for job candidates. *International Journal of Selection and Assessment, 11*, 113–120.

Cober, R. T., Brown, D. J., Blumental, A. J., Doverspike, D., & Levy, P. (2000). The quest for the qualified job surfer: It's time the public sector catches the wave. *Public Personnel Management, 29*(4), 479–494.

Cober, R. T., Brown, D. J., Keeping, L. M., & Levy, P. E. (2004). Recruitment on the Net: How do organizational Web site characteristics influence applicant attraction? *Journal of Management, 30*, 623–646.

Cober, R. T., Brown, D. J., Levy, P. E., Keeping, L. M., & Cober, A. B. (2003). Organizational websites: Website content and style as determinants of organizational attraction. *International Journal of Selection and Assessment, 11*, 158–169.

Collins, J. C. (2001). *Good to great: Why some companies make the leap . . . and others don't.* New York: HarperCollins.

Daft, R. L., & Lengel, R. H. (1986). Organizational information requirements, media richness and structural design. *Management Science, 32*, 554–571.

Dineen, B. R., Ash, S. R., & Noe, R. A. (2002). A web of applicant attraction: Person-organization fit in the context of Web-based recruitment. *Journal of Applied Psychology, 87*, 723–734.

Dineen, B. R., Ling, J., Ash, S. R., & DelVecchio, D. (2007). Aesthetic properties and message customization: Navigating the dark side of web recruitment. *Journal of Applied Psychology, 92*, 356–372.

Dineen, B. R., & Noe, R. A. (2009). Effects of customization on application decisions and applicant pool characteristics in a web-based recruitment context. *Journal of Applied Psychology, 94*, 224–234.

Galanaki, E. (2002). The decision to recruit online: A descriptive study. *Career Development International, 7*, 243–251.

Guion, R. M. (1998). *Assessment, measurement, and prediction for personnel decisions.* Mahwah, NJ: Lawrence Erlbaum.

Heneman, H. G., & Judge, T. A. (2006). *Staffing organizations* (5th ed.). Boston: McGraw-Hill.

Hogler, R. L., Henle, C., & Bemus, C. (1998). Internet recruiting and employment discrimination: A legal perspective. *Human Resource Management Review, 8*(2), 149–164.

Hunter, J. E., & Schmidt, F. L. (1982). *Personnel selection programs based on cumulative knowledge.* Presentation at the PTC fall conference on validity generalization, Newport Beach, CA.

Jackson, L. A., Ervin, K. S., Gardner, P. D., & Schmitt, N. (2001). Gender and the Internet: Women communicating and men searching. *Sex Roles, 44*, 363–379.

Judge, T. A., & Cable, D. M. (1997). Applicant personality, organizational culture, and organizational attraction. *Personnel Psychology, 50*, 359–394.

Karat, J. (1997). Evolving the scope of user-centered design. *Communications of the ACM, 40*, 33–38.

Kehoe, J. F., Dickter, D. N., Russell, D. P., & Sacco, J. M. (2005). e-Selection. In H. G. Guental & D. L. Stone (Eds.), *The brave new world of eHR* (pp. 54–103). San Francisco: Jossey-Bass.

Kristof-Brown, A. L., Zimmerman, R. D., & Johnson, E. C. (2005). Consequences of individuals' fit at work: A meta-analysis of person-job, person-organization, person-group, and person-supervisor fit. *Personnel Psychology, 58*, 281–342.

Kuhn, P., & Skuterud, M. (2000). Job search methods: Internet versus traditional. *Monthly Labor Review, 123,* 3–11.

Lyons, B. D., & Marler, J. H. (2011). Got image? Examining organizational image in Web recruitment. *Journal of Managerial Psychology, 26*(1), 58–76.

Marakas, G., Yi, M., & Johnson, R. (1998). The multilevel and multifaceted character of computer self-efficacy: Toward clarification of the construct and an integrative framework for research. *Information Systems Research, 9*, 126–163.

McCourt-Mooney, M. (2000). Internet briefing: Recruitment and selection—R&D using the Internet—Part III. *Journal of Managerial Psychology, 15,* 737–740.

McManus, M. A., & Ferguson, M. W. (2003). Biodata, personality, and demographic differences of recruits from three sources. *International Journal of Selection and Assessment, 11,* 175–183.

Mead, A., & Drasgow, F. (1993). Equivalence of computerized and paper-and-pencil cognitive ability tests: A meta-analysis. *Psychological Bulletin, 114*, 449–458.

Mohamed, A. A., Orife, J. N., & Wibowo, K. (2002). The legality of key word search as a personnel selection tool. *Employee Relations, 24*, 516–522.

Morrison, E. W., & Robinson, S. L. (1997). When employees feel betrayed: A model of how psychological contract violation develops. *Academy of Management Review, 22*, 226–256.

Naglieri, J. A., Drasgow, F., Schmit, M., Handler, L., Prifitera, A., Margolis, A., & Velasquez, R. (2004). Psychological testing on the Internet. *American Psychologist, 59*, 150–162.

Nielsen, J. (2000). *Designing Web usability.* Indianapolis, IN: New Riders.

PewInternet. (2006). *Internet activities.* Retrieved February 4, 2007, from www.pewinternet.org/trends/Internet_Activities_1.11.07.htm

Potosky, D., & Bobko, P. (2004). Selection testing via the Internet: Practical considerations and exploratory empirical findings. *Personnel Psychology, 57*, 1003–1004.

Reed, K., Doty, H. D., & May, D. R. (2005). The impact of aging on self-efficacy and computer skill acquisition. *Journal of Managerial Issues, 17*, 212–228.

Reed Company. (2003). *The Reed Recruitment Index report.* Retrieved June 1, 2007, from www.onrec.com/content2/news.asp?ID=1981

Rousseau, D. M. (1990). New hire perceptions of their own and their employer's obligations: A study of psychological contracts. *Journal of Organizational Behavior, 11*, 389–400.

Rozelle, A. L., & Landis, R. S. (2002). An examination of the relationship between use of the Internet as a recruitment source and student attitudes. *Computers in Human Behavior, 18*, 593–604.

Schmidt, F. L., & Hunter, J. E. (1998). The validity and utility of selection methods in personnel psychology: Practical and theoretical implications of 85 years of research findings. *Psychological Bulletin, 124*, 262–274.

Schneider, B., Goldstein, H. W., & Smith, D. B. (1995). The ASA framework: An update. *Personnel Psychology, 48*, 747–773.

Seminerio, M. (2001, April 24). E-recruiting takes next step. *eWeek, 18,* 16, 51–54.

Shaffer, D. J., & Schmidt, R. A. (2006). Personality testing in employment. In *Society of Human Resources Management legal report.* Retrieved February 21, 2007, from www.shrm.org/hrresources/lrpt_published/CMS_000991.asp

Society for Human Resource Management. (2004). *Merging tests with applicant tracking systems.* Retrieved June 12, 2008, from www.shrm.org/ema/library_published/nonIC/CMS_006199.asp

Society for Human Resource Management. (2008). *Online technologies and their impact on recruitment strategies: Using social networking websites to attract talent.* Alexandria, VA: Author. Retrieved September, 24, 2008, from http://www.shrm.org/Research/SurveyFindings/Articles/Documents/SNS%20staffing%20%20research%20Presentation Final.pdf

Society for Industrial and Organizational Psychology. (2003). *Principles for the validation and use of personnel selection procedures* (4th ed.). Bowling Green, OH: Author.

Stone, D. L., Lukaszewski, K. M., & Isenhour, L. C. (2005). e-Recruiting: Online strategies for attracting talent. In H. G. Gueutal & D. L. Stone (Eds.), *The brave new world of eHR* (pp. 22–53). San Francisco: Jossey-Bass.

Stone, D. L., Stone-Romero, E. F., & Lukaszewski, K. (2003). The functional and dysfunctional consequences of human resource information technology for organizations and their employees. In D. L. Stone (Ed.), *Advances in human performance and cognitive engineering research* (pp. 37–68). Greenwich, CT: JAI Press.

Tippins, N. T., Beaty, J., Drasgow, F., Gibson, W. M., Pearlman, K., Segall, D. O., & Shepherd, W. (2006). Unproctored Internet testing in employment settings. *Personnel Psychology, 59*, 189–225.

Ulrich, D. (2001). From e-business to e-HR. *International Human Resources Information Management Journal, 5,* 90–97.

U.S. Department of Labor. (1999). *Testing and assessment: An employer's guide to good practices.* Washington, DC: Author.

U.S. Equal Employment Opportunity Commission, U.S. Civil Service Commission, U.S. Department of Labor, & U.S. Department of Justice. (1978). Uniform guidelines on employee selection procedures. *Federal Register, 43*(166), 38295–38309.

Walker, H. J., Field, H. S., Giles, W. F., Armenakis, A. A., & Bernerth, J. B. (2009). Displaying employee testimonials on recruitment Web sites: Effects of communication media, employee race, and job seeker race on organizational attraction and information credibility. *Journal of Applied Psychology, 94*, 1354–1364.

Wanous, J. P. (1992). *Organizational entry.* Reading, MA: Addison-Wesley.

Williamson, I. O., Lepak, D. P., & King, J. (2003). The effect of company recruitment Web site orientation on individuals' perceptions of organizational attractiveness. *Journal of Vocational Behavior, 63,* 242–263.

Wright, P. M., & Snell, S. A. (1998). Toward a unifying framework for exploring fit and flexibility in strategic human resource management. *Academy of Management Review, 23*, 756–772.

Zusman, R. R., & Landis, R. S. (2002). Applicant preferences for Web-based versus traditional job postings. *Computers in Human Behavior, 18,* 285–296.

Chapter 13

Training and Development

Issues and HRIS Applications

Ralf Burbach

EDITORS' NOTE

Training is one of the major programs offered by HR departments and is an important aspect of an organization's talent management program. Organizations use training not only for skill and knowledge learning but also to develop employees for future positions. In addition, training plays an important role in the motivation of employees. It shows that the organization is concerned about the development of its employees and would like to retain them. However, training generally captures the largest portion of the HR departmental budget. Due to these heavy costs, the application of an HRIS to save money is very important. In the applications section of this chapter, you will learn how training can be made to be cost-effective through an HRIS that serves both as a more efficient transaction processor and as an aid to managerial decision making.

CHAPTER OBJECTIVES

After completing this chapter, you should be able to

- Discuss how training can be used as a source of competitive advantage
- Differentiate between training and development (T&D)
- Understand how training and development affect both learning and motivation
- Explain the steps in a systems model of training
- Understand the essential features of the culture of a learning organization

- Explain the factors that influence transfer of training
- Understand both the costs and the benefits metrics associated with training
- Discuss the critical importance of the evaluation of training
- Understand MIS, HRMS, and DSS (see Chapter 1) training applications
- Explain the advantages and disadvantages of Web-based learning
- Develop a practical application, using EXCEL, in the evaluation of training

HRIS IN ACTION

Midwestern Mighty Markets (Triple M)[1] is one of the largest supermarket chains in five states, with 275 store locations. The corporate director of training, June Grady, was hired externally and has been on the job for two months. She has inherited the job with little information about what had been happening in the past relative to training and the use of any computer-based technology to manage the training activities and programs. She has begun a careful examination of the training activities, particularly supervisory training since that is where the next higher-level managers will be identified. The annual budget for training has been $2.2 million, of which $1.1 million is devoted to supervisory training.

Supervisory training is one week in length and occurs on a monthly basis in each state at a central location. It is focused on training assistant department managers (e.g., produce, meat, and grocery) in the supervisory skills needed to be a department manager. Based on department managers' recommendations, assistant managers are sent to training at a central location in their state. However, all assistant managers across the states have the same training content and training activities. At the conclusion of the training, all trainees complete an evaluation of the training program based on their experiences.

The company has an HRIS software application developed by PeopleSoft and implemented three years ago. It is used for the management of all the training in the company. There are a number of reports that can be generated from the software, including attendance by states, stores, and departments within the stores. This information is useful for June, so she can make sure that training is occurring evenly across departments, stores, and states. Other reports are also available that can be sent to department and store managers as well as to the regional managers of Triple M.

June has been examining all these reports available from the HRIS software to determine if anything is missing. During her examination, she notices that no one has been accessing the reports summarizing the trainees' evaluations of the training programs. On further examination, she finds that some store managers receive these summary reports but rarely use them. Also, she discovers that there is an additional report that has been designed to be generated by the software. This report is based on evaluation data that are to be collected from department managers three months after the trainees have returned to their jobs. This report appears quite important since it asks the department managers to rate the trainees' job performance after they have completed training to determine any effects of the training.

June sees a serious problem with this lack of training-evaluation data collection and assessment; the trainees' post-training evaluations are not being analyzed by the available software, and, more important, the department managers' ratings of trainee job performance are not being completed. Therefore, even though the company owns sophisticated (and costly) software, it is not being used to evaluate the supervisory training programs. More seriously, June has no idea if the $1.1 million being spent on supervisory training has had any effect on the job performance of the trainees.

INTRODUCTION

The nature of work and the structure of organizations are rapidly changing. Internationalization, globalization, and changing customer expectations of service and quality standards require firms to improve and transform themselves perpetually to remain competitive. Emerging concepts such as the global marketplace, knowledge economy, knowledge worker, information age, and digital revolution underscore that an organization's ability to survive in a constantly changing business environment is founded on its capacity to generate new knowledge, to share knowledge, and to innovate continuously (Nonaka & Takeuchi, 1995; Porter, 1990; Senge, 1990). In the new global economy, knowledge is now the new lever for success, since knowledge potentially adds more value than the traditional factors of production—capital, raw material, and labor (Harrison, 2005). This new knowledge-based economy is

> directly based on production, distribution and use of knowledge and information. Knowledge is now recognised as the driver of productivity and economic growth, leading to a new focus on the role of information, technology, and learning in economic performance. . . . Employment in the knowledge-based economy is characterized by increasing demand for more highly skilled workers. . . . The knowledge-based economy is characterized by the need for continuous learning of both codified information and the competencies to use this information. (Organisation for Economic Co-operation and Development [OECD], 1996, pp. 3, 7, 13)

Knowledge is created by a firm's knowledge assets, that is, its **human capital**[2] (see OECD, 2001, p. 18), which has long been recognized as one of the key sources of competitive advantage (Grant, 1996; Prahalad & Hamel, 1990; Wright, Dunford, & Snell, 2001). Hence, the **learning, training, and development (LT&D)** of employees is now center stage in today's organizations to ensure long-term competitiveness, excellence, quality, flexibility, and adaptability. Changing work practices and new services and products necessitate new knowledge, competences, and skills. It may also be argued that today's organizations ought to learn faster and more effectively than their rivals in order to remain competitive. However, a range of other reasons exist as to why organizations train and develop their workforces—for instance, to enable employees to cope with daily workloads. T&D activities can also alleviate possible future skill shortages. High-commitment organizations train and develop their employees to foster employee motivation and satisfaction (Pfeffer, 1996, 1998). In a time when job security is diminishing and employability is of increasing value, employees place much greater emphasis on career prospects and career development in their choice of employer. This point is of particular relevance for specialist knowledge workers who are in short supply in a tight labor market. The strategic importance of individual and organizational learning and development is mirrored in the continued interest in the concepts of the **learning organization** and **organizational learning**. These terms are often used interchangeably. However, the learning organization is the ultimate state of organizational learning at which the organization is able to facilitate the learning of all its members and can continuously transform itself (Argyris & Schon, 1978; Pedler, Burgoyne, & Boydell, 1991). "It is the potential of organizational learning to enable organizations to reinvent themselves in order to compete in the changing and increasingly uncertain and competitive environment that is making it such an attractive proposition for many managers" (Burnes, 2004, p. 129).

Yet it has been argued that few firms, if any, have actually achieved this aim. Nonetheless, the notion of the learning organization illustrates that organizational learning is inextricably linked to individual LT&D. It is also closely linked to the notion of lifelong learning and continuous professional development. Employees at all levels of the organization will have to demonstrate their commitment to these, especially when they seek a new employer, pay increases, or promotions. T&D activities are thus closely allied with **performance management** and talent management. Most large organizations use human resource information systems (HRIS) to collect, store, and analyze T&D information. This information is generally contained in specialist talent management modules, T&D modules, and learning management systems to reflect the strategic importance of LT&D in the organization. This chapter examines the strategic implications of T&D before it covers the **systems model of training and development**. The section on the systems model will look in detail at its four stages—identifying T&D needs, designing T&D solutions, implementing T&D, and evaluating T&D. Then, training metrics and benefit analysis will be discussed. The next section investigates some HRIS applications in training and some implementation issues. The chapter concludes with a summary of the key issues.

TRAINING AND DEVELOPMENT: STRATEGIC IMPLICATIONS AND LEARNING ORGANIZATIONS

The introduction to this chapter has already alluded to a number of key terms associated with T&D. Some of the terms, such as *learning, training, development,* and *education,* are frequently used in combination and sometimes even, incorrectly, as substitutes. To comprehend the processes involved in LT&D, we must differentiate these key concepts. *Education* is aimed at developing, usually as part of a formal program of study, general knowledge, understanding, and moral values. *Training* refers to the planned acquisition of the knowledge, skills, and abilities (KSA) to carry out a specific task or job in a vocational setting. The purpose of training interventions is to attain a positive change in performance. *Development* is a continuous process of systematic advancement, of "becoming increasingly more complex, more elaborate and differentiated, by virtue of learning and maturation" (Collin, 2007, p. 266). Development in an organizational context ensures that employees possess the KSA required to fulfill future roles in the organization. Hence, development may be conceived as a lever for career development, succession planning, performance management, and talent management (Gunnigle, Heraty, & Morley, 2002). Training focuses on immediate job performance, whereas development centers on long-term, continuous changes of an individual's potential. Learning is defined as the process of assimilating new knowledge and skills in consequence of experience or practice that will bring about relatively permanent changes in behavior. Effective learning necessitates a capacity to integrate new knowledge with existing knowledge (Learning, 2007). However, the manner in which adults learn and are motivated to learn differs fundamentally from the ways in which children and adolescents learn. Andragogy, or the study of adult learning, purports that adults learn best when

1. They know the reasons for learning a new concept or skill
2. They are actively involved in creating or setting the learning activity
3. They can connect new learning to the knowledge and experience they have developed over time
4. Learning is problem centered
5. They believe a learning activity is immediately relevant to their job
6. They are internally rather than externally motivated to learn; in other words, they learn when they can see a benefit (Knowles, Holton, & Swanson, 2005)

Learning at an individual or organizational level is ineluctably linked to the creation and management of knowledge. Learning is the basis for any T&D activity. The outcomes of learning include skills, competencies, know-how or tacit knowledge, and higher-level cognitive and other skills (Collin, 2007). Skills are directly related to performance and the ability to carry out a task. It has been argued that new organizational realities require higher levels of cognitive skills. Bloom's taxonomy of learning, for example, identifies six increasingly higher levels of thinking—knowledge, comprehension, application, analysis, synthesis, and evaluation (Bloom, Engelhart, Furst, Hill, & Krathwohl, 1956). Competencies consist of KSA and the underlying characteristics of a person that allow the jobholder to perform a task effectively. The knowledge of employees is a tacit commodity, an intangible asset. It is associated with an understanding of and a constructive application of information (Grant, 1996). In a knowledge-based economy, organizations must become knowledge productive, and employees, knowledge workers and knowledge assets. Knowledge-intensive organizations are those that heavily depend on knowledge creation and knowledge sharing, such as firms with a significant research and development focus or consultancy firms. **Knowledge management (KM)** essentially consists of five separate activities, which are the acquisition, documentation, transfer, creation, and application of knowledge (Yahya & Goh, 2002). Whereas knowledge is generated by individuals, organizational knowledge and learning are the result of the combined learning of everybody in the organization and the acquisition of knowledgeable individuals (Grant, 1996).

Hence, if a firm's organizational culture rewards learning, it facilitates KM and the transformation of the firm into a knowledge organization (Mayo, 1998; Soliman & Spooner, 2000). The sharing, codifying, storing, and replicating of knowledge within the organization is greatly facilitated by information and communication technology (ICT). Consequently, KM focuses on the interaction of human beings and ICT and the subsequent creation of knowledge and, in addition, on the alignment of technology with people systems within a firm. The HR department plays a vital role in determining where, among employees, tacit knowledge exists, what type of knowledge is present, and whether and to what degree this knowledge is conducive to attaining present and future organizational goals (Soliman & Spooner, 2000). Should the HR function detect a gap between existing knowledge and the knowledge necessary to pursue strategic objectives, it can initiate procedures to remedy this shortfall through recruitment, socialization, and T&D initiatives. It is evident that the concepts of KM and organizational learning are closely related. Organizational learning is by no means a new concept. Argyris and Schon (1978) suggested a three-level model of organizational learning, consisting of single-loop, double-loop, and triple-loop learning. Single-loop learning is adaptive and focuses on the detection of deviations in performance from established organizational norms, practices, policies, and procedures. Double-loop learning questions the suitability of norms, practices, policies, and procedures that define performance standards. Triple-loop learning challenges the rationale of the organization with the aim of completely transforming it (Burnes, 2004). One of the most influential proponents of the learning organization is Peter Senge. In his book *The Fifth Discipline*, he puts forward five interrelated disciplines that an organization should cultivate among its employees to engender learning and success (Senge, 1990):

1. *Personal mastery:* individual growth and learning
2. *Mental models:* deep-rooted assumptions that affect the way in which employees perceive people, situations, and organizations
3. *Shared visions:* a shared view of the organization's future
4. *Team learning:* a shift from individual learning to collective learning
5. *Systems thinking:* or the "Fifth Discipline," which connects the previous disciplines (Burnes, 2004)

Other writers promote generic organizational characteristics that stimulate organizational learning. Cummings and Worley (2001), for instance, advocate a flat teamwork-based organizational structure to facilitate networking; the use of information systems to collect, process, and share information; human resource practices such as appraisals and rewards that reinforce learning; effective leadership that is supportive of organizational learning; and an organizational culture that encourages openness, creativity, and experimentation among members of the firm. A learning culture is one of the key levers for organizational learning, training, and development. Transfer of training is far more likely to occur in an environment where the basic assumptions, shared values, norms, and artifacts of an organization espouse successful LT&D, and where employees are encouraged to create, process, and share information and knowledge (Cummings & Worley, 2001). A T&D intervention can only be considered successful if transfer of training has occurred and a permanent change in behavior has taken place.

Systems Model of Training and Development

The approaches to T&D adopted by organizations are quite possibly as diverse as the organizations that employ them. The literature is teeming with different, sometimes competing, models, which mirror the approaches to T&D found in practice. One of the most frequently cited models is the systems or systematic approach. This formal or planned approach to workforce T&D consists of four interrelated and connected steps, which are illustrated in Figure 13.1. The steps are arranged as a cycle to highlight the cyclical and continuous nature of the process; the systems model, then, is conceptualized as an ongoing activity, in much the same way as is employee development. Thus, the model is applicable to both training and development. Its simplicity and clear structure make it ideally suited in the context of HRIS applications in this area. In addition, the model provides a rational foundation for the allocation of resources throughout the T&D process. However, the systematic model has also received some criticism *because* of its simplicity, because of the fact that it is a closed system, and because it does not take account of individual differences among the learners. Notwithstanding these criticisms, the model continues to find broad application, for instance, in the development of national training standards and, indeed, in many IT-based T&D applications that are designed based on the four steps (Stewart, 1999).

Identifying T&D Needs

The first step of the systems model is concerned with the identification of the learning and development needs of organizational members. The **training needs analysis (TNA)** is the key activity of the systematic approach and essentially serves to identify any discrepancies, the T&D "gap," between existing KSA and those required in the present and in the future. Thus, it ensures the integration of

Figure 13.1 The Systems Model of Training and Development

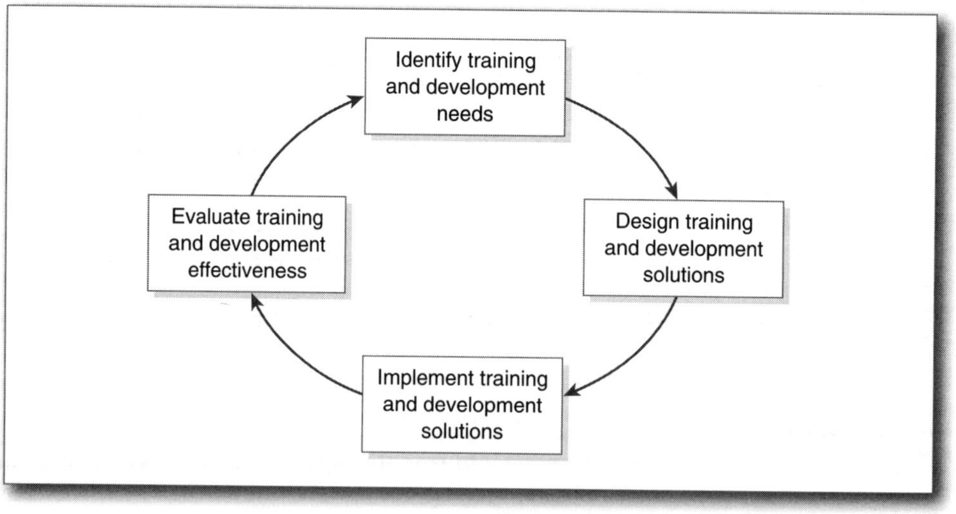

employee T&D activities with the business needs of the firm. Hence, the TNA must assess the validity of initiatives, it ought to assist in prioritizing T&D objectives and initiatives, and it has to be able to determine the actual training needs. Training needs may arise at three distinct levels (Boydell, 1983):

- At an organizational level (current and future employee T&D requirements that an organization has to fulfill in order to attain its strategic long-term objectives)
- At a job level (relevant KSA that are part of specific jobs)
- At a personal level (the competences required)

Because of the crucial importance and comprehensive nature of the TNA, many organizations employ an HRIS to collect, store, and analyze training needs data, thus ensuring that the resulting information is both timely and accurate. Data sources range from business objectives and statistics, at the organizational level, to job descriptions and output levels, at the job level, and staff appraisals, biographical data, and individual training records, at the personal level. Most HRIS can be configured to gather data from these and other sources. However, a host of specialist T&D software (discussed further on in this chapter) exists that will aid a firm in accomplishing its T&D activities. In the event, however, that the TNA highlights a considerable gap between existing and desired KSA, an organization may decide on external recruitment to hire individuals who already possess the required competencies. In that case, it will be of vital importance that the organization has access to skilled personnel and demographic data, which might provide some indication regarding the skill levels of the wider population and the environment in which the firm operates.

Developing T&D Initiatives

The second stage of the cycle focuses on the development of T&D initiatives, objectives, and methods that should be capable of meeting the three levels of needs identified during the first phase, the TNA. Organizations have a wide array of T&D methods at their disposal, and advances in and access to ICT and mobile technologies will further increase the number of methods and ways of content delivery available. Faced with an apparent overabundance of methods, how should organizations choose the ones most appropriate for their needs? A number of criteria will guide the decision-making process.

The effectiveness of individual learning plans and events ultimately hinges on the design of these T&D interventions. A learning activity can be considered successful if it leads to transfer of learning as well as a noticeable and permanent change in behavior in the trainees. The aim of the HRIS in this context is to compare employee training data with subsequent performance data. Successful learning events must achieve a "best fit" between

- the content of what is to be learned,
- the media through which content is delivered, and
- the method used to facilitate learning (see Figure 13.2).

With regard to individual learning, it is important to note that every individual has his or her preferred learning style and that these learning styles must be taken into consideration when one designs a training event to encourage learning transfer (explained below). Based on Kolb's (1984) learning cycle, which involves a concrete experience, reflective observation, abstract conceptualization, and active experimentation, Honey and Mumford (1992) developed four preferred learning styles—activist, reflector, theorist, and pragmatist.

In today's highly regulated working environments, it is also essential to attain internal and external consistency. Internal consistency is achieved if learning interventions are mutually supportive of one another and of the business objectives. External consistency is attained if T&D activities are aligned with external regulations (e.g., health and safety legislation), best practices in the industry, and the stipulations and standards of external training award bodies. The conditions for a successful learning event are illustrated in the **best-fit learning event model** in Figure 13.2.

T&D methods essentially fall into two broad categories—on the job and off the job, albeit the emergence of e-learning has somewhat diluted this distinction, as it can be either. **On-the-job training** usually involves peer observation and can be informal, structured, or unstructured, although successful learning outcomes are more likely to occur in a structured rather than an unstructured environment. Compared with **off-the-job training**, on-the-job training is relatively inexpensive. While off-the-job methods may provide greater exposure to expert knowledge, they may also be more time-consuming and may not encourage knowledge transfer. Table 13.1 lists a number of examples of T&D methods in each category.

e-Learning

e-Learning (also elearning, Elearning, or eLearning) is an umbrella term and broadly refers to any learning facilitated using electronic means. **e-Learning** can capitalize on a variety of delivery media depending on the approach taken:

- Printed media (including textbooks but also online text and online magazines and journals)

Figure 13.2 Best-Fit Learning Event Model

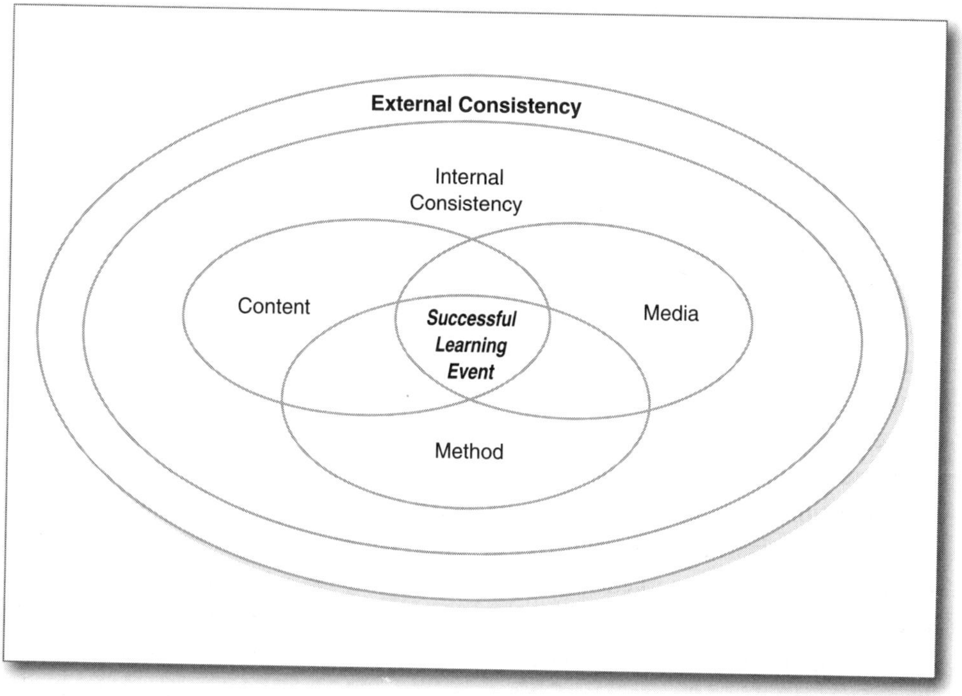

Table 13.1 Training Methods

On-the-Job Training Methods	*Off-the-Job Training Methods*
Observation Mentoring Coaching Job rotation Apprenticeship Self-directed learning	Simulation Role play Case study Business games External course or workshop Behavior modeling Placement Open, distance, or blended learning

- Audio (e.g., traditional audiotapes, CDs, MP3s, WAV, and other electronic file formats)
- Video (e.g., traditional videotapes, CD-ROMs, interactive videos, DVDs, video streaming, and satellite or cable transmissions)
- Other combined media, including hypermedia, collaborative software, or **social networking technology** (e.g., Web sites, discussion forums, e-mails, blogs, wikis, MySpace, YouTube, Twitter, Facebook, LinkedIn)

Other technologies used in e-learning encompass computer-aided assessments, animations, simulations, games, and electronic performance support systems (EPSSs). EPSSs are not learning technologies per se. However, they provide an electronic support infrastructure that allows employees to carry out their work. An EPSS would typically include assistants (e.g., Microsoft Office Assistant), wizards, knowledge bases, help, and advice functions.

Some of the media employed in e-learning may be interactive; that is, the learner interacts with the media. A number of e-learning methods to address different training needs are identified in Table 13.2. However, rapid developments in ICT also imply that many methods and approaches have a relatively short shelf life; that is, they quickly become obsolete (e.g., computer-based training). In addition, the distinction between some of these e-learning methods has become blurred, and the terminology can be confusing as terms are often used interchangeably.

The e-learning methods explained in Table 13.2 are arranged according to the extent to which they use the Internet, the degree to which they facilitate interaction between peer learners and instructors, and the degree to which computers are networked or not networked. **Web-based training (WBT)**, which is also called **Internet-based training (IBT)**, shows the highest level of interaction and networking. However, this does not imply that methods that rely on greater student interaction or that allow greater access to external resources are necessarily the better options—the choice of e-learning method will depend on the best fit with the training needs that ought to be addressed (see Figure 13.2).

An emerging issue in online learning is that of digital collaboration. The term *digital collaboration* denotes networking and communication via the Internet. Although digital collaboration is of vital importance in the effectiveness of virtual teams in the business world, online collaboration between learners also tends to increase learning and learning transfer. Intranet-based **collaborative technologies**, such as groupware (electronic meeting software), provide a company forum for tracking, sharing, and organizing information. Groupware combines e-mail, document management, and electronic bulletin boards and allows users to collaborate on projects and documents simultaneously. The most common groupware is Lotus Notes (Noe, 2002). However, Google Mail combined with Google Docs represents a free alternative. Internet-based collaborative technology, or social networking technology (e.g., blogs, wikis, or podcasts), plays an increasingly important role in informal peer-to-peer learning, which is much faster, more flexible, and more responsive than formal modes of training (Frauenheim, 2007). Collaboration and communication in this context may be synchronous or asynchronous. **Synchronous communication** refers to "real-time" or live communication using tools such as messenger services or

Table 13.2 e-Learning Methods

e-Learning Methods	*Explanation*
Computer-based training (CBT) or technology-based training, computer-managed instruction (CMI), computer-aided (assisted) instruction (CAI), computer-based learning (CBL)	Interactive training experience using a stand-alone computer, when no collaboration and access to external resources is necessary; media used include CD-ROMs, DVDs, interactive video
Multimedia-based training (MBT)	Training experience that combines text, colors, graphics, audio, and video to engage the learner; MBT can range from a simple graphical presentation of text to a complex flight simulation
Distance learning (or education)	Learner and tutor are in different locations; the approach uses both synchronous and asynchronous communication; the course provider usually provides online support and supplies students with a course pack, including printed and audiovisual materials; courses follow a predetermined curriculum and schedule
Open learning (or education)	Learner has complete control over how, what, when, where, and at what pace learning occurs; any type and combination of media may be used
Open distance learning (ODL)	Umbrella term that covers both open and distance learning
Virtual learning environment (VLE) or virtual classroom	Online environment in which learning takes place
Web-based training (WBT) or online learning (or education), Internet-based training (IBT)	Any training and learning that takes place online, that is, via the World Wide Web
Mobile learning	Any T&D offering that involves mobile technologies; mobile technologies include personal digital assistants (PDAs), cell/mobile phones, MP3 players

videoconferencing. These virtual classrooms operate in much the same way as traditional classrooms would.

However, not all collaboration can occur in real time, especially if learners are geographically dispersed across different time zones. While **asynchronous communication** still makes use of the Internet, communication is delayed, and learners access the learning spaces at their own convenience. Table 13.3 provides some examples of synchronous and asynchronous methods of e-learning.

Although it is important to make a distinction between different forms of collaboration, most e-learning combines various types of communication, collaboration, e-learning methods, and, in some cases, more traditional approaches to

Table 13.3 e-Learning Communication Typology

Synchronous	• Virtual learning environments (VLEs) • Instant messaging services • Audio- and videoconferencing • Digital chat rooms • Shared whiteboard applications • Application sharing
Asynchronous	• E-mail • Discussion forums or blogs • Threaded discussions • Self-paced learning

maximize learning transfer. Testing and assessment of e-learning may rely on traditional paper-based methods, the electronic submission of files, or interactive assignments (including online discussions). The combination of e-learning methods with traditional face-to-face methods is referred to as **blended learning**. According to industry reports, the use of blended learning in workplace training is rapidly increasing (Rossett & Frazee, 2006; Shaw & Igneri, 2006; Sparrow, 2004). This hybrid approach promises to combine the advantages of both traditional and e-learning approaches to training. For instance, one of the key issues in workplace training is the ability to apply new skills to the actual job. However, most online training does not provide for the application of new knowledge and skills, which is one of the key elements of Kolb's learning cycle. Blended learning, thus, allows the learner to apply new skills in a real-life situation, either in a classroom or on the job.

The development of e-learning programs and resources requires significant investments of time and money. However, the volatile nature of the global marketplace and the rapidly changing information needs of firms necessitate a different approach to e-learning. While standard e-learning solutions can take months to develop, **rapid e-learning (REL)** or just-in-time learning solutions may be developed in weeks, days, or even hours, depending on the complexity of materials to be created. Essentially, REL allows companies to produce a large amount of content, using limited resources, in a short time interval, and deliver this content in real time to a large number of people. Therefore, it is not surprising that industry observers predict significant increases in the REL market in years to come (Archibald, 2005; van Dam, 2005). REL has a number of key characteristics:

- It has a short development time.
- Subject matter experts (SMEs) act as the key source of content development.
- It can be created using standard presentation software.

- It allows for easy assessment and tracking of training.
- Auxiliary multimedia tools (including flash applications) can be used to enhance training experiences.
- Training units can be undertaken in minutes rather than hours.
- It can be synchronous as well as asynchronous (Bersin, 2005).

REL should ideally be used to deal with

- urgent necessary business and training needs,
- short shelf life of training,
- critical information needs and standard information broadcasts,
- training that is purely informational in nature,
- training that does not require mastery,
- prerequisite and introductory training, and
- training updates

but finds limited application for training in new skills and competencies (Bersin, 2005).

Although e-learning methods diverge on a number of levels, for instance, the level of interaction between learners, e-learning, in general, offers a range of advantages and disadvantages to the learner and to the organization. These are shown in Table 13.4. The key advantage of e-learning is flexibility; that is, it affords learners the choice of what, when, where, and how much is learned. The key disadvantages center on the lack of human contact and technological issues.

Despite the increasing global popularity of e-learning initiatives, they suffer from several shortcomings. Nunes, McPherson, Annasingh, Bashir, and Patterson (2009) identify several of these:

- Some of the most advertized advantages of e-learning, such as reductions in the travel and accommodation costs associated with face-to-face training, are not well accepted by learners. Often, trainees have to undergo e-learning in addition to their normal workloads, in the office, and subject to their usual daily work pressures.
- Another source of dissatisfaction with e-learning is its lack of human touch: the lack of interaction with knowledgeable trainers and the lack of socialization with fellow learners.
- Generic multimedia simulations without an organizational and work-specific focus tend to alienate learners.

Table 13.4 Advantages and Disadvantages of e-Learning

Advantages	*Disadvantages*
• Cost advantages compared with traditional methods • Improves computer skills • Self-paced • High degree of learner control • Choice of learning environment • Interactive • Easy tracking of learner progress and engagement • Real-time feedback • Consistent delivery method • Variety of formats and methods available • Consistent content • Unlimited access in terms of time and locale • Better support, help functions, knowledge base than other methods • Appeals to several senses simultaneously • Increased benefits through the combination with traditional training methods • Can be both synchronous and asynchronous • Accommodates different learning styles	• Basic computer skills necessary • Use of computers might cause apprehension • Not suitable for certain content • Privacy concerns if based online • Requires self-motivation to learn • Learners may feel isolated from instructors and peers • Lack of human contact in general • Technical difficulties impede access

- Organizations still tend to rely on the conservative "drill-and-practice" model and "force-fed instruction" and, in the process, ignore the social, informal, and collaborative aspects of learning.
- There is also less emphasis on learner-centered approaches that take advantage of social negotiation, on-the-job learning, on-demand learning, and peer support. New learning models are moving in the direction of "casual, instant, and informal" learning facilitated by Web 2.0 technologies, such as blogs, Webcasts, online conferencing, and **mobile learning** using mobile devices.
- There is little research that links e-learning to employee creativity, innovation, and adaptability—all of which are essential to any workforce in the 21st-century knowledge economy.
- Often, learners are pushed into e-learning without being properly equipped with the basic skills required for being successful in a networked learning environment. e-Learning may also ignore diversity considerations, as certain groups of employees, such as ethnic minorities, women, and older people, may not have the aptitude and confidence to learn in a computer-mediated environment.
- Finally, e-learning is currently serving the needs of mainly large organizations and has yet to address the learning needs of small and medium-sized enterprises.

Salas, DeRouin, and Littrell (2005) offer several research-based guidelines for designing e-learning packages. Even though these guidelines pertain to **distance learning**, they are relevant and useful for other e-learning methods as well:

- Only provide e-learning when you are sure it meets the organization's specific learning and development needs.
- Train learners on computer basics before offering computer-based training.
- Take into consideration human cognitive processes when designing e-learning programs.
- Enhance the learning experience by including graphics, texts, and learning games in the presentation of learning topics.
- Keep learners "engaged" by offering blended learning and allowing interaction among trainees and between trainees and facilitators.
- Offer trainees control over certain aspects of instruction, and guide them through the learning process by using tools, such as cognitive maps.

Implementing T&D

The third stage of the systems model of T&D involves the implementation of training. Although this stage is depicted as a separate phase of the training process, it is closely linked with the preceding stage, the design stage. Indeed, many book chapters on T&D consider both stages in unison. The reason for this is that the design of a training solution ultimately determines its implementation, as any issues and factors that could arise during the implementation phase should be anticipated at the design stage (Stewart, 1999). For instance, if an organization wanted to roll out e-learning to its entire workforce via the company intranet, the firm would have to ensure that every employee had access to the intranet. To ensure that the implementation phase runs smoothly, organizations ought to formulate an implementation plan that should specify

- the resources required,
- how the training should be carried out,
- who should facilitate the training, and
- the period within which the training should occur.

The requisite resources vary with the training method chosen. While traditional face-to-face training necessitates physical training rooms and equipment, e-learning requires initial investments in ICT. Available resources are normally set out in predetermined annual training budgets. The training design will provide answers to the questions of how, by whom, and by when training should be implemented.

The implementation of a T&D initiative can only be considered successful if transfer of learning has occurred.

Training Transfer

Positive and long-lasting changes in employee behavior and, ultimately, increased shareholder value can only be attained if training (or learning) transfer occurs. **Training transfer** is the continuous application of the KSA acquired during the training exercise. Various classifications of transfer of training exist depending on the context:

- Near versus far (how close the training task is to the actual job task)
- Specific versus general (transfer of skills versus transfer of principles)
- Positive versus negative (linked to the perception of the training experience)
- Lateral versus vertical (Hayashi, Chen, & Terase, 2005)

Lateral transfer is about the application of training to similar tasks at the same level of complexity, while vertical transfer implies analysis and synthesis, that is, the ability to apply training to more complex tasks (Gagné, 1985). Training transfer depends on a number of variables, which can be summarized under five headings (Baldwin & Ford, 1988):

1. Trainee characteristics (the trainee's predisposition to training)
2. Training design (the organization of the learning environment)
3. Work environment (the immediate factors at work that affect transfer)
4. Learning and retention
5. Generalization and maintenance (ensuring that the trainee is given the opportunity to continuously use the acquired KSA)

Only if the trainee possesses the necessary characteristics, the training design and workplace environment foster learning transfer, and the trainee is given ample opportunity to apply the training will learning and retention take place. In addition, it has been demonstrated that transfer of training is *critically* dependent on the organizational climate that supports the training transfer (Lance, Kavanagh, & Brink, 2002; Rouiller & Goldstein, 1993; Tracey, Tannenbaum, & Kavanagh, 1995; Velada, Caetano, Michel, Lyons, & Kavanagh, 2007).

Evaluating T&D

To assess whether a particular training initiative, method, or solution has met the training needs and objectives of the firm and whether transfer of learning has taken place, organizations must evaluate their T&D efforts. Training evaluation is not an isolated activity. It is part of the T&D cycle and must be considered alongside and aligned with **needs analysis**, design, and implementation to provide a holistic picture of the entire T&D process. Similar to the T&D cycle, the evaluation process should be viewed as cyclical. The steps in the evaluation process are illustrated in Figure 13.3.

The evaluation process commences with the needs analysis. Training needs must then be translated into measurable learning outcomes. Appropriate metrics must be identified against which outcomes can be measured. The next step involves the selection of an appropriate evaluation strategy. Not all training can be assessed in the same manner because of the diversity in training methods. Once an evaluation has been carried out, the results must be analyzed and fed back into the training process. This final step is omitted in many evaluation models, even though it is crucially important to use evaluation data to make decisions about

Figure 13.3 The Evaluation Process

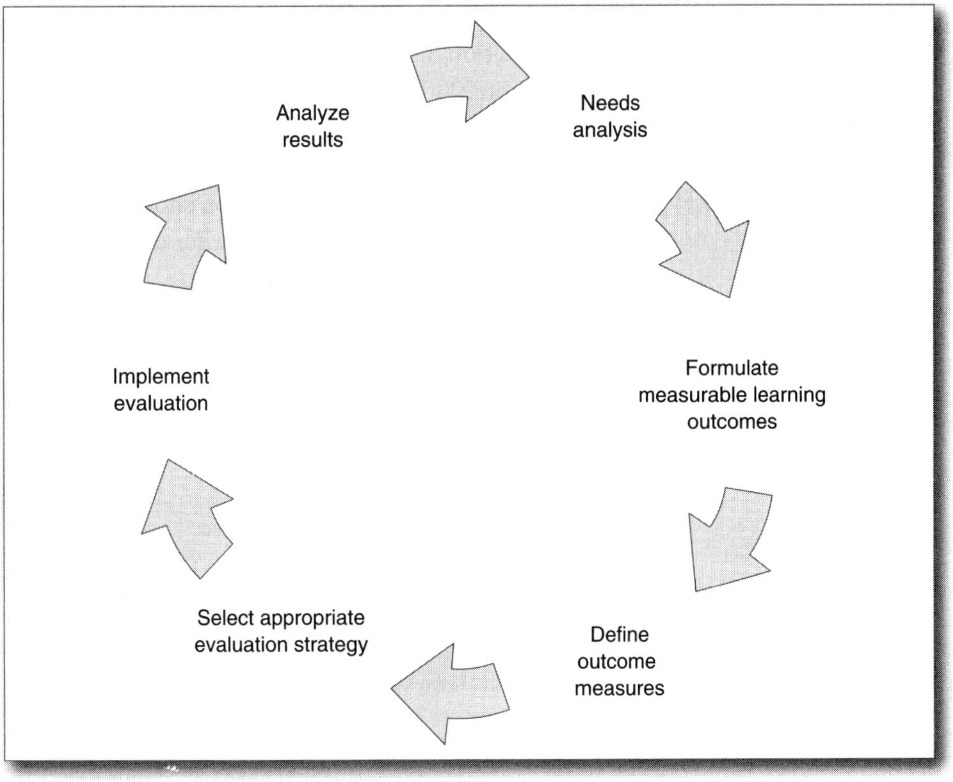

SOURCE: Developed from Noe (2002).

future training initiatives. An HRIS can be invaluable in supporting this process as it contains a vast amount of data related to training and performance that can form the basis of any T&D decision.

However, many organizations pay lip service to evaluation without having a clear concept of what evaluation means and what purpose it serves.

> People often confuse the process of monitoring, validation and evaluation. The purpose of monitoring is to take the temperature of a learning event from time to time, picking up any problems or emerging needs. Validation measures the achievement of learning objectives set for a learning initiative or process. Evaluation looks at the total value of that event or process, thereby placing it into its organizational context and aiding future planning. Faced with an evaluation task, there are four crucial questions to answer: why, who, when and how? (Harrison, 2005, p. 143)

Hence, the purpose of evaluation is manifold. Figure 13.2 shows that training initiatives must attain internal and external consistency to be effective. Thus, training is frequently validated under these aspects. Internal and external validations assess the degree to which stipulated T&D objectives are attained (Stewart, 1999). The purposes of evaluation discussed in the literature are plentiful (see, for example, Bramley, 1991; Gibb, 2002; Thomson, 2008) and range from the "very vague" to the "very specific" (Marsden, 1991). The primary purposes of evaluation could be summarized as in Table 13.5.

So what should be evaluated? As a rule, criteria for evaluation should be based on the training objectives (see Figure 13.3). In addition, the criteria ought to be

Table 13.5 Purposes of Evaluation

Summative	Quantitative in nature; establishes whether T&D program was effective, was efficient, has added value, and has met its objectives
Formative	Qualitative in nature; assesses how training, learning, and development can be improved, that is, how they could be made more efficient and effective
Learning	Quantitative and qualitative assessment of learner's post-training performance to evaluate whether learning transfer has occurred
Power and Politics	Subjective in nature; is used to serve the interests of specific stakeholders within the organization

SOURCE: Based on Easterby-Smith (1986).

relevant; that is, they should not be contaminated (biased) or deficient. However, criteria should also be reliable, practical, and discriminative. Training outcomes fall into a number of distinct categories. The number of training evaluation models in the literature seems almost infinite. Kirkpatrick (1960) suggests four levels of outcomes: reaction, learning, behavior, and results. Warr, Bird, and Rackham's (1970) CIRO framework also has four levels: context, inputs, reactions, and outcomes (immediate, intermediate, and ultimate). Easterby-Smith (1986) suggests a CAPIO framework comprising context, administration, process, inputs, and outputs. Finally, individual outcomes of training programs have been identified as falling within **Bloom's taxonomy** of learning domains (cognitive, psychomotor, and affective), which is one of the most widely used models to describe learning outcomes (Bloom et al., 1956; Bloom, Masia, & Krathwohl, 1964). A comparison of these and other frameworks reveals a significant overlap between these evaluation models, as well as between a number of the key learning outcomes contained within them.

The key objective of any evaluation process will be to assess the broad range of individual and organizational outcomes as well as return on investment (ROI). Hence, one of the key considerations will be whether a T&D program has had any measurable impact on the firm's bottom line, so as to justify training expenditure and training budgets. The following section will consider some of the complexities involved in establishing the costs and the actual benefits of T&D initiatives.

TRAINING METRICS AND COST-BENEFIT ANALYSIS

The costs involved in training can be established relatively easily. These overheads can be substantial and involve direct costs and indirect costs (Noe, 2002). (See Chapter 7 for information on cost-benefit analysis.) A considerable direct cost is the loss of production sustained through the absence of trainees from work for the duration of the training. e-Learning significantly reduces this element of direct costs, as trainees generally do not have to leave their place of work to participate in online training (provided they have access to a computer). Online courses may also be taken outside of work. In many cases, employees can avail themselves of online training through an intranet, which can be accessed from work and from home, thus allowing for greater flexibility at a reduced cost.

However, the actual benefits to the firm may be much more difficult to ascertain, as many of the benefits take a long time to materialize or can often be of an intangible nature. Moreover, it may prove almost impossible to isolate completely from other organizational variables the effects of training on performance. Ascertaining these effects is of great significance, though. In fact, this preoccupation with the quantification of the business benefits of training has frequently been described as the search for the "Holy Grail," and those organizations that evaluate training employ a number of different models and approaches to pursue this quest, including the balanced scorecard (Kaplan & Norton, 1992, 1993) and ROI (Phillips, 1996b). Russ-Eft and Preskill (2005) highlight three critical factors in HR development evaluation that complicate the assessment of training outcomes:

1. Evaluation occurs within a complex, dynamic, and variable environment.
2. Evaluation is essentially a political activity.
3. Evaluation ought to be purposeful, planned, and systematic.

Notwithstanding these factors, Phillips (1996a) advocates that any available post-training data should be analyzed and converted into monetary values to establish ROI. Phillips's (1996c, 2005) ROI methodology (or ROI process) produces six types of data, which are based on **Kirkpatrick's** (1960) **evaluation taxonomy**:

1. Reaction, satisfaction, and planned action
2. Learning and application
3. Implementation
4. Business impact (see Table 13.6)
5. ROI
6. Intangibles

The ROI method advocates five useful steps for converting hard (tangible) data and soft (intangible) data into monetary values:

1. Focus on a single unit of improvement in output, quality, or time.
2. Determine a value for each data unit.
3. Calculate the change in output performance directly attributable to training.
4. Obtain the annual amount of the monetary value of the change in performance.
5. Determine the annual value (the annual performance change times the unit value).

Having identified relevant data sources and applying these best practices, firms can use a number of approaches to quantify the relationship between training costs and benefits. These approaches are shown in Table 13.6. Organizations may use one or more of these ratios to determine the costs and benefits of planned and existing learning technology projects.

It is possible to enter basic values into a spreadsheet application to calculate the ratios listed in Table 13.6. However, the variety of possible outcomes from training, the variety of factors that affect these outcomes, and the variety of data to be collected to produce any meaningful results appear to make the evaluation process a rather tedious task that would be next to impossible to complete efficiently and effectively without the help of a computerized system. Most commercial HRIS can be customized to record, analyze, and report on the training metrics that have been identified by a firm. For instance, the system could be configured to collect information on the monetary benefits of T&D projects, such as increased production output or a reduced number of complaints, and compare this information with data collected on the costs of T&D projects. In addition, the satisfaction with or the success of particular training interventions could be assessed. T&D data will usually be stored in the T&D module of the HRIS. The human capital management (HRM) modules included in the HRIS of the largest ERP providers, for example SAP or Oracle, incorporate functionalities for creating employee development plans, competency management tools, and online learning environments, as well as numerous training metrics. In addition, many dedicated

Table 13.6 Cost-Benefit Approaches

Approach	*Explanation*
Benefit-cost ratio (BCR)	Monetary benefits of T&D projects Costs of T&D projects
Cost-benefit ratio (CBR)	Costs of T&D projects Monetary benefits of T&D projects
Payback period	Costs of T&D projects Annual savings
Return on investment (ROI)	Monetary benefits of T&D projects Costs of T&D projects

SOURCE: Sadler-Smith (2006).

T&D systems are commercially available. The following section will discuss the data elements and various HRIS applications used in the training function.

HRIS APPLICATIONS IN TRAINING

Traditionally, training software applications have been employed to record information associated purely with training administration purposes (Noe, 2002). Today, firms place much greater demands on training applications in terms of compatibility with existing systems, analytical functionality, and accessibility to meet business needs. The primary demand on any system, however, must be that it furnishes usable information to key decision makers to achieve both administrative and strategic advantages (Kovach, Hughes, Fagan, & Maggitti, 2002).

Hence, useful HRIS information should possess three key characteristics:

1. It must be presented in a user-friendly manner.
2. It must be meaningful and appropriate (Keebler & Rhodes, 2002).
3. It must be used effectively in the decision-making process to support an organization's overall business strategy (Kovach & Cathcart, 1999).

However, Kovach and Cathcart (1999) argue that HRIS do not need to be intricate or even computerized to serve the information needs of a business. Elementary HRIS training databases are easily set up using commercial or open-source desktop software (see Figures 13.4 and 13.5). These databases may then be used to collect, store, and analyze training-related HR information. The amount of data that can be stored, the manner in which it is collected, and the level of

Figure 13.4 Example of an HRIS T&D Database in Spreadsheet Format

HRIS Training & Development Application.xls

	A	B	C	D	E	F
1	Employee ID	Employee name	Training history	Certified skills & competencies	Professional memberships	Educational Qualifications
2	001	Joe Soap				
3	002					
4	003					
5	004					
6	005					
7						

Sheet1 / Sheet2 / Sheet3

analysis possible will depend on the application used. Table 13.7 shows the basic data elements an electronic T&D database should contain. The first column, "Data Element," shows the main categories of data elements, while "Subcategory 1" and "Subcategory 2" provide examples of the type of information these data elements could include.

Using these essential data elements, we could create a spreadsheet (see Figure 13.4). This basic database contains relevant training information and possesses limited search and reporting capabilities. Should a firm decide to upgrade to commercial training software, data stored in a spreadsheet can be imported into most training applications.

Clearly, both the amount of information that can be collected and stored using a spreadsheet and the level of analysis that this application permits are limited. Therefore, many organizations create bespoke databases, which offer greater possibilities regarding the collection and presentation of training data. These database applications allow users to run queries using customizable search criteria; they provide greater reporting options; and information on different screens can be linked to avoid multiple entry of data. An example of such a database, one that includes the data elements and subcategories of Table 13.7, is shown in Figure 13.5. As more functionality is desired, organizations can also use a more sophisticated learning management system (LMS) to collect and manage training data (see Figure 13.6).

Figure 13.5 Example of a Database

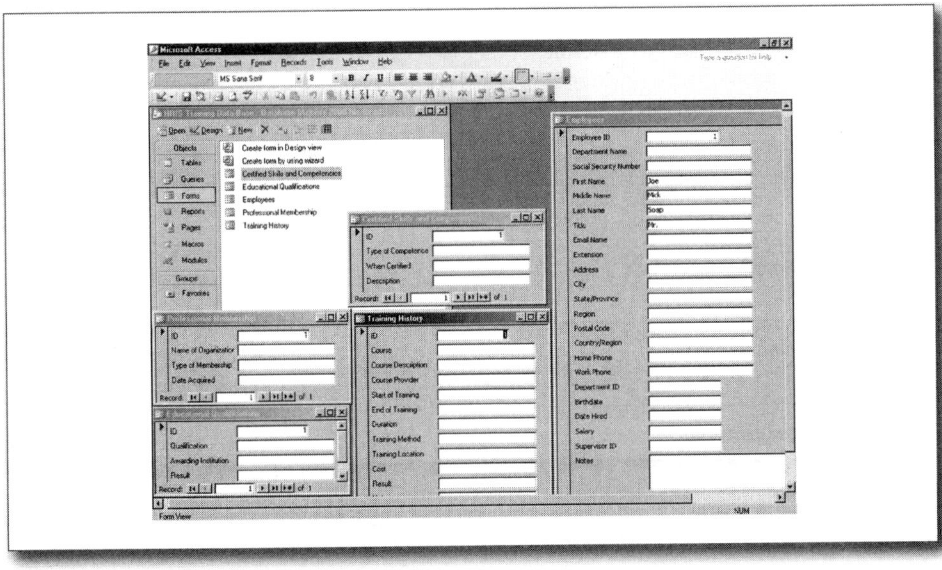

Table 13.7 Basic Data Elements for an HRIS Training Database

Data Element	*Subcategory 1*	*Subcategory 2*
Employee information	Employee ID	
	Employee name	Title
		First name
		Middle name
		Second name
	Social security number	
	Department	
	Position	
	Reporting to	
Training history (training course completed)	Date of training (start and end)	
	Training methods	(see above)
	Course (including description)	List of common courses
	Course provider	List of common providers
	Training location	In-house
		Out-of-house
	Result	
	Duration	
	Cost	
	Notes on performance	
Certified skills and competencies		
Professional memberships		List of professional organizations
Educational qualifications		

Figure 13.6 Training Module With OrangeHRM (an Open Source HRIS)

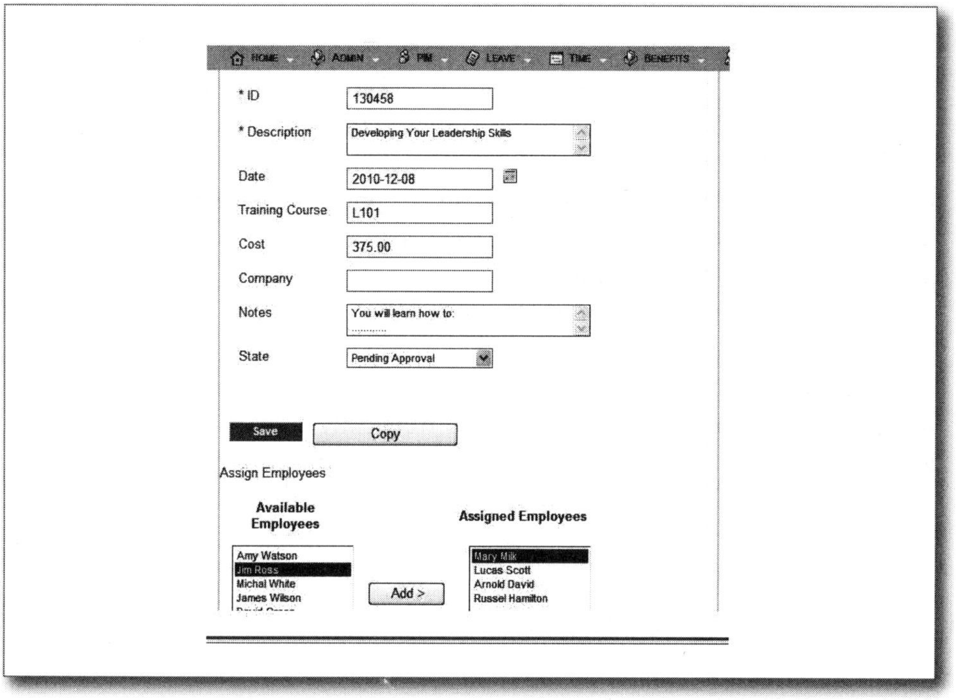

SOURCE: OrangeHRM (www.orangehrm.com). Reproduced with permission.

As firms grow in size, their need to manage training activities and training data more effectively and efficiently increases accordingly. A host of commercial systems service the broad spectrum of T&D, ranging from stand-alone training administration software to fully integrated expert systems. T&D software is available in many guises. The most common applications are discussed here.

HRIS/Learning Applications: Learning Management Systems

The vast majority of large organizations rely on fully integrated enterprise-wide systems, called enterprise resource planning (ERP) systems, to satisfy their information needs. An ERP system amalgamates the management information systems (MIS) capabilities from all functional areas in a business, for example, finance, production, marketing, and HRM, into a single integrated system. The ERP component that supports the HR function is commonly referred to as an HRIS. These data repositories for HR-related data typically comprise a number of modules, which in turn can support every area of HR, including T&D. Traditionally, firms used HRIS T&D applications and modules for administrative purposes only. The capabilities of today's HRIS T&D applications—learning management software that is usually bundled into a **learning management system (LMS)**—range from training administration to training and talent management. The uses and capabilities of an LMS are shown in the LMS classification presented in Table 13.8.

The use of administrative systems is restricted to transaction processing, including the calculation of training costs. Training management systems can facilitate the entire T&D process (see the systems model of T&D described previously) from TNA to training evaluation. A **learning content management system (LCMS)**, as the name implies, can be used to store and develop T&D content, such as multimedia files, templates for training courses, or assignments. It may also be employed to track training attendance and completion records or for quality assurance purposes. LCMS is frequently used in combination with REL. A **talent management system (TMS)**, sometimes referred to as a human

Table 13.8 Learning Management System Classification

Classification	*Uses and Capabilities*
Administration	• Basic employee and T&D records • Calculation of training costs • Administrative permissions (who has data access, who can enter data)
Training management (including learning content management)	• Scheduling and access to training courses • Setup of training courses and initiatives • Assignment of training based on skills and certification requirements • Authoring of training courses and initiatives • Online access to courses • Training evaluation • Tracking of training attendance and results • ROI measurement
Talent management	• KSA assessment • Performance reviews and appraisals • Recruiting • Succession planning • Career planning • Management development

SOURCE: Adapted from e-Learning Consulting (2007).

capital management system, is an integrated software suite that can comprise a range of applications, such as applicant tracking, succession and career planning, performance management, compensation and benefits management, and learning management. Talent management systems allow employees to create personal electronic *talent profiles,* which can be updated and usually reflect their KSA and goals. Organizations can use these data to generate information on the talent profile of the organization and to develop macro- and micro-level employee development plans. A large number of commercial learning management systems exist (see list of vendor Web sites in the appendix). These range from off-the-shelf products to server and Web-based enterprise solutions. The choice of system will be determined principally by an organization's LT&D needs, LT&D budget, and ICT capabilities. The reporting, analytical, and strategic potential of these systems will diverge accordingly. The degree to which learning management systems can assist strategic decision making may be assessed using Beckers and Bsat's (2002) decision support system (DSS) classification. Their model consists of five levels:

1. Management information systems (MIS)
2. Decision support systems (DSS)
3. Group decision support systems (GDSS)
4. Expert systems (ES)
5. Artificial intelligence (AI)

Each consecutive category offers the users more extensive reporting and analytical capabilities that can support strategic T&D decision making. MIS can be used to support T&D decision making at the operational, functional level of the organization. DSS and GDSS are designed to facilitate senior management decision making in the long term and relate to the overall mission and objectives of an organization. They are based on "what if" scenarios. Expert systems consist of a knowledge base, a decision-making function, and an interface. They replicate the decision-making capabilities of human experts. An example of a system that uses AI is an intelligent tutoring system (ITS). An ITS can be employed to tutor, coach, or empower employees. The advantages of these systems are that instruction can be aligned with learner needs, the system can respond to learner actions, and learner progress can be modeled (Noe, 2002). ES and AI aid strategic T&D decision making at the board level of the organization. However, capital investments in sophisticated HRIS T&D applications alone will not necessarily improve LT&D in the organization, nor will they lead to knowledge creation or organizational learning. Any HRIS project requires careful planning and ample resources (time, money, and expertise). Bonadio (2009) puts forward five key issues that could enhance the effectiveness of an LMS:

1. Employee development should be linked to learning delivery.
2. Learning activities ought to be aligned with business objectives.
3. Regulatory compliance must be maintained.
4. Learning effectiveness must be measured throughout the organization.
5. An integrated approach to employee onboarding (employee orientation) should be established.

HRIS T&D Applications: Implementation Issues

Many HRIS T&D projects fail to meet the expectations of key decision makers. The reasons for these failures are manifold. Some firms introduce a new TMS only because competitors have done so; yet, these companies may not have the necessary expertise to operate the system. Frequently, decision makers have false expectations of ROI or apply training metrics that merely focus on cost savings and fail to take note of intangible gains derived from T&D (see the section "Training Metrics and Cost-Benefit Analysis"). In other cases, the HRIS T&D application strategy is not aligned with training needs and the overall T&D, HR, and business strategies. Few organizations involve employees during the implementation stage of the HRIS, which can lead to underutilization and dissatisfaction with the system (Burbach & Dundon, 2005). For a variety of reasons (see "Disadvantages" in Table 13.4), many employees never actually complete the e-learning programs in which they are enrolled. Sometimes, disenchantment is simply the result of poor planning and the consequent incompatibility of various disjointed HR systems, albeit an increasing number of organizations purchase one or more items of their training management system from a single vendor to prevent these problems (Frauenheim, 2006). A number of authors have suggested success factors for the introduction of HRIS T&D applications (Gascó, Llopis, & González, 2004; Noe, 2002; Sadler-Smith, 2006) and for increasing e-learning completion rates (Frankola, 2001):

- Align e-learning strategy with T&D strategy, HR strategy, and overall business strategy.
- Create a corporate learning culture that fosters e-learning and the use of HRIS T&D applications.

- Assess HRIS T&D projects based on their suitability to meet the T&D strategy of the organization rather than the technical sophistication and elegant features of the system.
- Carefully plan HRIS T&D projects to guarantee compatibility with legacy systems, affordability in terms of budget allocations, and the existence of expertise to use the system.
- Involve line managers and employees in HRIS T&D projects to ensure greater buy-in.
- Match HRIS T&D applications and e-learning initiatives with their ability to meet training needs to encourage learning transfer.
- Establish a suitable evaluation strategy to assess the extent to which training technology meets training needs, and evaluate this fit regularly.
- Identify suitable T&D metrics that take account of all direct and indirect training outcomes.
- Promote the use of HRIS T&D applications and e-learning.
- Make managers accountable for the uptake of e-learning and for HRIS T&D utilization.
- Reward employees for their use of e-learning.
- Ensure that e-learning and T&D systems are user-friendly and provide quality information.
- Develop a data security policy for the T&D system and applications.
- Do not focus on only financial gains from HRIS T&D projects.
- Train managers and employees in the use of T&D technologies.

SUMMARY

This chapter highlighted the strategic importance of LT&D in an increasingly knowledge-intensive global economy. The discussion showed that it is important to distinguish between learning, training, and development to understand the processes that lead to the acquisition of knowledge, skills, and abilities (KSA). Other key concepts, such as knowledge management (KM) and the learning organization, were also explained. Knowledge creation, innovation, and organizational learning are inextricably linked to an organization's capacity to remain competitive. This chapter identified and explained various e-learning methods, their role in knowledge acquisition, and their advantages and disadvantages. Nonetheless, traditional face-to-face methods still carry considerable credence, which is reflected in the increasing use of blended learning, an approach that combines both traditional and online methods of learning. A careful analysis of training needs, various LT&D methods, and individual learning styles is necessary to ensure that transfer of learning occurs and that, ultimately, the strategic objectives of the organization can be attained. HRIS T&D applications are vitally important tools in pursuing a systematic approach to LT&D, which necessitates identifying training needs, designing LT&D solutions and methods, implementing these initiatives, and evaluating the effectiveness of training (including completing an assessment of ROI on training). As many LT&D outcomes are of an intangible nature or take a long time to materialize (note the definition of development in this context), it is inherently intricate to determine appropriate training metrics that may be employed to perform any meaningful CBA. The key is to analyze any available data. Notwithstanding these difficulties, a number of approaches to ascertain ROI using HRIS T&D applications were offered. This chapter also expounded on how an elementary T&D system can be created using a spreadsheet or database desktop application. A variety of HRIS T&D applications exist. Learning management systems may be embedded in an HRIS or ERP. These learning management systems vary considerably in their capacity to manage the training process, generate reports, or assist in strategic decision making. Talent management suites integrate a range of applications, including succession planning and learning management. Learning management systems with DSS and ES capabilities offer the greatest strategic value. However, the choice of system is contingent on the T&D needs of an organization, its budget, and its ICT capabilities. This chapter concluded with a discussion of the implementation of HRIS T&D applications.

KEY TERMS

asynchronous communication
best-fit learning event model
blended learning
Bloom's taxonomy
collaborative technologies
distance learning
e-learning
human capital
Internet-based training (IBT)
Kirkpatrick's evaluation taxonomy
knowledge management (KM)
learning content management system (LCMS)
learning management system (LMS)
learning organization
learning, training, and development (LT&D)
mobile learning
needs analysis
off-the-job training
on-the-job training
organizational learning
performance management
rapid e-learning (REL)
social networking technology
synchronous communication
systems model of training and development
talent management system (TMS)
training needs analysis (TNA)
training transfer
Web-based training (WBT)

DISCUSSION QUESTIONS

1. What is the systems model of T&D? Discuss how HRIS T&D applications can assist in carrying out the steps in the systems model.
2. Explain synchronous and asynchronous communication in relation to e-learning.
3. What are the advantages and disadvantages of e-learning?
4. How can HRIS T&D applications help firms foster organizational learning?
5. Explain how organizations should choose appropriate T&D methods.
6. What is transfer of training? What role does transfer of learning play in e-learning?
7. Explain the issues involved in establishing ROI for T&D initiatives. What role do HRIS T&D applications play in establishing ROI?
8. Outline how standard desktop applications such as a spreadsheet or database can be used to set up a basic T&D system.
9. Discuss the different types of HRIS T&D applications and their reporting and decision-support capabilities.
10. What issues might arise during and as a result of the implementation of HRIS T&D applications?

CASE STUDY

Meddevco (name changed) is a large multinational corporation that operates in the medical devices sector. The firm employs around 33,000 people in five divisions and has operations in 120 countries. A total of 66% of the multinational's revenue is generated from products that are less than two years old, and 80% of employees are working on products that are less than two years old. These figures illustrate the highly competitive and fast-paced nature of the medical devices sector. This sector is also characterized by high levels of regulatory control and a need to comply with industry norms. Meddevco is headquartered in the United States and Switzerland. The information needs of a firm of this size are substantial, and it would be next to impossible to collect, store, and analyze HR-related information without the use of a fully integrated global HRIS. Moreover, the diversity of the workforce, the multiplicity of skills required in the different divisions and to support the various product lines, and the pressure of compliance necessitate a perfectly orchestrated T&D effort. Needless to say, HRIS T&D applications play a major role in managing the T&D function. Meddevco uses an HRIS by PeopleSoft (now Oracle) to manage the majority of its global HR processes, including e-recruitment and performance appraisals. With regard to data entry into the system, the corporation operates a strict "no customization unless legally required" policy to ensure data compatibility across the system. In the United States, most HR services are centralized in an HR shared services center. The corporation has a dedicated HRIS center in Europe, and negotiations are ongoing to implement a European HR shared services model. The company uses a number of different payroll systems in Europe for compliance reasons. All employees in the corporation have access to a company intranet called My Meddevco, which also includes a learning portal that provides access to online training programs, which employees can use at work and at home. The intranet also includes a knowledge base and detailed company information, including a full listing of all employees and their job titles and locations. Employee transfers and promotions are also listed. A number of years ago, the corporation made the decision not to use the training module included in PeopleSoft and opted for a training management system called SABA to coordinate and manage training initiatives; for example, the recent rollout and training for the use of SAP (an ERP system) for production facilities was managed through SABA. In addition, Meddevco has recently commenced using the talent management module included in PeopleSoft to identify and track high-performing employees for promotion. Every employee is required to complete an online talent profile, which is similar to an online CV and which can be updated by the employee. The combination of systems and applications and the careful analysis of HR information contained therein allow the organization to develop and implement a global T&D strategy. However, the firm also faces some challenges arising from the use of these systems. As the organization largely grew through acquisition, a number of legacy systems still coexist with the global HRIS at some of its subsidiaries. Data compatibility issues also derive from the use of SABA, which is not part of PeopleSoft. In addition, the firm is also using SAP, and it is questionable whether Oracle (the owner of PeopleSoft) will support data exchanges with a system supplied by its chief competitor. Furthermore, because Meddevco did not involve the workforce in the implementation process of the TMS, employees are reluctant to complete their talent profiles. Moreover, the need to customize the HRIS locally to comply with the national legislation affecting Meddevco subsidiaries further complicates the collection and transfer of data within the global HRIS.

The example of Meddevco illustrates how large organizations employ HRIS to manage their workforces and how they leverage HR development through the use of HRIS T&D applications, learning portals, and specialized learning management systems. However, it is also apparent that careful planning is essential to avoid compatibility issues and to ensure a consistent global flow of HR- and T&D-related information.

Case Study Questions

1. What should Meddevco have done to avoid some of its problems?
2. How could Meddevco now solve the problems created by not involving employees during the implementation of the HRIS?
3. What else should Meddevco do now to improve the operation of its system?

Practical Exercise

Try to set up an interview with someone from a company such as FedEx, UPS, or Amazon with a view to discussing corporate training initiatives and the effects of these on employee retention, development, and performance. In particular, try to establish the role and integration of HRIS in the organization's training programs and how HRIS is being used to increase the efficiency and effectiveness of training initiatives.

NOTES

1. The company's name must remain confidential.
2. The bold terms in this chapter are included in the list of key terms. These terms cannot and do not purport to provide an exhaustive list of HRIS T&D applications. However, they furnish explanations of the key concepts discussed in this chapter. More extensive e-learning glossaries are available on the World Wide Web, for instance, from the American Society for Training and Development, or ASTD (www.learningcircuits.org/glossary), and from World Wide Learn (www.worldwidelearn.com/elearning-essentials/elearning-glossary.htm).

REFERENCES

Archibald, D. (2005). *Rapid e-learning: A growing trend.* Retrieved May 10, 2007, from www.learningcircuits.org/2005/jan2005/archibald.htm

Argyris, C., & Schon, D. A. (1978). *Organization learning II: Theory, method and practice.* Reading, MA: Addison-Wesley.

Baldwin, T. T., & Ford, J. K. (1988). Transfer of training: A review and directions for future research. *Personnel Psychology, 41*(1), 63–105.

Beckers, A. M., & Bsat, M. Z. (2002). A DSS classification model for research in HRIS. *Information Systems Management, 19*(3), 41–50.

Bersin, J. (2005). Making rapid e-learning work. *Chief Learning Officer, 4*(7), 20–24.

Bloom, B. S., Engelhart, M., Furst, E. J., Hill, W., & Krathwohl, D. (1956). *Taxonomy of educational objectives: Vol. 1. The cognitive domain.* New York: McKay.

Bloom, B. S., Masia, B. B., & Krathwohl, D. (1964). *Taxonomy of educational objectives: Vol. 2. The affective domain.* New York: McKay.

Bonadio, S. (2009). *HR field guide—5 tips to effective learning management.* Wayland, MA: Softscape.

Boydell, T. H. (1983). *A guide to the identification of training needs.* London: British Association for Commercial and Industrial Education.

Bramley, P. (1991). *Evaluating training effectiveness: Translating theory into practice.* London: McGraw-Hill.

Burbach, R., & Dundon, T. (2005). The strategic potential of human resource information systems: Evidence from the Republic of Ireland. *International Employment Relations Review, 11*(1/2), 97–118.

Burnes, B. (2004). *Managing change: A strategic approach to organisational dynamics.* Harrow, UK: Prentice Hall/Financial Times.

Collin, A. (2007). Learning and development. In J. Beardwell & T. Claydon (Eds.), *Human resource management: A contemporary approach* (5th ed.). Harlow, UK: Prentice Hall, Financial Times.

Cummings, T. G., & Worley, C. G. (2001). *Organization development and change* (7th ed.). Cincinnati, OH: South-Western College Publishing.

Easterby-Smith, M. (1986). *Evaluation of management, training, and development.* Aldershot, UK: Gower.

e-Learning Consulting. (2007). *Learning management systems.* Retrieved February 10, 2007, from www.e-learningconsulting.com/consulting/what/learning-management.html

Frankola, K. (2001). Tips for increasing e-learning completion rates. *Workforce, 80*(10), 56.

Frauenheim, E. (2006). Talent management software is bundling up. *Workforce Management, 85*(19), 35.

Frauenheim, E. (2007). Your co-worker, your teacher: Collaborative technology speeds peer-peer learning. *Workforce Management, 86*(2), 19–23.

Gagné, R. M. (1985). *The conditions of learning and theory of instruction* (4th ed.). New York: Holt, Rinehart & Winston.

Gascó, J. L., Llopis, J., & González, M. R. (2004). The use of information technology in training human resources: An e-learning case study. *Journal of European Industrial Training, 28*(5), 370–382.

Gibb, S. (2002). *Learning and development: Process, practices, and perspectives at work.* Basingstoke: Palgrave Macmillan.

Grant, R. M. (1996). Toward a knowledge-based theory of the firm. *Strategic Management Journal, 17*(10), 109–122.

Gunnigle, P., Heraty, N., & Morley, M. (2002). *Human resource management in Ireland* (2nd ed.). Dublin, Ireland: Gill & Macmillan.

Harrison, R. (2005). *Learning and development.* London: Chartered Institute of Personnel and Development.

Hayashi, A., Chen, C. C., & Terase, H. (2005). Aligning IT skills training with online asynchronous learning multimedia technologies [Electronic version]. *Information Systems Education Journal, 3*(26), 3–10. Retrieved June 10, 2007, from http://isedj.org/isecon/2004/2434/ISECON.2004.Hayashi.pdf

Honey, P., & Mumford, A. (1992). *Manual of learning styles* (3rd ed.). London: Peter Honey.

Kaplan, R. S., & Norton, D. P. (1992). The balanced scorecard: Measures that drive performance. *Harvard Business Review, 70*(1), 71–79.

Kaplan, R. S., & Norton, D. P. (1993). Putting the balanced scorecard to work. *Harvard Business Review, 71*(5), 134–140.

Keebler, T. J., & Rhodes, D. W. (2002). e-HR: Becoming the "path of least resistance." *Employment Relations Today, 29*(2), 57–66.

Kirkpatrick, D. L. (1960). Techniques for evaluating training programmes. *Journal of the American Society for Training and Development, 14,* 13–18, 25–32.

Knowles, M. S., Holton, E. F., III, & Swanson, R. A. (2005). *The adult learner: The definitive classic in adult education and human resource development* (6th ed.). San Diego: Elsevier.

Kolb, D. A. (1984). *Experiential learning: Experience as a source of learning and development.* Englewood Cliffs, NJ: Prentice Hall.

Kovach, K. A., & Cathcart, C. E. (1999). Human resources information systems (HRIS): Providing business with rapid data access. *Public Personnel Management, 28*(2), 274–282.

Kovach, K. A., Hughes, A. A., Fagan, P., & Maggitti, P. G. (2002). Administrative and strategic advantages of HRIS. *Employment Relations Today, 29*(2), 43–48.

Lance, C. E., Kavanagh, M. J., & Brink, K. E. (2002). Retraining climate as a predictor of retraining success and as a moderator of the relationship between cross-job retraining time estimates and time to proficiency in the new job. *Group and Organization Management, 27,* 294–317.

Learning. (2007). In *Encyclopædia Britannica.* Retrieved March 14, 2007, from www.britannica.com/eb/article-9369902

Marsden, J. (1991). Evaluation: Towards a definition and statement of purpose [Electronic Version]. *Australian Journal of Educational Technology, 7,* 21–28. Retrieved November 24, 2007, from http://www.ascilite.org.au/ajet/ajet7/marsden.html

Mayo, A. (1998). Memory bankers. *People Management, 4*(2), 34–38.

Noe, R. A. (2002). *Employee training and development* (2nd ed.). New York: McGraw-Hill.

Nonaka, I., & Takeuchi, H. (1995). *The knowledge-creating company.* New York: Oxford University Press.

Nunes, J. M., McPherson, M. A., Annasingh, F., Bashir, I., & Patterson, D. C. (2009). The use of e-learning in the workplace: A systematic literature review. *Impact: Journal of Applied Research in Workplace E-learning, 1*(1), 97–112.

Organisation for Economic Co-operation and Development. (1996). *The knowledge based economy.* Paris: Author.

Organisation for Economic Co-operation and Development. (2001). *The well-being of nations: The role of human and social capital.* Paris: Author.

Pedler, M., Burgoyne, J., & Boydell, T. (1991). *The learning company: A strategy for sustainable development.* Maidenhead, UK: McGraw-Hill.

Pfeffer, J. (1996). *Competitive advantage through people: Unleashing the power of the work force.* Boston: Harvard Business School Press.

Pfeffer, J. (1998). *The human equation: Building profits by putting people first.* Boston: Harvard Business School Press.

Phillips, J. J. (1996a). How much is the training worth? *Training & Development, 50*(4), 20.

Phillips, J. J. (1996b). ROI: The search for best practices. *Training & Development, 50*(2), 42.

Phillips, J. J. (1996c). Was it the training? *Training & Development, 50*(3), 28.

Phillips, J. J. (2005). The value of human capital: Macro-level research. *Chief Learning Officer, 4*(10), 60–62.

Porter, M. (1990). *The competitive advantage of nations.* New York: Free Press.

Prahalad, C. K., & Hamel, G. (1990). The core competencies of the corporation. *Harvard Business Review, 6*(3), 79–91.

Rossett, A., & Frazee, V. (2006). *Blended learning opportunities.* New York: American Management Association. Retrieved June 10, 2007, from www.amanet.org/blended/pdf/WhitePaper_BlendLearn.pdf

Rouiller, J. Z., & Goldstein, I. L. (1993). The relationship between organizational transfer climate and positive transfer of training. *Human Resource Development Quarterly, 4,* 377–390.

Russ-Eft, D., & Preskill, H. (2005). In search of the Holy Grail: Return on investment evaluation in human resource development. *Advances in Developing Human Resources, 7*(1), 71–85.

Sadler-Smith, E. (2006). *Learning and development for managers: Perspectives from research and practice.* Oxford, UK: Blackwell.

Salas, E., DeRouin, R. E., & Littrell, L. N. (2005). Research-based guidelines for designing distance learning. In H. G. Gueutal & D. L. Stone (Eds.), *The brave new world of eHR* (pp. 104–136). San Francisco: Jossey-Bass.

Senge, P. (1990). *The fifth discipline.* New York: Doubleday.

Shaw, S., & Igneri, N. (2006). *Effectively implementing a blended learning approach* (Eedo Knowledgeware White Paper). New York: American Management Association.

Soliman, F., & Spooner, K. (2000). Strategies for implementing knowledge management: Role of human resources management. *Journal of Knowledge Management, 4*(4), 337–345.

Sparrow, S. (2004). Blended is better. *Training & Development, 58*(11), 52–55.

Stewart, J. (1999). *Employee development practice.* London: Financial Times/Pitman.

Thomson, I. (2008). Evaluation of training. *Chartered Institute of Personnel and Development (CIPD).* Retrieved January 10, 2008, from http://www.cipd.co.uk/subjects/lrnanddev/evaluation/evatrain.htm

Tracey, J. B., Tannenbaum, S. I., & Kavanagh, M. J. (1995). Applying trained skills on the job: The importance of the work environment. *Journal of Applied Psychology, 80,* 239–252.

van Dam, N. (2005, January 28). e-Learning development at the speed of business. *Chief Learning Officer.* Retrieved May 10, 2007, from www.clomedia.com/content/anmviewer.asp?a=850&print=yes

Velada, R., Caetano, A., Michel, J. W., Lyons, B. D., & Kavanagh, M. J. (2007, December). The effects of training design, individual characteristics, and work environment on transfer of training. *International Journal of Training and Development, 11*(4), 282–294.

Warr, P., Bird, M., & Rackham, N. (1970). *Evaluation of management training.* Aldershot, UK: Gower.

Wright, P. M., Dunford, B. B., & Snell, S. A. (2001). Human resources and the resource based view of the firm. *Journal of Management, 27*(6), 701–720.

Yahya, S., & Goh, W.-K. (2002). Managing human resources toward achieving knowledge management. *Journal of Knowledge Management, 6*(5), 457–468.

Chapter 14

Performance Management, Compensation, Benefits, Payroll, and the Human Resource Information System

Charles H. Fay and Renato E. Nardoni

EDITORS' NOTE

This chapter is the fourth one involving an organization's talent management program and its utilization as aided by an HRIS. This chapter completes our look at the cycle of activities involved in talent management—planning and forecasting the need for talent (Chapter 11); recruitment and selection of talent (Chapter 12); and training for talent management (Chapter 13). Ultimately, the purpose of talent management is to achieve the organization's strategic goal of remaining competitive in its market through the effective management of its HR. The focus of this chapter is on management of employee performance in a systematic manner. This performance management system involves evaluation of both individual job performance and the reward system of the organization that supports the evaluation. The reward system of the organization involves the design, decision making, and administration of both compensation and benefits practices. The uniqueness of this chapter is its description of the design and operation of typical HRIS applications in the performance management, compensation, and benefits programs of the HRM function.

CHAPTER OBJECTIVES

After completing this chapter, you should be able to

- Understand the performance management (PM) cycle and the role of the HRIS in PM design, decision making, and administration
- Understand typical compensation practices and the role of the HRIS in compensation design, decision making, and administration
- Understand typical benefits practices and the role of the HRIS in benefits design, decision making, and administration
- Understand payroll systems and the role of the HRIS in payroll administration

HRIS IN ACTION

As Mark walked into his work area, he was fuming. "Those idiots in HR and payroll are really the gang that couldn't shoot straight," he announced to everyone in the vicinity. "What did they do now?" asked Marsha. "Don't tell me they got it wrong again!"

"They sure did," said Mark. "After I complained last month you'd think they would at least check to make sure they corrected their mistake. If I treated a customer this way I'd get fired!"

Mark's paycheck is wrong once again, and the story is a complicated one. It started with the performance review Mark had received from his boss the previous month. The review was good, and Mark had earned an "Exceeds standards" summary rating. Somehow, when an HR data-entry clerk entered the approved rating into the system an error was made, and "Does not meet standards" went into the compensation review system. The error snowballed, and Mark received no merit increase or bonus for the year. In fact, because of increased deductions for health coverage, his check was actually smaller than the one he had received two weeks earlier. Apart from the financial costs, Mark was psychologically shattered because his boss had discussed in their performance review meeting how good his performance was.

After his boss intervened, HR and payroll corrected the error and noted that Mark would receive the expected increase and a one-time adjustment for back pay. On the strength of that, Mark made additional financial commitments. When the latest check was direct deposited into Mark's bank account, the mistake had not been corrected, and a check Mark had written was returned for insufficient funds. Payroll's excuse? HR had not received the approved changes at least one week prior to check issuance—payroll's deadline for changes.

How can errors like this be avoided? They are not uncommon. A large state university in the Northeast makes salary adjustments to faculty who receive performance increases in two stages: The adjustment becomes part of the biweekly paycheck in late spring, and the adjustment for January 1 through late spring is paid out as a lump sum in summer. Last summer, the back-pay adjustment was considerably higher than it should have been because of a data entry error in the adjustment formula. No one caught the error until this year, when the university had to notify all faculty members that the back-pay adjustment for this year would be reduced by the excess adjustment received the previous year.

PM, compensation, benefits, and payroll are sensitive areas for most employees. The typical employee tends to "keep score" on his or her relationship with an employer through these systems. It is critical that information technology (IT) systems in these areas be flawlessly executed from the employee's perspective because getting the wrong (or no) paycheck sends a very bad message to the employee. Given the amounts of money involved, it is critical that IT systems in these areas be flawlessly executed from the employer's perspective as well.

In this chapter, we will provide an overview of PM, compensation, benefits, and payroll, so that you have an idea of the complexity that must be captured if the HRIS is to work well.

INTRODUCTION

Performance, rewards, and payroll systems focus on the basic exchange between employees and employers: Employees provide performance, and, in exchange, employers provide rewards, which are distributed via payroll systems. These systems also serve as good examples of several IT issues in human resources management (HRM). **Performance management (PM)** systems are usually entirely internal to the organization, but data must be linked to several other systems, including rewards, staffing, training and development, and career development. PM systems are used as working tools by managers and must, therefore, be inherently self-explanatory. Often, data are specific to the individual, although various summary measures must be comparable across subsets of employees or all employees.

In contrast, reward systems have both internal and external ties to multiple other information systems. Both pay and benefits must be linked (or linkable) to external survey data, legal requirement data, and internal systems such as budgeting and planning systems. Usage of parts of reward systems must be restricted to HR professionals, while other parts must be widely available to employees for self-queries. Most organizations consider rewards data to be highly confidential, so system security is critical. Reward systems data focus on the individual, small-group, unit, and organization levels for different purposes, and the same variable (e.g., value of a specific benefit, seniority, option value) may have to be defined, calculated, stored, and reported in multiple ways depending on the need.

In the case of payroll systems, flawless data integrity and even more flawless execution are critical. Anyone who has ever received an inaccurate paycheck will understand the frustration and anger that occur; a payroll system that is not flawless is an administrator's nightmare. Payroll systems must be linked to external data (e.g., federal and state requirements for minimum wage) and internal data (e.g., general ledger, benefit choices) and must be capable of incorporating constant change. The payroll system is generally used only by payroll specialists, but every employee "audits" his or her own results. One final aspect of payroll is that some summaries of payroll data are not likely to match summaries of the same variables used in compensation or other HR systems. Even in a question as seemingly simple as number of employees, there will be discrepancies in these data summaries. For example, the compensation system is likely to contain only currently active employees; benefits might also include employees on leave, retired employees, and those former employees who have elected continuation of benefits under the **Consolidated Omnibus Budget Reduction Act (COBRA)** of 1986; and payroll files will contain everyone for whom a check is cut.

Although the interrelationships between performance management, rewards, benefits, and payroll are clear, and it is obvious that the HRIS applications for these four functions need to interface seamlessly, it would be a mistake to assume that these four functions can be considered independently of other HR applications or, indeed, of any of the information systems operated by the organization. The HRIS must allow for all aspects of the employment relationship (including relationships with prospective and past employees) to be considered, analyzed, and acted on. Neither managers nor employees see the relationship between the organization and the employee through a single lens. In turbulent times, it is difficult to predict how information may need to be used. The potential must be there for any data sets currently collected by the organization to be retrieved and analyzed based on the requirements of the problems faced, not on the bin in which the data currently reside.

This chapter focuses on the data inputs, the typical reports that are generated, data outflows to other systems, and the ways that the IT system can provide decision support to organizations and managers in the areas of PM, rewards, and payroll. Before that discussion can be meaningful, however, a brief overview of each of the areas is necessary.

PERFORMANCE MANAGEMENT

Overview

Until recently, most discussion in organizations focused on the performance appraisal process. The emphasis was on getting the "best" appraisal format and training managers to "rate" employees using the format. Most research, whether by scholars or professionals, was on rating formats, rater error, and the training of raters. The assumption was that, if the correct format could be developed and managers were trained to use it, the resulting ratings would be accurate.

During the 1980s, professionals and some scholars became interested in a different goal: improving performance (Banks & May, 1999; Bernardin, Hagan, Kane, & Villanova, 1998). This interest led to a reconsideration of the whole performance process, and attention shifted to PM. The PM process consists of three parts: performance planning, **performance observation**, and providing **positive feedback** and/or **corrective feedback**. In support of this process, periodic performance summaries are developed to serve as a basis for performance planning for the next period while providing data for a variety of HR decisions, including rewards, staffing, training, and other decisions affecting the employee's relationship with the organization.

PM is now considered within the framework of "talent management," which encompasses all areas of HR that have to do with onboarding, developing, evaluating, and managing the workforce through all the normal cycles. PM is just one of the areas connected to others such as

- recruiting (external),
- staffing (internal),
- career management,
- 360° assessment,
- development management,
- retention management, and
- workforce planning.

The model of contemporary talent management is shown in Figure 14.1.

Note that many organizations today, although having installed expensive and expansive enterprise resource planning (ERP) systems, which were supposed to provide a single platform for all these integrated applications, found that it was necessary to add specialized talent management solutions from third-party vendors to achieve the necessary functionality.

The link from the resulting performance and compensation processes to the core payroll systems, however, still remains as an integral link between the ERP systems and the specialized talent management solutions. In the example given in the opening vignette, if there were an integrated talent management system linking the performance module and compensation, there would be no need for anyone to enter the performance rating into the compensation system since the performance rating would have already been there as a result of the approved employee review.

Figure 14.1 Model of Contemporary Talent Management

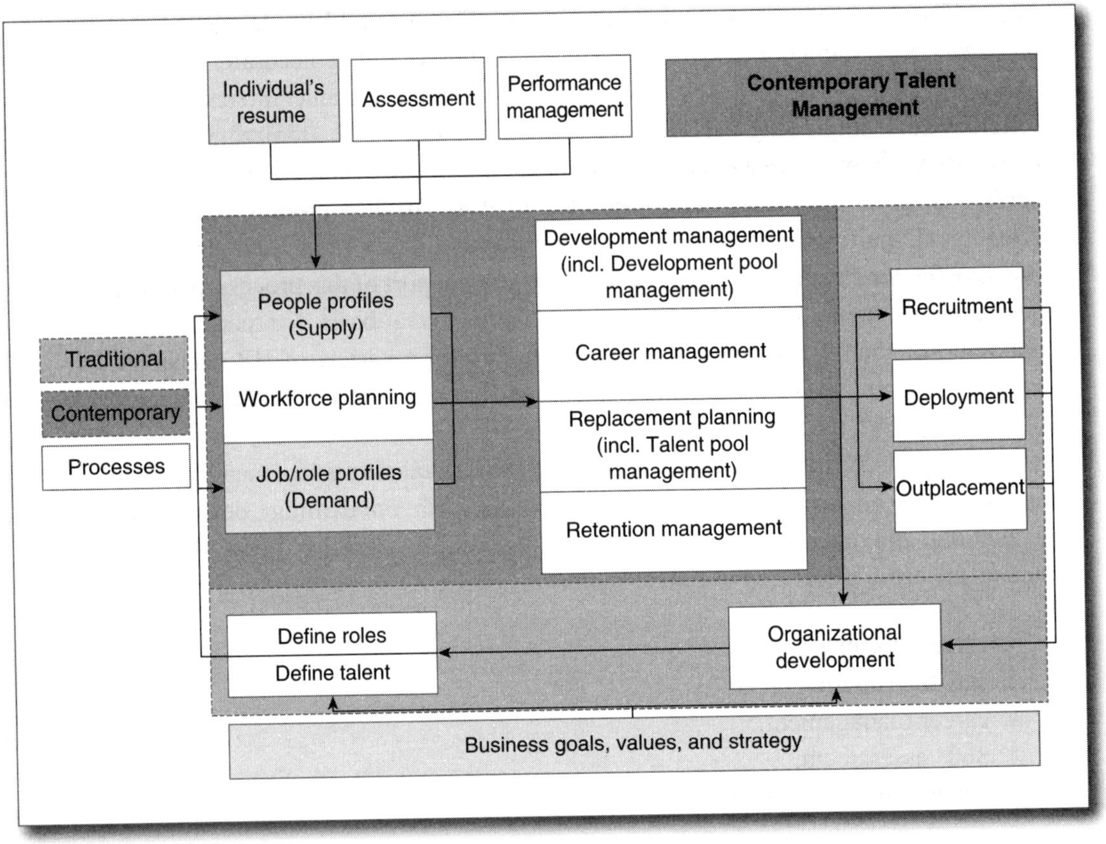

Performance Planning

Performance planning, like most management processes, must be constructed in such a way that any manager can do it, regardless of management style or skills. Better managers involve the employee collaboratively in all phases of the PM process, but the system is designed so that even directive managers can follow the process. This discussion assumes that the manager is more directive than collaborative.

The manager must first define what performance means in the case of a specific **direct report** (i.e., the employee whose job performance is being evaluated). At the broadest level, this definition of performance would encompass any employee who fills the job position. Another way to conceive the definition of performance is that it is the performance expected of a new employee in the position if the direct report were terminated. Ideally, this definition is based on a cascade of goals beginning with the organizational strategy and operating plan, with the immediate source being what the manager is expected to accomplish during the period and ending with the direct report's expected part of that accomplishment (Evans, 2001). The manager must then move from the general to the specific, usually expressed in terms of desired outcomes. This constitutes the performance dimensions for the direct report.

When outcomes are difficult to observe or measure, behaviors that are expected to lead to desired outcomes are added. For each performance dimension, the manager must develop specific outcomes and behaviors that will be used to measure the direct report's performance. For a performance dimension of budget management, an outcome might be "Stays close to budget for each budget category." A behavior on the same dimension might be "Checks expenditures against budget." After the measures are determined, the manager must set appropriate standards for each measure. The standard for "Checks expenditures against budget" might be "Checks expenditures against budget weekly." After defining standard performance, "Exceeds standards" and "Fails to meet standards" would be defined. The "Exceeds standards" level for "Checks expenditures against budget" might be "Checks expenditures against budget weekly; where discrepancies exceed 2%, checks those categories daily until discrepancies disappear." The "Fails to meet standards" level might be "Misses weekly check of expenditures against budget; allows discrepancies to continue without any follow-up." It should be noted that performance dimensions, measures, and standards are unique to each position, although attempts should be made to develop common standards for employees with identical job titles.

When performance dimensions, measures, and standards have been developed, the manager must communicate them to the direct report. The manager must make certain that the direct report understands measures and standards. The manager then gets the direct report to set goals for performance for the coming year. Note that goals and standards are not the same thing. The standard is what is expected of a fully job-knowledgeable employee who exerts normal effort. One purpose of PM is to get employees to set stretch goals, to be better than the standard. At the end of the goal-setting discussion, the direct report has agreed on some performance level as a goal. The set of performance measures, with standards and goals, becomes the performance "contract" for the period.

Formats

Most organizations define the performance instrument differently depending on the type or level of the employee. For example, a nonmanagement or clerical position may have a relatively standard set of criteria that requires little or no change year after year. On the other hand, management employees tend to use a format that combines both goals and objectives together with a competency evaluation. A well-designed performance application can automatically map the correct "format" based on the employee who has logged into the performance Web site.

For the management "format," the performance evaluation can reflect a weighting of a goal portion and the competency portion (i.e., 60% of the overall rating will be based on the goals results, while 40% will reflect the competency ratings). Also, within each of these sections, a specific performance level for each goal or competency might be rated. Therefore, the overall result could reflect a weighted calculation of each goal, competency, and section. Web-based performance systems can easily perform these calculations for the user. Even if the organization prefers that the employee and/or the manager actually determine the overall rating, the system can provide "advice" as to the reasonableness of the entered rating versus the underlying ratings.

Performance Period

During the performance period, the manager uses the performance contract as a benchmark for observing the direct report. When performance above standard is observed, the standard becomes the basis of positive feedback. When performance is below standard or below the goal set by the direct report, corrective feedback is used, again relying on the standard and on the goal set as the benchmarks for the performance observed. When discussion about performance is couched in terms of known measures, standards, and performance goals, feedback can be much more objective, and it is less likely to be seen as criticism of character. The direct report is not bad per se, but is simply not performing at the agreed-on level on one or more measures.

Periodic Performance Summary

At some point, a summary of performance during the period is provided to the direct report. In most organizations, this is an annual event, but some organizations have quarterly or semiannual performance summaries. At this point, the manager provides a summary of how the direct report has done on each performance measure and whether standards and goals have been met. In performance systems that offer both the employee and the manager Web-based input capabilities, periodic review of the employee's progress toward achieving goals is much easier. Once the employee self-assesses her or his own performance, the manager can also review each goal while viewing the employee's comments (see Figure 14.2 for an example).

Figure 14.2 Performance Planning and Rating Module Screen

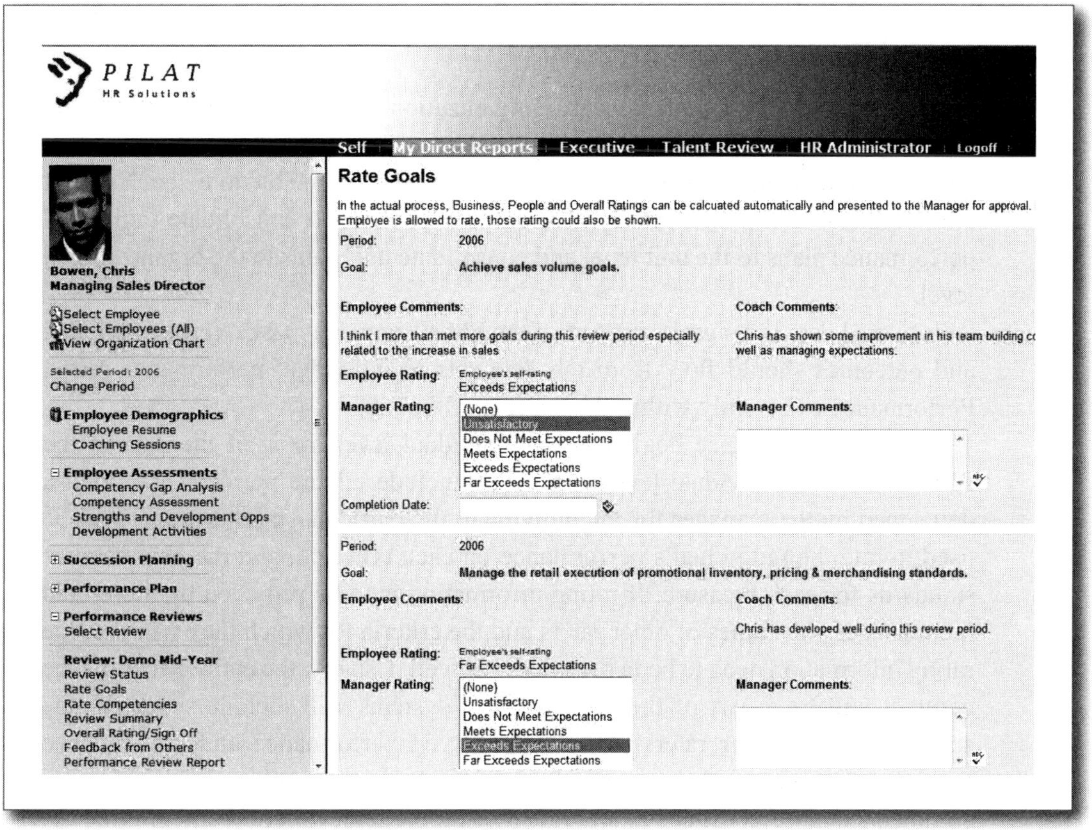

Consequences of achieving various performance levels are communicated, and planning for the next period's performance begins. If PM has been done correctly, the summary appraisal should have no surprises for the direct report. As shown in Figure 14.1, development is a critical component. One of the more important outputs of the performance process is an **individual development plan (IDP)** that is used to document any steps necessary to improve employee performance. Each employee should have an IDP.

The process described above applies to PM at the individual level. Yet most employees today work as an integrated part of one or more teams. The PM process does not change significantly for a team. It is usually easier to get outcome performance measures for a team than for an individual, and it is more difficult to get individual performance measures for a team member (Bing, 2004). Some organizations have elected to use team output as the primary outcome measure of performance for all team members and then develop a "team citizenship measure" for each team member.

Typical Data Inputs

Data inputs for PM systems include organizational-, job-, and individual-level data. Organizational-level data consist of links to organizational and unit goals and strategies and business plans. Performance plans should be able to tie back to unit and organizational plans; ideally, it should be possible to consolidate individual performance plans to the unit level and consolidate unit plans to the organizational level.

Job-level data is a significant part of the PM system. Key tasks, responsibilities, and outcomes should flow from job data sets to individual performance plans. Performance exists only within the context of the job.

Because performance begins at the individual level, most of the data in the PM system are individual-level data. Data include all the performance criteria developed by the manager for the individual, the particular measures that will be used to rate the individual's performance on each criterion, and the performance standards for each measure. If rating information is to be provided by more than the manager, the names of other raters and the criteria for which they will provide rating information need to be in the system as well. Usually, the entire performance contract will be a part of the system. Most systems will include space for the supervisor (and other raters) to enter observed performance and performance incidents. Contemporary systems allow both employees and managers to enter comments and observations at any time during the review period and provide the option of having all those comments swept into the final review, presenting them in a concatenated area for editing by users. There should also be space for documentation of positive and corrective feedback. While creating an IDP, many systems can recommend and provide a library of development activities that can be used to correct specific problems.

Performance management systems must interface with staffing and training applications. As an example, if certain jobs are hard to staff, the PM system will want to add the competencies required for that job so that more internal candidates can be surfaced. Similarly, training applications need to be coordinated with the PM system so that evaluation of training (and development) programs will be possible.

Typical Reports

The most important standardized reports produced by the HRIS are the performance contract and the annual summary appraisal for each employee. Other reports include aggregate performance data by unit and reports comparing aggregated unit performance with unit output (Cohen & Hall, 2005, p. 64). The HRIS needs to have the capability of archiving data so long-term performance trends for individuals and groups can be tracked. If competency assessments are used as a part of the review, the HR department can monitor systemic developmental requirements based on the aggregated competency results (e.g., those for business unit, location, or level).

Data Outflows

Performance data are used in many HRM decisions and will flow automatically into some processes or be available for others as needed. One automatic flow will be into compensation. Organizations with merit pay need performance distributions to construct a merit matrix. (Note that many performance applications are capable of having compensation functionality built in.) The performance measure used is the summary performance level for each employee. Performance data on various performance dimensions are used in decisions relating to promotion, layoffs, assignment to training programs, and developmental assignments. Performance data are also central to HR planning. Other applications that make use of performance data are training and development (so that training needs can be analyzed based on current weaknesses in employee performance) and staffing, where aggregated strengths and weaknesses of currently needed skills and competencies can trigger recruitment and staffing goals. In addition, performance processes utilizing competency assessment can be used by manpower planning applications to assist in forecasting future deficiencies based on required skill profiles.

Decision Support

The basic decision support system in the area of PM is the entire system. Having performance criteria, performance measures, performance standards, and recent performance documentation in a single place allows managers to keep track of how each direct report is doing and what interventions need to be made to improve performance (Evans, 2001). This self-service feature for managers makes the performance management module a management tool for daily use. All performance management documentation activities required of the manager can be dealt with through the system. Performance planning, documented observation of performance, feedback documentation, and the formal appraisal can all be developed on the system itself and stored there for future reference by managers. Similarly, the system can provide self-service for employees by allowing them to view the same data and use those data as a basis for deciding on areas where improvement is needed. Appropriate interfaces between the performance management module and training and development modules can lead either the manager or the direct report to training programs or other developmental activities based on the specific performance problems noted. Indeed, PM software can be categorized as either preformatted appraisal systems—systems that allow the development of customized appraisals—or systems that diagnose performance problems (Forrer & Leibowitz, 1991, pp. 104–106).

Flowers, Tudor, and Trumble (1997) note that such systems should allow managers to update information, serve as a support in conducting the appraisal interview, allow the creation of effective appraisal forms, and support all legal mandates relevant to performance appraisals. A system supporting multisource feedback appraisals such as **360° appraisals** is described by Meyer (1998).

Group performance can also be tracked and the data used for performance improvement; because most employees work as part of teams, there has been increased interest in measuring and managing team performance (e.g., Jones & Schilling, 2000). Stegner and Kofahl (2004) provide a case study of a process for group performance improvement that could not exist without heavy input from the HRIS. In some cases, systems tie closely with marketing and management information systems; Charles, Kurlander, and Savage (2000) describe a sales performance tracking system that keeps home office and sales personnel aware of results against quotas and suggests where efforts need to be made to enhance sales performance.

Finally, automated PM systems allow managers and HR managers to track the administrative aspects of PM: Have all managers completed performance contracts with their direct reports? Are summary appraisals done on time? Do ratings by a manager and the performance of the manager's unit jibe? These are questions that can be answered by the system. Additionally, performance ratings can be checked for possible bias against protected groups. This checking can include not only the ratings themselves but also their use in HR decisions. Under the *Uniform Guidelines on Employee Selection Procedures* (U.S. Department of Labor & U.S. Department of Justice, 1978), performance appraisals are considered "tests" when used for HR decisions, such as promotions, and are subject to the same validity and reliability requirements as other tests when they are found to have an adverse impact on protected groups.

Web-based systems can also provide a calibration tool for employee performance ratings that allows for a visual inspection of the distribution of ratings for a population. This calibration is often essential as a tie-in to the compensation process since performance ratings often dictate how much employees may receive for their annual merit review. The example of performance calibration presented in Figure 14.3 is part of a succession planning system being

Figure 14.3 Example of Relating Performance to Compensation

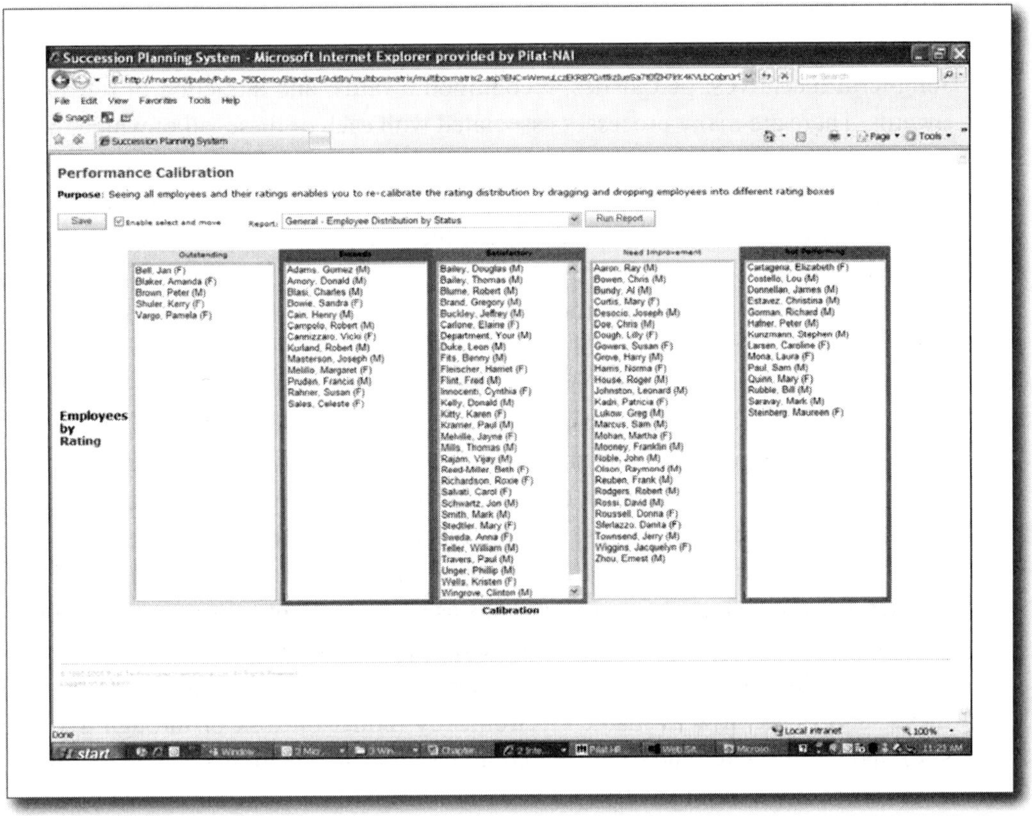

used by a large utility organization, a system that allows managers to view the distribution and even drag-and-drop employees within the ratings to adjust for any discrepancies.

COMPENSATION

Overview

Compensation is one of the most complex topics in HRM, and attempting to present an overview is ambitious. Organizations faced with the complexities of creating and administering compensation systems are increasingly turning to technology for help. Wright (2003, p. 55) estimates that a 12,000-person firm can save as much as $850,000 per year in administrative costs by automating compensation planning alone. Brink and McDonnell (2003) point out that nearly all processes used to design, communicate, and manage pay are moving toward Web applications.

The basic compensation system includes **base pay**, merit pay, short-term and long-term incentives, perquisites, recognition awards, and attraction or retention awards. There are many processes associated with each of these, all of which must be coordinated. If that were not enough, there are also special populations that have unique pay processes: executives, sales personnel, scientists and engineers, expatriates, unionized workers, and the whole panoply of temporary, contract, or part-time workers.

Base pay is built around two processes: **job evaluation** and market benchmarking. Job evaluation creates an internal hierarchy of value. In the most common form of job evaluation, a set of factors is developed that reflects characteristics that add value to work in the specific organization (e.g., the education required). Each factor is weighted by importance, and scales are developed. Every job that will be in the base pay system is evaluated on the set of scales, and a point score is calculated. Jobs are arranged by total points, and this forms the basis for a salary structure.

Market benchmarking is used to price the structure (or individual jobs). Market data are collected for as many jobs as possible. In most organizations, one or more surveys may be developed in-house to collect market benchmarks; but the bulk of benchmark data come from commercial and association surveys. Many of these surveys are now available electronically (either on disk or through a Web site) and can be integrated into the compensation information system. Entering data can be done through a Web site with a format that maximizes ease of data entry (Tobin, 2002). However, Web sites with salary data are not without problems; employees frequently access Web sites that may have unrepresentative data and argue that they are underpaid based on bad data (Menefee, 2000).

An employee is placed in the salary grade appropriate for her or his job. Each grade has a midpoint that serves as a proxy for all the jobs in that grade, and a range is built around that midpoint. (This range defines the minimum and maximum salary for jobs in that grade, usually ±20% from the midpoint.) Exact placement in the range is usually a function of performance and individual characteristics (quality of degree, experience).

The structure is adjusted each year based on market movements. If the market were to increase by 3%, for example, the midpoints would increase by 3% as well. However, not all employees receive a 3% increase if the organization uses a merit pay system. In a merit pay system, the size of the increase is a function of performance level and of where an employee is in the range: the higher the performance, the larger the increase and, generally, the lower the place in the range, the higher the increase. A merit matrix, developed to provide guidelines based on performance and place in the range, ensures that the total amount spent by the organization is no more than the specified percentage of payroll.

There are many forms of short-term **incentive pay**. Unlike merit pay, short-term incentive pay is rarely added to base pay and must be re-earned every year. Typical short-term incentive programs include bonuses, gain sharing, goal sharing, small-group incentives, and profit sharing. Short-term incentive programs usually have specific measures, set up prior to the beginning of the program, that will drive payout (profit sharing as an incentive is not typically covered by these measures). Gain sharing, for example, bases payouts on reductions in production costs due to more efficient use of labor. Specific preplanned formulas based on past production costs drive payouts. Bonus systems can be driven by preplanned criteria related to manufacturing, customer service, safety, or anything else that the company wishes to motivate employees to achieve. Profit sharing is usually retrospective, however; the board decides after the books have closed for the fiscal year that some percentage of profits will be shared with employees. In all cases, the measures driving short-term incentive payouts must be collected, either through existing measurement systems or through special systems designed for the purpose.

Long-term incentives are primarily based on organization stock, options to buy organization stock, or phantom (make-believe) stock. The goal of long-term incentives is twofold: to align the interests of employees with those of shareholders and to motivate aligned performance over periods of more than one year.

Perquisites are rewards that are a function of organizational status. Executive dining rooms, first-class or corporate jet air travel, and club memberships are examples. Perquisites frequently have tax consequences to the employee receiving them and, thus, must be included as part of the pay system. In the past several years, some organizations have transformed perquisites into incentive rewards based on performance; go to any Disney property, and you will see parking spaces near the employee entrance that are reserved for high performers.

Recognition awards are low-cost or no-cost awards that are retrospective: When an employee does something of note, he or she receives an award that may have little financial value but is psychologically rewarding. The use of Web sites in recognition programs, so that every employee can go online and find where he or she stands in comparison with other eligible employees, can greatly enhance the motivational impact of such programs (Perlmutter, 2002). **Attraction** or **retention awards** are one-time awards that are used to attract prospective employees to the organization or persuade them to remain with the organization. These awards may take the form of cash, stock options, benefits, or adjustments to benefits rules. The goal is to incur a one-time cost that does not drive up base pay.

Although the types of compensation already described are made up of multiple programs, it is critical that all compensation programs be integrated, so employees receive a single message about what adds value in the organization and the type of behavior and culture that is desired.

Compensation programs must also meet federal and state statutory and regulatory requirements. The **Fair Labor Standards Act (FLSA)** differentiates **exempt workers** and **nonexempt workers**; the organization must pay nonexempt workers at least the minimum wage, must pay for time worked in excess of 40 hours a week at an overtime rate of 1.5 times the normal pay, and must provide records to the federal government on hours worked and regular and overtime pay for all nonexempt workers. The **Office of Federal Contract Compliance Programs (OFCCP)** requires annual evidence of nonbias with respect to race and gender for similarly situated employee groups (SSEGs) and requires multiple linear regression analyses as evidence.

Typical Data Inputs

Compensation data inputs include internal, external, and generated data. Internal data include information about jobs (descriptions, specifications), people (performance, salary history), and organizational units (salary budget, job evaluation system). External data would include market survey data and information on rewards practices. Internal and external data would be combined and used to generate job evaluation results, salary structures, merit matrices, and a variety of reward guidelines. Incentive programs will require input data on whatever behavior or outcome is being encouraged; such data might include customer survey results, accident data, time-to-market data, or product quality data. Data from the staffing function can highlight problem areas, for example, jobs for which compensation may be too low.

Compensation for a special employee group usually requires data specific to that group. Executive compensation is likely to require organization-wide sales, productivity, profit, share price, market share, and other financial, market, and production data indicative of organizational success. Sales compensation systems may require data on quotas, sales, bonus or commission rates, and competitive market data. Gain-sharing programs require historical averaged data on labor costs as a proportion of value of production. Bargaining unit employee pay systems require data on contract specifics. For nonexempt employees, hourly rates and hours worked per week are required.

In short, there are very few data within the organization that might not be required by some part of the compensation system. As an example, a company that market-prices jobs will collect as much market data on wages as possible. Even so, it is unlikely that market data can be found for all jobs. The "market rate" for these jobs must be estimated. It is common to use multiple linear regression for this purpose. As much information about all jobs is collected as possible, using either job specification data or aggregate information from job incumbents. Some specific information that might be collected from the HRIS includes the average education level of job incumbents in each job, the average amount of training incumbents in each job have had, the average number of direct reports each incumbent in a job has, and so forth. Although logic guides the choice of which independent variables to use in the regression equation to predict market rates, the goal is to get the best prediction, so whatever variables end up providing the best prediction are the ones that will be used. Similarly, incentive programs may make use of any financial, market, or production data to determine whether bonuses should be paid and, if so, how much and to whom.

Typical Reports

There are a number of standard reports in the compensation arena; however, because of the sensitive nature of compensation information, they are not widely circulated. The most common reports include budget reports to managers showing how their actual compensation costs compare with the projected costs. Most organizations provide each employee with an "Annual Compensation Report" showing the total amount of money spent by the organization on the employee, including money spent on wage or salary, incentive pay, and the cost of benefits paid for by the organization. Similar reports, such as incentive reports that tell people how they are doing with respect to earning a specific incentive award, become much more effective when a Web site is used for communication (Stiffler, 2001).

Companies participating in wage surveys produce reports for use by surveying organizations. In some cases, a compensation analyst draws the data from the HRIS and enters them into the survey, but, in other cases, an automated application gathers data from the HRIS and enters them into the survey program.

A new report on the analysis of possible "systemic compensation bias" among "similarly situated employee groups" is now required by the U.S. OFCCP. This report will be due annually, along with the organization's EE0-1 Report.

Data Outflows

The primary data outflow from compensation modules is to payroll. Compensation analysts draw on the data for additional analyses, however. Managers preparing budgets draw on compensation data as they project costs over the next budget period. Benefits analysts draw on compensation data as they analyze probable future costs of wage-based benefits (pensions are usually a function of salary level while health benefits are largely independent of salary level).

Data are sent to federal, state, and local agencies, including taxing agencies, labor departments, and other units tracking wage data. Many organizations also provide data to firms conducting reward surveys.

Decision Support

The major rewards decision that has to be made about every employee is how much to pay that individual. Decision support systems in compensation are all aimed at that decision. Because of the complexity of compensation, though, a series of decisions must be made before a final compensation decision is made. Thus, there are decision support systems dealing with job evaluation, the use of market data, market pricing, building a salary structure, developing a merit matrix, and running incentive programs. Although much of this activity is carried out by compensation and other HR managers, other managers can do much of the work themselves if the system is set up correctly as a self-serve system. The most common areas that managers would handle themselves include salary budget planning, merit, promotional and other increases, and most incentive programs. Using Web-based compensation modules, managers can perform salary-planning functions much easier than was possible with paper-based processes. Data such as current salary, compa-ratio, and salary ranges can be viewed for all their employees at once; for international organizations, such systems can handle multicurrency requirements; and these systems can ensure that the total of the projected salary increases recommended by each manager does not exceed budgeting guidelines. Figure 14.4 depicts the work area of a Web-based application that enables managers to do compensation planning for their employees.

Koski (2003) describes a project that automated a worldwide employee bonus system; executives and managers got a self-service system, and compensation executives could keep track (in real time) of award amounts and payouts. Supported by computer and Web-based products, these processes generally offer advantages to the organizations using them (Zingheim & Schuster, 2005). Indeed, Zingheim and Schuster (2004) argue that Web management of pay and rewards is one of two great innovations in the rewards field.

Employees do not make many compensation decisions themselves, so self-service functions are largely restricted to providing information. Most companies now make salary structures available on the company intranet, and job postings typically provide either structure information or the salary grade of a job, so employees can look up what the range of pay for any job would be. The merit

Figure 14.4 Screen of Salary Review Module for Department Manager

Salary Review - USA

Budget Figures

Total Budget for United States: 14674
Budget Used: 13500.7
Budget Remaining: 1173.29

USA Merit Increase Matrix

The following table is used to determine the merit increase percentage based on the employee's Consolidated Rating and RSP scores.

Rating	RSP 70 - 100 (From)	RSP 70 - 100 (To)	RSP >100 - 130 (From)	RSP >100 - 130 (To)
10 - 24.9 Points	0	0	0	0
25 - 34.9 Points	0	0	0	0
35 - 44.9 Points	3	5	0	3
45 - 54.9 Points	5.5	7.5	3.5	5.5
55 - 70 Points	8	10	6	8

Employee Merit Increase

The local currency is: **US Dollar**. The Euro exchange rate is: **0.830220**.

Employee	Rating	Consolidated Rating	Range %	Current Salary Local	Current Salary	Merit Range From	Merit Range To	Merit Increase %	Merit Increase Amount	Salary with Merit	Adjustment Increase %	Adjustment Increase Amount	Salary with Adjustment	New RSP
Blasi, Charles	60	20	90.00	27,000.00	22,416.00	0.00	0.00	3.00	672.48	23,088.48	0.00	0.00	23,088.48	90.00
Flint, Fred	38	38	108.00	35,000.00	29,058.00	0.00	3.00	4.00	1,162.32	30,220.32	0.00	0.00	30,220.32	111.00
Rossi, David	43	43	101.00	36,500.00	30,303.00	0.00	3.00	5.00	1,515.15	31,818.15	0.00	0.00	31,818.15	104.00
Bowen, Chris	45	50	79.00	36,000.00	29,888.00	5.50	7.50	5.50	1,643.84	31,531.84	2.00	630.64	32,162.48	89.00
Steinberg, Maureen	56	56	85.00	45,000.00	37,360.00	8.00	10.00	8.00	2,988.80	40,348.80	0.00	0.00	40,348.80	92.00
Innocenti, Cynthia	59	70	90.00	73,000.00	60,606.00	8.00	10.00	8.00	4,848.48	65,454.48	0.00	0.00	65,454.48	98.00
				252,500.00	**209,631.00**				**12,831.07**	**222,462.07**		**630.64**	**223,092.71**	

matrix, average salary increases, average bonuses of various kinds, and other reward information are all posted by some companies. Most public sector salaries are publicly available under state and local "freedom of information" acts, and, in these cases, salaries (and total earnings) of specific employees are available; private organizations almost never post such information.

There can be difficulties with Web management of pay. Van De Voort and McDonnell (2003) point out that working "live" can create problems when numbers change during the process. As an example, if a manager is calculating merit pay and is working off a specific budget number, changes to that number by a senior manager can create confusion and bad decisions. The use of a frozen or static database ensures that everyone is working with the same data, formulae, and figures.

Other decision support systems deal with sales compensation. Cocks and Gould (2001) note that compensation software is critical in defining commission levels, designing compensation plans, and managing compensation, since all three areas require on-the-fly complex calculations on a repeated basis. Weeks (2000) notes that virtual sales teams in widely separated areas can be much more effective in maintaining customer satisfaction; only the Web allows the coordination between team members required to pull off this strategy, and it also allows sales compensation experts to audit and fine-tune the sales compensation system to maintain high motivation levels.

A whole set of applications relate to executive pay. Since the Enron scandal and the subsequent passage of the **Sarbanes-Oxley Act (SOX)**, compliance reports, including those dealing with executive pay, are required. SOX compliance is greatly supported by data from the HRIS ("How HRIS Can Help With SOX Compliance," 2005; Sherman, 2005). Additional regulations covering executive pay have come about as a result of the **Troubled Asset Relief Program (TARP)** of 2009 and the financial bailout of troubled financial services firms and automakers. More financial regulations are expected in 2011. The HRIS must be flexible enough to add any new fields required by these regulations and capable of running the audits required.

BENEFITS

Overview

A full discussion of benefits programs is beyond the scope of this chapter. There are five broad types of benefits programs in most U.S. organizations. Because some company-provided benefits in this country are government provided in other countries, a different typology would be required for organizations abroad.

The first set of benefits programs common in U.S. companies includes **pension plans** (both defined benefit and defined contribution), individual savings plans (such as Keoghs, **simplified employee pensions [SEPs]**, and **individual retirement accounts [IRAs]** and Social Security. Although few Americans think of Social Security as a benefit, the organization must fund contributions to Social Security just as an employee does. The goal of all these benefits programs is to ensure that the employee will have continuing income after retirement. The second set of benefits programs includes workers' compensation, unemployment insurance, long- and short-term disability insurance, and life insurance. The goal of these programs is to ensure that employees who cannot work (through no fault of their own) have some income until they can work again and to provide income protection to employees' families.

The third set of benefits programs includes medical and other health benefits, such as hospitalization and medical care insurance; surgical and major medical care insurance; long-term care; dental, vision, and hearing care insurance; and prescription drug coverage insurance. These benefits are designed to make sure that employees and their families are not bankrupted by illness or accident and can obtain preventative and curative care. The fourth area of benefits is paid time off and includes vacation, holidays, personal days, special purpose days (because of jury duty, bereavement, or military service, for example), and family leave. The purpose of paid time off is to allow employees to recharge their batteries, spend time with their families for celebrations, and participate in other significant life events.

The fifth and final category of benefits includes miscellaneous benefits such as dependent care, flexible working benefits (telecommuting, job sharing, compressed workweek), employee assistance programs, professional memberships, tuition reimbursement, holiday parties and gifts, subsidized cafeterias and gyms, legal advice benefits, and employee discounts. These benefits round out the benefits package and are typical of organizations found in the "best companies to work for" lists.

Benefits programs differ from compensation in two major ways. First, in the majority of organizations, employees pay part (or all) of the costs for most benefits. (Even when benefit costs are borne entirely by employees, group purchasing reduces the cost that the employee would pay for an equivalent self-purchased benefit.) Second, most organizations offer some flexibility in their benefits programs. All employees receive a core benefits package but then choose additional coverage or additional benefits, or both, up to the level of the total benefits package. (**Flexplans** also allow the employee to purchase additional coverage or benefits or both at cost.) These two characteristics of benefits programs make them relatively complex to administer; each employee in the organization may have a slightly different benefits package with a unique salary deduction profile. Things even get complicated with paid time off. Not only may different employee groups (e.g., bargaining units, executives) have different configurations for paid time off, but these configurations may also differ within groups based on seniority. In addition, many organizations have what is called a paid time off bank, through which employees can trade paid time off for cash or other benefits, can buy additional paid time off, or can donate paid time off to other employees (e.g., in cases of long-term illness). All this makes benefits programs extremely complex and difficult to administer.

Another major difference between benefits and compensation programs, one that strongly affects HRIS configuration, is the growing trend to outsource benefits programs and administration. Few parts of the typical compensation program are outsourced. The most common is the outsourcing of wage benchmarking. Although consultants are frequently used in compensation, they tend to work offline. In benefits, however, program design, benefit delivery, and program administration (including employee communications) are increasingly outsourced. As a result, the HRIS must interface not only with other internal systems, such as rewards and payroll, but also with the IT systems of other organizations. The necessity of establishing these interorganizational linkages introduces problems such as how to define fields, which fields can be included, what protocols for interaction to establish, and how to maintain security.

Legal requirements for benefits programs are also more stringent than those for compensation programs. Most benefits programs are influenced by the **Employee Retirement Income Security Act (ERISA)**, which grants benefits a tax-favored status. However, to qualify for favorable tax treatment, the benefit must meet stringent requirements. These include reporting to recipients of benefits and to the federal government, demonstrating that requirements for qualified status are met. In addition, many organizations offer nonqualified benefits to some employee groups, particularly to executives.

Typical Data Inputs

There are HRIS benefits modules with different purposes, and each requires a different type of data input. One set of functions focuses on the organization's relationship with current and prospective benefits vendors (of health insurance, for example). Inputs, in this case, will include aggregate data about the people to be covered, data outlining the relevant demographics for the covered groups, and data specifying the program coverage desired and cost limitations.

A second set of functions focuses on the internal management of benefits programs and will be used to track usage, employee choices (in the case of flex plans), and costs. Experience, usage, and costs will be fed into this program.

A third (and the most common) set of programs focuses on employee input about enrollment and other coverage choices, changes in coverage desired, and changes in employee status (e.g., addition of a dependent, change in marital status) that may affect coverage and employee costs. These programs may also allow employees to file claims with the organization. In these programs, many of which are Web based, employees feed in personal data, coverage choices, and other data relevant to their use of the benefit.

The fourth set of data placed into the system consists of the myriad federal, state, and local laws and regulations governing benefits practice. These laws and regulations provide decision support system "rules" for managers using the system.

Typical Reports

There are dozens of reports required by federal and state government units, including the IRS, units of the U.S. Department of Labor, other federal agencies, and similar units at the state level. The most common report is the annual benefits report to employees required for tax-qualified plans under ERISA. This report requires organizations to report to employees annually about certain benefit facts, such as vested pension levels. Most organizations have gone beyond the ERISA requirements and provide a report to each employee showing the total value of all compensation and benefits received by the employee during the year. This annual compensation report is the "rewards scorecard" for the employee. Ceccon (2004) estimates that putting this annual report online rather than distributing printed copies can save a company with 30,000 employees $678,000 in actual costs over five years and that productivity savings from reducing the amount of time employees use to find benefit account balances, pay information, and other rewards information on multiple sites or via phone calls to the HR department can save $625,000 per year. HR productivity increases net an annual savings of $30,000, and increased employee retention would reduce costs by $150,000 per year. With a five-year savings of $678,000 and an annual productivity savings totaling $805,000, Web reporting is clearly advantageous.

With Web-based access to benefits and other employee information, staff can view summary reports at any time, which, in many cases, eliminates the need for a company to produce expensive paper versions. With a Web-based system, an employee can, at his or her convenience, view his or her current benefits, salary, and other information directly (as shown in Figure 14.5) and decide to print a paper copy if one is needed. For an international company that distributes benefits or pay in multiple currencies, the system could normalize that data into a single currency.

Figure 14.5 Compensation and Benefits Planning Screen

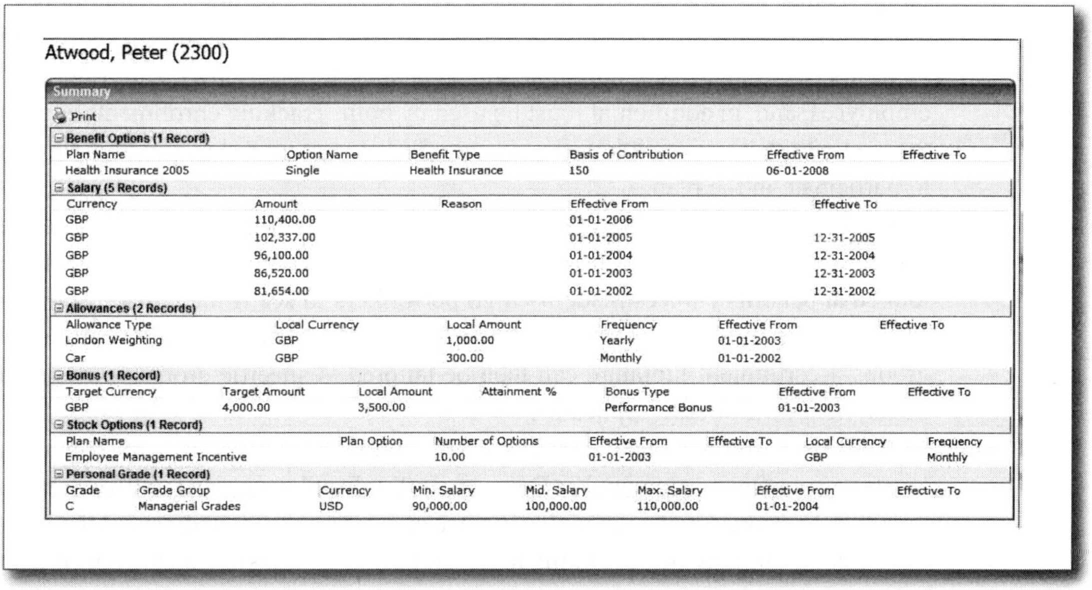
Atwood, Peter (2300)

Summary

Print

Benefit Options (1 Record)

Plan Name	Option Name	Benefit Type	Basis of Contribution	Effective From	Effective To
Health Insurance 2005	Single	Health Insurance	150	06-01-2008	

Salary (5 Records)

Currency	Amount	Reason	Effective From	Effective To
GBP	110,400.00		01-01-2006	
GBP	102,337.00		01-01-2005	12-31-2005
GBP	96,100.00		01-01-2004	12-31-2004
GBP	86,520.00		01-01-2003	12-31-2003
GBP	81,654.00		01-01-2002	12-31-2002

Allowances (2 Records)

Allowance Type	Local Currency	Local Amount	Frequency	Effective From	Effective To
London Weighting	GBP	1,000.00	Yearly	01-01-2003	
Car	GBP	300.00	Monthly	01-01-2002	

Bonus (1 Record)

Target Currency	Target Amount	Local Amount	Attainment %	Bonus Type	Effective From	Effective To
GBP	4,000.00	3,500.00		Performance Bonus	01-01-2003	

Stock Options (1 Record)

Plan Name	Plan Option	Number of Options	Effective From	Effective To	Local Currency	Frequency
Employee Management Incentive		10.00	01-01-2003		GBP	Monthly

Personal Grade (1 Record)

Grade	Grade Group	Currency	Min. Salary	Mid. Salary	Max. Salary	Effective From	Effective To
C	Managerial Grades	USD	90,000.00	100,000.00	110,000.00	01-01-2004	

Data Outflows

Data generated by benefits programs have to be transferred to payroll and accounting internally. Data are sent externally to benefits providers, outsourced benefits administrators, and a variety of federal, state, and local agencies. Aggregate data are provided to benefits survey firms.

The real-time transfer of data can result in large cost savings. Moynihan (2000) notes that AT&T saved $15 million when it switched to providing updated enrollment information to all its various health plans. Previously, tardy data transfer resulted in health plans denying coverage to employees who were in fact eligible and in claims being paid out to people who no longer worked for AT&T.

Decision Support

Decision support tools overlap to some extent with reports in the benefits arena because, frequently, these reports trigger the need to make changes to comply with federal, state, or local requirements. As an example, McCormack (2004) notes that the Family and Medical Leave Act (FMLA) has complicated the administration of employee leave. Many states have more stringent leave requirements than FMLA or the 40 other federal leave laws. A system that tracks these laws and can tell the HR manager exactly what the leave requirements are in a specific locality ensures compliance and minimizes the risk of lawsuits and fines.

Similarly, tax-qualified benefit plans are subject to federal bias regulations. In this case, "bias" refers to income level rather than protected group status. Federal policy is that tax laws should not underwrite benefits that are available only to highly paid employees. If an organization is to have a qualified 401(k) retirement plan, for example, the plan must be available to both low- and high-paid employees, and, in addition, it must be used by both. Tracking enrollments against those eligible for participation can trigger efforts to get more low-paid employees to participate in the plan.

When organizations offer flexible benefit plans, it is common to track the choices made by employees to guide plan development. A few organizations have looked at benefits choices made by high performers to see if they differ from the choices made by low performers. Others look at the choices made by protected groups. Recruitment literature can then be tailored to specific groups to ensure a better yield of desirable applicants.

Web-based services also offer decision support to employees deciding what levels of coverage to sign up for (Dawson, 1997). Employees can readily compare the cost of various levels of benefits service and more readily understand the cost-benefit trade-off that they are going to make. Similarly, transferring the enrollment process to the employees themselves can save the organization money (Teer, 1997). However, such savings are not likely to occur unless the system is easy to use for all employees, not just the technologically savvy (Ashley, 2006).

Self-service systems for managerial use in the benefits area are not frequent, as few managers have a role in benefits decisions concerning their direct reports. However, self-service systems for employees are increasingly relied on by employers to lessen the burden of benefits transactional administration. Employees typically make and change selections in flexible benefits plans through the company intranet. They can change beneficiaries or dependents as births, deaths, and divorces occur. They can increase tax-deferred or pretax contributions to various benefits categories such as 401(k) plans, health spending accounts, and similar programs. They may buy or sell vacation days from the paid time off (PTO) bank. They may transfer PTO days into their 401(k). (There are timing and contribution limits and other rules that must be observed, but these can be built into the application.) Employees can also find out the status of various benefits through self-service approaches. At least one organization allows employees to do "what-if" scenarios with respect to retirement: for example, "If I retired tomorrow, what would my pension be?"

The outsourcing of benefits creates additional issues for the HRIS. Some major corporations have outsourced all benefits. An extensive interface must be built connecting the organization's HRIS with the outsource firm's system. The benefits advisers at the outsource firm must have current, accurate data on the benefits status of every organizational employee to be able to answer questions and provide advice. Outside access raises security issues to a greater level of concern; benefits data (including hospital and other medical billing and psychiatric care and employee assistance program billing) are the most sensitive employee data held by the organization, and privacy standards (including Health Insurance Portability and Accountability Act requirements) must be met.

A whole range of decisions concerning benefits is made outside the HR department. Benefits costs are the most rapidly increasing part of labor costs, particularly costs for health care benefits and defined benefit pension plans. Consequently, senior executives (especially the CFO) are interested in the aggregate costs of the various benefits packages offered by the organization. However, determining these costs is complicated. For many benefits, such as workers compensation, cost is a function of experience; for others, such as insurance, cost depends on usage; and for others, such as health insurance and pensions, employee demographics are particularly significant. Therefore, the organization needs to be able to price current benefits packages and project costs based on expected demographic changes. It also needs to be able to run "what if" scenarios based on alternate benefit packages: What would we save over the next five years if we switched from a defined benefit pension to a cash balance plan? How would that compare to switching to a 401(k) with match?

PAYROLL

Overview

Payroll is the transactional process through which compensation is transferred to employees and federal, state, and local income and payroll taxes are withheld from employees' checks. It is also through payroll that any benefits costs borne by employees are withheld. Although some employees receive actual checks for net pay, it is more common, especially among large organizations, for direct deposits to be made to employees' bank accounts. Companies that outsource need to make sure that the compensation and benefits modules of the HRIS interface flawlessly with the provider's payroll input. Even when companies do payroll in-house, the payroll module is usually part of the accounting system rather than the HRIS, so it is critical that the interface between the HRIS and the payroll software work flawlessly (Walker, 1987).

In the majority of organizations, payroll is a function administered by finance or accounting rather than the HR department. HR departments feed compensation data and benefits coverage (and employees' coverage choices) to payroll, which makes sure that all appropriate federal, state, and local income and payroll taxes are withheld at the correct rate and that any deductions for benefits are also withheld at the correct rate. Payroll usually has the responsibility for keeping track of income and payroll tax rates and applicable salary levels. Payroll results are fed back into the general accounting system by payroll. Because labor costs are the largest variable cost for most organizations, it is critical for the organizations' financial well-being that payroll records be accurate and timely. Because the paycheck is a signal of the employment relationship and because many employees rely on their paychecks to meet bills that are due, it is critical that the payroll system deliver accurate and timely paychecks or bank transfers. Little will anger or demoralize an employee more than a missing or an inaccurate paycheck or transfer. In short, payroll is a transactional task that must be flawless.

Payroll is the most heavily outsourced HRM function. Great economies of scale can be achieved by a payroll processor with respect to keeping up with the intricate requirements of income and payroll tax deductibles or maintaining (and upgrading) software that ensures that payroll is accurate and completed in a timely manner. However, outsourcing companies do not work in a vacuum, and compensation and benefits functions must deliver data to the outsourcer, and the accounting and finance functions must receive data back from the outsourcer. Also, some companies argue that integrating the HR and payroll functions makes sense and saves data entry and labor costs while providing greater accuracy and timeliness (Gale, 2002).

Typical Data Inputs

Data entered into the payroll system from inside the organization include compensation data, benefits data, and other payroll addition data (e.g., special awards) and deductions data (e.g., union dues, wage garnishments for child support, credit union repayment installments). Time and attendance data are usually handled in a special module, and data from this module are also fed into payroll (Robb, 2004). Data external to the organization include federal, state, and local income and payroll tax rules that allow the organization to withhold appropriate amounts from each employee's paycheck. There may be payments made to individuals who are not active employees. Although these are usually taken care of in a separate COBRA module, there may even be payments from ex-employees for the continuation of benefits. The most frequent data input are change data. Every time a new employee goes on the payroll, an employee changes status, an employee makes benefits elections changes, governments change tax or withholding rates, or the organization makes changes such as pay increases, data reflecting the changes have to go into the payroll system. Many of these elections can be performed by employees themselves using the self-service capability of a Web-based payroll system. Through a direct entry screen (shown in Figure 14.6), the employee can enter or update any data that he or she controls, such as the number of exemptions or extra withholding, without the need for HR intervention. For an international company, the system could automatically present any financial data in whatever currency the employee requested.

In addition to internal and external data, the system generates data that it stores and uses over time. For example, in 2010, FICA (**Federal Insurance Contributions Act**, i.e., Social Security) taxes were withheld on the first \$106,800 of income and the maximum tax withheld for any employee was \$6,621. Payroll must keep a running total of FICA paid to date so that it does not deduct too much from the employee's paycheck.

Typical Reports

There are a number of standard payroll reports. These show—for the organization as a whole (or for subunits)—the actual amount paid to employees for a period

Figure 14.6 Screen Used for Entering Data for a Paycheck

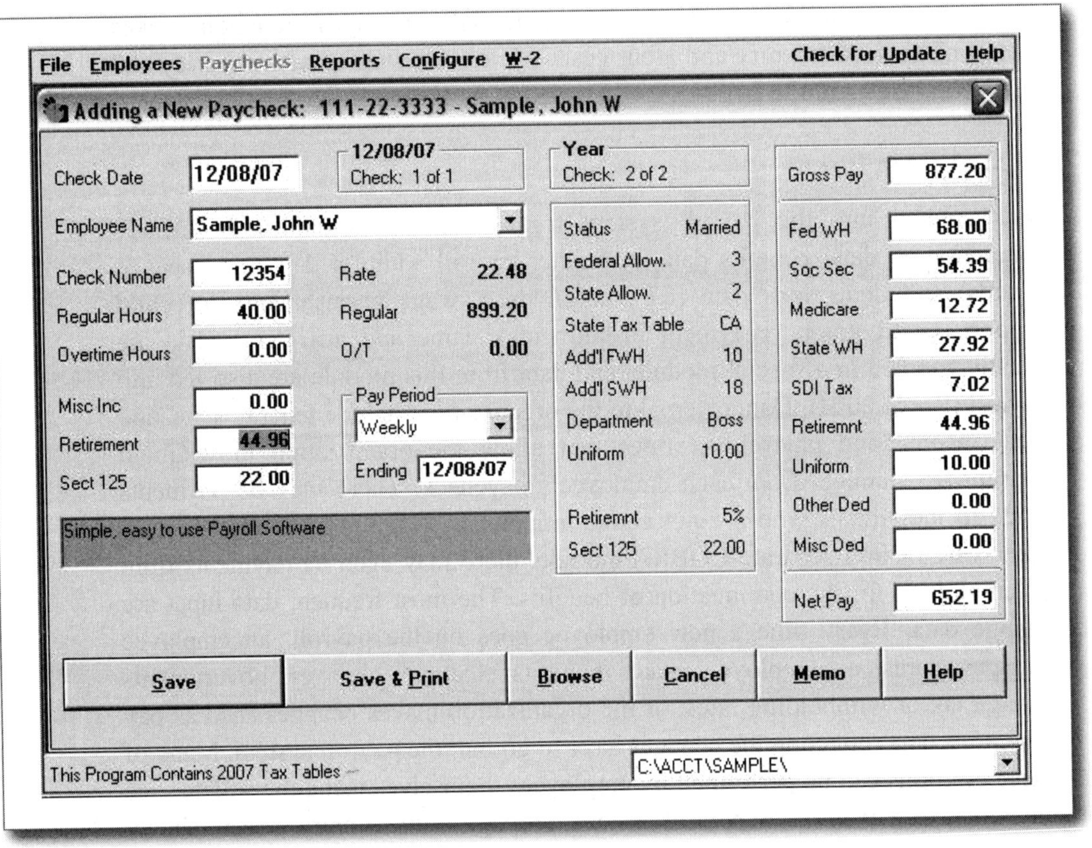

(and cumulatively) and the amounts deducted for various purposes. Reports go to federal, state, and local agencies, including taxing authorities, and to benefits providers. Employees receive reports with their paychecks or notices of deposit; the report shows gross pay and all deductions. Usually year-to-date accumulations are also provided.

Data Outflows

Payroll data go to accounting; federal, state, and local agencies; benefits outsourcing firms; and individual benefit program providers. These payroll data are the input for a variety of processes in those units, so it is critical that systems interface flawlessly. Interface becomes even more complicated as external systems communicate not only with payroll but also with compensation, benefits, and other HR systems.

Decision Support

Payroll data are not usually used by HR departments or line managers for decision-making purposes. They are used extensively for audit purposes. Employees, on the other hand, like to know from time to time how much money they have earned in a given year, how much income and payroll taxes have been paid, and the level of pretax and deferred tax contributions made for various benefits. This information can be made available through a self-service system. Similarly, a self-service system can allow employees to increase withholding or make other (limited) changes in their pay.

SUMMARY

The overall goal of this chapter was to provide the reader with a broad understanding of the role and focus of HRIS in supporting performance management, compensation, benefits, and payroll processes. The combined PM, compensation, benefits, and payroll systems constitute some of the most important parts of the HRIS. Money may not be at the forefront of how people talk about the organization and their linkages to it, but, if performance ratings result in lower than expected salary increases, bonuses are miscalculated, benefits elections are not implemented, or a paycheck is wrong or (worse still) not delivered, employees become vocal. Because pay and benefits constitute the largest variable cost to any organization and the largest cost overall to many organizations, it is critical that managers plan, track, and audit outlays on a real-time basis. A significant proportion of the data and reports owed to federal, state, and local agencies comes from the compensation, benefits, and payroll modules. The consequences of inaccurate, misleading, or missing data and reports include embarrassment, fines, and even jail time. And these are the risks associated with poor data from just the transactional part of these modules. Thus, one of the major purposes of an HRIS is to help organizations administer their performance management, compensation, benefits, and payroll systems.

A key part of strategic HR is aligning employee behaviors with the strategic intent of the organization. It is important to hire the best people and provide them with the training and development needed. Without PM, the success of hiring strategies is unknown, and, similarly, the need for training and development interventions is unknown. PM systems support the translation of corporate strategy into individual performance plans. Compensation and benefits systems can be used to hire the right people, retain the high performers, and motivate all employees to perform at a higher level. Compensation can also be used to motivate poor performers out of the organization. As systems technology has progressed, managers have become better able to enhance the performance of their direct reports and to tailor compensation and benefits programs to attract, retain, and motivate the best. Thus, the importance of understanding the central role of an HRIS in assisting managers in making key decisions regarding performance, compensation, benefits, and payroll cannot be underestimated.

KEY TERMS

attraction awards
base pay
Consolidated Omnibus Budget Reduction Act (COBRA)
corrective feedback
direct report
Employee Retirement Income Security Act (ERISA)
exempt workers
Fair Labor Standards Act (FLSA)
Federal Insurance Contributions Act (FICA)
flexplans
incentive pay
individual development plan (IDP)
individual retirement account (IRA)
job evaluation
market benchmarking
nonexempt workers
Office of Federal Contract Compliance Programs (OFCCP)
pension plans
performance management (PM)
performance observation
performance planning
perquisites
positive feedback
recognition awards
retention awards
Sarbanes-Oxley Act (SOX)
simplified employee pension (SEP)
360° appraisals
Troubled Asset Relief Program (TARP)

DISCUSSION QUESTIONS

1. Discuss how a manager might make sure that the performance plan for each of her direct reports was driven by organizational strategy and the business plan. How can information systems support this goal?
2. Merit increases require a single "performance" number, while most incentive plans have multiple and varying performance measures. How can the PM system meet both needs?
3. Compensation strategy includes how competitive the organization wants to be, the number of different compensation systems the organization wants to have, the mix of various reward and benefit components, and the basis of increases. Discuss the data

inflows required if an organization wanted to automate its compensation design and administration processes.

4. Both PM and benefits information systems make provisions for employee access and input. What access would you provide in each of these systems, and what leeway would you provide employees in reading, entering, and changing data?

5. A lot of compensation information is available to employees today on the Web (e.g., www.salary.com), and much of it is inaccurate. How can an organization assure employees that they are fairly compensated (assume they are) when public data suggest otherwise?

6. Flexible benefit plans are common today. Discuss ways in which employers can ensure that employees make good choices about the benefits and benefit levels that they choose within the benefits information system itself.

7. Payroll and benefits are commonly outsourced. Discuss which parts of PM, compensation, benefits, and payroll you would consider outsourcing, justifying your views.

CASE STUDY: GRANDVIEW GLOBAL FINANCIAL SERVICES, INC.

Grandview Global Financial Services is an international corporation providing multiple financial services. Although it is one of the smaller players in the field, the firm has about 20,000 employees worldwide. Corporate strategy has focused on serving a niche market comprised of high net worth individuals, providing them with all the wealth management services they require. These services include investments, insurance, banking, real estate, financial planning, and related services.

The linchpin making all these services work well is the quality of the employees—the degree to which they are motivated to provide "over-the-top" attention to clients' needs. Clients have come to expect this level of service regardless of where they might happen to be and regardless of the time. Because of clients' high expectations, every employee is expected to provide flawless service.

As it has expanded globally, Grandview has hired employees from all the countries in which it does business. While all employees are expected to speak English, business is conducted in nine different languages in 45 locations. Grandview has invested heavily in developing a uniform corporate culture but has not succeeded in doing so in all locations.

One difficulty has been the PM and reward systems. Each geographic area developed its own PM tools, which reflect the national culture and the past experiences of local employees. There are a variety of systems using different performance criteria. Most of the PM materials are in Microsoft Word. Some of the systems seem to work all right, while others do not. None of the systems are coordinated, except to the extent that final performance ratings are sent to the Grandview corporate HR department. There has been enormous push back and noncompliance with PM policies from the employees because of the difficulty of the paper performance process as well as the nine different languages being used worldwide.

Rewards systems are similarly localized. Base pay, incentive systems, and benefits have grown up in each geographic location in accord with local market practices, laws, and customs. The complexity and number of Excel spreadsheets needed to manage the financial targets and the resulting compensation plans for that many employees have created perceived and actual inequities. It is difficult to transfer employees across geographic areas because of the different systems in place, and awareness that employees in different locations have very different terms and conditions has created morale problems.

Corporate HR has PM and rewards modules in its HRIS covering U.S. employees, but this takes care of only about 60% of Grandview's employee population. An executive rewards module does cover about 2,000 senior executives worldwide, but all foreign data are sent from different locations and entered into the module at headquarters. Part of the historic reason for this process involves the legal requirements concerning privacy of information in the EU and some other locales; it is easier to get executives to grant permission for the transmission of specific data when those data are used to calculate stock option awards and other executive incentive payments granted by the corporation.

Corporate HR would like to move away from local systems and institute a corporate-wide system that relies neither on Word documents for performance reviews nor on Excel spreadsheets for the resulting compensation plans that result from the overall performance ratings. It was thought that common systems for PM and rewards would support a more unified culture and help translate Grandview's corporate strategy into individual performance plans worldwide.

The ideal system would be a Web-based, multilingual, integrated PM and compensation system. The PM system would be accessible by managers and their direct reports and would be tied to corporate strategy and the current business plan. Managers and their direct reports could access the system at any time to see performance criteria, measures, and standards and to look at current progress against standards. The rewards and benefits modules, while based on local law and customs, would be standardized with respect to process, fostering a more uniform rewards culture. It is critical to HR managers that the technology selected be flexible enough so that yearly changes to the application could be made efficiently and legal requirements in different locations could be accommodated, as well as changes in those requirements.

Because the performance goals are based on financial targets and employees' merit and incentive payments are directly related to employee performance as well as Grandview's overall results, all necessary functionality for the compensation process should be built into the performance system. At year end, results should be able to be imported directly from corporate financial systems and used to generate performance reviews and compensation plans for the employees. The resultant pay increases and bonus payments would be fed directly into the payroll system already in use by Grandview in the United States and abroad. The system administrators should be able to ensure worldwide compliance with the performance process directly from the system through a variety of reports.

Case Study Questions

1. What is the role of PM in establishing and maintaining corporate culture?
2. What is the role of compensation and benefits in establishing and maintaining corporate culture?
3. Since laws, labor markets, and customs relevant to PM, compensation, and benefits differ from country to country, does it make sense to try to maintain a common global process for managing each of these areas?
4. Given all the cross-country differences, why would a global organization want to have a common HRIS?
5. How should Grandview go about implementing a global PM system?
6. How should Grandview go about implementing a global rewards system?
7. How should Grandview go about implementing a global benefits system?
8. How should Grandview go about implementing a global HRIS to manage these functions?

REFERENCES

Ashley, D. (2006). Intuitive technologies increase employee adoption of human resource solutions. *Compensation & Benefits Review, 38*(1), 62–68.

Banks, C. G., & May, K. E. (1999). Performance management: The real glue in organizations. In A. I. Kraut & A. K. Korman (Eds.), *Evolving practices in human resource management: Responses to a changing world of work* (pp. 118–145). San Francisco: Jossey-Bass.

Bernardin, H. J., Hagan, C. M., Kane, J. S., & Villanova, P. (1998). Effective performance management: A focus on precision, customers, and situational constraints. In J. W. Smither (Ed.), *Performance appraisal: State of the art in practice* (pp. 3–48). San Francisco: Jossey-Bass.

Bing, J. W. (2004). Metrics for assessing human process on work teams. *IHRIM Journal, 8*(6), 26–31.

Brink, S., & McDonnell, S. (2003). e-Compensation. In *The e-merging technologies series go-to-guide* (pp. 4.1–4.18). Burlington, MA: IHRIM Press.

Ceccon, A. (2004). The real value statement: Aggregating pay and benefits on the Internet. *Compensation & Benefits Review, 36*(6), 53–58.

Charles, E. W., Kurlander, P., & Savage, B. (2000). Tracking sales performance. *ACA News, 43*(3), 38–41.

Cocks, D. J., & Gould, D. (2001). Sales compensation: A new technology-enabled strategy. *Compensation & Benefits Review, 33*(1), 27–31.

Cohen, A. J., & Hall, M. E. (2005). Automating your performance and competency evaluation process. *WorldatWork Journal, 14*(3), 64–70.

Dawson, S. (1997). Leveraging an intranet for employee self-service: A Q & A with Unisys corporation. *IHRIM.link, 2*(3), 54–65.

Evans, E. M. (2001). Internet-age performance management: Lessons from high-performing organizations. In A. J. Walker (Ed.), *Web-based human resources: The technologies and trends that are transforming HR* (pp. 65–82). New York: McGraw-Hill.

Flowers, L. A., Tudor, T. R., & Trumble, R. R. (1997). Computer-assisted performance appraisal systems. *Journal of Compensation and Benefits, 12*(6), 34–35.

Forrer, S. E., & Leibowitz, Z. B. (1991). *Using computers in human resources: How to select and make the best use of automated HR systems.* San Francisco: Jossey-Bass.

Gale, S. F. (2002). How three companies merged HR and payroll. *Workforce, 81*(1), 64–67.

How HRIS can help with SOX compliance. (2005). *HR Focus, 82*(10), 7, 10.

Jones, S. D., & Schilling, D. J. (2000). *Measuring team performance: A step-by-step, customizable approach for managers, facilitators, and team leaders.* San Francisco: Jossey-Bass.

Koski, L. (2003). Executive/manager self-service: Stat Street Corporation's annual incentive program. *Compensation & Benefits Review, 35*(2), 21–25.

McCormack, J. (2004). Compliance tools: Technology can help HR stay on the right side of the law. *HR Magazine, 49*(3), 95–98.

Menefee, J. A. (2000). The value of pay data on the Web: Nominal or real? *Workspan, 43*(9), 25–28.

Meyer, G. (1998). 360 on the net: A computer toolkit for multirater performance feedback. *HR Magazine, 43*(11), 46–50.

Moynihan, J. J. (2000). HIPPA compliance offers human resource department savings. *Healthcare Financial Management, 54*(3), 82–83.

Perlmutter, A. L. (2002). Taking motivation and recognition online. *Compensation & Benefits Review, 34*(2), 70–74.

Robb, D. (2004). Marking time. *HR Magazine, 49*(7), 111–115.

Sherman, E. (2005). Use technology to stay in SOX compliance. *HR Magazine, 50*(5), 95–99.

Stegner, R., & Kofahl, B. (2004). Case study: Human performance improvement model at work. *IHRIM Journal, 8*(6), 18–20.

Stiffler, M. A. (2001). Incentive compensation and the Web. *Compensation & Benefits Review, 33*(1), 15–19.

Teer, M. S. (1997). Surfing for benefits. *IHRIM.link, 2*(3), 66–74.

Tobin, N. (2002). Can technology ease the pain of salary surveys? *Public Personnel Management, 31*(1), 65–77.

U.S. Department of Labor & U.S. Department of Justice. (1978). Uniform guidelines on employee selection procedures. (1978). *Federal Register, 43*(166), 38290–39309.

Van De Voort, D. M., & McDonnell, S. W. (2003). Computers and compensation. In W. A. Caldwell (Ed.), *The compensation guide* (pp. 21–32). Minneapolis, MN: Thomson/West.

Walker, A. J. (1987). *HRIS development: A project team guide to building an effective personnel information system.* New York: Van Nostrand Reinhold.

Weeks, B. (2000). Setting sales force compensation in the Internet age. *Compensation & Benefits Review, 32*(2), 25–42.

Wright, A. (2003). Tools for automating complex compensation programs. *Compensation & Benefits Review, 35*(6), 53–61.

Zingheim, P. K., & Schuster, J. R. (2004). What's the next great pay and reward innovation? Business value, paying for skill, and the Internet! *IHRIM Journal, 8*(5), 47–50.

Zingheim, P. K., & Schuster, J. R. (2005). Evaluating human resource pay and reward computer and Web products. *Compensation & Benefits Review, 37*(5), 42–45.

Chapter 15

HRIS and International Human Resource Management

Michael J. Kavanagh and John W. Michel

EDITORS' NOTE

Chapter 1 emphasized the emergence of the global marketplace as one of the most important trends in the field of HRM. In particular, Figure 1.2 in Chapter 1 indicates that the system model of organizational functioning centered on an HRIS exists within each country's national cultural environment. This cultural envelope of a country indicates there will be differences between countries, and these differences will influence HR programs and practices. In this chapter, some of the significant differences between **domestic-only HRM** and **international human resource management (IHRM)** in **multinational enterprises (MNEs)** are covered, and some of the additional HRM issues involved in an international organization are also described. To understand the operation of multiple companies in the global marketplace, we identify the different organizational structures that exist. The importance of the influence of national culture on the external environment in which the firm competes for market share is highlighted. The external environment also has a major impact on the IHRM department's activities and program—that is, the management of the human capital of a firm. This impact, in terms of its effects on IHRM programs, is discussed. Naturally, these added international issues and additional complexities pose significant challenges for the design, development, implementation, and use of an HRIS in a global company, and the ways in which these challenges are met will be covered.

CHAPTER OBJECTIVES

After completing this chapter, you should be able to

- Understand the differences between domestic-only[1] and international HRM
- Identify the types of organizational forms used for competing internationally
- Understand the different types of employees who work in MNEs
- Discuss the staffing process for individuals working in MNEs
- Understand the problems that handling expatriates poses for the IHRM department
- Describe the training needs of and programs for international assignees
- Reconcile the difficulties of home-country and host-country performance appraisals
- Identify the characteristics of a good international compensation plan
- Understand the modifications necessary for using HRIS applications in IHRM

HRIS IN ACTION

Skylor Electronics,[2] an MNE with headquarters in Seattle, Washington, was having considerable difficulty with **expatriate failure** in its overseas subsidiaries. Although there were a number of failures in the **European Union (EU)** countries, the largest failure rate was in its subsidiary in China. The vice president for HR, Marvin Russell, was deeply concerned since the costs of expatriate failure were very high, from $145,000 in the EU to over $400,000 in China. These comprised the direct costs, that is, dollars lost. The indirect costs of having the expatriate return early from the assignment were also quite heavy in terms of the negative image it created for the company in the local economy. In fact, the plant manager for one of the subsidiaries in China refused to accept any more American expatriates until they "could function in the Chinese culture."

HR Vice President Marvin Russell was looking for answers to this problem, and he called a meeting with Director of Overseas Operations Elaine Peterson and Director of Career Development Bill Seamon. Elaine was also quite upset with this expatriate failure because it was very disruptive in terms of meeting production deadlines and maintaining quality. Bill did not understand why there was a problem since he, along with Director of Training Dawn Fisher, had expatriates attend a three-hour orientation meeting that provided information on their destination countries. As Bill noted, each expatriate saw a 45-minute film, which was followed by a question-and-answer period. Then, the expatriate was given written material on the country.

Marvin indicated that he had spoken directly to several expatriates who returned early to determine the reason for the high failure rate. In general, each former expatriate had mentioned "not being prepared" for the new country and its culture. This experience of "culture shock" was most severe for the failed expatriates from China. After some discussion, it was clear that no one really knew what all the problems were with the expatriate failure problem and that no systematic data existed to help understand the problem. Marvin directed Bill and Dawn to investigate this problem and to provide a report in two weeks. Elaine indicated that she would provide a member of her staff to help with this investigation.

Two weeks later, Bill and Dawn presented their report to Marvin and Elaine. The gist of the report was that the predeparture training for the expatriates and their families was completely inadequate. In fact, there was no training for expatriates' families, and one of the most common problems that led to the premature return of the expatriate was that the spouse was extremely unhappy. Bill and Dawn proposed a predeparture, two-week training program for potential expatriates and their families as well as a trip, paid by the company, to the country where the expatriate was to be assigned. When Marvin objected to the costs of this program, Bill and Dawn were able to show by completing a cost-benefit analysis (CBA), as described in Chapter 7, that the costs saved by reducing expatriate failure exceeded the costs of the predeparture training program.

INTRODUCTION: INCREASING IMPORTANCE OF INTERNATIONAL HUMAN RESOURCE MANAGEMENT (IHRM)

As noted in Chapter 1, the **globalization of business** is one of the major changes in the world of work. Tsui (2007) notes that exports as a percentage of world gross domestic products (GDP) increased from 11.6% in 1970 to 30.7% in 2006. Further illustrating this change, the competitive environment for businesses is the topic of a recent executive action report from The Conference Board (Iyer, 2005), which raised this question: "Globalization: Will Your Company Be Left Standing?" This question provides evidence for the impact that globalization is having worldwide.

Perhaps one of the major changes in the world's business economy has been the formation of regional free-trade zones. The passage of the **North American Free Trade Agreement (NAFTA)** in 1994 established the world's largest free market, increasing trade between Mexico, the United States, and Canada. Subsequently, the EU was formed and includes more than 25 member countries (a membership that's still growing) engaged in free trade. Other trade agreements, such as the **Association of Southeast Asian Nations (ASEAN)**, the **East Asia Economic Caucus (EAEC)**, the **Asia-Pacific Economic Cooperation (APEC)**, and the **South Asian Association for Regional Cooperation (SAARC)**, have improved trading relationships in Asia. One can only expect that there may be an African, and perhaps a Middle Eastern, free-trade zone in the future.

As illustrated in the diagram in Chapter 1 (see Figure 1.2), organizational functioning is contained *within* **a national culture envelope**. There is little doubt that the external environment for global business is significantly affected by the country in which it occurs, that is, the host country. The host country and its culture will affect all the factors in the **external environment**: government regulations, labor market, societal concerns, technology, HRM research, and competition. As noted by Bartlett (2002),

> The most important corporate transformation in 75 years is taking place right now. It will radically change human resource management and its role in the organization. . . . Behind this transformation are numerous forces, such as privatization, deregulation, the information revolution, and above all, globalization. (p. xi)

Many of the issues raised by the globalization of business and, in turn, by changes in the IHRM function are clearly caused by factors in the external environment. However, there are still **internal issues** to consider in the effective globalization of an MNE. As noted by Beaman (2002), "The heritage of the industrial age prevents many organizations from creating the organizational structures, operational infrastructures, HR policies, and company cultures required to effectively function in the global economy" (p. v). As will be covered in this chapter, there has been considerable progress in handling these internal issues, and much of it has come from the implementation of an HRIS in these MNEs.

There are a variety of factors that have led to the increased globalization of business and the increased importance of the IHRM function. These factors include the following: (1) a dramatic increase in global competition; (2) deregulation in the United States, Germany, and other industrialized countries, which has changed the domestic business environment in those countries; (3) an increase in international mergers and acquisitions; and (4) an increased awareness of the existence of talented human capital throughout the world. Globalization means managing human resources worldwide.

One cannot overlook that one of the major factors related to a firm's choosing to have an international presence is the availability and cost-effectiveness of computer technology. Computer technology has had a major influence on the acquisition and use of physical and financial resources, as well as greatly enhancing the marketing capabilities of MNEs. However, the most important impact of computer technology has been in HRM. Improved communications, worldwide recruiting and selecting, and better talent and performance management programs tied to career planning are only a few of the HR programs in MNEs that have been improved by the use of computer technology. In this chapter, we will examine the characteristics of MNEs and the management of people within these enterprises. In addition, we will be covering the various ways in which computer technology and a well-developed HRIS have affected the field of IHRM.[3]

Types of International Business Operations

In today's global economy, organizations tend to compete based on different levels of participation in international markets (Noe, Hollenbeck, Gerhart, & Wright, 2006). International business operations differ primarily by their level of global participation on a continuum from an international corporation to a global corporation. Although many organizations have only limited global scope, a growing number, such as Dell and Microsoft, have a large number of personnel and facilities throughout the world (Bohlander & Snell, 2007). The following section provides a brief description of the general types of international business operations described by their level of global participation.

International Corporation

An **international corporation** uses its existing core competencies to expand operations into foreign markets (Bohlander & Snell, 2007). These organizations compete in the global marketplace by exporting existing products and eventually opening facilities in other countries. While their corporate headquarters reside in the parent country, international corporations have foreign operations in one or more host countries. Companies operating as international corporations include Honda, General Electric, and Procter & Gamble (see Bohlander & Snell, 2007).

This type of international business operation presents various unique challenges for the HRM function of the organization. Two issues particularly relevant to international corporations are the host country's legal system and the host country's national culture. A legal issue might arise because of a country's minimum wage, for example. In some countries, the minimum wage is relatively high, driving up labor costs (Noe et al., 2006). Examples of cultural differences affecting international corporations are communications and morale problems.

Multinational Corporation

A **multinational corporation** is a more complex international business operation. Multinational corporations operate as fully autonomous units in multiple countries, in an attempt to capitalize on lower production and distribution costs (Bohlander & Snell, 2007; Noe et al., 2006). An example of a multinational corporation is General Motors (GM). While GM's headquarters and some of its operations are located in the United States, many of its manufacturing facilities have been relocated to places such as Mexico and China with the goal of reducing production costs by paying lower employee wages. Locating facilities to China has allowed GM to sell to the Asian markets with reduced distribution costs. The HRM issues experienced by multinational corporations are similar to those encountered by international corporations, but exacerbated.

One approach taken by multinational corporations has been to hire expatriates from countries other than the parent country to help with staffing and management issues (Noe et al., 2006). However, according to Noe and others (2006), although hiring expatriates from other countries has its advantages, it often requires greater cross-training of cultural and managerial skills.

Global Corporation

Global corporations are similar to multinational corporations; however, the **global corporation** integrates its worldwide operations through a centralized home office (Bohlander & Snell, 2007). Multinational corporations produce and distribute identical products and services worldwide. Global corporations, on the other hand, emphasize flexibility and mass customization to meet the needs of differing customer groups worldwide (Noe et al., 2006). Ford represents an example of a global corporation. Ford offers two different lines of automobiles, one to its American consumers and the other to its European consumers. For example, it meets the need of European consumers for smaller, more fuel-efficient cars by offering the Ka—a car similar to Daimler's smart car.

Because of this integrative international focus, global corporations must manage their human resources through a transnational HRM system. This type of system is characterized by three attributes: (1) it is essential that HR decisions be made from a global rather than a national perspective, (2) it is important that the company's management be composed of people from all over the world, and (3) it is imperative that decision-making and planning processes include people from a variety of cultures and backgrounds (Noe et al., 2006).

The type of international business operation chosen by the corporation will inevitably influence the way in which the organization manages its human resources. It is feasible to conceptualize organizations on a continuum based on their level of global participation, from the domestic corporation representing the lowest level of global participation to the global corporation representing the highest level of global participation. With this in mind, we provide in the following sections of this chapter a discussion of issues surrounding the management of human resources internationally. Although these distinctions among MNEs are important, the actual structure of the MNE determines its effectiveness. There is no "best structure" that fits the distribution and marketing needs of all MNEs. Perhaps having a flexible approach to structure is the best way to manage an MNE.

Going Global

For international and multinational corporations, becoming a global corporation is an important step. Beaman (2009) calls this decision "**going global**." Jeitosa

Group International, in collaboration with the **International Association for Human Resource Information Management (IHRIM)**, completed a survey of 97 multinational organizations from diverse industry sectors that focused on the factors that lead an MNE to "go global." The survey was designed to answer these questions:

1. How does an organization decide when it should go global?
2. How does it determine whether or not its HR department and HRIS[4] are ready?
3. Are its business and HR functions capable of supporting a move to a global level for the organization?

As depicted in Figure 15.1, there are a number of challenges that organizations face when going global. The figure presents the percentage of survey respondents

Figure 15.1 Top Challenges Organizations Face in Going Global

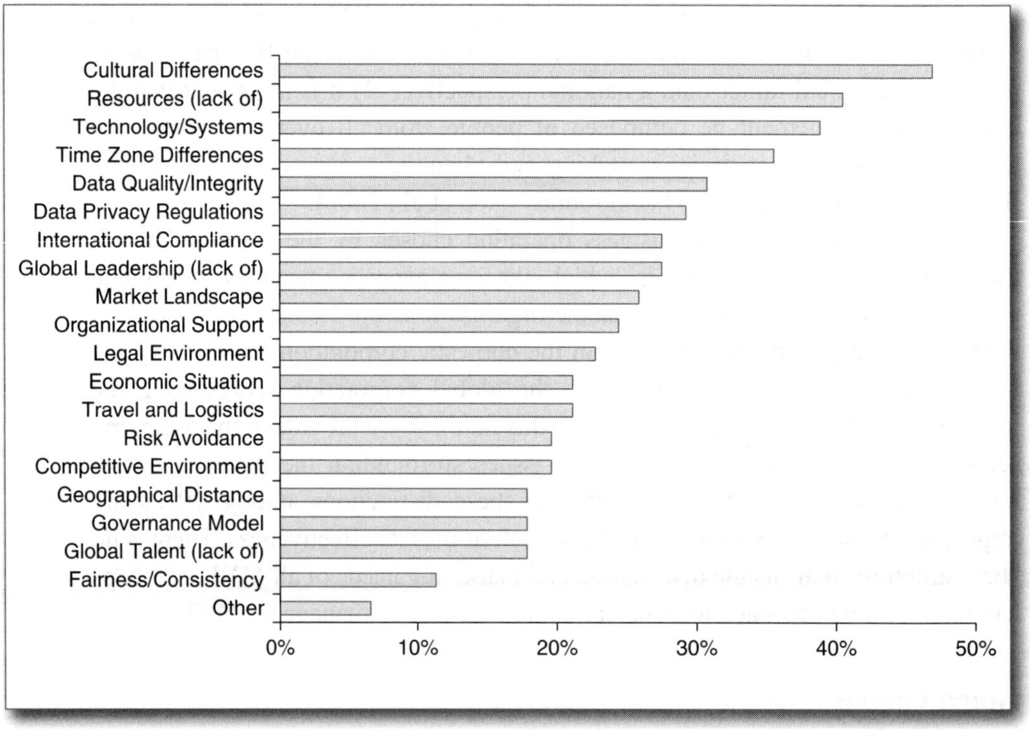

SOURCE: Beaman (2009, p. 3). Reprinted with permission.

who felt a particular factor was challenging. The top four—cultural differences (47%), lack of resources (40%), technology/systems issues (39%), and time zone differences (35%)—are among the top IHRM-related challenges facing global organizations (Adler, 2002; Briscoe & Schuler, 2004; Dowling & Welch, 2005; Evans, Pucik, & Barsoux, 2002). However, it is important to note that the remaining issues are quite significant for organizations moving to a global status. Many of them are the result of organizations being established in countries whose circumstances and cultures are different from those of the home country. For example, data quality, data privacy, international compliance, the legal environment and economic situation of host countries, and risk avoidance are all factors that have been, or will be, covered in this chapter to describe the complexity and managerial issues that MNEs face when they expand to a global status.

As well as asking about the challenges faced by organizations going global, the survey also queried the respondents about the successes they experienced during this transition. Figure 15.2 contains the percentage of respondents in terms of the top successes they experienced. It is interesting to note that the top successes were in the area of cultural diversity/appreciation (52%), since cultural differences were the top challenge faced by organizations going global (see Figure 15.1). One could possibly conclude that organizations anticipating going global recognize the challenge of this process and thus put more resources and time into handling this

Figure 15.2 Top Successes Organizations Experience in Going Global

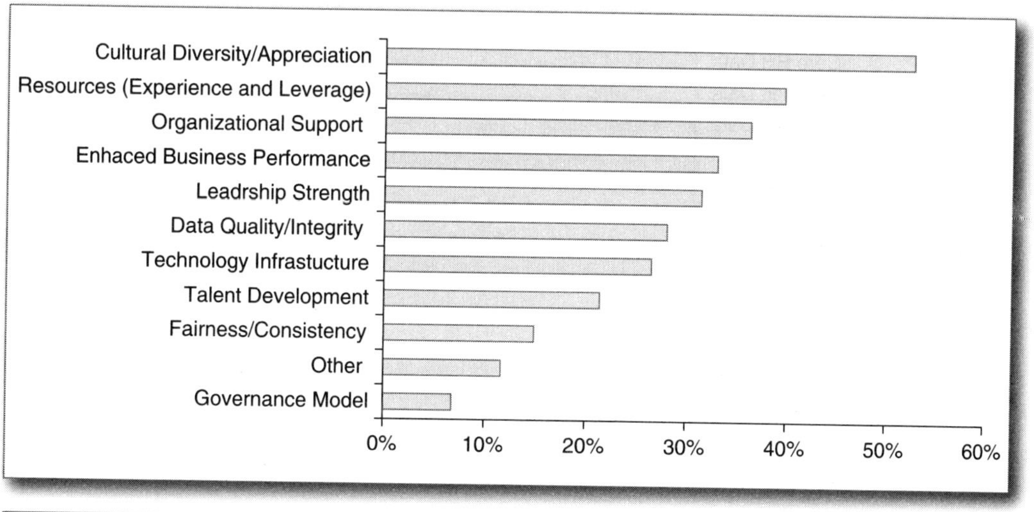

SOURCE: Beaman (2009, p. 5). Reprinted with permission.

issue. The other successes in Figure 15.2, in general, could reflect an understanding by management that leadership strength, organizational support, experience resources, and talent development are quite important for the transition to global status and thus have received increased attention.

The survey also asked the respondents what HR **global data** was being maintained in their HR systems. It is interesting to note that the core HR data, which was referred to as the basic employee information module (BEIM) in Chapter 10, ranks first in terms of the percentage of respondents who indicated that this HR core global data was in their systems. As noted by Beaman (2009), "As expected, the majority of global data maintained is in the core HR (86%) and compensation (71%) areas—the most basic types of information and the most mature areas of HR systems deployment" (p. 4). Note that performance (45%) and payroll (42%) global data are maintained by just less than half of the respondents, whereas talent and benefits have the least global HR data.[5]

One conclusion is that becoming a global organization is complex and challenging. Beaman (2009) concludes the report as follows:

> The world of globalization is complex, but comprehensible; it is daunting, yet exciting; it is challenging and achievable! Studying the leading practices of others who have "gone global" before is an effective way to avoid the traps and to develop a path forward. Globalization is a journey, not a destination. (p. 19)

Figure 15.3 Global Data Maintained in HR Systems

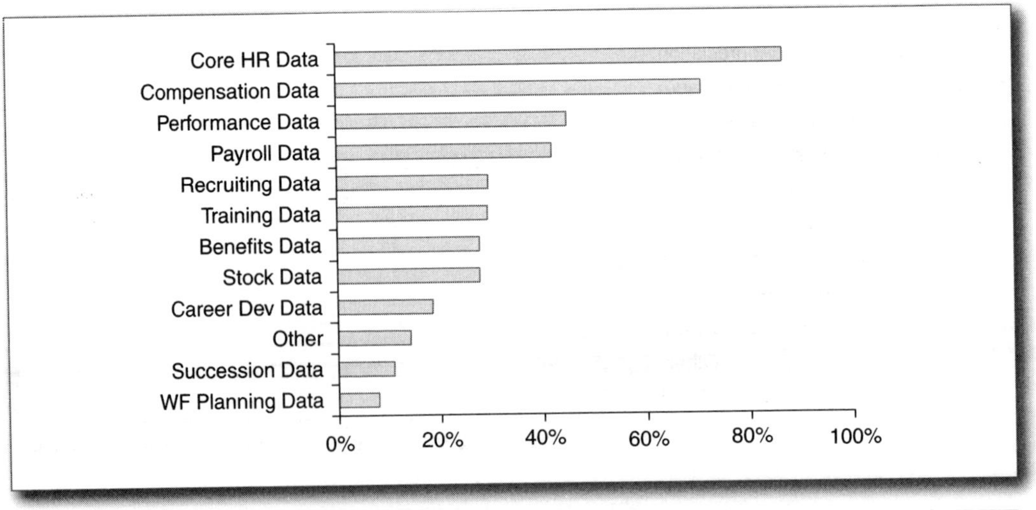

SOURCE: Beaman (2009, p. 4). Reprinted with permission.

The difficulties involved in managing the workforce of any MNE, including a global one, are covered in the remainder of this chapter.

Differences in HRM in MNEs

Even though there were a number of different types of international business operations described in the previous section, for convenience, these types will all be referred to as multinational enterprises (MNEs). As one might expect, there are significant differences in HRM programs and practices between a domestic enterprise and an MNE. Most organizations start out as domestic corporations (Noe et al., 2006). Because the domestic organization only operates in one labor market, managing its human resources is much easier than is the case for organizations operating in multiple countries. MNEs operate in multiple countries and must have information on the labor markets in all the countries in which they do business.

Another obvious difference is that there are three types of employees in a typical MNE, as opposed to one type in a domestic firm. These MNE employees include **parent-country nationals (PCNs)**, **host-country nationals (HCNs)**, and **third-country nationals (TCNs)**. PCNs are from the country in which the corporate headquarters of the MNE is located, while HCNs are from the countries where subsidiaries are located. Obviously, TCNs are employees from countries other than the parent or host countries. In spite of these differences in the types of employees hired by a domestic enterprise and an MNE, the major programs of HRM, for example, talent management and compensation, exist in both domestic and international organizations. However, the fact that an MNE competes in multiple countries versus the single-country orientation of a domestic company contributes to the complexity of IHRM.

An example of this complexity for the IHRM function is that, although operating in multiple countries provides a larger labor pool for the organization, it makes the talent management process multifaceted since applicants from different countries will have very different levels of education and experience. In particular, applicants from third world countries likely have very little formal education and less experience with technology. While these applicants can work in entry level or less technical positions, they will require greater training and preparation if the organization wants to promote them. In a similar fashion, compensation levels and policies will differ between home country and other MNE employees. It is likely that home-country employees will demand higher salaries and more benefits than other employees. MNEs will have to use IHRM systems to manage these different compensation policies. Other factors affect the complexity of IHRM. Dowling and

Welch (2005) argue that the complexity of international HR management can be attributed to six factors:

- More HR activities: An HR department in an international firm must be concerned with activities that would not be part of an HR department in a domestic firm, for example, relations with host governments; differences in labor laws and guidelines in the host country; and administrative details of the employees, such as international taxation, international relocation, orientation, and language training.

- The need for a broader perspective: The HR department and managers in MNEs need a broader worldview in dealing with PCNs, HCNs, and TCNs and a recognition of both the cultural differences among employees and the differences in work ethic and practices in the employees' home countries.

- More involvement in employees' personal lives: The IHRM department is more involved in the lives of employees in the areas of taxation, education, and even banking services. It also has to address the issue of visas and housing arrangements for PCNs (expatriates) and TCNs.

- Changes in emphasis of HR programs, such as compensation, managerial style, and tolerance of employee diversity, as the workforce mix of expatriates and locals varies. The immense pool of talent available to MNEs means a varying mix of PCNs, HCNs, and TCNs in the workforce. Consequently, a number of different languages will often be spoken. This situation would dictate language training to support a common language for employees and to improve communication in the working environment.

- Risk exposure: The IHRM department must be aware of the risks to its employees and keep them apprised of any significant problems (e.g., terrorist threats, impending war, environmental disasters). It must be prepared for any necessary evacuation of employees.

- Broader external influences: Many factors can affect the operation and activities of IHRM in multiple countries, such as government regulations and relations, the labor market, societal concerns, and the level of technology.

Managing Different Types of Employees in MNEs

Managing in the global business environment creates unique complexities for managers—especially expatriate managers. These complexities have been created due to the mix of PCNs, HCNs, and TCNs. In the past, organizations have relied on expatriates as a major source of staffing for their overseas operations (Schuler

& Tarique, 2007). Although the diversity of its workforce will depend on the type of international business operation adopted by the MNE, more and more, MNEs are shifting from an expatriate-focused workforce to a global workforce. Beaman (2008), discussing the organization of IHRM in MNEs, centralized versus decentralized, argues that "it is only by first 'thinking locally' to truly understand the needs of our local business communities, and then 'acting globally' to seamlessly knit together diverse business functions and (HR) systems into a holistic, global approach that we can build an effective, efficient and competitive organization" (p. 6).

In addition, it is important for management to understand the cultural differences between expatriates and the host- and third-country workforce. A study conducted by Inform Group of 79 international companies found that only 14% reported they were ready for the future use of this mixed group of potential employees in terms of their workforce planning (Babcock, 2007; see Chapter 11 for HRP). Understanding cultural differences can make it easier for managers to relate to and manage their global workforce. Some of the most important cultural factors include education, politics and law, and economics (see Bohlander & Snell, 2007).

Global Diversity and Inclusion

As previously noted, the globalization of business and corporations has been one of the major changes in the world of work. MNEs, in their search for human talent, are focused on a worldwide labor market. Organizations are recognizing the importance of having a global approach to the management of employees in order to remain competitive in the global marketplace, particularly when the MNEs are in need of additional employees to meet business needs. This search for new employees must take account of cultural differences in multiple countries by recognizing the importance of developing greater cross-cultural competence in their employees. In order to survive, organizations must manage differences so that employees from all backgrounds can be heard, be understood, and be able to work together productively. This organizational program and effort is known as managing diversity and inclusion of employees.

In a recent study measuring the degree of **global diversity and inclusion** within countries of the world, 546 senior executives of MNEs were surveyed and 40 senior executives in North America, Europe, Asia, and Latin America were interviewed to determine the extent to which various countries support diversity and inclusion in their organizations (Society for Human Resource Management [SHRM], 2009). The entire survey had questions focused on the opinions of the executives about the support for diversity and inclusion in the organizations in various countries of the world, reflecting the need for locating the human talent that is critical to the survival of MNEs. The Society for Human Resource Management (SHRM) commissioned the Economist Intelligence Unit (EIU), a subsidiary of The Economist Group, to conduct this international study on diversity and inclusion (SHRM, 2009). As noted in the introduction to the report, "Driven by a need to compensate for talent shortages—and compete in an increasingly diverse marketplace—companies are extending their recruiting and promotion efforts to groups that traditionally were under-represented or not present at all" (p. 5). According to the report, "This study was launched to provide a deeper understanding of Diversity and Inclusion issues on a global scale, and to offer insight into Diversity and Inclusion best practices worldwide" (p. 3).

The arguments for increased diversity and inclusion have their basis in equal employment legislation. However, two additional reasons for increasing diversity and inclusion in an MNE are (1) the moral issue of discrimination in hiring and promotion on the basis of gender and race and (2) the business case that increasing diversity and inclusion will improve the financial position of the MNE. The business case simply states that, if the consumer population is diverse, then it behooves an MNE to have a diverse workforce.

The EIU also researched the diversity readiness of 47 countries to create the **Global Diversity Readiness Index (DRI)**, an online spreadsheet tool that is available on the SHRM Web site (www.shrm.org/diversity). The DRI is used to rank the 47 countries on 39 separate indicators, which combine to create diversity scores on five categories. Using this tool, we can see the overall rankings in these five categories on a single page. A high ranking on the DRI indicates a higher degree of readiness to manage diversity and foster inclusion for that country. Individual country profiles show all the indicators of diversity and inclusion for each surveyed country on all of the diversity and inclusion indices. The importance of this tool is obvious for an MNE seeking to enter a new country by establishing a sales office or a production plant; if a country has a reputation (or cultural value) to support workplace diversity and inclusion, it is likely that it will be easier for MNEs to find available talent within the country. Finally, the DRI can help global managers understand the prevailing attitudes and values of the countries in which their companies are located.

Education

Having a workforce of PCNs, HCNs, and TCNs means the educational level of the workforce will be highly varied. It is important for managers to understand and deal with the human capital needs of a highly diverse workforce made up of individuals (1) coming from different cultural backgrounds, (2) possibly speaking different languages, and (3) having different educational experiences. These education differences require that managers provide a supportive work environment for their employees. One important aspect of support is training on (1) cultural differences, (2) verbal and nonverbal communication, and (3) specific skill sets particular to the employee's job.

Political and Legal Systems

The political and legal systems within the host country will affect the type of HR practices that can be used (Noe et al., 2006). The laws and regulations of the host country are determined in part by the societal norms of that country. For example, the United States has created laws governing issues such as equal employment opportunities and fair pay standards (Noe et al., 2006). However, these laws are specific to the United States and do not exist in other countries. In addition, free speech is a **cultural norm** in the United States and is protected by law. It is acceptable for organizations and individuals to speak out against the government if they do not like certain government regulations or taxes or if they think they are being unfairly treated. However, in other parts of the world, it may be highly inappropriate, and possibly dangerous, for organizations to speak out against the government.

Economic System

The economic system of the host country is one determinant of the way in which HR programs and practices are used. This economic system affects human capital primarily through its compensation system (Noe et al., 2006). Countries such as Germany, Switzerland, and Japan have strong educational systems and provide employees with good wages. In comparison, third world countries such as Sri Lanka, Afghanistan, and Haiti have poorer educational systems and provide substantially lower compensation to their workforces. A study by the U.S. Department of Labor (2002) indicates that the average compensation for employees in the manufacturing sector in Sri Lanka was \$0.42 per hour, compared with \$21.33 per hour for manufacturing employees in the United States. If the workforce of an MNE in Sri Lanka were composed of employees from both Sri Lanka and the United States, an equity issue might arise and must be managed effectively.

HR PROGRAMS IN GLOBAL ORGANIZATIONS

International Staffing

The complexities inherent in managing a global organization make staffing an especially important part of the IHRM system. When staffing for managerial and nonmanagerial positions, the MNE needs to determine if personnel will be selected from the home-country, host-country, or third-country talent pool.

As described by Bohlander and Snell (2007), each of these employee groups provides a different advantage for the MNE. A common issue for all of these employee groups, however, is the underutilization of and lower pay for female employees (Adlung, 2010). Adlung found that, in a number of European countries, females received approximately 25% less salary than their male counterparts. This point suggests that MNEs should emphasize hiring female employees and paying them fairly. Adlung suggests that companies could utilize an integrated talent management system such as PeopleSoft, TalentSoft, or SuccessFactors to leverage this untapped talent pool and reduce the salary gap between male and female employees.

Selecting Global Managers: Managing Expatriates

One of the most difficult, but important, responsibilities of the IHRM function is the selection of managers from the parent country for assignments in host countries.

Most of the literature on this topic is focused on the selection of expatriates, whether they are PCNs, HCNs, or TCNs. The reason expatriates can be from any of these three categories is that, at the managerial level in an MNE, these individuals will move from country to country. Thus, the term **expatriate** will be used to designate global managers, regardless of the home country. To understand the difficulty in selecting expatriates, we will discuss in this section (1) the **cultural environment of countries**, (2) expatriate failure and its causes, and (3) selection criteria and procedures for expatriates.

The Cultural Environment of Countries

One of the most important aspects of an expatriate's job that will significantly affect performance is his or her interaction with the local government and people of a country. Because of this interaction, most expatriates will experience **culture shock** as they move from country to country within an MNE. Culture shock can be mild, for example, for a German manager who relocates to a subsidiary plant in France, or quite severe, for example, for an Australian manager who moves to a subsidiary in Egypt. Thus, one of the most important tasks of the IHRM department is to gather information about the culture of countries where the MNE does business to try to estimate the cultural differences between the home countries of employees and the countries where they may be assigned. An HRIS can be very useful in that it can serve as a repository of this information, and, thus, **cultural profiles of countries** can be quickly generated.

Further emphasizing the importance of a country's culture, Briscoe and Schuler (2004) state,

> Knowledge about and competency in working with country and company cultures is the most important issue impacting the success of international business activity. And possibly the area of business that is most impacted by cultural differences is the human resource function. (p. 114)

Culture, as defined by Hofstede (1991), "is the collective programming of the mind which distinguishes the members of one group or category of people from another" (p. 6). Hofstede's research was the first systematic study of the dimensions of national culture, and he identified five dimensions on which the cultures of countries differ. In addition to Hofstede's work, other studies have examined differences in national culture (GLOBE Research Team, 2002; Trompenaars, 1992). Trompenaars, like Hofstede, found five distinct cultural factors that differentiated country cultures, while the Global Leadership and Organizational Behavior Effectiveness (GLOBE) research project categorized countries on nine cultural dimensions. Regardless of which study we examine, all authors agree that the cultural environment of a country has a strong effect on the management of employees and should be considered when selecting expatriates.[6]

To define the culture of a country, Bohlander and Snell (2007) list the following elements that will differentiate countries in terms of their cultural environment for international business: (1) education/human capital, (2) values/ideologies, (3) social structure, (4) religious beliefs, and (5) communication. Information gathered in these five categories could be used to create profiles of the cultural environment of countries in which the MNE does business. It is most important to emphasize that this information could be stored electronically in the HRIS and maintained by the IHRM department. Both of the major IT platforms, Oracle PeopleSoft (www.peoplesoft.com/corp/en/public_index.jsp) and SAP (www.sap.com/usa/index.epx), have this capability, or it can be customized by the MNE.

A final note on country culture: it will have an *effect on all the activities and programs* of the IHRM function, including selection, training, compensation, and performance management.

Expatriate Failure and Causes

Expatriate failure is defined as the return of an expatriate to the home country before the period of the assignment has been completed. Thus, expatriate failure represents an error in a selection decision. There is such an emphasis on expatriate failure because of its costs to the MNE. These costs are both direct and indirect. Direct costs include the actual money spent on selecting and training, relocation costs for the expatriate (and family), and salary. These costs can be quite substantial. However, indirect costs can frequently be higher than direct costs. Indirect costs are harder to quantify, but they could include loss of market share in the country, negative reactions from the host country's government, and possible negative effects on local employee morale. For example, expatriate failure could lead a local host government to insist that, in the future, only an HCN fill the position. Finally, there will be the indirect costs experienced by the returning expatriate in terms of personal failure, loss of respect by peers, and possibly negative influences on future promotions.

What are the causes of expatriate failure? Although there has been considerable research on this topic, the answer is not completely clear. It is safe to say that one cannot generalize from the research results to every expatriate situation; however, the results do provide a guide to the information that should be collected during the selection of expatriates. In general, one could state that the major factor affecting expatriate failure is the *inability to adjust to the new situation and culture* by the expatriate and her or his family.

In terms of specific reasons for expatriate failure, Dowling and Welch (2005) cite the global surveys of the Organizational Research Counselors (ORC) (2002) and the GMAC Global Relocation Services and Windham International (2002). The problems reported by expatriates and companies in these surveys were

- spouse/partner dissatisfaction,
- inability to adapt,
- difficulties with family adjustment in the new location,
- difficulties associated with different management styles,
- culture and language difficulties, and
- issues associated with the accompanying partner's career development.

Similarly, Briscoe and Schuler (2004) indicate that "a number of surveys and studies have found that the most important factors in the early return of expatriates . . . lie in the inability of their families (and/or themselves) to adjust to the foreign environment" (p. 242). The clear implication of these findings is that the expatriate's family or partner must be considered in the selection decision process.

Selection Criteria and Procedures for Expatriates

In selecting expatriates, IHRM professionals should remember that the selection process is an exchange between the organization and the employee. Furthermore, the prospective expatriate's family must be involved in the exchange. In terms of the utility of selection, that is its cost-effectiveness (covered in Chapter 12), making a mistake is extremely costly. IHRM professionals must be cognizant of the causes of expatriate failure when developing the selection procedures, for example, tests or interviews, and also have an understanding of the cross-cultural issues in the evaluation and recommendation of employees for an expatriate assignment.

The factors involved in the selection of expatriates can be divided into two general categories—individual and situational (Dowling & Welch, 2005). In the individual category are technical ability, **cross-cultural suitability**, and family requirements. Technical ability is quite clear and would include both managerial and technical skills. The person selected must be technically proficient in his or her field (e.g., electrical engineering) and also must have a good performance record as a manager. Technical ability is very important to the selection process, as indicated by the results of the ORC worldwide survey (2002), in that 72% of responding firms used it as the first screening criterion in their selection procedure. In selection terms, technical ability would be the *absolute minimum* requirement for the first screening of prospective employees for the assignment. Note that technical incompetence or poor performance is not mentioned as a cause of expatriate failure; however, job-related factors could possibly cause premature departure—for example, the nature of the job not being as described or the expatriate being unable to transfer technical or managerial skills to the new assignment.

The second individual factor, cross-cultural suitability, has several aspects. It could include language ability, cultural empathy, adaptability, and a positive attitude toward the assignment in the specific country being considered. Although technical ability is very important for success in the assignment, cross-cultural suitability is equally important since a number of the causes of expatriate failure are directly related to this factor.

The third individual factor, family requirements, has a great deal to do with the success of the expatriate's assignment. In all the research and surveys on causes for expatriate failure, the poor adjustment of the accompanying spouse or partner and children has been well documented as one of the major causes of expatriate failure. Although it is appropriate to use standard testing and interview techniques to assess the technical ability and cross-cultural suitability of potential expatriates, evaluation of these factors means the involvement of the family. Interviewing the candidate's spouse or partner and children regarding the assignment is frequently done. In addition, most MNEs have learned to build in a preassignment visit for the expatriate candidate and his or her family as part of the selection process. This involvement of the entire family in the selection process has become a common practice for MNEs. In fact, if there are two possible locations for the assignment, companies may encourage a preassignment visit to both countries.

With regard to the general factors that affect the assignment situation, Dowling and Welch (2005) list country and cultural requirements, language, and MNE requirements. Country and cultural requirements could include work permits and visas. Generally, the work permit is given to the expatriate, and the accompanying spouse or partner may not be permitted to work. As for the children, there may not be schools that would be acceptable, particularly if the children do not speak the language of the host country. In some expatriate assignments, the children either receive language training or there is a school in which their native language is spoken. The opportunity for the spouse or partner and the children to learn another language is sometimes seen as a benefit of the international assignment. Of course, this relates to the second factor of language. Difficulties in language are a major barrier to cross-cultural communication; thus, this is a very important factor for the expatriate and the family. Fortunately, many companies offer language training to the entire family prior to departure for the assignment. The final factor, MNE requirements, could involve getting permission from the host country for the selection of any expatriate. This is common in joint international ventures. Other factors could be the duration and type of assignment. When the duration of the assignment is for only two to three months or the assignment is in a "high-risk" country, the family members usually would not accompany the expatriate.

Selection of expatriates is a critical function of IHRM, particularly in MNEs where expatriate assignments are used to "groom" managers for higher levels of management. Many of the factors to consider in selecting expatriates and the factors causing expatriate failure are handled by training. However, the software applications available can greatly reduce the time required to make this process work. The next section focuses on training in the MNE, primarily the training of expatriates.

Training and Development of Expatriates

This section will focus primarily on training and career development for expatriates. As was done in the previous section, all managers in an MNE will be considered as expatriates since their career assignments and development typically mean that they will move from country to country. Training and development activities and programs in MNEs also include nonmanagerial employees of all types—PCNs, HCNs, and TCNs. Because traditional training and development were covered in detail in Chapter 13, most kinds of typical organizational training (e.g., orientation or technical training) will not be discussed. However, the use of an HRIS and its applications (covered in Chapter 13) will still be discussed. In fact, the training applications that are a part of the HRIS will be very useful for training expatriates. Not only will the expatriates' personal, work experience, and skills information stored on the HRIS be easily accessible but also the results of the training in terms of expatriate success or failure can be recorded. This information should be useful for future expatriate selection.

The corporate IHRM department has responsibility for all training; however, this responsibility is usually decentralized by delegating it to the MNE's subsidiaries. There may be training programs developed at the headquarters of the MNE, but it is unusual for these IHRM professionals at headquarters to deliver programs to the subsidiaries when it can be done more economically by the local IHRM professionals. Most of this local training for nonmanagerial employees will vary by different geographic locations of the MNE. Therefore, some cross-cultural training for nonmanagerial employees who are not HCNs will be necessary, for example, language training; but again, Chapter 13 covers the approach and design of these training programs.

This section will cover expatriate training in detail and will be divided into the following subsections: (1) the purpose of expatriate training, (2) **predeparture training** and the repatriation of expatriates, and (3) **transfer of training**.

Purpose of Expatriate Training

The dual purpose of any training program is to inform and motivate employees. Even training that is focused on learning a manual skill, for example, keyboarding, has both knowledge and motivational aspects. Clearly, the employee is learning a new skill, but with the proper training method, the employee can be encouraged to be more productive; and with the improved skill, the employee may be happier in the job. In addition to these two purposes of training, the first specific purpose of expatriate training is to supplement the selection process and assist the expatriate and her or his family in adjusting to the new situation. It must be emphasized that selection of expatriates is never perfect. Why else would there be expatriate failure? Thus, the training program content for expatriates is based on both the selection criteria identified above and the causes of expatriate failure.

The second specific **purpose of expatriate training** is economic. Recall that the expatriate brings both technical and managerial expertise to the subsidiary when there are no HCNs ready to fill the positions. In addition, the expatriate assignment is used by MNEs as a career development process for managers. Thus, the MNE has significant economic reasons for using expatriates. When one calculates the potential **direct and indirect costs of expatriate failure**, the amount of the investment increases. The MNE makes a major investment in selecting employees for placement in its subsidiaries, and training programs are another IHRM element used to protect that investment.

Predeparture Training

It should be noted that predeparture training programs do not focus on the technical ability of the expatriate, unless there are new technical or managerial skills necessary for the assignment, for example, the introduction of new technology. Because one of the major causes of expatriate failure is the dissatisfaction of or the lack of adjustment by the employee's spouse, partner, or family, the inclusion of these people in predeparture training is very important. To assist the adjustment of the expatriate and his or her family to a new culture, predeparture training typically includes training in cultural awareness, language, and practical matters regarding daily living in the new culture. Most MNEs will also include preliminary visits as a part of predeparture training.

Another element in predeparture training that is highly recommended is **repatriation** training. Formal repatriation is the process that occurs as the expatriate and family return to their homeland. However, recent research and literature has indicated that the repatriation process should begin before the person leaves the home country. The expatriate may find on return that the situation that was expected in the home country (e.g., a promotion to a new position) is not available; and thus, the expatriate will seek other employment. This problem of losing expatriates during the repatriation process has been well documented in the literature (Black, 2000; Feldman & Tompson, 1993; Poe, 2000; Solomon, 1995). There is considerable discussion in the recent literature on the design and implementation of repatriation programs that suggests that companies need to begin repatriation training prior to the expatriate leaving the home country—in predeparture training—rather then waiting for the return of the expatriate (Briscoe & Schuler, 2004; Dowling & Welch, 2005; Evans et al., 2002), and most companies consider repatriation as part of the career development program of the MNE.

Training in cultural awareness, language, and practical matters regarding daily living in the new culture constitutes the predeparture training that the expatriate and family will attend. It is important to recall that expatriate selection is a two-way street. The expatriate still has the right to decline the assignment. Thus, the predeparture training both informs and attracts, which are the two purposes of training. There are a large number of topics that can be included in predeparture training. The topics listed in Table 15.1 make up a possible content for the predeparture program. Note that this list could change depending on the host and parent countries involved.

Transfer of Training

The idea that the predeparture training program could change as a function of the two countries involved has been recognized by scholars, and several models

Table 15.1 Topics for Predeparture Training

1. Cultural values and religions
2. Web sites for country information
3. Country history, recommended readings, videos,* and achievements in the country
4. Classical literature describing the country's history, its folkways, and heroes and heroines
5. Information about other HCN expatriates in the country
6. Information on job opportunities for spouses and partners
7. Descriptions of the educational facilities and opportunities for families
8. Current news about the country, particularly its relationship to the parent country
9. Traditional family roles of father, mother, and children
10. Locations for shopping and shopping hours
11. Dominant language of country; extent of bilingualism in country
12. Nonverbal gestures and their meanings
13. Political structure, particularly as it affects the operation of the MNE
14. Descriptions of currency, temperature variations, transportation, hours of business
15. Sightseeing, including historic, artistic, and important cultural locations that would appeal to all the family

NOTE: This is a very general list, which will vary from country to country.

*Videos should be made available to expatriates and their families, either to review or to keep.

have been proposed to provide guidelines on predeparture training programs (Mendenhall, Dunbar, & Oddou, 1987; Tung, 1981, 1998). These researchers argue that predeparture training should not be viewed as "one size fits all" but rather that the training design and program should be contingent on other factors in the expatriate assignment. According to Tung (1981, 1998), the two factors that most affect predeparture training design are (1) the dissimilarity between the expatriate's native country and the host culture—low to high—and (2) the expected amount of interaction between the expatriate and members of the host country—low to high. Based on an analysis of these two factors, Black and Mendenhall (1989) argue that the design of the training program can then vary on three dimensions: (1) the training methods used, (2) the level of training rigor, and (3) the duration of the training program. For example, if both the dissimilarity between the expatriate's native country and the host culture and the expected amount of interaction between the expatriate and members of the host country are quite high, then the predeparture training should be rigorous and the length of training should be one to two months. In this situation, the training methods would attempt to immerse the expatriate in the host country's culture through assessment centers, simulations, sensitivity training, and extensive language training. As mentioned earlier, the use of the HRIS to analyze the success or failure of these training programs will enable the MNE to make more effective decisions about expatriates and their training in the future.

Performance Appraisal in MNEs

Performance appraisal is an important process for documenting the performance of employees, determining areas for development, deciding on pay increases and promotional opportunities, and giving employees the opportunity to express their views (Von Glinow, Drost, & Teagarden, 2002). The type of performance appraisal conducted and its content depend on the specific job requirements and personal attributes of the person being appraised (Schuler, Budhwar, & Florkowski, 2002). This is particularly true when we compare the appraisal of expatriates with that of HCN and TCN employees. The section in Chapter 14 on performance evaluation and performance planning covers a number of HRIS applications that could be used for performance appraisal in an MNE. Naturally, the inclusion of plants with a diverse employee population in multiple countries creates considerable complexity, particularly when the results of the appraisals are being used to move managers from country to country. However, most vendors of HRIS products have packaged software applications available that can be modified for local conditions in each specific country.[7]

Appraising Expatriate Performance

Important considerations in the appraisal of an expatriate's performance are who should conduct the appraisal and what performance criteria are specific to the expatriate's situation (Bohlander & Snell, 2007). The first question is who should complete the performance appraisal. Typically, the performance of employees is appraised by their supervisors. Expatriate managers are geographically distanced from their parent-country supervisors, and, as a result, supervisors who are located in the parent country cannot observe the day-to-day activities of these employees (Dowling & Welch, 2005). Therefore, managers of expatriates tend to base their evaluations of the person on the objective criteria used for other employees in similar positions located in the parent country. A potential problem with this type of assessment is that the parent-country manager does not have direct information or observational data about the more subjective performance criteria, such as the expatriate manager's leadership skills or performance within the context of the subsidiary (Borman & Motowidlo, 1993). Moreover, the supervisor located in the parent country may not be aware of culturally bound biases that constrain the job performance of the expatriate manager.

Because of these complexities, it may be most appropriate to obtain multiple ratings of the expatriate's performance through the use of a 360° feedback system (Dowling & Welch, 2005). Ratings of the expatriate manager's performance could be garnered from his or her superiors, peers, and subordinates in the expatriate assignment, as well as from the expatriate himself or herself. This would provide a clearer picture of the expatriate's total job performance. In fact, in a study of 58 U.S. multinational firms, Gregersen, Hite, and Black (1996) found that 81% of the companies used more than one rater when assessing the job performance of expatriate employees.

What Performance Criteria Should Be Appraised?

As with managers in domestic assignments, it is important to evaluate the specific job-related competencies of the expatriate manager. However, assessing the competence of an expatriate is somewhat more complex in that there are qualities unrelated to their jobs that they need to possess to perform their roles effectively (Schuler et al., 2002). In addition to typical task and contextual performance behaviors, expatriates should be assessed on other criteria, such as cross-cultural interpersonal skills; sensitivity to differences in the norms, laws, and cultures of various countries; and the ability to adapt to uncertain and unpredictable circumstances. Since expatriates are working in a new culture, they will face new experiences that may be vastly different from their experiences in the United States. As a result, it is important that the HR department of the parent country recognize the impact of these aspects of the expatriates' experience in their performance appraisals.

Appraising Host- and Third-Country Nationals' Performance

Appraising the performance of HCNs and TCNs is somewhat different from appraising the performance of domestic employees in the United States. It is important for PCNs to be sensitive to cultural differences when appraising performance. For example, in Japan, discussing the negative aspects of an employee's performance may be taken as an insult (Dowling & Welch, 2005). Because "saving face" is so important in Japan, discussing the negative attributes of an employee may cause that employee to distrust the manager. To deal with these cultural differences, organizations should employ HCNs to assist in the development and administration of performance appraisals (Dowling & Welch, 2005). HCNs know what type of information is culturally sensitive. Unlike expatriates, they are less likely to be perceived as outsiders. This perception is important since performance evaluations are used to determine pay increases and promotional decisions, training opportunities, and dismissal decisions.

Finally, these appraisals can help identify individual performance problems that can be solved by training.

Managing International Compensation

The management of compensation[8] in an MNE is one of the most complex but critically important functions of the IHRM department. Its complexity comes from having a mix of PCNs, HCNs, and TCNs within one company and, thus, having to handle wage, salary, and benefits information that differs across countries. As a result, the IHRM compensation manager must be aware of differences in taxation, labor laws affecting compensation and benefits, currency fluctuations, and cost-of-living differences within and between countries where the MNE has a presence. The criticality of compensation and benefits management by the IHRM rests, in part, on the effects that salary and benefits have on employee motivation. In spite of differences across countries regarding the motivational factors in the workplace, money seems to be consistently at the top of the list.

The other reason for the critical importance of compensation management in subsidiaries is its link to the strategy of the MNE. To help us understand some of the important elements and dynamics of compensation in an MNE, this section will cover (1) the objectives of international compensation, (2) the components of international compensation, and (3) two approaches to international compensation.

The Objectives of International Compensation Policy

Actually, the objectives of a compensation policy in an MNE are similar to those in a domestic company. It has been fairly well established in the management research literature that compensation administration is closely related to the strategy of the firm. For example, if the company has forecasted increased sales in the next year and thus has determined a need for new employees with specialized skills, it may be necessary to pay above the labor market's "going salary rate" in order to get the best available individuals. This necessity would be especially true when information from the labor market indicates that there is a shortage of people in a particular country having the skills needed for the target job—for example, computer programmers. Similarly, when the labor market statistics indicate that there is an abundance of people with the skills necessary for a specific job, it would be recommended that the compensation level match the labor market values.

As in a domestic firm, the *first objective* for an MNE is to align its compensation administration with the strategy of the firm. Of course, compared with the domestic firm, this alignment is much more complex for the MNE. It requires the MNE to have accurate and up-to-date labor market compensation information for all the countries in which it has a presence. This requirement is one of the most powerful advantages of having an HRIS with labor market information for the IHRM department. Labor market statistics, such as average compensation as well as forecasted shortages and surpluses for jobs, are available for most countries and can be stored in the HRIS. The applications in the computer software that produce analyses of these data would be quite similar to those described in Chapter 14. However, it is clear that the reports generated from the HRIS would be much more complex in an MNE since multiple countries would be involved.

The *second objective* of compensation administration in an MNE, as in a domestic firm, is to affect employee motivation in several ways. It must motivate employees to (1) join the firm, (2) be productive while members of the firm, and (3) stay with the firm. Employee motivation, then, is an important objective of an MNE's international compensation policy, which is complicated since multiple cultures are involved. Although most cultures see monetary rewards as motivational, there are clear differences across world cultures in terms of the other factors that motivate employee behaviors. For example, the meaningfulness of the work may be very important in some cultures, whereas the opportunity for promotion would be most important in other cultures.

The *final objective* of compensation policy for an MNE is that it must be perceived as fair by the employees. This notion of fairness or equity has been shown to be a powerful motivator of human behavior (Colquitt, Conlon, Wesson, Porter, & Ng, 2001), and it may be the most important objective of an international compensation policy. Given the mix of employees from different companies (PCNs, HCNs, TCNs), *perceived or real* differences in wages or benefits between groups of employees could lead to considerable dissatisfaction among the less privileged groups and consequently affect the retention of employees.

The Components of International Compensation

The components of an international compensation system are very similar to those of a domestic program. The major components are a base salary and a set of benefits. However, extra pay premiums would be much more complex for an MNE. For example, there may be a foreign-service or hardship premium for expatriates, whether they are from the parent or a third country. Other premiums could be based on the "risk level" of the assignment in the country. Although most domestic companies give cost-of-living allowances (COLAs) based on where one works (e.g., rural vs. urban locations), MNEs must also use between- and within-country COLAs to have an equitable compensation system. These considerations, along with the other compensation issues discussed, make managing the compensation system a "nightmare" for the IHRM department. Having the employee, country, and compensation/benefits data in an HRIS means that IHRM professionals have the ability to access important information quickly for making both policy and operational decisions about compensation in an MNE.

Two Approaches to International Compensation

The IHRM textbooks mentioned earlier in this chapter (Briscoe & Schuler, 2004; Dowling & Welch, 2005; Evans et al., 2002) all discuss two approaches to international compensation—the **going-rate** and the **balance-sheet approaches**. In the going-rate or **host-country approach** (Bohlander & Snell, 2007), the base salary for international employees is tied to the salary levels in the host country. For example, an expatriate would earn pay that is comparable with the salaries of employees in the host country. Thus, the compensation levels for employees would depend on wage surveys of (1) local nationals (HCNs), (2) expatriates of the same nationality, and (3) expatriates of all nationalities (Dowling & Welch, 2005). For low-pay countries, the base pay and benefits could be supplemented with additional payments. It should be obvious that HRIS applications for compensation based on the going rate would be useful for establishing initial compensation levels, particularly for expatriates. Having this database would also be quite useful for handling complaints by any MNE employee regarding the equity of his or her compensation. Computer-based compensation applications are available from the major providers of software platforms such as Oracle PeopleSoft or SAP.

The second approach to compensation policy, the balance-sheet approach, has as its goal the maintenance of a home-country living standard plus a financial inducement for accepting an international assignment. As Dowling and Welch (2005) note, "The home-country pay and benefits are the foundation of this approach; adjustments to home package to balance additional expenditure in the host country and financial incentives (expatriate/hardship premium) are added to make the package attractive." Although this approach would appear to be more attractive to the expatriate, it has a disadvantage for the IHRM department—it can be very complex to administer. Software applications and reports from an HRIS can assist in untangling these objective, and probably perceived, inequalities, but IHRM professional and line managers are still required to explain these programs to employees.

In sum, compensation is probably the most difficult and complex of the HR programs to implement and administer in an MNE. However, it is critically important to the equity exchange (or psychological contract) between the company and its employees. Ergo, it can affect employee motivation. Interactions between employees and their immediate supervisors in a domestic enterprise or an MNE regarding compensation have the greatest impact on motivation of the employees. Having an HRIS produce the needed data and information on the equity of compensation among employees is a tremendous boon to employee relations.

HRIS APPLICATIONS IN IHRM

Introduction

It should be apparent from the previous sections of this chapter that management, and HRM in particular, in an MNE is exceedingly more complex than in a domestic firm. As business becomes more global, ignoring its international aspects would be foolish. International companies functioning in the 1970s through the 1990s were hampered by the lack of sources for, and the slowness of transmission of, important HR information for effective management decisions. However, with the current technologies available, difficulties in executing the basic HR functions of planning, recruiting, selecting, training, and managing performance in MNEs have been reduced.

Specific HRIS applications for MNEs have been noted previously, mostly in concert with two software platforms, Oracle PeopleSoft and SAP. Not only are these the only software providers available for software applications in the IHRM field, but they are also good starting points for the interested student. Thus, this last section of this chapter will focus on broader issues in the application and use of an HRIS in IHRM. Problems and potential solutions will be examined[9] and discussed briefly under three topics: (1) organizational structure for effectiveness, (2) IHRM-HRIS administrative issues, and (3) HRIS applications in MNEs.

Organizational Structure for Effectiveness

The issue of the *most effective* structure for the operation of an HRIS in an MNE has been a "moving target." The most common advice regarding the management of an MNE has been to "**think global, act local.**" This advice applies to the total management process of an MNE—its strategy, operations, finance, marketing, and HR—and has been followed religiously for many years in international management. However, Beaman (2008) has provided arguments for a different approach, at least in terms of the development and use of an HRIS in international organizations. As she states,

> I maintain that we have been going about globalization the wrong way. The slogan, "Think Global, Act Local" . . . is completely the inverse of what we should be doing with our HRIT [synonym for HRIS] organizations. Rather, it is only by first "thinking locally" to truly understand the needs of our local business communities, and then "acting globally" to seamlessly knit together diverse business functions and systems into a holistic, global approach that we can build an effective, efficient and competitive organization. (p. 6)

A well-established piece of advice in the management literature has been that "structure does not drive success—people do." So to build an organizational structure for an HRIS in an MNE, we should consider Beaman's very reasonable suggestion.

IHRM-HRIS Administrative Issues

Service-Oriented Architecture (SOA)

It may be repetitive, but it is important to reexamine some of the HRIS approaches covered in Chapter 10 in terms of HRIS applications in an MNE. These applications can be much more useful in an international firm than in a domestic one. One of the most important approaches for handling administrative issues in an MNE is the use of a service-oriented architecture (SOA). As discussed in Chapter 10, an SOA "is a paradigm for organizing and utilizing distributed [computing] capabilities that may be under the control of different ownership domains . . . providing a uniform means to offer, discover, interact with and use capabilities to produce desired [business] effects" (OASIS, 2006, p. 8). SOA is focused on providing a service for a function that is well-defined, self-contained, and context and platform independent, a function that adds value to the organization's business purpose rather than simply being focused on the technology itself. In effect, SOA is a collection of internal and external services that can communicate with each other by point-to-point data exchange or through coordination among different services to achieve a business purpose. As a result, an SOA can combine multiple business functions from different organizational departments, for example, production, marketing, and HR, that have similar electronic transactions (such as change of address or salary level) into a central procession unit. SOAs were created when it was discovered that the various departments of organizations (marketing, finance, operations, R&D, and HR) were storing the same basic information on employees. Creating an SOA was a way to use the IT capabilities of an organization more efficiently.

Outsourcing, Offshoring, and Insourcing

MNEs were the first organizations to outsource many of their jobs that required low levels of skills (e.g., call centers). Outsourcing in HR had been done for years, for example, using Automatic Data Processing, Inc. (www.adp.com/corporateLanding) for payroll administration. However, the HR departments in the 1990s were looking to outsource other programs (recruiting and selection) to supposedly save money for their operations. Thus, using the Internet for outsourcing HR programs became a reality (Gueutal & Stone, 2005; Walker, 2001). Most of these approaches failed for a variety of reasons; the major one had to do with the privacy and confidentiality of employees' personal data. Still, because of the tremendous financial benefits if the MNE could use outsourcing or offshoring, these practices continued. Another major problem, however, was that many companies outsourced or offshored HR functions that were a critical part of the primary business of the organization, for example, talent management. Thus, many companies reverted to insourcing certain business processes, particularly those in the HR department.

Data Privacy and Security

The general cautions and guidelines for maintaining data privacy and security given in Chapters 3, 10, and 15 also apply to MNEs. In addition to the normal safeguards used in a domestic company, the MNE has to create additional ones to be in compliance with security and privacy laws and regulations in different countries. As noted by Harris (2002), 36 countries in the world have legislation governing the manner in which personal information can be collected and handled. The Safe Harbor program, negotiated by the European Commission and the U.S. Department of Commerce, is an attempt to create a single set of privacy regulations regarding the use and transfer of personal information. These regulations represent a compromise between the American and European approaches to privacy issues with personal data. Regarding privacy and security in an MNE, Harris (2002) suggests the following:

> Adopting a global approach to employee privacy issues, and building an internal culture of respect for privacy, is the best course of action open to a multinational corporation that wants to act as a global employer in the current regulatory environment surrounding the collection and use of personal information. (p. 198)

HRIS Applications in MNEs

As discussed in this chapter, most of the HRIS applications for a domestic company can be used for MNEs. However, some modifications are necessary due to the complexity of the database in an MNE. In today's global environment, access to data from any physical location in the world is increasingly important. Teams of employees may be stationed in Thailand, India, and the United States. As covered in Chapter 2, two issues arise when data are shared across wide geographic locations. These are (1) managing the day and time of a transaction and (2) determining where to store the various components of the business application, DBMS, and database.

To deal with the date and time issue, developers of DBMS such as Oracle, MS SQL Server, and IBM DB2 are building the capability to deal with recording dates and times according to the time zone in which the data originated. So, for example, if a database is stored in London and an employee records a transaction while sitting at a terminal in Los Angeles, in addition to the time (say 1 PM in Los Angeles), the time zone (–08:00 from Greenwich Mean Time) is also stored with the transaction.

As part of a global information system design, organizations have chosen to break their business applications and DBMS into components, often called "tiers." More detail on tiers was covered in Chapter 3. Traditional client-server architectures broke an application into two tiers, typically with the **user interface** and some business logic on the user's computer, such as a PC (the client), and the database and mainstream parts of the application stored on a server. In today's global environment with high-speed data networks, **N-tier architectures** exist with databases and applications being distributed among many different computers around the world. So if, for example, you are in an Internet café in Bangkok trying to get information about your benefit election, the hosting computer may be in London and the data may be located on a computer in Chicago. In sum, computer networks are created that provide instant access to these operational data, allowing real-time decision-making capabilities regardless of one's physical location.

A centralized database allows a company to confine its data to a single location and, therefore, to more easily control data integrity, updating, backup, queries, and access. A company with many locations and telecommuters, however, must develop a communications infrastructure to facilitate data sharing over a wide geographical area. The advent of the Internet and a standardized communication protocol made the centralized database structures and geographically dispersed data sharing feasible.

The database structures and system architectures we have discussed would be very useful to a multinational enterprise. Consider the differences between a compensation database for a domestic corporation operating in a single labor market and for an MNE. The multinational's compensation database would include labor market data for all countries in which the MNE has a presence, for example. Also, a great number of the modifications to an HRIS in an MNE would be driven by the different labor laws and regulations of the various host countries. As noted, there is software available for IHRM, but the use of this software demands that the database be accurate and timely. Being able to create and access reports based on employee data, and do it quickly, requires that the data be accurate and up-to-date—an axiom that has been emphasized throughout this book.

SUMMARY

Globalization is a reality. Twenty-five years ago it was the reality primarily for major corporations such as GE and IBM. Now, it has become increasingly important for midsize firms—the fastest growing group in all countries. This chapter has examined the implications of this globalization on the HRM function in MNEs and has documented the explosion of the HRM function into a separate field, IHRM. How IHRM has become increasingly complex by expanding on the traditional HR functions of selection, training, and compensation was also covered. The complexity of having a diversity of employees (PCNs, HCNs, TCNs) and of contending with the varying laws and practices of host countries dictated that MNEs abandon the paper-and-pencil system for computer technology.

The advantages of having employee information stored, manipulated, and reported using computer technology were discussed relative to the use of these capabilities in multiple IHRM programs. However, some of the more critical information that an HRIS can store, analyze, and produce reports on is contained in the cultural and legal profiles of countries. This information is valuable in all the activities and programs of the IHRM department and significantly influences the management of the many parts of an MNE.

KEY TERMS

Asia-Pacific Economic Cooperation (APEC)

Association of Southeast Asian Nations (ASEAN)

balance-sheet approach

cross-cultural suitability

cultural environment of countries

cultural norm

cultural profiles of countries

culture shock

direct and indirect costs of expatriate failure

domestic-only HRM

East Asia Economic Caucus (EAEC)

European Union (EU)

expatriate

expatriate failure

external environment

global corporation

global data

global diversity and inclusion

Global Diversity Readiness Index (DRI)

globalization of business

going global

going-rate approach

host-country approach

host-country nationals (HCNs)

internal issues

International Association for Human Resource Information Management (IHRIM)

international corporation

international human resource management (IHRM)

multinational corporation

multinational enterprises (MNEs)

N-tier architectures

national culture envelope

North American Free Trade Agreement (NAFTA)

parent-country nationals (PCNs)

predeparture training

purpose of expatriate training

repatriation

South Asian Association for Regional Cooperation (SAARC)

"think global, act local"

third-country nationals (TCNs)

transfer of training

user interface

DISCUSSION QUESTIONS

1. Describe the differences between domestic and international HRM.
2. What are the different types of organizational forms that corporations use for international operations?
3. What are the three types of employees who work in MNEs? Explain how an HCN could change to become a TCN in an MNE.
4. Describe the staffing process in an MNE. How does it differ from that of a domestic-only corporation?
5. What are the causes of expatriate failure?

6. Describe a training program for expatriates. Why is it recommended that the family of the expatriate also receive training?
7. Which method is best for completing performance appraisals for each of the three different types of employees in an MNE?
8. What are the objectives of an international compensation plan?
9. What are the modifications necessary for using HRIS software applications that are designed for domestic companies in an MNE?

CASE STUDY

A large MNE in the cookware industry was having difficulties maintaining its market share due to a number of mergers among other competing firms in the industry. The MNE, with corporate headquarters in Canada, had production plants in 15 countries and a company presence[10] in a total of 29 countries. Although the firm had a number of competitors, its product was considered as having the highest quality—the Mercedes of cookware. The firm was family owned and founded in 1937. The most pressing problem was how the firm could stay competitive in the marketplace and stop decreases in sales. Naturally, it was highly desirable to increase sales beyond annual averages, but, first, the firm had to change something to stabilize its place in the market.

Examining the problem, the CEO and the corporate board, consisting of all the corporate vice presidents as well as the CEOs of all the international locations, concluded that it was necessary to reduce operating costs by 5% to 6% to remain competitive. Thus, it was decided to determine if these cost savings could be achieved in operations, raw materials, finances, or HR.

The MNE managers examined the latest production technology in their industry. The firm discovered that its technology was fairly current and the few technological changes available would only help decrease costs by less than 1%. However, these modifications to their current technology were very expensive and did not appear to have a favorable return on investment (ROI).

Trying to obtain better financing was nearly impossible since the MNE had very favorable financing currently. The same was true for raw materials, since a decision to use cheaper materials would greatly reduce the quality of the company's products.

As a result, the management of the MNE asked the IHRM department for some suggestions as to how personnel costs could be trimmed. However, there was one constraint established by tradition in the company. The MNE had never had a layoff of employees in its history, and the CEO refused to use this option to reduce personnel costs. One of the complicating factors was the different labor legislation as well as the very different cultures in the 29 countries in which the MNE did business.

Case Study Questions

1. How would you approach a solution to this problem for the MNE?
2. Assuming that reducing personnel costs is the best, and probably only, way to reduce overall corporate costs, what specific programs would you suggest to reduce costs? Why?
3. How would an HRIS for the MNE aid in finding HR programs to help solve this problem? What would be the important data to access in the HRIS for all the units and divisions of the MNE to determine feasible HR programs?
4. Are the problems of reducing personnel costs for an MNE different from those for a domestic-only company? Explain.

NOTES

1. For convenience, domestic-only corporations will be referred to as domestic corporations.
2. The company and individual names used are fictitious.
3. This chapter cannot cover all the literature and issues in the field of IHRM. However, for the interested reader, there are excellent and comprehensive textbooks available on IHRM (Adler, 2002; Briscoe & Schuler, 2004; Dowling & Welch, 2005; Evans et al., 2002).
4. In the paper by Beaman (2009), human resources information technology (HRIT) is used instead of HRIS. However, we feel these two terms are interchangeable.
5. There are 24 more charts and figures in this report (Beaman, 2009), and the interested student can access it by going to the Jeitosa Group International Web site (http://www.cedarcrestone.com/research.php).
6. Readers interested in more information on the culture of countries can access any of the works cited in this paragraph.
7. Readers are referred to the Web sites for Oracle PeopleSoft or SAP for information on these applications for international companies.
8. In this chapter, compensation will refer to the entire wages, salaries, benefits, and extra allowances available in an MNE.
9. It is difficult to target exactly where the IT, HR, or HRIS fields are in terms of their development at any specific time. Thus, this section will provide only a snapshot of the field when this chapter was written.
10. A company presence for an MNE means that the firm has at least a sales office in the country.

REFERENCES

Adler, N. J. (2002). *International dimensions of organizational behavior.* Cincinnati, OH: South-Western.

Adlung, I. C. (2010, March). The male-female salary gap. *Regional HR update: Europe, HRinsights*. New York: Jeitosa Group International.

Babcock, P. (2007). Workforce planning remains largely unaddressed global challenge. *SHRM India*. Retrieved October 10, 2010, from http://www.shrm.org/hrdisciplines/staffing management/Articles/Pages/WorkforcePlanningGlobalChallenge.aspx

Bartlett, C. (2002). Foreword. In K. Beaman (Ed.), *Boundaryless HR: Human capital management in the global economy.* Austin, TX: IHRIM Press.

Beaman, K. (Ed.). (2002). *Boundaryless HR: Human capital management in the global environment.* Austin, TX: Rector Duncan & Associates.

Beaman, K. (2008). Think local, act globally: The collaborative transnational HRIT organization. *IHRIM.link, 12*(6), 6, 10.

Beaman, K. (2009). *2009–2010 global readiness report.* New York: Jeitosa Group International & IHRIM.

Black, J. S. (2000, January/February). Coming home. *HR World,* 30–32.

Black, J. S., & Mendenhall, M. (1989). A practical but theory-based framework for selecting cross-cultural training methods. *Human Resource Management, 28*(4), 511–539.

Bohlander, G., & Snell, S. (2007). *Managing human resources* (14th ed.). Mason, OH: Thomson South-Western.

Borman, W. C., & Motowidlo, S. J. (1993). Expanding the criterion domain to include elements of contextual performance. In N. Schmitt & W. C. Borman (Eds.), *Personnel selection in organizations* (pp. 71–98). San Francisco: Jossey-Bass.

Briscoe, D. R., & Schuler, R. S. (2004). *International human resource management* (2nd ed.). London: Routledge.

Colquitt, J. A., Conlon, D. E., Wesson, M. J., Porter, C., & Ng, K. Y. (2001). Justice at the millennium: A meta-analytic review of 25 years of organizational justice research. *Journal of Applied Psychology, 86*(3), 425–445.

Dowling, P. J., & Welch, D. E. (2005). *International human resource management: Managing people in a multinational context* (4th ed.). Mason, OH: Thomson South-Western.

Evans, P., Pucik, V., & Barsoux, J. (2002). *The global challenge: Frameworks for international human resource management.* New York: McGraw-Hill.

Feldman, D. C., & Tompson, H. B. (1993). Expatriation, repatriation, and domestic geographical relocation: An empirical investigation of adjustment to new job assignments. *Journal of International Business Studies, 24*, 507–529.

GLOBE Research Team. (2002). *Culture, leadership, and organizational practices: The GLOBE findings.* Thousand Oaks, CA: Sage.

GMAC Global Relocation Services & Windham International. (2002, October). *Global relocation trends 2002 survey report.* New York: Author.

Gregersen, H. B., Hite, J. M., & Black, J. S. (1996). Expatriate performance appraisal in U.S. multinational firms. *Journal of International Business Studies, 27,* 711–738.

Gueutal, H. G., & Stone, D. L. (Eds.). (2005). *The brave new world of e-HR.* San Francisco: Jossey-Bass.

Harris, D. (2002). Managing data privacy in global systems. In K. Beaman (Ed.), *Boundaryless HR: Human capital management in the global environment* (pp. 173–199). Austin, TX: Rector Duncan & Associates.

Hofstede, G. (1991). *Cultures and organizations.* New York: McGraw-Hill

Iyer, R. (2005, December). *Globalization: Will your company be left standing?* (Report No. A-0171-05-EA). New York: The Conference Board.

Mendenhall, M., Dunbar, E., & Oddou, G. (1987). Expatriate selection, training, and career-pathing: A review and critique. *Human Resource Management, 26,* 331–345.

Noe, R. A., Hollenbeck, J. R., Gerhart, B., & Wright, P. M. (2006). *Human resource management: Gaining a competitive advantage* (5th ed.). New York: McGraw-Hill Irwin.

Organizational Research Counselors. (2002, September). *Dual careers and international assignments survey.* Retrieved March 20, 2011, from https://www.orc-netsafe.com/surveys/dual.cfm (Name changed to ORC Worldwide in 2003 and to Mercer in 2010.)

Organization for the Advancement of Structured Information Systems (OASIS). (2006, May). *OASIS reference model for service oriented architecture 1.0.* Retrieved April 7, 2007, from www.oasis-open.org/committees/download.php/18486/pr-2changes.pdf

Poe, A. C. (2000, March). Focus on international HR: Welcome back. *HR Magazine,* 94–105.

Schuler, R., Budhwar, P. S., & Florkowski, G. W. (2002). International human resource management: Review and critique. *International School of Management Review, 4*(1), 41–70.

Schuler, R., & Jackson, S. (2005). A quarter-century review of human resource management in the U.S.: The growth in importance of the international perspective. *Management Revue, 16,* 11–35.

Schuler, R., & Tarique, I. (2007). International human resource management: A North American perspective, a thematic update, and suggestions for future research. *International Journal of Human Resource Management, 18,* 717–744.

Society for Human Resource Management. (2009). *Global diversity and inclusion: Perceptions, practices and attitudes*. Alexandria, VA: Author.

Solomon, C. M. (1995, January). Repatriation: Up, down, or out. *Personnel Journal,* 21–26.

Tarique, I., Schuler, R., & Gong, Y. (2006). A model of multinational enterprise subsidiary staffing composition. *International Journal of Human Resource Management, 17,* 207–224.

Trompenaars, F. (1992). *The seven cultures of capitalism.* New York: Currency Doubleday.

Tsui, A. S. (2007). From homogenization to pluralism: International management research in the academy and beyond. *Academy of Management Journal, 50,* 1353–1364.

Tung, R. (1981). Selecting and training of personnel for overseas assignments. *Columbia Journal of World Business, 16,* 68–78.

Tung, R. (1998). A contingency framework of selection and training of expatriates revisited. *Human Resource Management Review, 8*(1), 23–37.

U.S. Department of Labor. (2002). *International comparisons of hourly compensation costs for production workers in manufacturing.* Washington, DC: Bureau of Labor Statistics. Retrieved March 21, 2008, from http://www.bls.gov/

Von Glinow, M. A., Drost, E. A., & Teagarden, M. B. (2002). Converging on IHRM best practices: Lessons learned from a globally distributed consortium on theory and practice. *Human Resource Management, 41,* 123–140.

Walker, A. J. (Ed.). (2001). *Web-based human resources.* New York: McGraw-Hill.

Part V

Special Topics in HRIS

Chapter 16

Information Security and Privacy in HRIS

Yuk Kuen Wong and Mohan Thite

EDITORS' NOTE

This chapter expands on the information security and privacy issues in HRIS described in Chapter 3 (system considerations) and Chapter 10 (HR administration). Many organizations mistakenly believe that the biggest threat to information security is from outside. This chapter explains how present and past employees can pose a greater threat in the light of the emergence of collaborative and convergent technologies, and what HR managers can do to safeguard information security and privacy in collaboration with IT departments. It describes the importance, legal aspects, and best practices in maintaining and promoting safe information-handling procedures.

CHAPTER OBJECTIVES

After completing this chapter, you should be able to describe

- The importance of information security and privacy in today's technology-intensive and information-driven economy
- The important components of and threats to information security
- The legal requirements pertaining to information security and privacy
- Best practices in safe information-handling procedures

HRIS IN ACTION

In an article titled "Why Security Matters Now," Brenner (2009), using data from the seventh annual *Global State of Information Security Survey* conducted by *CIO* and *CSO* magazines and PricewaterhouseCoopers, identifies the following technology trends and how they impact information security:

- The promise and peril of social networking:

  In the last few years, social networking sites, such as Twitter, Facebook, and LinkedIn, have become a way of life for people both at work and away from work. What worries firms is the ease with which users could share customer data or sensitive company activities that might be subject to phishing scams. While firms do not want to block access to these sites because of their potential business benefits, they are struggling to find the right balance between security and usability. Nearly a third of respondents in the survey monitor what employees are posting to external blogs and social networking sites. Firms mainly use Web content filters to keep data behind the firewall, the most secure version of Web browser and security products that are compatible with Web 2.0. Some experts believe that social networking security problems are more cultural than technological. Therefore, educating employees about what is appropriate to share is crucial.

- Jumping into the cloud, sans parachute:

  Cloud computing services, such as software as a service (SaaS), and the virtualization technology that enables them offer many benefits (see Chapter 17); however, any attempt to get into the cloud should follow a well-considered security strategy. The key security risks of cloud computing, as identified by survey respondents, relate to fears about vendors in terms of their ability to enforce security policies, inadequate training and IT auditing, access control at the provider site, ability to recover data, and ability to audit the service providers. Both clients and providers of cloud services need to address the risks associated with the technical, operational, and organizational changes that could result as a consequence of the implementation of these technologies. Sometimes, if the physical and cloud-based assets are poorly configured, the flaws can be easily found and exploited by attackers. Because there are many clouds that are not federated, security in the cloud is a matter of managing a variety of risks across multiple platforms.

- Insourcing security management:

  Attacks on data have increased faster than any other security exploit, and the top targets include databases, file-sharing applications, laptops, removable media, and backup tapes. Thirty-one percent of respondents rely on security outsourcers, such as **managed security service providers (MSSPs)**; however, the trend today is to manage security in-house by taking control of application firewalls, encryption management, and patch management. One reason for this trend is the current state of chaos in the security market, with security vendors experiencing a seeming avalanche of corporate mergers and acquisitions.

- New corporate commitment:

  With the increasing realization that security can't be ignored, more companies are investing in security technologies and hiring chief information security officers (CISOs). Cybercrime and security breaches cost firms an average of US $833,000 per year, and the results are serious: a compromised corporate brand or reputation, stolen intellectual property, defaced Web pages, and direct financial losses, through fraud, for example. Firms are responding with multiple initiatives and a renewed commitment to information security.

INTRODUCTION

The history of information security can be traced back to World War II (Kizza, 2007, pp. 101–116), when the physical protection of information, with barricades and armed guards controlling access, was introduced in the military. Today, with the rapid growth of and advancements in information and communication technologies, most organizations can afford to deploy powerful computers in their workplaces to conduct their business (Pfleeger, 2006). The Internet and mobile technologies have enhanced the interconnectivity of many computers and information systems. With the widespread use of electronic data processing, online processing, and data exchange through the Internet, mobile technology, wireless access points, and home computers, there is an urgent need for better control mechanisms to protect company information (Dhillon, 2004; Freeman, 2007).

For the past two decades, it has been argued that an information revolution is taking place that is having a significant impact on all aspects of company life (Neuberger, Andrew, & Levetown, 2004). If applied effectively within strategic human resource management, information can result in the realization of significant corporate benefits; indeed, it has been contended that "information is the lifeblood of the company" (Confederation of British Industry, 1992, p. 2). It can be argued that information is vital to the success of the business, as it contributes directly to the employee's performance and the company's operational performance and financial health (Kotulic & Clark, 2004). However, information will only be recognized as a vital organizational resource if employees can readily gain access to the information they require. Many employees are desperate to gain access to the information they need. Unfortunately, as a consequence of the high incidence of **security breaches**, many companies are failing to provide consistently the information resources that their employees require (Von Solms & Von Solms, 2004).

Enterprise resource planning (ERP) systems seamlessly integrate application systems of different business functions, such as finance, HR, logistics, and customer relationship management. The major risks of these systems, particularly when they are Web enabled, are the security risks occasioned when confidential enterprise data is handled. With regard to an HRIS, sensitive information includes employee personal details, pay and benefits history, medical records, and disciplinary records. Firms have to pay close attention to what employee data is collected, stored, manipulated, used, and distributed—when, why, and by whom. This attention is necessary to address information security as well as privacy concerns and to comply with legislative safeguards.

Many organizations, including governments, financial institutions, hospitals, and private businesses, amass a great deal of **confidential information** about their employees, customers, and suppliers (Dhillon, 2004). These data are stored electronically and transmitted across networks. Human resource managers must make every effort to ensure that their information resources maintain data integrity, confidentiality, and availability. However, the increasing integration of HRIS both within and among companies, coupled with the growing value of corporate information resources, has made information security management a complex and challenging undertaking (Gerber, Von Solms, & Overbeek, 2001). Indeed, it is estimated that "security breaches (internal and external) affect 90% of all businesses every year, and cost some $17 billion" (Austin & Darby, 2003, p. 121). Moreover, protective measures can be very expensive: "The average company can easily spend 5% to 10% of IT budget on security" (Austin & Darby, 2003, p. 123). One increasingly important mechanism for protecting corporate and employee information, in an attempt to prevent security breaches, is the formulation and application of an information security policy in HRIS (Gordon & Loeb, 2004; Hone & Eloff, 2002). **Information security in HRIS** means protecting information in the HRIS from unauthorized access, use, disclosure, disruption, modification, or destruction. The objectives of information security are to ensure confidentiality, integrity, and **availability of information** (Pfleeger, 2006).

COMPONENTS OF INFORMATION SECURITY

Three main principles of information security are to achieve confidentiality, integrity, and availability of data (see Figure 16.1) within an HRIS. The HRIS is composed of three components—hardware, software, and communications—as mechanisms of protection in a client-server architecture design at physical, personal, and organizational levels (Freeman, 2007; International Organization for Standardization [ISO], 2000; Lippert & Swiercz, 2005). Security procedures and policies are essential, as they

Figure 16.1 Components of Information Security

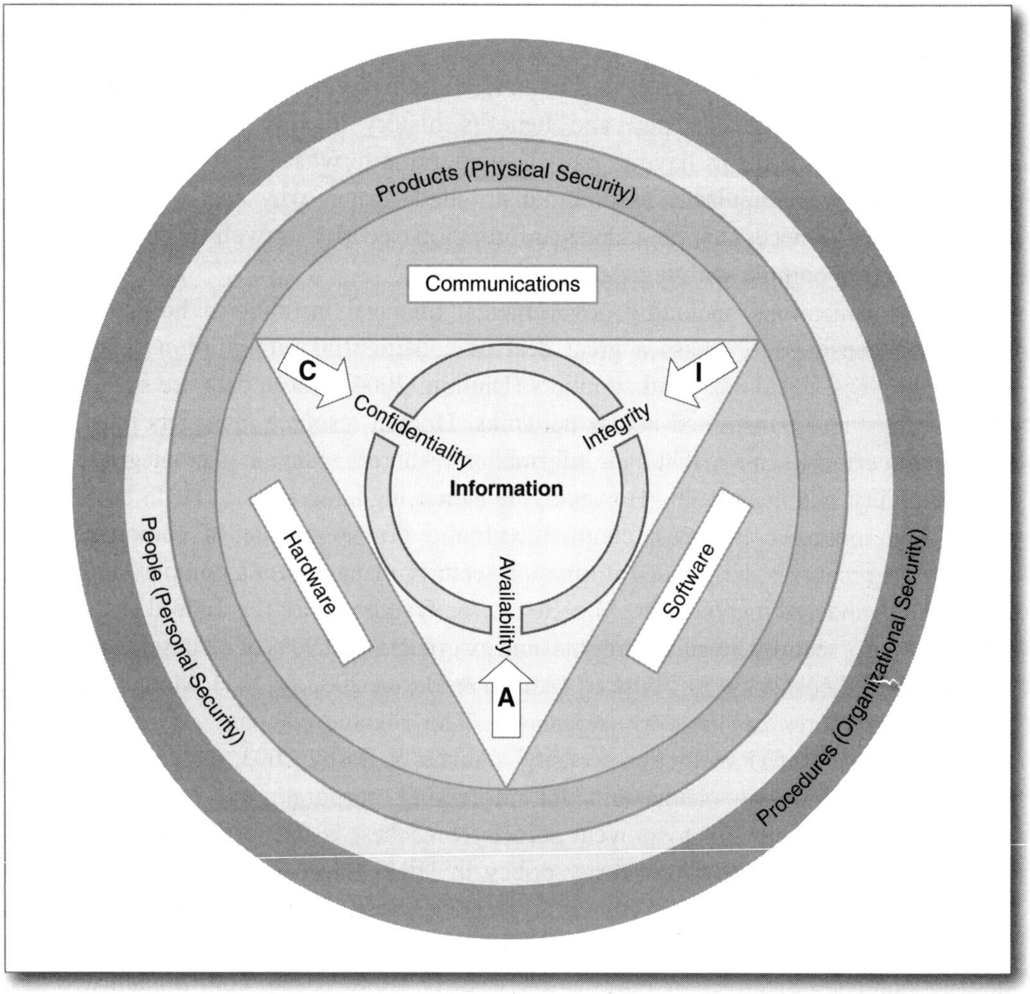

SOURCE: Wikipedia (2007).

provide guidelines to employees on how to use the HRIS to ensure security of information within the organization (Doherty & Fulford, 2003).

Confidentiality

Confidential information must be accessed, used, or disclosed only by authorized users (Lippert & Swiercz, 2005; Townsend & Bennett, 2003). Confidentially is important but not sufficient by itself for maintaining the privacy of the employees' personal details. See Chapter 10 for an extensive coverage of privacy laws.

Integrity

Integrity refers to safeguarding the accuracy and completeness of information and processing methods by ensuring that data cannot be modified without authorization (Sadri & Chatterjee, 2003).

Availability

Information availability means that authorized users must be able to process and access the information when required (Ashbaugh & Miranda, 2002). Employees need to fulfill their obligations to the contract for using the HRIS. Common techniques such as digital signatures and passwords are used to establish authenticity and non-repudiation in HRIS (Townsend & Bennett, 2003).

LEGAL REQUIREMENTS FOR INFORMATION SECURITY

Governments, at various levels, in most of the developed countries have enacted several laws and regulations to safeguard information security and data protection. Some of these legal requirements from Europe and North America are listed below (Kizza, 2007; Townsend & Bennett, 2003; Wikipedia, 2007):

- Personal Information Protection and Electronics Document Act: The act was enacted in Canada to support and promote electronic business by protecting personal information that is collected, used, or disclosed in certain circumstances.
- California Security Breach Information Act, SB 1386: This law in the state of California requires organizations to notify customers or employees when unencrypted personal information has been compromised, stolen, or lost.
- Computer Misuse Act, 1990: The act was proposed to make computer crime (e.g., hacking or cyber-terrorism) a type of criminal offence in the United Kingdom.
- The European Union Data Protection Directive (EUDPD): This directive requires that all EU members must adopt national regulations to standardize the protection of data privacy for citizens throughout the European Union.
- Health Insurance Portability and Accountability Act: This act requires health care providers, insurance companies, and employers to safeguard the security of health information. It sets national standards for electronic health care transactions.

THREATS TO INFORMATION SECURITY

When confidential information about employees, business partners, or customers falls into the hands of competitors, such a breach of security could lead to business losses, law suits, or even bankruptcy (Townsend & Bennett, 2003). Protecting organizational information is an essential element of a company's security policy (ISO, 2000), and, in many countries, it is also a legal requirement and part of corporate social responsibility (Ball, 2001).

The following are the common **security threats**:

- *Human error:* When an HRIS is not well designed, developed, and maintained and employees are not adequately trained, there is a high potential threat of security breaches. Research suggests that human errors, such as incorrectly entered data or accidental destruction of existing data, constitute security threats to the availability, accessibility, and **integrity of information**.
- *Damage by employees:* One of the concerns overlooked by HR managers is that information may be damaged by disgruntled employees. A recent survey suggested that a third of companies felt that their information security was at risk from disgruntled employees (Ernst & Young, 2003).
- *Misuse of computer systems:* One of the predominant internal security threats is employees' unauthorized access to or use of information, particularly when it is confidential and sensitive.
- *Theft:* The value of information can be much higher than the price of hardware and software. With contemporary advances in technological developments, a relatively small computer chip (e.g., a USB device) can easily store up to 120 GB of data.
- *Computer-based fraud:* There is growing evidence that computer-based fraud is widespread. Over 90% of companies have been affected by computer-based fraud, such as data processing or data entry routines that are modified (Garg, Curtis, & Halper, 2003).
- *Viruses, worms, and Trojans:* These are common external security threats and often come in e-mail attachments (De Campeaux, 2002). They have the capability to replicate themselves automatically across systems and networks, as well as typically delivering mischievous functionality or damaging data.
- *Hackers:* Another significant threat is the penetration of organizational computer systems by **hackers**. A hacker is defined as someone who accesses a computer or computer network unlawfully. Such attacks, often termed "intrusions" (Austin & Darby, 2003, p. 122), can be particularly dangerous because, once the hacker has successfully bypassed the network security, he or she is free to damage, manipulate, or simply steal data at will. Related to

this aspect of security threat is cyber-terrorism, incorporating, for example, unlawful attacks designed to intimidate (Austin & Darby, 2003). Cyber-terrorists usually send a threatening e-mail stating that they will release some confidential information, exploit a security leak, or launch an attack that could harm a company's systems or networks. Cyber-terrorism—leveraging of an information system, particularly via the Internet—is intended to cause physical, real-world harm or severe disruption of a system's infrastructure (Hinde, 2003). In one such scenario, a person with high-level computer and network skills is hired to break into a specific computer or computer network to steal or delete data and information.

- *Natural disasters:* Typical forms of natural disasters are floods, earthquakes, fires, and lightning strikes, which destroy or disrupt computing facilities and information flow.

Managing these security threats, risks, and vulnerabilities requires a proactive information security plan (Lippert & Swiercz, 2005). Organizations must address the blurring of the security perimeter and seek to develop a security-conscious culture in employees, a culture supported through the leadership of senior executives, including HR managers.

ROLE OF HR IN INFORMATION SECURITY

Information security issues are no longer solely the domain of the IT department and IT managers. To have effective information security in place, HR managers need to align information security with their HR objectives. To do this, they must eliminate the hierarchical layers between the functional managers, who have historically viewed information security as a technology issue and not an HR issue. Having the active involvement of senior management in security-related decisions is crucial in establishing this alignment. Companies need to back up their talk about the importance of protecting their valuable organizational and employee information (digital assets) by investing in information security. Too often, it requires a security breach, a competitor being attacked, or a regulatory mandate for the HR department to take action. Even then, core HR objectives are ignored, and a temporary fix is applied to the problem. Measured, proactive spending is less costly in the long run than reactive spending, which is often overspending in response to an incident.

Many HR managers still tend to think that security threats refer to external security breaches (e.g., virus outbreaks or malicious hackers). However, HR managers should focus more on the less obvious threats, such as those posed by **disgruntled employees** and ex-employees, by network links to business partners who don't have proven or trustworthy systems, by employee misuse of computers, and by insecure network access points set up by employees. These may not only cause serious damage but also destroy a company's reputation and increase its long-term costs. The growing complexity of employees' profiles (part-time, casual, and full-time employees; contractors; ex-employees; and employees of business partners) makes the problem even worse. Wipawayangkool (2010) suggests that, with organizations enabling the more strategically active role of HRM through a combination of selection, training, and pay practices, they could more effectively handle people issues in information security management (ISM), particularly security awareness and insider threats, and possibly sustain their competitive advantage.

The best practices for handling information in HRM/HRIS include the following (Canavan, 2003; David, 2002; Tansley & Watson, 2000):

- Adopt a comprehensive information security and privacy policy.
- Store sensitive personal data in secure HRIS and provide appropriate encryption.
- Dispose of documents properly or restore computer drives and CD-ROMs.
- Build document destruction capabilities into the office infrastructure.
- Conduct regular information security practice training for all employees.
- Conduct privacy "walk-throughs," and make spot checks on proper information handling.

Kovach, Hughes, Fagan, and Maggitti (2002) and Grundy, Collier, and Spaul (1994) suggest the following additional measures:

- The careful selection of staff with due regard to their honesty and integrity
- The raising of information security awareness among staff and ensuring that employees know and understand the company's security policies
- Measures to address the personal problems of employees, such as gambling and drug addiction, which might lead them to indulge in computer abuse for financial gain
- Access to effective grievance procedures, since the motivation for much computer abuse is retaliation against management

INFORMATION SECURITY MANAGEMENT FOR HRIS

A well-known information security management standard is **ISO/IEC 27002** (ISO, 2000), as stipulated by the International Organization for Standardization and the International Electrotechnical Commission (Dresner & Wood, 2007;

Freeman, 2007). This security management process consists of administrative/procedural, logical/technical, and physical controls (see Table 16.1) and constitutes a best practice recommendation (Department of Broadband, Communications and the Digital Economy [DBCDE], 2007; Freeman, 2007).

Information Privacy

Privacy is a complex construct and is influenced by a variety of disciplines, such as ethics, economics, management, and law. Privacy comprises ethical, moral, and legal dimensions and has assumed greater importance with the increased adoption of the Internet and Web 2.0 technologies. The ethical aspect of privacy includes the issue of **electronic surveillance**. An important consideration in the understanding of privacy is the "centrality of the issue of control . . . specifically, the individual's need to have control over . . . personal information" (McParland & Connolly, 2008, p. 118). For the individual, information security has a significant effect on privacy, which is viewed very differently in different cultures. Trust is important in ensuring privacy in the sense that individuals need to feel confident that their personal information will not be used without their consent and will not be given to third parties.

Privacy is a human value consisting of four elements (Kovach & Tansey, 2000):

- Solitude: The right to be alone without disturbances
- Anonymity: The right to have no public personal identity
- Intimacy: The right not to be monitored
- Reserve: The right to control one's personal information, including the methods of dissemination of that information

There is a tenuous relationship between employee privacy concerns and organizational needs (Ball, 2001; Kovach & Tansey, 2000). Fair information policies suggest that employees have the right to know how their personal information is used, to prevent the use of personal information by other parties (e.g., governments, insurance companies), and to take reasonable precautions to prevent misuse of their personal information (Camardella, 2003; Kovach & Tansey, 2000). The human resource literature mainly focuses on invasion of privacy perceptions and procedures for handling information about the hiring process, from job application to hiring decision (Kovach et al., 2002). An important element in the success of managing this personal information is the HRIS, a database of personal information about each employee and job applicant. Because of the authority given to them to access and use HRIS information, HR managers must be aware of the ethical and legal issues associated with both the creation and use of personal information in the HRIS (Kovach & Tansey, 2000;

Table 16.1 Information Security Program for HRIS

Information Security	*Descriptions*
Control Types	*To mitigate a risk, it is recommended that the following control strategies be used in designing an HRIS:*
Administrative	• Administrative control (also known as procedural control) consists of policies, procedures, standards, and guidelines. An administrative control is developed from the information security framework for managing people and organizational operations. Some of these policies, procedures, and guidelines are regulated by laws. Examples of administrative controls include the corporate security policy, password policy, hiring policies, and disciplinary policies.
Logical	• Logical control (also referred to as technical control) regulates access to information in HRIS. For example, passwords, network- and host-based firewalls, network intrusion detection systems, access control lists, and data encryption are logical controls. The common problem of logical controls is access privileges when an employee's job duties change or he or she is transferred to another department. The access privilege required by the new role is frequently added onto his or her already existing access privilege, which may no longer be necessary or appropriate.
Physical	• Physical controls refer to the physical environment, such as computer facilities in the workplace. Separation of duties ensures that an individual cannot complete a critical task by himself or herself. For example, an employee who submits a reimbursement request should not also be able to authorize payment. An HR manager who manages the employees' database should not manage the finance database—these roles and responsibilities must be separated from one another.
Security classification for information	• An important aspect of information security and risk management is recognizing the value of information and defining appropriate procedures and protection requirements for it. Classification of information to be assigned should take into account how much value that information has to the organization. All employees in the organization must be trained in the classification schema and should understand the required security controls and handling procedures for each classification. The HR department plays a significant role in the process.
Access control	• Access to protected information must be restricted to people who are authorized to access the information. Control techniques such as identification and authentication are important for the HRIS. The most common access control technique is user name and password. HR managers need to ensure the obligations of employees using the HRIS.
Cryptography	• Cryptography is a computer technique to ensure that sensitive information is only read and used by authorized employees. There have been significant academic research and technological developments in cryptography.
Defense in depth	• To fully protect the information during its lifetime, each component of the information processing system must have its own protection mechanisms. The building up, layering on, and overlapping of security measures is called "defense in depth." The strength of any system is no greater than its weakest link. When using a defense-in-depth strategy, should one defensive measure fail, there are other defensive measures in place that continue to provide protection.

SOURCE: Department of Broadband, Communications and the Digital Economy (2007).

Sadri & Chatterjee, 2003). The information privacy concerns related to HRIS include (1) what types of employee information can be collected and stored in the system and (2) who can access and update the information (Noe, Hollenbeck, Gerhart, & Wright, 1994; Sadri & Chatterjee, 2003). It is recommended that organizations should only collect and store information based on sound and valid business reasons (Hubbard, Forcht, & Thomas, 1998).

Because organizations are accountable and liable for their information practices and procedures, it is prudent to ensure that the collection, maintenance, use, and dissemination of personal information is *necessary, lawful, current,* and *accurate* (Camardella, 2003). By focusing on the purpose for and amount of data collected, HR managers can minimize privacy-based litigation in their organizations while maintaining high ethical standards. There are a number of common privacy violations, including violation of Internet usage, intentional misuse of information, interception of information, and information matching. As the HRIS is integrated with many other information systems, Web sites, and databases, employees can use the information-matching technique to generate the specific information they want. The difficulty with information matching is that no one may know what the profiles built from the matched information will be used for or who will use them.

In recent times, governments have moved to enact legislation to protect an individual's right to privacy. You may recall that Chapter 10 provides a detailed description of U.S. federal and state laws on privacy, with particular reference to HRIS.

The major privacy concerns include determination of what types of employee information should be stored on the system and who can access and modify information in the HRIS databases (Camardella, 2003). Following are some of the best practices that HR managers should consider to secure information security and privacy (Noe et al., 1994; Pfleeger, 2006):

- Train users on how to securely use and handle the equipment, data, and software.
- Train employees to "log off" personal computers after they are through using them.
- Do not allow passwords to be shared. Change passwords frequently.
- Run software through a virus detection program before using it on the system.
- Ensure that backup copies, data files, software, and printouts are used only by authorized users.
- Make backup copies of data files and programs.
- Ensure that all software and mainframe applications include an audit trail (a record of the changes and transactions that occur in a system, including when and who performed the changes).

- Use edit controls (such as passwords) to limit employees' access to data files and data fields.
- Have employees take responsibility for updating their employee records themselves via the self-service system.

Another critical issue with regard to workplace privacy is **employee monitoring**, including electronic surveillance. This practice can involve monitoring employee use of the telephone, Web, computer, electronic mail, and video. In using various electronic gadgets, employees leave "digital footprints," and surveys indicate that a majority of employers will monitor these footprints. Please refer to the Web site of the Privacy Rights Clearinghouse (http://www.privacyrights.org) for more on the nature of employee monitoring and its legal and ethical ramifications.

SUMMARY

The chapter begins with establishing the need for security, particularly with the emergence of new technologies that offer exciting possibilities but also bring with them considerable risks to information security and privacy. It describes the main components and principles of information security, namely confidentiality, integrity, and availability. The legal requirements to maintain information security are briefly discussed. Various threats to information security, from both within and outside the organization, are identified. The HR professionals have an important responsibility in ensuring information security in terms of recruitment, training, and employee monitoring. Some of the best practices in this regard are highlighted. A robust information security program needs to consider administrative, logical, and physical controls, using information classification, access control, **cryptography**, and **defense in depth** as effective tools. The concept of privacy in an organizational context is then presented, and some of the best practices in this regard are highlighted.

KEY TERMS

availability of information
confidential information
cryptography
defense in depth
disgruntled employees
electronic surveillance
employee monitoring
hackers
information security in HRIS
integrity of information
ISO/IEC 27002
managed security service providers (MSSPs)
privacy
security breaches
security threats

DISCUSSION QUESTIONS

1. Why are information security and privacy important considerations in the design, development, and maintenance of HRIS?
2. List and discuss the major information security and privacy threats to organizations.
3. What are the important goals and considerations of information security?
4. Identify the important legal provisions governing information security and privacy in your country.
5. What is the role of HR professionals in information security and privacy management?
6. What are some of the best practices to manage information security and privacy in terms of procedural, technical, and physical controls?

CASE STUDY: PRACTICAL APPLICATIONS OF AN INFORMATION PRIVACY PLAN

XYZ University is a medium-sized tertiary education provider in the state of Queensland, Australia. In undertaking its normal business of teaching, learning, and research, the university collects, stores, and uses "personal information," that is, anything that identifies a person's identity.

With respect to students, this information may include, among other things, records relating to admission, enrollment, course attendance, assessment, and grades; medical records; details of student fees, fines, levies, and payments, including bank details; tax file numbers and declaration forms; student personal history files; qualifications information; completed questionnaire and survey forms; records relating to personal welfare, health, equity, counseling, student and graduate employment, or other support matters; records relating to academic references; and records relating to discipline matters.

The bulk of this information is retained in the student management information systems and in the file registry. Academic and administrative staff, at various levels, have access to these records only as required to carry out their duties. Portions of the information held in university student records are disclosed outside the university to various agencies, such as the Australian Taxation Office; the Department of Education, Employment and Workplace Relations; other universities; consultant student services providers; Department of Immigration and Citizenship; and overseas sponsorship agencies.

The university has a well-documented information privacy policy in accordance with the community standard for the collection, storage, use, and disclosure of personal information by public agencies in Queensland. The policy relies on the 11 principles developed in the Commonwealth Privacy Act of 1988. These principles broadly state the following:

- Personal information is collected and used only for a lawful purpose that is directly related to the collector's function.
- Before the information is collected, the individual concerned should be made aware of the purpose, whether it is required by law, and to whom the information will be passed on.
- Files containing personal information should be held securely and protected against loss; unauthorized access, use, modification, or disclosure; or any other misuse.
- Personal information can only be disclosed to another person or agency if the person concerned is aware of it and has consented and the disclosure is authorized or required by law.
- Personal information should not be used without taking reasonable steps to ensure that it is accurate, up-to-date, and complete.

Presented below are three scenarios in which you need to decide how to apply the privacy policy and principles. The following scenarios were sourced from the Griffith University Privacy Plan (http://www.griffith.edu.au/about-griffith/plans-publications/griffith-university-privacy-plan/pdf/privacy-training-guide.pdf). The link to the privacy plan itself is www.griffith.edu.au/ua/aa/vc/pp. A complete statement of the relevant privacy principles can be found at www.dva.gov.au/health_and_wellbeing/research/ethics/Documents/ipps.pdf.

Scenario 1

Roger, a photocopier technician, has been asked to repair an office photocopier that just broke down while someone was copying a grievance matter against an employee of the agency. The officer who was copying the file takes the opportunity to grab a cup of coffee and leaves Roger in the photocopy room while the photocopier cools down. While waiting, Roger flips through the file and realizes that the person against whom the grievance was made lives on the same street as he does.

Scenario 2

Tom telephones a student at home about attending a misconduct hearing. The student is not at home; however, the student's partner, Christine, answers the phone. She states that she knows all about the misconduct hearing but asks for clarification of the allegations. When pressed, Tom provides further details. Tom feels comfortable about providing this information to Christine because she is the student's partner, and she has already told Tom that she knows all about her partner's misconduct hearing.

Scenario 3

Brad works in a student administration center, and Janet is a student. They know each other, as they used to attend the same high school. Occasionally, they get together at the university to have coffee and chat about mutual friends. Brad knows that Janet's birthday is coming up because Janet happened to mention that she'll be another year older in the near future. Brad decides to access the student information system to find out Janet's date of birth and home address. A few weeks later, Janet receives a birthday card from Brad sent to her home address.

Case Study Questions

With regard to the above scenarios, you need to decide

1. what information privacy principles (IPPs) have been breached,
2. how, and
3. what you would do to address the situation.

REFERENCES

Ashbaugh, S., & Miranda, R. (2002). Technology for human resources management: Seven questions and answers. *Public Personnel Management, 31,* 7–20.

Austin, R. D., & Darby, C. A. (2003, June). The myth of secure computing. *Harvard Business Review, 81*(6), 121–126.

Ball, K. S. (2001). The use of human resource information systems: A survey. *Personnel Review, 30*(6), 677–693.

Brenner, B. (2009, October 16). Why security matters now. *CIO*. Retrieved September 30, 2010, from http://www.cio.com.au/article/322362/why_security_matters_now/

Camardella, M. J. (2003). Electronic monitoring in the workplace. *Employment Relations Today, 30*(3), 91.

Canavan, S. (2003). *An information security policy: A development guide for large and small companies*. Bethesda, MD: SANS Institute. Retrieved March 20, 2011, from http://www.sans.org/reading_room/whitepapers/policyissues/information-security-policy-development-guide-large-small-companies_1331

Confederation of British Industry. (1992). *IT: The catalyst for change*. London: Author.

David, J. (2002). Policy enforcement in the workplace. *Computers and Security, 27*(6), 506–513.

De Campeaux, D. (2002). Taking responsibility for worms and viruses. *Communications of the ACM, 45*(4), 15–16.

Department of Broadband, Communications and the Digital Economy. (2007). *Secure your information: Information security principles for enterprise architecture*. Retrieved February 23, 2008, from http://www.dbcde.gov.au/__data/assets/pdf_file/0017/70622/Secure-Your-Information_CIOCSO.pdf

Dhillon, G. (2004). The challenge of managing information security. *International Journal of Information Management, 24,* 3–4.

Doherty, N. F., & Fulford, H. (2003, May 18–21). Information security policies in large organisations: Developing a conceptual framework to explore their impact. In M. Khosrow-Pour (Ed.), *Information technology and organizations: Trends, issues, challenges and solutions* (pp. 1052–1053). Hershey, PA: Idea Group.

Dresner D. G., & Wood, J. (2007). Operational risk: Acceptability criteria. In *Proceedings of the Third International Symposium on Information Assurance and Security* (pp. 301–306). Los Alamitos, CA: IEEE.

Ernst & Young Security Survey. (2003). *Global Information Security Survey 2003.* Southampton, UK: Author.

Freeman, E. H. (2007). Holistic information security: ISO 27001 and due care. *Information Systems Security, 16*(5), 291–294.

Garg, A., Curtis, J., & Halper, H. (2003). Quantifying the financial impact of information security breaches. *Information Management and Computer Security, 77*(2), 74–83.

Gerber, M., Von Solms, R., & Overbeek, P. (2001). Formalizing information security requirements. *Information Management and Computer Security, 9*(1), 32–37.

Gordon, L. A., & Loeb, M. P. (2004). *Economics of information security.* New York: Springer.

Grundy, E., Collier, P., & Spaul, B. (1994). Auditing personnel: A human resource approach to information systems control. *Managerial Auditing Journal, 9*(6), 10–16.

Hinde, S. (2003). Cyber-terrorism in context. *Computers and Security, 22*(3), 188–192.

Hone, K., & Eloff, J. H. P. (2002). Information security policy, international security standards say? *Computers and Security, 21*(5), 402–409.

Hubbard, J. C., Forcht, K. A., & Thomas, D. A. (1998). Human resource information systems: An overview of current ethical and legal issues. *Journal of Business Ethics, 17,* 1319–1323.

International Organization for Standardization. (2000). *Information technology: Code of practice for information security management, ISO 17799.* Geneva, Switzerland: Author.

Kizza, J. M. (2007). *Ethical and social issues in the information age.* London: Springer-Verlag.

Kotulic, A. G., & Clark, J. G. (2004). Why there aren't more information security research studies. *Information & Management, 41,* 597–607.

Kovach, D. K. A., & Tansey, K. (2000). The balance between employee privacy and employer interests. *Business and Society Review, 105*(2), 289–298.

Kovach, K. A., Hughes, A. A., Fagan, P., & Maggitti, P. G. (2002). Administrative and strategic advantages of HRIS. *Employment Relations Today, 29*(2), 43–48.

Lippert, S. K., & Swiercz, P. M. (2005). Human resource information systems (HRIS) and technology trust. *Journal of Information Science, 31*(5), 340–353.

McParland, C., & Connolly, R. (2008). Technology-related privacy concerns: A critical assessment. *The Business Review, 9*(2), 117–124.

Neuberger, M. J., Andrew, S., & Levetown, A. S. (2004). Special employment considerations to ensure the security of your IT department. *Employment Relations Today, 31*(1), 35.

Noe, R. A., Hollenbeck, J. R., Gerhart, B., & Wright, P. M. (1994). *Human resource management: Gaining a competitive advantage.* Burr Ridge, IL: Irwin.

Pfleeger, C. P. (2006). *Security in computing.* Englewood Cliffs, NJ: Prentice Hall.

Sadri, J., & Chatterjee, V. (2003). Building organisational character through HRIS. *International Journal of Human Resources Development and Management, 3*(1), 84–98.

Tansley, C., & Watson, T. (2000). Strategic exchange in the development of human resource information systems (HRIS). *New Technology Work and Employment, 15*(2), 108–122.

Townsend, A. M., & Bennett, J. T. (2003). Human resources and information technology. *Journal of Labor Research, 24*(3), 361–363.

Von Solms, B., & Von Solms, R. (2004). The ten deadly sins of information security management. *Computers and Security, 25,* 371–376.

Wikipedia. (2007). *Information security.* Retrieved February 17, 2008, from www.wikipedia.org

Wipawayangkool, K. (2010, August 12–15). *Strategic role of human resource management in information security management.* Paper presented at the 16th annual Americas Conference on Information Systems, Lima, Peru.

Chapter 17

THE FUTURE OF HRIS

EMERGING TRENDS IN HRM AND IT

MICHAEL J. KAVANAGH, MOHAN THITE, AND RICHARD D. JOHNSON

EDITORS' NOTE

In Chapter 1, the history of HRM was discussed along with its eventual merging with the field of IT, thus creating a new field of study and managerial practice—human resource information systems (HRIS). This book has provided information on the development and implementation of an HRIS. Most of the HRIS development and sophistication began in the United States, but these systems have spread rapidly throughout the industrialized countries of the world. The question to be answered here is where the field of HRIS is going in the future. Forecasting the future is always difficult. One can expect evolutionary, rather than revolutionary, changes in the HRIS field. This chapter will discuss some of these trends in the field of HRIS.

CHAPTER OBJECTIVES

After completing this chapter, you should be able to

- Discuss the short-term future trends in HRM
- Discuss the long-term future challenges for HRM and tactics to handle them
- Explain the impact of future trends in IT/IS and workforce technologies on the operation of an HRIS
- Understand how HR and IT/IS are combining for future HRIS business applications

INTRODUCTION

Before we analyze future trends in HRIS, it is appropriate to revisit how we got here. In Chapter 1, we tracked the evolution of HR and HRIS with a particular focus on a systems perspective. Others have also suggested similar models highlighting the systems perspective of HRIS (Mayfield, Mayfield, & Lunce, 2003). In the subsequent chapters, we had an in-depth look at the entire system development life cycle (SDLC) of an HRI system that included planning, analysis, design, implementation, and maintenance (Chapters 2–5). We also looked at the specific applications of HRIS in some of the core functions of HRM (Chapters 8–15).

There is no doubt that technology has radically altered the world of work. Today, one can work anytime and anywhere, using any device, possibilities that have globalized the workplace and given it a 24/7 work cycle. Enabled by enterprise resource planning (ERP) software, organizational functions such as production, supply chains, marketing, customer relations, finance, and HR are now more integrated than ever in the pursuit of organizational success. Although HR has evolved from an administrative to a strategic focus, transactional activities, such as HR administration, legal compliance, and benefits management, still consume a major portion of HR resources. The move to e-HR, though, has helped greatly in shifting HR professionals toward more value-added transformational activities by enabling the automation of routine, transactional activities.

With the increasing focus on Strategic HRM and developments in technology, HR professionals are deploying innovative technology solutions to address their core challenges, such as talent management and workforce metrics and analytics (Haines & Lafleur, 2008). Multinational enterprises are leveraging human resource information systems to align their information technology, processes, and people to successfully replicate their HR policies and practices across global operations (Morris et al., 2009). Some enterprises also use HRIS for effective disaster planning and recovery during various crises, such as terrorist attacks and natural disasters (Hurley-Hanson & Giannantonio, 2008).

However, the contribution of technology to Strategic HRM has been limited, and some research indicates that HR professionals view ERP vendors as "over promising and under delivering" in this area (Dery & Wailes, 2005). It is important to remember that technology is only an enabling tool and not a solution or panacea for HR-related problems. Instead, the successful implementation of an HRIS depends on many different factors, such as the organizational culture, leadership and managerial competence, and the fit of the technology with organizational processes. In addition, many organizations fail to implement technology successfully because of their inherent rigidity, inertia, and resistance to change (Lengnick-Hall & Lengnick-Hall, 2006). Sometimes, there can also be certain "unintended negative consequences" within the process of realizing the potential of an HRIS; problems "related to the various ways in which different organizational stakeholders and groups engage with, enact, subvert, or avoid the technology or its planned objectives . . . can undermine its anticipated value to the HR function and organization more generally" (Grant, Newell, & Kavanagh, 2010, p. 4).

Until recently, the major HRIS products were expensive, monolithic, and rigid—providing little flexibility—and, consequently, only large organizations could afford to buy and deploy them. However, with its increasing capability and affordability, technology has largely had a positive impact on the HRM function, particularly at the transactional level, and now it is largely up to the HR profession to exploit technology's potential fully by taking it to the next level of transformational impact. And we're just getting started. The future of the field of e-HR will be driven by changes in HRM, HRIS, and internationalization. We briefly touch on the trends affecting each in this chapter.

FUTURE TRENDS IN HRM

Forecasting the future is, in general, quite difficult and even more so in HRM. Although one can examine past trends and extrapolate to the future, there can be unexpected contingencies, such as the financial crisis of 2008–2009. Also, changes in laws, directives, and guidelines from governmental agencies can strongly affect the future of HRM and HRIS. In fact, any significant changes in the environmental factors depicted in Figure 1.2 could cause major changes in the operation of HRM and an HRIS in organizations. To examine any future trends in the HR field, one must look within and between countries, since labor laws differ from country to country and, thus, could have a significant impact on any new developments in HRM for that country. However, the international HRM literature presents some similar trends across countries (e.g., a focus on the cost effectiveness of HR programs). An update on the future trends in HRM and HRIS in the United States will be discussed next in this chapter. However, there will also be discussion of trends in HRM, IT, and HRIS in multinational enterprises (MNEs). It is important to remember that countries may differ somewhat in terms of specific future trends within their culture.

SHRM Expert Panels

Since 2005, the Society for Human Resource Management (SHRM) has convened expert panels to discuss future trends in the HRM field. For the 2010 update, members of the panels were asked to examine the 2009 report to see if the future trends outlined there needed revision (Clark & Schramm, 2009). There were 12 panels, which focused on areas such as **corporate social responsibility and sustainability (CRS)**, employee health, safety and security, ethics, globalization, human capital measurement and HR metrics, technology and HR management, and workplace diversity. As can be seen, the panels covered most of the areas of the HRM function in organizations. On the basis of the work of the panels, 11 broad future trends important for HRM were identified. Each trend is listed below along with two verbatim statements by the expert panels describing the importance of that trend (Clark & Schramm, 2009).[1]

1. The impact of the **global recession**[2] on business strategy and employees
   a. Talent management [globally] continues to be a high priority and must be more efficient than before while leveraging cost awareness and monitoring demands for key positions. (p. 5)
   b. A new approach is needed to develop global workforce cultures, with better understanding of transnational teams, online collaboration, globalization and **business process transformation**. (p. 5)
2. The influence of social networking, especially as it relates to recruiting
   a. Social networking increasingly will affect the work done by HR departments—for example, recruiting and selection, employer branding, innovation initiatives—necessitating the creation of appropriate boundaries between business interests, ethics and employee privacy. (p. 4)
   b. Organizations increasingly are adopting **viral recruiting** and social media for employer brand messaging (e.g., Facebook, Twitter). (p. 8)
3. The continuing importance of **work/life balance** as employees deal with multiple caring responsibilities and, in some cases, multiple paid jobs
   a. Work/life balance issues will continue to influence employee stress levels.
   b. Work/life considerations will require increased attention from HR to address issues related to employees' overall health, retirement planning, financial health and the effects of the increase in the number of employees holding multiple jobs in addition to their primary employment. (p. 4)

4. The need for measurement of results and the development and standardization of key HR metrics
   a. There will be an increasing demand by organizations to measure and assess the value of their human capital and the HR activities, initiatives and practices that support it. (p. 6)
   b. The increasing need to use business intelligence, visualization and workforce planning technologies to support data integration, reporting, analysis and presentation challenges HR and HRIS professionals to evolve their HR technology platform and show the return of implementing these technologies. (p. 6)

5. The growing need for organizations to demonstrate a commitment to ethics, sustainability and social responsibility
   a. There is a growing need to incorporate the ethical values of an increasingly diverse and global workforce. (p. 5)
   b. Organizations increasingly will be subject to external scrutiny and expectations, leading to a greater separation between companies that implement and embrace CRS [corporate social responsibility and sustainability] as a way of doing business and those that use it only as a public relations tool. (p. 4)

6. Safety issues, particularly workplace aggression and the potential impact of a global disease pandemic
   a. A growth in the incidence of workplace aggression will influence employee safety policies. (p. 4)
   b. Safety compliance issues will increase and demand more attention from HR. (p. 4)

7. The importance of globalization and integrating markets
   a. The economic crisis and fewer existing business opportunities will create a high demand on the global HR function to demonstrate greater agility and contribute strategic guidance. (p. 5)
   b. **Global mobility** of high-value workers continues as multinational companies restrict new hires and relocate talented employees from within their existing workforce. (p. 6)

8. Continued emphasis on performance management
   a. There is a renewed focus on performance management and on performance and process improvement. (p. 7)

b. Increased demand for HR metrics may bring about a widely accepted set of analytic measures and methods—global standards—to describe, predict and evaluate the quality and impact of HR practices and the productivity of the workforce. (p. 6)

9. The ongoing need for skilled employees and concerns about the ability of the U.S. education system to produce the needed skilled workers of the future
   a. Education and job mismatch will increase as employees return to college and graduate school, but for degrees for jobs that are not in demand, i.e., white-collar jobs as opposed to skilled trade jobs where demand may increase. (p. 5)
   b. Workforce planning will be affected both by the education system's ability to produce qualified workers and by changes in retirement patterns. (p. 7)

10. Demographic change and its impact on diversity and labor availability
    a. Economic challenges have disrupted **workforce demographics** (delayed retirement, lack of new skilled workers, etc.) and affected employee engagement. (p. 7)
    b. There is a differentiation of rewards among different employee segments, as increasingly one size will not fit all, given several generations in the workforce and increasingly diverse ethnic and cultural demographics. (p. 8)

11. The implications of government legislation
    a. There is an increased government intervention in employer-provided compensation and benefits through expanded regulations that affect private-sector compensation, paid time off, health benefits and retirement plans. (p. 8)
    b. Governmental involvement in setting the CSR agenda will increase in both regulatory and legislative arenas. (p. 4)

Future Trends and Challenges

Another poll conducted by SHRM surveyed 449 HR professionals, from both U.S.-based companies (72%) and multinational organizations (28%), regarding the specific challenges they expected to face over the next 10 years (SHRM, 2010). Almost half of those responding indicated that "obtaining human capital and optimizing on human capital investments" is the top investment challenge they face. The most commonly noted key to meeting the related challenges of "attracting, retaining and rewarding the best people" was the ability of organizations to provide employees with the flexibility to balance life and work (58%). Here are the other findings that were endorsed by over 20% of respondents:

- Creating an organizational culture where trust, open communications and fairness are emphasized and demonstrated by leaders (47%).
- Having jobs designed to provide employees with meaningful work that has a clear purpose in meeting organizational objectives (40%).
- Demonstrating a commitment to employee development (29%).
- Offering a higher total rewards package (i.e., total compensation and benefits package) than organizations that compete for the same talent (23%). (p. 1)

The common themes across these two surveys are the importance of talent management, **organizational culture**, and compensation in a global business environment. The first study (Clark & Schramm, 2009) focused on trends in HR without any consideration of how to manage the trends forecasted for only *one year*. The second survey specifically asked how HR was going to survive the challenges over the next *ten years*.

In terms of the issues for MNEs, these organizations face the challenges of globalization and of managing data for a global workforce. For example, in a recent study by Jeitosa Group International and IHRIM (Beaman, 2009), the survey respondents indicated that three important challenges facing them as they move toward a global workforce are (1) how to ensure **data quality and integrity** (31%), (2) concerns about **data privacy** and the associated (and often inconsistent) country regulations (29%), and (3) **international compliance** (27%) (p. 3).

Although shared services have been around for more than a decade, another trend in IHRM is the growing use of these services, with 32% of organizations recently surveyed indicating that they have a global **shared-services center** (Beaman, 2010). The shared-services approach refers to the centralization of all HR services into one location rather than having separate HR staff in different locations and divisions. Sharing services provides economies of scale and scope and helps to centralize knowledge and expertise and make both available to all divisions.

A final trend in HRM on which we briefly touch is the virtualization of work. No longer are employees confined by physical or temporal space. Employees can conduct work anywhere and at any time. "The **virtual workspace** can be defined as an environment where employees work away from company premises and communicate with their respective workplaces via telephone or computer devices" (Lockwood, 2010, p. 1). For example, one of the authors has recently taught a class in which a student was part of a virtual team. His team consisted of six members on four continents, none of whom had physically met. Together, they were responsible for ensuring that a global corporation's database systems were "constantly up" and free of errors. They had to coordinate global schedules to hold monthly meetings to ensure that the team was meeting targets and schedules. Yet, they had to do this while never working in the same physical space! Managing in this geographically dispersed environment creates challenges in leadership, in the effectiveness of communication, in technology, and in procedures for conducting virtual meetings and ensuring appropriate HR management. For example, Figure 17.1 lists several keys to managing virtual meetings successfully. Given the growing use of virtual teams, organizations will increasingly need to be aware of the benefits and pitfalls of managing employees in the virtual workplace.

Figure 17.1 Tips for Effective Virtual Meetings and Management

Prepare and distribute agendas in advance; ensure agendas reflect input requested from participants.
Initiate meetings with "roll call" of all participants; review agenda, meeting objectives and timeframe.
Identify the key roles of facilitator and scribe.
Position participants in locations "free" of distractions or background noise.
Promote climate of collaboration and inclusion; encourage every attendee to participate and express his or her view.
Encourage participants to effectively use available technology.
Conduct meeting evaluation at the close of the session.
Establish expectation for distribution of the meeting minutes.
Establish "next steps" and make follow-up assignments.

SOURCE: SHRM interview with Global Dynamics, Inc. (www.global-dynamics.com), as presented in Lockwood (2010).

As seen by these forecasted HR trends, which present both domestic and global challenges, managers of HR are facing a complex future world. Although all of the studies previously described focus on different issues, there are common themes across all: the importance of human capital, organizational culture, and compensation in a global business environment. It is interesting to note that these common themes were identified as playing a role in the future of HR in 2011 as well as 10 years from now. Thus, how managers respond to this complexity will be aided by advances in both HR practice and the technology that supports it (e.g., HRIS). Accordingly, the next section of this chapter covers future trends in the fields of IT/IS and HRIS.

FUTURE TRENDS IN IT/IS AND HRIS

In the first edition of this book, we started this section as follows: "When examining future trends in HRIS, it is impossible to separate the future trends in IT/IS without relating them to the field of HRM" (Kavanagh & Thite, 2009, p. 413). If anything, this statement is more accurate today than when the first edition of this book appeared. The knowledge economy is being profoundly influenced not only by the intensity but also by the speed of technological evolution. Information technologies have been steadily evolving and improving from mainframes to client servers and now to Internet/Web interfaces (Collective HR Solutions, 2010; Macy, 2010; Roberts, 2006). Network communication technologies (broadband and wireless), convergence technologies (e.g., cell phones and PDAs), collaborative tools (e.g., Web 2.0, portals), **service-oriented architecture (SOA)**, rich Internet application (RIA), and business intelligence HR software systems are some of the notable developments that have affected the field of HRIS and its related technologies. Apart from achieving better coordination and integration of different systems within an enterprise, these technologies are empowering both employers and employees to deploy, share, and use their knowledge for the common benefit of their company. One of the most critical aspects of the emerging technology is a focus on more efficient and accurate decision making, also a primary focus throughout this book. For example, the goal of intelligent HR software is to replace the traditional approach to decision making with an approach that makes a better decision in the most efficient manner. Obviously, this technology can help organizations improve their use of human capital and increase their competiveness in the market. We next briefly discuss the changes in technology that will have a large impact on the HRIS and the delivery of HR functionality.

Software as a Service (SaaS) and the Cloud

Traditionally, HRIS implementations were large, time-consuming, and expensive undertakings. Whether implementing a large-scale system such as an enterprise resource planning (ERP) system or a smaller system focused on one HR function, an organization would often work with vendors and consultants to purchase and install hardware and software on its premises. This "on-premise" approach to acquiring software was the dominant and often the only approach available to organizations. Traditional software development models are being replaced by "on-demand" software plans, which see the company or customer leasing access to as few or as many HR functions as it wishes to access. This approach to accessing software has been called **software as a service (SaaS)** (Zeidner, 2007). With SaaS, small and medium companies are now able to access HRIS capabilities that were previously only available to large organizations. These companies currently comprise the largest customer pool for new HRIS packages.

The newest trend in delivering software to companies is **cloud computing**. With cloud computing, HRIS functionality is delivered to companies via the Web. For the company, there is no hardware to purchase or software to install. Employees can also access the software anywhere they have a Web browser. As with SaaS, companies are able to adopt only the amount of functionality currently needed and then scale up to additional functionality. Momentum toward cloud computing is growing. For example, IBM is ready to offer the Federal Community Cloud, a secure cloud environment designed for federal agencies, and Lockheed Martin recently unveiled the Starfire Mission Ready Cloud™. The growing popularity and strengths of SaaS and cloud computing should lead to more organizations rethinking their HRIS delivery strategies. These new "rent" versus "buy" decisions should become more common in the next few years (Johnson & Gueutal, 2011).

Service-Oriented Architecture

One of the major problems during this technological evolution has been the frustration associated with frequent system upgrade cycles. SOA may be a solution, as it converts monolithic and static systems into modular and flexible components. According to Roberts (2006), "The big change in enterprise software that will impact everything from financials to HR is standards-based, service-oriented software (SOA)" (p. 104). The self-contained services in an SOA are loosely coupled, like a set of Lego pieces, and can be reconfigured to suit a particular business process and end-user application rather than being hard-coded together, as they were in the past.

SOA is about "efficient modular design and deployment, and reusable software is at the heart of the architecture" (Macy, 2007). SOA offers several advantages to end users, who can change the business process when needed and purchase or develop only those applications that are involved in the new processes. This approach is much better than working around the existing system or purchasing a package from a vendor based on predetermined processes and applications. Thus, under SOA, the business process dictates the IT system to be used and not the other way round. In the long run, this will reduce technology costs and should improve productivity. The use of SOA in talent management is covered in Chapter 10.

In Chapter 10, XML-enhanced SOA was also discussed. Whether SOA delivers what it promises depends on how the major companies in the ERP market respond. For example, having acquired PeopleSoft and JD Edwards, Oracle may need to integrate its own systems before harnessing the potential of SOA. Oracle Fusion and SAP's NetWeaver, the two strategies adopted by Oracle and SAP around SOA, will play an important role in how HRIS technology evolves in the future. In addition, Workday, a new firm in the IT/IS and HRIS field, is developing a product built around a document-centric data structure, like Google (Roberts, 2006).

Web 2.0

This term refers to a second generation of Web-related services focusing on creativity, collaboration, and sharing, in contrast to traditional isolated information silos. **Web 2.0** users not only access information but also generate, share, and distribute new content. According to Dario de Judicibus, "Web 2.0 is a knowledge-oriented environment where human interactions generate content that is published, managed and used through network applications in a service-oriented architecture" (as quoted in Deloitte Consulting LLP, 2008).

Examples of Web 2.0 technology include the following (McKinsey & Company, 2007):

- Social networking sites (e.g., chat rooms, MySpace, Facebook)
- Wikis (publicly available collaborative Web dictionaries enabling users to contribute to online documents or discussion)

- Blogs (short for Web logs, i.e., online journals or diaries hosted on a Web site, both personal and corporate)
- Mash-ups (software composed of two or more composite applications—e.g., pulling up a rental car booking site within an airline booking site)
- Podcasts (audio or video recordings)
- RSS (rich site summary) feeds (e.g., news items)
- Personal Web sites
- Peer-to-peer networking (P2P; sharing files, e.g., text, music, and videos)
- Collective intelligence (sharing knowledge to tap the expertise of a group)
- Web services (Web-enabled instant communication between users to update information or conduct transactions—e.g., a supplier and a retailer updating each other's inventory systems)

Web 2.0 has also encouraged businesses to promote user collaboration to share knowledge and to communicate with business partners, such as suppliers and outsourcing providers. With an emphasis on sharing, Web 2.0 can dramatically change the way in which employees communicate with each other and with customers. Using Web 2.0 will require the HR department to pay greater attention to the legal, ethical, and security implications of information exchange.

Social Networking

As noted in the previous section, **social networking** is one of the features of Web 2.0. Social networks such as Facebook, MySpace, blogs, and wikis are personal in nature and vary in the extent to which organizations have adopted them. Although these networks were originally developed to enhance social connections, organizations are increasingly harnessing the power of social networking in the workplace. For example, tools such as wikis are being used by organizations to harness and centralize employee knowledge. Some companies are even requiring that employees contribute to the company wiki, making these contributions a formal component of various jobs. Blogs are not only used to share information within the company and with external stakeholders but also to communicate organization culture and personality.

In addition, companies are using Facebook and Twitter to help expand their HR brand and attract employees to the organization. Many companies, such as IBM and Deloitte, are making social networking a central component of how they bring new employees into the organization, connecting them with current employees and easing their transition into the company.

Companies are also using social networks to connect employees and share information. For example, EMC Corporation uses its social business network,

EMC/One, to generate ideas from its employees for its annual innovation contest. After the employees post their innovation ideas on EMC/One, they can also vote for the best idea (Roberts, 2010). At AT&T, senior HR managers use its social business network, tSpace, to identify employees with special skills or knowledge, such as the ability to read or speak a foreign language. Of course, as Roberts notes, there is the possibility that some organizations may use these networks inappropriately. However, part of this problem is controlled by the fact that social business networks require employees to use their full names, and companies have strict policies regarding a code of conduct for employees.

Enterprise Portals

Enterprise portal is the general term used to refer to the ways in which individuals can interact with each other. **Enterprise portals** can be information portals, collaboration portals, expertise and knowledge portals, operation portals, **social business networks**, or a combination of all of these. Within an HRIS, employee and manager self-service portals are powerful examples of the potential use of such portals (see Chapter 10). In the context of portals, two of the most commonly used standards are WSRP (Web Services for Remote Portlets) and JSR (Java Specification Request), although, as described in the previous section, companies are beginning to adopt software necessary to build social business networks. One very important implication regarding the establishment and use of enterprise portals is their effect on the family-work conflicts that dual wage earners face. Being able to respond to and, it is hoped, solve work problems from one's home will be increasingly important in the future.

Open Source Software

As discussed throughout this text, traditionally, vendors developed software following a very structured approach. Software is often released in formal cycles, and, in each cycle, new functionality is added and errors from previous releases are fixed. Each cycle, then, culminates with a release date. In addition, vendors will often stop supporting older releases as they place more resources into newer releases. The software developed in this way is copyrighted, and the source code is neither open nor available for others to enhance. This approach to software development has been criticized by some software developers as increasing the cost of software, stifling innovation, and encouraging developers to make previous versions obsolete (requiring companies to then upgrade).

In response to these concerns, some software developers have agreed to a different approach to the development of software called open source. In an open source approach to software development, the developers make the source code available for anyone to see and to change. This means that other companies or developers can then expand on the product or easily develop complementary products. **Open source software** also costs much less than traditional (or proprietary) software, and is sometimes provided for free. Open source products are available for a wide variety of organizational needs. Examples of open source products include Linux (an operating system), Apache (a Web server that plays a central role in the operation of the Web), OpenOffice (a free alternative to Microsoft Office), and MySQL (a database product). The major risk facing organizations considering open source adoption is the long-term viability of the product as the continued success of these products depends on the continuing interest of the developers. But, in many areas where needs are common across organizations, open source products are finding strong support.

Open source software should grow in importance for human resources in the near future. For example, many HR vendors such as Workday, Taleo, and Journeyx use open source software in support of their product offerings. In addition, companies are starting to emerge that offer open source HRIS. Some of these are integrated and some are more function specific. For example, TimeTrex is open source software for time and attendance management, and OrangeHRM offers a more integrated suite. These products are targeted at small- to medium-sized businesses. Central to these companies' business model is not the sale of the software itself. Instead these companies focus on providing support services and customization support. The business model thus changes from one of continual updates for profit to one of developing a long-term relationship with clients.

FUTURE TRENDS IN WORKFORCE TECHNOLOGIES

The many future trends in the HRM, IT/IS, and HRIS fields can easily lead to confusion for organizations, management, vendors, and employees. A solution to this confusion has been proposed by Carden (2009), and we agree wholeheartedly—technology should serve strategic goals. Carden notes that the increasing competition by organizations to improve their profitability has often led to the conclusion that *new technology will solve these issues*, but the reality is more complex than that. Organizations that are most successful are those who are able to leverage the technology that most closely links to a strong business strategy. With the recent global recession, the increasing pressure to remain competitive and survive has led to companies adopting technology to carefully diagnose what *strategic goals* the adoption of technology could support. "Even the most sophisticated software is rendered powerless without a solid business strategy behind it" (Carden, 2009, p. 20). Thus, as we consider the changes in workforce technologies, it is important to keep in mind that how effectively organizations are able to harness the power of these new technologies will depend on how well they link it to their HR strategy.

In the first edition of this book, we noted that Henson (2005) had made the following predictions about the future of workforce technologies:

- the technology of the future will be both collaborative and connected;
- there will be increased and more widespread use of intelligent self-service via employee portals;
- there will be increased use of HR scorecards coupled with workforce analytics and decision trees;
- there will be increases in process automation and the use of online analytical processing (OLAP) for processing raw data;
- faster and cheaper access to accurate real-time HR information will be possible due to advancements in communication tools; and
- the worker of the future will be able to work anywhere, any time, and on any device, which will not only help work-life balance but also turn the workplace into a 24/7 cycle.

As we examine the recent state of workforce technologies, we agree with Henson. Surprisingly, many of these predictions mentioned in 2005 have already been realized. Therefore, we decided to conclude this chapter by reporting the results of the latest *CedarCrestone 2010–2011 HR Systems Survey* (CedarCrestone, 2010) on "HR Technologies, Service Delivery Approaches, and Metrics."[3] The purpose of this survey was to provide "a worldwide benchmark of workforce technologies adoption and the value achieved from their use," so CedarCrestone broadened its "coverage scope for both HR technologies and emerging technologies . . . to explore over 40 applications concerning adoption, deployment options, vendor outlook, value achieved, and expenditures" (p. 1). The results of this systems survey are depicted in Figure 17.2.

Figure 17.2 How Respondents Spend Time and Budget (Percentage of Respondents)

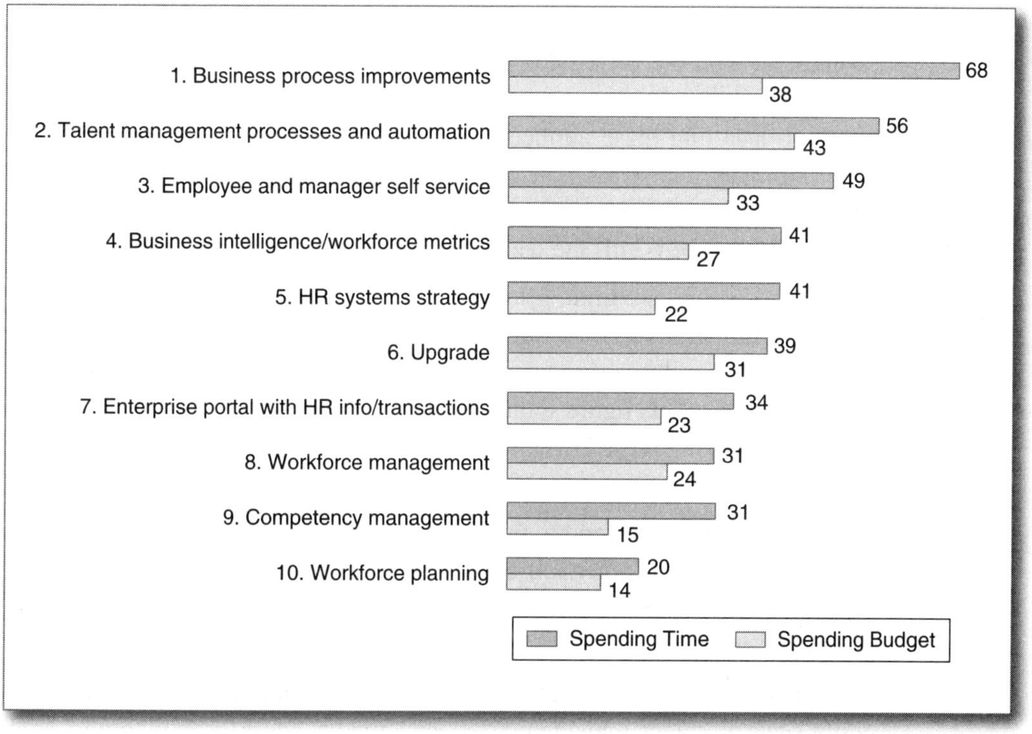

SOURCE: *CedarCrestone 2010–2011 HR Systems Survey: HR Technologies, Service Delivery Approaches, and Metrics*, 13th Annual Edition (CedarCrestone, 2010).

Data for this report were collected in 2010 from 1,289 respondents representing more than 20 million employees. The sample represents companies from throughout the globe including North America, Europe, Asia, and Australia. The major findings of this study are as follows:

1. As was reported in the first edition of this book, organizations that have more automation across all categories of technologies outperform those organizations with less automation on the important productivity measures of net income growth, sales growth, and sales per employee.
2. Due to recent economic conditions, the market was quite unstable for the organizations represented in the survey sample. However, the respondents in the survey reported that their organizations have had strong recoveries, and they forecasted a 100% growth in HRIS talent management, social media,[4] and analytics and planning applications.

3. Organizations reported that business process improvement through techniques such as Six Sigma (Chapter 8) for recruiting new employees was their top initiative.
4. Consistent with our discussion of SaaS earlier in the chapter, organizations are increasingly choosing to rent access to applications instead of purchasing and installing these applications on site. This growth was noted to be even stronger than was indicated in CedarCrestone's last survey (2009). However, although sales are forecast to decrease in the next year, on-premise licensed software is still the leader across all HRIS applications.
5. Organizations are continuing to invest in applications across all HR functions. Administrative HRIS software for core HR record keeping, payroll, and benefits is still the dominant class of technology, with worldwide average use at 90%. This figure should not be a surprise to the reader, as we have been emphasizing these HRIS functions throughout this book, especially in Chapter 10.
6. There is a continuing trend to use new "service delivery" applications, such as employee and manager self-service systems, portals, HR help desks, and workforce life cycle management; this trend is expected to grow during the next three years.
7. The major increase in the use of technology to support HR will focus on tools such as talent management, social media, workforce planning, and workforce analytics, with over 90% growth in the next three years.
8. Among organizations that have installed multiple talent management applications, that is, those for acquiring, developing, and retaining employees, those companies with four or more applications installed outperformed those companies with three or fewer applications in terms of higher net income growth, sales growth, and sales per employee.
9. Organizations have begun preparing to use service-oriented architecture (SOA) to automate business processes such as applicant tracking. As discussed earlier in this chapter, SOA provides an overall service that is well defined, self-contained, and context and platform independent and that adds value to the organization's business purpose.
10. Finally, the survey focused on choices and investments that are providing a strong return to companies. These choices include the following:
    - **Focus on Career Development.** It is not simply technology that makes a difference for employees. By leveraging technology and HR practices, organizations that actively support employee professional development will find that employee loyalty will increase and turnover will be reduced.

- **Use Workforce Optimization Technologies.** There is continued growth of organizations adopting workforce planning and workforce analytics. Organizations that have adopted these applications outperform those that have not.
- **Choose an Integrated ERP-based Talent Management Solution.** For the third year in a row, organizations pursuing a strategy that integrates multiple HR functions into a software solution have had the best financial performance out of all those firms participating in the study.
- **Adopt Social Networking.** Early evidence suggests that the adoption of social networking by organizations is leading to lower costs and improved organizational agility and responsiveness.

SUMMARY

As noted early in this chapter, forecasting the future is very difficult. One reason for this difficulty is that the field of HRIS is not just about what might become technically possible. It is, essentially, about systems that serve humans and human enterprise. Students focusing on understanding the field of HRIS must never forget the human issues involved in developing and implementing an HRIS. The field of HRIS continues to evolve, and it is important for those studying it not only to understand what is occurring today but also to look at the environmental and technological forces that will affect it in the coming years. If there is one central theme of our look toward the future, it is the importance of HR policies matched with organizational change and technology; this alignment will have the greatest impact on the future success of HRIS and the organizations investing in these systems. For example, one of the findings from the CedarCrestone survey was the emphasis on change management—to which an entire chapter of this book was devoted (see Chapter 9). Technology is not a substitute for managerial competence and employee discretionary behavior (Armstrong, 2005). It can only be a messenger, not a message. It is also impractical to expect information systems to supplant the soft functions of the HR department, such as an online electronic tutor replacing a good executive coach (Stanton & Coovert, 2004). In sum, technology is extremely important in the field of HRIS, but people are simply more important.

KEY TERMS

business process transformation
cloud computing
corporate social responsibility and sustainability (CRS)
data privacy
data quality and integrity
enterprise portals
global mobility

global recession
international compliance
open source software
organizational culture
service-oriented architecture (SOA)
shared-services center
social business networks
social networking
software as a service (SaaS)
viral recruiting
virtual workspace
Web 2.0
work/life balance
workforce demographics
workforce optimization technologies

NOTES

1. Selected specific examples of the general trends will be covered here. The main trends quoted here can be found in Clark and Schramm (2009, p. 4). Interested readers can access the entire document at http://www.shrm.org/Research/FutureWorkplaceTrends/Documents/09-0700 Workplace panel_trends_sympFINAL Upd.pdf.
2. The bold font used here and for some other quoted phrases has been applied by the editors to highlight key terms.
3. We are reporting only part of the results of this survey due to its length; however, the entire survey may be obtained from CedarCrestone (http://www.cedarcrestone.com/whitepapers/CC_2010-2011_HRS_Survey_WP.pdf).
4. This finding echoes the description of social business networking discussed in an earlier section of this chapter.

REFERENCES

Armstrong, G. (2005). Differentiation through people: How can HR move beyond business partner? *Human Resource Management, 44*(2), 195–199.

Beaman, K. (2009). *2009–2010 Going global readiness report.* New York: Jeitosa Group International and the International Association for Human Resource Information Management (IHRIM).

Beaman, K. (2010, March). Shared services: Environmental factors. *HRinsights*. New York: Jeitosa Group International.

Becker, B. E., & Huselid, M. A. (2006). Strategic human resources management: Where do we go from here? *Journal of Management, 32*(6), 898–925.

Carden, M. (2009). Strategy first, technology second. *IHRIM.link, 14*(2), 20–22.

CedarCrestone. (2009). *CedarCrestone 2009–2010 HR systems survey: HR technologies, service delivery approaches, and metrics* (12th annual ed.). Alpharetta, GA: CedarCrestone, Inc.

CedarCrestone. (2010). *CedarCrestone 2010–2011 HR systems survey: HR technologies, service delivery approaches, and metrics* (13th annual ed.). Alpharetta, GA: CedarCrestone, Inc.

Clark, M., & Schramm, J. (2009). *Future insights: The top trends according to SHRM's HR subject matter expert panel.* Alexandria, VA: Society for Human Resource Management, SHRM Research Department.

Collective HR Solutions. (2010, April). *HR technology implementation value survey.* San Francisco: Author.

Deloitte Consulting LLP. (2008, October 10). The maturing human network: Can you find me now? *ComputerWeekly.com*, sec. 4, para. 3.

Dery, K., & Wailes, N. (2005). Necessary but not sufficient: ERPs and strategic HRM. *Strategic Change, 14*, 265–272.

Grant, D., Newell, S., & Kavanagh, M. (2010, August). *Realizing the potential of an HRIS: Unintended consequences, human agency and the HR function.* Paper presented at the annual meeting of the Academy of Management Symposium, Montreal, Canada.

Haines, V. Y., & Lafleur, G. (2008). Information technology usage and human resource roles and effectiveness. *Human Resource Management, 47*(3), 525–540.

Henson, R. (2005). The next decade of HR: Trends, technologies and recommendations. In H. G. Gueutal & D. L. Stone (Eds.), *The brave new world of eHR* (pp. 255–292). San Francisco: Jossey Bass.

Hubbard, J. C., Forcht, K. A., & Tomas, D. S. (1998). Human resource information systems: An overview of current ethical and legal issues. *Journal of Business Ethics, 17*, 1319–1323.

Hurley-Hanson, A. E., & Giannantonio, C. M. (2008). Human resource information systems in crises. *Proceedings of the Academy of Strategic Management, 7*(1), 23–27.

Johnson, R. D., & Gueutal, H. G. (2011). *Transforming HR through technology: The use of eHR and human resource information systems in organizations* (SHRM Effective Practice Guidelines Series). Alexandria, VA: The SHRM Foundation.

Kavanagh, M. J., & Thite, M. (Eds.). (2009). *Human resource information systems: Basics, applications, and future directions.* Thousand Oaks, CA: Sage.

Lawler, E. E. (2005). From human resource management to organizational effectiveness. *Human Resource Management, 44*(2), 165–169.

Lengnick-Hall, C. A., & Lengnick-Hall, M. L. (2006). HR, ERP and knowledge for competitive advantage. *Human Resource Management, 45*(2), 179–194.

Lockwood, N. R. (2010). *Successfully transitioning to a virtual organization: Challenges, impact and technology.* Alexandria, VA: Society for Human Resource Management, HR Content Program, SHRM Research.

Macy, J. (2007, March). Welcome to the Web 2.0 age. *HR Monthly*, pp. 36–37.

Macy, J. (2010, March). HR technology: IDE and modern application development. *HRinsights.* New York: Jeitosa Group International.

Martin, E. (2008, February/March). Creating the HR value proposition. *IHIM.link, 13*(1), 22–23.

Mayfield, M., Mayfield, J., & Lunce, S. (2003). Human resource information systems: A review and model development. *Advances in Competitiveness Research, 11*(1), 139–151.

McKinsey & Company. (2007, March). How businesses are using Web 2.0: A McKinsey global survey [Electronic version]. *The McKinsey Quarterly.* Retrieved March 20, 2011, from http://www.mckinseyquarterly.com/How_businesses_are_using_Web_20_A_McKinsey_Global_Survey_1913

Morris, S. S., Wright, P. M., Trevor, J., Stiles, P., Stahl, G. K., Snell, S., Paauwe, J., & Farndale, E. (2009). Global challenges to replicating HR: The role of people, processes and systems. *Human Resource Management, 48*(6), 973–995.

Roberts, B. (2006). New HR systems on the horizon. *HR Magazine, 51*(5), 103–107.

Roberts, B. (2010). Developing a social business network. *HR Magazine, 55*(10), 54–60.

Shrivatsava, S., & Shaw, J. B. (2003). Liberating HR through technology. *Human Resource Management, 42*(3), 201–222.

Society for Human Resource Management. (2010). *SHRM poll identifies top HR challenges for next 10 years.* Alexandria, VA: Society for Human Resource Management. Retrieved October 10, 2010, from http://www.shrm.org/Publications/HRNews/Pages/Challenges10years.aspx

Stanton, J. M., & Coovert, M. D. (2004). Guest editors' note: Turbulent waters: The intersection of information technology and human resources. *Human Resource Management, 43*(2/3), 121–125.

Ulrich, D., & Smallwood, N. (2005). HR's new ROI: Return on intangibles. *Human Resource Management, 44*(2), 137–142.

Zeidner, R. (2007). *SAAS identified as leading trend in HR tech* (SHRM White Paper). Alexandria, VA: Society of Human Resource Management.

APPENDIX

ADDITIONAL RESOURCES

Internet Resources

A collection of change theory sites: http://www.comminit.com/en/taxonomy/term/36%2C25

Academy of Management: http://www.aomonline.org/

Advantiv (DecisionDirector® software): www.advantiv.com

American Society for Training and Development: www.astd.org

Association of Change Management Professionals: www.acmp.info

Being First, Inc.—a change leadership development and transformational change consulting firm with lots of free resources for change leaders and consultants: www.beingfirst.com/

CedarCrestone: http://www.cedarcrestone.com

Change Management Learning Center: www.change-management.com

Economic Research Institute: www.erieri.com

Employee Benefit Research Institute (EBRI): www.ebri.org

Expert Choice: www.expertchoice.com

Gartner, Inc.—an information technology research and advisory company: www.gartner.com

The Hackett Group—a company offering business best practices, business benchmarking, and transformation consulting services: www.thehackettgroup.com

Hay Group—a global management consulting firm: www.haygroup.com

HR-Guide: www.hr-guide.com

Human Factors and Ergonomics Society: www.hfes.org

International Association for Human Resource Information Management: www.ihrim.org

International Foundation of Employee Benefit Plans: www.ifebp.org

Jeitosa Group International—a consultancy firm specializing in global human resource technology and management: www.jeitosa.com

Kaiser Associates—an international strategy consulting firm: www.kaiserassociates.com

Maritz—a sales and marketing services company specializing in employee motivation: www.maritz.com

Mercer—a company specializing in benefits administration: www.mercer.com

Organization for the Advancement of Structured Information Systems (OASIS): www.oasis-open.org

Salary.com—a tool to find salary data: www.salary.com

SalaryExpert.com—a tool providing reports on salaries and cost of living from compensation professionals: www.salaryexpert.com

PwC Saratoga—a firm specializing in the measurement and benchmarking of human capital: www.pwc.com/us/en/hr-saratoga

Six Sigma—a firm providing information on Six Sigma as a change process as well as educational opportunities in Six Sigma. The registration is free: www.isixsigma.com

Society for Human Resource Management: www.shrm.org

Society for Industrial & Organizational Psychology (SIOP): www.siop.org

Structured Analysis Wiki: http://yourdon.com/strucanalysis/wiki

Themanager.org provides an excellent collection of topics on change management: www.themanager.org/Knowledgebase/Management/Change.htm

Towers Watson—a firm offering solutions in the areas of employee benefits, talent management, rewards, and risk and capital management: www.towerswatson.com

U.S. Department of Labor: www.dol.gov

U.S. Department of Labor, Bureau of Labor Statistics: www.bls.gov

Wageweb.com: www.wageweb.com

WorldatWork (was ACA)—a nonprofit focusing on global human resources issues: www.worldatwork.org

Vendor Software:

www.cornerstoneondemand.com
www.orangehrm.com
www.oracle.com
www.outstart.com
www.plateau.com
www.saba.com
www.sap.com
www.sumtotalsystems.com

Additional Readings

Abrahamson, E. (2004). *Change without pain.* Boston: Harvard Business School Press.

Adler, N. J. (2002). *International dimensions of organizational behavior.* Cincinnati, OH: South-Western.

Adler, S. (1987). Toward the more efficient use of assessment center technology in personnel selection. *Journal of Business and Psychology, 2,* 74–93.

Aguinis, H., Henle, C. A., & Beaty, J. C. (2001). Virtual reality technology: A new tool for personnel selection. *International Journal of Selection and Assessment, 9,* 70–83.

Alavi, M., & Leidner, D. E. (2001). Research commentary: Technology-mediated learning—A call for greater depth and breadth of research. *Information Systems Research, 12*(1), 1.

Allen, E. T., Melone, J. J., Rosenbloom, J. S., & Mahoney, D. F. (2007). *Retirement plans: 401(k)s, IRAs and other deferred compensation approaches.* New York: McGraw-Hill.

Anderson, N. (2003). Applicant and recruiter reactions to new technology in selection: A critical review and agenda for future research. *International Journal of Selection and Assessment, 11,* 121–136.

Armstrong, M. (2006). *Performance management: Key strategies and practical guidelines* (3rd ed.). London: Kogan Page.

Armstrong, M., & Stephens, T. (2005). *A handbook of employee reward management and practice.* London: Kogan Page.

Bartram, D. (2006). Testing on the Internet: Issues, challenges, and opportunities in the field of occupational assessment. In D. Bartram & R. K. Hambleton (Eds.), *Computer-based testing and the Internet: Issues and advances* (pp. 13–37). San Francisco: Wiley.

Bauer, T. N., Truxillo, D. M., & Paronto, M. E. (2004). Applicant reactions to different selection technology: Face-to-face, interactive voice response, and computer-assisted telephone screening interviews. *International Journal of Selection and Assessment, 12,* 135–148.

Bauer, T. N., Truxillo, D. M., Tucker, J. S., Weathers, V., Bertolino, M., Erdogan, B., & Campion, M. A. (2006). Selection in the information age: The impact of privacy concerns and computer experience on applicant reactions. *Journal of Management, 32,* 601–621.

Beaman, K. (Ed.). (2002). *Boundaryless HR: Human capital management in the global environment.* Austin, TX: Rector Duncan & Associates.

Beatty, R. W., Huselid, M. A., & Schneier, C. E. (2003). New HR metrics: Scoring on the business scorecard. *Organizational Dynamics, 32*(2), 107–121.

Bebchuck, L., & Fried, J. (2004). *Pay without performance: The unfulfilled promise of executive compensation.* Cambridge, MA: Harvard University Press.

Becker, B. E., & Huselid, M. A. (2006). Strategic human resource management: Where do we go from here? *Journal of Management, 32*(6), 898–925.

Beer, M., & Nohria, N. (2000). *Breaking the code of change.* Boston: Harvard Business School Press.

Bieg, B. J. (2007). *Payroll accounting 2007.* Mason, OH: Thomson/South-Western.

Braddy, P. W., Meade, A. W., & Kroustalis, C. M. (2006). Organizational recruitment website effects on viewers' perceptions of organizational culture. *Journal of Business and Psychology, 20,* 525–543.

Bridges, W. (2003). *Managing transitions: Making the most of change.* Cambridge, MA: Da Capo Press.

Buckley, P., Minette, K., Joy, D., & Michaels, J. (2004). The use of an automated employment recruiting and screening system for temporary professional employees: A case study. *Human Resource Management, 43,* 233–241.

Burke, W. W. (2007). *Organization change: Theory and practice.* Thousand Oaks, CA: Sage.

Business & Legal Reports (BLR). (2007). *2007 survey of employee benefits.* Old Saybrook, CT: Author.

Cappelli, P. (2001). Making the most of online recruiting. *Harvard Business Review, 79,* 139–146.

Carr, D. K., Hard, K. J., & Trahant, W. J. (1996). *Managing the change process.* New York: McGraw-Hill.

Cascio, W. F. (2000). *Costing human resources: The financial impact of behavior in organizations* (4th ed.). Boston: Kent.

Chan, D., & Schmitt, N. (2004). An agenda for future research on applicant reactions to selection procedures: A construct-oriented approach. *International Journal of Selection and Assessment, 12,* 9–23.

Cohen, D. S., & Kotter, J. P. (2005). *The heart of change field guide.* Boston: Harvard Business School Press.

Conner, D. R. (1992). *Managing at the speed of change.* New York: Villard Books.

Conner, M. L. (2002). How do I measure return on investment (ROI) for my learning program? *Learning and training FAQs.* Retrieved April 5, 2008, from www.learnativity.com

D'Aprix, R. (1996). *Communicating for change.* San Francisco: Jossey-Bass.

Dennis, A. R., Wixom, B. H., & Roth, R. M. (2006). *Systems analysis and design* (3rd ed.). Hoboken, NJ: Wiley.

Dineen, B. R., & Noe, R. A. (2009). Effects of customization on application decisions and applicant pool characteristics in a web-based recruitment context. *Journal of Applied Psychology, 94,* 224–234.

Dowling, P. J., & Welch, D. E. (2005). *International human resource management: Managing people in a multinational context* (4th ed.). Mason, OH: Thomson South-Western.

Duck, J. D. (2001). *The change monster: The human forces that fuel or foil corporate transformation and change.* New York: Crown Business.

Ellig, B. R. (2002). *The complete guide to executive compensation.* New York: McGraw-Hill.

Ensher, E. A., Nielson, T. R., & Grant-Vallone, E. (2002). Tales from the hiring line: Effects of the internet and technology on HR processes. *Organizational Dynamics, 31,* 224–244.

Epstein, J., & Klinkenberg, W. D. (2001). From Eliza to Internet: A brief history of computerized assessment. *Computers in Human Behavior, 17,* 295–314.

Epstein, J., Klinkenberg, W. D., Wiley, D., & McKinley, L. (2001). Insuring sample equivalence across Internet and paper-and-pencil assessments. *Computers in Human Behavior, 17,* 339–346.

Feldman, D. C., & Klaas, B. S. (2002). Internet job hunting: A field study of applicant experiences with on-line recruiting. *Human Resource Management, 41,* 175–192.

Fitz-enz, J. (1995). *How to measure human resources management* (2nd ed.). New York: McGraw-Hill.

Fitz-enz, J., & Davidson, B. (2002). *How to measure human resource management* (3rd ed.). New York: McGraw-Hill.

Flannery, T. P., Hofrichter, D. A., & Platten, P. E. (1996). *People, performance, and pay.* New York: Free Press.

Galpin, T. J. (1996). *The human side of change.* San Francisco: Jossey-Bass.

Gane, C., & Sarson, T. (1979). *Structured systems analysis.* Englewood Cliffs, NJ: Prentice Hall.

Gerhart, B., & Rynes, S. L. (2003). *Compensation: Theory, evidence, and strategic implications.* Thousand Oaks, CA: Sage.

Gilley, J. W., Quatro, S. A., Hoekstra, E., Whittle, D. D., & Maycunich, A. (2001). *The manager as change agent.* Cambridge, MA: Perseus.

GLOBE Research Team. (2002). *Culture, leadership, and organizational practices: The GLOBE findings.* Thousand Oaks, CA: Sage.

Grant, D., Newell, S., & Kavanagh, M. J. (2010, August). *Realizing the potential of an HRIS: Unintended consequences, human agency and the HR function.* Symposium presented at the annual meeting of the Academy of Management, Montreal.

Gueutal, H. G., Marler, J. H., & Falbe, C. M. (2007). Skill sets for the e-HR world. *IHRIM Journal, 11*(2), 9–15.

Gueutal, H. G., Stone, D. L., & Salas, E. (2005). *The brave new world of eHR: Human resources in the digital age.* San Francisco: Jossey-Bass.

Harris, M. M. (2006). Internet testing: The examinee perspective. In D. Bartram & R. K. Hambleton (Eds.), *Computer-based testing and the Internet: Issues and advances* (pp. 115–133). San Francisco: Wiley.

Hiatt, J. M. (2006). *ADKAR: A model for change in business, government, and our community.* Loveland, CO: Prosci Learning Center Publications.

Hornik, S., Johnson, R. D., & Wu, Y. (2007). When technology does not support learning: Conflicts between epistemological beliefs and technology support in virtual learning environments. *Journal of Organizational and End User Computing, 19*(2), 23–46.

Hornke, L. F., & Kersting, M. (2006). Optimizing quality in the use of web-based and computer-based testing for personnel selection. In D. Bartram & R. K. Hambleton (Eds.), *Computer-based testing and the Internet: Issues and advances* (pp. 115–133). San Francisco: Wiley.

Huang, F., & Cappelli, P. (2010). Applicant screening and performance-related outcomes. *American Economic Review, 100,* 214–218.

Jellison, J. M. (2006). *Managing the dynamics of change.* New York: McGraw-Hill.

Johnson, R. D., & Gueutal, H. G. (2011). *Transforming HR through technology: The use of eHR and human resource information systems in organizations* (SHRM Effective Practice Guidelines Series). Alexandria, VA: The SHRM Foundation.

Johnson, R. D., Gueutal, H., & Falbe, C. (2009). Technology, trainees, metacognitive activity and e-learning effectiveness. *Journal of Managerial Psychology, 24*(6), 545–566.

Johnson, R. D., Hornik, S. R., & Salas, E. (2008). An empirical examination of factors contributing to the creation of successful e-learning environments. *International Journal of Human-Computer Studies, 66,* 356–369.

Jones, J. W., & Dages, K. D. (2003). Technology trends in staffing and assessment: A practice note. *International Journal of Selection and Assessment, 11,* 247–252.

Jones, S. D., & Schilling, D. J. (2000). *A step-by-step, customizable approach for managers, facilitators, and team leaders.* San Francisco: Jossey-Bass.

Kotter, J. P. (1996). *Leading change.* Boston: Harvard Business School Press.

Kotter, J. P., & Cohen, D. S. (2002). *The heart of change.* Boston: Harvard Business School Press.

Lievans, F., & Anseel, F. (2007). Creating alternate in-basket forms through cloning: Some preliminary results. *International Journal of Selection and Assessment, 15,* 428–433.

Marler, J. H., Liang, X., & Dulebohn, J. H. (2006). Training and effective employee information technology use. *Journal of Management, 32,* 721–743.

Marshak, R. J. (2006). *Covert processes at work.* San Francisco: Berrett-Koehler.

Meade, J. G. (2003). *The human resources software handbook: Evaluating technology solutions for your organization.* San Francisco: Jossey-Bass.

Milkovich, G., & Newman, J. (2007). *Compensation.* New York: McGraw-Hill.

Nadler, D. A. (1998). *Champions of change.* San Francisco: Jossey-Bass.

Piskurich, G. M. (2003). *The AMA handbook of e-learning.* New York: AMACOM.

Potosky, D., & Bobko, P. (2004). Selection testing via the internet: Practical considerations and exploratory empirical findings. *Personnel Psychology, 57,* 1003–1034.

Risher, H., & Fay, C. H. (Eds.). (1995). *The performance imperative: Strategies for enhancing workforce effectiveness.* San Francisco: Jossey-Bass.

Rynes, S. L., & Gerhart, B. (Eds.). (2000). *Compensation in organizations: Current research and practice.* Thousand Oaks, CA: Sage.

Salgado, J. F., & Moscoso, S. (2003). Internet-based personality testing: Equivalence of measures and assessees' perceptions and reactions. *International Journal of Selection and Assessment, 11,* 194–205.

Searle, R. H. (2006). New technology: The potential impact of surveillance techniques in recruitment practices. *Personnel Review, 35,* 336–351.

Sitzmann, T., Kraiger, K., Stewart, D., & Wisher, R. (2006). The comparative effectiveness of web-based and classroom instruction: A meta-analysis. *Personnel Psychology, 59,* 623–664.

Smith, M., & Smith, P. (2005). E-selection: Computer-based assessment and interpretation. In M. Smith & P. Smith (Eds.), *Testing people at work* (pp. 220–237). Malden, MA: Blackwell.

Smither, J. W. (Ed.). (1998). *Performance appraisal: State of the art in practice.* San Francisco: Jossey-Bass.

Stone, D. L. (Ed.). (2003). *Advances in human performance and cognitive engineering research* (Vol. 3). New York: JAI Press.

Stone, E. F., & Stone, D. L. (1990). Privacy in organizations: Theoretical issues, research findings, and protection strategies. In G. Ferris & K. Rowland (Eds.), *Research in personnel and human resources management* (Vol. 8, pp. 449–511). Greenwich, CT: JAI Press.

Van Rooy, D. L., Alonso, A., & Fairchild, Z. (2003). In with the new, out with the old: Has the technological revolution eliminated the traditional job search process? *International Journal of Selection and Assessment, 11,* 170–174.

Wallace, J. C., Tye, M. G., & Vodanovich, S. J. (2000). Applying for jobs online: Examining the legality of Internet-based application forms. *Public Personnel Management, 29,* 497–503.

Weichmann, D., & Ryan, A. M. (2003). Reactions to computerized testing in selection contexts. *International Journal of Selection and Assessment, 11,* 215–229.

Williamson, I. O., Lepak, D. P., & King, J. (2003). The effect of company recruitment website orientation on individuals' perceptions of organizational attractiveness. *Journal of Vocational Behavior, 63,* 242–263.

WorldatWork. (2007). *The WorldatWork handbook of compensation, benefits & total rewards.* New York: Wiley.

Zingheim, P. K., & Schuster, J. R. (2000). *Pay people right!* San Francisco: Jossey-Bass.

GLOSSARY

Ability test A standardized test of personal skills. An example is the Watson-Glaser Critical Thinking Appraisal that measures critical thinking skills. It is a multiple-choice reasoning test in which the examinee reads a short- or medium-length passage and draws logical conclusions about the statements, choosing the answer that makes the best logical sense. Many other ability tests are similar in appearance and format to educational tests that are familiar to students (e.g., the Scholastic Aptitude Test [SAT], the Miller Analogies Test [MAT], and the Graduate Record Examination [GRE]).

Action-research model A process model of the management of change in organizations. The basis of this model is the interaction of managerial or organizational action and research that both evaluates the action taken and provides data for future planning of the change effort.

Aesthetic features of Web site The overall stylistic or innovative features of a Web site, such as contrasting colors, pictures, animation, and playfulness, that keep the user engaged while navigating through multiple Web pages.

Affirmative action plan (AAP) A written report detailing how an employer actively seeks to hire and promote individuals in protected classes. For employers with government contracts totaling $50,000 or more, the Office of Federal Contract Compliance Programs (OFCCP) requires that an AAP be completed.

Age Discrimination in Employment Act (ADEA) The 1967 federal legislation prohibiting illegal discrimination in employment against individuals 40 years of age and older.

Americans With Disabilities Act (ADA) The 1990 federal legislation prohibiting illegal discrimination in employment against individuals with disabilities. A disability is defined as a physical or mental impairment that substantially limits one or more major life activities.

Application server Software that delivers specific applications, such as a recruiting plan, to computers in the HR department, typically through the Internet and using the HTTP.

Application service provider (ASP) A third-party firm that hosts and provides access to a bundle of one or more software application services from a central location to multiple clients via the Internet. Clients pay a subscription fee, which generally entails data management and software upgrades. ASPs are often considered a cost-effective way for organizations to manage their information requirements. Many learning management systems are ASP based; that is, access to applications is available through ASPs.

Asynchronous communication Two-way communication in which transmission does not take place in real time. Examples include e-mail or Internet discussion forums. It is useful for collaboration across different time zones.

Attributes Characteristics of the entity in a relational database. For example, an employee has a name, address, phone number, education, and so on.

Availability of information This means that the authorized users must be able to process and access the information when required.

Backsourcing The effort to bring functionality that had previously been outsourced back in-house.

Balanced scorecard A means of measuring strategic organizational performance that gives managers a chance to look at their company from the perspectives of stakeholders, including external customers, employees, and shareholders.

"Balance sheet" compensation An approach for expatriate compensation that has as its goal the maintenance of a home-country living standard plus a financial inducement for accepting an international assignment.

Bandwidth This term refers to the rate and volume of data transfer, measured in bits per second.

Base pay The pay received by an employee as the reward for being employed. The employee will make at least this much unless fired. Base pay for some workers is stated in terms of pay per hour; for others, it is stated in terms of annual pay.

Benchmarking (also known as *best-practice benchmarking* or *process benchmarking*) A process used in management, and particularly in human resources management, to evaluate various aspects of the HR function, both activities and programs, usually within a firm's own market sector.

Best of breed (BOB) An approach to acquiring HRIS capabilities where the company will pick the best application to support each functional area of HR. Thus, the technology architecture combines the best-fit products from multiple vendors.

The Big 3 The three main questions for any HRIS-related project: Where are we now? Where are we going? How are we going to get there?

Blended learning As the term implies, it "blends" various approaches to learning and could incorporate, for instance, face-to-face, formal, informal, and online learning methods.

Boundary-spanning function Any HR management activity or program that must interface directly with the external environment of the organization to be effective.

Business application A set of one or more computer programs that serve as an intermediary between the user and the DBMS (database management system) while providing the "functions" or "tasks" that the user wants performed.

Business intelligence (BI) A broad category of business applications and technologies that provide users with timely and easy access to key organizational data stored in databases or data warehouses. BI applications include the activities of decision support systems, query and reporting, statistical analysis, forecasting, and data mining. The data analysis enabled by BI can range from simple queries to complex mathematical and statistical data mining techniques.

Business process reengineering The analysis and redesign of work flow to improve an organization's efficiency and effectiveness. Also, see **Six Sigma**.

Business process transformation The fundamental rethinking of how a business operates, in which the business redesigns its processes to improve its global competitiveness. Global companies must transform themselves to develop global workforce cultures, with better understanding of transnational teams, online collaboration, and globalization and standardization of their HR processes, such as recruiting.

Business requirements definition The process that occurs when an organization analyzes an HR system, whereby it determines and documents its current and future needs. These needs become the targets or goals that the new system will attempt to satisfy. Business requirements definition is similar to a **needs analysis**.

Change agent (also known as *change leader*) A person who is responsible for leading an organizational change or someone who is influential and can communicate and motivate others to accept a change by informal means.

Change management A structured approach to changing the mindset and perceptions of individuals, groups, and organizations to accept and implement new ideas and processes in an organization.

Civil Rights Act Title VII The 1964 federal legislation prohibiting illegal discrimination in employment based on individuals' race, sex, religion, or national origin. The act also defines and prohibits sexual harassment.

Client-server A term to describe the software and hardware configuration that divides a business application into two tiers, typically with the user interface and some business logic on the user's computer, such as a PC (the client), and the database and mainstream parts of the application stored on a server.

Cloud computing The newest trend in delivering software to companies through hosted software services that are on demand, elastic, and fully managed by the provider. Cloud-based computing platforms deliver scale and cost savings. With cloud computing, HRIS functionality is delivered to companies via the Web. For the company, there is no hardware and software to install.

Column-level security This type of security in an HR database would restrict specific information on employees, for example, age or gender, that makes up a column of information in employees' records.

Commercial off-the-shelf (COTS) software Prewritten or developed software or hardware products that already exist for purchase.

Competency A combination of some set of knowledge, skills, and abilities. Many industrial psychologists equate competencies with traits.

Confidential information Information that must be accessed, used, or disclosed only by authorized users.

Configuration (also **fit-gap**) This process consists of systematically working through every HR process and matching each of those to each of the integral HRIS processes. The result is an understanding of where organizational processes and the software processes mesh (fit) and where they do not (gap). Any gaps that are identified need to be closed either through modification of organizational processes or by software customization.

Content information The degree to which the Web site hosts relevant information that the user deems valuable and informative in nature.

Context level diagram The highest-level data flow diagram that contains the least amount of detail. It is used to represent the system, its boundaries, and the external entities that interact with the system.

Corporate culture An organization's collective values, beliefs, experiences, and norms that shape the behavior of the group and the individuals within it.

Corporate social responsibility and sustainability (CRS) A form of corporate self-regulation that demonstrates a commitment to ethics, sustainability, and social responsibility. There is an increasing need to incorporate the ethical values of an increasingly diverse and global workforce.

Corrective feedback In performance management, information fed back to an employee pointing out the discrepancy between observed performance and a performance standard. The purpose is to solve any performance problem and increase performance level.

Cost-benefit ratio (CBR) A measurement that expresses the benefits of an HR project (e.g., implementation of an HRIS) as the numerator and the costs as the denominator; thus values greater than one indicate a favorable ratio. The CBR for any HR or IT project will estimate the effects of the project on the company's "bottom line."

Country's culture This refers to the history, myths, traditions, values, religious beliefs, communications, and social structure of a country.

CPM chart A method for analyzing a project that calculates the starting and ending times for each activity and determines which activities are critical to the completion of a project (called the *critical path*) and which activities have "float time" (are less critical).

Critical path The sequence or project network with the longest overall duration determining the shortest time possible to complete the project.

Cross-cultural suitability This term refers to an attribute of an expatriate. It could include language ability, cultural empathy, adaptability, and a positive attitude toward the assignment in the specific country being considered.

Cross-tab query This query performs calculations on the values in a field and displays the results in a datasheet.

Cryptography The encoding and decoding of computer messages, which ensures that sensitive information is read and used only by authorized employees.

Cultural norm A specific belief, attitude, or behavior that is defined as right or wrong, correct or incorrect, within a given culture in a country. Cultural norms are part of the cultural environment of a country.

Culture shock The feeling of uneasiness and discomfort experienced when going from one culture to another as well as the adjustment that occurs in a relatively short time when moving from one country to another.

Current analysis The process of analyzing the current state of existing HR processes, technologies, and capabilities. This analysis addresses the **Big 3** questions.

Customization The modification of a software product to match specific organizational processes or needs.

Database A permanent, centralized collection of interrelated data items that can be processed by one or more business applications.

Database management system A set of software applications that supports the processes of creating and managing the physical database, managing the data in the database (e.g., insert, read, update, and delete data from the database); maintaining data integrity and security; and preventing data from being lost by providing backup and recovery capabilities.

Data flow DFD (data flow diagram) component that represents the flow of data within the system. An arrow indicates the direction of flow, and the name of the flow indicates the type of data.

Data flow diagram (DFD) Graphical tool that represents the flow of data through a system and the various processes that manipulate or change the data.

Data migration The process of transferring employee data between storage types and computer systems or software applications.

Data mining The sophisticated statistical analysis of large data sets to identify recurring relationships and patterns. For example, data mining an employee database might reveal that most employees reside within a group of particular zip codes.

Data store A DFD (data flow diagram) component that represents the temporary or permanent storage of data within the system. A data store is represented by an open-ended rectangle in the data flow diagram.

Data warehouse A repository of a company's electronically stored data, which is specifically designed to facilitate reporting and analysis for decision making. Data warehouses are often copies of production (e.g., in use) databases that are stored separately for quick analysis.

Decision support systems (DSS) Software applications that are designed to support business professionals in their decision-making process. One such approach is the use of "what-if" analysis through which managers are able to review and compare various business scenarios and assess the benefits of one problem solution against other solutions.

Defense in depth To protect information fully during its lifetime, each component of the information processing system must have its own protection mechanisms. The building up, layering on, and overlapping of security measures is called *defense in depth*.

Direct costs of expatriate failure These costs include the actual money spent on selecting and training, relocation costs for the expatriate (and family), and the salary of the expatriate.

Direct report The direct report is the employee whose job performance is being evaluated. At the broadest level, this definition of the performance would include any employee who fills the job position, that is, it describes the job performance expectations for any position in the organization.

Economic feasibility System feasibility assessment tool that focuses on the financial and economic benefits and costs that a new system would bring to the organization.

Electronic data processing (EDP) The automation of business processes to perform routine, standardized sets of transactional activities.

Enterprise application integration (EAI) A framework that uses the architectural principles of software and computer systems to integrate a set of disparate software applications. It is the software that allows different functional software applications such as employee selection and employee compensation to work together.

Enterprise resource planning (ERP) software A set of integrated applications, or modules, that carry out the most common business functions, including human resources, general ledger, accounts payable, accounts receivable, order management, inventory control, and customer relationship management. ERP modules are integrated primarily through a common set of definitions and a common database.

Entity An external person, department, or agent that interacts with the system through receiving or sending data. An entity is represented as a square on the DFD (data flow diagram).

Equal Employment Opportunity (EEO) The condition in which all individuals have an equal chance for employment, regardless of their race, color, religion, sex, age, disability, or national origin, as established in federal legislation and the U.S. Constitution and its amendments (13 and 14).

Exempt Not subject to the provisions of the Fair Labor Standards Act. See **Nonexempt**.

Expatriate A parent-country national (PCN) employee assigned to a subsidiary of a multinational enterprise (MNE) in another country.

Expatriate failure The return of expatriates prior to the completion of their overseas assignments.

eXtensible Markup Language (XML) A markup language or set of rules for encoding an electronic document.

Fair Labor Standards Act (FLSA) The 1938 federal legislation that established a minimum wage for hourly workers, set the rate of pay for overtime work beyond the defined workweek of 40 hours, prohibited oppressive child labor by restricting hours of work for children below 16 years, and listed hazardous occupations too dangerous for children.

Family and Medical Leave Act (FMLA) The federal legislation that requires organizations with 50 or more employees to provide up to 12 weeks of unpaid leave after childbirth or adoption, to care for a seriously ill family member, or for an employee's own serious illness.

Field An attribute of an entity that is stored in a table. It appears as a column.

File-oriented data structures Data-processing systems that performed record-keeping functions that mimicked the existing manual procedures. Thus, electronic data were stored in computers much the same way as they were stored in paper-based filing systems.

Firewall A device or set of devices that will permit or deny all computer traffic between computers with different security requirements based on a set of rules.

Fit-gap See **Configuration**.

Flexplan (also known as **cafeteria plans**) A benefits plan in which an employee is provided with some core set of benefits and can then add on some dollar amount of additional benefits paid for by the providing organization.

Force-field analysis A useful technique for looking at all the advantages and disadvantages of a proposed change.

Foreign key The primary key from one table that is stored as an attribute in another table. It represents a common key between two tables that is used to form a relationship between the two tables.

Form An object in a database that you can use to maintain, view, and print records in a more "structured" manner.

Functional experts Employees with extensive knowledge of HR and IT processes. These employees can sometimes be referred to as the power users because of these skills.

Future-oriented competency modeling To consider the future needs of a particular department or role type.

Gantt chart A popular type of bar chart that illustrates a project schedule. It provides a graphical representation of the duration of tasks against the progression of time in a project.

Gap analysis An assessment of the differences between the current state of affairs in the organization and the desired future state.

Global Diversity Readiness Index (DRI) An online spreadsheet tool that is available on the SHRM Web site (www.shrm.org/diversity). The DRI is used to rank 47 countries on 39 separate indicators, which combine to create diversity scores in five categories.

Going-rate or **host-country compensation** An approach to expatriate compensation that ties the base salary for international employees to the salary levels in the host country. For example, an expatriate would earn pay that is comparable with that earned by employees in the host country.

"Go live" The first day the new software is used to manage the organization.

Hierarchical access A set of access rules that provides differential security for employees at different levels or roles in the organization.

High-performance employees (HIPERs) In a talent management approach, the employees who are considered to be performing well in their current role.

High-potential employees (HIPOs) In a talent management approach, the employees who have the potential to develop further and wish to do so.

Host-country nationals (HCNs) Employees of the MNE who are citizens of a country in which a branch or subsidiary is located, but where the organization's headquarters is located in a different country.

HR functional expert Those who provide expertise about what HR data are needed for HR programs, how the HR process maps should be interpreted, and what data are required for decision making.

HRIS Human resource information systems; systems used to acquire, store, manipulate, analyze, retrieve, and distribute information regarding an organization's human resources.

HRIS functionality The number of programs or functions—such as recruiting, compensation, and job analysis—that are operational using the specific HRIS configuration, as well as the features of these programs that enhance their usability and capacity to affect outcomes.

HRM Human resource management; an integral part of the organizational system dealing with strategies, policies, and practices that aim to attract, develop, and retain high-quality intellectual capital.

HR metrics Measures used to evaluate the functioning of HR programs and as benchmarks for the total HRM department.

Human capital This encompasses "the knowledge, skills, competencies and attributes embodied in individuals that facilitate the creation of personal, social and economic well-being" (OECD, 2001, p. 18, cited in Chapter 13, this volume).

Human capital management (HCM) Another term used for **talent management**.

Human resource management decision system (HRMDS) A specific type of decision support system (DSS) that focuses on generating reports of different types, levels, and frequencies to assist HR managers in their decision-making processes.

Human resources planning (HRP) A systematic approach to estimating the future needs of a company for human capital in terms of labor and supply.

Hypertext Markup Language (HTML) The predominant markup language for Web pages. It provides a means to describe the structure of text-based information in a document—by denoting certain text as links, headings, paragraphs, lists, and so on—and to supplement that text with *interactive forms,* embedded *images,* and other objects.

Implementation The selection, installation, and population of an information technology system.

Implementation team The team working with the project manager to complete the actual software implementation.

Incentive pay Compensation provided for some performance achievement. Unlike merit pay, it is not added to base pay but is a one-off reward that must be re-earned to be received again.

Indirect costs of expatriate failure Indirect costs are harder to quantify than direct costs, but they could include loss of market share in the country, negative reactions from the host-country government, and possible negative effects on local employee morale.

Information According to the *Oxford English Dictionary,* information is the act of informing or giving form or shape to the mind. Information provides "structure" and "meaning" to abstract data and is of potential value to organizations.

Information privacy A human value consisting of four elements that refer to human rights, namely, solitude, anonymity, intimacy, and reserve. Information privacy concerns come to play wherever personally identifiable information is collected, stored, and used.

Information security Ensuring the confidentiality, integrity, and availability of information.

Information security in HRIS Protecting information in the HRIS from unauthorized access, use, disclosure, disruption, modification, or destruction.

Integrity of information Integrity means data must be created, modified, or deleted only by the authorized users.

Internal rate of return (IRR) A capital budgeting metric that is the annualized effective compounded return rate that can be earned on an investment; it is an indicator of the efficiency of an investment.

International Association for Human Resource Information Management (IHRIM) The professional organization for specialists in both human resources and human resources technology.

International human resource management (IHRM) The profession and practice of HRM within an international or global corporation.

Internet service portals A Web portal that functions as a point of access to information on the World Wide Web.

IT architecture The basic hardware, software, and networking infrastructure of the organization.

Job analysis The process of systematically obtaining information about jobs by determining the duties, tasks, or activities of jobs, from which a set of KSA (knowledge, skills, and abilities) can be estimated.

Job description The product of a job analysis. It contains the complete description of a job and includes the necessary duties, tasks, and activities and define the working contract between the employee and the organization.

Job evaluation A rating or ranking system designed to create an internal hierarchy of job value. In many organizations, job evaluation results form the basis of the salary structure.

Job forecasting Planning for future work requirements to determine the number and range of specific jobs required.

Knowledge, skills, and abilities (KSA) The requirements for each job in the organization. These provide the basis for HR planning and for the recruitment and selection of new employees.

Knowledge test A multiple-choice training posttest of knowledge of the tools, machines, and equipment used at a factory, designed to measure how well the new hire has learned essential job information taught in classroom training.

Kotter's process of leading change This model provides two key lessons: first, that the change process goes through a series of phases, each lasting a considerable period of time, and second, that critical mistakes in any of the phases can have a devastating impact on the momentum of the change process.

Learning management system (LMS) A software application or Web-based technology that allows the creation, delivery, and management of learning resources and content. An LMS can perform a variety of functions, including training administration, performance management, competency management, skills-gap analysis, or resource allocation.

Legacy system A large, outdated computer system or application that is still being used, often because of the high cost of replacing such a system. The cost of maintaining such systems, which increases over time, is often a key driver for a new system investigation.

Legal and political feasibility A system feasibility assessment tool that focuses on the legal issues associated with the implementation of a new system and any political impacts that would emerge from its use.

Level 0 diagram The first-level DFD (data flow diagram) that outlines the major processes (functions) of the system, the basic sequence of these processes, the basic data stores, and the external entities that interact with the system.

Lewin's change model One of the earliest and key contributions to organizational change, Lewin's framework serves as a general model for understanding planned change.

Load balancing A technique in computer networking that spreads work between computers, network links, or CPUs, in order to get optimal resource utilization from the network.

Logical design A phase in the SDLC (system development life cycle) in which a new system is designed without regard to the technology (e.g., hardware, software, networking) in which it will be implemented.

Logical model A model of the system that graphically illustrates what the system does, independent of any technological architecture (e.g., hardware, software, networking).

Long-range planning An examination of the organization's information needs in light of its long-range strategy. Typically, it looks beyond the present, usually focusing on information needs in the future—that is, 1, 5, and 10 years from now.

Magnetic Ink Character Recognition (MICR) As defined by the American National Standards Institute (ANSI), it is the common machine-language specification for the paper-based payment transfer system. It consists of magnetic-ink-printed characters of a special design that can be recognized by high-speed magnetic recognition equipment (www.whatismicr.com).

Maintenance The ongoing task of operating and maintaining a new system after the initial implementation, including auditing, updating, and upgrading.

Management information systems (MIS) A type of information system designed to provide detailed data to aid managers in performing day-to-day activities.

Management reporting systems Software that (1) focuses on information aimed at middle managers; (2) integrates transaction-processing data by business function such as manufacturing, marketing, and human resources; and (3) provides reporting of summarized data.

Management sponsor The senior manager who is ultimately responsible for the successful completion of a project.

Market benchmarking A compensation practice designed to provide labor market rates for jobs in an organization. The labor markets may be local, regional, national, or global. The underlying rationale is that an organization should pay for a job roughly what other employers in the relevant market pay to attract and retain employees.

Merit pay A system providing increases to base pay based on merit or performance. Once merit pay is awarded, the employee receives it until he or she leaves the organization.

Middleware The general term for any computer programming that serves to "glue together" or mediate between two separate and often already existing programs.

MS Access A small scale, relational database management system (DBMS) that integrates both database application software and DBMS software into one.

Multinational enterprise (MNE) A term applied to any organization that has a business presence in more then one country. A multinational enterprise is also called a multinational corporation.

Nadler's congruence model An organizational performance model that is built on the view that organizations are systems and that only if there is congruence ("fit") between the various organizational subsystems can we expect optimal performance.

Navigability (of a Web site) The overall ease with which a user can browse through multiple Web pages to locate topics of interest.

Needs analysis In the analysis of an HR system, the process by which an organization determines and documents its current and future system needs. These needs become the targets or goals that the new system will attempt to satisfy. See also **business requirements definition**.

Nonexempt Subject to the requirements of the Fair Labor Standards Act. Employers of nonexempt employees must pay them at least minimum wage, pay overtime of 1.5 times the base pay rate for every hour worked in one week in excess of 40 hours with 2.5 allowed for meals, keep track of hours worked, and file reports with the U.S. Labor Department demonstrating compliance.

N-tier architectures The software and hardware configurations in which databases, applications, and other resources are distributed among many different computers around the world.

Occupational Assessor® software Software developed and supported by the Economic Research Institute (ERI), which was founded in 1987 to provide compensation research to organizations and consultants in the form of published reports and survey software.

Occupational Safety and Health Act (OSHA) The 1970 law that authorizes the federal government to establish and enforce occupational safety and health standards for all places of employment affecting interstate commerce.

Offshoring An organization's use of groups outside of its home country (e.g., India, Ireland, or China for U.S. corporations) to provide services (e.g., HR call centers) to achieve strategic organizational goals.

Online recruiting (also known as *Web-based recruiting*, *Internet-based recruiting*, *cyber recruiting*, and *e-recruiting*) The use of the Internet in attracting job seekers to a company's job openings.

Operational feasibility System feasibility assessment tool that focuses on how well the new system will fit within the organization and can be used to consider issues such as development schedule, extent of organizational change, and user responses to the system.

Optical Character Recognition (OCR) The translation of images of handwritten or printed text into computer-editable text, usually by a scanner.

Outsourcing An organization's use of an outside group to provide services—from a few services (e.g., recruiting, compensation processing) up to a broad set of services (e.g., all HR functions)—to achieve strategic organizational goals.

Parent-country nationals (PCNs) Employees of the multinational organization (MNE) who are citizens of the country in which the parent, or headquarters, of the MNE is located.

Payback period A capital budgeting metric that calculates the number of years required for the flow of benefits returned by an investment to equal the cost of the investment.

Performance appraisal A retrospective system noting how an employee has performed during a previous period. Performance appraisal data usually form the basis for merit pay.

Performance criterion An outcome, behavior, or competency used in the performance management (or appraisal) process. Performance criteria are the factors on which an employee's performance is rated.

Performance management A managerial process designed to improve employees' job performance. Performance management is broader than performance appraisal because it focuses on planning for performance, providing performance feedback to an employee, and rewarding changed job performance behavior.

Performance standard The level of a performance criterion a fully job-knowledgeable employee who makes a reasonable effort should achieve.

Perquisite A reward based on job status. In the past, these were usually reserved for executives (corporate jet, executive dining room, special parking), but now they are frequently used as performance rewards for other workers.

Phase containment The process of identifying and fixing problems early in the system development life cycle so as to avoid costly rework later.

Physical design A phase in the SDLC (system development life cycle) in which a new system is designed with particular focus on how the hardware, software, networking, activities, and so on will be implemented.

Position analysis questionnaire A specific technique for completing a job analysis. There is a software package that automates this approach to job analysis.

Positive feedback Remarks made by a manager to a direct report concerning observed performance and designed to reinforce efforts leading to high performance.

Power user The most demanding user of HRIS who will use a large amount of the system functionality.

Primary key An attribute that is used to uniquely identify each record in a table. For example, each employee has an employee ID that is unique (i.e., only one person has a particular number).

Process A business function or activity through which data are created, manipulated, or transformed. A process is represented on a DFD (data flow diagram) by a square with rounded edges

Process mapping The systematic documentation of organizational processes that directly relate to the ongoing project.

Program (or project) evaluation and review technique (PERT) A method for analyzing the tasks involved in completing a given project, the time needed to complete each task, and the minimum time needed to complete the total project. Once the PERT analysis is completed, a Gantt chart can be constructed to guide the project.

Project charter A planning document that defines the scope of, and provides a basic "rule book" to facilitate completion of, a software implementation project.

Project concept This describes the key stakeholders and seeks to ensure that the right questions are asked so that the right problem is solved.

Project creep The addition of functionality beyond what was defined in the project scope. It is also called *scope creep*.

Project manager The person chosen by an organization to be responsible for the planning, execution, and evaluation of an HRIS implementation project.

Project proposal (also called a **project charter**) A description of the objectives and performance targets (e.g., cost, time, scope) for the HRIS project.

Project scope The portions of the information system that need to be completely operational to satisfy the needs of the various customers, employees, and senior management.

Project sponsor Often, a member of the steering committee whose organizational unit has provided the fiscal resources for the development and implementation of the HRIS.

Psychological contract Employees' beliefs about the reciprocal obligations and promises between them and their organizations.

Qualified The status of a benefits plan with respect to favorable tax treatment. A qualified plan cannot discriminate in favor of the highly paid by design or in practice.

Query A question you ask about the data stored in a database. For example, you may want to know which employees live within a specific zip code.

Rapid e-learning (REL) (also called *just-in-time learning/training* and *on-demand learning*) The essence of REL is the ability to develop and deliver tailor-made e-learning content swiftly (within weeks, days, or hours) and inexpensively to a large number of learners and to track their learning progress in order to stay abreast of rapidly changing knowledge and information needs. The responsibility for content creation lies with the subject matter experts themselves. REL tools require only limited audiovisual expertise, as they incorporate easy-to-use presentation software. REL solutions may be either synchronous (real time) or asynchronous (on demand). As REL modules can be very short (30 minutes or less), they are convenient and are easily "digested" by the learners.

Recognition award Any reward (whether cash or noncash) with the primary purpose of celebrating the specific performance achievements of individuals or groups. A group implementing a new HRIS, for example, might be treated to a party upon the successful completion of an important segment of the project. The cash value of the award is less important than the psychological value, even if the award has significant cash value.

Record A row in a table that represents an "instance" of the entity. For example, in an employee table, each row contains data about a particular employee, and each column contains data that represent an attribute of that employee, such as name, phone number, and e-mail address.

Reengineering The process of implementing the right technology infrastructure and streamlining the business processes.

Regression analysis A statistical procedure that provides predictions of future states of the firm based on the history of the firm. For example, changes in market share for a company's product can be linked with the number of employees. Thus, future expected changes in market share (an increase) could be used to estimate the number of new employees needed.

Relational database A type of database that stores data in tables with each table representing one "entity" in the real world and the information associated with that entity stored only in that table. Tables are related to each other through a common attribute or key.

Relationships These are created by having the same attribute in two separate tables within the database. The relationships are created by matching the value of the attribute in each table. Most often, this is done by taking the **primary key** of one table and including it in the related table.

Repatriation The process that occurs as the expatriate and family return to their homeland. It is critically important that repatriation programs be established since there is a readjustment (reverse culture shock) when individuals return to their home cultures.

Reports Formatted presentations of data that help employees and managers make business decisions. Data are drawn from a table, multiple tables, or queries that are created as a printout or to be viewed on screen. Data displayed in a report are dynamic, reflecting the latest data from the tables on which the report is based.

Request for proposal (RFP) A document that solicits potential consultants or vendors to submit proposals and bids for proposed work.

Resistance to change A common response to any major change initiative; individuals reject all or part of the change and strive to maintain the status quo.

Return on investment (ROI) A capital budgeting metric in which the flow of benefits that result from an investment is compared with the cost of the investment, usually in the form of a ratio, using the cost of the investment as the denominator. ROI is generally expressed as a percentage of the total benefits less total costs over the total costs, and it is usually determined by the following formula:

$$\frac{\text{Total benefit} - \text{Total costs}}{\text{Total costs}} \times 100 = \text{ROI}$$

Return on investment in training A financial measure of the total benefits of training (anything that adds directly or indirectly to the bottom line of the organization as a result of training) compared with the total costs of training, including direct and indirect costs. Direct costs involve any costs directly related to training, for example, trainer's or instructor's fees, equipment and facility rental, and production and purchase of training materials. Indirect costs are not directly associated with the delivery of training, for example, administrative support or office supplies.

Row-level security This is similar to column-level security. It refers to a set of rules that define who can access (or is prohibited from accessing) information on specific employees; for example, a supervisor can access information on the employees in his group but not on employees under a different supervisor.

Scenario planning This identifies possible alternative futures, for example, how different roles may develop in terms of a career structure or possible routes to a senior management or senior specialist position.

Selection ratio The number of candidates who, based on the assessment, are chosen for the job divided by the number of candidates who are assessed.

Select query This query allows you to ask a question based on one or more tables in a database.

Self-service portal A single sign-on electronic access point from which an employee or manager can access and manage personal or other relevant organizational information.

Service-oriented architecture (SOA) A structure for organizing and utilizing distributed computing capabilities that may be under the control of different ownership domains.

75% rule If a package can meet approximately 75% of your needs, that is quite good.

Shared-service center (SSC) A technology-enabled centralized group designed to provide excellent service to internal customers at reduced costs.

Short-range planning Typically, planning for the next year—that is, deciding what systems and projects fall within the immediate window for action.

Single data truth All enterprise data can be accessed by all users wherever and whenever needed.

Six Sigma The streamlining of operations through business process reengineering, which is useful for streamlining HR programs and processes.

Skills test A practical exercise or simulation that tests the candidate's effectiveness in performing an activity or job function, for example, data entry speed and accuracy or using Microsoft Word software.

Social business networks A type of enterprise portal built to provide tools for employees to connect, coordinate, and communicate within a specific company *only*.

Society for Human Resource Management (SHRM) The largest worldwide professional organization for HR practitioners and academics.

Software as a service (SaaS) An approach to accessing software that allows small and medium companies to access HRIS capabilities that were previously only available to large organizations. Cloud computing is the latest type of SaaS.

Sourcing partner An external firm that partners with a company to provide some of its HR functionality, for example, recruitment or benefits management. Sourcing partners require certain information to complete these tasks, such as information about vacant positions including position description, job specifications, desired candidate competencies, potential salary range, and contact information. The information provided is limited to specific searches for open jobs and is updated as needed.

Steering committee A committee usually composed of the project manager, the senior-management member who is the project sponsor, and the lead employee from each involved area (e.g., lead systems analyst, lead database administrator). Also on the steering committee are HR functional experts, whose role is to provide expertise about what HR data are needed, how the HR process maps should be interpreted, and what data are required for decision making.

Strategic HRM The strategic alignment of the HR management function with organizational goals. It aims to harness the potential of people as a key competitive advantage through the use of their creativity and innovation.

Structured Query Language (SQL) A command (i.e., programming) language used in processing, modifying, and querying data in relational database systems.

Synchronous communication "Real-time" or live communication using tools such as messenger services or videoconferencing.

System development life cycle (SDLC) A formal process through which a system is analyzed, redesigned, and implemented. The SDLC will include phases such as analysis/evaluation, design/improvement, development, implementation, and maintenance of the system.

System investigation The early planning and diagnosis to examine the feasibility of a new system. A business case for change is developed and, if favorable (e.g., return on investment is compelling), leads to the initiation of an HRIS project.

Tables A collection of organized data within a database that stores information about entities. One table is created for each entity. Attributes are stored as the columns (also called fields) in the table. For example, an employee table would have data on the following characteristics: employee ID, first name, last name, street address, city, state, social security number, and so on. Each of these characteristics represents an attribute or field of the table.

Talent diversity The selection and development of employees who will provide diversity of thinking about increasing the performance of the organization.

Talent management (human capital management) A strategic approach to the recruitment, selection, training, development, and management of employees, including the management of their performance and promotion, to meet the strategic objectives of a firm and, thus, improve the organization's competitiveness in the marketplace.

Technical feasibility A system feasibility assessment tool that focuses on the technical capability of the organization and the availability of the technology necessary to implement a new system.

Tests and assessments Job-related decision-making tools that provide information about candidates that organizations use to make choices about their people. The terms *test, assessment, selection tool,* and *selection procedure* can be used interchangeably. Examples may include polygraphs, work samples, and inventories.

"Think global, act local" The most common advice regarding the management of an MNE has been to "think global, act local." This advice applies to the total management process of an MNE—its strategy, operations, finance, marketing, and HR—and has been followed religiously for many years in international management. Beaman has argued that this approach is completely the inverse of how we should be developing and managing our global HRIS projects.

Third-country nationals (TCNs) Employees of the MNE who are citizens of a country other than the parent or host country.

360° appraisal Any system in which employee performance is rated by managers, peers, subordinates, and (possibly) outsiders and the employee as well.

3-Tier architecture A type of computer architecture in which a client computer interacts with two (or more) servers. One server usually maintains the database and data while the other server manages the processing logic.

Traditional HR Traditional functions of an HR department, such as recruitment and training. They can add strategic value to the organization depending on how they are conducted.

Transactional capabilities The capability and capacity of the HRIS to process routine activities, for example, change of addresses for employees. (See Chapter 1 or 10 for more details.)

Transactional HR Routine, day-to-day activities of the HR department, such as record keeping, that are important but add little value to the competitive position of the organization.

Transaction cost theory The idea that organizations can choose to purchase the goods and services they need in the competitive marketplace or make those goods and services internally.

Transaction processing systems Business applications that focus on processing operational data and whose main functions are (1) data storage, processing, and flows at the daily operational level and (2) efficiency, accuracy, and speed.

Transformational HR High-value-added programs or functions in the HR department, such as cultural change, which can significantly affect the strategic direction and long-term viability of the organization. A simple example would be a training program for marketing department employees designed to increase sales, and its effects.

Trend analysis The process of collecting information and analyzing it to identify a pattern, or *trend,* in the information. For example, in HR planning, it could be used to determine if particular age or gender groups of employees had higher turnover rates.

2-Tier architecture The most basic type of computer hardware infrastructure in which a computer server provides information to a client computer.

U.S. Department of Labor's O*Net database (http://online.onetcenter.org) A database containing job descriptions for a large number of jobs in a variety of industries. It is a good starting point for a job analysis project.

User acceptance The willingness of a user of a system to employ the new technology for all its intended purposes.

User interface The communication boundary between the hardware device (e.g., computer, PDA, kiosk) and the user of that hardware. It is the point at which the user interacts with the system, providing inputs and receiving information or feedback from the system.

Validity coefficient A statistical correlation that indicates the correspondence between test scores and job performance or some other important work outcomes.

"Vanilla" The version of the software to be implemented without customization is referred to as the "vanilla" version.

Vendor A company that specializes in making or selling commercial software for purchase by other companies. In the HR context, they are the firms that sell prepackaged software to support the various functional areas of HRM.

Virtual private network (VPN) This term refers to the creation of a "private" computer network across a public network (e.g., the Internet) through the use of software controls. It can provide organizations with the privacy they seek without forcing them to build a separate network infrastructure for just their data or system.

Virtual workspace A work environment where the employees of a company work away from company premises and communicate with their respective workplaces via telephone or computer devices.

Web site usability The extent to which users are able to use a Web site effectively. Web usability is often viewed as being comprised of a number of dimensions, including navigability, content and display of information, aesthetics, and ease of use.

Web 2.0 The second generation of Web-related services, focusing on creativity, collaboration, and sharing in contrast to traditional isolated information silos.

Work breakdown structure A definition of the order in which activities, tasks, and jobs are to be performed that also establishes specific check or monitoring points.

Work packages These define what must be done, by whom, using what resources, in what time, and at what cost to complete the HRIS project.

Work simulation An in-basket exercise in which the examinee must examine a variety of types of information (correspondence, reports, and other information) and also interact with simulated coworkers, employees, or other business associates (whether computer simulated or role-played by actors over the telephone or in person). The examinee is evaluated on a variety of dimensions, from accuracy and the quality of decisions to work-related competencies, interpersonal skills, and other personal attributes.

Author Index

Subject Index

About the Editors

Michael J. Kavanagh is currently Professor Emeritus of Management at the State University of New York at Albany. He also serves on the faculty of the Lorange School of Business Administration, Zurich, Switzerland. He is past editor of *Group & Organization Management* and a fellow of the American Psychological Association, the American Psychological Society, the Society for Industrial and Organizational Psychology, and the Eastern Academy of Management. He has been involved in the HRIS field since 1982. He established the HRIS MBA program at the University at Albany in 1984 and has taught numerous courses in the field of HRIS. In 2006, he received the Award for Career Excellence from the International Association for Human Resource Information Management (IHRIM). He received his PhD in industrial/organizational psychology from Iowa State University in 1969.

Mohan Thite is an Associate Professor at Griffith Business School, Griffith University, Brisbane, Australia. He has more than 25 years' experience as an HR professional, both in industry and in academia. He is a fellow of the Australian Human Resources Institute. He has been teaching HRIS for several years. His research interests include strategic HRM in the knowledge economy, HRIS, and HRM in multinational corporations from emerging economies. His publications include a book on *Managing People in the New Economy* (Sage, India), a coedited book on HRM in the business process outsourcing industry in India, book chapters, and articles in international journals such as *Work, Employment, and Society,* the *International Journal of HRM*, and the *International Journal of Project Management*.

Richard D. Johnson is an assistant professor of management at the University at Albany, State University of New York. His research interests are human resource information systems, the psychological and sociological impacts of computing, computer self-efficacy, e-learning, and issues surrounding the digital divide. His research has appeared in several journals such as *Information Systems Research,* the *Journal of Applied Social Psychology,* the *Journal of the Association for Information Systems*, and the *International Journal of Human-Computer Studies.* He is a certified Human Resource Information Professional and teaches courses on human resources and HRIS as part of the University at Albany's nationally recognized MBA concentration on HRIS. He received his PhD from the University of Maryland, College Park.

About the Contributors

Bradley J. Alge is Associate Professor of Management at the Krannert School of Management at Purdue University. Currently, he teaches courses in organizational behavior, technology, and human capital management and has spent the past 10 years teaching HRIS in Krannert's graduate programs. He has received distinguished teaching recognition at both the graduate and the undergraduate levels. He is also an accomplished researcher. Winner of the Jay Ross Young Faculty Scholar Award, he conducts research on leadership, motivation, team dynamics, prosocial and antisocial work behaviors, creativity, and technology. His research has been published in top-tier outlets, including the *Journal of Applied Psychology*, *Personnel Psychology*, *Organizational Behavior and Human Decision Processes*, and *Research in Personnel and Human Resource Management*. He serves on the editorial boards of *Organizational Behavior and Human Decision Processes* and the *Journal of Management*. He received his PhD in organizational behavior and HRM from The Ohio State University.

Michael D. Bedell is a professor of management, MBA Program Director, AACSB Accreditation Director, and past Bautzer University Advancement faculty member at California State University, Bakersfield. He has previously worked in the banking industry as a TQM expert focused on improving service quality. He has worked for a *Fortune* 500 retailer in corporate organizational development, and his responsibilities included developing and validating selection methods, implementing a PeopleSoft HRIS, and training merchandising teams. His research and consulting interests are centered on HRIS, HR metrics, and HR strategy with a focus on small or family businesses. He is a member of numerous professional and academic organizations. He received his PhD in human resource management with a minor in operations management from Indiana University in 1996.

Salvatore M. Belardo is Professor Emeritus of Information Technology Management at the University at Albany. He has been a visiting professor at the Copenhagen School of Business, the Graduate School of Business Administration in Zurich, Switzerland, and the University of Maryland. He has worked with a number of firms, including General Electric, Unilever, Novartis, and Orell Füssli, and has developed information systems for a number of public agencies, including the U.S. Coast Guard, the New York State Department of Transportation, and the U.S. Department of State. He has published widely in a number of top journals, including *Management Science*; *Decision Sciences*; *IEEE Transactions on Systems, Man, and Cybernetics*; and the *Journal of Management Information Systems*. He has been recognized for his contributions to the field of decision support systems. He has written and edited several books, including *Simulation in Business and Management* and *Innovation Through Learning*. He received his PhD in management information systems from RPI in 1981.

Ralf Burbach is the campus coordinator of the Wexford Campus of the Institute of Technology, Carlow, Ireland, where he previously lectured. He has also lectured at the National University of Ireland, Galway, and the Galway-Mayo Institute of Technology, Ireland. He has previously taught courses in organizational behavior, organizational change, industrial relations, strategic human resource management, international human resource management, and HRIS. He is a chartered member of the Chartered Institute of Personnel and Development, the United Kingdom's and Ireland's leading professional body for HR professionals. He has been carrying out research into HRIS since 2001, including a government-funded project on HRIS use in small enterprises. His current research interests include global HRIS, e-HRM, talent management systems, and international and comparative HRM.

Michael L. Canniff has worked in the IT field for more than 15 years, beginning with IBM as a software engineer and, most recently, as Vice President, Development for Acuitrek. His time in the field also includes several years of developing leading-edge Internet-based products and solutions as Director of Development for PeopleSoft. Currently, he is the acting chief technology officer with San Joaquin Regional Transit and provides strategic research for software companies such as SAP. He has specialized his career research in the areas of enterprise application integration and electronic commerce systems. He implemented cross-product XML integration standards while at PeopleSoft. He has published several papers on electronic commerce and business process management best practices.

Kevin D. Carlson is Associate Professor and Director of Graduate Studies in the Department of Management at Virginia Tech. He has published research on a wide variety of topics related to the measurement and evaluation of individual, process, and organizational effectiveness. His work has been published in the *Journal of Applied Psychology*, *Personnel Psychology*, the *Journal of Management*, the *IHRIM Journal*, and *Personnel Review*, and he has presented papers to the Academy of Management, the Society for Industrial and Organizational Psychology, and the International Association for Human Resource Information Management (IHRIM). He is an associate editor for *Human Resource Management*, a member of the editorial board for the *Academy of Management Learning and Education*, and a member of the board of directors of IHRIM. His current research addresses how to use HR metrics and workforce analytics to enhance organizational performance.

David N. Dickter is Senior Manager, Talent Assessment at PSI. He is a consultant to *Fortune* 500 companies for the selection, assessment, and development of individuals at all levels. Previously, he was in the corporate organization effectiveness group at AT&T. His experience also includes personnel selection and research roles at Educational Testing Service and the United States Air Force. He has published and presented research and practical papers on selection and technology, turnover, decision making, and various other human resources topics. He received his PhD in industrial/organizational psychology from The Ohio State University.

James H. Dulebohn is an associate professor of human resource management and associate director at Michigan State University's School of Human Resources and Labor Relations. His research interests include decision making, HRIS, compensation and benefits, and HR systems. His articles have appeared in journals, including the *Academy of Management Journal*, *Personnel Psychology*, the *Journal of Management*, the *Journal of Risk and Insurance*, *Organizational Behavior and Human Decision Processes*, *Research in Higher Education*, and others. He has consulted for a variety of organizations, including Dow Chemical, Monsanto, Raytheon, TIAA-CREF, the State of Illinois, the State of Texas, and Marriott. He also served on PeopleSoft's Academic Advisory Committee and on the editorial board of the Society of Human Resource Planning. He earned his PhD and master's degrees from the University of Illinois at Urbana-Champaign.

Charles H. Fay is currently a professor of human resource management at the School of Management and Labor Relations, Rutgers University. He has taught undergraduate and graduate courses in rewards management, performance appraisal, HRIS, statistics, and labor economics. He has also taught rewards management, performance management, and HRIS in several executive and management education programs in the United States, Singapore, Malaysia, and Indonesia. His research focuses on rewards and performance management. He is the coauthor of several books, including *The Performance Imperative*, *New Strategies for Public Pay*, and *The Executive Handbook on Compensation*. He was a presidential appointee to the Federal Salary Commission and served as a consultant to the Bureau of Labor Statistics on the National Compensation Survey. He has earned certified compensation professional status from WorldatWork (formerly the American Compensation Association). He has served as an expert witness on compensation issues before the Presidential Emergency Board numerous times and testified before Congress on compensation and performance management issues. He has a PhD in management and organization behavior from the University of Washington.

Barry D. Floyd is currently Professor of Information Systems at California Polytechnic State University. He has designed and developed enterprise application software as well as consulted on ERP implementation projects. He has presented at conferences and published articles on incorporating ERP systems into the business curriculum. His teaching efforts include courses on database design, systems analysis and design, e-commerce, enterprise resource planning, and HRIS. He received his PhD in computer and information systems from the University of Michigan.

Linda C. Isenhour is currently Associate Professor of Management at Eastern Michigan University, where she develops and teaches courses in HR and technology. Her research interests include recruitment, cultural values, strategic human resource management, and human resource information systems. She has published articles and book chapters on HRM and technology, recruitment, HRM and cultural values, and HRM and privacy. In addition, she has presented scholarly papers to the Academy of Management, the Society of Industrial and Organizational Psychology, the Southern Management Association, and the Western Business and Management Association. A member of the Academy of Management, the Southern Management Association, and the Society for Human Resource Management, she has also earned certification as a Global Professional in Human Resources (GPHR) from the Society of Human Resource Management.

Kevin M. Johns is a business development and sales executive at IBM Corporation. His career with IBM began in 1982, and he has worked in sales, systems engineering, and consulting services, covering the major clients of IBM in multiple industries such as telecommunications, life sciences, insurance, and government. Presently, he is responsible for global business partner alliances that sell industry solutions to joint clients. These solutions include ERP, CRM, HCM, and business intelligence (BI) systems. He has experience with ERP applications such as SAP and PeopleSoft. Recently, he has been a lecturer at the Rutgers School of Management and Labor Relations. He teaches a course in HRIS and covers project management skills necessary for successful HR implementations along with HR lab exercises in SAP. He received his undergraduate degree in economics and his MBA from Rutgers University.

Jerard F. Kehoe received his doctorate in quantitative psychology in 1975 from the University of Southern California. He joined AT&T in 1982 where he had responsibility for selection programs in manufacturing, customer service, sales, technical, management, and leadership jobs, assuming overall leadership and direction of that function in 1997. In September 2003, Jerry founded Selection & Assessment Consulting and serves as president. Dr. Kehoe has been active professionally, with several publications, chapters, and conference presentations on selection and assessment topics, including computerized testing, fairness, scoring strategies, cut scores, and test validity. In 2000, he edited the Society for Industrial and Organizational Psychology's Professional Practice Series volume, *Managing Selection in Changing Organizations: Human Resource Strategies.* In 2001–2003, he served on the SIOP subcommittee that revised the *Principles for the Validation and Use of Employment Selection Procedures.*

Kimberly M. Lukaszewski is an associate professor of management at the State University of New York at New Paltz. Her research is focused on electronic human resources, privacy, and diversity issues. Her work has been published in journals such as the *Human Resource Management Review*, the *Journal of Business and Psychology*, the *Journal of Business Issues*, the *Journal of the Academy of Business Education*, the *Business Journal of Hispanic Research*, and the *International Association for Human Resources Information Management Journal.* She has written various book chapters published in the *Handbook of Workplace Diversity*, *The Brave New World of eHR: Human Resources Management in the Digital Age*, *The Influence of Culture on Human Resource Management Processes and Practices*, *The Handbook of Human Resource Management Education*, and *Advances in Human Performance and Cognitive Engineering Research.* She received her MBA in HRIS and her PhD in organizational studies from the University at Albany.

Brian D. Lyons is an assistant professor of management in the Raj Soin College of Business at Wright State University. His research interests center on Web recruitment, counterproductive work behavior, and investigating the validity of selection tools in nontraditional employment contexts (professional athletics). His research has been mentioned in the press (Atlanta Journal-Constitution) and appeared in journals such as *Human Performance*, the *Journal of Occupational and Organizational Psychology*, the *International Journal of Selection and Assessment*, and the *Journal of Managerial Psychology*. He received his PhD in organizational studies from the University at Albany, State University of New York.

Janet H. Marler is Associate Professor and Chair of the Management Department at the State University of New York at Albany. Prior to earning a PhD from Cornell University's School of Industrial and Labor Relations, she held several senior executive positions in the financial services industry. Her research centers on the strategic use of HRIS, alternative and flexible work arrangements, and compensation strategy and has been published in leading scholarly journals and books. A leader in the use of ERP systems technology in the classroom, she teaches executive MBA programs in HRIS, HR, and compensation strategy.

John W. Michel is an assistant professor of management at Towson University. His research interests include customer service management, leadership and influence processes, supportive and fun workplace practices, employee selection and retention, and the utilization of HRIS in HRM. He received his PhD in organizational studies from the State University of New York at Albany in 2007.

Renato E. Nardoni is President of Nardoni Associates, Inc.—now known as Pilat HR Solutions, the internationally known succession planning and 360-degree assessment software company. He has consulted with clients such as Merrill Lynch, The World Bank, ConocoPhillips, Nike, Ericsson, RIM, Marriott, IBM, Exelon, Wellpoint Health, Philip Morris, Johnson & Johnson, Chase Manhattan, and AT&T. He has served on the board of directors of the New York IHRIM chapter and was the editor of its newsletter. He has been contributing editor to personnel magazines and computers in personnel. He spent more than 17 years with AT&T in a variety of IT, financial, and human resource positions. In 1982, as a founder of Human Resource Technologies, he designed and developed one of the first commercially available PC-based HRIS products.

Romuald A. Stone is a professor of civilian leader development at the Army Management Staff College, Fort Belvoir, VA. He is also an online faculty member in the Keller Graduate School of Management. He has held previous professional appointments at James Madison University and George Mason University. His research and writings include numerous strategy case studies and practitioner-oriented articles. He is the coauthor of *Managing Organizational Change*, a change management textbook. His work has appeared in the *Academy of Management Executive*, *Psychological Reports*, the *Journal of Management Education*, *Computers in Human Behavior*, *Educational and Psychological Measurement*, *Business Horizons*, *Employment Relations Today*, the *SAM Advanced Management Journal*, and the *Journal of Applied Management and Entrepreneurship*. As a practitioner, he has more than 20 years of experience as a trainer and consultant in the areas of organizational management and leadership. He received his DBA from Nova Southeastern University in 1990.

Karen Bruner Upright is currently Systems Manager, Procter & Gamble–Global Flavor & Fragrance in Cincinnati, Ohio. She holds several professional designations from the International Foundation of Employee Benefit Plans, including Certified Employee Benefits Specialist (CEBS). She has been involved in HRIS for the past 10 years, focusing on defined benefit pension plans. She spoke on the topic of *Information Security: Protecting a Firm's Most Valuable Assets* at the 2006 symposium of the International Society of Certified Employee Benefit Specialists in Toronto, Ontario, Canada. She earned an MBA from Purdue University and holds a BS in computer science from Florida State University.

Yuk Kuen Wong is currently working at Macquarie University, Australia. Her research work (information management and quality control) is internationally recognized by leading organizations, such as the ICSE (International Conference on Software Engineering). Her recently published research book on quality controls has been listed across disciplines in a number of institutions. She has previously worked at the University of New South Wales and the University of Technology, Sydney. Her teaching areas include data communications, information management and controls, information and computer security, information technology management, system auditing, global data networks, data management, and project management. Before her academic appointments, she worked in the areas of enterprise resource planning systems implementation, systems and business processes reengineering, and e-business solutions. She is a founding member of the Association for Information Systems Special Interest Group on IT/IS in Asia-Pacific and a member of the Association for Information Systems, the Association for Computing Machinery, the Institute of Electrical and Electronics Engineers, and the IEEE Communications Society.

Cheryl R. Wyrick is Professor and Chair of the Management and Human Resources Department at California State Polytechnic University, Pomona, where she has taught HR information systems, benefits, and training and development and other HR courses. She served on the university's project team that implemented PeopleSoft and, in addition, conducted training that introduced the HR staff to strategic metric analyses. She has designed HRIS instructional materials for use in undergraduate courses. She has presented and written on the topic of metrics and technology. An active volunteer, she has held various leadership positions in HR professional associations, including the Society for Human Resource Management, where she served on the HR technology management expertise panel. She is currently a member of the HRCI Board of Directors.